ORGANIZED
CRIME

TENTH EDITION

HOWARD ABADINSKY
St. John's University

WADSWORTH
CENGAGE Learning·

Australia • Brazil • Japan • Korea • Mexico • Singapore • Spain • United Kingdom • United States

Organized Crime, Tenth Edition
Howard Abadinsky

Senior Publisher: Linda Schreiber-Ganster

Senior Acquiring Sponsoring Editor: Carolyn Henderson-Meier

Assistant Editor: Rachel McDonald

Assistant Editor: Virginette Acacio

Associate Media Editor: Andy Yap

Senior Marketing Manager: Michelle Williams

Marketing Coordinator: Jack Ward

Marketing Communications Manager: Heather Baxley

Manufacturing Planner: Judy Inouye

Rights Acquisitions Specialist-Image and Txt: Broyer Roberta

Art and Cover Direction, Production Management, and Composition: PreMediaGlobal

Cover Designer: Riezebos Holzbaur/Brieanna Hattey

Cover Image: Brian Hagiwara & Michel Stevelmans

For product information and technology assistance, contact us at
Cengage Learning Customer & Sales Support, 1-800-354-9706

For permission to use material from this text or product, submit all requests online at **www.cengage.com/permissions**. Further permissions questions can be emailed to **permissionrequest@cengage.com**

Library of Congress Control Number: 2012933004

ISBN-13: 978-1-133-04963-0

ISBN-10: 1-133-04963-X

Wadsworth
20 Davis Drive
Belmont, CA 94002-3098
USA

Cengage Learning is a leading provider of customized learning solutions with office locations around the globe, including Singapore, the United Kingdom, Australia, Mexico, Brazil and Japan. Locate your local office at **www.cengage.com/global**.

Cengage Learning products are represented in Canada by Nelson Education, Ltd.

For your course and learning solutions, visit **www.cengage.com**.

Purchase any of our products at your local college store or at our preferred online store **www.cengagebrain.com**.

Printed in the United States of America
2 3 4 5 6 7 16 15 14 13

Brief Contents

Contents

Chapter 13   Organized Crime in Labor, Business, and Money Laundering   307

Preface

Ever dynamic, organized crime continues to change, with efforts to combat one aspect of the phenomenon, the American Mafia, reaching high levels of prosecutorial success and a resulting decline in importance. Meanwhile, criminal organizations operating on a global scale have become more sophisticated and more threatening, and additional crime groups have been added to the pantheon we refer to as organized crime. This edition reflects changes that have occurred and updates information and analyses of organized crime and efforts to deal with it.

The decline in political order and deteriorating economic circumstances have led to a growing underground economy that habituates people to working outside the legal framework. Easy access to arms, the massive flow of emigrants and refugees, and the normal difficulties involved in accomplishing meaningful international cooperation are working to the advantage of criminal organizations. And the "rise of better-organized, internationally based criminal groups with vast financial resources is creating a new threat to the stability and security of international systems" (Godson and Olson 1995: 19). "Many international and transnational criminal organizations are continuing to expand their networks and links with other criminal organizations throughout the world, allowing the larger organizations to become increasingly powerful, technically sophisticated and global in their approach" (*INTERPOL at Work* 2003: 17). Added into this mix is the global problem of terrorism as organized crime and criminal organizations with political goals overlap.

ORGANIZATION

- *Chapter 1*, Introduction to Organized Crime, explores definitional issues related to organized crime and the structural characteristics of criminal organizations, *networking, credentialing, and brokerage*. The chapter looks at the differences and connections between terrorism and organized crime.

- *Chapter 2*, Development of Organized Crime in the United States shows how the success of the Robber Baron in amassing great fortunes via an "ends-justifies-the-means" credo paved the way for the criminal organizations that emerged out of Prohibition. The "incubator" provided by corrupt political machines aided development of these organizations. With repeal, national syndication remained enabling organized crime leaders to coordinate involvement in other areas of profit, from labor racketeering to drug trafficking.

- *Chapter 3*, The American Mafia examines the history and current state of Italian-American organized crime, focusing on two areas of strength: New York and Chicago.

- *Chapter 4*, Explaining Organized Crime examines relevant sociological, psychological, and biological theory in an effort to explain the existence of organized crime and its ability to continue despite societal changes and the concerted efforts of law enforcement.

- *Chapter 5*, Italian Organized Crime and the Albanian Connection begins with a discussion of Southern Italy followed by an examination of the *Mafia, Camorra, 'Ndrangheta*, and *Sacra Corona Unita* with its ties to Albania and war in the Balkans.

- *Chapter 6*, Latin American Organized Crime examines Colombian and Mexican criminal organizations—especially the upsurge of violence in Mexico—Dominican, Salvadoran (MS-13), and prison-based Latino criminal organizations.

- *Chapter 7*, Black Organized Crime examines West African, Jamaican, and African-American crime groups.

- *Chapter 8*, Asian Organized Crime discusses the yakuza of Japan, Chinese Triads, and related criminal organizations, domestic and international.

- *Chapter 9*, Russian Organized Crime, examines organized crime in both the former Soviet Union and émigré crime in the United States.

- *Chapter 10*, Outlaw Motorcycle Clubs explores the biker world and examines the most prominent of the outlaw clubs: Hell's Angels, Bandidos, Outlaws, Pagans, Mongols, and ties to the American Mafia.

- *Chapter 11*, Organized Crime: "Goods and Services" begins with a discussion of: "goods and services" or extortion? The chapter discusses illegal gambling, loansharking, theft, fencing, cyber-crime, and trafficking in persons, arms, and counterfeit products.

- *Chapter 12*, Organized Crime and Drug Trafficking examines the history of drugs of abuse in the United States and explores international and domestic drug trafficking, the mix of politics and foreign policy implications, and major source areas in Latin America, the Far East, and the Middle East.

- *Chapter 13*, Organized Crime in Labor, Business, and Money Laundering notes the pioneering role of labor racketeer Lepke Buchalter and examines both labor and business racketeering—often opposite sides of the same coin.

- *Chapter 14*, Organized Crime: Statutes examines and explains the primary statutes used against organized crime and the history that led to their enactment. Most important is Racketeer Influenced and Corrupt Organizations (RICO) section of the Organized Crime Control Act of 1970.

- *Chapter 15*, Organized Crime: Law Enforcement reviews problems inherent in responding to organized crime, and looks at all of the federal agencies that have responsibility for combating organized crime and their techniques.

NEW IN THIS EDITION

Each chapter in the 10th Edition now opens with a high-interest vignette to make the chapter material more relatable for students. Also included for the first time are chapter learning objectives, which are linked to comprehensive bullet-point summaries at the ends of chapters in addition to an extensive set of end-of-chapter review questions. Crucial chapter updates include the following:

- **Chapter 1.** The patron-client model has been replaced with a focus on *networking, credentialing, and brokerage* and there is an expansion of the differences between and the connection between terrorism and organized crime.

- **Chapter 2.** Combines and streamlines versions of Chapters 3 and parts of Chapter 4 from the ninth edition

- **Chapter 3.** Combines Chapters 4 and 5 from the ninth edition, reflecting the reduced importance of Italian-American organized crime, focusing on two areas of strength: Chicago and New York.

- **Chapter 4.** Biological theory has been added as part of the effort to explain organized crime and its participants.

- **Chapter 5.** Updated with an expanded discussion of Southern Italy, *Mafia, Camorra, 'Ndrangheta,* and *Sacra Corona Unita.* There is additional material on Albanian organized crime and its ties to the *Sacra Corona Unita* and war in the Balkans.

- **Chapter 6.** Material on Colombian and Mexican criminal organizations has been updated to reflect their current status and the significant upsurge in organized crime-related violence in Mexico.

- **Chapter 7.** Reorganized and updated material on West African, Jamaican, and African-American crime groups, especially Chicago's Black P. Stone Nation.

- **Chapter 8.** Updated with new information on Japanese and Chinese organized crime.

- **Chapter 9.** Reorganized and updated with new material on Russian organized crime in both the former Soviet Union and the United States.

- **Chapter 10.** Reorganized with a generic discussion of outlaw motorcycle clubs and then a discussion of the five most important clubs. Updated, with two outlaw clubs added: the Pagans, who have ties to the American Mafia, and the Mongols, an especially violent organization that has expanded rapidly with chapters inside and outside the United States.

- **Chapter 11.** Additional material on extortionate practices and deletion of material on horse-race bookmaking in favor of the far more popular sports betting; maintaining numbers gambling but deleting policy betting that is rare. Dated material has been deleted and the chapter contains additional material on cyber-crime, and, most importantly, trafficking in persons, as well as arms and counterfeit products. Statutes dealing with human trafficking are in Chapter 14.

- **Chapter 12.** Updates information on international and domestic drug trafficking; Oxycontin has been added.

- **Chapter 13.** Material on pioneering labor racketeer Lepke Buchalter has been moved from Chapter 4 in the 9/e. and new material on both labor and business racketeering has been added.

- **Chapter 14.** The Kefauver Committee, the McClellan Committee, the President's Commission on Law Enforcement and Administration of Justice, and the President's Commission on Organized Crime, have been moved from Chapter 3 in the 9/e, to this chapter, linking their efforts with subsequent legislation. The Sherman Anti-Trust Act and Landrum-Griffin Act have been added as well as additional material on drug trafficking statutes. Identity theft and related statutes have been added as well statutes dealing with human trafficking. Electronic surveillance statutes appear in this chapter while techniques and problems in electronic surveillance appear in Chapter 15.

- **Chapter 15.** Additional agencies have been added, such as the Treasury Department's *FinCen,* and the chapter now includes all federal agencies with a role in organized crime law enforcement.

ABOUT THE AUTHOR

Howard Abadinsky is professor of criminal justice at St. John's University. He was an inspector for the Cook County, Illinois, Sheriff for 8 years and a New York State parole officer and senior parole officer for 15 years. He is the founder of the International Association for the Study of Organized Crime and served as a consultant to the President's Commission on Organized Crime. The author has a B.A. from Queens College of the City University of New York, an M.S.W. from Fordham University, and a Ph.D. in sociology from New York University. He is the author of several books, including *The Criminal Elite: Professional and Organized Crime; The Mafia in America; Probation and Parole*, 11th edition; *Law and Justice*, 6th edition; and *Drug Use and Abuse*, 7th edition.

Caralyn Bishop-Abadinsky

Dr. Abadinsky encourages comments about his work and can be reached at St. John's University, 8000 Utopia Parkway, Jamaica, NY 11439; abadinsh@stjohns.edu.

Organized crime and terrorists interact in *Ciudad del Este*, Paraguay.   AP Photo/Jorge Saenz

Introduction to Organized Crime

"During the past 15 years, technological innovation and globalization have proven to be an overwhelming force for good. However, transnational criminal organizations have taken advantage of our increasingly interconnected world to expand their illicit enterprises.

"Criminal networks are not only expanding their operations, but they are also diversifying their activities, resulting in a convergence of transnational threats that has evolved to become more complex, volatile, and destabilizing. These networks also threaten U.S. interests by forging alliances with corrupt elements of national governments and using the power and influence of those elements to further their criminal activities. In some cases, national governments exploit these relationships to further their interests to the detriment of the United States."

—*President Barack Obama (National Security Council 2011: i).*

This chapter we will examine transnational organized crime that the president finds so problematic.

Conventional wisdom recognizes that garden variety conventional crime is different from *organized* crime; that Jesse James and Al Capone—criminals both—are remarkably different. The James Gang ended with Jesse's death in 1882, while the Capone organization (Chicago Outfit)—despite his imprisonment in 1932 and subsequent death as an invalid in 1947—is with us in the twenty-first century. Thus, *perpetuity* is a variable that can distinguish organized from conventional crime. While the crime portfolio of Jesse James and his ilk was rather limited (robbing banks, stagecoaches, and trains), "the criminality of persons in organized crime differs from that of conventional criminals because their organization allows them to commit crimes of a different variety [labor racketeering, for example] and on a larger scale [smuggling planeloads of cocaine, for example] than their less organized colleagues" (Moore 1987: 51). Organization permits a scope of activities unavailable to conventional criminals, while providing a vehicle for criminal interaction and coordination on a regional, national, and international level.

Attempts to define organized crime, however, have met with only limited success, and no generally accepted definition has emerged. While there is a great deal of discussion about organized crime groups and their activities, a review of the subject in the law enforcement and academic literature reveals it is difficult to determine what exactly is being discussed (Loree 2002).

The FBI defines organized crime as "any group having some manner of a formalized structure and whose primary objective is to obtain money through illegal activities. Such groups maintain their position through the use of actual or threatened violence, corrupt public officials, graft, or extortion, and generally have a significant impact on the people in their locales, region, or the country as a whole." The United Nations Convention Against Transnational Organised Crime (Article 2(a)) states that an "organised criminal group shall mean a structured group of three or more persons, existing for a period of time and acting in concert with the aim of committing one or more serious crimes or offences established in accordance with this Convention, in order to obtain, directly or indirectly, a financial or other material benefit."

ATTRIBUTES OF ORGANIZED CRIME

More than three decades ago, I began teaching in western North Carolina and noticed "dream books," which are publications associated with numbers gambling. The state had a religion-based conservative attitude toward gambling, and at the time permitted only bingo by nonprofits for modest prizes. (North Carolina established a lottery in 2005.) Through a friendship with the Asheville Chief of Police, I was given access to department gambling records and officers in the gambling enforcement unit. I also spoke to my students, many of whom were law enforcement officers. There was, indeed, an extensive bolita (a type of lottery) network throughout the county, and it had been operating for many years. *Organized crime or crime that is organized?* I discovered there had never been any violence associated with bolita. Even people who accumulated gambling debts that they failed to pay were not physically harmed or even threatened—they were blackballed, no longer permitted to play bolita. As we will see, instrumental violence is an essential feature of organized crime. In its absence, there can be crime that is organized, but not *organized crime*.

Although there is no generally accepted definition of organized crime, there are a number of attributes identified by law enforcement agencies and researchers as indicative of the phenomenon. Offering these attributes has a practical dimension: they provide a basis for determining if a particular group of criminals constitutes *organized crime* and, therefore, needs to be addressed in a way different from the way one would approach terrorists or groups of conventional criminals or a group of persons that forms for the immediate commission of a single offense.

Organized crime:

- Absence of political goals
- Is hierarchical
- Has a limited or exclusive membership
- Constitutes a unique subculture
- Perpetuates itself
- Exhibits a willingness to use illegal violence
- Is monopolistic
- Is governed by explicit rules and regulations

Let us examine each of these attributes.

1. *Absence of political goals.* The goals of an organized crime group are money and power whose procurement is not limited by legal or moral concerns. An organized crime group is not motivated by social doctrine, political beliefs, or ideological concerns. While political involvement may be part of the group's activities, the purpose is usually to gain protection or immunity for its illegal activities. This distinguishes organized crime from groups of persons who are organized and violating the law to further their political agenda, such as nationalist or terrorist groups. Organized crime members are not potential suicide bombers. Indeed, they typically find terrorism incomprehensible: Why would anyone take extreme risks without the prospect of personal financial gain? Why confront authorities instead of evading or corrupting them? (Bovenkerk and Chakra 2004).

A group whose primary goal is political or ideological may consider their mission no longer relevant and, rather than disband, become an organized crime group. A group, or simply some of its members, may find personal and pecuniary goals outweighing ideology and drift across the amorphous divide between political and organized crime, for example, violent groups in Northern Ireland supporting (loyalists) and opposing (republicans) British rule, or Marxist guerillas in Latin America. Like cars that can run on gas or electricity, a criminal organization may also be a hybrid; that is,

combine pecuniary crime with ideologically driven behavior (Dishman 2005).

2. *Hierarchical.* An organized crime group has a vertical power structure with at least three permanent ranks—not just a leader and followers—each with authority over the level beneath. The authority is inherent in the position and does not depend on who happens to be occupying it at any given time.

3. *Limited or exclusive membership.* An organized crime group significantly limits membership. Qualifications may include ethnic background, kinship, race, criminal record, or similar considerations. Those who meet the basic qualification(s) for membership usually require a sponsor, typically a ranking member, and must also prove qualified for membership by their behavior—for example, willingness to commit criminal acts, obey rules, follow orders, and maintain secrets. There is a period of apprenticeship that may range from several months to several years. If the group is to remain viable, there must be considerably more persons who desire membership than the organized crime group is willing to accept. Exclusivity of membership serves to indicate that belonging is indeed something to be valued.

While *membership* can refer to being part of a specific group, such as the Genovese Family or the Hell's Angels, it can also entail a more amorphous attachment to a criminal network (*underworld*), such as that which characterizes much Russian organized crime in the United States (discussed in Chapter 9). Membership indicators include bonding rituals such as initiation ceremonies and distinctive group icons on clothing, jewelry, and tattoos. In the absence of specific indicators, the question of membership can be viewed subjectively: Does the person view himself as being part of a particular criminal organization? Is the person recognized by others in the underworld as part of a criminal organization? Membership provides a basis for *credentialing,* discussed later.

In British Columbia, electronic surveillance revealed the well-established Hell's Angels (HA) expressing concern over a loosely organized criminal group called the "UN," as in United Nations, an apparent reference to its diverse membership. The HA wanted to know if the UN had any specific identifying markers, such jackets or tattoos, indicating membership. If they did, in the opinion of the HA, that would make the UN a more formidable competitor in the drug business. (A UN logo eventually appeared on clothing and jewelry of members. In 2009, the reputed leader of the UN was sentenced in a Seattle federal court to thirty years imprisonment for cross-border drug trafficking.)

4. *Constitutes a unique subculture.* Members of organized crime frequently view themselves as distinct from conventional society, which they typically view with derision if not contempt, and therefore not subject to its rules. A group structured around various not necessarily criminal dynamics (e.g., military, athletic) may develop into a criminal organization when members come to realize that the application of their resources, such as instrumental violence, offers a source of considerable income.

There is a "Chicken-or-the-egg, which came first?" dimension. For example, during Prohibition (1920–1933), did a criminal subculture develop around bootlegging, or did members of an existing criminal subculture enter the trade? Or both? In either event, a subcultural base provides the flexibility necessary for criminal entrepreneurs to switch enterprises. For example, after repeal of Prohibition, bootleggers moved to drug trafficking and labor racketeering.

5. *Perpetuates itself.* An organized crime group constitutes an ongoing conspiracy designed to persist through time, that is, beyond the life of the current membership. Permanence is assumed by the members, and this provides an important basis for attracting qualified persons, thus perpetuating the group's existence. The strength of this attribute often depends on the depth of the subcultural orientation manifested by the group. Cressey (1969: 263) states that in order for an organized crime group to survive, it must have "an institutionalized process for inducting new members and inculcating them with the values and ways of behaving of the social

system." American Mafia groups in many cities ceased to be viable when they could no longer interest young males of Italian heritage to enter their ranks, while the outlaw biker subculture remains strong, providing sufficient numbers to ensure continuity.

6. *Willingness to use illegal violence.* In an organized crime group, violence is a readily available and routinely accepted resource. Access to private violence is an important dimension that allows the group to actively pursue its goals. The use of violence is not restricted by ethical considerations but controlled only by practical limitations.

7. *Monopolistic.* An organized crime group eschews competition. It strives for hegemony over a particular geographic area (a metropolitan area or section of a city), a particular "industry," legitimate or illegitimate (for example, gambling, drug trafficking), or a combination of both (for example, loansharking in a particular area or the wholesale cocaine market in a city). A monopoly, of course, restrains "free trade" and increases profits. An organized crime monopoly is maintained by violence, by the threat of violence, or by corrupt relationships with law enforcement officials. A combination of both methods, violence and corruption, may be employed.

Although an organized crime group may strive for a monopoly, this may not be possible given the nature of competing groups or the type of industry, for example, drug trafficking. In 1995, when Maurice ("Mom") Boucher, head of Nomads chapter of the Montreal Hell's Angels, attempted to assert control over the city's drug market, he encountered a serious impediment—Vito Rizzuto, a Bonnano crime Family captain with his own murderous Montreal crew. Given the danger of conflict, Boucher chose diplomacy and negotiated a deal with Rizzuto (Lamothe and Humphreys 2006).

Moreover, territoriality is more closely associated with localness rather than the broader reach of transnational criminal organizations (Reuter and Petrie 1999). In Chapter 6, for example, we will examine Mexican organizations that, although associated with a particular geographic area (for instance, the "Juárez cartel"), do not expend resources defending geographic hegemony—they do use extreme violence to assert control over transshipment points.

8. *Governed by rules and regulations.* An organized crime group, like a legitimate organization, has a set of rules and regulations that members are expected to obey. In organized crime, however, a rule-violating member is not fired but, more likely, fired upon.

Were one forced to limit a definition of organized crime to only *two* variables, they would be: *nonideological* and *instrumental violence.*

These attributes are arrayed in a structure that enables the criminal organization to achieve its goals—money and power. A criminal group will pass through stages of development (Gottschalk 2009), and, if sufficiently stable, at some point mature into an organization with most, if not all, of these attributes. A number of criminal organizations have many, if not all, of the attributes that have been discussed. Some are domestic, while most examined in this book are transnational in scope or have important organizational or business ties overseas. Some have links to terrorism. While some (e.g., Albanese 2011) object to distinguishing criminal organizations on the basis of ethnicity, members of criminal organizations often share an ethnic identity. This could be the result of geographic proximity or kinship, but "birds of a feather" do tend to flock together, and it is not unusual for criminals, organized or not, to refer to criminal organizations in ethnic terms.

Organized Crime as a Bureaucracy

The corporation, the police, and the military are examples of bureaucracies, that is, a mode of organization essential for efficiently carrying out large-scale tasks. All bureaucracies are rational organizations sharing a number of attributes:

- A complicated hierarchy
- An extensive division of labor
- Positions assigned on the basis of competence

- Responsibilities carried out in an impersonal manner
- Extensive written rules and regulations
- Communication from the top of the hierarchy to persons on the bottom via a chain of command

As an entity, club, business, or criminal organization continues to expand, at some point it needs to adopt the bureaucratic style of organization. For example, a "mom and pop grocery" need not have any of the attributes of a bureaucracy. The owners and workers are related, and the structure is informal and kinship-based. If the business expands—the owners establish many groceries—a formal hierarchy becomes necessary, as do skilled persons and a division of labor: there will be written rules and regulations dealing with such matters as work hours, sick leave, vacation time, and manner of dress, and directives will be transmitted via the hierarchy. As the distance between the hierarchy and its agents increases, the ability to monitor agents decreases—they could engage in embezzlement and/or behave in ways likely to attract law enforcement attention, to which they may respond by becoming informants (Varese 2011).

A criminal organization structured along bureaucratic lines has inherent weaknesses:

- Communication from top management to operational-level personnel can be intercepted.
- Generating and maintaining written records endangers the entire organization.
- Successful infiltration at the upper level can jeopardize the entire organization.
- Death or incarceration of command personnel can leave dangerous gaps in operations.
- The absence of personal ties makes betrayal more likely.

That explains why, in contrast to the bureaucratic ideal, criminal organizations generally prize loyalty over competence.

Many aspects of bureaucracy are impractical for criminal organizations because they must be concerned with the very real possibility that communications are being monitored. The use of the telephone must be limited (often only to arrange for in-person meetings), and written communication is to be avoided. Information, as well as orders, money, and other goods, is more secure when transmitted on an intimate, face-to-face basis. Lengthy chains of command, a characteristic of modern bureaucracy, are impractical for criminal organizations, and this limits the span of control. Randall Collins (1975) points out that control is a special problem for which bureaucracies develop to overcome. Joseph Albini (1971: 285) notes that the bureaucratic model would be a relatively easy target to move against: "All that would be necessary to destroy it would be to remove its top echelon." The need to exercise effective command and control over a far-flung criminal enterprise "is the feature that law enforcement can use against them, turning their strength into a weakness. The communications structure of international organized crime operating in the United States is, therefore,

the prime target for drug law enforcement" (Marshall 1999: 5).

Compartmentalization. These deficiencies can be offset by the use of a compartmentalized form of bureaucracy (see Figure 1.1), wherein persons at the operational/street level are organized into cells and know only other members of their cell. In some criminal organizations, cell members may not even know for whom they are working. If a cell is lost as the result of law enforcement infiltration, for example, the organization can continue to function uninterrupted and the cell is eventually replaced. Cells are bundled under the direction of a controller who is not in direct contact with and may not even know the other controllers. A controller who is lost is quickly replaced by the central command operating out of an area of relative safety, such as another country.

A criminal organization can manifest a bureaucratic structure with ranks and levels of authority,

Central command: Located in a relatively safe haven, the central command oversees and coordinates operations through the controllers.

Controller: Responsible for overall operations of the several cells within a region, the controller reports to central command via cell phone or Internet.

Cell: Compartmentalization involves cells with about ten members, each operating independently—members of one cell typically do not know members of other cells. Operating within a geographic area, the head of each cell reports directly to a controller.

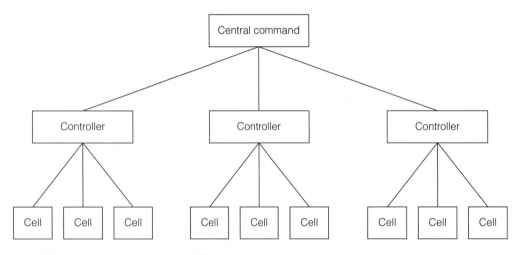

F I G U R E 1.1 Compartmentalized Criminal Organization

VALUE OF A BAD REPUTATION

Police in Vancouver, Canada, in a surveillance van watched a line of parked motorcycles outside a bar. Some bikes had the logo of the Hell's Angels and on one of those sat a fat wallet with a broken chain attached. They watched as people walked by, glanced at the bikes and the wallet, and moved on. Several hours later, when the owner of the bike appeared, the wallet was still there, undisturbed.

---

while economic activities may be divorced from the formal structure. In such cases, every member of the organization can have a slot on the "company chart" while their business activities are independent, conducted solo or in partnerships with members and nonmember associates, and not dependent on the formal structure. In these instances, the member is an independent entrepreneur who may have financial and other obligations to the organization—for example, aiding members in conflict with outsiders—but his income-generating activities are not under direction of the hierarchy. He enjoys a *franchise*, a grant of authority to engage in business activity under the aegis of the organization, such as the Hell's Angels or the Gambino Family.

Franchise/Credentialing

Franchise provides a sense of entitlement and *credentials* that enable the possessor to engage in criminal activity knowing that he will be supported and protected by the franchisor—the criminal organization granting the franchise. He will be protected from other criminals and have access to the network in which the organization is embedded. He will be able to traverse the criminal underworld in relative safety.

Criminals who are part of a recognizable (by other criminals) organization have the credentials necessary to negotiate transactions those without an organizational affiliation would find difficult if not impossible to accomplish. Some organizations use "trademarks" to confirm membership, such as the death head logo of the Hell's Angels, which is in fact a registered trademark. Unauthorized use of a trademark can be painful (forcible removal of a death head tattoo) or even fatal. Russian *vory* and Japanese *yakuza* use similar trademarks.

In the dangerous and anarchic world of crime, organizational affiliation provides a form of *credentialing* by reputation, encouraging networking that facilitates cooperation between criminals that might not otherwise occur. The willingness of criminals to cooperate requires a level of trust that can explain the need for bonding rituals used by groups as diverse as the Mafia, Triads, *vory*, and outlaw motorcycle clubs (von Lampe and Johansen 2004). Credentialing promotes business relationships between criminals who do not enjoy a history of interaction; locally, for example, members of outlaw motorcycle clubs and the American Mafia, or globally, for example, Russian criminal organizations and Latin American drug cartels.

In the Hobbesian world inhabited by criminals, the member of an organization with sufficient martial capacity—the *value of a bad reputation*—can offer services typically reserved for government such as contract enforcement and adjudication of disputes. Indeed, the degree of sophistication characterizing a criminal organization can be measured by the degree to which members provide contract and arbitration services to criminals and sometimes legitimate entrepreneurs looking for a swifter, more reliable form of justice. In places where the legal system places onerous burdens on plaintiffs, such as Russia and Japan, the collection of legitimate debts is frequently contracted out to members of criminal organizations whose reputation for violence can expedite the collection process.

Credentialing also permits members of a criminal organization to enforce extralegal social norms ranging from restraining boisterous behavior to requiring a young man to marry the

POINT OF CONVERGENCE

The bar on Roosevelt Avenue in the Jackson Heights section of the New York City borough of Queens was a few blocks from the apartment house where I lived; it was known as a place for "Mafia types." The bar was crowded when three strangers entered and the bartender asked what he might serve them. They drew handguns and announced a holdup. The bartender asked them to remain calm and offered the money in his register—everyone paid cash in this bar. One of the men took the cash and then decided to rob the customers. He gave his handgun to a confederate and moved toward the closest customer, order-ing him to hand over his wallet. The customer, his hands raised, let go a powerful punch that knocked the robber to the floor—and all hell broke loose. Guns appeared and bullets started flying—in the direction of the remaining robbers, one of whom was felled by the gunfire. In the chaos, the bartender locked the front door so when the third robber sought to exit, he did so by jumping through a plate glass window. The police followed a bloody trail and he was arrested. The bartender opened the door for the officers who found two men, one with bullet wounds, the other with broken bar stools covering his lifeless body.

young lady he impregnated. In Chicago, when the police failed to adequately respond to complaints about reckless driving by young men in the Grand Avenue section, several residents went to see their neighbor "Judge Joey," Joseph ("The Clown") Lombardo. This ranking member of the Outfit resolved the problem with a few carefully chosen words to the young men. In British Columbia, the son of a female friend of a member of the Hell's Angels was being harassed by a gang of students at his high school. Wearing the full regalia of the Hell's Angels, the member visited the school and explained there was a choice: the principal could do something about the matter or the Hell's Angel would. The principal sent for the gang members, whom he introduced to the Hell's Angel. The harassment quickly ended.

Criminal Networks and Brokers

A network consists of a collection of connected points or junctures. A criminal network typically functions within a subcultural environment—an "underworld"—whose habitués range from members of criminal groups to persons with marginal employment (e.g., bouncers at sex-oriented establishments, professional gamblers) to a variety of part- and full-time criminals with varying degrees of skill and success. There may be "knock-around guys" who, while not routinely involved in crime, are not averse to criminal opportunity, such as trafficking in stolen property. The subcultural environment also contains persons who are ostensibly legitimate but enjoy frequenting places "on the wild side."

A criminal network has *points of convergence* where participants congregate. "Hangouts," or places that welcome their patronage—bars, restaurants, social clubs, nightclubs, gyms—may be owned or under the control of criminal entrepreneurs. Some locations may cater to a particular subculture, such as a "biker bar." While they serve primarily as places for socialization, hangouts provide opportunity to advance business interests.

The subculture contains gaps between persons with complementary resources and information. They require a third party: a broker who, typically for remuneration, can fill the gap by constructing a "social bridge" and connecting otherwise isolated individuals (Xia 2008). The role of a broker is enhanced if he is properly credentialed and can thereby provide an umbrella of protection and act as a guarantor (akin to title insurance in real estate) for a transaction. Thus the New Jersey crime Family captain remained outside of his house while the individuals he had introduced (a thief with valuable merchandise and a businessman in a position to profitably dispose of the merchandise) negotiated. Each understood that they would be bound by whatever was agreed upon: to do otherwise would raise the ire of the guarantor and likely be fatal.

"The difficulties identifying partners," notes Diego Gambetta (2009: 6) "keep much potential crime at bay. Making identification is arguably the most powerful deterrent against crime that the force of law brings about, by discouraging the countless dormant criminals who refrain from acting unlawfully for fear of being caught when searching or advertising." A person with information of value to professional burglars or hijackers, such as the employee of an insurance firm, a warehouse worker or teamster with information about expensive electrical equipment, could not ordinarily make profitable use of this information. The credentialed criminal can serve as the "yellow pages," acting as a catalyst for a great deal of crime that in his absence is unlikely to occur.

Criminal network participants have ties to conventional persons, parents, siblings, other relatives, or neighbors. The criminal network extends into conventional society, linking the criminal and the legitimate, often via a broker with ties to both "worlds," as in this vignette from New York City.

He owned two factories, one modern and efficient, the other antiquated and a drain on his profits. Unable to sell it for a reasonable amount, he recognized that the best possible outcome would be for the inefficient factory to experience a fire for which he could collect insurance. But, he was a businessman, not an arsonist.

In a casual conversation with his employees' union representative, he expressed a wish for a factory fire. The rep replied that such wishes could be made to come true—was he interested? An affirmative reply set in motion a connect between the otherwise legitimate businessman and the criminal network of the union rep. He contacted a member of the Genovese crime Family who through his network was able to provide a "torch," a professional arsonist. The scheme also required a professional burglar who could enable the arsonist to gain entrance into the factory without tripping an alarm. The Genovese member was able to team up the arsonist with a professional burglar. While his imprimatur enabled the scheme, the Genovese

member who made the referrals avoided direct contact with the criminal participants and left the businessman to explain their assignments. The factory burned to the ground leaving no evidence of arson, allowing its owner to collect insurance and pay an agreed upon fee to the participants, a percentage of which was given to the Genovese Family boss who played no role in the scheme.

TRANSNATIONAL ORGANIZED CRIME AND TERRORISM

"Changes in the global economy and in international political alignments have greatly benefited the criminal underworld" (Viano, Magallanes, and Bridel 2003: 3). Unprecedented openness in trade, finance, travel, and communication has created economic growth and wellbeing; it has also given rise to massive opportunities for criminal organizations (UNODC 2010). "The traditional Mafia type organization—which is linked to its territory and which exercises pressing control over the entities in its territory by means of intimidation and extortion tactics—has gradually expanded to include new opportunities deriving from the globalization of markets and the widespread distribution of technologies" (Patrignani 2009: 64). A hierarchical structure linked to a specific territory will be unable to implement in an optimal manner the tasks required for large-scale drug, arms, and human trafficking. This has spurred the growth alliances with criminal groups operating across national boundaries.

The collapse of the Soviet Union was a pivotal historical event that intertwined with the rapid expansion of global markets—"money, goods and people have circulated with a rapidity and facility which were once unthinkable…. Whether in the developed or in the developing world, criminal organizations' scope of action and range of capabilities are undergoing a profound change" (Violante 2000: x). Furthermore, note Roy Godson and William Olson (1995: 19), the decline in political order and deteriorating economic circumstances

TRANSNATIONAL ORGANIZED CRIME (TOC)

Transnational organized crime refers to those self-perpetuating associations of individuals who operate transnationally for the purpose of obtaining power, influence, and monetary or commercial gains, wholly or in part by illegal means, while protecting their activities through a pattern of corruption and/or violence, or while protecting their illegal activities through a transnational organizational structure and the exploitation of transnational commerce or communication mechanisms. There is no single structure under which transnational organized criminals operate; they vary from hierarchies to clans, networks, and cells, and may evolve to other structures. The crimes they commit also vary. Transnational organized criminals act conspiratorially in their criminal activities and possess the following characteristics:

- In at least part of their activities they commit violence or other acts which are likely to intimidate, or make actual or implicit threats to do so.

- They exploit differences between countries to further their objectives, enriching their organization, expanding its power, and/or avoiding detection or apprehension.
- They attempt to gain influence in government, politics, and commerce through corrupt as well as legitimate means.
- They have economic gain as their primary goal, not only from patently illegal activities but also from investment in legitimate businesses.
- They attempt to insulate both their leadership and membership from detection, sanction, and/or prosecution through their organizational structure.

(National Security Council 2011: ii)

---

have led to a growing underground economy that habituates people to working outside the legal framework. Easy access to arms, the massive flow of emigrants and refugees, and the normal difficulties involved in accomplishing meaningful international cooperation are working to the advantage of criminal organizations. And the "rise of better-organized, internationally-based criminal groups with vast financial resources is creating a new threat to the stability and security of international systems."

Chapter 2 will show how Prohibition acted as a catalyst for the unprecedented mobilization of criminal organizations and the cooperative ventures of syndication. The international trade in liquor altered the heretofore local scope of most criminal organizations, whetting the appetite for further innovative opportunities and fueling the trade in heroin. The expanded capacity of contemporary criminal organizations derives from intensification of goods traditionally traded by organized crime, in particular, drugs, arms, and sex workers. In each case, the country of destination is different from that of its origins. Consignments transit across national boundaries and

even oceans. As is the case with legitimate trade, arrangements need to be made that involve the use of banks, finance houses, and customs formalities, and require ongoing relationships with criminal organizations of different countries. "These commercial necessities have created solid international relations between all of the most dangerous criminal organizations" (Violante 2000: ix). The new face of organized crime, notes Angela Patrinani, (2009: 65), "is increasingly similar to a transnational commercial company combining rigid hierarchies and territorial rooting with flexible structures that are easily adaptable to changing circumstances. Commercial specialization has been repudiated in favor of the simultaneous trade and supply of different categories of illegal goods and services."

Migration, legal or illegal, broadens the reach of existing criminal networks. Although most migrants, including many of those who enter their destination country illegally, are generally law-abiding, among them are inevitably affiliates of a variety of criminal networks. "These people bring with them their crime-related skills and knowledge as well as their criminal contacts. Chinese, Nigerian, Italian and Russian groups are well-known examples of network proliferation through migration" (UNODC 2010: 34).

The globalization of organized crime created a nexus with terrorism. "In years past, TOC was largely regional in scope, hierarchically structured, and had only occasional links to terrorism. Today's criminal networks are fluid, striking new alliances with other networks around the world and engaging in a wide range of illicit activities, including cybercrime and providing support for terrorism" (*Strategy to Combat Transnational Organized Crime* 2011: 3).

Just as there is no accepted definition of organized crime, *terrorism* also defies a universally accepted definition. Indeed, "many definitions of terrorism are, in fact, encoded political statements" (Combs 2003: 7). Title 22 of the *United States Code*, section 2656f(d), defines terrorism as "premeditated, politically motivated violence perpetrated against noncombatant targets by subnational groups or clandestine agents, usually intended to influence an audience." The Federal Bureau of Investigation defines terrorism as "the unlawful use of force or violence against persons or property to intimidate or coerce a government, the civilian population, or any segment thereof, in furtherance of political or social objectives."

As opposed to organized crime, terrorism is inherently political, and as such it is relative to one's political view. Because the term is pejorative, terrorism is a label most likely to be attached to the violent activities of political opponents. One person's terrorist is another person's freedom fighter: The British view of George Washington in contrast with that of revolutionary Americans. Terrorists are nonstate actors whose intention is to "intimidate an audience larger than their immediate victims, in the hope of generating widespread panic and, often, a response from the enemy so brutal that it ends up backfiring by creating sympathy for the terrorists' cause. Their targets are often ordinary civilians, and even when terrorists are trying to kill soldiers, their attacks often don't take place on the field of battle" (Lehmann 2001: 73).

There is also confusion over the terms *terror* and *terrorism:* "The object of military force, for example, is to strike terror into the heart of the enemy, and systematic terror has been a basic weapon in conflicts throughout history" (White 2006: 3). While the tactics of terrorists can appear to be the same as those of military action, such as bombings and hostage taking, their targets are frequently noncombatants. (Of course, the same can be said of the nuclear bombs dropped on Japanese cities in 1945.) For the terrorist, injury to the innocent "is not an undesirable accident or by-product [euphemistically called "collateral damage"], but the carefully sought consequence of a terrorist act" (Combs 2003: 12).

Terrorists often choose their targets at random and thus there are few if any precautions potential victims can take. They exploit noncombatant deaths as a means to advertise their cause. Terrorists do not expect governments to capitulate; indeed, their activities are frequently designed to elicit an overreaction that will aid in winning hearts and minds (Danner 2005). Although a number of American Mafia Families probably benefited from the building of the World Trade Center, they were not looking to advertise their role or make a political statement. And with the exception of Colombia, "rarely do the large established crime organizations link with terrorist groups, because their long-term financial interests require the preservation of state structures" (Shelley et al. 2005: 1). Indeed, many traditional organized crime groups are politically quite conservative and supportive of their host governments, for example, Japanese *yakuza* (discussed in Chapter 8), Sicilian Mafia (discussed in Chapter 5), and the American Mafia (discussed in Chapter 3). The infamous Medellín drug cartel in Colombia used terrorist tactics in their battle with the Marxist revolutionary group known as M-19.

However defined, the various categories of terrorism may overlap, whether they are domestic or international, left- or right-wing, separatist or religious. The Ku Klux Klan and other hate groups, self-styled militia groups, and survivalists are domestic and right wing, while right-wing

"Skinheads" and Neo-Nazis are active in Europe. The Weather Underground in the United States used violence during the 1970s to express left-wing views, while the Red Army did the same in Germany, Italy, and Japan; and the separatist *Euzkadita Askatasuna* (ETA) uses violence against Spain in an effort to establish a Marxist independent Basque state. Al-Qaeda is the best-known example of a religious and international terrorist group whose activities often begin in one country and take place in another.

There are also terrorists that defy easy categorization, such as "ecoterrorists" of the Earth Liberation Front and Animal Liberation Front who use violence to promote animal rights and preserve wilderness. Some observers refer to state-sponsored terrorism to describe such events as the Khmer Rouge slaughter in Cambodia during the 1970s, the Serbian militia massacres of Muslim men and rape of Muslim women in Bosnia during the 1990s, and the massacres of Tutsis by government-supported Hutus militias in Rwanda during the 1990s. But terrorism can be carried out by a single person, such as Ted Kaczynski ("The Unabomber"), who was arrested in 1996, while organized crime by definition requires organization.

In some parts of the world, such as the Balkans, breakaway areas of the former Soviet Union, and Latin America, organized crime and terrorist organizations share the same geography (usually conflict zones), and membership can overlap with individuals belonging to both terrorist and organized crime groups (Shelley et al. 2005). Criminal networks and terrorist networks may be or become intertwined, as in *Ciudad del Este*.

Ciudad del Este (CDE), or "City of the East," provides a microcosm of the nexus between organized crime and terrorism. This remote Paraguayan city is the center of a triborder area with Brazil and Argentina where border controls barely exist—a free trade zone for contraband infested with criminals and terrorists. Originally a village, this rapidly expanding city of some 250,000 people was developed under the military dictatorship of Julius Stroessner (1954–1989),

AP Photo/Jorge Saenz

Moussa Hamdan arrested in Ciudad del Este in 2010 for financing Hezbollah terrorist activities.

who turned Paraguay into a haven for fugitives, including Nazi war criminals (Shelley et al. 2005). "*Ciudad del Este* is an oasis for informants and spies; peddlers of contraband (largely cheap East Asian goods) and counterfeit products; traffickers in drugs, weapons, and humans (prostitutes, including women and children forced into prostitution); common criminals; mafia organizations; and undocumented Islamic terrorists" (Hudson 2010: 10).

Organized crime groups of all types thrive in the triborder area. It is a meeting place for the *yakuza* (discussed in Chapter 8) as well as Colombian and other Latin American crime groups (discussed in Chapter 6) who pass illegal drugs through the area on their way to the ports of Brazil, Argentina, and Uruguay, and then into the United States and Europe. Chinese Triads such as the Fuk Ching, Big Circle Boys, and Flying Dragons (discussed in Chapter 8) are well established and believed to be the main force behind organized crime in the area (Shelley et al. 2005).

CDE is also a center of operations for several terrorist groups, including al-Qaeda, Hezbollah, Islamic Jihad, Gamaa Islamiya, and FARC (discussed in Chapter 6). Lebanon-based Hizballah clearly derives a quite substantial amount of income from its various illicit activities in CDE (Hudson 2003). Although local structures used by both terrorist and criminal organizations may overlap, cooperation is ad hoc. "There is no indication of any significant organizational overlap between criminal and terrorist groups" (Shelley et al. 2005: 61).

In some cases, terrorists imitate the organized criminal behavior they see around them, borrowing techniques. This can lead to more intimate connections, particularly in places of poor governance, ethnic separatism, or a tradition of criminal activity, such as in failed states, war regions, prisons, and some urban neighborhoods (Shelley and Picarelli 2005). "It is not particularly uncommon for terrorist groups to recruit some of their members among criminal elements, particularly among individuals who may have special skills or common criminals who can contribute to its goals in instrumental, training, and other matters" (Préfontaine and Dandurand 2004: 16). Terrorist and organized criminal groups share some attributes, in particular, organizational structure such as compartmentalization. Terrorist groups and criminal organizations often have similar requirements for moving people, money, and matériel across borders and often operate under a similar set of contingencies. Terrorists are increasingly turning to criminal networks to generate funding and acquire logistical support (*Strategy to Combat Transnational Organized Crime* 2011).

FBI Director Robert S. Mueller, III (2011) notes the link between transnational organized crime and terrorism. "If a terrorist cannot obtain a passport, for example, he will find someone who can. Terrorists may turn to street crime—and, by extension, organized crime—to raise money, as did the 2004 Madrid bombers. Organized criminals have become 'service providers.' Could a Mexican group move a terrorist across the border? Could an Eastern European enterprise sell a Weapon of Mass Destruction to a terrorist cell? Likely, yes. Criminal enterprises are motivated by money, not ideology. But they have no scruples about helping those who are, for the right price."

In 2007, Italian investigators confirmed a disturbing trend: the growing link between terrorism and organized crime. They revealed that al Quaeda was using the Neapolitan Camorra, with its extensive network and expertise in forging documents, to move its operatives through Europe to safe houses in such cities as Paris, London, Berlin, and Madrid. If trouble arises, Camorra's alliances enable al Quaeda operatives to exit Naples via one of the many trains leaving the city's main station, or via speedboats—the same vessels the Camorra uses to traffic cigarettes, drugs, and other contraband (Chepesiuk 2007).

Yury Fedotov, Executive Director of the United Nations Office on Drugs and Crime (UNODC), points out: "Today, the criminal market spans the planet, and in many instances criminal profits support terrorist groups. Globalization has turned out to be a double-edged sword. Open borders, open markets, and increased ease of travel and communication have benefited both terrorists and criminals. Thanks to advances in technology, communication, finance and transport, loose networks of terrorists and organized criminal groups that operate internationally can easily link with each other. By pooling their resources and expertise, they can significantly increase their capacity to do harm" (From UNODC Press release, March 16, 2011. Reprinted by permission of the United Nations Secretariat, Publications.).

Once terrorists and other criminals start to work together, they naturally begin to buy and sell services and goods from each other. It is more efficient to outsource a service (such as passport forgery) to an established specialist than to try to master the necessary techniques. If these business relationships progress beyond individual transactions, in the next stage the two groups begin working together more regularly and begin to share each other's goals as well as working methods. A symbiotic relationship, as seen in the Russian region of Chechnya, discussed in Chapter 9, develops where there is no hard-and-fast line between Chechen organized crime and Chechen rebels fighting a terrorist war against Russian sovereignty over their homeland (Shelley and Picarelli 2005). The Albanian Kosovo Liberation Army (KLA) in the former Yugoslavia forged links with drug traffickers and international criminals, then used these connections, as well as contributions from Albanian emigrant communities abroad, to fund its paramilitary campaign against Serbian authorities.

Although the Revolutionary Armed Forces of Colombia (FARC)–controlled safe haven, or *despeje*, is situated between two of Colombia's largest coca cultivation areas, it is not considered a major area for coca cultivation or drug trafficking. Many FARC units throughout southern Colombia raise funds through the extortion ("taxation") of both legal and illegal businesses, the latter including the drug trade (discussed in Chapters 6 and 12). Similarly, in return for cash payments, or possibly in exchange for weapons, some units protect cocaine laboratories and clandestine airstrips in southern Colombia. FARC units may be independently involved in limited cocaine laboratory operations, and some are more directly involved in local drug trafficking activities, such as controlling cocaine base markets. At least one prominent FARC commander has served as a source of cocaine for a Brazilian trafficking organization. FARC cocaine was also shipped to the Hell's Angels in Amsterdam via Curacao in the Dutch Antilles (Sher and Marsden 2006).

Taliban insurgents in Afghanistan have been using heroin to finance their efforts. In 2005, Afghan drug lord Baz Mohammad was extradited to the United States, where he is accused of heading an organization that controlled poppy fields in Afghanistan, heroin-processing plants in Pakistan, and a trafficking network that smuggled millions of dollars worth of drugs into the United States. In partnership with the Taliban, Mohammad told supporters they would be committing jihad by selling heroin to Americans (Zambito 2005b; McFadden 2005). A tribal warlord allied with the Taliban, Bashir Noorzai, was tricked into traveling to New York where in 2005 he was arrested and, in 2008, convicted of smuggling $50 million dollars worth of heroin into the United States (Associated Press 2008a).

In Southeast Asia's Golden Triangle, there is a long-standing tradition of using heroin trafficking to support insurgencies (discussed in Chapter 12). According to the Director of the Office of National Drug Control Policy: "Almost half of the State Department's list of known terrorist organizations are known to have, at one point or another, trafficked in drugs" (Walters 2003: 9). This gives rise to the term *narcoterrorism,* terrorist acts carried out by groups directly or indirectly involved in cultivating, manufacturing, transporting, or distributing illegal drugs. The links between terrorist organizations and drug traffickers can take many forms, ranging from facilitation, protection, transportation, and taxation, to direct trafficking by the terrorist organization itself in order to finance its activities. Traffickers and terrorists have similar logistical needs in terms of matériel and the covert movement of goods, people, and money.

Relationships between drug traffickers and terrorists are mutually beneficial. Drug traffickers gain from access to terrorists' military skills and weapons supply; terrorists gain a source of revenue and expertise in illicit transfer and laundering of proceeds. Both bring corrupt officials whose services provide mutual benefits, such as greater access to fraudulent documents, including passports and customs papers. Drug traffickers may also gain considerable freedom of movement when they operate in conjunction with terrorists who control large amounts of territory (Beers and Taylor 2002).

Elyssa Pachico (2011: 2) points out that the fight against terrorism and that against organized crime have important parallels and overlaps. In Latin America, for example, "politically motivated groups like the FARC are increasingly taking on the characteristics of criminal gangs, while organized criminal groups, most notably Mexico's cartels, are threatening the state and carrying out such large-scale attacks that some describe them as insurgent."

THE NUCLEAR CONNECTION

There is concern that organized crime groups, particularly Russian criminal organizations, have become involved in smuggling nuclear material that they are willing to sell to the highest bidder. However, few actual cases of sale of nuclear contraband have been recorded in the former Soviet Union or in the West, and even fewer of them involved the confiscation of material that could actually be used to make nuclear weapons (Préfontaine and Dandurand 2004). Indeed, trafficking in bogus radioactive materials is a scam perpetrated by Russian criminal groups (Varese 2011).

Organized Crime and Terrorism: Similarities and Dissimilarities

Like Colombian drug cartels, terrorist groups are frequently organized along compartmentalized lines. Similar to Italian and Asian organized crime groups, terrorist organizations such as al-Qaeda use sponsorships, apprenticeships, and initiation ceremonies. Like organized crime, terrorist groups have a need to launder their financial assets. The Provisional Irish Republican Army, for example, is reported to have become expert at money laundering through a portfolio of front businesses in Belfast (Chrisafis 2005).

"Roughly speaking, politically motivated groups are interested in the subversion of the status quo, while criminally motivated ones have an important stake in maintaining it, so that they can keep operating" (Kolliarakis 2010: 92). The differences between terrorist organizations and organized crime groups rest on means and ends. While both engage in organized criminal activity to support themselves, terrorists use their funds to further political ends, to overthrow governments and impose their worldview. Organized crime instead seeks to form a parallel government while coexisting with the existing one. Organized crime groups are not motivated by an ideology, while terrorist groups try to give their activities an altruistic aura to justify their acts and to solicit people's sympathy for their cause. Frank Hagan (2006) refers to this as *political* crime, committed for ideological purposes. Organized crime groups prefer to carry out their activities secretly, while terrorists seek to maximize media coverage and to promote their message and publicize their goals. While organized crime groups typically place significant restrictions on membership, terrorists actively recruit and typically enjoy sympathy from a segment of the population that identifies with their goals. Thus, whether an individual is a patriot or a terrorist is not a relevant issue with respect to organized crime.

Terrorist groups and drug trafficking organizations often rely on cell structures to accomplish their respective goals. This enhances security by providing a degree of separation between the leadership and the rank and file. In addition, terrorists and drug traffickers use similar means to conceal profits and fund-raising. They use informal transfer systems such as "hawala" (discussed in Chapter 13), and also rely on bulk cash smuggling, multiple accounts, and front organizations to launder money. Both make use of fraudulent documents such as passports and other identification to smuggle goods and weapons. Both fully exploit their networks of trusted couriers and contacts to conduct business. To increase communications security they use multiple cell phones and encrypted emails and are careful about what they say on the phone. The methods used for moving and laundering money for general criminal purposes are similar to those used to move money to support terrorist activities. Countries and jurisdictions with poorly regulated banking structures allow both terrorist organizations and drug trafficking groups to use online transfers and accounts that do not require disclosure of owners (Beers and Taylor 2002).

One striking dissimilarity is the suicide bomber frequently used by Jihadist terrorists—unlikely (understatement) to be used by organized crime. A radical British Muslim is quoted as saying: "Even if my own family were killed by a Jihadist bomb, I would say it is the will of Allah" (Powell 2005: 56). "Organized crime's business is business. The less attention brought to their lucrative enterprises, the better. The goal of terrorism is quite the opposite. A wide-ranging public profile is often the desired effect" (Cilluffo 2000: Internet). Organized crime groups enjoy the shadows and do not seek to publicize their activities for public consumption. Al-Qaeda, on the other hand, distributed a videotape depicting their second-in-command cutting off the head of an American journalist. However, at times, organized crime groups have used high-profile terror tactics, such as those perpetrated by Pablo Escobar in Colombia and the Sicilian Mafia's attacks on the Uffizi Galleries in Florence. In these instances, the goal was to intimidate governments into changing policies antithetical to organized crime. For organized crime groups, notes Thomas Sanderson (2004: 56), terrorism may serve as a tactic, "whereas criminal activities may become a permanent necessity for terror groups lacking sufficient sources of funding."

In sum, terrorist organizations and organized crime groups differ on means and ends. Both engage in organized criminal activity such as drug trafficking to support themselves, but terrorists use their funds to further political ends, to overthrow governments and impose their worldview. Organized crime instead seeks to corrupt government to gain immunity for their crimes. Rather than destruction, criminal organizations frequently form a parallel government while coexisting with the existing one. While members of organized crime are not motivated by an ideology and generally identify themselves as criminals, terrorist groups try to give their activities an altruistic aura to justify their acts and to solicit people's sympathy for their cause. Organized crime groups prefer to carry out their activities secretly, while terrorists seek to maximize media coverage to promote their message and publicize their goals.

Law enforcement resources diverted to fighting terrorism dilute government efforts against organized crime. But greater surveillance of our borders to fight terrorism also benefits efforts against drug smuggling. There is a parallel between the Organized Crime Control Act of 1970 and the USA Patriot Act (both discussed in Chapter 14) enacted in the wake of the September 11, 2001 destruction of the Twin Towers. Both provide the federal government with extraordinary powers justified by "clear and present dangers," and both have been used against persons devoid of ties to organized crime or terrorism. For example, a Patriot Act provision that authorizes "secret warrants" permits federal agents to search a home without immediately notifying the target that they have been there has "been used in a wide variety of cases beyond terrorism, including child pornography, drug trafficking and organized crime" (Lichtblau 2005b: 19).

As Frank Bovenkerk (2011: 263) points out, "Terrorism can turn into organized crime." A terrorist group may abandon its political goals or the use of violence to achieve these goals. In either instance, some members no longer restrained by ideological ends may find that their skills lend themselves to achieving more personal goals—greed replaces ideology. A transformation occurs as individual skills developed as terrorists and the advantages of organization are mobilized in the pursuit of pecuniary interests: terrorists become organized crime. There is evidence of this transformation in Northern Ireland where the Irish Republican Army has relinquished violence as an organizational tool. This may be occurring in Colombia where FARC guerillas become increasingly involved in drug trafficking and lose sight of their original ideological motivation. Glenn Curtis and Tara Karacan (2002: 4) refer to this as "fighters turned felons." If, for example, drug trafficking proves lucrative beyond the immediate goal of paying for arms, the "pure" ideology of a terrorist group "may be diluted and some parts of the organization may 'wander off' into conventional criminal activity." Chris Dishman (2005: 237) adds that when terrorist groups use financial incentives to recruit and retain militants, they may find that persons who join to make money "will quickly set ideological goals to the side if it affects profits."

SUMMARY

1. Understand the difficulty in defining organized crime and know its attributes:
   - There is no generally accepted definition of organized crime
   - Organized crime has eight attributes:
     1. Has no political goals
     2. Is hierarchical
     3. Has a limited or exclusive membership
     4. Constitutes a unique subculture
     5. Perpetuates itself
     6. Exhibits a willingness to use illegal violence
     7. Is monopolistic
     8. Is governed by explicit rules and regulations
2. Know the salient features of a bureaucracy:
   - Bureaucracy is essential for efficiently carrying out large-scale tasks.
   - Bureaucratic organizations exhibit a complicated hierarchy and an extensive division of labor, assign positions on the basis of skill, carry out responsibilities in an impersonal manner, and have extensive written rules and regulations, and communicate via a chain of command.
   - Whenever an entity, club, business, or criminal organization continues to expand, at some point it will have to adopt the bureaucratic style of organization.
   - Many aspects of bureaucracy are impractical for criminal organizations because they must be concerned with the very real possibility that communications are being monitored.
   - In the compartmentalized form of bureaucracy, persons at the operational/street level are organized into cells and know only other members of their cell.
   - A criminal organization can manifest a bureaucratic structure, while economic activities are divorced from the formal structure.
3. Be familiar with the concepts of franchising, credentialing, points of convergence, and the role of a broker:
   - Franchises provide a sense of entitlement, enabling the possessor to engage in criminal activity with the knowledge that he or she will be supported and protected by the criminal organization granting the franchise.
   - A network consists of a collection of connected points or junctures; a criminal network typically functions within a subcultural environment—an "underworld."
   - A criminal network has *points of convergence* where participants congregate.
   - *Credentialing* enables criminals to negotiate transactions that those without an organizational affiliation would find difficult if not impossible to accomplish.
   - With the proper credentials, a criminal entrepreneur can profit by acting as a broker, that is, a person who connects otherwise disconnected parts of a network.
4. Understand transnational organized crime:
   - Traditional Mafia-type organizations are linked by territory and exercise control over the entities in their territories by means of intimidation.
   - The collapse of the Soviet Union and the expansion of global trade provides opportunity for criminal organizations capable of operating across national boundaries.
   - This has spurred the growth of alliances with criminal groups operating across national boundaries.
   - Global organized crime is similar to a transnational commercial company.
   - Migration broadens the reach of existing criminal networks.
5. Know the similarities and differences between organized crime and terrorism and the connection between organized crime and terrorism:
   - Terrorism is inherently political.
   - Terrorists often choose their targets at random.
   - Organized crime does not seek the overthrow of governments.

- Organized crime and terrorist organizations share the same geography. Membership can overlap and have similar needs for weapons and money laundering services.

- Both organized crime and terrorists may use compartmentalization.

REVIEW QUESTIONS

1. What is the generally accepted definition of organized crime?

2. What are the eight attributes of organized crime?

3. What are the characteristics of a bureaucratic organization?

4. When an organization expands, why does it tend to become bureaucratic?

5. What are the impractical aspects of a bureaucracy for a criminal organization?

6. What are the advantages of compartmentalization for a criminal organization?

7. How can criminal organization manifest a bureaucratic structure while its economic activities are divorced from the formal structure?

8. How is the concept of *franchise* applicable to organized crime?

9. In a criminal network, what is meant by points of convergence?

10. How does *credentialing* aid members of a criminal organization?

11. How can a credentialed criminal act as a broker?

12. How do traditional "Mafia-type" organizations differ from global criminal organizations?

13. What factors led to the expansion of global organized crime?

14. How is global organized crime similar to a transnational commercial company?

15. How has migration impacted on organized crime?

16. How does terrorism differ from organized crime?

17. How is terrorism similar to organized crime?

18. What is a hybrid organization?

Dutch Schultz, from street thug to "Beer Baron of the Bronx".   © TopFoto/The Image Works

Development of Organized Crime in the United States

In their typical methodical approach to murder, the victim had been tailed for a week. As he walked to a Bronx subway station on the morning of July 25, 1939, right on schedule, five members of a Murder, Inc. hit team drove by, did a U-turn, and approached the victim from behind. One of the men stepped out onto the running board and emptied a .32 revolver into his back. It was a classic Murder, Inc. hit, save for one thing—it was the wrong guy. The outrage that followed the murder of a classical music publisher with a wife and two daughters signaled the beginning of the end of Murder, Inc. (David Krajicek 2010).

Murder, Inc. represents the apex of organized crime in the United States, when the major chieftains financed a unit of assassins who, although operating out of Brooklyn, carried out murders throughout the country. The history leading up to this development will be discussed in this chapter.

CHAPTER 2 WILL ENABLE THE READER TO UNDERSTAND:

- The pioneering role of the "Robber Barons" in American criminal history
- The connection between immigration and urban politics
- The importance of the saloon in urban machine politics
- The connection between upperworld and underworld
- The connection between reform and nativism in American politics
- The vital role of Prohibition in the development of organized crime
- "Murder, Inc." as a symbol of the cooperation between criminal organizations
- How the findings of the Kefauver Committee influenced views of organized crime

The intertwining of urban machine politics and Prohibition provided Irish, Jewish, and Italian immigrants unparalleled criminal opportunity to climb the "queer ladder of social mobility." But it was the Robber Barons who helped enrich the fertile soil necessary for the growth of organized crime in the United States and whose spiritual legacy lives on in twenty-first-century corporate crime.

THE ROBBER BARONS

"Al Capone," notes Michael Woodiwiss (1987: 8), "was not the first ruthless entrepreneur to combine with thugs, gunmen, and government officials and carve out an illegal fortune. But the expression—'organised crime'—was not commonly used until the 1920s and the Prohibition era when academics and newspaper editors found it to be a convenient new label for an old phenomenon." While contemporary organized crime has its roots in Prohibition (1920–1933), unscrupulous American businessmen, such as Astor, Drew, Gould, Sage, Rockefeller, Stanford, and Vanderbilt, provided role models and created a climate conducive to its growth. These earlier generations of predatory Americans with English, Scottish, Scandinavian, and German ancestry paved the way for later generations of Irish, Jewish, and Italian criminals who, in turn, are being emulated by criminals of Asian, African, Hispanic, and Russian ancestry. Rampant—that is, uncontrolled—capitalism, a feature of nineteenth-century America, is now being experienced by the former Soviet Union and it too has spawned a class of "Robber Barons" and organized crime that we will examine in Chapter 9.

John Jacob Astor

John Jacob Astor (1763–1848) arrived from Germany penniless and died the richest man in America; in today's value he was worth $78 billion (Klepper et al. 1998). He was "the first great self-made millionaire whose career whetted the ambitions of a host of young Americans" (Rugoff

1989: 40). The Astor fortune was based on alcohol and fraud: Drunken Native Americans were systematically cheated by agents of Astor's American Fur Company. When the victims complained to the government, Astor's agents resorted to violence. When the Indians retaliated, troops were sent to quell the "Indian disorder." In addition to exploiting Native Americans, Astor succeeded in forcing his employees in the western wilderness to buy from company-owned stores at exorbitant prices. By the time they returned east, most employees were actually in debt to Astor (Myers 1936; Rugoff 1989).

Astor was able to monopolize the fur trade and "was never prosecuted for the numerous violations of both penal and civil law invariably committed at his direction and for his benefit. With the millions that rolled in, he was able to command the services of the foremost lawyers in warding off penalties of law, and also to have as his paid retainers some of the most noted and powerful politicians of the day" (Myers 1936: 103). For example, he paid Lewis Cass, then governor of the territory of Michigan, $35,000 for unexplained services. David Loth (1938: 104) notes that the money was well invested. Later, as secretary of war, "Cass was to hear, and dismiss, many charges of corruption, extortion, trespass and violence against the [American Fur] company and its representatives." The money gained through lawlessness and violence against Native Americans in the western fur trade was used for real estate speculation in New York, where easily corrupted officials helped Astor become America's greatest "slumlord," extracting money from poor immigrants for the privilege of living in the vilest of tenement housing. The Astor-inspired slums became a spawning ground for organized crime.

Cornelius Vanderbilt

Cornelius Vanderbilt (1794–1877) came from a small farming family on Staten Island (now part of New York City). He parlayed profits from a ferryboat venture into shipping and shipbuilding, and at age 47, the "Commodore" was a rich man. The government of Nicaragua had given his Accessory Transit Company a monopoly over transportation across the isthmus connecting the two great oceans. In 1853, while Vanderbilt was on a European vacation, two members of his board of directors, in accord with business practices of the day, usurped control of Accessory Transit. Vanderbilt retaliated by setting up a competing line and, by cutting prices, forced the two directors to withdraw. They retaliated by financing an insurrection in Nicaragua, where Accessory Transit was chartered. The revolutionary forces, led by an American adventurer, achieved a great victory. Early in 1856, the Vanderbilt charter was canceled and Vanderbilt's property was confiscated.

Vanderbilt responded that summer by persuading the governments of Honduras, San Salvador, and Costa Rica to form an alliance against Nicaragua. Then, on Vanderbilt's orders, two American mercenaries led an invasion of Nicaragua. By the end of the first year the invasion force was progressing quite well; then the Nicaraguans counterattacked. Vanderbilt thwarted the offensive by persuading the State Department to send in the U.S. Marines, who succeeded in deposing the revolutionary government, and Vanderbilt's charter was restored (Andrews 1941). Even Mario Puzo's fictitious godfather did not use "muscle" on this scale.

Like many other successful businessmen of the era, Vanderbilt was a "war profiteer." During the Civil War he acted as an agent for the Union Army, securing unfit and rotting vessels for the transportation of federal troops at exorbitant prices. However, his primary interest was civilian transportation, and Vanderbilt moved from shipping to railroads. Striving for monopoly, he gained control of the Hudson River and Harlem lines and forced the competing New York Central to sell out. In 1866 he sought to complete his transportation stranglehold by taking over the Erie Railroad which ran from Jersey City to Lake Erie, a direct competitor. Vanderbilt, however, was ambushed by the Erie Ring, comprising three of America's greatest pirate capitalists: Daniel Drew, James Fisk, and Jay Gould.

The Erie Ring

As part of a scheme to fleece Vanderbilt, the Erie Ring secretly authorized the issue of ten million new shares of Erie stock while Vanderbilt was busy buying up shares to gain control of the Erie Railroad. The more stock he purchased, the more stock was printed by the ring, which declared their actions in accord with the First Amendment—"freedom of the press." In 1868, after Vanderbilt realized he had bought more Erie stock than was known to exist and still did not control the line, an obliging New York Supreme Court judge, part of the notoriously corrupt "Tweed Ring," signed an injunction against further issue of Erie stock. The judge also ordered the ring to return to the treasury one-fourth of what they had already issued. "When Vanderbilt needed a court order in a hurry or a special bill or a joker in a franchise, he could rely on the 'Boss' [Tweed] to have it in stock" (Loth 1938: 196). William M. Tweed was the head of Tammany Hall, an organization that dominated New York City politics and government for more than one hundred years (discussed later).

The judge's injunction drove up the price of Erie stock but did not stop the ring. They had "their judge" issue a counter-injunction, and chaos swept Wall Street. Trading in Erie stock was suspended by the stock exchange, but not before Vanderbilt had lost between $5 and $7 million (a significant sum in those days). He responded by having "his judge" issue contempt-of-court arrest warrants for the members of the ring.

The Erie Ring withdrew all its combined funds from New York banks, took all its securities and documents from safes, and crossed the Hudson River to Jersey City with their printing press—out of range of Boss Tweed. Arriving just ahead of pursuing sheriff's deputies, Gould, Drew, and Fisk set up headquarters in Jersey City where they were guarded by their own railroad police and cooperative city police officers. Cannons were mounted on piers to thwart any landings from New York, and the ring counterattacked by reducing fares to Buffalo, undercutting the hard-pressed Vanderbilt line. Vanderbilt retaliated by ordering a band of thugs into New Jersey. The Erie Ring fled to New York where the field of battle shifted to the state capital. In Albany, the ring spread $1 million worth of "good will" in an effort to legalize its theft of the Erie from Vanderbilt. Jay Gould even "drew the 'Boss' away from the Commodore's New York Central by the present of a block of Erie stock, a directorship and a retainer of many thousands as counsel" (Loth 1938: 197). Vanderbilt joined the fray but soon grew tired of trying to satisfy state legislators' seemingly insatiable appetites for bribe money. The ring achieved a "legislative victory," and Vanderbilt sued for peace. In return for $4.5 million he relinquished his interest in the Erie, and the arrest warrants were quashed (Josephson 1962; Rugoff 1989).

Daniel Drew

The oldest member of the Erie Ring, Daniel Drew, was born in Carmel, New York, in 1797. An illiterate raised in poverty, Drew began his business career as a cattle drover, buying cattle on credit from New York farmers and driving them to market for sale. He often failed to pay his debts and was forced to move operations to Ohio, where he perfected the technique that resulted in the term *watered stock*. His cattle were kept thirsty by a liberal diet of salt and very little water. Before arrival at the drover's market, the cattle were allowed to quench their thirst, increasing their poundage accordingly. With money thus earned, Drew purchased a tavern and became a moneylender, a steamship owner, and a stockbroker. He gained notoriety by his comments on the advent of the Civil War: "Along with ordinary happenings, we fellows on Wall Street now have in addition the fortunes of war to speculate about, and that always makes great doings on the stock exchange. It's good fishing in troubled waters" (O'Connor 1962: 51).

Drew became treasurer and virtual dictator of the Erie Railroad. He would issue stock for new steel rails and other vital equipment and divert the money for his own speculative investments. As a result, the Erie's "schedules were fictional, its rolling stock ruinous, and its rails so weak and chipped as to invite derailment" (Swanberg 1959: 24). For his own enrichment, Drew ran what had been considered a technological marvel, the Erie Railroad, into the ground (Ackerman 1988). In 1866, the line was in financial trouble and borrowed $3.5 million from Drew. As collateral, he received 28,000 shares of unissued stock and $3 million in convertible bonds. The securities had been entrusted to him only as collateral; they were not to be sold. Drew converted the bonds into 30,000 shares of stock and, with Jim Fisk as his broker, began selling short—speculating that the price of the stock would go down. To ensure that this would happen, Drew dumped all 58,000 shares on the market and realized a profit of almost $3 million (at a time when most workers earned less than $25 a week and New York State legislators were paid $300 a year).

Drew, an ardent Methodist churchgoer, was responsible for the founding of the Drew Theological Seminary in New Jersey, now part of Drew University. As a pious fraud, notes Milton Rugoff (1989), Drew offered to endow the seminary with $250,000 but wound up giving the institution only the 7 percent interest on this amount. He founded a brokerage firm, but the panic of 1873 wiped out his fortune. Whereas Cornelius Vanderbilt died leaving an estate valued at $90 million (today's value: $95.9 billion) and a university named in his honor, Drew died a pauper in 1879 (Swanberg 1959).

James Fisk

James Fisk, Jr., was born in Vermont in 1834 to a family of English ancestry. He left home at age 15 to join the circus, returning a few years later to join his father as an itinerant peddler. His success at this trade led to a job as a salesman for Jordan, Marsh and Company of Boston. During the Civil War, Fisk acted as an agent for Marsh to the Union Army, lobbying congressmen and generals with lavish entertainment and liberal spending. This led to lucrative contracts for Marsh and advancement for the young Fisk. While other young men were dying by the thousands for the Union, Fisk was making Marsh a fortune through a smuggling operation that moved southern cotton to the northern mills of Jordan Marsh. At the end of the war, a grateful Marsh presented Fisk with a bonus of $65,000. Fisk took his Civil War profits and used them to swindle buyers of Confederate bonds in Europe. After the fall of Richmond, he sold short to Englishmen who did not know that the Confederacy had collapsed.

Although he successfully avoided military service during the Civil War—when a man could get killed—in peacetime he and his fortune assumed command of a National Guard militia unit. "The Ninth New York," notes Richard O'Connor (1962: 116), "was up for sale; without transfusions of men and money it would have to be disbanded." The newly elected Colonel Fisk, in uniform and astride his horse, rode at the head of his militiamen during the Orangemen parade of 1871. When the English loyalists were attacked by a mob of Irish Catholics, Fisk reacted by throwing away his sword and fleeing. Three of his militiamen died in the fighting, and the colonel prudently absented himself from their funeral.

Known as a bon vivant, Fisk was murdered in 1872 by the paramour of his favorite mistress, the actress Josie Mansfield. He left an estate valued at $1 million. Although his wife was reputed to be worth $2 million, in 1912 she died a poor woman living on an income of $50 a month from some rental property (Swanberg 1959).

Jay Gould

The third member of the Erie Ring, Jay Gould (1836–1892), was born in Roxbury, New York, the son of a poor farmer. The Golds (the original family name) had roots in America dating back to 1674, when the family first settled in Connecticut (Klein 1986). At age 16, having a neat hand and a good head for figures, the future member of the Erie Ring was working as a clerk for a village storekeeper. He discovered that his employer had negotiated to buy a piece of property for $2,000. Gould secured a loan from his father, purchased the land for $2,500, and sold it to his employer for $4,000. Taking advantage of positions of trust was to become the basis for Gould's early financial success. At age 20, he took $5,000 he had accumulated and entered the leather market in New York.

Gould was befriended by a wealthy businessman who, impressed with the young man's ability, provided him with $120,000 to establish a large tannery in Pennsylvania. "Early in life," writes Maury Klein (1986: 43), "he revealed a talent for charming people." According to Matthew Josephson (1962), the company did well, but the owner in New York was receiving no profits—Gould was systematically diverting the funds for his own speculative investments. (Klein states, however, that there is no evidence to support this conclusion.) When the investor arrived in Pennsylvania, he found the books in disarray. Fearing for his investment, he offered to sell the company to Gould for only $60,000—money that Gould didn't have. Gould found other backers, paid off the original owner, and continued to divert funds for his own use until the new owner attempted to physically take back his property. Using hired thugs and idle workers, Gould resisted the effort until officers of the law finally ousted him (Josephson 1962). Klein states that Gould was blameless and that his financial backer used the hired thugs, Gould relying on the tannery's workers. However, Klein admits, "Jay came out of the episode in better financial shape than when he began it. The tannery may have lost money, but Jay did not" (1986: 60).

Gould entered the railroad business, first buying mortgage bonds of the Rutland and Washington Railroad. For ten cents on the dollar Gould was able to gain controlling interest in this small, bankrupt line. He then hired men with managerial ability, improved the railroad's rolling stock, and consolidated it with other small lines whose stock he had also purchased. By complex stock manipulations, Gould was able to drive up the price of his holdings. He then purchased a controlling interest in the Cleveland and Pittsburgh Railroad, using profits from bond speculation, and manipulated the line's stock to an all-time high. Gould then sold it to the Pennsylvania Railroad Company (Myers 1936). His next great enterprise involved him as part of the Erie Ring in its battle with Cornelius Vanderbilt.

In 1869, the United States had an unfavorable balance of trade. To trade successfully, American importers had to pay European exporters in gold. Gould discovered that there was only about $15 million in gold in the New York market, and he plotted to corner that market. Gould already owned $7 million worth of gold, and using the Erie's resources and that of his backers, he could easily absorb the outstanding $15 million and drive the price of gold sky high. Only one ingredient of Gould's plan remained to be dealt with— President Ulysses S. Grant. The president had the power to release some of the $100 million in gold reserves, which the federal government did periodically in the interest of fostering trade and commerce. Gould attempted to influence the president through a financial relationship with Grant's brother-in-law. He also had stories placed in newspapers that the government was going to refrain from releasing any gold reserves. These activities, in addition to his and Jim Fisk's feverish buying, caused a "bull market," and the price of gold skyrocketed (Loth 1938).

Gould discovered, however, that Grant had not been influenced—the president would not permit the price of gold to rise freely. Gould began to sell off his gold. Suddenly, on September 24— known as "Black Friday"—the price of gold plummeted. Enraged mobs of investors sought to lynch Gould and Fisk, who were protected by their paid thugs from the Erie line. Gould, of course, made a handsome profit—$1 million—from the entire venture (Swanberg 1959; Rugoff 1989). In 1886 the Knights of Labor demanded a minimum wage of $9 a week. Gould responded with wholesale firings at one of his holdings and the union called a strike. Violence broke out, and with the help of private detectives and strikebreakers, Gould broke the strike and the union (Rugoff 1989).

When Gould died he left an estate whose value in today's dollars was $42.1 billion (Klepper et al. 1998). His progeny, however, fought costly legal battles over the estate and frequently mismanaged what they inherited. Nevertheless, the last surviving son, Howard, who died in 1959, left an estate of more than $62 million to twenty-eight relatives (O'Connor 1962). On January 3, 1984, the *New York Times* reported that the jewelry collection of the late daughter-in-law of "railroad magnate Jay Gould" would be auctioned at Christie's. The widow of Jay Gould's youngest son had a jewelry collection insured for more than $100 million, in addition to an art collection of 120 works by van Gogh, Renoir, Monet, Degas, Goya, and others of like quality. The bulk of the estate went to the Gould Foundation to promote Franco-American friendship (Reif 1984). The Gould family also provided generous endowments to New York University (NYU), where Frank, Jay's youngest son, graduated in 1899; his eldest daughter, Helen, graduated from the NYU Law School for Women in April 1895. Several of the school's buildings bear the Gould name.

Leland Stanford

The railroading tradition of Vanderbilt, Drew, Fisk, Gould, and Sage was not reserved for the eastern portion of the United States. But in the West there was none of the cutthroat competition that pervaded the East. Leland Stanford was born in Watervliet, New York, in 1824. In 1852, after a fire destroyed his law office in Wisconsin, Stanford moved to California, where he became involved in Republican politics. Elected governor in 1861, Stanford approved four public grants totaling millions of dollars for the construction of a transcontinental railroad line—he was president of the Central Pacific Railroad. With three colleagues he formed the Pacific Association and used their combined assets, $200,000, prudently—but not to build a railroad: The money was "laid out in bribes to Congressmen or others with influence" in the nation's capitol. Loth (1938: 159) states: "The Central Pacific had thrown its $200,000 upon Congressional waters and lo! it had returned in the form of a land grant for 9,000,000 acres and a loan of Federal bonds for $24,000,000."

The Central Pacific would run from the ocean to as far as it could reach in a race east, with the Union Pacific racing west. The lines linked up in 1869. For every mile of track, the lines received a subsidy from the government. This did not satisfy Stanford and his associates. They intimidated local governments into providing millions of dollars by threatening to have the line bypass their communities. San Francisco, for example, provided $550,000 (Myers 1936; Josephson 1962). Nevertheless, Stanford was elected to the U.S. Senate by the legislature in 1885 and reelected in 1890. In 1885, he established Leland Stanford, Jr., University—now known as Stanford University—in memory of his son, who had died in 1884 at age 15 (R. White 2011). Stanford died in 1893 worth over $18 billion in today's dollars (Klepper et al. 1998).

John D. Rockefeller

John D. Rockefeller (1839–1937) was born in Richford, New York, the son of a vendor of "patent medicines" (which had no patent and frequently

This late nineteenth century cartoon reflects popular attitudes toward one of the most powerful and ruthless "Robber Barons," oil monopolist John D. Rockefeller balances the world in the palm of his hand.

© Bettmann/Corbis

contained cocaine and opium). A studious, hardworking youngster, at age 16 he secured a job as a bookkeeper for a produce merchant. He saved his meager earnings and became a successful commodities broker, buying and selling grain and produce. During the Civil War, Rockefeller made a fortune selling grain to the military while avoiding conscription. In 1862, he invested in a technique to extract kerosene from crude oil and in 1865 sold his share in the produce business to devote all his time and money to oil. His remarkable success in the oil business was aided by the Vanderbilt-owned railroad, which shipped the Rockefeller oil at a discount. A portion of the shipping costs were rebated—"kickbacks"—allowing Rockefeller to undercut his competitors.

In 1870, Rockefeller and Henry Flagler incorporated the Standard Oil Company, and during the following year they conspired to control the entire oil industry in the United States. First they obtained the Pennsylvania charter of a defunct corporation that had been authorized to engage in a plethora of business activities—the South Improvement Company (SIC). Then, in collusion with railroad officials, shipping rates were doubled while the increase for the SIC was rebated. By 1872, Rockefeller was intimidating rival oil companies into selling out to SIC. An "oil war" resulted as independent oil dealers fought the SIC by refusing to sell their oil to the Rockefeller-controlled refineries. The oil boycott hurt the railroads, which rebelled against Rockefeller and the Pennsylvania legislature eventually revoked the SIC charter (Lloyd 1963).

The great monopolist struck again, this time conspiring with refinery owners to gain control over the setting of railroad oil shipping rates. The owners of the fifteen strongest oil firms in the United States swore an oath of secrecy and became part of what became known as the "Standard Oil Conspiracy." In league with the railroads, they controlled the delivery of oil, forcing competitors to sell out to Standard or pay exorbitant shipping costs that would render them noncompetitive. Those who were stubborn enough to resist were harassed with price wars and, if that didn't work, dynamite. The Rockefeller trust—Standard Oil—extended its vertical control of the oil industry to include pipelines, oil terminals, and direct marketing. By 1876

Standard Oil controlled 80 percent of the oil production in the United States.

In 1877, a great oil boom threatened to break the Standard Oil monopoly. Rockefeller fought the new independents by refusing them use of railroads, pipelines, and storage facilities. The independents organized and fought back, financing the construction of the Tidewater Pipe Line to break Rockefeller's control over railroad rates. They attacked Standard Oil in the courts, and Flagler and Rockefeller were indicted in Pennsylvania for conspiracy in restraint of trade.

Undaunted, Rockefeller built a rival pipeline, slashed prices, attacked Tidewater credit in the money market, and convinced "his judges" to enjoin the issue of Tidewater bonds. In the finest tradition of direct action, Standard Oil operatives plugged up Tidewater pipelines. Under siege, Tidewater finally capitulated and was bought out by the National Transit Company, which was owned by Standard Oil (Lloyd 1963). By 1890, the Rockefeller trust controlled about 90 percent of the petroleum production in the United States, a situation that led to the passage of the Sherman Anti-Trust Act (discussed in Chapter 14) that same year. Nevertheless, by 1913, Rockefeller was worth $189.6 billion in today's dollars (Klepper et al. 1998).

John D. Rockefeller died in 1937. His legacy lives on in the University of Chicago, Rockefeller University, and the Rockefeller Foundation. His descendants have served as governors of New York, Arkansas, and West Virginia, U.S. senator from West Virginia, and vice president of the United States.

Conclusion

What does this sampling of "Robber Barons" add up to, what are we to conclude? First, we must understand that the United States, as the Eisenhower Commission[1] pointed out, is quite a violent country. Important aspects of U.S. history have hinged on the use of violence, both figurative (for example, "financial piracy") and literal (for example, the use of gunmen, thugs, private police, law enforcement agents, the National Guard, and the military), to further *private* ends. This legacy continues as evidenced by the economic crisis fostered by the finance industry.

Lincoln Steffens noted in 1902 that the "spirit of graft and of lawlessness is the American spirit" (1957: 8). With the western frontier closed, with the wealth of the "Robber Barons" institutionalized and their progeny firmly in control of the economy, there was only modest opportunity for the poor but ambitious adventurers of our urban frontiers. Among these later immigrants—Irish, Jewish, Italian—some have sought to innovate, not on the grand scale of the Vanderbilts, the Goulds, and the Rockefellers, but in a manner more consistent with available opportunity. Many found this opportunity in the politics and vice of urban America beginning in the latter half of the nineteenth century.

IMMIGRATION AND URBAN POLITICS

Immigration into the United States, except for brief depressions, grew dramatically in the years from 1820 to 1850, particularly in urban areas. During those three decades, the population of cities in the East and West quadrupled—New York's population rose to half a million (Bennett 1988). Immigrants and their offspring comprised more than two-thirds of the population of the largest cities in the Northeast and more than three-quarters of the population of New York, Boston, and Chicago (Buenker 1973).

These urban immigrants found employment in the most dangerous, monotonous, and poorly paid industries; women and children often labored as well. They were forced into slum housing reserved for their own ethnic group. Their culture, customs, and religious beliefs and practices were subjected to

---

1. National Advisory Commission on the Causes and Prevention of Violence (1969); see also Graham and Gurr (1969).

virulent attack by Americans of earlier stock. "Beset by hostility and discrimination on virtually all sides, the immigrant gradually found that he possessed at least one commodity that some native Americans coveted: his vote" (Buenker 1973: 3). A new breed of broker—the political boss—emerged to channel these votes into a powerful entity known as the "machine."

The necessities of urban America required construction workers, street cleaners, police, and firemen, and service workers of all kinds, thus providing the immigrant with his livelihood and the political boss with patronage (Hofstadter 1956). During the 1880s, for example, New York's Tammany Hall had more than 40,000 municipal jobs at its disposal (Erie 1988). "The immigrant, in short, looked to politics not for the realization of high principles but for concrete and personal gains, and he sought these gains through personal relationships. And the boss, particularly the Irish boss, who could see things from the immigrant's angle but could also manipulate the American environment, became a specialist in personal relations and personal loyalties" (Hofstadter 1956: 182).

Organized crime in America "is the product of an evolutionary process extending more than a century" (Tyler 1962: 89). The roots of organized crime can be found in the politics of urban America before Prohibition, in the patron–client network known as the political machine. The underpinnings of this phenomenon are found in immigrant America and in the role of the Irish.

The Irish

There are strong historical parallels between the repression suffered by Sicilian peasants (discussed in Chapter 5) and that endured by their Irish counterparts. In both cases, this helped shape their culture. Ireland fell under foreign domination in the twelfth century, although it was not until the latter half of the sixteenth century and the reign of Elizabeth I (1558–1603) that England tried to impose Protestantism on the largely Catholic Irish. England used the religious dispute to seize large

tracts of the most fertile land in Ireland. Thousands of Protestant Lowland Scots (and to a lesser extent, English) were encouraged to settle in Northern Ireland, and they soon owned most of the land. In the south, Oliver Cromwell crushed an Irish rebellion in 1649 and parceled out two-thirds of the land to his soldiers and followers (Shannon 1989). Ireland was reduced to a "country of peasants who were constantly oppressed by excessive rents, taxes, and tithes, and for whom poverty was a general condition" (Levine 1966: 5). Before Queen Elizabeth's rule, people of the island identified themselves as followers of a particular local chieftain; afterward, they viewed themselves as Irish.

Paradoxically, this environment of misery gave rise to a culture of hospitality and openhandedness. The Irish looked forward to opportunities for social gatherings—even events as sad as death which meant gathering for an "Irish wake." As in southern Italy, a certain attitude developed: Let outsiders, the government, and the world be damned (Shannon 1989). Finding no justice in the formal system of government imposed by the British, the Irish turned to informal mechanisms, bargaining and negotiating for favorable outcomes. The Irish resorted to secret and open organizations on local and national levels as part of their continuous efforts to deal with British oppression. When the franchise was extended to Ireland, the Irish were caught up in the corrupt politics fostered by the British, and they became a thoroughly politicized people (Levine 1966).

Two centuries of personal experience with Anglo-Saxon (British) Protestant government led to a disdain for law among the Irish and provided the knowledge and skill that enabled them to serve an important role in the rough-and-tumble politics of America's urban areas. "The Irish political personality was shaped by confrontation with British imperialism and colonialism. In their efforts to free themselves from anti-Catholic Penal Laws and to achieve national independence, the Irish learned to compete within the context of the Anglo-Saxon political system. They became particularly adroit in the techniques of mass agitation, political organization, confrontation, and liberal, democratic politics" (McCaffrey 1976: 8).

English policy reduced the Irish to abject poverty. "Unless an Irish labourer could get hold of a patch of land and grow potatoes on which to feed himself and his children, the family starved." When the Irish potato crop failed (1845–1847) because of a fungus, there was widespread famine that resulted in the deaths of about 1.5 million people (Woodham-Smith 1962: 32). The workhouses, supported by taxes on landowners, were overflowing and they encouraged and sponsored Irish immigration to the United States as a way of easing their tax burden (Wyman 1984).

Once in the United States, the Irish tended to settle in urban areas. Uneducated and often illiterate—the British had denied them educational opportunity—Irish immigrants secured employment as unskilled laborers (McCaffrey 1976). But, "Irish immigrants came to America with a live political tradition" (Shannon 1989: 15): They "were the world's greatest experts in the art of warfare without confrontation. They could make alliances without formal conferences, agreements, or treaties that would leave a record. They could act in concert without giving commands but with a clear understanding of who was in charge. These were the lessons they had learned while living under repression. It did not take very long to learn how to apply their underground tactics to a democracy" (Reedy 1991: 22).

Between 1840 and 1844, about a quarter of a million people from mostly Catholic districts in Ireland entered the United States (Bennett 1988). In a single decade, 1845–1854, almost 1.5 million Irish immigrants entered the United States, and from 1855 until the turn of the twentieth century three million more arrived. They constituted the first large-scale immigration to the United States of a group since the arrival of Anglo-Saxon Protestants in the 1600s and 1700s. And "although generally peasants in their homeland, most of the new arrivals lacked either the resources or the desire to resume agrarian life. Arriving at a time when available land was scarce and agriculture mechanized, most sought work as unskilled laborers in

the burgeoning industrial metropolises" (Buenker 1973: 2); only 6 percent would become farmers (Erie 1988). "By 1870, while only about 10 percent of the country's twenty-nine million native-born whites lived in the big cities, 42 percent of the nation's 1.8 million Irish-born lived in the twenty-five cities with populations greater than 50,000" (Erie 1988: 25). By 1850, more than one-third of New York City's population was Irish (Shannon 1989).

In the United States the Irish found themselves restricted from upward mobility, which was reserved for middle-class Protestants. In response, Irish immigrants remained in close-knit neighborhoods, where they joined the Democratic Party as an outlet for social and economic advancement. However, "instead of using politics as an avenue to integration into the middle class, politics enveloped the Irish, and the Irish social structure became an integral part of the process of recruiting other Irishmen into both the party and government. As the Irish swarmed into city politics, political office was recognized as the career among them, and politics became the secular extension of their essentially religious identity" (Levine 1966: 5).

Irish Catholic immigrants distrusted the public education system, which was dominated by Protestants: "Most Irish took a dim view of the usefulness of education and left its destiny in the hands of the clergy" (Levine 1966: 87). Although Catholic parochial education promoted Irish solidarity, it did not encourage secular intellectual pursuits and higher education. "Before World War I, few Irish boys and girls went on to secondary schools and before World War II few of them enrolled in college" (McCaffrey 1976: 82).

Politics and government employment provided the most readily available road to social mobility. Irish success in politics coincided with a decrease in the substantial crime rate among Irish immigrants, that is, until Prohibition in 1920 suddenly offered a new fast track to economic—albeit crime-based—success. "The Irish, the most numerous and advanced section of the immigrant community, took over the political party (usually the Democratic Party) at the local level and converted it into virtually a parallel system of government" (Shannon 1989: 62). The Irish clan system welded the Irish into a community capable of acting in concert while disregarding the formal governmental and legal structure (Reedy 1991).

Irish success in politics was also advanced by their ability to speak English, knowledge of government, and the timing of their arrival in the United States. They were also "community-minded, gregarious by nature, fond of visiting and talking" (McCaffrey 1976: 65); "the Irish have, in fact, been a highly social people, gregarious above everything" (Woodham-Smith 1962: 266). The Irish were also "neutral outsiders in the traditional ethnic antipathies and hostilities which the Central and East European ethnic groups brought to America from their homelands. A Chicago politician notes: "A Lithuanian won't vote for a Pole, and a Pole won't vote for a Lithuanian. A German won't vote for either of them—but all three will vote for a 'Turkey,' an Irishman" (Rakove 1975: 33). And there was the Irish connection to the saloon, a refuge from overcrowded slum dwellings. "For many years the saloon was as important a link in the communications process of the Irish social structure as was the parish church" (Levine 1966: 119). "Irish politicians used Catholic solidarity as a voting base, saloons as political clubs" (McCaffrey 1976: 140).

THE SALOON AND THE MACHINE

Throughout much of urban America, the saloon was a center of neighborhood activity, an important social base for political activity, and saloonkeepers became political powers in many cities. "Part of the appeal of the saloon was due to the social services it provided. In saloons files of newspapers in several languages were available along with cigars, mailboxes for regular patrons, free pencils, paper, and mail services to those wishing to send letters, and information on employment. Saloons provided a warm fire in the winter, public toilets, bowling alleys, billiard tables, music, singing, dancing, constant conversation, charity and charge accounts,

quiet corners for students, and special rooms for weddings, union meetings, or celebrations. No other institution provided such a variety of necessary services to the public" (Engelmann 1979: 4).

City government was fragmented and power was dispersed. The city was divided into wards or districts, which were both electoral and administrative units containing relatively small numbers of people. The police and police (lower) courts operated on the ward or district level (Haller 1990a). These wards or districts were divided into electoral precincts. In this environment saloonkeepers were in a position to influence their customers and their votes—they could deliver their precincts and thus control the wards or districts. It was only a slight exaggeration to jest that in New York the easiest way to break up a meeting of Tammany Hall leaders was to open the door and shout: "Your saloon's on fire."

The Constitution does not provide for or even make mention of political parties. Indeed, the Founders perceived the political party as an unnecessary, if not divisive, element in the democratic process. Because of this constitutional omission, political parties enjoyed the same degree of autonomy as any other voluntary association, despite the reality that a political party often determined the outcome of an election. Until the late 1880s, a political party was a private association and as such determined its method for nominating candidates. The methods used lacked state control; they were informal and often effectively disenfranchised the electorate.

Throughout most of the nineteenth century, each political party provided its own ballots and ballot boxes at the general election—previously, a voter stated his preference in a voice vote. Parties printed their own ballots, called "tickets," in different colors. Voters chose one and placed it in the ballot box under the careful eye of party workers. This system virtually precluded "split-ticket" voting and facilitated the buying of votes, because party workers could readily see which ballot a voter cast. This system enabled ward politicians, often with the help of street-corner boys and gangs that proliferated in urban ghettos, to deliver lopsided votes that helped the machine to dominate a city. Politicians employed the gangs for legitimate purposes such as distributing campaign literature, hanging posters, and canvassing for votes. Gang members were also used as "repeaters" (who voted early and often) and as sluggers, who attacked rival campaign workers and intimidated voters. "Elections were held at odd hours in odd places, including bars and brothels. Voters were seldom informed of their franchise, and there was frequent intimidation of voters whose loyalties were suspect" (Johnston 1982: 46). With a small following and a willingness to engage in "political hardball," machine politicians could easily win power. "Powerful ward chieftains were often rewarded with a share of the patronage commensurate with their district's share of the total party vote" (Erie 1988: 26).

From 1888 to 1890, states began providing the ballots for general elections, placing party labels on these ballots. This made the ballot secret and gave formal recognition to political parties, but only the major ones. Laws were enacted to restrict third-party access to the new ballot. The treatment of political parties as public entities provided legal justification for government control of the primary elections that followed: "By 1896 all states but one had statutory regulations for nominating candidates for elective office" (Epstein 1986: 166).

The machine politician was usually a popular figure who, in the days before social welfare programs, provided important services to loyal constituents—jobs, food, and assistance in dealing with public agencies, including the police and the courts. All that he asked for in return were votes and a free hand to become wealthy in politics. To the impoverished and powerless ghetto dweller, this was a small price to pay for services that would otherwise not be available. And even when such services became available through government agencies during the Great Depression, the loss of self-respect that this entailed discouraged many from applying. On the other hand, the precinct captain "asks no questions, exacts no compliance with legal rules of eligibility and does not 'snoop' into private affairs" (Merton 1967: 128).

The very personal nature of the machine is highlighted by one day in the life of George Washington Plunkitt, a Tammany district leader at the turn of the twentieth century who died a wealthy man in 1924 at the age of 82 (Riordon 1963: 93):

- 2:00 A.M. Aroused from sleep by ringing on his doorbell; went to the door and found a bartender, who asked him to go to the police station and bail out a saloonkeeper who had been arrested for violating the excise law. Furnished bail and returned to bed at three o'clock.

- 6:00 A.M. Awakened by fire engines passing his house. Hastened to the scene of the fire, according to the custom of the Tammany district leaders, to give assistance to the fire sufferers, if needed. Met several of his election district captains who are always under orders to look out for fires, which are considered great vote getters. Found several tenants who had been burned out, took them to a hotel, supplied them with clothes, fed them, and arranged temporary quarters for them until they could rent and furnish new quarters.

- 8:30 A.M. Went to the police court to look after constituents. Found six drunks. Secured the discharge of four by a timely word with the judge, and paid the fine of the other two.

- 9:00 A.M. Appeared in Municipal Court. Directed one of his district captains to act as counsel for a widow against who dispossess proceedings had been initiated and obtained an extension of time. Paid the rent of a poor family about to be dispossessed and gave them a dollar for food.

- 11:00 A.M. At home again. Found four men waiting. One had been discharged for neglect of duty, and wanted the district leader to fix things. Another wanted a job. The third sought a place on the Subway and the fourth was looking for work. The district leader spent nearly three hours fixing things for the four men, and succeeded in each case.

- 3:00 P.M. Attended the funeral of an Italian. Hurried back to make his appearance at the funeral of a Hebrew constituent and later attended Hebrew confirmation ceremonies in the synagogue.

- 7:00 P.M. Went to the district headquarters and presided over a meeting of election district captains.

- 8:00 P.M. Went to a church fair.

- 9:00 P.M. At the clubhouse again. Listened to the complaints of a dozen pushcart peddlers who said they were persecuted by the police and assured them he would go to Police Headquarters.

- 10:30 P.M. Attended a Hebrew wedding. Had previously sent a handsome wedding present to the bride.

- Midnight. In bed.

And no job was too unpleasant or demeaning for Democratic machine alderman Charley Weber of Chicago, as newsman Len O'Connor (1984: 117) reports:

> When he hung up the phone, Charley looked at me with sadness and said, "That woman's lived in the ward for more than twenty years and she's Republican. Now she's got a dead rat in the alley behind her house—and she don't call no Republican to come over and take care of her dead rat; she calls the alderman."
>
> "So what are you going to do, Charley?"
>
> "What can I do?" he replied. "I got to go over there, like I said, and pick up her rat and find a good garbage can with a top on it and, well take care of it."
>
> "With one phone call," I said, "you could get somebody to do this."
>
> "You crazy?" he said. "It's a good chance, dealin' with the rat. This woman'll be peekin' out the kitchen window and see the alderman drive up in his Cadillac and get out and pick up her dead rat and drive away with it. She'll tell everybody."

Robert Merton points out that the "political machine does not regard the electorate as an amorphous, undifferentiated mass of voters. With keen sociological intuition, the machine recognizes that the voter is a person living in a specific neighborhood, with specific personal problems and personal wants. Public issues are abstract and remote; private problems are extremely concrete and immediate. It is not through the generalized appeal to large public concerns that the machine operates, but through the direct quasi-feudal relationships between local representatives of the machine and voters in their neighborhood" (1967: 128). "There is nothing satanic about the Chicago machine," notes one newsman. "The basis of its success has always been the machine's dedication to a policy of doing little favors for the people. If a humble householder is getting the runaround from City Hall when he complains about a crew from the Department of Streets and Sanitation smashing up his curbing, a ward committeeman who learns of this will instantly raise hell with 'somebody downtown' and get the curb fixed. The widow who is struggling to make ends meet will get a food basket delivered from the ward office" (O'Connor 1984: 114).

The very personal nature of the machine was noted back in 1931: "In the midst of the current depression, an Irish alderman named Moriarity distributed unleavened bread [matzah] to hundreds of Jewish families in his district, so that they might keep the feast of Passover. This will not cost him any votes" (McConaughy 1931: 312). A Tammany district leader in Manhattan at the turn of the century understood the business of being a political leader: "His job was to see that politics in his district were run efficiently for the purpose for which primarily politics existed. That purpose was to look after the welfare of individuals who resided in the district.... Almost any family was likely to want something. Perhaps the father had died and there was not money enough for the funeral. Perhaps one of the boys had been arrested, justly or unjustly. Perhaps a man who had a job on the police force had been dropped or moved to an undesirable location. Perhaps laborers had to be placed in the street cleaning department, or a transfer effected for one of his constituents from one department to another, or an increase in salary negotiated" (Hapgood and Moskowitz 1927: 41).

And when challenged, the machine could fight back with "hardball" tenacity. Besides voter fraud, machines used repression to weaken their opponents. "Irish party bosses were famous for the ingenuity with which they systematically weakened labor and socialist parties. Machine-controlled bureaucrats and judges denied parade and meeting permits. The party's plug-uglies armed with brass knuckles waded into peaceful assemblies. Opposition leaders were frequently arrested on trumped-up charges. For insurgent Jews and Italians, the Irish machines specialized in rigorous enforcement of Sunday closing laws and in punitive denial of business permits" (Erie 1988: 11). By 1890, most big-city Democratic machines were controlled by Irish bosses. In New York, Irish immigrant Richard Croker led the infamous Fourth Avenue Tunnel Gang and, in 1886, at age 44, Tammany Hall which commanded 90,000 precinct workers and 40,000 jobs (Stevenson 2006).

UPPERWORLD AND UNDERWORLD

The machine leader was a master at keeping his ward or district organized, a broker par excellence who was in a key position to perform services for both the captains of industry and the captains of vice. The machine leader mediated between unorganized urban masses, the underworld, and the upperworld. The machine could deliver franchises, access to underdeveloped land sites, government contracts, tax abatements, and other special considerations (Steffens 1931). Once entrenched, the Irish machine bosses quickly built alliances with older-stock business interests (Erie 1988).

In Chicago, corrupt and inefficient government was promoted by business interests: "All factions, Republican and Democratic, were the handmaidens of the business interests" (Gosnell 1977: 8). "Populous and efficient as the underworld is, it could not wield the influence it does if it were not for its financial and political alliance with the inhabitants of Chicago's upperworld…. The deal is that the underworld shall have a 'liberal government' and a 'wide open town' and its upperworld

allies shall be permitted to plunder the public treasury and appropriate wealth belonging to the people" (Dobyns 1932: 8).

In most cities, particularly Chicago, Kansas City, New York, Philadelphia, Pittsburgh, and St. Louis, "the rough and tumble ward and city bosses allowed the private utilities and favor-seeking men of wealth as well as the purveyors of vice to exploit the great mass of citizens" (Douglas 1974: ix; also Steffens 1957). Merton (1967: 135) notes the irony: "The supporters of the political machine include both the 'respectable' business class elements who are, of course, opposed to the criminal or racketeer, and the distinctly 'unrespectable' elements of the underworld."

"Just as the political machine performs services for 'legitimate' business, so it operates to perform not dissimilar services for 'illegitimate' business: vice, crime and rackets" (Merton 1967: 132). Actually, the relationship between the racketeer and the machine was symbiotic. "Not only are the contributions from the underworld interests an important item in the campaign funds of the dominant party, but the services of the underworld personnel are also significant. When word is passed down from the gangster chiefs, all proprietors of gambling houses and speak-easies, all burglars, pick-pockets, pimps, fences, and their like, are whipped into line. In themselves they constitute a large block of votes, and they frequently augment their value to the machine by corrupt election practices" (Gosnell 1977: 42). As I was reminded many times while living in Chicago in the late twentieth century, death does not preclude the deceased from casting a vote.

In Kansas City, Missouri, a professional criminal (Audett 1954: 120) writes that he received his orders from gangster chief John Lazia, who was an important part of the Pendergast political machine. He looked up vacant lots: "I looked them up, precinct by precinct, and turned them lists in to Mr. Pendergast—that's Tom Pendergast, the man who used to run Kansas City back in them days. When we got a precinct all surveyed out, we would give addresses to them vacant lots. Then we would take the addresses and assign them to people we could depend on—prostitutes, thieves, floaters, anybody we could get on the voting registration books. On election days we just hauled these people to the right places and they went in and voted—in the right places."

In return for "delivering the vote," the ward boss was rewarded with patronage and recognized as lord of his area in a system that resembled feudalism. He appointed, directly or indirectly, police officials in his area, so he was in a position to protect vice activity (gambling, prostitution, liquor-law violations), which he "licensed."

In Kansas City, James Pendergast began his political career as a saloonkeeper. He became a dominant power in the First Ward, and his ability to deliver the vote enabled him to provide police protection for organized gambling. The police acted on his behalf, forcing independent operators to join the gambling combine or get out of business. Between 1900 and 1902, Pendergast named 123 of the 173 policemen on the Kansas City force. The Pendergast machine, under brother Tom, received the support of the gang bosses, and they in return secured police protection (Dorsett 1968). This led to the Election Day outrage of 1934. Despite an estimated 50,000 to 100,000 fake registrations, the machine was taking no chances (Steinberg 1972: 307):

> In the streets that morning, long black limousines cruised slowly past voters on their way to the polls and created an atmosphere of fright, for none of the cars had license plates and their passengers looked like gangsters. One of the cars did more than cruise. When it rolled past the opposition's headquarters in downtown Kansas City, seven shots were fired through the big window, though miraculously no one inside the crowded office was hit by a bullet. Another car pulled up at the ninth ward center of the opposition, and its passengers rushed inside to beat several persons with blackjacks.

With repeat voters, the beating of opposition voters, guns and baseball bats at polling places, the Pendergast machine won an overwhelming victory; four persons were killed and dozens beaten.

In Chicago, "the police department generally, and the [38] district stations in particular, were parts of the Democratic political machine. The department was a source of patronage jobs, and alderman and ward committeemen controlled law enforcement in their districts. In effect, each alderman functioned as the mayor of a community, with the district captain acting as his chief of police. Alderman would choose their own captains and controlled promotions, assignments, and transfers of personnel" (Bopp 1977: 91).

In New York, "in each district of the city, saloon keepers, owners of houses of prostitution, grocers who wanted to obstruct sidewalks, builders who wanted to violate the building regulations of the City, paid tribute at election time to the district leaders, who turned the money over to the general campaign fund of Tammany Hall. The organization collected not only from those who wanted to violate the laws, but also from those who wanted to live peacefully without having the windows of their shops smashed by the district leader's gang, or without being unnecessarily molested by the police" (Werner 1928: 293–294; Lardner and Reppetto 2000). And the Tammany-controlled district attorney was no better than the police: The district attorney's office "was a dumping ground for machine loyalists who could be trusted not to upset any of these arrangements" (Steinberg 2003: 775).

In Chicago, Kansas City, New York, and elsewhere, gambling operators paid heavily for protection, with the understanding that an occasional police raid would have to be staged "for appearances." The raiding squads were careful not to damage furniture or equipment, and policemen obligingly guarded the resort while the gambling operators and their customers made a brief, perfunctory appearance before a friendly magistrate before returning to the gaming house to resume play (Commission on the Review of the National Policy Toward Gambling 1976). An extraordinary Kings County (Brooklyn) Grand Jury, which sat for four years (1938–1942) investigating police corruption in that borough, found bookmaking and policy operations flourishing. Furthermore, the police had "a tendency to make unfounded arrests in order to create a record of apparent efficient law enforcement," and they had a "practice of presenting the evidence in such a manner that a conviction cannot possibly result." An "examination of the plainclothes policemen who were assigned to gambling cases in Kings County during the period covered by this investigation revealed that in all except a few cases the assignment to plainclothes work on gambling violations was accompanied by a distinct change in financial status" (Supreme Court of the State of New York 1942: 5–6).

A special grand jury in Philadelphia in 1928 found that certain members of that city's police department received $2 million in bribes annually (Haller 1985b). The National Commission on Law Observance and Enforcement concluded (1931: 45): "Nearly all of the large cities suffer from an alliance between politicians and criminals. For example, Los Angeles was controlled by a few gamblers for a number of years. San Francisco suffered similarly some years ago and at one period in its history was so completely dominated by gamblers that three prominent gamblers who were in control of the politics of the city and who quarreled about the appointment of the police chief settled their quarrel by shaking dice to determine who would name the chief for the first two years, who for the second two years, and who for the third."

The political machine organized and mobilized urban immigrants and workers into a political force through which it dominated city government. Control of government, in particular the police, enabled the machine to protect vice entrepreneurs and gang leaders who reciprocated with financial and voting support. Control of government enabled the machine to provide special favors to the captains of business and industry who reciprocated with financial support. Control of public and private sector jobs, and funds with which to provide social services, strengthened machine support among the urban masses (Figure 2.1).

REFORM AND NATIVISM

In cities dominated by machine politics, the same ones that would spawn organized crime, a pattern

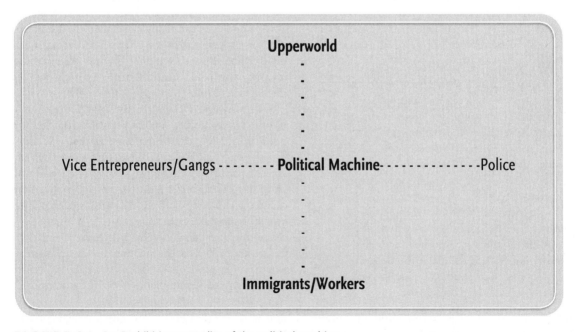

FIGURE 2.1 Pre-Prohibition centrality of the political machine

of corruption-reform-corruption-reform was often interspersed with investigations and widely publicized hearings. It is important to recognize the political motivation, and the not-insignificant degree of hypocrisy, behind many of these exposés and reform efforts. In New York, investigations were often initiated by upstate, rural, Protestant Republican interests against downstate (New York City) urban, Catholic and Jewish Democrats. In 1894, for example, the New York State Senate appointed a special committee, five Republicans and two Democrats, headed by Senator Clarence Lexow of (heavily Republican) Rockland County, to investigate charges of vice and corruption leveled by the (Presbyterian) Reverend Charles H. Parkhurst. The hearings revealed a sordid tale of corruption. However, the recommendations of the committee, given its findings, were actually quite modest, because they were designed not to correct the problem but rather to enable Republicans to share in the rich patronage created by the Democratic machine (Fogelson 1977). The threat of investigation and public disclosure was often used to secure the support of city politicians for legislation favored by rural or big business interests. Corruption was real and often rampant, but many of the efforts purporting to deal with it were just as corrupt—morally, if not legally.

Reform was typically fostered by business leaders for their own ends: "The machine leaders had to be paid to defeat legislation opposed by business interests: municipal ownership, labor legislation, adequate health regulations, better schools, new parks, decent housing, aid to the needy.... Businessmen in politics were eager without bribes to oppose anything that raised taxes or threatened private enterprise. They wanted to stop paying graft, but keep all the favors graft bought. They demonstrated that the perennial demand for business methods in government was as logical as a cry that penitentiaries ought to be run by criminals" (Loth 1938: 280).

In Chicago, dishonest, corrupt, and inefficient government was actually promoted by business interests: "All factions, Republican and Democratic, were the handmaidens of the business interests" (Gosnell 1977: 8). "Reform" was frequently a favorable label applied by newspapers to the efforts of two, sometimes overlapping, interest groups: businessmen and white, Anglo-Saxon Protestants, whose voting strength was in rural America. "Most immigrant voters realized instinctively that honesty, efficiency, and economy in government would do nothing to alleviate their condition and could severely cripple the system's ability to dispense favors" (Buenker 1973: 26).

Reformers were often part of the rampant *nativism* that at times intertwined with social Darwinism. Nativism helped tie urban dwellers—immigrants in general, Catholics (and often Jews) in particular—to the political machine. Attitudes of extreme religious prejudice have a long history in our country, dating back to the first colonists. Settlers came to the New World in search of religious freedom, but they sought only *their* religious freedom. Virulent anti-Catholicism was such an important part of Colonial America that in the seventeenth century, mass could not be publicly celebrated anywhere in Colonial America except in Pennsylvania. In 1834, a mob of Protestant workmen in Charlestown, Massachusetts, ransacked and burned a convent, the first fruit of Catholic educational enterprise in New England (Bennett 1988). Samuel Morse (1791–1872), distinguished painter, inventor of the telegraph code, and son of a prominent minister, wrote, "We are the dupes of our hospitality. The evil of immigration brings to these shores illiterate Roman Catholics, the tools of reckless and unprincipled politicians, the obedient instruments of their more knowing priestly leaders"[2] (quoted in Bennett 1988: 40). In contrast, the machine politician "cultivated the immigrant's ethnic pride by defending him against nativist attack, observing his customs, and concerning himself with conditions in the homeland" (Buenker 1973: 5). The most successful campaign waged by nativist interests involved prohibiting the beverages most favored by immigrants.

---

2. Morse was also a strong defender of slavery.

PROHIBITION

The acrimony between rural and urban America, between Protestants and Catholics, between Republicans and (non-Southern) Democrats, between "native" Americans and more recent immigrants, and between business and labor reached a pinnacle with the ratification of the Eighteenth Amendment in 1919. Efforts at limiting or prohibiting alcohol consumption, however, date back to the earliest days of our republic. Residents of the United States have traditionally consumed large quantities of alcoholic beverages. In 1785, Dr. Benjamin Rush, surgeon general of the Continental Army and a signer of the Declaration of Independence, wrote a pamphlet decrying the use of alcohol. The pamphlet helped fuel the move toward prohibition and inspired in 1808 the establishment of the first temperance society whose cause was supported by Protestant churches throughout the country (Hamm 1995).

The temperance movement made great progress everywhere in the country, often accompanying nativist sentiments that swept over the United States during the late 1840s and early 1850s. In 1869, the Prohibition Party attempted, with only limited success, to make alcohol a national issue. In 1874, the Women's Christian Temperance Union (WCTU) was established, and in 1893 the Anti-Saloon League was organized. Around the turn of the twentieth century, both groups moved from efforts to change individual behavior to a campaign for national prohibition. The WCTU was handicapped because its members lacked the franchise—women could not vote until 1920. After a period of dormancy, the prohibition movement was revived in the years 1907–1919 (Humphries and Greenberg 1981). By 1910, the Anti-Saloon League had become one of the most effective political action groups in U.S. history. It had mobilized America's Protestant churches behind a single purpose: to enact national prohibition (Tindall 1988). In 1915, nativism and Prohibitionism fueled the rebirth of the Ku Klux Klan, which spread into northern states and exerted a great deal of political influence, including

control of state politics in Indiana (see Tucker 1991). During World War I, anti-German feelings, already strong, were made more intense because brewing and distilling were associated with German immigrants (Cashman 1981).

Prohibition was accomplished by the political efforts of an economically declining segment of the American middle class. "By effort and some good luck this class was able to impose its will on the majority of the population through rather dramatic changes in the law" (Chambliss 1973: 10). Andrew Sinclair (1962: 163) points out, "In fact, national prohibition was a measure passed by village America against urban America." We could add: much of Protestant America against Catholic (and, to a lesser extent, Jewish) America. "Thousands of Protestant churches held thanksgiving prayer meetings. To many of the people who attended, prohibition represented the triumph of America's towns and rural districts over the sinful cities" (Coffey 1975: 7; Gusfield 1963). Prohibition reflected not only revulsion at drunkenness and contempt for the drinking immigrant masses, but also represented an assault on the pleasures and amenities of city life (Bennett 1988).

Big business was also interested in Prohibition; alcohol contributed to industrial inefficiency, labor strife, and the saloon that served the interests of machine politics. Workmen's compensation laws also helped stimulate business support for temperance. Between 1911 and 1920, forty-one states had enacted workmen's compensation laws. "By making employers compensate workers for industrial accidents the law obligated them to campaign for safety through sobriety. In 1914 the National Safety Council adopted a resolution condemning alcohol as a cause of industrial accidents" (Cashman 1981: 6).

The Eighteenth Amendment to the Constitution was ratified in 1919 and ten months later, over a veto by President Woodrow Wilson, Congress passed the Volstead Act. The act strengthened the language of the amendment and defined all beverages containing more than 0.5 percent alcohol as intoxicating. Although prohibitionists believed that primary enforcement would come at the state and local level, the Volstead Act provided for federal enforcement and the Prohibition Bureau, an arm of the Treasury Department, was created. Local enforcement was unenthusiastic and inconsistent, and the Prohibition Bureau soon became notorious for employing agents on the basis of political patronage (Hamm 1995).[3] This patronage provision helped pass the act, and almost 18,000 federal jobs were exempted from Civil Service restrictions: "The clause had been passed by dry votes in Congress. The lobbyists who cracked the whip over the legislators later explained that Congress had insisted upon the exemption in return for passage of the Volstead Act" (Loth 1938: 346). The treasury agent who brought down Al Capone commented that the "most extraordinary collection of political hacks, hangers-on, and passing highwaymen got appointed as prohibition agents" (Irey and Slocum 1948: 5).

In addition to being inept and corrupt, Prohibition Bureau agents were a public menace: They ran up a record of being killed (by 1923, thirty had been murdered) and for killing hundreds of civilians, often innocent women and children. By 1930, the figure rose to eighty-six federal agents and two hundred civilians killed. Prohibition agents set up illegal roadblocks and searched cars; drivers who protested were in danger of being shot. Agents who killed innocent civilians were rarely brought to justice—when they were indicted by local grand juries, the cases were simply transferred, and the agents escaped punishment (Woodiwiss 1988).

The bureau was viewed as a training school for bootleggers, because agents frequently left the service to join their wealthy adversaries. The Treasury Department was headed by the banking magnate Andrew Mellon (1855–1937), a man who had millions invested in the liquor trade before Prohibition and was not interested in enforcing the new law (Sinclair 1962). Neither were most local police agencies and very little money was allocated to enforce the most

sweeping criminal law ever enacted in the United States (Asbury 1950). Ten days after the Eighteenth Amendment went into effect, three Prohibition agents were indicted in Chicago for bribery and selling seized liquor to bootleggers. And it got worse. Prohibition agents escorted liquor trucks and helped smugglers unload cargoes: "On salaries averaging less than three thousand dollars a year, prohibition agents bought country homes, town houses, city and suburban real estate, speedboats, expensive automobiles, furs, and jewelry for their women, and fine horses; many reported to work in chauffeur-driven cars." One agent had been a worker on a garbage truck before being appointed: "He worked three months as an agent and then took a six-month leave so that he and his wife could tour Europe" (Irey and Slocum 1948: 6). It was not until 1930, that Prohibition Bureau agents were placed under civil service procedures (Gottschalk 2006).

Herbert Packer (1968: 263) reminds us that people do not necessarily respond to new criminal prohibitions by acquiescence. He points out that resistance can be fatal to the new norm; moreover, when this happens "the effect is not confined to the immediate proscription but makes itself felt in the attitude that people take toward legal proscriptions in general." Thus, primary resistance or opposition to a new law such as Prohibition can result, secondarily, in disregard for laws in general: *negative contagion*. During Prohibition, a "general tolerance of the bootlegger and a disrespect for federal law were translated into a widespread contempt for the process and duties of democracy" (Sinclair 1962: 292). This was exemplified by the general lawlessness that reigned in Chicago:

> Banks all over Chicago were robbed in broad daylight by bandits who scorned to wear masks. Desk sergeants at police stations grew weary of recording holdups—from one hundred to two hundred were reported every night. Burglars marked out sections of the city as their own and embarked upon a course of systematic

---

3. In 1923, New York repealed a statute that had incorporated Prohibition into state law, thereby placing the burden of alcohol law enforcement on federal agents.

plundering, going from house to house night after night without hindrance…. Payroll robberies were a weekly occurrence and necessitated the introduction of armored cars and armed guards for the delivery of money from banks to business houses. Automobiles were stolen by the thousands. Motorists were forced to the curbs on busy streets and boldly robbed. Women who displayed jewelry in nightclubs or at the theater were followed and held up. Wealthy women seldom left their homes unless accompanied by armed escorts.

Every year until Prohibition was repealed, the murder rate rose, going from 6.8 per 100,000 persons in 1920 to 9.7 in 1933 (Chapman 1991).

In the ninety days preceding the date the Eighteenth Amendment became effective, $500,000 worth of bonded whiskey was stolen from government warehouses, and afterward it continued to disappear (Sinclair 1962). Less than one hour after Prohibition went into effect, six armed men stole $100,000 worth of whiskey from two Chicago boxcars. In February 1920, a case of whiskey purchased in Montreal for $10 could easily be sold in New York for $80 (Coffey 1975). In fact, Canadians began making so much money from Prohibition that provinces with similar laws soon repealed them (Sinclair 1962). The heavily Catholic state of Rhode Island refused to ratify Prohibition and its 400 miles of coastline soon became awash with boats bringing in liquor from Canada. Newport, Rhode Island, is barely two hundred nautical miles from Nova Scotia and Yarmouth where the Bronfman brothers, owners of the Seagram liquor empire, sold legal liquor at 65 cents a gallon to smugglers who resold it in the United States for $7 a gallon (Krajicek 2007).

A limited amount of beer and wine could be made under the Prohibition law for personal or religious consumption and almost immediately, stores sprang up selling hops, yeast, malt, cornmeal, grains, copper tubing, crocks, kettles, jugs, bottle tops, and other equipment for home distilling and brewing. Within one week of the onset of Prohibition, portable stills were on sale throughout the country (Asbury 1950; Kavieff 2000). This legal loophole was soon exploited for commercial purposes by organized crime.

ORGANIZED CRIME

Until Prohibition, gangsters were merely errand boys for the politicians and the gamblers; they were at the bottom of a highly stratified social milieu. The gamblers were under the politicians, who were "kings" (Katcher 1959). Prohibition changed the relationship among the politicians, vice entrepreneurs, and gang leaders. Before 1920, the political boss acted as a patron for the vice entrepreneurs and gangs: He protected them from law enforcement, and they gave him financial and electoral support. The onset of Prohibition, however, unleashed an unsurpassed level of criminal violence, and violence is the specialty of the gangs. Physical protection from rival organizations and armed robbers was suddenly more important than was protection from law enforcement. Prohibition turned gangs into empires (Logan 1970).

Arthur Flegenheimer—"Dutch Schultz"—provides an outstanding example of how the opportunities afforded by Prohibition turned thugs into wealthy "beer barons." At the beginning of Prohibition, Schultz, a street tough, worked for a trucking company whose owner went into the beer business. In 1928, Schultz became a partner in a Bronx speakeasy. He bought trucks and garages and, aided by a vicious crew of gunmen, became a major beer distributor. Schultz expand into the territories of rival beer businesses. One unfortunate was kidnapped, severely beaten, hung by his thumbs, and eventually blinded—sending a message that was not lost on other recalcitrant beer distributors. Schultz soon controlled Prohibition-related businesses and politics in an area that stretched

> ## Changes in the Social Order
>
> **Pre-Prohibition**
> Machine Politicians
> Vice Entrepreneurs
> Gangs
>
> **Prohibition**
> Gangs
> Machine Politicians
> Vice Entrepreneurs

FIGURE 2.2 Prohibition changes the social order

from the Bronx to Uptown Manhattan. With Prohibition "pumping money into mob pockets, power shifted from men with votes to men with money and guns" (Pietrusza 2003: 302).

Although America had organized crime before Prohibition, it "was intimately associated with shabby local politics and corrupt police forces"; there was no organized crime activity "in the syndicate style" (King 1969: 23). The "Great Experiment" was a catalyst that caused organized crime, especially violent forms, to blossom into an important force in American society. Prohibition mobilized criminal elements in an unprecedented manner. Pre-Prohibition crime, insofar as it was organized, centered around corrupt political machines, vice entrepreneurs, and, at the bottom, gangs. The competitive violence of Prohibition turned the power structure upside down. It also led to a new level of criminal organization (Figure 2.2).

In order to be profitable, the liquor business, licit or illicit, demands large-scale organization. Raw material must be purchased and shipped to manufacturing sites. This requires trucks, drivers, mechanics, warehouses, and laborers. Manufacturing efficiency and profit are maximized by economies of scale. This requires large buildings where the whiskey, beer, or wine can be manufactured, bottled, and placed in cartons for storage and distribution to wholesale outlets or saloons and speakeasies. If the substances are to be smuggled, ships, boats, and their crews are required, as well as trucks, drivers, mechanics, laborers, and warehouses. And there is the obvious need to physically protect shipments

through the employment of armed guards. "As illegal entrepreneurs," notes Mark Haller (1985a: 142), bootleggers "also had to learn to use legal institutions to service their illegal enterprises, they had to learn banking to handle their money, insurance to protect their ships, and the methods of incorporation to gain control of chemical and cosmetics companies from which they diverted industrial alcohol. They also dealt with varied legitimate companies to purchase trucks, boats, copper tubing, corn sugar, bottles, and labels." Businessmen who had previously been involved in the legal liquor industry did not remain in business during Prohibition; this left the field open to opportunistic amateurs, often violent young men who had heretofore been left behind in the race for economic success. Bootlegging "was a relatively open field of endeavor and allowed ambitious young Italians and Jews (as well as some Poles and Irishmen) to catapult to quick success" (Haller 1974: 5). It brought Jewish criminals into prominence.

Toughened by the ethnic conflicts of urban America and endowed with a cohesion forged by centuries of anti-Semitism, Jewish criminals found a niche in gambling and labor racketeering. By the second decade of the twentieth century, however, opportunities afforded by America released an entrepreneurial spirit that had been bottled up in the ghettos of Eastern Europe and gave free rein to the Jewish pursuit of education—the Jewish criminal was being pushed to the fringes of the past. Then came Prohibition and the fast-track opportunities presented brought the Jewish criminal to the fore: "During Prohibition, 50 percent of the nation's leading bootleggers were Jews, and Jewish gangs bossed the rackets in some of America's largest cities" (Rockaway 1993: 5).

Prohibition encouraged cooperation between gang leaders from different ethnic groups and various regions—*syndication*. Legal or illegal, the liquor business is international in scope. Smuggled rum and whiskey from Canada, the Caribbean, and Europe had to be moved across the Great Lakes or from the Atlantic onto beaches along the East Coast. Shipments then had to be trucked intra- and interstate to warehouses at distribution points. At each juncture the shipment required political and physical protection. Only the criminal organization dominant in the local area could provide such protection. Syndication arose out of these needs, and a number of meetings between important organized figures have been documented: "Meetings were held for a number of reasons—to settle disputes, choose successors for slain or deposed leaders, divide local or regional markets, or discuss production, supply, and distribution problems. Some gatherings consisted of Italian criminals and limited their discussions to problems of interest to them. Others involved only Jews or Irish or some other ethnic group; still others were formed of members of a variety [of] ethnic syndicates" (Nelli 1976: 212).

With the onset of the Great Depression (1929) and the subsequent repeal of Prohibition (1933), the financial base of organized crime narrowed considerably. Many players dropped out: Some went into legitimate enterprises or employment; others drifted into conventional criminality. Bootlegging, as noted earlier, required trucks, drivers, mechanics, garages, warehouses, bookkeepers, and lawyers—skills and assets that could be converted to noncriminal endeavors. For those who remained in the business, reorganization was necessary. "When Prohibition ended in 1933, bootleggers were still young men—generally in their thirties—yet with wealth and nationwide contacts that had grown out of their bootlegging enterprises. In addition to their liquor interests, they already had substantial investments in restaurants, nightclubs, gambling, and other profitable businesses. In the 1930s and 1940s, then, they used their national contacts, diverse interests, and available capital to cooperate in a variety of entrepreneurial activities, legal and illegal" (Haller 1974: 5–6). The *Browne-Bioff Episode* provides an example.

Willie Bioff was a small-time Chicago racketeer who specialized in shakedowns of kosher butchers. He went into partnership with George Browne, a local official of the International Alliance of Theatrical Stage Employees (IATSE), whose members included motion picture projectionists and other movie theater employees. The two began extorting money from theater chains under the threat of "labor trouble." With Prohibition ending, the Chicago Outfit was searching for new areas of profit, and Frank Nitti soon "muscled in" on the scheme, first as a 50-percent partner and eventually as a 75-percent partner. In 1932, Browne unsuccessfully ran for the presidency of the international union. Then, in 1934, Nitti arranged for Browne to gain the support of major East Coast gangsters Lucky Luciano and Lepke Buchalter in New York and Longie Zwillman of New Jersey, and Browne was elected president of the IATSE (Nelli 1976). The convention that elected Browne was pervaded with "such an atmosphere of intimidation that opposition wilted" (Johnson 1972: 329).

Browne appointed Bioff to a union position, and the two increased their extortion activities, this time on a nationwide scale. They were able to extort money from Hollywood film studios such as RKO and Twentieth Century-Fox under the threat of closing down theaters throughout the country (Johnson 1972). The scheme ended in 1941, when the brother of the Twentieth Century-Fox chairman of the board was indicted for income-tax evasion. In exchange for leniency, he disclosed the activities of Bioff and Browne. Bioff was eventually sentenced to ten years, Browne to eight. As a result of their cooperation, important members of the Outfit were convicted.[4]

---

4. In 1955, living under an assumed name, Bioff left his Phoenix home and entered his pickup truck. A moment later, Bioff and the truck went up in a tremendous explosion—a dynamite bomb had been wired to the starter.

Three years later, all were paroled in a scandal that rocked the administration of President Harry Truman.

Some entrepreneurial bootleggers simply continued in the newly legitimate liquor trade. Sam Bronfman moved the main office of the Seagram Company from Canada to New York and paid $1.5 million in taxes that the United States said he owed on Prohibition-era shipments. Taking advantage of the start-up time American distillers needed to get back into business, Seagram flooded the country with Canadian whiskey (Allen 1998). His bootlegging confederate, Lewis Rosenstiel, continued to operate Schenley Distillers Company. The Reinfeld syndicate—Joe Reinfeld and New Jersey crime boss Longie Zwillman—became Renfield Importers. Joseph P. Kennedy, father of a future president, moved from bootlegging to head Somerset Importers (Fox 1989).

Just before the end of Prohibition, gang leaders began meeting throughout the United States in anticipation of the new era. In 1932, the Chicago Police Department detained a number of gangsters, including Paul Ricca of the Capone syndicate, Lucky Luciano, and Meyer Lansky of New York, for questioning. In 1934, the major leaders of organized crime in the East gathered at a New York hotel, with Johnny Torrio (discussed in Chapter 3) presiding. They came to an understanding: "Each boss remained czar in his own territory, his rackets unmolested, his local authority uncontested. In murder, no one—local or imported—could be killed in his territory without his approval. He would have the right to do the job himself or permit an outsider to come in—but only at his invitation. In fact, no lawlessness on an organized scale could take place in his domain without his sanction and entire consent, unless he was overruled by the board of governors." Now each mob leader "had behind him not just his own hoods, but a powerful amalgamation of all hoods. Every gang chieftain was guaranteed against being interfered with in his own area—and against being killed by a rival mobster" (Turkus and Feder 1951: 99).

"A second meeting was called in Kansas City to hear from the Western executives. The Capone crowd from Chicago and the Kansas City mob liked the idea. Reports came from Cleveland and Detroit that the Mayfield Gang and the Purple Mob wanted in. Boston and Miami, New Orleans and Baltimore, St. Paul and St. Louis—all flocked to the confederacy of crime, until it was nationwide" (Turkus and Feder 1951: 99). Hank Messick (1967: 32) adds, "The country was divided into territories. Wars ended between regional groups, between religious groups, between national groups." There are several significant indications of this cooperation: the founding of modern Las Vegas (discussed in Chapter 11), labor racketeering on a national level (discussed in Chapter 13), and Murder, Inc.

Murder, Inc.

The setting is the East New York–Brownsville section of Brooklyn, a Jewish neighborhood, and the adjoining Italian neighborhood of Ocean Hill. The story begins in the spring of 1930, when Abe ("Kid Twist"—from the twisted chocolate candy he favored) Reles, Martin ("Bugsy") Goldstein, and Herschel ("Pittsburgh Phil") Strauss decided to take over the neighborhood rackets dominated by the three Shapiro brothers, Irving, Meyer, and Willie. The boys from East New York–Brownsville secretly teamed up with a crew from Ocean Hill, all of who had worked as strong-arms for the Shapiros. An attempt to kill the three brothers while they were checking the inventory at their brewery failed, and the Shapiros responded (Ross 2003).

In 1930, a member of the Reles group was killed, and Reles and Goldstein were wounded. Meyer Shapiro then abducted Reles's girlfriend, whom he beat and raped. The Reles group struck back. During 1930 and 1931, eighteen attempts were made on Meyer Shapiro's life—number nineteen was successful. Brother Irving's demise followed, and Willie was abducted, severely beaten, and buried alive. The Reles group took over gambling, loansharking, and prostitution in the East New York–Brownsville section, and they soon became involved in labor racketeering. Their specialty, however, was murder.

The "Boys from Brooklyn" were used as staff killers by the newly formed confederation of organized crime leaders that emerged from Prohibition. They took orders from labor racketeer Lepke Buchalter and Mafia boss Albert Anastasia and received a retainer to be "on call" whenever the occasion arose—and it arose often. In a ten-year period they murdered more than 80 persons in Brooklyn alone. They were so efficient that gang leaders from across the country made use of their services, and Paul Kavieff (2006) reports that the Boys from Brooklyn murdered about a thousand persons nationally.

There were full-dress rehearsals; getaway routes were carefully checked. A "crash car" followed the stolen vehicle containing the actual killers in the event of a police pursuit. Guns were rendered untraceable, although ropes and ice picks were often the preferred weapons. One of the group's members describes the "contract system" (Berger 1940: 5): "The 'trooper' [killer] is merely directed to take a plane, car, or train to a certain place to meet 'a man.' The man 'fingers' [points out] the victim for the trooper, who kills him when it is convenient. The trooper then leaves town immediately, and when local hoodlums are questioned, their alibis are perfect."

In 1940, several of the "Boys" were indicted for the 1933 murder of a 19-year-old who had been "convicted" of talking to the authorities. Quite to the surprise of the Brooklyn district attorney's office, one of the group's members agreed to become a government witness. Reputedly the toughest of the "Boys," Abe Reles, upon being granted immunity from prosecution, began to disclose the sensational details of Murder, Inc. His information and subsequent testimony led to the conviction and electrocution of seven men. Before any case could be made against Albert Anastasia, Reles had an accident: On November 12, 1941, while under constant police guard, he fell out of the sixth-floor window of the Coney Island Half-Moon Hotel. His death remains officially unexplained.

Murder, Inc. was an "experiment" gone astray, placing too much knowledge into the hands of a small group of low-level psychopaths, eventually becoming a threat to syndicate leaders. This aspect of bureaucracy—specialization/division of labor—was not to be repeated.

THE KEFAUVER CRIME COMMITTEE

The importance of organized crime as a national political issue was recognized by Tennessee Senator Estes Kefauver in 1950. The five-term member of Congress had been elected to the Senate in 1948 despite vigorous opposition from the political machine headed by notorious "Boss" Ed Crump of Memphis. On January 5, 1950, Kefauver introduced a resolution "to investigate gambling and racketeering activities" by a special subcommittee. The crime committee was established by Senate resolution, but not without a fight. Bosses of big-city machines were concerned that an investigation might look into their activities. Further, the chairman of the Judiciary Committee, Pat McCarren of Nevada, was apparently worried about the impact of an investigation on his native state, so he held Kefauver's bill captive for several months. On April 6, 1950, the gambling boss of Kansas City, Missouri, and one of his men were murdered in a Democratic Party clubhouse. This helped spur passage of the Kefauver legislation, and on May 10, 1950, the senator became chair of the Special Committee to Investigate Organized Crime in Interstate Commerce, launching the first major congressional investigation into the phenomenon (Moore 1974). This was made all the more dramatic by a new element in public hearings—television:

> One factor, television, was largely responsible for fixing the public consciousness upon this one investigation…. For the first time millions of Americans (some 20 million by one estimate) observed the periodic outbursts of drama and boredom that comprised a congressional hearing as it unfolded. Americans gaped as the denizens of other worlds—bookies, pimps, and gangland enforcers, crime bosses and their slippery lawyers—marched across their television screens. They watched and were

impressed by the schoolmasterish Estes Kefauver, the dignified Tennessean who was the committee's first chairman, as he condemned criminals and the system of ineffective law enforcement, graft, and popular apathy that permitted them to thrive. (Wilson 1975: 353)

The first hearing was conducted on May 26, 1950, and before Kefauver's term as chair ended on May 1, 1951, the committee heard more than six hundred witnesses in fourteen cities. This whirlwind of activity led the committee to conclude that "there is a sinister criminal organization known as the Mafia operating throughout the country with ties in other nations in the opinion of the committee. The Mafia is the direct descendant of a criminal organization of the same name originating in the island of Sicily" (Kefauver 1951a: 1). The Mafia, according to Kefauver (1951b: 19), is "the shadowy international organization that lurks behind much of America's organized criminal activity." In fact, the committee's final report contained a great deal of nonsense. The committee tied organized crime and the Mafia, thereby equating Italians with organized crime (Moore 1974).

SUMMARY

1. Be familiar with the pioneering criminal role of the "Robber Barons":
   - "Robber Barons" such as Astor, Vanderbilt, Drew, Fisk, Gould, Stanford, and Rockefeller, engaged in crime on an unparalleled level, providing models for immigrant-based crime that followed.
2. Know the connection between immigration, the saloon, and urban machine politics:
   - There are strong historical parallels between the repression suffered by Sicilian peasants and that endured by their Irish counterparts.
   - Irish success in urban politics is explained by their ability to speak English and familiarity with electoral democracy, in addition to cultural attributes.
   - Throughout much of urban America, the saloon was a center of neighborhood activity, an important social base for political activity, and saloonkeepers became political powers in many cities.
3. Appreciate the connection between the upperworld of commercial interests and the underworld, and the influence of nativism on efforts at reform:
   - The machine leader served as a broker between urban masses, businessmen, and government, and between the upperworld and the underworld.
   - Reform was often connected to nativism.
4. Be familiar with the role of Prohibition in the development of organized crime and the changes that occurred with the repeal of Prohibition:
   - Prohibition altered the relationship between the political machine and gangs.
   - Prohibition led to an unparalleled level criminal organization.
   - Prohibition encouraged cooperation between gang leaders from different ethnic groups and various regions—*syndication*.
   - When Prohibition ended, organized crime moved into labor racketeering on a national level, and cooperated in the founding of modern Las Vegas.
   - Murder, Inc. was an outcome of the cooperation between criminal organizations.
5. Appreciate how the Kefauver Committee influenced views of organized crime:
   - The Kefauver committee tied organized crime and the Mafia, thereby equating Italians with organized crime.

REVIEW QUESTIONS

1. Who were the "Robber Barons" and how did they provide models for the organized crime that followed their rise to power and wealth?

2. What is the connection between urban machine politics and immigration?

3. What are the parallels between the repression suffered by Sicilian peasants and that endured by their Irish counterparts?

4. What explains Irish success in urban politics?

5. What was the connection between urban politics and the saloon?

6. What was the broker role played by political machine leaders?

7. Why was the machine politician usually a popular figure among immigrants?

8. What was the connection between the political machine and the underworld?

9. How did this role change with Prohibition?

10. How did Prohibition lead to criminal syndication?

11. What was the connection between reform and nativism?

12. Why did business interests favor reform?

13. What was the relationship between *negative contagion* and Prohibition?

14. Why did Prohibition result in an unparalleled level of criminal organization?

15. How did organized crime change with the repeal of Prohibition?

16. What was "Murder, Inc." and how does it provide an example of interethnic cooperation in organized crime?

17. What did the Kefauver Committee conclude?

Crime bosses Lucky Luciano of New York and Al Capone of Chicago

The American Mafia

Early in the morning of January 20, 2010, FBI agents and other law enforcement officers arrested nearly 130 members and associates of the American Mafia in the largest nationally coordinated organized crime takedown in FBI history. Included were members of New York's Five Families, the DeCavalcante Family of New Jersey, and the Patriarca Family of New England. They were charged with murder, drug trafficking, arson, loansharking, illegal gambling, witness tampering, labor racketeering, and extortion. The American Mafia "may have taken on a diminished criminal role in some areas of the country, but in New York, the Five Families are still extremely strong and viable," said Dave Shafer, an assistant special-agent-in-charge who supervises FBI organized crime investigations in New York (FBI press release January 20, 2011).

While the power and influence of the American Mafia has declined, it remains a dangerous entity in the Northeast and Chicago, two areas that will be examined in this chapter.

CHAPTER 3

CHAPTER 3 WILL ENABLE THE READER TO UNDERSTAND:

- The connection between the cultural attributes of Sicilian immigrants and the development of the American Mafia

- The role of the "Castellammarese War" in American Mafia history

- Historical differences between the American Mafia in New York and Chicago

- The importance of Johnny Torrio and Al Capone in the development of organized crime in Chicago

- The connection between political reform and organized crime violence in Chicago

- The structure of the American Mafia in New York and that in Chicago

As noted in Chapter 2, organized crime in the United States has a history that encompasses cities in every region of the country. However, outside of the Northeast and Chicago, there are few or no vestiges of the formidable criminal organizations that evolved out of Prohibition. The Irish, Jewish, and Italian communities from which these criminal organizations drew the bulk of their personnel failed to provide a continuous supply of replacements necessary for their survival. As discussed in Chapter 2, the Irish found success in politics, and although Jewish immigrants and their progeny played a vital role in the development of organized crime, by the third generation, Jews had moved out. Italian-American communities were sufficiently large enough to provide adequate replacement personnel in only a few cities, such as New York and Chicago, the focus of this chapter. Even there, those aspiring to membership in the American Mafia are a tiny fraction of the Italian-American community now solidly part of America's middle class and whose members are well-represented in the ranks of professionals and public officials. Why this tiny fraction remains interested in being "wiseguys" is explored in Chapter 4.

The American Mafia is unique: "No other criminal organization has controlled labor unions, organized employer cartels, operated as a rationalizing force in major industries, and functioned as a bridge between the upperworld and the underworld" (Jacobs, Friel, and Raddick 1999: 128).

THE MAFIA IN NEW YORK

Between 1891 and 1920, 4 million Italians entered the United States, the overwhelming majority coming from the *Mezzogiorno*—the area south of Rome—in particular, Sicily, Naples, and its surrounding Campania area, and the province of Calabria (Gallo 1981). Every important Italian-American organized crime figure has had cultural roots in the *Mezzogiorno* (discussed in Chapter 5). These poor immigrants encountered an economy shaped by the Astors, the Rockefellers, and the Vanderbilts, in which powerless people had little opportunity. Facing enormous social and economic hardship exacerbated by nativism, they "found work in the city's construction crews, laboring as ditch diggers, hod carriers, and stone cutters. As long as they had strong arms, it did not matter if they could not speak English or operate a complex machine" (Gallo 1981: 44).

By early 1900, about 500,000 (mostly southern) Italians lived in New York City, in the most deprived social and economic circumstances. Italian immigration "made fortunes for speculators and landlords, but it also transformed the neighborhood into a kind of human ant heap in which suffering, crime, ignorance and filth were the dominant elements" (Petacco 1974: 16). The Italian immigrant provided the cheap labor vital to the expanding capitalism of that era. As with earlier generations of immigrants, a small number sought to succeed by bending and breaking both moral and legal codes. Being relative latecomers, they could not imitate the scions of earlier generations, the Robber Barons, who had already, by "hook or crook," secured a place in society. Instead, they adapted their southern Italian culture to the American experience.

"Functional deficiencies of the official structure," notes Robert Merton (1967: 127), "generate an alternative (unofficial) structure to fulfill existing needs somewhat more effectively." Randall Collins (1975: 463) adds, "Where legitimate careers are blocked and resources available for careers in crime, individuals would be expected to move in that direction." Thus, Collins notes, the prominence of Italians in organized crime is related to the coincidence of several historical factors: "The arrival of large numbers of European immigrants from peasant backgrounds who demanded cultural services that the dominant Anglo-Protestant society made illegal; the availability of a patrimonial form of military organization that could be applied to protecting such services; and the relatively late arrival of the Italians in comparison with other ethnic groups (for example, the Irish) who had acquired control of legitimate channels of political and related economic mobility" (1975: 463).

"In order to beat rival organizations," notes Luigi Barzini (1965: 273), "criminals of Sicilian descent reproduced the kind of illegal groups they had belonged to in the old country and employed the same rules to make them invincible." Richard Gambino (1974: 304) concludes that, although southern Italian characteristics do not predispose people toward crime, "where the mode of life has been impressed onto organized crime it has made it difficult to combat effectively the criminal activity" (1974: 297).

Among these immigrants were *mafiosi* who established protection regimes in every American city that had a sizable Sicilian population, "feeding off the common laborer's honest toil and claiming to serve as a means of easing adjustment to American society" (Nelli 1976: 136). The Mafia "was imported by Sicilian immigrants, who reproduced it in the cities in which they settled, as a ritual brotherhood consisting of loosely linked but otherwise independent and uncoordinated 'families' organized hierarchically" (Hobsbawm 1969: 686). Mafia groups "served important social as well as financial functions. The group produced a sense of belonging and of security in numbers. This function was at least in part through the use of initiation ceremonies, passwords and rituals, and rules of conduct with which members must abide" (Nelli 1976: 138). "The fertile criminal soil of the United States," notes John Dickie (2004: 164), "was one of the rare environments into which the mafia's method could be transferred wholesale." Groups of *mafiosi* were also involved in the manufacture of low-cost, high-proof, untaxed alcohol, a business that prepared them well for Prohibition, and enabled them to break out of the bounds of their "Little Italys" and into the wider community—bootlegging was an equal opportunity employer.

One of Francis Ianni's (1972: 57) informants describes a Mafia gang operating in Brooklyn in 1928: "All the old Sicilian 'moustaches' used to get together in the backroom of the club—it was a *fratallanze* [brotherhood] and they used to call it *Unione Siciliana*. They spent a lot of time talking about the old country, drinking wine and playing cards. But these were tough guys too, and they were alky cookers [bootleggers] and pretty much ran things in the neighborhood. They had all of the businesses locked up and they got a piece of everything that was sold."

The *Unione Siciliana* emerged in nineteenth-century New York as a lawful fraternal society designed to advance the interests of Sicilian immigrants. Branches were established wherever new colonies of Sicilians expanded. With Prohibition, gangsters began to infiltrate and pervert the association. With an expanding criminal front, *Unione* leaders became natural catalysts for any racketeers seeking to widen their influence and profit potentials.[1] Membership included clannish old-world criminal types who stressed the maintenance of the cultural traditions of the Sicilian Mafia, and a younger Americanized faction anxious to increase business operations through cooperative agreements even with non-Italians. "The *Unione* of the 1920s became the object of power struggles, with both orientations contending at local, regional, and national levels for more advantageous posts. This struggle terminated in 1931 in the Castellammarese War" (Inciardi 1975: 115).

CASTELLAMMARESE WAR

By 1930, there were two major Mafia factions in New York, one headed by Giuseppe ("Joe the Boss") Masseria operating out of the Little Italy of East Harlem, and the other by Salvatore Maranzano whose business office was in midtown Manhattan. Prohibition had enabled the Mafia gangs to break out of the bounds of "Little Italy" and operate in the wider society—booze-hungry Americans were not fussy about the source of their liquor. The struggle for domination of Italian-American organized crime in New York became known as the Castellammarese War because Maranzano and many of his supporters came from the small Sicilian coastal

---

1. In Italy, the Freemasons reportedly played a similar role: Mafia bosses and members became members to enhance their relationships with business and political leaders (della Porta and Vannucci 1999; Paoli 1999).

town of Castellammare del Golfo. The Maranzano group consisted mainly of Sicilians, especially the "moustaches," Old World types, many of whom had fled from Mussolini's persecution of *mafiosi* (discussed in Chapter 5). After his own escape, Maranzano helped smuggle many of his compatriots into the United States, and they supported their *padrone*. The Masseria group had both Sicilian and non-Sicilian members, including Lucky Luciano and Gaetano Lucchese (Sicilians), Vito Genovese (Neapolitan), and Frank Costello (Calabrian). Through ties developed by Luciano, they were allied with non-Italians such as Meyer Lansky and Ben ("Bugsy") Siegel. As the war turned against Masseria—the Maranzano forces were reinforced by a continuing supply of Sicilian exiles—five of his leading men, led by Luciano, went over to the other side.

On April 15, 1931, Masseria drove his steel-armored sedan, a massive car with plate glass an inch thick in all of its windows, to a garage near the Nuova Villa in the Coney Island section of Brooklyn. He then walked to the restaurant for a meal and a card game with Luciano. It was Masseria's last meal ("Racket Chief Slain by Gangster Gunfire" 1931). Luciano excused himself and went to the washroom: "Joe the Boss was shot as he sat at the table. As Masseria died, he still clutched the ace of diamonds, and that, in years to come, became a symbol of impending death to all good Mafia members" (Messick 1973: 54). The Castellammarese War was over.

It did not take long for Maranzano to irritate many of his followers, particularly the more Americanized gangsters such as Luciano. Joseph Bonanno, who was born in Castellammarese del Golfo, was a staunch ally of Maranzano. In his autobiography Bonanno points out that the new Mafia boss was out of step with the times. "Maranzano was old-world Sicilian in temperament and style. But he didn't live in Sicily anymore. In New York he was advisor not only to Sicilians but to American Italians. Maranzano represented a style that often clashed with that of the Americanized men who surrounded him after the war. It was difficult, for example, for Maranzano even to communicate effectively

with many of these men, for they only understood American street cant" (Bonnano 1983: 137–38).

On September 10, 1931, four men carrying pistols entered a suite at 230 Park Avenue, the Grand Central Building, in New York City. "One of them ordered the seven men and Miss Frances Samuels, a secretary, to line up against the wall. The others stalked into the private office of Salvatore Maranzano. There was a sound of voices raised in angry dispute; blows, struggling, and finally pistol shots, and the four men dashed out of the suite." Maranzano was found with "his body riddled with bullets and punctured with knife wounds" ("Gang Kills Suspect in Alien Smuggling" 1931: 1). The killers are believed to have been Jews (who Maranzano and his bodyguards would not recognize) sent by Lansky and Siegel at the behest of Luciano. Because the killers flashed badges, Maranzano and his bodyguards apparently believed them to be federal immigration agents who had visited him before as part of an investigation into the smuggling of Sicilians into the country. They attempted to kill him silently with knives, and when Maranzano fought furiously to save his life, they shot him.

Lucky Luciano

With the deaths of Masseria and Maranzano, Lucky Luciano became the most important American Mafia figure in New York, a status he would enjoy until 1935. In that year, investigators for special prosecutor Thomas E. Dewey discovered an extensive prostitution network that, although independent at one time, had been subject to extortion by a member of the Luciano Family. In a single raid, Dewey's investigators arrested prostitutes, madams, and "bookers" (pimps). They were pressured and cajoled into testifying against Luciano, who protested that he had no knowledge of or involvement in the extortion activities. Dewey charged that acting on behalf of Luciano, two hundred bordellos and three thousand prostitutes were organized into a $12-million-a-year business. In fact, the witnesses tying Luciano to prostitution were not credible, and this enterprise was not even a good moneymaker for the syndicate (Powell 2000). "Dewey's argument seemed to be that Luciano was a prostitution overlord but even if he was not, he still was a menace to society" (Stolberg 1995: 128).

Luciano chose to take the stand in his own defense—a bad decision, as it turned out. Dewey was able to trap him in lies about his criminal record. In 1936, Luciano was found guilty of sixty-one counts of compulsory prostitution and sentenced to a term of thirty to sixty years in prison, despite an arguably weak case and a pervasive feeling that Luciano was actually convicted of being "notorious" (Powell 2000).

Luciano languished in Clinton State Prison at Dannemora, New York, while war raged in Europe and the Pacific. By 1942, German submarines operating in U.S. coastal waters had sunk 272 U.S. ships. It was suspected that information on American shipping was being leaked to the Germans by people employed in eastern ports.[2] It was also suspected, incorrectly, that German submarines were receiving supplies from American fishing boats. The specter of sabotage was raised when the luxury liner *Normandie*, which had been refitted as a naval vessel, rolled over in flames while harbored in the Hudson River. (In fact, renamed the U.S.S. *Lafayette*, the *Normandie* was accidentally set ablaze by workers using acetylene torches.)

Luciano was transferred to a prison closer to New York City where he met with naval intelligence officers. Through Meyer Lansky, the word went out: In addition to ordering port workers and fishermen to "keep alert," crime figures helped place intelligence operatives in key areas by supplying them with union cards and securing positions for them on the waterfront, on fishing boats, and in waterfront bars, restaurants, and hotels. Crime figures also provided another important service. At the request of naval officials, they prevented strikes and

other forms of labor unrest that could interrupt wartime shipping (Campbell (1977; Costanzo 2007). There was no sabotage, and waterfront workers became careful about what they said lest they reveal the kind of goods that were being unloaded, loaded, and their destination.

In 1945, Dewey, now governor of New York, received a petition for executive clemency on behalf of Luciano, citing his efforts during the war. The following year, Dewey announced that Luciano would be released from prison and deported to Italy. Luciano left the United States on February 9, 1946. Before the end of the year, however, he was in Havana holding court with the elite of New York's underworld. U.S. pressure on Cuba compelled Luciano to return to Italy in 1947, where he died of a heart attack in 1962.

In the aftermath of the Castellammarese War, five Mafia Families emerged in New York: *Bonanno*, *Colombo* (originally the Profaci Family), *Gambino* (originally the Mineo Family), *Genovese* (originally the Luciano Family), and *Lucchese* (originally the Reina Family).

The New York Families have been subjected to successful prosecution aided by a breakdown in discipline and loyalty. There have there been dozens of made-guy turncoats and by 2004, the heads of all five Families were incarcerated. As former FBI supervisory agent Lin DeVecchio (2011: 158) notes: "Today … you make an arrest and everybody rolls over."

THE STRUCTURE OF THE AMERICAN MAFIA: NEW YORK MODEL

At the center of the New York model is the boss—the *paterfamilias*, who may be assisted by an underboss (*sottocapo*) and counselor/advisor (*consigliere*). In a structure that resembles a model of the universe, the boss is surrounded by clients, for example, captains (*capiregime*), to whom he acts as a patron. The captains are surrounded by members or soldiers (*soldati*), to whom they act as patrons. This crime unit is tied together in a network that

---

2. Coastal cities such as New York, Atlantic City, and Miami, fearing a loss of tourist trade, refused to enforce blackouts, creating a neon shooting gallery for German submarines: "The U-boats nightly lay in the wait on the seaward side of the shipping lanes and picked off their sharply silhouetted victims at will" (Kennedy 1999: 68).

includes nonmember associates who are clients of each of the members, including the boss and captains (see Figure 3.1). In the American Mafia, each of the bosses is connected (by kinship, friendship, mutual respect) to every other boss. This structure represents what Richard Scott (1981) refers to as a *natural system*: Members are not necessarily guided by their organization's goals, but they share a common interest in the survival of the system and engage in collective activities informally structured to secure this end. In organized crime as a natural system, the organized crime unit is more than an

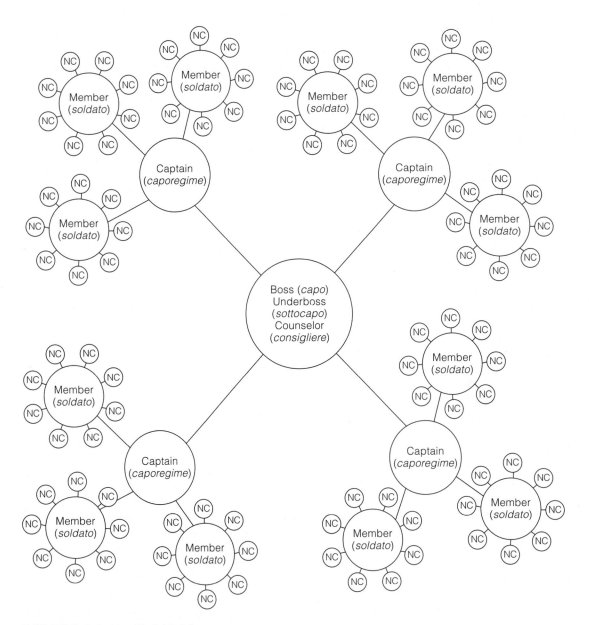

FIGURE 3.1 New York Model

instrument for attaining defined goals; it is fundamentally a social group attempting to adapt and survive in a dangerous environment. In New York, the basic unit is the Family, or *borgata*. However, the actual name by which a group is known may vary. In New England, for example, it is the "Office," in Chicago, "The Outfit." Although any number of members may be related, the term *Family* does not imply kinship by blood or marriage. Each crime unit is composed of members and associates.

Membership

Although part of a particular crew, each member is an independent entrepreneur—not an employee—who receives no salary from the group. Instead, each member of a Mafia Family, a "made guy," has been accorded a valuable franchise, a sense of entitlement that enables him to engage in a virtual smorgasbord of criminal activity with the knowledge that he will be supported and protected by the Family. Violent and aggressive, he is constantly on the prowl for moneymaking opportunities, sharing a portion (roughly 15 percent) of all profits from crime with his captain who in turn shares his earnings with the boss. In return, he will be protected by the Family from other criminals and has unlimited access to the network in which the Family is enmeshed. His reputation as a "made guy" serves to instill fear, a valuable resource in the otherwise anarchic world of criminals. Even when a made guy engages in legitimate business, he enjoys advantages: Unions may avoid pressing demands, security costs are minimized (dangerous to victimize a made guy), and competitors can be intimidated.

In a typical pattern, a made guy will attract nonmembers who are eager to associate with him, to become "connected," because an associate enjoys some of the status and connections that the crime Family enjoys. In a discussion with an associate, a new member of the Colombo Family reported on his recent change in status: "Since I got made I got a million fuckin' worshippers hanging around" (Iannuzzi 1993: 172). The member-as-patron thus sits at the center of a network of nonmember clients that constitutes an action-based unit for coordinated criminal activities. If the member is able to generate considerable income, he gains greater status in the Family and can become a candidate for advancement to *caporegime*. If successful associates are Italian, they become candidates for membership.

In criminal circles, the importance of membership is revealed by the numerous terms and phrases used to indicate membership status: "made guy" (the Sicilian Mafia refers to a newly initiated member as being "made into a man" [Paoli 2003]), "wiseguy," "button" or "receiving his button," "being straightened out," "goodfella," "amico," and "friend of ours." And there is an initiation ceremony. Testifying before a senate subcommittee ("Russian Organized Crime" 1996: 46), Anthony ("Gaspipe") Casso,[3] imprisoned former underboss of the Lucchese Family, stated:

> To become a "made" member, you would have to be sponsored by a captain of the family, who would bring you to the boss of the family and sponsor you to become a "made" member. They have a ceremony with the boss, the *consigliere,* and the underboss present at the time, and the captain who brings you in. They prick your trigger finger and make it bleed, and then they put a little on a piece of paper; they set it on fire and you burn it in your hand, and you repeat after them that you will never betray La Cosa Nostra, or you will burn like the paper is burning in your hand. And your life does not belong to you anymore; your life belongs to them.

In 1989, two electronic eavesdropping devices were placed in the basement ceiling of a house in Medford, Massachusetts, a Boston suburb. The bugs recorded the initiation of four men into the crime Family then headed by Raymond Patriarca, Jr., who presided at the ceremony.

---

3. For a journalistic biography of Casso, see Carlo (2008).

The prospects were introduced to the gathered Family members, and the *consigliere* asked each to individually take an oath in Italian/Sicilian (translated): "I want to enter into this organization to protect my family and to protect all of my friends. I swear not to divulge this secret and to obey with love and *omertá*." He was then assigned to a *caporegime*.

Each candidate was asked which finger he shoots with, and that finger was pricked to draw blood. A holy card with the image of the Patriarca family saint was burned. The prospect was told that he was required to keep secrets and could not leave the Family unless he was dead. Some details of mob protocol and rules were explained: to introduce other members as "a friend of ours" and associates as "a friend of mine"; if ordered, to kill anyone who betrays the Family, even if he is your brother; to respect the female relatives of other members—under penalty of death; to memorize the chain of command; to keep your *caporegime* informed of your whereabouts; to remember that all crime Families in America are related; and to avoid kissing other members in public—too conspicuous.

Michael Franzese,[4] a captain in the Colombo Family, reports a two-stage process. First, he was formally proposed—taken by an old-time member to meet the Family boss, who explained the rules: "After the meeting, my name, along with those of the other potential inductees, was circulated around the other four Families" (Franzese and Matera 1992: 124). Franzese was then assigned to a *caporegime* for a probationary period of nearly a year. In 1975 he was formally inducted in a ceremony similar to those already described.

Former NYPD detective Ralph Salerno (with Tompkins 1969) reports that recruitment into organized crime involves the careful study of neighborhood youngsters by those who control membership. A potential recruit must exhibit a recognition of the authority of the organization and a willingness to perform various criminal and noncriminal functions (usually minor at first) with skill and daring and without asking questions. Robert Woetzel (1963: 3) points out: "The standards of the teenage gang from which the potential criminals come are the same as those of an adult conspiracy": a code of loyalty and exclusive "turf" (territory). The gang boy may also have a criminal record and an antisocial attitude, which indicate that he is a "stand-up" kid, the proper credentials for a career in organized crime.

Raymond Martin, a former ranking officer with the NYPD, describes why recruitment is made easy in certain Italian neighborhoods in Brooklyn (1963: 61):

> On so many street corners in Bath Beach, in so many luncheonettes and candy stores in Bensonhurst, boys see the mob-affiliated bookies operate. They meet the young toughs, the mob enforcers. They hear the tales of glory recounted—who robbed what, who worked over whom, which showgirl shared which gangster's bed, who got hit by whom, the techniques of the rackets and how easy it all is, how the money rolls in. What wonder is it that some boys look forward to being initiated into these practices with the eagerness of a college freshman hoping to be pledged by the smoothest fraternity on campus. With a little luck and guts, they feel, even they may someday belong to that splendid, high-living band, the mob.

The centrality of the neighborhood for providing a pool of organized crime aspirants cannot be overemphasized. In these areas, there is a "romanticization of the mob"—young "wannabes" copy the styles of their notorious idols and are eager to ingratiate themselves with made guys. As one recruit, raised in the organized crime neighborhood of Brooklyn's East New York–Brownsville section, recounts, "At the age of twelve my ambition was to be a gangster. To be a wiseguy. To me being a wiseguy was better than being president of the United States. It meant power among people who

---

4. Michael's father, John ("Sonny") Franzese, when he was arrested in 2008 at age 89 for racketeering, was identified as underboss of the Colombo Family.

had no power. It meant perks in a working-class neighborhood that had no privileges. To be a wise-guy was to own the world. I dreamed of being a wiseguy the way other kids dreamed about being doctors or movie stars or firemen or ball players" (Pileggi 1985: 13).

An undercover FBI agent describes the day an associate was "made"—initiated as a member of the Bonanno crime Family (Pistone 1987: 64): "When he came back, he was ecstatic, as proud as a peacock. 'Getting made is the greatest thing that could ever happen to me,' he said. 'I've been looking forward to this day ever since I was a kid.' … That night we partied together for his celebration. But now every-body treated him with more respect. He was a made guy now." After completion of his initiation, Jimmy ("the Weasel") Fratianno "was so excited that he could feel his legs tremble." Becoming a member of the Los Angeles crime Family of Jack Dragna "made him a special person, an inheritor of enor-mous power. It was something he had wanted for as long as he could remember" (Demaris 1981: 3).

To be eligible for membership, a young man (there are no female members) must be of Italian descent. As Gambino Family underboss Sam Gravano states, "Years and years ago, you had to be Italian on both sides. Then it became that you only had to be that on your father's side. Not your mother's. Because they say you are what your father is, you carry his name. Like John Gotti's wife is part Russian Jew. So his son, John Junior, got made, right? He's part Italian and part Russian Jew" (Maas 1997: 84). One source reports that this change in qualifica-tions occurred in 1975 as a response to recruiting difficulties experienced by the New York Families (Volkman 1998). The requirement of having an Ital-ian heritage, no matter how defined, limits the supply of prospective members.

The prospective member requires a sponsor and must have a history of successful criminal activity or possess certain skills required by the group. They can be roughly divided between the "earners" and the "shooters." The earners have proven their mettle by financial success, while shooters, such as Jimmy Fratianno, possess the ability to execute persons in an efficient,

impersonal, and dispassionate manner (Demaris 1981). However, every potential member is expected to participate in a murder—although not necessarily as the actual executioner. Such participa-tion serves to more closely bind the person to the ongoing conspiracy that is organized crime, and it precludes government agents from becoming members. Peter Maas (1997: 46) points out that even though committing a murder—"making your bones"—was not a prerequisite for induction into *Cosa Nostra*, more often than not, it would happen. "Murder was the linchpin of *Cosa Nostra*—for con-trol, for discipline, to achieve and maintain power. For made members and associates, it was an everyday, accepted fact of life." Sam and Chuck Giancana (1992) state that in Chicago, a guy didn't necessarily have to kill someone to be made if he had powerful friends to protect him from such dirty work. There is also evidence that one can get credit for killing some-one by assisting in the murder rather than carrying out the killing itself. An organized crime group is particularly interested in criminals who have proven to be moneymakers, "earners" who can increase the group's income. In 1988, the former underboss of the Cleveland Family testified before a congressional committee:

> My name is Angelo Lonardo. I am 77 years old, and I am a member of the La Cosa Nostra. I am the underboss of the Cleveland organized crime Family. I became a member of La Cosa Nostra in the late 1940s, but have been associated with the organization since the late 1920s. When I was "made" or became a member of La Cosa Nostra, I went through an initiation ceremony. I later learned that to be proposed for membership in La Cosa Nostra, you would have to have killed someone and stood up to the pressure of police scrutiny. Today, you do not have to kill to be a member, but just prove yourself worthy by keeping your mouth shut or by being a "stand-up" guy. However, if you are called upon to kill someone, you have to be prepared to do it.

According to FBI recordings released at the 1992 trial of John Gotti, in New York, the "making" of prospective members requires passing the list around to other Families. But this is complicated by the very informality that characterizes organized crime—men are typically known only by their nicknames, which may not be precise enough to identify a particular person for such an important function as determining fitness for membership. In fact, just before a ceremony for the making of new members, Sam Gravano reported to *consigliere* Frank Locascio that "I don't have it right, Frank. I don't have their last names. I don't have the proper spellings. I ain't got the, the guys all down" (recorded January 4, 1990). At his 2005 sentencing hearing, Bonanno Family boss-turned-informant Joseph Massino was asked by a federal judge for the real names of people against whom he had testified. "I don't know their proper names," Massino replied.

Because of their acquisitive and violent nature, members of organized crime can easily come into conflict with members of the same or another organized crime unit. The more members a group has, the greater the likelihood of conflict—too many made guys in search of too few moneymaking opportunities. Under such circumstances, members are more likely to become involved in high-risk ventures that can be a threat to the safety of the group. This dynamic places natural limitations on membership. Furthermore, each new member is a potential threat to the security of the group—a potential informant—so new members are selected with caution and great care. A prospective member may have to serve the group for many years before achieving membership status. During the 2006 trial of John Gotti, Jr. (for ordering the beating of radio personality and head of the Guardian Angels Curtis Sliwa—he was not convicted), a member of the Gambino Family testified that there is a ceiling on how many members each of the five New York Families can initiate—someone has to die (Hartocollis 2006).

Membership, compared with some type of associate status, provides rewards associated with being an "insider." As one member told me, "A made guy is considered more honorable," meaning that there is a greater level of trust—and respect. Only members will be allowed to attend certain important meetings and be privy to important conversations and information, and information is an important basis of power. The basic mechanism for resolving disputes is arbitration—a *sitdown* or *table*—and a nonmember needs a member to represent him. A nonmember associate in a dispute with a made guy is at a distinct disadvantage—a disadvantage that can be life-threatening. This can become balanced if the associate is an "earner"—a source of substantial funds.

Considerable "psychic gain" accrues with membership. Within criminal and certain legitimate circles, being "made" conveys a great deal of prestige, if not fear. The President's Commission notes that although a soldier is the lowest-ranking member of the organization, "he is a considerable figure on the street, a man who commands respect and fear" (PCOC 1986c: 44). In testimony before the commission, a witness elaborated:

> [Q:] How did you come to know that Greg Scarpa [soldier in the Colombo crime Family] is a "made" individual while someone in his crew is not "made"?
>
> [A:] Conversation—you could just see the way that everybody answers to him; I mean, he has a club on 13th Avenue [in Brooklyn] and everyone comes up to him, and no one—they don't double park their car without getting his permission, so to say. In other words, no one does anything without getting his permission. So you could just see the respect he gets.

A number of otherwise legitimate persons are attracted by the mystique that surrounds organized crime. Popular sources report that many young women are attracted to organized crime figures and to the bars and nightclubs that are owned or frequented by them. For similar reasons young men may aspire to membership in organized crime—reasons that go beyond economic advantages—out of a desire to be part of the mystique reinforced by media representations such as *The Godfather* trilogy,

Goodfellas, and *The Sopranos*; they serve as an unintended medium for recruitment.

There are also important disadvantages associated with membership. Law enforcement agencies take great interest in a criminal if they discover he is a made guy. Any insult or assault on a member requires that he kill the offender. He is also required to obey the orders of his boss, even if this means participating in the murder of a complete stranger or perhaps a close friend or relative. But, of course, the member is protected by the boss, who will respond to any attack on one of his soldiers as a personal affront, a fundamental lack of respect, requiring mobilization of the group's resources for violence. It is the ready availability of private violence that makes the organized crime group a viable entity.

The continuation of the American Mafia depends on the ability of crime units to recruit new members, which, in turn, depends upon the availability of a pool of qualified applicants. For at least some crime groups, this is becoming more difficult. On January 4, 1990, John Gotti, boss of the Gambino Family, was recorded by the FBI decrying the paucity of qualified candidates for membership to *consigliere* Frank Locascio:

> And where we gonna find them, these kinda guys? Frank, I'm not being a pessimist. It's gettin' tougher, not easier. We got everything that's any good. Look around, ask your son someday, forget who you are, what you are. Talk to your son like his age. Put yourself in his age bracket, and let him tell you what good kids in the neighborhood other than the kids that are with you. Or good kids in the neighborhood other than with him. You know what I'm trying to say? I told you a couple of weeks ago, we got the only few pockets of good kids left.

Crews

Members and associates are organized into crews, semi-independent units nominally headed by a *caporegime*, a *capodecina*, a street boss, or even a soldier.

Crews generate finances, which they share with their crew chief, who shares it with the *caporegime* or with the boss. These crews have been described in a number of popular books on organized crime. FBI agent Joseph Pistone (1987: 51–52),[5] in his undercover role, describes the crew of a soldier in the Bonanno Family, whose "headquarters" was the back room of a store stocked with expensive clothing—stolen merchandise:

> Although these were lower-echelon guys in the mob, they always had something going. They always had money. They were always turning things over. They always had swag around…. You name it, they stole it. Jilly's crew would hit warehouses, docks, trucks, houses…. There wasn't one hour of one day that went by when they weren't thinking and talking about what they were going to steal, who or what or where they were going to rob…. The mob was their job.

The crew headed by Paul Vario,[6] a *caporegime* in the Lucchese crime Family, used a drab, paint-flecked storefront cabstand and dispatch office in Brooklyn as its headquarters. Nicholas Pileggi (1985: 35) notes that the Vario crew did most of the strong-arm work for the Lucchese Family. "At the cabstand there were always young tough guys ready to go out and break a few heads whenever Paul gave the order and killers who were happy to take on the most violent of assignments." The persons in Vario's crew "had always been outlaws. They were the kids from the neighborhood who were always in trouble. As youngsters they were the ones invariably identified as toughs by the police and brought into the precinct for routine beatings, whenever some neighborhood store burglary or assault moved the station house cops into action."

The crew headed by John Gotti, a *caporegime* and later boss of the Gambino Family, was headquartered

---

5. Pistone's exploits became the subject of a book and movie, *Donnie Brasco*. The Bonanno Family captain who had permitted the agent's penetration was found murdered, his hands symbolically cut off.
6. Vario, played by Paul Sorvino in the movie *Goodfellas*, died in prison while serving a 15-year sentence.

at the Bergin Hunt and Fish Club, a (very) private storefront in the Ozone Park section of the New York City borough of Queens: "The Bergin men were good customers in the small cafes and stores operating on slim margins. Around his neighbors, Gotti acted like a gentleman; around him they acted as though he were a successful salesman. He began saluting the community with Fourth of July fireworks displays and barbecues; some residents began saluting him by alerting the club when men resembling undercover detectives were around" (Mustain and Capeci 1988: 112). The fireworks display was reportedly not appreciated by important wiseguys who considered it part of a pattern by Gotti of drawing unnecessary attention to organized crime.

The Boss

Although he is at the center of the universe of an American Mafia unit, the boss does not have a complete overview of the decentralized activities of his members. In the past the boss was usually a senior citizen—it takes many years to gain the respect of members and the knowledge and connections needed by the group. It is a sign of weakness that some *Cosa Nostra* bosses are relatively young, as well as volatile and violent. Some Families are being ruled by a troika of elder captains; "taking the seat," being identified as the boss, is apparently too risky given the law enforcement attention it attracts.

Typically, the boss operates out of a fixed location: a restaurant, a private club, or his own business office. Raymond Patriarca, Sr., the New England crime boss who died of natural causes in 1984 at age 76, operated out of his vending-machine business, the National Cigarette Service, in the Federal Hill section of Providence, Rhode Island. Vincent Teresa (and Renner 1973: 95) states that the entire area around Patriarca's headquarters was an armed camp: "It was impossible to move through the area without being spotted and reported." Throughout

AP Photo/David Cantor

John Gotti, right, arrives at court on the morning of February 9, 1990. The jury continued to debate charges that Gotti ordered the assault on John F. Connor, former vice president of Carpenters Union Local 608. Attorney Gerald Schargel follows Gotti and his brother Peter Gotti, at left.

LITTLE ITALY

The historic Little Italy of lower Manhattan encompasses about two dozen square blocks, but few actual Italians. According to the latest census, of the neighborhood's 8,600 residents, about 5 percent identify themselves as Italian, none of whom were been born in Italy. While there are plenty of Italian restaurants and an annual Feast of San Gennaro, most residents are of Asian origin; the National Park Service designates the area as the Chinatown and Little Italy Historic District (Robert 2011).

the day, Patriarca received visitors, sometimes legitimate persons asking for a favor, usually to resolve a dispute, but more frequently "a parade of the faithful bearing tithes, cold cash for the middle drawer in the dirty back room of a cigarette vending-machine business in a run-down section of Providence. It could be the receipts from a wholly owned subsidiary or rent from a franchise. In a complex maze of interests, he completely controlled some markets, especially those involving gambling, loansharking, and pornography, and dabbled in others such as truck hijacking and drug trafficking in which free-lancers negotiated fees to do business" (O'Neill and Lehr 1989: 43).

The boss of the Genovese Family in New York operated out of an Italian restaurant in lower Manhattan, to which he was driven every day from his home in Long Island by a chauffeur-bodyguard. In the back of the restaurant was a table reserved for him. Persons having business with the boss would come in all day long and sit at the table for varying periods. Strangers were not welcome in the restaurant, which was located in the heart of an Italian neighborhood dominated by the Genovese Family. There was no place to park; all parking spaces were taken by members of the Family or their associates. Anyone walking in the area who was not recognized would be reported to the Family members at the restaurant. If a stranger entered the restaurant, he or she was told that a reservation was needed—but the restaurant refused to take reservations (Abadinsky 1983). Joseph Colombo, whose crime Family bears his name, operated out of a neighborhood real estate firm, Cantalup Realty Co., in the Bensonhurst section of Brooklyn. He was on the books as a licensed real estate salesman—the licensing

test was fixed (Cantalupo and Renner 1990). Gambino Family boss John Gotti operated out of the Ravenite Social Club at 247 Mulberry Street in lower Manhattan's Little Italy; every Wednesday, Gotti would hold court at a gathering of Family captains. To avoid electronic surveillance Gotti would discuss business on the street or in an apartment upstairs from the club; however, the apartment was bugged by the FBI (Coffey and Schmetterer 1991).

A boss has a number of men who report directly to him. They carry messages and perform assignments as necessary; they also physically protect the boss. In many crime groups, particularly those in New York, where five Families—and one from New Jersey—operate, most of the activities of Family members are not under the direct or indirect supervision of the boss. He often finds out about many of the activities of members only as the result of periodic briefings by the captains.

Crime boss Joseph Bonanno (with Lalli 1983: 157) describes how he operated as "Father" of his Family:

> Internal disagreements between Family members were solved at the grassroots level by group leaders or by the consigliere. A Family member's personal or business problems were usually handled in this manner, and the problem rarely had to be brought to my attention.
>
> On the other hand, if a Family member wanted to go into business with a member of another Family, such an association would need the approval of the Fathers of the respective Families. A Family member's relations with non-Family members was his own affair.

Other than meeting with other Fathers and meeting with group leaders within my Family on an ad hoc basis, being a Father took up relatively little of my time. Family matters were largely handled by the group leaders under me. Indeed, there were many Family members I never met. If I convened a Family meeting, I met only with the group leaders, who in turn passed the information to the people in their groups.

Peacekeeping, notes Bonanno, was his main responsibility as head of the Family. Given the violent nature of "made guys," this is a crucial responsibility. According to the PCOC (1985a), the Family boss is also responsible for making all important decisions on trial strategy when a Family member is the defendant. This responsibility is for protecting Family interests during the trial.

Crime boss Carlo Gambino would often conduct briefings in a moving car to reduce the possibility of surveillance. Very important or sensitive operations, such as those that could result in conflict with other crime Families or attract undue law enforcement attention, are cleared with the boss in advance. And, as noted earlier, in all but the smallest units, the boss will be assisted by an underboss (*sottocapo*) and a counselor/advisor (*consigliere*).

The boss, like many other members of a crime Family, has investments in illegitimate and legitimate enterprises, often in partnership with other members of his own or other crime groups or with nonmember associates. He receives a portion of the illegal earnings of all of the members of his Family. A soldier will share his earnings with his captain, who will pass on a portion to the boss. A captain will expect 15 percent of an ongoing business, such as loansharking or extortion, but more from a particular score, such as a hijacking. According to undercover FBI agent Joe Pistone (2004: 36), a greedy captain "will take 50 percent of whatever is waved under their noses" and he must provide the boss with whatever amount is requested. "All the captains of the Family must make weekly payments to the boss, and the amount of these payments is completely at the whim and discretion of the boss." The captain has to produce that

amount every week, and when "he falls short, the captain usually goes nuts and terrorizes his soldiers and demands they increase their payments to him."

Sitting in the back of his restaurant headquarters, the head of the Genovese Family would receive visitors who passed sealed envelopes filled with money to his bodyguard—their show of respect (Abadinsky 1983). As opposed to bureaucratic organizations, the money goes only in one direction—upward. When the boss gives someone money, it is for investments on which a substantial return is expected, or violence is guaranteed.

The boss demands absolute respect and total obedience. His working day is spent in exchanges with many people. With a word or two, a sentence, a shake of the head, a smile, or a gesture, he can set in motion a host of activities and operations involving dozens, if not hundreds, of persons. The boss is treated with a great deal of deference. People rise when he enters the room, and they never interrupt when he is speaking. If they are close, a kiss on the boss's check is considered an appropriate gesture of respect. If the boss rises, all rise. If the boss rises and embraces an individual, this is considered a great honor, often reserved only for other bosses.

The intensity of government surveillance and prosecution of organized crime during the last four decades has made the position of boss less desirable than in the past. As a result, filling the position may be difficult because those most qualified—men with good incomes and low profiles—may also be those who are most reluctant to undergo the law enforcement scrutiny that comes with the position. In such circumstances, the boss may be a relatively weak figure, with strength concentrated in the captains heading crews of earners.

The weakness of current Mafia Families is highlighted by the meteoric rise of Carmine Sessa, who admitted to eleven murders. Inducted into the Colombo Family in 1987, three years later he was *consigliere,* and three years after that a government witness testifying against fellow Family members (Capeci 2003). In 2011, in a historic first, the head of the Bonanno Family, Joseph C. Massino, often reputed to be last of the old-time bosses, was in federal court testifying as a cooperating witness.

The Commission

Crime bosses are linked in a rather informal arrangement known as the "commission," The commission, reports Bonanno (with Lalli 1983: 159), can arbitrate disputes. Having no direct executive power, however, it has to depend on influence: "It had respect only insofar as its individual members had respect. In 1986, in what became known as the "Commission Case" (*United States v. Salerno,* 85 Cr. 139, SDNY, 1985), a number of New York bosses were convicted of conducting the affairs of "the commission of La Cosa Nostra" in a pattern of racketeering that violated the RICO statute (discussed in Chapter 14). The case revealed the role of the commission in New York:

- Regulate and facilitate relationships between the Families

- Promote and facilitate joint ventures between Families

- Resolve actual and potential disputes between Families

- Regulate the criminal activities of the Families

- Extend formal recognition to newly chosen Family bosses and resolve leadership disputes within Families

- Authorize the execution of Family members

- Approve of the initiation of new members into the Families

The power of approving the initiation of new members keeps Family size stable and prevents wholesale initiation, which would be likely in times of intra-Family conflict. During the struggle to lead the Colombo Family (1991–1993), for example, the commission would not permit either faction to initiate new members and thereby gain an advantage over its opposition.

Rules

Even though the American Mafia does not have written rules, it has an elaborate set of norms that govern behavior. Francis Ianni (1972) argues that

RULES OF THE AMERICAN MAFIA

- Report any failure to show respect to one's patron immediately.
- Violence must be used, even if only of a limited type, to ensure respect.
- Never ask for surnames.
- Never resort to, or even threaten, violence in a dispute with a "made guy."
- Do not use the telephone except to arrange for a meeting place, preferably in code, from which you will then travel to a safe place to discuss business.
- Avoid mentioning specifics when discussing business— for example, names, dates, and places—beyond those absolutely necessary for understanding.
- Keep your mouth shut—anything you hear, anything you see, stays with you, in your head; do not talk about it.
- Do not ask unnecessary questions. The amount of information given to you is all you need to carry out your instructions.

- Never engage in homosexual activities.
- If your patron arranges for two parties to work together, he assumes responsibility for arbitrating any disputes between the parties.
- The boss can unilaterally direct violence, including murder, against any member of his Family, but he cannot engage in murder-for-hire, that is, make a profit from murder.
- The boss cannot use violence against a member or close associate of another Family without prior consultation with that Family's boss.
- The principal form of security in the American Mafia is an elaborate system of referral and vouching. Vouching for someone who turns out to be an informant or undercover officer entails the death penalty.

Sources: Abadinsky (1981a, 1983); Capeci (2003); Coffey and Schmetterer (1991); D. Jacobs (2002); transcripts from the 1992 trial of John Gotti.

the rules of the American Mafia are actually standards of conduct based on the traditions of southern Italy, particularly the concept of family loyalty. However, my research (Abadinsky 1981a, 1983) indicates that the rules are not traditional but quite rational and sometimes counter to southern Italian tradition. For example, loyalty to the crime Family supersedes loyalty to one's own blood family. According to the rules, if required by the boss, a member must participate in the murder of a relative (usually by helping to "set him up"). When Vincent Siciliano (1970: 74) discovered who had killed his father, he swore vengeance but later found out that the hit had been "authorized," the killers carrying out Family orders. Finding one of the killers at a restaurant, Siciliano told him: "Look, I came here to talk to you. I want to apologize about the noise I was making." His father's murderer responded: "Hey, don't worry about it. I know how you felt about your father. I understand. There are no hard feelings, Vinnie." In Philadelphia, Frank ("Chickie") Narducci was killed on orders of Family boss Nicky Scarfo; yet his sons, Philip and Frank, Jr., continued to work as enforcers for Scarfo (Anastasia 1991). After John Gotti had *caporegime* Thomas Gambino's uncle, Paul Castellano, murdered, Gambino continued to report and show respect to Gotti, who became boss of the Gambino Family.

This is all contrary to the southern Italian credo *sangu de me sangu* ("blood of my blood"), which actually means *famiglia* (family) above all: *o tortu o gridu difenni i to* ("right or wrong, defend your own" kin). Actually, the rules of the American Mafia have succeeded in preventing the emergence of a violent southern Italian tradition: vendetta, the irrational blood feud that is bad for business. Since the 1930s, there have been no "wars" between traditional organized crime groups, although there has been a great deal of intragroup violence.

Analysis of the Structure

The structure of New York Mafia Families is only loosely coupled to its criminal activities. It is rather fluid, similar to that of the real estate development business: "A great deal of illegal activity within the illegal industries is not routine production and distribution carried on under the auspices of a specific firm, but instead the result of many ad hoc deals and projects" (Moore 1987: 54). The firms (crews) in New York are not consistently in one business but are intermittently in several. They are organized not as a "production line" but as a "job shop." Annelise Anderson (1979) found that the formal organizational structure of the Philadelphia crime Family was not the same as its economic structure. There was a relatively clear hierarchy within the Family—boss, underboss, captains, soldiers—but its income-generating activities were based on several smaller operationally independent crews involved in gambling and loansharking. This structure, notes Ronald Goldstock (Stone 1992: 29), is less like a corporation and more like a government: "In a corporation, people at the bottom carry out the policies and perform tasks assigned to them by the executives at the top. In the Mob, the people at the bottom are the entrepreneurs. They pass a percentage of their income upward as taxes in return for government-type services: resolution of disputes, allocation of territories, enforcement and corruption services." Anderson (1979: 46) argues that the most threatening aspect of this type of organized crime is the "group or organization's capacity for forming a quasi-government, giving it a competitive advantage."

THE AMERICAN MAFIA IN CHICAGO

Organized crime in the Windy City—a nickname that refers to its politicians, not its weather—differs from that in New York City by degree. The connection between politics and the dominant criminal organization has been extraordinary both for its intensity and longevity. Chicago has also been remarkable for the extent to which persons of various ethnicity have been integrated into the dominant criminal organization, now known as "The Outfit."

When Chicago was incorporated as a town in 1833, it was little more than an Indian trading post.

Immigration, usually by steamship, increased with the breaking of ground for the Lake Michigan–Illinois River Canal in 1836. By 1855, Chicago was the terminus of ten railroad trunk lines and eleven branch lines and was the country's greatest meatpacking center and grain port (Asbury 1942). The boom naturally attracted adventurers, gamblers, pimps, prostitutes, and other undesirables.

The Civil War brought further prosperity to Chicago, but it also brought thousands of soldiers and the gambling establishments and brothels that were patronized by large numbers of unattached young men on military leave. At this time, Chicago became known as "the wickedest city in the United States" (Asbury 1942: 6). But not until Mike McDonald became established could vice in Chicago be said to be truly *organized*.

Mike McDonald

The origins of organized crime in Chicago can be traced to the mayoralty election of 1873, in which Mike McDonald backed the victorious candidate for mayor (Nelli 1969). "McDonald, the gambling boss of Chicago, demonstrated that under effective leadership the gamblers, liquor interests, and brothel keepers could be welded into a formidable political power" (Peterson 1963: 31). The election pitted reformers who insisted on the enforcement of Sunday closing "blue laws" against a party, organized by McDonald, whose ranks were swelled by Irish and German immigrants (Flinn 1973). Until McDonald, gambling had been rather unorganized in Chicago, and so were politics. When his candidate won the election, "McDonald had Chicago in his back pocket" (Sawyers 1988: 10). From then until his death in 1907, McDonald controlled mayors, congressmen, and senators. His newspaper, the *Globe*, often influenced the outcome of elections, and he also owned the elevated railroad line in Chicago (Wendt and Kogan 1974). Any gambler who wanted to operate outside of the red-light districts had to see Mike to arrange to pay over a large proportion of his income for division among the police, various city officials, and the members of McDonald's syndicate. As a close friend and chief

advisor of mayors, and as a leader of the Cook County Democratic organization, McDonald was the boss of Chicago (Asbury 1942).

Reform hit Chicago in 1893 at a time when a rich and powerful McDonald had lost interest in maintaining his vast political-gambling empire, His political mantle was picked up by Michael ("Hinky Dink") Kenna and John ("Bathhouse") Coughlin; gambling went to Mont Tennes (Asbury 1942; Sawyers 1988).

Mont Tennes inherited much of the gambling empire left by Mike McDonald. Writing in 1929, John Landesco stated (1968: 45): "The complete life history of one man, were it known in every detail, would disclose practically all there is to know about syndicated gambling as a phase of organized crime in Chicago in the last quarter century. That man is *Mont Tennes*." Anyone wanting to enter the gambling business had to apply to the Tennes ring. He controlled the wire service and paid politicians and the police; gamblers who paid Tennes received race results immediately and protection from police raids (Landesco 1968).

With the advent of Prohibition, however, the level of violence in organized crime increased dramatically. In the end, Tennes became an associate of the Capone organization, but withdrew from this "shotgun marriage" and retired about 1927, a millionaire (Smith 1962). Tennes died of a heart attack in 1941 (Pietrusza 2003).

"Hinky Dink" and "The Bath"

McDonald's saloon-headquarters was located in the Levee District of Chicago's notorious First Ward. With his backing, a "Mutt and Jeff" team became the political "Lords of the Levee": John ("Bathhouse") Coughlin, a powerfully built six-footer, and Michael ("Hinky Dink") Kenna, a diminutive organizational genius. Born in the First Ward to Irish immigrant parents in 1860, Coughlin began his political career as a rubber in the exclusive Palmer Baths, where he met wealthy and powerful politicians and businessmen. These contacts helped him when he opened his own bathhouse and soon other bathhouses. Among his customers were important politicians, and the Bath (a nickname he enjoyed) became a Democratic precinct captain and president of the First Ward Democratic Club.

In 1892, Coughlin was elected alderman from the First Ward, one of thirty-five city wards. The First Ward, in addition to the Levee, contained the city's central business district, "the Loop" (so-called because of the elevated train line circling the area). The city council that Coughlin joined was literally selling out the city of Chicago. The "boodles," schemes through which city privileges were sold, made the $3-a-meeting alderman's position quite lucrative.

Kenna was born in the First Ward in 1858 and became a successful saloonkeeper (despite being a nondrinker) and, of course, a politician. He worked hard in First Ward Democratic politics as a saloon-based precinct captain and eventually became friendly with the Bath. With Kenna as the mastermind, the two men organized the vice entrepreneurs of the First Ward, established a legal fund, and forged an alliance with the mayor. Eventually they "found themselves in possession of a thriving little syndicate" (Wendt and Kogan 1974: 81).

After the mayor was murdered by a disgruntled job seeker, the Bath and Hinky Dink provided his successor with his margin of victory. When a depression swept the country in the winter of 1893, Kenna provided care for eight thousand homeless and destitute men, who did not forget this kindness. They registered in the First Ward and were brought back for each election. Coughlin and Kenna were also assisted by the police of the ward and the Quincy Street Boys, who included some of the toughest and most feared hoodlums of the First Ward. Actually, notes John Landesco, in 1929, the use of street gangs in politics became widespread in Chicago (1968: 184–185): "The young of the immigrant group, beginning with the child at play in the street, were assimilated uncritically into all of the traditions of the neighborhoods in which they lived. Street gangs were their heritage, conflict between races and nationalities often made them necessary—conflict and assimilation went on together. The politician paid close attention to them, nurturing them with favors and using them

for his own purposes. Gang history always emphasizes this political nurture. Gangs often became political clubs."

The ability of Coughlin and Kenna to deliver the vote was key to their power. Majorities in the First Ward were so overwhelming they could affect city, county, and even state elections. And as their power grew, it became necessary to be "licensed" by Kenna and Coughlin to do business in the First Ward. In 1897, they skillfully engineered the Democratic nomination for Carter Henry Harrison, son of the murdered mayor. In the First Ward they delivered a vote of five to one, and Kenna was elected to the city council. However, Harrison eventually allied himself with reformers and moved against the Levee, which cost him the vital support of the First Ward and led to the 1915 election of Republican William Hale ("Big Bill") Thompson.

Thompson's victory in 1915 was based on his demagogic appeals. In German and Irish neighborhoods he attacked the British; in German-hating Polish neighborhoods he attacked the Germans; and when addressing Protestant audiences he warned that a vote for his Catholic opponent was a vote for the Pope. He promised the reformers strict enforcement of the gambling laws, and he promised the gamblers an open town. Thompson received strong support in the black wards, and many Harrison Democrats deserted the party to support the Republican.

"During the last few months of Mayor Harrison's final term Chicago was probably as free from organized vice as at any time in its history" (Asbury 1942: 309). With the election of Thompson, "the spoils system swept over the city like a noxious blight, and city hall became a symbol for corruption and incompetence" (Merriam 1929: 22). "Within six months he had violated every campaign promise but one. He did keep Chicago wide open" (Kobler 1971: 57). Despite these excesses, Big Bill was reelected in 1919. In 1923, with Prohibition in full swing, and despite the support of Al Capone, Thompson was defeated by reformers. In 1927, running on a pledge to let the liquor flow again in Chicago, Thompson was swept back into office for a third term. In 1931,

Thompson was defeated by Anton J. Cermak, the founder of what has since been called the "Cook County Democratic Machine."

Jim Colosimo

Like Mont Tennes, Coughlin and Kenna soon felt the power of gangsterism in the First Ward. With Thompson in charge of city hall, the power of the Bath and Hinky Dink was reduced considerably. Political-police protection had to be negotiated directly from "the hall"—individual Democratic aldermen had little or no influence with Big Bill. One precinct captain, a man who had aided Coughlin and Kenna in capturing the growing Italian vote of the First Ward, began to assert control over the Levee.

James ("Big Jim" or "Diamond Jim") Colosimo was 10 years old when his father brought him to the United States from Calabria, Italy. He spent all but three years of the rest of his life in the Levee, the waterfront district of Chicago. Beginning as a newsboy and bootblack, by the time he was 18, Colosimo was an accomplished pickpocket and pimp. In the late 1890s, after several close brushes with the law, he obtained a job as a street cleaner and by 1902 had been promoted to foreman. Known as the "white wings" because of their white uniforms, sweepers were organized by Colosimo into a social and athletic club that later became a labor union. Kenna appointed Colosimo a precinct captain in return for delivering the votes of his club, a position that brought with it virtual immunity from arrest (Asbury 1942).

In 1902, Colosimo married a brothel keeper and began to manage her business. In 1903, he helped organize a gang of "white slavers," an operation that brought girls, often as young as 14, from many American and European cities—turnover was good for business (Asbury 1942). Most were willing entrants to the business of house prostitution, but others were lured by false promises of domestic employment or some other duplicity, such as promises of marriage. Once in Chicago, the recruiters turned the girls over to specialists, who would drug, rape, and humiliate the girls for days. After being

thus "broken in," they were sold as chattel to brothel keepers, who would restrict their contacts with the outside world.[7] Colosimo opened several brothels and a string of gambling houses. He also owned the nationally famous restaurant, Colosimo's Café, which attracted luminaries from society, opera, and the theater (Nelli 1969). He was the "first Italian-American gangster to cross over from the underworld to the fringes of respectability" (Repetto 2004: 56). "By the middle of 1915, Colosimo was the acknowledged overlord of prostitution on the South Side, and because of his political power was almost as important in other sections of the city" (Asbury 1942: 314).

Colosimo flaunted his success: "He wore a diamond ring on every finger, diamond studs gleamed in his shirt front, a huge diamond horseshoe was pinned to his vest, diamond links joined the cuffs, and his belt and suspender buckles were set with diamonds" (Asbury 1942: 312). All this attracted attention, some of it unwelcome. In 1909, Colosimo, like many other successful Italians, became the target of Black Hand[8] extortion threats. In response, he brought Johnny Torrio to Chicago. Some sources refer to Torrio as Colosimo's nephew, whereas others report that he was a distant cousin of Colosimo's wife, Victoria.

Johnny Torrio

Torrio was born near Naples in 1882, and his parents settled on New York's Lower East Side. Using brains rather than brawn, Torrio became the leader of the James Street Boys, which was allied with the infamous Five Points Gang. He later moved operations to Brooklyn and entered into a partnership with Frankie (Ioele or Uale) Yale, a member of the Five Points gang who became a notorious gang leader in

---

7. These activities led to the enactment of the Mann Act in 1910, making it a federal crime to transport females interstate for "immoral purposes."

8. *La Mano Negro*, or Black Hand, consisted of individuals or small gangs of extortionists preying on Italian immigrants who had achieved a level of financial success. Victims would receive a crude letter or note demanding money and signed with a skull or black-inked hand (Lombardo 2002a, 2004).

Coney Island. Though Torrio, a happily married man, did not smoke, drink, or consort with women, he was the right man for the job. Shortly after arriving in Chicago, Torrio lured three Black Handers into an ambush, where gunmen shot them to death. His Chicago career was underway (McPhaul 1970; Schoenberg 1992). Torrio's usefulness extended to overseeing brothels and gambling operations for Colosimo. Eventually, Colosimo left Torrio in charge of his operations.

Back in New York, Frankie Yale hired a heavy-fisted member of the Five Points gang to deal with obstreperous customers in his saloon. On one occasion, however, the young bouncer made an offensive remark to a young girl in the saloon, which led to a four-inch scar courtesy of her irate brother and his pocketknife. The young Five Pointer was prone to be overexuberant in carrying out his responsibilities—a suspect in two murders, his third victim was on the critical list when Yale thought it best that Alphonse ("Scarface") Capone leave New York. Al Capone arrived in Chicago at a fortuitous time, 1919, the year before Prohibition went into effect. Although Capone first worked as a bouncer, Torrio began to give him important responsibilities (McPhaul 1970). Then came Prohibition.

With the onset Prohibition, "the personnel of organized vice took the lead in the systematic organization of this new and profitable field of exploitation. All the experience gained by years of struggle against reformers and concealed agreements with politicians was brought into service in the organizing and distribution of beer and whiskey" (Landesco 1968: 43). Colosimo, however, was fearful of federal enforcement efforts and wanted to stay away from bootlegging (McPhaul 1970). Torrio and Capone chafed at this reluctance; not only would it deny access to untold wealth, but would also enable competing racketeers to grow rich and powerful. On May 11, 1920, Diamond Jim was found in the vestibule of Colosimo's Cafe—he had been shot to death. "After Colosimo's death, John Torrio succeeded to the First Ward based Italian 'syndicate' throne, which he occupied until his retirement in 1925. An able and effective leader, Torrio excelled as a master strategist and organizer and quickly built up an empire which far exceeded that of his predecessor in wealth, power, and influence" (Nelli 1969: 386).

As an organizer and administrator of underworld affairs, Torrio is unsurpassed in the annals of American crime. He conducted his criminal enterprises as if they were legitimate businesses. "In the morning he kissed his wife good-by and motored to his magnificently furnished offices on the second floor of the Four Deuces [saloon/gambling house/brothel]. There he bought and sold women, conferred with the managers of his brothels and gambling dens, issued instructions to his rumrunners and bootleggers, arranged for the corruption of police and city officials, and sent his gun squads out to slaughter rival gangsters who might be interfering with his schemes." His workday over, "Torrio returned to his Michigan Avenue apartment and, except on rare occasions when he attended the theater or a concert, spent the evening at home in slippers and smoking jacket, playing cards with his wife or listening to phonograph records" (Asbury 1942: 320–321).

Torrio-Capone Organization

As in New York, Prohibition enabled men who had been street thugs to become crime overlords. Outside of the First Ward, various gangs ruled over sections of Chicago, where they pushed aside the local aldermen and parlayed crime and politics into wealth and power. On the North Side, the gang headed by Dion O'Banion controlled the 42nd and 43rd Wards. O'Banion controlled the Irish vote much as Colosimo controlled the Italian vote in the First Ward. Despite his sordid background, including several shootings in public view, in 1924, a banquet was held in O'Banion's honor by the Cook County Democratic organization. It seems that O'Banion had decided to swing his support to the Republicans because the reform-minded Democratic mayor was insisting that laws against many of O'Banion's activities be enforced. Democratic officials made speeches in his honor and even presented O'Banion with a platinum watch—to no avail. O'Banion and the votes of his wards went to the Republicans. O'Banion was a regular church-goer and loved flowers. This led him to purchase a florist shop and become gangland's favorite florist (Asbury 1942; Landesco 1968). He would soon clash with the Torrio-Capone organization.

Late in the summer of 1920, Torrio held long conferences with the major gang leaders in Cook County and persuaded them to abandon predatory crime in favor of Prohibition-related activities. To facilitate operations, the city and county were divided into spheres of influence. In each, an allied gang chieftain was supreme, with subchiefs working under his direction. "A few of these leaders themselves owned and operated breweries and distilleries, but in the main they received their supplies from Torrio and were principally concerned with selling, making deliveries, protecting shipments, terrorizing saloonkeepers who refused to buy from the syndicate, and furnishing gunmen for punitive expeditions against hijackers and independents who attempted to encroach upon Torrio territory" (Asbury 1942: 324–325).

Torrio also moved to extend the suburbanization of his business and by 1923 had expanded beer and bordello operations well beyond his South Side stronghold into towns west and southwest of Chicago. He toured the Cook County suburbs, and when a location was decided upon, the neighborhood people were canvassed. If they were agreeable, Torrio agents would provide rewards: a new car, a house redecorated or painted, a new furnace, mortgage payments. The local authorities were then approached and terms negotiated (Allsop 1968). Most of this was accomplished peacefully—but then there was Cicero.

When You Smell Gunpowder, You're in Cicero

Adjacent to Chicago's Far West Side is the suburban city of Cicero (current population about 55,000). In 1923, reform hit Chicago and the mayoralty went to Democrat William Dever. He ordered the police to move against the rampant vice in Chicago, but corruption was too deeply ingrained to be easily pushed aside. However, with the Democrats in control of Chicago, the Republicans were fearful of a reform wave that would loosen their control of the suburban areas of Cook County. As a result, a local

Republican leader made a deal with Al Capone while Torrio was on vacation in Italy. In return for helping the Republicans maintain control in Cicero, Torrio would be given a free hand in that city (Allsop 1968).

In the election of April 1924, the Capone brothers, Al and Frank, led a group of two hundred Chicago thugs into Cicero. They intimidated, beat, and even killed Democrats who sought to oppose the Republican candidates. Some outraged Cicero officials responded by having a county judge deputize seventy volunteer Chicago police officers, who entered Cicero and engaged the Capone gangsters. In one incident, Chicago police saw the Capone brothers, Charlie Fischetti (a Capone cousin), and a Capone gunman standing by the polls with guns in their hands ushering voters inside. In the ensuing exchange of gunfire, during which the police were probably mistaken for rival gunmen, Frank Capone was killed (Schoenberg 1992). Despite this, the Capone candidate was overwhelmingly reelected mayor of Cicero (Kobler 1971).

Capone moved his headquarters from Chicago to Cicero, where he took over the Hawthorne Inn with a little help from his friends—they opened fire at the owner "while shopping housewives and local tradesmen threw themselves behind cars and into doorways in the horizontal position that was becoming an identifiable posture of Cicero citizens" (Allsop 1968: 62–63). At the Hawthorne Inn, Capone ruled with an iron hand. When the Cicero mayor failed to carry out one of his orders, Capone went to city hall, where he personally knocked "his honor" down the steps and kicked him repeatedly as a policeman strolled by (Allsop 1968). Corruption problems in Cicero continued into the twenty-first century.

THE CHICAGO WARS

The election of a reform mayor in Chicago had unanticipated consequences. It created an unstable situation and encouraged competitive moves by various ganglords. When Thompson lost to Dever in 1923, the system of political/police protection broke down, and in the ensuing confusion Chicago became a battleground. The most significant feud was between the Torrio-Capone syndicate and the forces headed by Dion O'Banion.

In 1924, the North Side O'Banion forces began to feud with the fearsome South Side Genna brothers and O'Banion hijacked a load of Genna liquor. The Gennas bristled, but Torrio restrained them and attempted to negotiate a peaceful settlement. In that same year, O'Banion swindled Torrio and Capone out of $500,000, selling them his share in a brewery he knew was going to be raided by the police. This indicated that Torrio had lost control of the police under Mayor Dever. Emboldened by the lack of a response from Torrio, and apparently mistaking caution for fear, O'Banion went around boasting about how he had "taken" Torrio: "To hell with them Sicilians" was a phrase O'Banion gunmen quoted when they told the story in underworld circles (Asbury 1942). This was a serious violation of respect and the response was inevitable.

On November 10, 1924, Mike Genna and two Sicilian immigrants who worked for the Gennas entered the O'Banion flower shop on the Near North Side. O'Banion was busy preparing flower arrangements for the funeral of Mike Merlo, president of the *Unione Siciliana*, who had died of natural causes a few days earlier. What the florist didn't know was that Merlo had been exerting his influence to keep the Gennas and Torrio from moving against O'Banion. Merlo abhorred violence and got along very well with O'Banion—but now he was dead (Kobler 1971). "Hello, boys, you want Merlo's flowers?" a porter told the police he heard O'Banion say to the three men. Torrio had placed an order for $10,000 worth of assorted flowers, and Capone had ordered $8,000 worth of roses. While shaking O'Banion's hand, Mike Genna suddenly jerked him forward and seized his arms. Before he could wriggle free and reach for any of the three guns he always carried, O'Banion was hit by five bullets. A sixth, the coup de grâce, was fired into his head after he fell to the floor. The war that followed took many lives and

ended on St. Valentine's Day, 1929 (Allsop 1968; Asbury 1942; Kobler 1971).

The O'Banion forces, under the leadership of Earl Wajciechowski, a Pole better known as "Hymie Weiss," struck back. Torrio left Chicago one step ahead of Weiss gunmen and early in 1925, Capone's car was raked with machine-gun fire. His driver was wounded, but Capone and his bodyguards were not hit. Capone began traveling in a specially built armored Cadillac limousine. Later that year, twelve days after his return to Chicago, Torrio was critically wounded while shopping with his wife. In the fall of 1925, he went to Italy for a visit, leaving Chicago and his organization to Capone (Landesco 1968).

Torrio emerged as part of organized crime in New York, where he apparently received some type of senior advisory status. He worked in partnership with a number of leading New York organized crime figures, including Dutch Schultz, with whom he was a partner in the bail bond business, and Frank Costello (Peterson 1983). He later received a two-and-a-half-year sentence for income tax evasion (Irey and Slocum 1948). Some sources credit Torrio with inspiring the formation of a national crime syndicate in 1934 (Messick 1967; Turkus and Feder 1951). Torrio suffered a heart attack while in a barber's chair in Brooklyn and died on April 16, 1957. His death went unnoticed by the media until May 8, when the *New York Times* ran a story: "Johnny Torrio, Ex-Public Enemy 1, Dies; Made Al Capone Boss of the Underworld." Torrio was described as a real estate dealer at the time of his death.

Weiss gunmen made a dozen attempts to kill Capone, and they nearly succeeded in 1926. The street in front of Capone's Cicero headquarters was filled with a lunch-hour crowd, and Capone was eating at a restaurant next door when "eleven automobiles filled with Weiss gangsters drove slowly past the Hawthorne Inn and began firing machine-guns, automatic pistols, and shotguns. After the roar of the attack had subsided, bullet holes were found in thirty-five automobiles parked at the curb. Inside the hotel, woodwork and doors had been splintered, windows shattered, plaster ripped from walls, and furniture wrecked in the office and lobby." Capone, however, was uninjured, although one of his bodyguards was hit in the shoulder. Among the many injured bystanders, a woman sitting with her infant son was struck by flying glass. Capone paid the physicians who saved her sight (Asbury 1942: 358–359).

Soon afterward, two gunmen armed with submachine guns, who had been waiting for three days, opened fire on Hymie Weiss and his four companions as they approached their headquarters above the O'Banion flower shop. Weiss was hit ten times. He and one of his companions died; the others survived. Weiss, at age 28, reportedly left an estate worth $1.3 million (Allsop 1968).

Gang wars are "bad for business," so in 1926, in the middle of the mayhem and murder, a truce was called. Weiss was dead by that time, and the O'Banion forces were led by George ("Bugs") Moran. The assembled gang chieftains divided up the city and the county, with the largest shares going to the Capone organization and Moran gang.

In 1928, Capone clashed with Frankie Yale. Capone had discovered that Yale—his one-time Brooklyn boss and the person responsible for protecting Capone's liquor shipments as they were trucked west to Chicago—was actually behind a series of hijackings (Kobler 1971). A black sedan followed Yale's new Lincoln as it moved down a Brooklyn street. As the sedan drew near, shots were fired, and Yale sped off with the sedan in pursuit. The end came with a devastating blast of gunfire that filled Yale's head with bullets and buckshot ("Gangster Shot in Daylight Attack" 1928). He was 35 years old.

During the first few months of 1929, while a peace agreement was in effect (at least in theory), Bugs Moran had been hijacking Capone's liquor, owned jointly by Capone and the (predominantly Jewish) Purple Gang of Detroit. Capone gave orders and went off to enjoy the Florida sun at his palatial fourteen-room estate on Miami's Palm Island. On February 14, St. Valentine's Day, Capone entertained more than one hundred guests on Palm Island: gangsters, politicians, sports writers, and show-business personalities. They all enjoyed a hearty buffet and an endless supply of champagne (Galvan 1982).

Meanwhile, back in Chicago, six of Bugs Moran's men, and an optometrist who liked to associate with gangsters, were waiting at a North Side warehouse to unload a shipment of hijacked liquor from Detroit. A Cadillac touring car with a large gong on the running board, similar to those used by detectives, stopped outside, and five men, two wearing police uniforms, entered the warehouse. Once inside, they lined up the seven men against the warehouse wall and systematically executed them with Tommy guns. One of the victims lived nearly three hours with fourteen bullets in him but refused to tell the police who was responsible for the shooting. Bugs Moran was not in the warehouse at the time, even though the "St. Valentine's Day Massacre" had been arranged in his honor. He arrived late, and seeing the "police car," left. It was later learned that the killers thought Moran was among the victims; lookouts had mistaken one of the seven for the gang's leader (Koziol and Estep 1983). The killers were never caught; it was suspected that they were brought in from Detroit or St. Louis where Capone had ties with "Eagan's Rats" (Kavieff 2000). The affair was apparently arranged by South Side hit man and Capone bodyguard James DeMora, who some sources refer to as Vincenzco Gibaldi, but who is better known as "Machine-Gun Jack McGurn."[9] For a long time it was generally believed that *real* policemen were the actual killers (Kobler 1971).[10]

Although the wrath of Bugs Moran continued, his gang withered. The man who handled brothels and "immoral cabarets" for Moran was gunned down in 1930. Less than three months later, Moran's

---

9. The Moran gang had twice tried to kill McGurn, and on one occasion he was seriously wounded. Believed responsible for killing at least twenty-two people, McGurn used to place a nickel in the hands of his victims. He was responsible for the 1927 attack on comedian Joe E. Lewis, during which his vocal cords were slashed and his tongue lacerated. Lewis, then a nightclub singer, had left McGurn's club for employment at another speakeasy. The Lewis story was told in the Frank Sinatra motion picture *The Joker Is Wild*. Seven years after the massacre, on the eve of Valentine's Day, McGurn was machine-gunned to death in a Chicago bowling alley. The two killers left a comic Valentine card next to his ruined body.

10. The old garage at 2122 North Clark Street was demolished in 1967.

partner and president of the *Unione Siciliana*, Joe Aiello, met the same fate. Moran left Chicago and eventually returned to more conventional crime. In 1946, he was sent to prison for robbing a tavern employee of $10,000 near Dayton, Ohio. After ten years, Moran was released from prison, and a few days later was arrested for bank robbery. On February 26, 1957, the *New York Times* reported that Moran died while serving his sentence in the federal penitentiary in Leavenworth, Kansas ("Bugs Moran Dies in Federal Prison" 1957).

Al Capone's Chicago

In May of 1929, after attending a national crime conclave in Atlantic City, Capone decided to go to jail to avoid the wrath of the Bugs Moran gang and any number of Sicilians who had vowed to kill him to avenge the vicious beating deaths of three of their countrymen, whom Capone suspected of disloyalty. He arranged to be arrested by a friendly detective in Philadelphia on a firearms violation. Although the maximum sentence was one year, Capone anticipated a sentence of about ninety days, enough time to let things cool down in Chicago. His arrest, however, generated a great deal of media attention, and the judge imposed the maximum sentence, twelve months; he was released from his comfortably furnished cell in 1930, two months early, for "good behavior." Although he continued to live with his family in a modest red-brick, two-flat house at 7244 South Prairie Avenue, the former saloon bouncer from Brooklyn was now the most powerful person in Chicago, thanks to Prohibition.

The Depression severely reduced the income of the Capone organization. New areas of profit were sought by the chieftains of organized crime who had grown wealthy in gambling and bootlegging. Until 1929, business and labor racketeering was only a sideline for most top gangsters such as Capone. However, as liquor sales fell off with the onset of the Depression, gang leaders were faced with a restless army of young and violent men whom they were committed to paying anywhere from $100 to $500 per week (Seidman 1938). Capone also recognized by 1928 that Prohibition would probably last only a few more years; new sources of income would be needed.

During Prohibition, numerous forms of racketeering flourished in Chicago: The small businesses of the city were generally marginal and intensely competitive. To avoid cutthroat competition, businessmen formed associations to make and enforce regulations illegally limiting competition. "Many of the associations were controlled, or even organized by, racketeers who levied dues upon association members and controlled the treasuries; they then used a system of fines and violence to insure that all businessmen in the trade joined the association and abided by the regulations" designed to keep prices uniform and high (Haller 1971–72: 225–226).

The Capone organization moved into racketeering on a grand scale and took over many rackets then prevalent in Chicago. In 1928, the Cook County state's attorney listed ninety-one Chicago unions and business associations under gangster control, and these gradually came under the control of the Capone organization—the gangsters who controlled racketeering in Chicago proved no match for the Capone forces (Kobler 1971; Seidman 1938). It was the same in other cities. In Detroit, for example, the Purple Gang took over labor racketeering through a reign of terror. The Capone organization "controlled a score of labor unions, most of them officered by ex-convicts, and as many protective associations. To build up this phase of the Capone syndicate operations, and to hold in line the businesses already conquered, bands of gunmen and sluggers hijacked and destroyed truckloads of merchandise, bombed stores and manufacturing plants or wrecked them with axes and crowbars, put acid into laundry vats, poured corrosives onto clothing hanging in cleaning and dyeing shops, blackjacked workers and employers, and killed when necessary to enforce their demands or break down opposition" (Asbury 1942: 366–367).

Capone's Downfall

The Depression severely reduced the income of the Capone organization, and a special team of federal investigators, headed by Eliot Ness and dubbed "the Untouchables," began to move against Capone distilleries, breweries, and liquor shipments. The most important event for Capone, however, was a 1927 U.S. Supreme Court decision (*United States v. Sullivan,* 274 U.S. 259) that upheld the Internal Revenue Service's contention that even *unlawful* income was subject to income taxes, the Fifth Amendment guarantee against self-incrimination notwithstanding. The tax evasion case against Capone was initiated in 1929 by the Special Intelligence Unit of the Treasury Department, a low-key agency that avoided publicity. A nearsighted special agent who never carried a firearm was put in charge of the investigation. He brought Capone down with a pencil.

Capone stood trial for having a net income of $1,038,654 during the years 1924 to 1929 for which he failed to pay income tax. In 1931, he was found guilty of income-tax evasion and received sentences totaling eleven years. In 1932, his appeals exhausted, Capone entered the federal prison in Atlanta. He was transferred to Alcatraz in 1934, where he was found to be suffering from syphilis. For several years Capone refused treatment. Early in 1938 he began showing symptoms of paresis and was transferred out of Alcatraz. Capone was released in 1939, his sentence shortened for good behavior, and by then he was suffering from an advanced case of syphilis. He headed for his winter home on Palm Island, Florida, and, after living years as an invalid, died in 1947 of pneumonia following a stroke.

THE OUTFIT

The Capone organization "can best be described *not* as a hierarchy directed by Al Capone but rather as a senior partnership involving four men, who in turn entered into a variety of partnerships to run specific enterprises." These four—Al Capone, his brother Ralph, Al's boyhood friend Frank Nitti, and Jake Guzik, Capone's accounting wizard—each received one-sixth of the income that they derived from their various enterprises. The rest was for the maintenance of their central headquarters with its personnel—mostly clerks and gunmen. "The senior partners, in turn, invested money and, when possible, provided political protection for an expanding and diverse group of enterprises" (Haller 1974: 11).

When Prohibition ended, Capone was in prison and the country was several years into the Great Depression. These changes affected organized crime in Chicago. At the height of his power, Capone is reputed to have had seven hundred gunmen under his control (Palsey 1971). This expensive army was no longer necessary; the Capone syndicate, consolidated under what became known as the Outfit, had an unchallenged monopoly on organized crime in Chicago, maintained with minimal force and a great deal of political influence.

The city's First Ward remained at the center of the Outfit's political influence, which reached into towns and villages of suburban Cook County. Frank Nitti ran the Outfit with the help of Capone's brothers Ralph and Matt, Capone cousins Charlie and Rocco Fischetti, Paul de Lucia (better known as Paul "the Waiter" Ricca), Anthony ("Joe Batters") Accardo, Jake Guzik, a Jew, and Welshman Murray Humphreys. The Chicago Crime Commission points out that the Outfit "has been somewhat unique in its willingness to deal with and, indeed, grant considerable responsibility to non-Italians." For many years, Humphreys, was the Outfit's chief political fixer and troubleshooter, and he was succeeded by Gus ("The Greek") Alex ("Spotlight" 1981).

Nitti was born in Sicily in 1889 and brought to the United States at 2 years of age. Known as "The Enforcer" for his role in dealing with internal discipline and external enemies of the Capone organization, Nitti began his career as a barber fencing stolen goods on the side. He had been a boyhood friend of Capone in New York and a fellow member of New York's Five Points gang— he followed Capone to Chicago (Napoli 2004). Although physically unimposing, he had Capone's confidence and became his second in command (Schoenberg 1992). In 1943, Nitti, who had been in poor health, feared prosecution for a nation-wide extortion scheme involving the motion picture industry (Demaris 1969): Brown-Bioff Episode (discussed in Chapter 2). On the day an indictment was handed down by a New York grand jury, Nitti committed suicide with a .32 revolver (Koziol and Baumann 1987).

In 1955, fearing further federal prosecution as head of the Outfit, Accardo and his aging partner, Paul Ricca, looked for someone to take over the day-to-day operations of the Outfit. They turned to Sam Giancana (Brashler 1977; Peterson 1962).

Sam Giancana

Christened Momo Salvatore, Sam Giancana was born in Chicago, in 1908, to Sicilian immigrants and raised in the notorious "Patch" of the Taylor Street neighborhood. Abused as a child, Giancana dropped out of school at age 14. Living mostly in the streets, he became a member of the "42 Gang"— a group that even other criminals of that day viewed as "crazy." They specialized in truck hijacking and auto theft, becoming notorious for their level of violence (Brashler 1977; Giancana and Giancana 1992; Landesco 1933). Fellow members of the 42s would also gain prominence in the Outfit. Although the gang was periodically involved in politics and union organizing as "muscle," their primary activity centered around conventional and often reckless criminality. Deaths, via the police or rival criminals, and imprisonment eventually brought an end to the 42s (Brashler 1977).

As an adolescent, Mooney (Giancana's nick-name) served as a gunman for Al Capone. Arrested dozens of times and indicted on several occasions for felonies, not a single case reached the trial stage—"friendly" judges are the explanation. In one murder indictment, the prosecution witness was murdered before the trial. In 1929, however,

Giancana's "luck" finally ran out, and he received a one-to-five-year sentence for burglary. Drafted by the army in 1943, Giancana was rejected for being a "constitutional psychopath" with an "inadequate personality and strong antisocial trends" (Demaris 1969: 8; Giancana and Giancana 1992).

Giancana's specialty for the 42s was being a "wheelman"—driving a getaway car. This eventu-ally earned him a position as chauffeur for "Machine Gun" Jack McGurn and later Paul Ricca. His Outfit connection, however, was no advantage in rural Garden Prairie, where Giancana was convicted of bootlegging in 1939. (The Outfit continued in the alcohol business after Prohibition, selling backwoods-still whiskey bottled as imported or quality domestic brands to saloonkeepers eager to improve their profits.) Giancana served three years in the federal prison at Terre Haute, Indiana, where he met Eddie Jones, a wealthy black num-bers operator. Jones and his brothers were major gambling and political figures in the city's African American areas (Chepsiuk 2007). Jones, who had pled guilty to income-tax evasion in 1939, told Giancana about the large amount of money he and his brother George had made in this enterprise, which had been dismissed by leading white gang-sters as "penny-ante." Since Prohibition, blacks had dominated the numbers business in Chicago (Haller 1990b). When Giancana was released from prison in 1942, Jones financed his entry into the jukebox and vending machine business and became his part-ner in a variety of gambling enterprises centered in the African American areas of the city's South Side.

Giancana repaid his benefactor by advising Ricca and Accardo of the lucrative black numbers operation and requesting permission to take it over using his crew of 42s (Brashler 1977). After Jones's release from Terre Haute in 1946, he was kid-napped and held for ransom in Giancana's new sub-urban home in Oak Park. After his family made a payment of $100,000, Jones was released and fled to Mexico with his brother, leaving Teddy Roe in charge of the business. Roe proved to be a tougher opponent than Jones and did quite well for six years—his income tax returns indicating an income of more than $1 million a year—but he was feeling heat from Giancana. After a campaign of intimidation, murder, beatings, and bombings, Roe became the last holdout from Giancana's takeover of the South Side numbers racket. Aiding Giancana's efforts were the police, who raided Roe's policy wheels. In 1951, Roe successfully fended off a kidnapping attempt, killing one assailant and wounding a second, but in 1952, he was ambushed and cut down by a shotgun blast. Sam Giancana had become a principal player in Chicago organized crime. Money from the numbers enabled Giancana to branch out into other enterprises, and his organizational skills and murderous crew allowed him to prosper. In 1955, Giancana was in charge of the Outfit's day-to-day operations (Brashler 1977; Giancana and Giancana 1992; Roemer 1995).

Giancana lived a high-profile social life, something that had become anathema to the now-modernized leaders of organized crime. He had a widely publicized romance with Phyllis McGuire (of the singing McGuire sisters) and a public friendship with Frank Sinatra. He even shared a girlfriend with President John F. Kennedy. Giancana generated a great deal of publicity when he secured an injunction against the FBI's intensive surveillance of his activities. In 1965, he was imprisoned for a year for contempt, refusing to testify before a federal grand jury after being granted immunity from prosecution (Peterson 1969). Following his release, Giancana sought refuge in Mexico. His daughter states that her father was forced into exile by Ricca and Accardo (Giancana and Renner 1985). Giancana remained in Mexico until 1974, when Mexican immigration agents dragged him to a waiting car, drove him 150 miles, and pushed him across the border into the waiting arms of FBI agents. He was then brought to Chicago for grand jury investigations.

The organization was running smoothly without Giancana—Accardo[11] had apparently resumed active control—and Giancana's subsequent return to Chicago was apparently not welcomed by the Outfit leadership. In 1975, Giancana was shot to death at close range in his suburban Chicago home by someone he apparently knew and obviously trusted. Even in death, controversy about Giancana continued. It was disclosed that in 1960, the Central Intelligence Agency had contacted John Roselli, a Giancana lieutenant, to secure syndicate help in assassinating Fidel Castro. Syndicate leaders had reason to dislike Castro, and they had contacts in Cuba and with exiles in South Florida. The plot apparently never materialized; in 1976, Roselli's body was found in an oil drum floating in Miami's Biscayne Bay.

In 1986, top leaders of the Outfit were convicted of skimming $2 million from gambling casinos in Las Vegas—portrayed in the 1995 Martin Scorsese film, *Casino*—except Accardo, who had assumed senior and semi-retired status.

Outfit Street Crews

In contrast to New York's separate crime Families, the Chicago Outfit has traditionally been organized on the basis of separate street crews associated with particular geographic areas. But as Jeff Coen (2009: 5) noted, "they weren't so much geographic territories as seats of power." The Chinatown crew, for example, also known as the 26th Street crew, had gambling agents as far away as Rockford, sixty miles northwest of Chicago.

There is evidence of criminal specialization among the various street crews, although it appears currently that various forms of gambling are a primary activity of each. Many of these criminal specializations are related to ecological aspects of each area. For example, the North Side contains Rush Street, Chicago's adult nightclub entertainment district, and the North Side/Rush Street crew is noted for its vice operations: prostitution, pornography, and liquor law violations. The 26th Street area contains a large number of railroad yards and associated shipping and trucking terminals, providing an opportunity for cargo theft and truck hijacking. Chicago Heights, located on the southern edge of the Chicago metropolitan area, has a reputation for automobile theft and chop shop operations, which became a major business for the Chicago Heights crew. This specialization did not prevent members

---

11. Tony Accardo died of natural causes in 1992.

of other crews from cartage theft: In 2001, the Chicago police uncovered an elaborate fencing operation whose source was goods stolen by members of the Grand Street and Elmwood Park crews from semi-trailers parked in railway freight yards (Ferkenhoff and Vogell 2001).

The American Mafia:
The Chicago Model

Organized crime in Chicago differs from that in New York in that the Outfit has always been a cooperative venture with other groups, although Italians have been dominant. There is an absence of independent entrepreneurs. In the "Family Secrets" trial, Outfit member-turned-government-witness Nick Calabrese reported being paid $3,000 a month during the 1980s "to kill people," an amount raised to $5,000 when he completed a double homicide (Coen 2009). Important decisions are made at the executive level. In a truly hierarchical organization, the decision to move into a new business or new territory is determined at the top; and so, for example, when the Outfit decided to get into the lucrative video poker machine business, an important question had to be answered: Should distribution be controlled centrally, or should each crew be allowed to distribute in its own territory? The boss, apparently in consultation with his advisors, decided on decentralization (Herion 1998).

The Outfit is led by a boss who at various times has actually been akin to a chief executive officer responsible to one or more persons constituting an informal board of directors. This was the case during the leadership of Sam Giancana, who reported to Tony Accardo and Paul Ricca. Accardo served as something analogous to a powerful president who appoints the prime minister. Assisted by a committee of older and influential members who assume some type of senior status, the boss controls three area bosses. Each area boss has responsibility for a particular part of "Chicagoland"—Cook County and the surrounding collar counties area. He oversees the activities of street bosses who direct the day-to-day activities of crew members.

While each of the crews is associated with a particular geographic area, these areas have undergone change over the years. In addition, there are subgroups nominally attached to crews. Thus, major gambling operations are the responsibility of a specialty crew whose members report to the Outfit hierarchy, rather than a street boss. Further complicating the picture is the custom of referring to a crew by the name of its current street boss or the primary residence of the street boss by federal officials, the Chicago Crime Commission, and even Outfit members themselves. Members of the various crews are not necessarily familiar with members of the other crews.

Each street crew, for the most part, acts independently of the other crews, and each street boss, assisted by (two or more) lieutenants, is responsible for supervising the activities of his crew. The head of the Outfit settles disputes between the crews and is responsible for relations with those outside the organization such as corrupt public officials and other crime groups. A street boss may also be involved in activities, such as labor racketeering, on an "industry" rather than a territorial basis. For example, Vincent Solano was boss of the North Side as well as president of Local 1 of the Laborers Union.

In Chicago, made guys are supervisors, and the people they supervise (associates) begin working for $500 a week in an entry-level position; an investigator (O'Rourke 1997) compared this to starting out as a ballplayer in the minor leagues. Salaries are kept on a par across crews, apparently to avoid competition or jealousy. Associates are assigned to activities for which they are equipped: Someone with numbers skills would, for example, work as a clerk for a bookmaker; someone with a tough-guy reputation would be assigned to collections. The clerk can earn additional income by recruiting customers and will even be allowed to have his own bettors for whom he is responsible. If he becomes very successful, he will be allowed to start a bookmaking business of his own. The collector for a loan shark can earn half of the vigorish (interest) of loans he has arranged. There is little crossover; clerks, for example, would not be used as collectors or vice versa. There are also special people "kept on the shelf," provided with moneymaking opportunities to have them available for "heavy work"—murder (Moriarity 1998).

Outfit employment is not exhausting work, often requiring only a few hours a day. A worker may also hold a legitimate job, for example, employment with the city Streets and Sanitation Department or (in the past) the county sheriff. Indeed, Outfit employment is often geared to keeping people busy so they remain tied to the Outfit—for some, crime may not pay (a great deal), but the hours are great! A successful bookmaker who also ran nightly gaming rooms (which were fixed—loaded dice, marked cards, magnetized roulette wheels) was asked why he did not give up the more time-intensive bookmaking for the time-limited and lucrative gaming rooms: "What would I do all day?" (Herion 1998; Moriarity 1998). "Some of the mob's worst hit men and goon enforcers were on the public payroll. Usually they did not even show up to punch in" (Cooley 2004: 113).

But every Outfit guy is on call. "It's worse than the FBI or the military. If they get a call at three in the morning: 'Go see Howard and collect some money; give him a whack or break his legs,' they can't say 'I'm busy.' They've got to do it." And they can be called to a meeting at any time: "Refusing to go to a meeting is a killing offense. It's the way they test loyalty. They call him in—call him in for 'a cigar,' where they get their ass chewed out by the boss. It's an easy way to set someone up for a murder. If you don't show up you got a problem; if you do show up …" (O'Rourke 1997).

Outfit Membership

Each crew is composed of made guys and associates who are said to be "connected" or "Outfit guys." The street boss and his lieutenants, if they are of Italian heritage, are made guys. Everyone else connected to the crew is an associate (although they are commonly referred to as "members" of a crew). There is some disagreement about the various terms used to describe positions within the Outfit. According to virtually all sources, the Outfit does not use terms common to the New York Families, such as *consigliere*, *caporegime*, or *Cosa Nostra*. And there is little evidence of an initiation ceremony involving oaths of secrecy and obedience, the drawing of blood, and the burning of a saint's portrait. To the extent that there is a ceremony, it appears to be more like a luncheon at which the person is introduced by the boss as a made guy. "In Chicago, according to informants, they do not go through an old-country style initiation and they kind of laugh at that. If you talk to guys actually going out bombing places, collecting the tax, threatening people, someone like that is going to laugh and say 'We don't do that in Chicago.' You become a made guy by being nominated by your boss because you have a history of making lots of money, a good earner. It's unclear if, like in the old days, you actually have to participate in a murder. Obviously, if you participated in a hit, either as the killer or getaway driver, you've made your bones and that helps your reputation" (O'Rourke 1997).

There is evidence, however, that the traditional ceremony was used by some crews in the past. In court testimony, a government informant related that the Taylor Street crew made people "the old way," and testimony in the "Family Secrets" trial (discussed later) revealed an induction ceremony for the 26th Street crew with cut fingers and the burning of a saint's picture. Such persons may have gone through two ceremonies: one with the Outfit boss, and another with his street boss.

In any event, there are definite distinctions between being a made guy and being an associate. In the Chicago Outfit, made guys hold supervisory (or senior advisory) status; everyone else is a worker, with a few important exceptions. Persons who have proven their value to the Outfit have sometimes been given important responsibilities even in the absence of Italian heritage. Being "made" also conveys important status: "Being a made guy grants certain rights and privileges that nobody else gets. You get a cut of the pie. You can order other people to do things. You get to work in a closed circle and you profit from it more so than everybody else. When you are a made guy, you are a guy that gets the money. All the rest of those guys get just a little shred. But there aren't that many made guys" (O'Rourke 1997). And there is considerable "psychic gain." Within criminal and certain legitimate circles, being "made" conveys a great deal of prestige, if not fear.

The requirement of being Italian has helped to prevent infiltration of the organization. It has also ensured that members of the Outfit share the same values. Many of the Southern Italian and Sicilian immigrants who were attracted to organized crime subscribed to the code of *omertá* and had lived under a Mafia dominated social order, both of which facilitated their participation in organized crime. The requirement of being Italian accomplishes a similar goal. Though the average recruit today has never been exposed to the Mafia, many have been raised in neighborhoods where the Outfit is part of the social structure, ensuring that potential recruits have been exposed to values supportive of organized crime.

Today, however, many Italian Americans, wiseguys among them, reside in suburbs where the critical core of street corner boys no longer exists. The traditional storefront social clubs are rare; often they are places where elderly Italians—Outfit guys among them—gather to talk, tell tales of the old days, and play cards or dominos. But certain traditions supportive of organized crime, such as cultural deviance (discussed in Chapter 4), continue to exist among some families even in the suburbs: "Their time frame is short and dishonesty is something that someone else has defined. They don't see anything wrong, when they need a suit for the kid, when someone graduates from high school, they go down the street to see 'Louie' and take care of it. If someone gets into trouble, they know who to go to, who the fixer is" (Risley 1998).

Italian-American young men are being raised in more comfortable surroundings than their predecessors' ghetto experiences. A few—the Outfit does not require many replacements for its considerably streamlined operations—may fantasize about being part of the "mob," being a wiseguy. If they have a connected relative, or perhaps a neighbor with whom they are close, they may be given an opportunity to be a clerk or a collector. Though many members of the Outfit are related by blood and marriage, the sons of Outfit members are rarely found in the ranks of Chicago organized crime. As lawyers and accountants, they are sometimes found working for the same union locals traditionally associated with the Outfit, or they may be defense attorneys in Outfit cases. And until recently, the Chicago Outfit had been free of the made-guy-turned-informant syndrome affecting crime Families in New York.

The size of the Outfit today is markedly smaller than the version once ruled by Al Capone. There are about a hundred made guys and four working crews—down from the traditional six (Coen 2009). Nevertheless, outside of predominantly black and Hispanic neighborhoods, the Outfit has been able to maintain hegemony over gambling and related activities in an area ranging from southern Wisconsin to northern Indiana. They have been able to do this in recent years using considerably less violence. Perhaps this is to be expected from the nature of Outfit leaders who haven't "come up from the streets" and who seem to prefer competitive business strategies rather than intimidation.

The Outfit's political base in the First Ward has been destroyed. From the 1870s to 1990, Chicago's First Ward remained a seemingly untouchable political link to organized crime. That changed in 1990, when indictments were announced against First Ward politicians and gangsters, most of who were subsequently found guilty. The First Ward case was developed by the FBI through the use of a corrupt lawyer acting as a mole and the placing of an electronic bug in a restaurant frequented by First Ward politicians (Cooley and Levin 2004). In 1992, Mayor Richard J. Daley put an end to the long and sordid political reign of the First Ward: In redrawing aldermanic districts, the Loop—the central business district—and the Michigan Avenue shopping area were placed in the 42nd Ward, and a new First Ward was created from parts of neighboring wards to ensure the election of a Latino alderman.

In the past, aspiring Outfit members cut their teeth on theft, particularly from interstate truck and train shipments; today, gambling and its related activities—taking bets, collecting receipts, servicing video poker machines—is the route to membership. Gambling is crucial to the Outfit; it provides considerable income and gives members something to do (they have considerable leisure time) while networking and socializing. The Outfit continues to be involved in the red light districts that appear in certain suburbs; and through control of unions, the Outfit is able to provide favored businessmen with a competitive edge, for example, by investing union funds. A number of Chicago union locals whose officers in the past were Outfit members or associates now have the sons and grandsons of these officials holding the same positions. (Herguth 2004).

The most significant convictions involving members of the Chicago Outfit in the last few years have involved persons on the "heavy" side, that is, those associated with violence. As a result, it appears the Outfit leadership has made a decision to stay away from business operations most likely to require violence. In recent years, there have been few murders related to organized crime. The thug side of the Outfit led to the most important federal case in decades, dubbed "Operation Family Secrets."

Family Secrets

The success of the Chicago Outfit in avoiding having made guys become informants ended in a most spectacular way—the ultimate betrayal of son against father, brother against brother (*United States v. Calabrese et al.,* 2 Cr. 1050, 2006). Frank Calabrese, an Outfit loan shark with a particularly violent reputation, was raised in the Outfit neighborhood surrounding the intersection of Grand Avenue and Ogden Street on Chicago's South Side. Expelled from school for fighting, he eventually went to work for Angelo LaPietra, and as Angelo rose in the Outfit, so did Frank. Nick Calabrese, Frank's younger brother, graduated from high school and served honorably in the Navy, but nevertheless became an important part of his brother's crew. Frank's son, Frank Calabrese, Jr., who also participated in some of his father's activities, in an effort to secure leniency, secretly provided information to law enforcement. Frank, Jr.'s cooperation with the government included recording incriminating conversations with his father who was incarcerated at the time. In 2004, after being confronted by the FBI with evidence of his role in a murder, Nick agreed to become a witness against his older brother. In 2007, he pled guilty to planning or carrying out fourteen murders. Frank Calabrese, Sr., was sentenced to life in prison in 2009 for his role in eighteen gangland slayings in the Chicago area dating back to 1970. Nick received twelve years and Frank, Jr., entered the Witness Security Program.

SUMMARY

1. Appreciate the connection between the cultural attributes of southern Italian immigrants and the development of the American Mafia:
   - Outside of the Northeast and Chicago, there are few or no vestiges of the formidable criminal organizations that evolved out of Prohibition.
   - Every important Italian-American organized crime figure has had cultural roots Southern Italy.

   - Italian criminals adapted their culture to organized crime in the United States.
2. Know the connection between the *Unione Siciliana*, the Castellammarese War, and the emergence of the Five Families in New York:
   - The *Unione Siciliana* emerged in nineteenth-century New York as a legitimate fraternal society designed to advance the interests of Sicilian immigrants. With Prohibition,

gangsters began to infiltrate and pervert the association.

- The Castellammarese War between the two major Mafia factions in New York ended with murder of Joseph Masseria.
- In the aftermath of the Castellammarese War, five Italian-American crime Families emerged, and they continue to maintain distinct identities: Bonanno, Colombo, Gambino, Genovese, and Lucchese.

3. Understand the structure of the New York Mafia Families:
   - Each member of a New York Mafia Family is an independent entrepreneur who shares a portion of his income with the hierarchy.
   - Membership eligibility requires Italian descent on your father's side, a sponsor, and a history of successful criminal activity or possess certain skills required by the group, an "earner" or a "shooter."
   - Law enforcement agencies take great interest in a criminal if they discover he is a made guy. Any insult or assault on a member requires that he kill the offender. He is required to obey the orders of his boss, even if this means participating in the murder of a complete stranger or perhaps a close friend or relative.
   - Members and associates are organized into crews, which are semi-independent units.
   - Members are not under the direct or indirect supervision of the boss, and he does not have a complete overview of the decentralized activities of members.
   - Given the violent nature of "made guys," peacekeeping is a primary responsibility of a boss.
   - Family bosses are linked in a rather informal arrangement known as the "commission."
   - American Mafia rules are contrary to the Southern Italian credo that places family above all else.
   - The formal organizational structure of a Mafia Family is not the same as its economic structure.

4. Appreciate the historical differences of the American Mafia in New York and Chicago:

- Chicago has been remarkable for the extent to which persons of various ethnicity have been integrated into the dominant criminal organization.
- Prior to Prohibition, vice operations were well-organized in Chicago and enjoyed political-police protection.
- Prohibition enabled violent young men in neighborhoods throughout Chicago to become crime overlords—control of violence became more important than control of politics.

5. Understand how political reform in Chicago led to an increase in violence:
   - The key figure in this new configuration was Johnny Torrio aided by his partner Al Capone.
   - The election of a reform mayor in Chicago broke down the stable system of police/political protection that resulted in the competitive violence of the "Chicago Wars."

6. Know how organized crime in Chicago changed with the end of Prohibition:
   - By the 1930, the Capone organization dominated the Chicagoland area.
   - With Prohibition ending and the onset of the Great Depression in 1929, leading gangsters began to look for new opportunities that they found in labor and business racketeering.
   - The expensive army of gunmen necessary during Prohibition, was no longer necessary when it ended—consolidation ensued.

7. Understand the differences between the structure of the American Mafia in New York and Chicago:
   - Chicago differs from New York in that the Outfit has always been a cooperative venture with other groups and there is an absence of independent entrepreneurs.
   - Each Outfit crew is composed of made guys and associates who are said to be "connected." The street boss and his lieutenants, if they are of Italian heritage, are made guys. Everyone else connected to the crew is an associate.
   - In the Chicago, made guys hold supervisory (or senior advisory) status.

REVIEW QUESTIONS

1. Why outside of the Northeast and Chicago, are there few or no vestiges of the formidable criminal organizations that evolved out of Prohibition?

2. What explains the prominence of Italians in American organized crime?

3. How did Prohibition impact *mafiosi* in the United States?

4. What was the *Unione Siciliana* and what was its relationship to organized crime?

5. What was the cause of the Castellammarese War and how did it end?

6. What are the advantages of being a "made guy" in a Mafia Family?

7. What are the membership requirements?

8. What are the disadvantages of membership?

9. What is a Mafia "crew"?

10. What are the responsibilities of the Family boss?

11. What is the role of the "commission"?

12. How are American Mafia rules contrary to Southern Italian culture?

13. In what way is the formal organizational structure of a Mafia Family not the same as its economic structure?

14. How did Prohibition change the relationship between politicians, vice entrepreneurs, and practitioners of violence?

15. What skills did Johnny Torrio bring to Chicago?

16. What was the critical change that resulted in the competitive violence of the "Chicago Wars"?

17. How did organized crime change in Chicago with the end of Prohibition?

18. How does organized crime Chicago differ from that in New York?

Assassinated Bonanno Family underboss Carmine Galente.   AP Photo

Explaining Organized Crime

According to the theory of "Ethnic Succession," organized crime in the United States has been a device for achieving social mobility by disadvantaged segments of the population. With social and economic success, the formerly disadvantaged exit crime in favor of conventional lives. This has affected the American Mafia that has difficulty attracting prospective members from traditional "mob neighborhoods" such as the Pleasant Avenue section of East Harlem and the southwest Brooklyn neighborhood of Bensonhurst.

In the summer, "Fat Tony" Salerno, boss of the Genovese Family, could often be found sitting in front of his pet shop on Pleasant Avenue, which during the Harlem riots of the 1964 was left strangely unmolested. "Fat Tony" is gone—he died in prison in 1992—and so is the mob. The five social clubs are no more and Pleasant Avenue, a short street, spanning just six blocks from 114th Street to 120th Street, is no longer an Italian enclave, but a black, Puerto Rican, and Mexican one (Fernandez 2010).

When I worked in Bensonhurst during the late 1960s, the well-maintained homes characteristic of the area had sidewalks that were washed-down several times a week by homeowners. An outsider—and only an outsider would do this—who dropped an empty pack of cigarettes was politely asked to pick it up. Failure to comply meant an unpleasant confrontation with some of the area's less genteel residents. Today, on Bath Avenue, Bensonhurst's main commercial strip, the wiseguy social clubs are gone and it is nearly impossible to find any trace of its mob past (Fernandez 2007).

Ethnic Succession and other theories of organized crime will be discussed in this chapter.

Organized crime has been subjected to only limited attempts at explanation—explanations beyond immoral people in pursuit of personal gain. This chapter will examine relevant theories in sociology, psychology, and biology. As sparse as the sociological literature is on organized crime, psychology provides even less, though some psychological theories offer insight. Biology, in particular neurology (brain science), offers an understanding of problematic behavior and will be examined for insight into persons who are part of organized crime.

THE SOCIOLOGY OF ORGANIZED CRIME

Although sociologists have offered a number of theories to help explain crime and criminal behavior, rarely have these been directed specifically at organized crime. Nevertheless, some sociological theories of crime and deviance provide insight into organized crime, and they will be examined in this chapter.

The Strain of Anomie

Building on a concept originated by the nineteenth-century French sociologist Émile Durkheim (1951), in 1938—during the Great Depression—Robert K. Merton set forth a social and cultural explanation for deviant behavior in the United States. To Merton, organized crime is a normal response to pressures exerted on certain persons by the social structure—the strain between goals and means. Goals, he points out, are economic, and he argues that there is an American preoccupation with economic success—*pathological materialism*. During the 1830s, a visitor from France, Alexis de Tocqueville (1966: 536) wrote: "It is odd to watch with what feverish ardor the Americans pursue prosperity and how they are tormented by the shadowy suspicion that they may have not have chosen the shortest route to get it." According to Merton, in America it is the goal that is emphasized, not the means, which are at best only a secondary consideration. "There may develop a disproportionate, at times, a virtually exclusive stress upon the value of specific goals, involving relatively slight concern with the institutionally appropriate modes of attaining these goals" (1938: 673).

This being the case, the only factors limiting goal achievement are technical, not moral or legal: "[E]mphasis on the goals of monetary success and material property leads to dominant concern with technological and social instruments designed to produce the desired result, inasmuch as institutional controls become of secondary importance. In such a situation, innovation [such as organized crime] flourishes as the range of means employed is broadened" (Merton 1938: 673). Thus, in American society, "the pressure of prestige-bearing success tends to eliminate the effective social constraint over means employed to this end. 'The-ends-justifies-the-means' doctrine becomes a guiding tenet for action when the cultural structure unduly exalts the end and the social organization unduly limits possible recourse to approved means" (1938: 681). The activities of earlier capitalists, the unscrupulous "Robber Barons" (discussed in Chapter 2), exemplify the spirit that Merton refers to as *innovation*. Taking advantage of every (legitimate and illegitimate) opportunity, these men became the embodiment of the great American success story. However, the opportunity for economic success is not equally distributed, and the immigrants who followed these men to America found many avenues from "rags to riches" significantly limited if not already closed.

Some immigrants recognized that the cards were stacked against them, and as a result, organized crime flourished. Writing several years before Merton, Louis Robinson (1933: 16) spoke of an American credo according to which "we dare not or at least will not condemn the criminal's goal, because it is also our goal. We want to keep the goal ourselves and damn the criminal for pursuing it in the only way he knows how."

> The methods which criminals use in attaining our common goal of wealth may, of course, differ from those that the non-criminal classes use. But this is to be expected. They are probably not in a position to employ our methods. We can think of a variety of reasons why a man without capital or without education or without industrial skill or without this or that advantage or handicapped by any one of several factors which anyone could easily name would be forced to seek the common goal by means differing from those employed by another man better situated or endowed. In other words, he would *play the game differently*. (1933: 15–16; emphasis added)

Anomie results when numbers of people are confronted by the contradiction between goals and means and "become estranged from a society that promises them in principle what they are deprived of in reality" (Merton 1964: 218). Despite numerous success stories, "We know in this same society that proclaims the right, and even the duty, of lofty aspirations for all, men do not have equal access to the opportunity structure" (1964: 218). Yet those with ready access to success ("born with a silver spoon") *and* those who are at a distinct disadvantage are constantly exposed to the rewards of "fame and fortune" by the mass media. For some, particularly the disadvantaged, anomie is the result. Merton states there are five modes of individual adaptation to this phenomenon: conformity, ritualism, rebellion, retreatism, and innovation. We are concerned only with the last adaptation—*innovation*—that includes organized criminal activity for those who would *play the game differently*.

British sociologists Ian Taylor, Paul Walton, and Jock Young (1973: 97) summarize the anomic condition in the United States: "The 'American Dream' urges all citizens to succeed whilst distributing the opportunity to succeed unequally: the result of this social and moral climate, inevitably, is innovation by the citizenry—the adoption of illegitimate means to pursue and obtain success." However, "routine" pedestrian criminal acts do not lead to any significant level of economic success. Innovation, then, is the adoption of sophisticated, well-planned, skilled, organized criminality.

Although *strain* can help explain why some persons from disadvantaged groups become involved in organized crime, it fails to provide a satisfying explanation for the continued existence of the American Mafia. In other words, even though poverty and limited economic opportunity can certainly impel one toward innovative activities, they do not explain why middle-class youngsters become involved in organized crime or why crimes by the wealthy and the powerful—for example, massive savings and loan industry fraud, securities fraud, insider trading, collusive agreements—continue to be a problem in the United States. Perhaps the mindset we are referring to as "wiseguy" transcends socioeconomic boundaries. In fact, organized criminal activity on a rather outrageous scale, for example, by Robber Barons, without necessarily being connected to conditions of *strain*, has been an important part of American history.

A question remains: Why do some persons suffering from anomie turn to criminal innovation, whereas others do not? Edwin Sutherland, the "father" of American criminology, provides an answer: *differential association*.

Differential Association

According to Sutherland (1973), all behavior—lawful and criminal—is learned. The principal part of learning occurs within intimate personal groups. What is learned depends on the intensity, frequency, and duration of the association. When these variables are sufficient and the associations are criminal, the actor learns the techniques of committing crime and the drives, attitudes, and rationalizations that add up to a favorable precondition to criminal behavior. The balance between noncriminal and criminal behaviors is tipped in favor of the latter.

Learning the techniques of sophisticated criminality requires the proper environment—ecological niches or *enclaves* where delinquent or criminal subcultures (discussed later) flourish and this education is available. In a capitalist society, socioeconomic differentials relegate some persons to an environment wherein they experience a compelling sense of strain—anomie—as well as differential association. In the environment where organized crime has traditionally thrived, strain is intense. Conditions of severe deprivation are coupled with readily available success models and associations that are innovative, such as racketeers and drug dealers. This makes certain *enclaves* characterized by social disorganization and delinquent or criminal subcultures spawning grounds for organized crime:

> Various types of people tend to seek out others like themselves and live close together. Located within these distinctive clusters are specialized commercial enterprises and institutions that support the inhabitants' special ways of life…. Each distinctive group, along with its stores and institutions, occupies a geographic area that

becomes intimately associated with the group. Through this linkage, areas acquire symbolic qualities that include their place names and social histories. Each place, both as a geographic entity and as a space with social meaning, also tends to be an object of residents' attachments and an important component of their identities. For example, people living in Little Italy or Chinatown think of themselves as Italian or Chinese, but their place of residence is also a prominent part of their self-concepts…. [The] enclave has some characteristics of a subculture, in which a group of people shares common traditions and values that are ordinarily maintained by a high rate of interaction within the group. (Abrahamson 1996: 1, 3)

Instead of conforming to conventional norms, some persons, through differential association, organize their behavior according to the norms of a delinquent or criminal group to which they belong or with which they identify. This is most likely to occur in environments characterized by relative social disorganization, where familial and communal controls are ineffective in exerting a conforming influence. In certain areas—enclaves with strong traditions of organized crime, be they in Chicago, Juárez, Medellín, Odessa, or Sicily—young persons stand a greater chance of being exposed to criminal norms. In these areas persons exhibiting criminal norms are often well integrated into the community, and such areas are the breeding ground for delinquent subcultures and prospective entrants into organized crime (Kobrin 1966).

Subcultures and Social Disorganization

Culture refers to a source of patterning in human conduct: it is the sum of patterns of social relationships and shared meanings by which people give order, expression, and value to common experiences. The strength of a culture is determined by the degree of commitment of its members: culture is a valued heritage. A *subculture* "implies that there are value judgments or a social value system which is apart from a larger or central value system. From the viewpoint of this larger dominant culture, the values of the subculture set the latter apart and prevent total integration, occasionally causing open or covert conflicts" (Wolfgang and Ferracuti 1967: 99). "Subcultures are patterns of values, norms, and behavior which have become traditional among certain groups. These groups may be of many types, including occupational and ethnic groups, social classes, occupants of 'closed institutions' [for example, prisons and mental hospitals] and various age grades." They are "important frames of reference through which individuals and groups see the world and interpret it" (Short 1968: 11).

Central to the issue of culture versus subculture are *norms*, "group-held prescriptions for or prohibitions against certain conduct" (Wolfgang and Ferracuti 1967: 113). Norms are general rules about how to behave and expectations that are predictive of behavior. These rules and expectations are approved by the vast majority of a society, which provides rewards or punishments for conformity or violation. "The 'delinquent subculture' is characterized principally by conduct that reflects values antithetical to the surrounding culture" (1967: 110). Subcultural theory explains criminal behavior as learned; the subcultural delinquent has learned values that are deviant—ideas about society that lead to criminal behavior. A number of studies indicate that delinquent youths hold values that differ markedly from those of nondelinquents. Indeed, they may view their criminal behavior as morally wrong, but this is not the controlling attitude. Being right or wrong in terms of the wider society is simply not a guidepost for behavior. Nonconventional behavior such as the ability to fight, to win at gambling, to "hold one's liquor," is admired and, thus, reinforced (Elliott, Huizinga, and Ageton 1985).

The connection between subcultural deviance and organized crime was revealed in an interview with an experienced investigator:

> They saw the Outfit [Chicago organized crime] guys, and gave them deference. It's in the culture. They don't grow up to believe this is wrong; it's a perverted sense of values: Knockin' down an old lady to take her purse; killing the clerk at the store for a few bucks, that's wrong. But everything to do with organized crime is perfectly acceptable. They know it's illegal, but who cares.... There's one group, for example, who we first noticed in 1990, '91, who call themselves the "Boys in the 'hood." There are about fifty or sixty of them, many of whom are now associates of the street crews. We had some as young as sixteen, but usually eighteen, nineteen, and usually from Elmwood Park, Melrose Park, the Northwest Side of Chicago [a residential area with many Italian Americans, and police officers and firefighters]. They were doing any scam that the Outfit would let them do—major burglaries, jewelry thefts, drug sales, credit card fraud. Many of them are relatives of Outfit members. Many of them now—they're in their twenties—work for the Elmwood Park [Taylor Street] crew. (Scarmella 1998)

Clifford R. Shaw and Henry D. McKay, sociologists at the University of Chicago, used that city as a laboratory for their study of patterns of criminality during the 1920s and 1930s.[1] They found that certain clearly identifiable neighborhoods maintained a high level of criminality over many decades despite changes in ethnic composition. Thus, although one ethnic group replaced another, the rate of criminality remained constant. What was it about the environment of these neighborhoods that made them criminogenic?

According to Shaw and McKay (1972: 72), such neighborhoods are characterized by attitudes and values that are conducive to delinquency and crime, particularly organized crime:

---

1. Despite the prominence of organized crime in Chicago during this period, the University of Chicago sociologists did not show much scholarly interest in the phenomenon (Reynolds 1995).

The presence of a large number of adult criminals in certain areas means that children there are in contact with crime as a career and with the criminal way of life, symbolized by organized crime. In this type of organization can be seen the delegation of authority, the division of labor, the specialization of function, and all the other characteristics common to well-organized business institutions wherever found....

The heavy concentration of delinquency in certain areas means that boys living in these areas are in contact not only with individuals who engage in proscribed activity but also with groups which sanction such behavior and exert pressure upon their members to conform to group standards. (1972: 174)

A disruption of the social order is associated with high rates of delinquency in a community, the result of a breakdown in mechanisms of social control. In many U.S. cities around the turn of the century, the social order was disrupted by the combined interactive effects of industrialization, immigration, and urbanization. Deviant traditions developed and competed with conventional norms; in some communities, deviant norms won out. Once established, these norms took root in areas that, according to Shaw and McKay, are characterized by attitudes and values that are conducive to delinquency and crime, thus creating a subculture of crime. The attitudes and values, as well as the techniques of organized criminality, are transmitted culturally. "Delinquent boys in these areas have contact not only with other delinquents who are their contemporaries but also with older offenders, who in turn had contact with delinquents preceding them, and so on back to the earliest history of the neighborhood. This contact means that the traditions of delinquency can be and are transmitted down through successive generations of boys, in much the same way that language and other social forms are transmitted" (1972: 174).

Back in the 1920s, John Landesco (1968) found that organized crime in Chicago could be explained by the prevalence of social disorganization in the wider society (during the period of Prohibition) and by the distinct social organization of urban slums from which members of organized crime emerge. "Once a set of cultural values is created and established—either because of economic factors or intellectual or moral transformations—they tend to become autonomous in their impact. From that point on, they can influence human relations independently of their original sources. And since they are, as a rule, accepted uncritically and through the most inadvertent process of socialization, they are regarded as normal and inevitable within each cultural system" (Saney 1986: 35).

In other words, the roots and culture of particular neighborhoods explain why gangsters come from clearly delineated areas "where the gang tradition is old" (Landesco 1968: 207) and where adolescents, through differential association, can absorb the attitudes and skills necessary to enter the world of adult organized crime. Indeed, in such neighborhoods, organized crime can provide a level of social control—limiting predatory crime, for example—that would otherwise be absent. At night, in an organized crime–dominated neighborhood in Brooklyn, a young woman did not realize she was being followed as she approached the door to her home. The young man following her did not realize that he was being watched. His attempt at a knifepoint robbery was foiled by several large men who quickly carried him up the stairs. An observer recalls: "I could make out the small roof wall on the front of the building—it was made of brick—and then I saw the guy launched right over it into the air. He hung there for just a second, flailing arms like a broken helicopter, and then he came down hard and splattered all over the street" (Pileggi 1990: 40). As ex-FBI agent Joe Piston notes: "Neighborhoods that are dominated by wiseguys are considered to be under the protection of these wiseguys. There are far fewer robberies, rapes, or muggings in wiseguy neighborhoods than even the safest precincts of the city" (Pistone 2004: 76).

Inadequate familial socialization prevents some persons from conforming to the conventional norms of the wider society. Through differential association, some of these persons organize their behavior according to the norms of a delinquent or criminal subculture with which they identify or to which they belong. This is most likely to occur in environments characterized by relative social disorganization, where familial and communal controls are ineffective in exerting a conforming influence. In his classic study of Chicago street gangs originally published in 1927, Frederic Thrasher (1968: 270) notes: "Experience in a gang of the predatory type usually develops in the boy an attitude of indifference to law and order—one of the basic traits of the finished gangster." Thrasher (1968: 273) points out: "If the younger undirected gangs and clubs of the gang type, which serve as training schools for delinquency, do not succeed in turning out the finished criminal, they often develop a type of personality which may well foreshadow the gangster and the gunman." In the Chicago of the Prohibition era, there was no hard-and-fast dividing line between gangs of boys and youths, and adult criminal organizations (1968: 281): "They merge into each other by imperceptible gradations."

To survive, an organized crime group must have "an institutionalized process for inducting new members and inculcating them with the values and ways of behaving of the social system" (Cressey 1969: 263). Donald Cressey notes: "In some neighborhoods all three of the essential ingredients of an effective recruiting process are in operation: inspiring aspiration for membership, training for membership and selection for membership" (1969: 236). In his research, Gerald Suttles (1968) refers to areas from which members of organized crime have typically emerged as *defended neighborhoods*: recognized ecological niches whose inhabitants form cohesive groupings and seal themselves off through the efforts of delinquent gangs, restrictive covenants, and a forbidding reputation. Such neighborhoods have traditionally provided the recruiting grounds that ensure the continuity of organized crime.

In such communities, the conventional and criminal value systems are highly integrated. Leaders of organized criminal enterprises "frequently maintain membership in such conventional institutions of their local communities as churches, fraternal and mutual benefit societies, and political parties" (Kobrin 1966: 156). Formal and informal political, economic, and religious ties provide both illegitimate and legitimate opportunities. These leaders are able to control violent and delinquent behavior in their domain—they are effective instruments of social control. "Everyone," particularly would-be miscreants, "knows" not to "mess around" in certain neighborhoods. And those who do not "know" have suffered serious consequences—selling drugs in one Chicago suburb, for example, resulted in mutilated corpses. In the Italian area of New York's Greenwich Village, "street corner boys" enforced the social order—made sure the streets were safe. And their self-appointed role was backed by the formidable reputation of the neighborhood's organized crime figures. For this protection, neighborhood residents reciprocated by providing "wiseguys" with a "safe haven" (Tricarico 1984).

Nicholas Pileggi (1985: 37–38) describes a defended neighborhood in Brooklyn:

In Brownsville–East New York wiseguys were more than accepted—they were protected. Even the legitimate members of the community—the merchants, teachers, phone repairmen, garbage collectors, bus depot dispatchers, housewives, and old-timers sunning themselves along the Conduit Drive—all seemed to keep an eye out to protect their local hoods. The majority of the residents, even those not directly related by birth or marriage to wiseguys, had certainly known the local rogues most of their lives. There was the nodding familiarity of neighborhood. In the area it was impossible to betray old friends, even those old friends who had grown up to be racketeers.

The extraordinary insularity of these old-world mob-controlled sections, whether Brownsville–East New York, the South Side of Chicago, or Federal Hill in Providence, Rhode Island, unquestionably helped to nurture the mob.

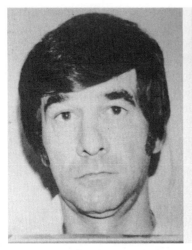  

Outfit members Paul Schiro (left), Frank Calabrese, Sr. (center), and Joseph ("Joey the Clown") Lombardo have been implicated in more than a dozen murders.

Recruitment into organized crime is made viable because "in the type of community under discussion boys may more or less realistically recognize the potentialities for personal progress in the local society through success in delinquency. In a general way, therefore, delinquent activity in these areas constitutes a training ground for the acquisition of skill in the use of violence, concealment of offense, evasion of detection and arrest, and the purchase of immunity from punishment" (Kobrin 1966: 156).

Robert Lombardo, a former organized crime investigator and ranking Cook County police official, points out that prospective members of organized crime "typically come from communities which share collective representations and moral sentiments which allow them to recognize the pursuit of a career in the underworld as a legitimate way of life" (1979: 18; 1994a). Young men from these areas dress in a certain style—"gangster chic"—and congregate in social clubs and night spots where they are able to associate with the men who have already been allowed entry into organized crime. They are ready and eager to show their mettle by accepting assignments from "goodfellas."

Even those who have moved to suburban locations—if they accept the "wiseguy" credo—gravitate back to the 'hood. In Chicago this phenomenon has been referred to as the "suburbanization

of the mob"—young men who have known only middle-class living conditions becoming part of organized crime. Like the members of outlaw motorcycle clubs discussed in Chapter 10, these young men are attracted to a subcultural lifestyle, not necessarily by the potential financial rewards offered by organized crime. For example, Salvatore ("Solly D.") DeLaurentis (b. 1938), who was raised in the Taylor Street neighborhood in Chicago, aspired to be a "gangster"—a term he uses to describe himself—since his earliest days. But his family moved out to suburban Lake County, and Solly D. found himself cut off from his career path: Lake County lacked the critical mass of older criminals and their young associates/wannabes. So DeLaurentis gradually made connections back in the old neighborhood and eventually became a member of the Outfit crew in charge of Lake County. (He is serving an eighteen-year sentence for a racketeering conviction.)

In Chicago, even senior members of the Outfit who reside in suburban locations frequent the restaurants, nightspots, and social clubs back in the 'hood. James D. ("Jimmy D.") Antonio, ranking member of the Grand Avenue crew, resided in suburban Skokie. But until his death in 1993 from an auto accident, he operated a storefront social club in the Grand Avenue neighborhood, which sponsored a boys' baseball team for neighborhood youths (O'Brien 1993). But many "mob neighborhoods" are changing. In one of them, a southwest Brooklyn area known as Bensonhurst whose main commercial strip is Bath Avenue, it is nearly impossible to find any trace of its mob past (Fernandez 2007).

According to Irving Spergel (1964), in such communities life in organized crime is considered acceptable and therefore a legitimate aspiration for young persons. Although these communities provide an appropriate learning environment for the acquisition of values and skills associated with the performance of criminal roles, integration into organized crime requires selection and tutelage in the process of acquiring recognition—and only a select few are given recognition by those who control admission. Entry into organized crime is characterized by *differential opportunity*.

Differential Opportunity

In agreement with Merton, Richard Cloward and Lloyd Ohlin (1960) noted that American preoccupation with economic success, coupled with socioeconomic stratification, relegates many persons to an environment wherein they experience intense strain: "Many lower-class male adolescents experience extreme deprivation born of the certainty that their position in the economic structure is relatively fixed and immutable—a desperation made all the more poignant by their exposure to a cultural ideology in which failure to orient oneself upward is regarded as a moral defect and failure to become mobile as proof of it" (1960: 107).

Conditions of severe deprivation with extremely limited access to ladders of legitimate success result in collective adaptations in the form of delinquent subcultures. Cloward and Ohlin distinguish three types:

1. *Retreatist subculture*: Activities in which drug usage is the primary focus; the anomic condition leads the sufferer to reject the goal of economic success in favor of a more easily obtainable one—the "high."
2. *Conflict subculture*: Gang activities devoted to violence and destructive acting out as a way of gaining status. As with retreatists, the anomic condition leads to a rejection of economic success in favor of a more easily obtainable goal.
3. *Criminal/rackets subculture*: Gang activity devoted to utilitarian criminal pursuits, an adaptation that begins to approximate organized crime.

Anomie alone, note Cloward and Ohlin, is not sufficient to explain participation in organized crime: what is necessary is cultural transmission (Shaw and McKay) through differential association (Sutherland). However, Cloward and Ohlin point out that illegitimate opportunity for success, like legitimate opportunity, is not equally distributed throughout society (1960: 145): "Having decided that he 'can't make it legitimately,' he cannot simply choose from an array of illegitimate means, all equally available to him." In other words, access to criminal ladders of success is no more freely available than are noncriminal alternatives:

> Only those neighborhoods in which crime flourishes as a stable, indigenous institution are fertile learning environments for the young. Because these environments afford integration of different age-levels of offender, selected young people are exposed to "differential association" through which tutelage is provided and criminal values and skills are acquired. To be prepared for the role may not, however, ensure that the individual will ever discharge it. One important limitation is that more youngsters are recruited into these patterns of differential association than the adult criminal structure can possibly absorb. Since there is a surplus of contenders for these elite positions, criteria and mechanisms of selection must be evolved. Hence a certain proportion of those who aspire may not be permitted to engage in the behavior for which they have prepared themselves. (Cloward and Ohlin 1960: 148)

The increasing scale and complexity of modern life has altered the social structure of urban communities. Greater social mobility has marked the end of many ethnically defined and defended neighborhoods. Racket subcultures vanish as residents became educated, find well-paying jobs, and move to the suburbs. But in some suburbs—think of where television's "Tony Soprano" lives—the tradition has moved with its adherents.

Although various types of conventional crime are open to everyone, "things are somewhat more complicated where organized crime in concerned" (Kleemans and de Poot 2008: 74). In organized crime, social relations are of greater importance, and illegal business relationships have to be built up: "Not everyone has suitable social ties and building up such relationships takes time and energy" (2008: 75). This is of particular importance in criminal activities that are transnational: smuggling drugs, arms, stolen vehicles, human trafficking for sexual exploitation, and money laundering. The very complexity of transnational organized crime may require going beyond one's own social circle. This is facilitated by the *credentialing* discussed in Chapter 1, and acquiring credentials requires affiliation with a known and respected (at least in criminal circles) criminal organization. In some (perhaps many) cases, however, persons with specific skills or occupations, such as those involving transportation and finance, may be drawn into a criminal organization through a serendipitous social relationship with an organized crime network—*social opportunity* (Kleemans and de Poot 2008). Such persons are relatively late starters who do not follow a career path from juvenile delinquency to adult crime.

In neighborhoods where the organized crime tradition continues, or among persons who have access to a requisite social network, why do young people who have the opportunity choose not to become contenders for positions in organized crime? *Social control theory* offers an explanation.

Social Control Theory

Social control refers to those processes by which the community influences its members toward conformance with established norms of behavior. Social control theorists argue that the relevant question is not, "Why do persons become involved in crime, organized or otherwise?" but rather, "Why do most persons conform to societal norms?" If, as control theorists generally assume, most persons are sufficiently motivated by the potential rewards to commit criminal acts, why do only a few make crime a career? According to social control theorists, "delinquent acts result when an individual's bond to society is weak or broken" (Hirschi 1969: 16). The strength of this bond is determined by external and internal restraints. In other words, external and internal restraints determine whether we move in the direction of crime or of law-abiding behavior.

External restraints include social disapproval linked to public shame and/or social ostracism and fear of punishment. In other words, people are typically deterred from criminal behavior by the possibility of being caught and the punishment that can result, ranging from public shame to imprisonment (and, in extreme cases, capital punishment). In neighborhoods or among subcultural groups with moral sentiments favorable to organized crime, such public shame/social ostracism is ineffective. Only the threat of imprisonment can offer a deterrent.

The strength of official deterrence—force of law—is measured according to two dimensions: risk versus reward. *Risk* involves the ability of the criminal justice system to detect, apprehend, and convict the offender. The amount of risk is weighed against the potential rewards. Both risk and reward, however, are relative to one's socioeconomic situation. In other words, the less one has to lose, the greater is the willingness to engage in risk. In the words of a Bob Dylan song (*Like a Rolling Stone*), "When you ain't got nothin', you got nothin' to lose." And the greater the reward, the greater is the willingness to engage in risk. This theory explains why persons in deprived economic circumstances would be more willing to engage in criminal behavior. However, the potential rewards and a perception of relatively low risk can also explain why persons in more advantaged economic circumstances would engage in remunerative criminal behavior such as corporate crime.

Internal restraints include what psychoanalytic theory refers to as the *superego* (discussed later): an unconscious, yet powerful, conscience-like mechanism that provides a sense of guilt. According to Sigmund Freud, conscience is not something that is a part of us from the very beginning of our lives. It is a controlling mechanism that develops out of the relationship with, and influence of, our parents. In the adult who experienced "healthy" parental relationships as a child, the superego takes the place of the controlling parental function. Dysfunction during early stages of childhood development, or parental influences that are not normative, result in an adult who is devoid of prosocial internal controls; some refer to this as psycho- or sociopathology, or antisocial personality disorder (ASP), characterized by a combination of antisocial behavior and emotional detachment (discussed later).

Ethnic Succession

During the decades following World War II, organized crime underwent considerable change. It became increasingly clear that in the United States, organized crime was dominated mainly by Italians—the Irish, except for small pockets in New York and Boston, were no longer involved. And although the sons of Jewish immigrants played a vital role in organized crime, by the third generation, the Jews had moved out. Jackson Toby (1958: 548) explains:

> Jews and Italians came to the United States in large numbers at about the same time—the turn of the century—and both settled in urban areas. There was, however, a very different attitude toward intellectual accomplishments in the two cultures. Jews from Eastern Europe regarded study as the most important activity for an adult male. The rabbi enjoyed great prestige because he was a scholar, a teacher, a logician. He advised the community on the application of the Written and Oral Law. Life in America gave a secular emphasis to the Jewish reverence for learning. Material success is a more important motive than salvation for American youngsters, Jewish as well as Christian, and secular education is better training for business and professional

careers than Talmudic exegesis. Nevertheless, intellectual achievement continued to be valued by Jews—and to have measurable effects. Second-generation Jewish students did homework diligently, got high grades, went to college in disproportionate numbers, and scored high on intelligence tests. Two thousand years of preparation lay behind them.

Immigrants from southern Italy, on the other hand, tended to regard formal education either as a frill or as a source of dangerous ideas from which the minds of the young should be protected. They remembered Sicily, where a child who attended school regularly was a rarity. There, youngsters were needed … only to help on the farm. Equally important was the fact that hard-working peasants could not understand why their children should learn classical Italian (which they would not speak at home) or geography (when they would not travel in their lifetimes more than a few miles from their birthplace). Sicilian parents suspected that education was an attempt on the part of Roman officials to subvert the authority of the family. In the United States, many southern Italian immigrants maintained the same attitudes. They resented compulsory school attendance laws and prodded their children to go to work and become economic assets as soon as possible. They encouraged neglect of schoolwork and even truancy. They did not realize that education has more importance in an urban-industrial society than in a semi-feudal one. With supportive motivation from home lacking, the second-generation Italian boys did not make the effort of Jewish contemporaries. Their teachers tried to stuff the curriculum into their heads in vain. Their lack of interest was reflected not only in low marks, retardation, truancy, and early school leaving; it even resulted in poor scores on intelligence tests. They accepted their parents' conception of the school as worthless and thereby lost their best opportunity for social ascent.

The pool of available candidates for membership in organized crime dwindled in Jewish communities. In Italian communities it remained adequate enough; the large-scale organizations needed to profit from Prohibition were no longer necessary. In Chicago, for example, during the height of Prohibition, Al Capone is reputed to have employed 700 gunmen for an organization that involved thousands of persons, while contemporary estimates of the size of the Chicago Outfit have ranged only as high as 130. The largest of the crime Families, the Genovese Family of New York, is estimated to have no more than 400 members. These core members, however, have associates, and the total number of criminal actors participating directly or indirectly in a crime group's enterprises is many times the size of the core membership at any given time.

Noting the small size of the American Mafia and the absence of armed retainers, Peter Reuter (1983: xi) has concluded: "My analysis suggests that the Mafia may be a paper tiger, rationally reaping the returns from its reputation while no longer maintaining the forces that generated the reputation." He theorizes that having established a dominant position, an unchallenged monopoly of force, the Mafia can depend on its fearsome reputation, an asset that can be substituted for personnel costs that would be incurred by maintaining armed forces. Reuter states that challenges to Mafia power in black and Hispanic communities have not "generated any effort by the Mafia to assert control through superior violence" (1983: 136; also 1995). Reuter theorizes that this may result from the lack of available force or simply from a cost-benefit analysis that militates against its use—excessive force attracts law enforcement attention and is bad for business in general. But outside of the Chicago and New York greater metropolitan areas, the American Mafia is largely absent.

Reuter notes that challenges to the Mafia outside of black and Hispanic communities have not been noticeable. The structure of Italian-American organized crime groups provides an explanation. As noted in Chapter 3, business activities are typically decentralized, often franchised, while violence is not. The Mafia is often "invisible"; that is, members usually avoid directly operating illegal enterprises such as gambling or marginal businesses such as "topless bars" or "strip joints." Instead, they often finance or "license" such enterprises, sometimes receiving payments for restricting entry or competition, sometimes providing no service—simple extortion. How would a competing group set out to deal with this operation? The most obvious method would be a direct attack on its members. But they do not reside, meet, or otherwise assemble in significant numbers, and they may be unknown to anyone except persons intimately involved in the local criminal underworld. The decentralized nature of the organization would render a frontal assault unproductive. While a number of members and associates could be killed here and there, the net effect would be analogous to punching an empty bag.

Any group with the temerity to undertake this challenge would require the resources necessary to sustain an "army in the field" for an indefinite period. Elderly members would probably head for condominiums in South Florida and Palm Springs, California, but remaining behind would be a cadre of young men whose sole function would be to murder those mounting the challenge to the group's supremacy. They could be reinforced with hired assassins from other groups. As Reuter (1983: 133) notes: "Large numbers of young men in major American cities are willing to accept paid employment as violence disputants." Rational criminals with martial skill would be inclined to side with an organization with proven staying power—the Mafia—rather than take a chance with a seemingly reckless new group.

As Nicholas Gage (1971a: 113) points out, *The Mafia Is Not an Equal Opportunity Employer*: "No door is more firmly locked to blacks than the one that leads to the halls of power in organized crime." He states that Irish, Jewish, and Italian mobsters have tended to recruit and promote from within their own ethnic groups, while cooperating with one another. Organized crime is no less stratified than the wider "legitimate" society, and the dominant groups in both have always been white. This leads to the issue of *ethnic succession* in organized crime.

Daniel Bell (1964) refers to crime as an American way of life, "A Queer Ladder of Social Mobility." He points out that the "jungle quality of the American business community, particularly at the turn of the century, was reflected in the mode of 'business' practiced by the coarse gangster elements, most of them from new immigrant families, who were 'getting ahead' just as Horatio Alger had urged" (1964: 116). Francis Ianni (1974) notes that this "queer ladder" had organized crime as the first few rungs:

> The Irish came first, and early in this century they dominated crime as well as big-city political machinations. As they came to control the political machinery of large cities they won wealth, power and respectability through subsequent control of construction, trucking, public utilities and the waterfront. By the 1920s and the period of prohibition and speculation in the money markets and real estate, the Irish were succeeded in organized crime by the Jews, and Arnold Rothstein [see box], Lepke Buchalter and Gurrah Shapiro

---

ARNOLD ROTHSTEIN AND THE RATIONALIZATION OF CRIME

"A. R.," or "the Brain," as author Damon Runyon called him, was born in New York in 1882 and "set new and historic standards in the development of organized crime in America" (Lacey 1991: 50). He "transformed criminal activity from a haphazard, often spontaneous endeavor into one whose hallmarks—specialized expertise, administrative hierarchy, and organizational procedure—correspond to the classic sociological model of a bureaucracy. Thus, Rothstein's illegal business had a definite administrative structure based on specific skills; competence and not ethnic pedigree determined one's rank and, of course, one's position in his outfit" (Joselit 1983: 143).

© Bettmann/Corbis

> Rothstein's office ... in the middle of the midtown business district, employed a staff comparable to that of any large (and legitimate) commercial firm, replete with secretaries, bookkeepers, and legal counsel.... A decision to enter some new illegal venture tended to be based not on personal motives of revenge or power but on strictly commercial considerations: the amount of profit to be made and the length of time it would take to make it. Finally, by investing the money he earned through illegal channels into legal enterprises such as real estate and the theater, Rothstein made it difficult to ascertain where the illegal enterprise left off and the legitimate one began. (Joselit 1983: 44)

[discussed in Chapter 13] dominated gambling and labor racketeering for over a decade. The Jews quickly moved into the world of business and the professions as more legitimate avenues to economic and social mobility. The Italians came next.... (1974: 13–14)

According to this thesis, each successive immigrant group experienced *strain* to which some members reacted by *innovating* in accord with a tradition that had been established by earlier American entrepreneurs—the "Robber Barons." Ethnic succession results when a group experiences success in crime, and legitimate opportunities thereby become more readily available. Strain subsides, and the group moves out of organized crime, creating an opportunity for innovation for the succeeding immigrant group. According to this thesis, persons involved in organized crime are not committed to a deviant subculture but are merely using available, albeit illegal, opportunity to achieve economic success. Letizia Paoli and Peter Reuter (2008) state that blocked opportunity and the "queer ladder" may also explain participation in organized crime by members of the immigrant community in Europe.

Almost four decades ago, Francis Ianni stated that ethnic succession is continuing, that "the Italians are leaving or being pushed out of organized crime [and] they are being replaced by the next wave of migrants to the city: blacks and Puerto Ricans" (1974: 14). Although they might not have been obvious to Ianni when he was conducting his research in New York, today we would have to add Albanians, Chinese, Colombians, Dominicans, Jamaicans, Mexicans, Nigerians, Russians, and outlaw motorcycle clubs. According to the ethnic succession thesis, involvement in organized crime is simply a rational response to economic conditions: Organized crime can be understood as a rational choice for responding to anomie.

Other theorists reject this one-dimensional view. Organized crime, they argue, provides important psychic rewards and meaningful social structures. Young Italian-American males from middle-class circumstances continue to be drawn by the allure of the American Mafia—a romantization of the mob kept alive in certain neighborhoods—enclaves—and reinforced by media representations. Being "connected" brings prestige, and in the social environment inhabited by wiseguys—bars, restaurants, nightclubs—a privileged status is evident. The "wannabe" outlaw is socialized into an exciting world where he eagerly adopts the attitude, behavior pattern, and even the clothing styles exemplified by wiseguys.

An example was the rise of a notorious gang of Italian-American hoodlums in the Pleasant Avenue section of Harlem. Dubbed the Purple Gang, apparently after the murderous Detroit (Jewish) mob of Prohibition days, they were used as "muscle" and executioners in many gangland murders, and their reputation for violence made them very useful to the Mafia leadership. The Purple Gang has been involved in numerous rackets, particularly drug trafficking, which is facilitated by their contacts with young men of other ethnic backgrounds who have access to importation quantities of heroin and cocaine. In his study of some members of the Purple Gang, Peter Lupsha (1983) found that they tend to have been born between 1946 and 1951 and to be third-generation Italian Americans who are related by blood and marriage. Even though they come from the Pleasant Avenue neighborhood, most reside in the Bronx or suburban Westchester County. "They are now, like many New York suburbanite businessmen, commuters to the old neighborhood for work, money, and visiting rather than residents" (1983: 76). Many Purple Gang members have been "made"—inducted into membership in traditional organized crime Families in New York. Similar groups have been identified.

Journalist Mike McAlary (1998) followed the exploits of a group of young Italian Americans known as the "Tanglewood Boys"—they used the Tanglewood Shopping Center in suburban Yonkers, New York, as a hangout. Six of the postadolescent gangsters had fathers who were members of New York's organized crime Families. The Tanglewood Boys committed armed robberies and murders, some for personal reasons, others for reasons related to business.

In Queens, the "Giannini crew" consisted of young men who worked for three New York City crime Families—their hangout is the Caffe Giannini on Fresh Pond Road in Ridgewood. They began their criminal careers in the late 1980s as a violent street gang affiliated with an older set of men, the Ridgewood Boys, some of whom had ties to organized crime. Federal officials describe the group as a "farm team" for organized crime. In 2001, when one of the Giannini crew, age 28, pled guilty to racketeering, he described several murders as if they were trips to the dry cleaners (Feuer 2001). One of the crew members, whose father is serving a life sentence for his involvement in the "Pizza Connection" heroin case (discussed later), became a made guy in the Bonanno Family (Marzulli 2005a). Anthony ("Ace") Aiello was described by the Family boss as "Luca Brasi," a reference to the hulking and murderous enforcer in the *Godfather* novel and film. In 2005, Aiello, 28, was arrested in Syracuse while a fugitive following the 2004 murder of a mob associate (Marzulli and Lemire 2005). Another Queens crew of young "wannabes," dubbed the "Young Guns," reported to a Gambino Family *capo* and worked in New York and Florida. In addition to armored car and bank robberies, crew members were responsible for at least four murders (McPhee 2003).

In New York, an organized crime insider explained to the writer that although older wiseguys may try to hide organized crime affiliations from their offspring, the sons and daughters discover the truth during adolescence. He noted that without any encouragement—and even with discouragement—from their fathers, some of these young men take advantage of their fathers' reputations to form crews of organized crime aspirants. Why? They are attracted by the allure of organized crime—of wiseguy chic and lifestyle.

Entry into organized crime, states Peter Lupsha (1981: 22), is not based on blocked aspirations, that is, on anomie or strain. Rather, it "is a rational choice, rooted in one perverse aspect of our values; namely, that only 'suckers' work, and that in our society, one is at liberty to take 'suckers' and seek easy money." The wiseguy attitude is exemplified by Paul ("Paulie") Vario, a powerful *caporegime* in the Lucchese Family. Vario associate Henry Hill (Pileggi 1985: 20) reports:

> Paulie was always asking me for stolen credit cards whenever he and his wife, Phyllis, were going out for the night. Paulie called stolen credit cards "Muldoons," and he always said that liquor tastes better on a Muldoon. The fact that a guy like Paul Vario, a *capo* in the Lucchese crime family, would even consider going out on a social occasion with his wife and run the risk of getting caught using a stolen credit card might surprise some people. But if you knew wiseguys you would know right away that the best part of the night for Paulie came from the fact that he was getting over on somebody.

With a great deal of insight, Pileggi (1985: 36) captures the wiseguy attitude toward society: "They lived in an environment awash in crime, and those who did not partake were simply viewed as prey. To live otherwise was foolish. Anyone who stood waiting his turn on the American pay line was beneath contempt." According to this view, organized crime comprises a deviant subculture to which members have a commitment that is not mitigated by the absence of strain. As one Gambino crime Family member told a reporter: "We don't want to be part of your world. We don't want to belong to country clubs" (Brenner 1990: 181). Benjamin ("Lefty") Ruggiero of the Bonanno Family explained: "As a wiseguy you can lie, you can cheat, you can steal, you can kill people—*legitimately*. You can do any goddamn thing you want, and nobody can say anything about it. Who wouldn't want to be a wiseguy?" (Pistone 1987: 330). As former undercover FBI agent Joe Pistone (2004: 9) points out:

> Wiseguys exist in a bizarre parallel universe, a world where avarice and corruption are the norm, and where the routines

that most ordinary people hold dear—working good jobs, being with family, living an honest life—are seen as the curse of the weak and the stupid. Wiseguys resemble us in many ways, but make no mistake, they might as well be from another planet, so alien and abnormal are their thoughts and habits.

Ianni (1972) describes the "Lupollos," his pseudonym for the Italian organized crime Family he studied, whose core members are all related by blood or marriage. In the fourth generation, "only four out of twenty-seven males are involved in the family business organization. The rest are doctors, lawyers, college teachers, or run their own businesses" (1972: 193). Ianni argued that ethnic succession continues (1974: 12): "We shall witness over the next decade the systematic development of what is now a scattered and loosely organized pattern of emerging black control in organized crime into the Black Mafia." Gus Tyler (1975: 178) did not find Ianni convincing, claiming that Ianni's evidence "consists of a pimp with a stable of seven hookers, a dope pusher, a fence who dabbles in loan sharking and gambling, a con man who gets phony insurance policies for gypsy cabs, and a numbers racketeer, etc." Tyler points out that, although these activities are "organized," they are not in a class with white organized crime either qualitatively or quantitatively. Indeed, early in his (1974) book, Ianni reports that the brother and partner of the aforementioned "dope pusher," actually a large-scale heroin dealer in Paterson, New Jersey, was found sans genitals—a "message" from the "White Mafia." A similar result obtained in Newark, New Jersey, when the Black Panthers attempted an incursion into a numbers operation that was under the patronage of the Lucchese Family (Raab 2005).

As for blacks and Latinos replacing Italians in organized crime, Lupsha (1981) argues that black and Latino groups have only succeeded in controlling markets that Italian-American groups have discarded because of poor risk-to-profit ratios. Lupsha (1981: 22) questions the "ethnic succession" thesis.

He argues that despite Ianni's (1972; 1974) limited findings, Italian organized crime figures who have gained economic status are not leaving organized crime and, in many instances, their progeny have followed them into organized crime. This view certainly has empirical support—there are dozens of contemporary American Mafia members whose children have followed them into "the life."

In New York, young men raised in comfortable middle-class circumstances have advanced into organized crime in a most violent way. Roy DeMeo of Brooklyn, for example, a second-generation American of Neapolitan heritage, became a loan shark while still in his teens. His uncle was a star prosecutor in the Brooklyn District Attorney's Office. But at age 32, to protect an extortion scheme run with his partner, a member of the Gambino Family, Roy committed his first murder—a solo job using a silencer-equipped pistol. He subsequently put together a crew of active criminals from the (middle-class) Canarsie section of Brooklyn. Their first murder victim, a car dealer who was testifying against them before a Brooklyn grand jury, was kidnapped, stabbed repeatedly, and dismembered. The medical examiner who handled the case, Dr. Dominick DiMaio, did not know that his cousin Roy DeMeo—his branch of the family spelled the name differently—was responsible for the murder. DeMeo was initiated into the Gambino Family, and his crew eventually killed and usually dismembered an estimated 200 persons; most of the bodies were never found. In fact, contrary to mob custom, Roy DeMeo added murder-for-hire to his repertoire and, against the edict of the Gambino Family boss, dealt in cocaine. One of DeMeo's leading assassins was arrested and began providing evidence against the Gambino Family. Soon afterward, in 1983, at age 42, DeMeo was the victim of a volley of shots fired into his head at close range (Mustain and Capeci 1992; Capeci 2003).

A meeting between John Gotti, boss of the Gambino Family, and Vincent ("Chin") Gigante, boss of the Genovese Family, revealed their different attitudes toward offspring following them into organized crime. Gambino underboss Sam Gravano

---

DEMEO'S "BROOKLYN BUTCHER SHOP"

Killings typically took place in a Brooklyn apartment. When the victim arrived, he would be shot with a silencer-equipped gun, and a towel was wrapped around his head to stop the blood. He would then be stabbed in the heart to stop the blood from pumping, and the body would be placed in the shower to bleed him. He was then placed on a pool liner in the living room, dismembered, and wrapped in plastic bags that were placed in cardboard boxes and taken to a nearby dump (Capeci 2003).

---

reports: "One thing I'll never forget from that meeting, was John telling Chin in sort of a proud way that his son, John Junior, had just been made. Chin said, 'Jeez, I'm sorry to hear that'" (Maas 1997: 239–40).[2] A journalist quotes Colombo Family *caporegime* Salvatore ("Big Sal"—350 pounds) Miciotta: "Only a real *gavone* [lowlife] wants for his kids what we got…. Idiots and wannabes are who's attracted to this life now" (Goldberg 1999: 27). The shrinking of Italian neighborhoods, notes Ronald Goldstock, former director of the New York State Organized Crime Task Force, "results in a lack of gangs, which means that there are no minor leagues to supply the majors" (Goldberg 1999: 71).

Though many young men appear to enjoy playing the wiseguy role—often outfitted with large pinkie rings, gold chains, and other symbols of gangster chic—many are neither bright nor tough.[3] As journalist George Anastasia notes, "they value form over substance" (1998: 25). The long neighborhood-based apprenticeships through which organized crime chooses the cream of the "wannabes" are history. Those accepted into membership are often not the tough, street-smart, stand-up kids of yesteryear, but rather social failures and potential informants quick to play "I've got a secret"—turn on their closest associates to avoid incarceration. Psychiatrists would point out that psychopaths and sociopaths have a weak sense of loyalty. Anthony ("Gaspipe") Casso recalls his first murder, committed at the behest of the Lucchese Family: "For me it was just business. I didn't know the guy. I'd never seen him before. He had to go. That's all I knew. That's all I needed to know" (Carlo 2008: 83). Faced with a long prison term, Casso, a Lucchese Family underboss, became a government informant.

New York Mafia Families have been riddled with informants from top to bottom: Bonanno Family underboss Salvatore ("Good Looking Sal") Vitale, at 56, for example, became a cooperating witness against his brother-in-law, Family boss Joseph Massino. And in 2005, Massino, long regarded as the last of the old-time bosses—tough, vicious, and low profile—but facing a death penalty for murder, became an informant against members of his own crime Family.

As noted in Chapter 3, even in Chicago, where made guys have not heretofore become informants, things are changing. In the "Family Secrets" case, Frank Calabrese, Jr. became a witness against his father and as did Frank senior's brother Nick, all made guys in the Outfit (Warmbir, Herguth, and Main 2005).

A development affecting ethnic succession in organized crime is the arrival of relatively large numbers of southern Italian immigrants into the New York metropolitan area beginning in the 1960s—"Zips."

---

2. In 2002, the son of Vincent Gigante was indicted for acting as intermediary for his father who was allegedly running the Genovese Family from prison. The following year, Andrew, at 46, was sentenced to two years in prison for extorting $90,000 from a businessman. His guilty plea also included a fine of $2 million. He was ordered by the court to desist from any future business activity at the New York City waterfront district (Marzulli 2003).

3. Some, however, do have a college education. Two older "players," Thomas Gambino, son of boss Carlo Gambino and a caporegime in that crime Family, and Jack Tocco, boss of the Detroit crime Family, are college graduates.

Zips

The connection between the criminal organizations of southern Italy—Mafia, Camorra, 'Ndrangheta, Sacra Corona Unita (discussed in Chapter 5)—and the American Mafia are the *Zips*, recent immigrants from the *Mezzogiorno*. (The term "Zip" is an allusion to the immigrants' rapid speech in Italian dialect.) Many are *mafiosi* fleeing intense pressure from Italian law enforcement and murderous factional conflicts between competing Mafia, Camorra, and 'Ndrangheta groups. "Their entry into the United States was made particularly easy by the reversal of a restrictive immigration statute that had discriminated against southern and eastern Europeans" (PCOC 1986c: 53). Any number are related to members of the American Mafia in New York. According to police sources in New York City, some of these Zips have been admitted to membership in American Mafia Families, and many more are operating in their own associations independent of, but in cooperation with, traditional crime groups. They have

Capomafioso Tommaso Buscetta, witness in the Pizza Connection case

been particularly active in drug trafficking. Using drug profits, Zips have opened strip malls containing bakeries, tobacco shops, cafes, newspaper stands, and limousine service storefronts. They are essentially reproducing the small-scale neighborhood life in which organized crime has traditionally felt most comfortable.

The American Mafia has a demand for criminal labor, particularly in the highly rewarding but dangerous enterprise of drug trafficking. Southern Italy has provided a vast labor market for American Mafia drug trafficking operations. "In southern Italy, *mafia* and *camorra* groups can rely on a 'reserve army' of individuals prepared to endanger their own—and other people's—lives in the execution of especially risky and violent tasks, because the problems of inner-city environment and youth unemployment are growing continually worse in the *Mezzogiorno*, so that the supply of criminal labour is continually increasing" (Arlacchi 1986: 194).

Ties between the American Mafia and the Zips were highlighted during the "Pizza Connection" case concluded in 1987. Former Sicilian Mafia boss Tommaso Buscetta was a prosecution witness in the trial of twenty-two defendants.[4] A Mafia group headed by Gaetano Badalamenti, then 64, an ousted *capomafioso* from Cinisi, Sicily, was found to have supplied heroin with a total value in excess of $1.6 billion to a group headed by Salvatore ("Totò") Catalano, then 46, a captain in the Bonanno crime Family of New York. Catalano[5] arrived in the United States from Sicily in 1961 and headed a crew of Zips in the Knickerbocker Avenue section of Brooklyn. The Sicilian defendants purchased morphine base in Turkey and processed it in Sicily. Pizza parlors in the United States owned by the defendants were used to facilitate the drug trafficking.

Two men implicated in the case were with Bonanno crime Family underboss Carmine Galente in a Brooklyn restaurant when he was shot down in

---

4. For an exciting journalistic look at the "Pizza Connection" investigation, see Blumenthal (1988b); also Alexander (1988).

5. Catalano is serving a 45-year federal sentence. Badalamenti, at 80, died in 1987 while serving a 45-year sentence.

1977. Baldo Amato[6] (born in 1952) and Cesare Bonventre (born in 1951), both Zips and cousins of Joseph Bonanno, for whom the Family is named, helped set up Galente's murder on behalf of Family boss Phil Rastelli.[7] Sicilian-born Gerlando Sciascia, at 65, a major heroin dealer and Bonnano Family *caporegime* in charge of a crew of Zips, was shot at close range in 1999, and his body dumped on a Bronx street (Capeci 1999b). In 2006, the *New York Daily News* reported that the acting head of the Bonanno Family is Sicilian-born Sal ("The Ironworker") Montagna, age 35 (Marzulli 2006). In 2011, the newspaper reported that the new head of the Gambino Family is Sicilian-born Domenico Cefalu, a low-profile ex-con who resides with his mother in Bensonhurst, Brooklyn (Marzulli 2011b).

One of the important Zip drug organizations was led by several Sicilian cousins of Carlo Gambino and headquartered in Cherry Hill, New Jersey:

> Although related to the late crime boss Carlo Gambino of New York, the New Jersey Gambino drug operations are independent from the New York family. There are direct lines of communication and influence based on actual blood ties between the New Jersey Gambinos and other traditional organized crime families in New York. Gambino family members own significant interests in the pizza industry in South Jersey and parts of Pennsylvania. These businesses have been used for concealing illegal immigrants, for laundering money, and for storing drugs. They are known to have employed illegal aliens and other nonfamily members who were more experienced in drug trafficking to smuggle heroin into and transport it within the United States. (PSI 1983a: 134)

The Zips and their American counterparts "share similar customs, criminal philosophies and a common heritage. The prototype of the crime Family is identical in each system" (PCOC 1986c: 53). In criminal and law enforcement circles, however, their "Old World" ways have earned the Zips more fear and respect than their American counterparts. Just how many Zips are in the United States is not clear, but they are believed to be concentrated in the Northeast, particularly in the New York City area. Other groups are known to be located in Boston, Buffalo, Chicago, Philadelphia, Houston, and Dallas.

The ranks of the American Mafia have been thinned by successful federal prosecutions using the Racketeer Influenced and Corrupt Organizations (RICO) statute (to be discussed in Chapter 14)—particularly the long, double-digit sentences typically handed down. Whether or not the Italian-American community and the Zips will be able to provide sufficient replacements to keep the American Mafia viable in the years to come remains an open question. In the meantime, new criminal groups are emerging that may prove to be more powerful and difficult to combat than those of the American Mafia. Gary Potter (1994) concludes that, historically, "ethnic succession" appears to be a dubious concept. Instead, he argues, new groups become part of organized crime, but they do not necessarily *replace* the older groups. This would appear to be the case with members of Italian-American organized crime, whose strong subcultural orientations have resisted changes in their economic status. In later chapters we will examine these emerging criminal organizations.

Prohibition was the turning point that allowed Jews and Italians to ascend the crooked ladder provided by participation in organized crime. In the United States, culture conflict between earlier and later immigrants created a demand from the latter for goods and services outlawed by the former. This led to the creation of gambling syndicates and infamous criminal organizations of the Prohibition era. Today, alcohol and various forms of gambling are legally available in most areas of the country, but the outlawing of certain chemicals

---

6. In 2006, Amato, 54, was sentenced to life imprisonment for two 1992 murders.

7. In 1984, the body of Bonventre was found stuffed into two barrels in a Garfield, New Jersey, warehouse.

enjoyed by a large minority of the population provides continuing incentive and opportunity for
criminal innovation. Though the Jews, largely in
New York, were the next group to dominate organized crime, they soon turned to business and the
professions. Prohibition affected the Italian gangsters in a manner different from earlier immigrant
groups. Before Prohibition, ethnic organized crime
was restricted to the local community. Prohibition
encouraged the creation of city- and regional-wide
criminal organizations that allowed Italian gangsters
to consolidate their power and keep it longer.
Eventually, however, the more than two-dozen
American Mafia groups throughout the country
melted down to a handful operating in the Northeast and the Chicago area. The once formidable
"Smaldone Family" of Denver, for example, no
longer exists. A retired city police captain explains
why: "They had two problems; one, they couldn't
recruit, they didn't have the Italian community
here to recruit from, and they kept their own families out of it" (Kreck 2009: 244).

THE PSYCHOLOGY OF
ORGANIZED CRIME

While sociological theories may help identify
societal variables that motivate involvement in
organized crime, they fail to explain why only a
small fraction of persons exposed to such variables
actually become criminals. Why do people exposed
to the same milieu react differently? Psychology, a
discipline that focuses on the individual, provides
some answers.

Clinical Psychology/
Psychoanalytic Theory

Clinical psychology is based, to various extents,
on psychoanalytic theory, a body of work fathered
by Sigmund Freud (1856–1939). Over the years
the theory has undergone change, although

Freud's basic contribution, his exposition of the
importance of phenomena of the unconscious
in human behavior, remains. Personality is strongly
influenced by determinants in the unconscious
that develop early in life. Simply put, this
concept argues that the most important determinants of our behavior are not available to our
conscious thought (Cloninger 2004). These determinants evolve during early stages of psychological
development.

A delicate balance is maintained by unconscious forces as a person experiences various
sociocultural and biological aspects of existence.
When the balance is upset, the psyche passes
from the normal to the psychoneurotic or the
psychotic (mental illness). That a fine line exists
between the normal and the neurotic and between
the neurotic and the psychotic is basic to psychoanalytic theory. In fact, only a difference of degree
separates the "normal" from the "abnormal."
The degree to which there is a malfunctioning
in psychic apparatus is the degree to which a
person is "abnormal" or "sick," that is, socially
dysfunctional.

Central to the psychoanalytic explanation for
crime is the *superego*, a conscience-like mechanism
whose function is to restrain the person from antisocial behavior. According to August Aichhorn
(1963: 221), "the superego takes its form and con-
tent from identifications which result from the
child's effort to emulate the parent. It is evolved
not only because the parent loves the child, but
also because the child fears the parent's demands."
If the superego does not attain full strength, the
person is more likely to act on primitive impulses,
often of a violent nature. Persons with an *antisocial
personality disorder* (ASPD) have a poorly developed
superego—they are sometimes referred to as
psychopaths or sociopaths[8]—who are restrained
only by the fear of punishment that alone cannot
exercise adequate control over antisocial impulses.
Such persons suffer little or no guilt as a result of

---

8. There is disagreement over these terms within psychology and psychiatry.

ORGANIZED CRIME AND GRATUITOUS VIOLENCE

"But you know, Paul, I think some guys just take so much pleasure from breaking heads that they'd almost rather not get paid"—*Caporegime* Joe

("Piney") Armone to Gambino Family boss Paul Castellano (quoted in O'Brien and Kurins 1991: 243–44).

FAMILY RELATIONS

Lefty Ruggiero, a member of the Bonanno Family, purchased a black squirt gun shaped like a submachine gun that he handed to his young grandson. "Now you can be a tough guy like

your granddad. You can be a shooter when you grow up, just like me." Lefty had murdered his son-in-law, the boy's father, for "doing drugs" (D. Jacobs 2002: 150).

MURDEROUS INDIFFERENCE

Sicilian *mafiosi* "do not usually feel any sense of guilt or sorrow when they kill somebody who is not a mafia member ... since they do not consider the

victim to be a human being and therefore do not view him as worthy of emotional involvement" (Paoli 2003: 84–85).

engaging in socially harmful behavior. They are characterized by a combination of antisocial behavior and emotional detachment (Black 1999) exemplified by a willingness to murder persons against whom they harbor no animosity. The nonfiction character portrayed by Joe Pesci in the movie *Goodfellas* exemplifies this type of personality, as does the DeMeo faction of the Gambino Family discussed earlier. Gambino Family underboss Sammy Gravano recalls his first murder—he shot a close friend in the back of the head on orders from the Colombo Family: "Am I supposed to feel remorse? Aren't I supposed to feel something? But I felt nothing like remorse. If anything, I felt good. Like high. Like powerful, maybe even superhuman. It's not that I was happy or proud of myself. Not that. I'm still not happy about that feeling. It's just that killing came so easy to me" (Maas 1997: 52).

"The most disturbing symptom of ASPD is often aggression, expressed in shades from quiet intimidation to explosive violence.... His actions may be sudden and unpredictable, but more likely they are deliberate, purposeful, and designed for maximum impact" (Black 1999: 47). The psychopathic criminal is totally without conscience, capable of unspeakable acts, and shows no external signs of psychoses or neuroses. Daniel came to the bar for his wife: "You've got two kids at home who need dinner and we need you to get out of here." When she said she wanted to have another drink with her friends, members of the Mongols motorcycle club, they intervened. "Fuck you then bitch, and fuck the Mongols." Daniel headed for the door but was intercepted. Mongols beat and stabbed him, and his life ended facedown on the pavement (Queen 2005).

Gregory Scarpa, a member of the Colombo Family known as "The Grim Reaper," was suspected (correctly) of being an FBI informer because of his uncanny ability to avoid arrest and prosecution. One member of his crew recalls (Connolly 1996: 50): "We all suspected something, but a few days later we were in the club with Greg and a guy he hated. We're talking and joking, and out of nowhere, Greg whips out a piece and shoots the guy in the head.... The guy's brains were all over me! My ears were ringing from the gunshot. Cool as he can be, he told us to roll the body in the rug and get rid of it. Nobody distrusted Greg after that day." Giovanni Brusca—the Sicilian *mafioso* who flipped the switch resulting in the death of prosecutor Giovanni Falcone and his wife (discussed in Chapter 5)—was asked by a psychiatrist how many people he had killed. Typical of *mafiosi*, he could not remember: "Certainly more than 100, but less than 200" (Maran 2009: 54).

In sum, criminal behavior is related to the superego function, which is a result of an actor's relationship to parents (or parental figures) during early developmental years. Parental deprivation through absence, lack of affection, or inconsistent discipline—or parental influence that is deviant—stifles the proper development of the superego. Parental influence weakened by deprivation during childhood development will result in an adult unable to adequately control aggressive, hostile, or antisocial urges.

Behavioral Psychology/ Learning Theory

Central to behavioral psychology is that all behavior is shaped by its consequences. Behavior is acquired through operant conditioning—a method of learning through positive and negative reinforcement that results from interaction with the environment. Through operant conditioning, an association is made between a behavior and a consequence for that behavior. If a person's "aggressive behavior has been rewarded, at least part of the time, no further explanation in terms of internal needs is necessary"; the person simply learns to behave aggressively (Nietzel et al. 2003: 47).

According to learning theory, antisocial behavior is the result of learning—that is, positive and negative reinforcement—directly from others (for example, peers) or the failure to learn how to discriminate between competing norms, both lawful and unlawful, because of inappropriate reinforcement. When conforming behavior is not adequately reinforced, a person can more easily be influenced by competing, albeit antisocial, sources of positive reinforcement (for example, money and excitement from criminal behavior). The environment inhabited by organized crime is awash with reinforcement for antisocial behavior, while conventional, conforming behavior is frequently ridiculed.

Biology of Human Behavior

The human body consists of cells organized into tissues. Specialized cells along the surface of the body receive information about the environment that is translated into electrochemical signals that we experience as sight, sound, smell, and touch. Information from the internal and external environment—collectively known as *stimuli*—is received by the central nervous system (CNS), consisting of the brain and the spinal cord, whose cells—neurons—send information to a specific processing center of the brain.

The brain, a dense mass weighing about three pounds and consisting of ten to fifty billion anatomically independent but functionally interrelated neurons ("brain cells"), is connected to the spinal cord by fibers and cells (the peripheral nervous system) that carry sensory information and muscle commands to the rest of the body. "This single organ controls all body activities, ranging from heart rate and sexual function to emotion, learning and memory" (Society for Neuroscience 2002: 5). After receiving and processing information, the brain sends commands to muscles and glands.

Neurons contain about one hundred different neurotransmitters, which are chemicals that when activated bind to receptors of an adjoining neuron in a "lock and key" action. Each neurotransmitter has a receptor site designed to receive it, triggering a particular response. Excitatory neurotransmitters such as dopamine, epinephrine, or norepinephrine trigger "fight or flight" mechanisms in response to perceived danger; endorphins produce a calming effect and aid in controlling pain and stress. A delicate balance of chemicals keeps information flowing to the brain, keeping humans alive and functioning.

The human brain is at great risk from biochemical imbalances, particularly as related to antisocial behavior. Those whose central nervous system quickly habituates to incoming stimuli owing to a neurotransmitter malfunction are most apt to be reinforced for engaging in antisocial behavior and less likely to learn alternative behavior patterns. Subjectively, such people regard many ordinary environments as boring and unpleasant and would therefore be more motivated than most people to seek novel and/or intense sensory stimulation. The behavior of such people includes impulsivity and risk taking (Ellis 1990).

Neurotransmitter levels are controlled by chemicals known as monoamine oxidases (MAO). Some individuals have elevated MAO, which lowers the levels of excitatory neurotransmitters, causing a state of depression. Easily bored persons may suffer from MAO-overload. This condition could induce risk-taking, engaging in sports, mountain climbing, or skydiving, for example, or crime. Low MAO activity is an apparent precursor for psychopathology and criminality. Furthermore, low MAO persons exhibit a tendency toward aggressive outbursts, often in response to anger, fear, or frustration. Several studies report relationships between MAO deficiency and abnormal aggressive behavior in males (Brunner et al. 1994; Ellis 1991; Sunderwirth 1985).

The neurotransmitter dopamine has received special attention because of its role in the regulation of mood and affect and its role in motivation and reward processes. This neurotransmitter is associated with regions of the brain that, among other important functions, produce the sensations associated with such pleasures as eating and sex. Dopamine is constantly released in small amounts in order to "keep the receiving cells in each brain region functioning at appropriate intensities for current demands—neither too high or too low" (Nestler 2005: 5).

A variant of the dopamine receptor (D^4) is associated with novelty seeking; people with this genetic factor tend to be extroverted, quick-tempered, impulsive, and easily bored (Angier 1995). They possess a gene that makes them especially responsive to dopamine, and this is believed related to participation in dangerous, though not necessarily criminal activities, such as boxing and motorcycle racing (Koerber 1997).

Persons with low levels of the neurotransmitter serotonin are more inclined toward aggression and violence than those with normal amounts. Because of this link, serotonin level is a rough predictor of criminal behavior. While the correlation between serotonin and crime is clear, it is unclear whether the environment influences the serotonin level. It is also possible that serotonin levels (and other biological factors) have roots in social conditions, such as extreme poverty and accompanying malnutrition.

"Environmental factors can alter the expression of genes involved with the way the brain works and responds to the environment, thus influencing the behavior of the individual" (Volkow 2006: 70). Thus, not all persons with genes associated with risk-taking engage in violent criminal behavior, although they might be inclined toward violent behavior that is not criminal. Contrast members of SEAL Team 6 who killed Omar bin Laden with Boston mobster Whitey Bulger (discussed in Chapter 15), who murdered at least 19 persons.

While sociology helps explain why persons in certain environments would be motivated to get involved in organized crime, most people similarly situated do not become involved. Perhaps, then, what is needed for involvement is the right environment coupled with the relevant psychological elements, as well as a particular genetic predisposition.

SUMMARY

1. Sociological theories that help explain organized crime:
   - There is a paucity of theories in sociology and psychology explaining organized crime.

   - According to Robert Merton's version of anomie, organized crime is a normal response to pressures exerted on certain persons by the social structure—the strain between goals and means.

- In the environment where organized crime has traditionally thrived, strain is intense.
- Conditions of severe deprivation coupled with readily available success models such as racketeers and drug dealers make certain *enclaves* spawning grounds for organized crime.
- According to Merton, American culture is characterized by pathological materialism.

2. Sociological theories that help explain organized crime, Sutherland's differential association:
   - According to Sutherland's theory of differential association all behavior—lawful and criminal—is learned within intimate personal groups. When the associations are criminal, the actor learns the techniques of committing crime and the drives, attitudes, and rationalizations that add up to a favorable precondition to criminal behavior.
   - Learning the techniques of sophisticated criminality requires the proper environment— ecological niches or *enclaves* where delinquent or criminal subcultures flourish and this education is available.

3. Sociological theories that help explain organized crime, subcultures:
   - Subcultural theory explains criminal behavior as learned through differential association by youth to whom being right or wrong in terms of the wider society is not a guidepost for behavior.
   - According to Shaw and McKay's view of criminal subcultures, the presence of a large number of adult criminals in certain areas means that children there are in contact with crime as a career, symbolized by organized crime.

4. Sociological theories that help explain organized crime, social disorganization, differential opportunity, and social control:
   - Social disorganization the result of the combined interactive effects of industrialization, immigration, and urbanization,

result in the development of deviant traditions that once established can create their own, albeit, extra-legal, forms of social control.

- Members of organized crime have typically emerged from the recruiting grounds of *defended neighborhoods*, recognized ecological niches whose inhabitants form cohesive groupings, and seal themselves off through the efforts of delinquent gangs, restrictive covenants, and a forbidding reputation.
- Conditions of severe deprivation with extremely limited access to ladders of legitimate success result in collective adaptations in the form of delinquent subcultures. one of which is *the rackets subculture* in which gang activity is devoted to utilitarian criminal pursuits, an adaptation that begins to approximate organized crime.
- Since there is a surplus of contenders for positions in organized crime, a certain proportion of those who aspire may not be permitted to engage in the behavior for which they have prepared themselves.
- According to social control theory, delinquent acts result when an individual's bond to society is weak or broken.
- External and internal restraints determine whether we move in the direction of crime or of law-abiding behavior. *External restraints* include social disapproval linked to public shame and/or social ostracism and fear of punishment. *Internal restraints* include what psychoanalytic theory refers to as the *superego*: an unconscious, yet powerful, conscience-like mechanism that provides a sense of guilt.

5. Sociological theories that help explain organized crime:
   - The pool of available candidates for membership in organized crime dwindled in Jewish communities. In Italian communities it remained adequate enough; the large-scale organizations needed to profit from Prohibition were no longer necessary.

- Daniel Bell refers to crime as an American way of life, "A Queer Ladder of Social Mobility." Francis Ianni notes that this "queer ladder" had organized crime as the first few rungs.
    - Each successive immigrant group experienced *strain* to which some members reacted by *innovating* in accord with a tradition that had been established by earlier American entrepreneurs—the "Robber Barons."
    - Ethnic succession results when a group experiences success in crime, and legitimate opportunities thereby become more readily available. Strain subsides, and the group moves out of organized crime, creating an opportunity for innovation for the succeeding immigrant group.
    - Organized crime comprises a deviant subculture to which members have a commitment that is not mitigated by the absence of strain.
    - A development affecting ethnic succession in organized crime is the arrival of relatively large numbers of southern Italian immigrants into the New York metropolitan area during the 1960s—"Zips."

6. Psychological theories help explain organized crime:
    - Central to the psychoanalytic explanation for crime is the *superego*, a conscience-like mechanism whose function is to restrain the person from antisocial behavior.
    - Persons with an *antisocial personality disorder* have a poorly developed superego and are restrained only by the fear of punishment that alone cannot exercise adequate control over antisocial impulses. Such persons suffer little or no guilt as a result of engaging in socially harmful behavior.
    - According to learning theory, antisocial behavior is the result of positive and negative reinforcement—directly from others (for example, peers)—or the failure to learn how to discriminate between competing norms, both lawful and unlawful, because of inappropriate reinforcement.
7. The influence of brain chemistry in explaining the behavior of those in organized crime:
    - Brain chemistry can help to explain violent behavior.

REVIEW QUESTIONS

1. How does Merton's theory of anomie explain organized crime?
2. Why is America characterized as suffering from pathological materialism?
3. What is the connection between differential association and organized crime?
4. What does it mean that "organized crime is not an equal opportunity employer"?
5. What qualities of the delinquent subculture correlate well with the prerequisites of organized crime?
6. What is meant by the "defended neighborhood"?
7. How does social control theory explain the emergence of organized crime?
8. What is the theory of ethnic succession?
9. How have the "Zips" impacted on ethnic succession?
10. Why did "Jewish organized crime" end while the American Mafia continues?
11. How does psychology explain the behavior of persons in organized crime?
12. What is the connection between the superego and anti-social personality disorder?
13. What is the connection between brain chemistry and violent behavior?

Capomafioso Luciano Liggio of Corleone, Sicily. © Bettmann/Corbis

Italian Organized Crime and the Albanian Connection

A major Camorra boss who had been a fugitive since 2002 was discovered in the Spanish town of Marbella, on the Costa del Sol. He had originally fled to Tangier, Morocco, where he started a relationship with a Moroccan woman. When she got pregnant, they moved to Marbella. She posted two photographs of her pregnant self on Facebook for relatives and friends. In one photo, she posed in front of a sign for a well-known beach in Marbella; the other in front of a popular local Italian restaurant that displayed the national symbol of Spain. With that information, Spanish police were able to monitor her email, and after following her for several days were able to arrest the Camorra boss (Cerruti 2011).

The Camorra will be discussed in this chapter.

CHAPTER 5 WILL ENABLE THE READER TO UNDERSTAND:

- The unique history and culture of southern Italy
- How the Mafia developed
- The influence of Mussolini and World War II on the Sicilian and American Mafia
- Differences between the traditional Sicilian Mafia and the *Nuovo Mafia*
- Differences between the Mafia and the Camorra
- Differences between the *'Ndrangheta* and the Mafia
- The origins of the *Sacra Corona Unita* (SCU) and its ties to Albanian criminal organizations
- History and geography resulted in close ties between the SCU and the Balkans, particularly Albania
- The characteristics of Albania and the culture in which criminal organizations developed

In this chapter we begin our examination of organized crime on the global scene, sometimes referred to as transnational organized crime. Our focus will be on criminal organizations that have affected, or have the potential to affect, the United States. We will begin our examination of four of these criminal organizations—*Mafia, Camorra, 'Ndrangheta,* and the *Sacra Corona Unita* (with its Albanian connection)—which have their roots in southern Italy, the *Mezzogiorno.*

THE *MEZZOGIORNO*

The southern Italian experience, which dates back more than a thousand years, led to the development of a culture that stresses the variables necessary for survival in a hostile environment. "To be respected in traditional southern Italian societies," notes Letizia Paoli (1999: 19), "meant to be entitled to the deference of others that came from the ability to use violence." The southern Italian developed an ideal of manliness, *omertá,* that includes noncooperation with authorities, self-control in the face of adversity, and the *vendetta*—"*blood washes blood*"—which dictated that any offense or slight to the *famiglia* (family) had to be avenged, no matter what the consequences or how long it took. Neither government nor church was to be trusted. The only basis of loyalty was *famiglia*—"blood of my blood" (*sangu de me sangu*). "The *famiglia* was composed of all of one's blood relatives, including those relatives Americans would consider very distant cousins, aunts, and uncles, an extended clan whose genealogy was traced through paternity. The clan was supplemented through an important custom known as *comparático* or *comparaggio* (godparenthood), through which carefully selected outsiders became, to an important (but incomplete) extent, members of the family" (Gambino 1974: 3).

The family patriarch, the *capo di famiglia,* arbitrated all ambiguous situations. The family was organized hierarchically: "One had absolute responsibilities to family superiors and absolute rights to be demanded from subordinates in the hierarchy" (Gambino 1974: 4). "The family, first

source of power, had to be made prosperous, respected, and feared with antlike tenacity; it was enlarged (like dynasties of old) by suitable marriages, strengthened by alliances with families of equal status, by negotiated submission to more powerful ones, or by establishing domination over weaker ones. In the *famiglia,* physical aggression was rewarded and the strongest member of the domestic group assumed the dominant status" (Barzini 1977: 36).

The *Mezzogiorno,* literally *midday,* but a nickname for southern Italy (Paoli 2003), never enjoyed a Renaissance, remaining mired in feudalism and dependant on agriculture; a legacy of political, social, and economic repression; and exploitation (Putnam 1993). A succession of foreign rulers ended in 1860 with a revolution against (Spanish) Bourbon rule that eventually united Italy. For the people of the *Mezzogiorno,* however, little changed. Instead of foreign repression, the *contadini* (peasants) were repressed by other Italians: "The political foundation of the new Italian state was an alliance between the northern industrial bourgeoisie and the southern landed aristocracy" (Chubb 1982: 16). The *Mezzogiorno,* with a population of about 20.8 million persons (out of a population of 59 million), continues to lag far behind northern Italy (and the rest of western Europe) in economic development. The rate of unemployment is roughly three times that of the north (Naravane 2008). About half of all murders committed in Italy take place in the *Mezzogiorno*—Campania, Puglia, Calabria, and Sicily—although the population of these four southern regions accounts for less than 30 percent of all Italians (Maffei and Betsos 2007).

Vast government spending in the *Mezzogiorno,* often on useless building projects that provide patronage opportunities, became a vehicle for infiltration. "By corruption and physical intimidation, Mafia-controlled firms took their share of public contracts, either directly or through subcontracts and dummy companies." This approach has aided the spread of the Mafia phenomenon beyond its traditional areas "to towns and provinces that had once been free of organized

---

NOT JUST THE *MEZZOGIORNO*

"The shrugged shoulder is real, a daily reminder here that part of Italy's charm rests in the fact that it does not much care for rules. Italians can be downright poetic about it, this inclination to dodge taxes, to cut lines, to erect entire neighborhoods without permits or simply to run red lights, while smoking or talking on the phone" (Fisher 2007: 3).

---

crime. In many areas, democracy as we know it ceased to exist" (Stille 1993: 63). And the *mafioso* adds nothing of value to his environment: "Even in Medellín of the cocaine barons [discussed in Chapter 6], the Escobar clan and the Gavirias wanted an ultra-modern airport, a futuristic elevated metro system, and first-class hospitals. But in Cosa Nostra's Sicily, in the *'Ndrangheta's* Calabria, in the Camorra's Naples, yesterday's ragamuffins turned into today's gang bosses exploit without putting anything back in except the frills and fancies of fly-by-night consumerism" (Siebert 1996: 81)—and garbage.

Campania has become northern Italy's garbage dump, where waste management firms controlled by the Camorra (discussed later) arrange for the shipping of garbage, often toxic, from northern Italy and other European Union countries to illegal dump sites throughout the province. Campania has become so flooded with illegal exogenous trash that provincial waste must be shipped to Germany for disposal at great cost to local industry, and the military has been called in to aid in waste management (DiManno 2011; Saviano 2007).

Fear of organized crime discourages business investment and increases the cost of credit that serves the interests of Mafia loan sharks (Bohlen 1997). At the end of 2007, Italy's largest cement company announced that it was closing its Sicilian operations rather than give in to Mafia demands for protection money.

The south "was brought into the Italian nation dragging its feet as the new government issued edict after edict that affected the southerners adversely" (Mangione and Morreale 1992: xv). This history led to the development of three different types of criminal organization. "The volatile urban criminality of the Neapolitan Camorra was very different from the old rural mafia's activities in the Sicilian hinterland, and the Calabrian *'Ndrangheta* was another thing again. But in each case a parasitic criminal class had inserted itself in the interstices between rulers and the ruled, exploiting both" (Robb 1996: 37). The Mafia—whose members refer to it as *Cosa Nostra*—and the *'Ndrangheta* "were an outgrowth of a section of the middle class which had been licensed to use violence by the ruling classes of the day and were founded on codes of honour, secrecy and silence." The Camorra was "an association of the poorest classes for whom crime was a means of survival and was neither secretive nor elitist." A fourth criminal organization, *Sacra Corona Unita*, is more recent, its expansion dating back to the 1970s because of "a desire by the other three criminal groups, at different times and for different motives, to have a consolidated criminal base on Apulia's long southeastern seaboard" (Jamieson 2000: 11).

Whether Mafia, Camorra, *'Ndrangheta*, or *Sacra Corona Unita*, these criminal organizations have the capacity to act as brokers extraordinaire, "to create bridges among dissimilar networks and to promote horizontal and vertical cooperation with diverse actors," between politicians and businessmen, businessmen and union officials, or conventional criminals and the providers of such services as fencing stolen property (Sciarrone 2010: 192). Across southern Italy, the government dissolved dozens of town councils because of their corrupt relationships with Mafia, Camorra, and *'Ndrangheta* clans (Jamieson 2000).

SICILY AND THE MAFIA

The largest island in the Mediterranean Sea, Sicily lies almost at its center. As such, it was a bitterly fought over prize colonized by commercial powers: Greeks, Romans, Arabs, the Normans, and, during the Napoleonic Wars, the British. In the twelfth century, rule passed to a German dynasty, then to the French, the Austrians, and, finally, Spain under the Bourbons. "Until the nineteenth century, aristocratic families controlled Sicilian life more or less independently of whatever conqueror happened to be ruling at any given time" (Orlando 2001: 10). In 1860, Italy was freed of foreign rule and united by Giuseppe Garibaldi (1807–1882), but for the exploited Sicilians, little changed. Although his success was via Sicily and the *Mezzogiorno*, Garibaldi handed over all of his territorial gains to the king of Piedmont. Instead of foreigners, Sicily was ruled by Vittorio Emmanuel II of the House of Savoy, a monarch from northern Italy. Sicilian young men fleeing conscription into the Piedmontese-controlled army became bandits.

The new Italian state was unable to establish a monopoly over the use of force in Sicily and, instead, violence became democratized as a "whole range of men seized the opportunity to shoot and stab their way into the developing economy.... Officials complained that what they called these 'sects' or 'parties'—sometimes they were merely extended families with guns—were making many areas of Sicily ungovernable" (Dickie 2004: 58). Unwilling or unable to impose law and order, the government in Rome turned a blind eye through successive regimes as powerful Mafia clans maintained a uniquely Sicilian form of order—brutal, at times protecting the property of the landed elite, at other times protecting outlaws (Schneider et al. 2005).

The government in Rome imposed a tax policy on the island that had the "overall effect of taking money out of Sicilian agriculture for investment in the north" (Finley, Smith, and Duggan 1987: 186). Landowners escaped heavy taxation, which fell disproportionately on the peasants (Catanzaro 1992). Eventually the aristocracy collapsed in Western Sicily and the administration of their lands fell to middlemen called *gabelloti*,

estate managers who had gained the reputation of *uomi inteso*—"strong men" (Orlando 2001). The *gabelloto* ruled over the estate—*latifondo*—with brute force, protecting it from bandits, peasant organizations, and unions. He was assisted by *famiglia*, *amici* (friends), and *campieri* (lawfully armed mounted guards). The *campieri* were hired because they were *uomini di rispettu*, "men of respect," meaning they were quick to use violence and people feared them. An important—that is, widely feared—*campiere* could become a *gabelloto*. On the Eastern half of the island there was no system of absentee landlords and, therefore, no need for *gabelloti* (Maran 2008).[1]

The *gabelloto* was a patron to his peasants who labored on the *latifondo*; he controlled access to scarce resources, in particular farming land, and he acted as a mediator between official power and government and the peasantry, a position he maintained by the exercise of force. In league with the landlords, he fought land reform, labor unions, and revolution (Servadio 1976). Peasants revolted in many parts of the *Mezzogiorno*, and an 1866 uprising in Palermo required an expeditionary force to quell it.

The *gabelloto* did not usually perform his overseer's functions in person—often he did not even show up on the estate that had been entrusted to his custody. "He simply allowed his name to be mentioned, with the declaration that the estate was under his protection" (Catanzaro 1992: 28). John Dickie (2004: 133) writes that "*Gabelloti* were such pivotal figures in Sicily's violent economy that it was often assumed that being a *mafioso* and being a *gabelloti* were the same thing. It is more accurate to say that joining the Mafia enabled a *gabelloto* to do his job better." Important *mafiosi* were *gabellotti*, the line between the two often invisible.

Mafia

Explanations of the term *mafia* come from Sicilian historical and literary works that link its root and

---

1. According to Paoli (2003), there was no fully developed Mafia Family in Eastern Sicily until the 1970s,

meaning to elements prevailing within Sicilian culture: "The word *mafia* is apparently Sicilian-Arabic derived from terms meaning to protect and to act as guardian; a friend or companion; to defend; and preservation, power, integrity, strength, and a condition that designates the remedy of damage and ill." In sum, *mafia* means "protection against the arrogance of the powerful, remedy to any damage, sturdiness of body, strength and serenity of spirit, and the best and most exquisite part of life" (Inciardi 1975: 112–113).

Luigi Barzini (1965: 253) separates *mafia* as a state of mind from Mafia as an illegal secret organization. The former (*mafia*) is shared by all Sicilians, the honest and the criminal: that "they must aid each other, side with their friends, and fight the common enemies even when the friends are wrong and the enemies are right; each must defend his dignity at all costs and never allow the smallest slight to go unavenged; they must keep secrets and beware of official authorities and laws." The anti-Mafia Sicilian author Leonardo Sciascia notes the dichotomy: "When I denounce the *mafia*, at the same time I suffer, since in me, as in any Sicilian, there are still present and vibrant the residues of feeling *mafioso*. So by struggling against the *mafia* I also struggle against myself" (quoted in Siebert 1996: 57).

Barzini points out that the two (Mafia and *mafia*) are closely related, and that Mafia could not flourish without *mafia,* which represents a general attitude toward the state: "A *mafioso* did not invoke State or law in his private quarrels, but made himself respected and safe by winning a reputation for toughness and courage, and settled his differences by fighting. He recognized no obligation except those of the code of honor or *omertá* (manliness), whose chief article forbade giving information to the public authorities" (Hobsbawm 1976: 92). As a nineteenth-century observer notes, the *mafioso* dresses modestly; his manner of speech is the same. When confronted with a greater power, he "makes himself seem naïve, stupidly attentive to what you are saying. He endures insults and slaps with patience. Then, the same evening, he shoots you" (Giuseppe Alongi quoted in Dickie 2004: 85). Or,

he will wait patiently for months or for years for an opportunity to avenge humiliation and thereby makes himself unconquerable.

Groups of *mafioso* adopted standardized rituals in the 1870s with an initiation ceremony similar to that used by American Mafia Families discussed in Chapter 3. At the center is the *padrino* or *capomafioso*, around whom other *mafiosi* gather, forming a *cosca*. The word *cosca* refers to the leaves of an artichoke, the *capomafioso* being the globe's heart. The Mafia evolved as a ritual brotherhood structured in the form of clans or *cosche* (plural of cosca) divided by sector or activity and geographical area (Hobsbawm 1976; Jamieson 2000; Schneider et al. 2005).

Because kinship can strengthen cohesion, sons, brothers, nephews, and other relatives are frequently admitted to *cosca* membership. In Mafia families it is almost obligatory for boys to consider a criminal career. But there is also a matter of talent. If a *mafioso's* son lacks the *fegato* (guts), he is allowed to go his own way (Schneider et al. 2005). Familial ties, however, can conflict with members' obligation of obedience to the *capomafioso*. In dramatic fashion, *mafiosi* are sometimes forced to prove where their loyalty ultimately lies; they are offered a choice: Kill a relative or die with him (Dickie 2004). Some *cosche* have rules against too many relatives (Schneider et al. 2005).

Once initiated into the *cosca*, the *mafioso* became a *compadre*, a practice based on the custom of *comparático* (fictional kinship or godparenthood). A ceremony of affiliation creates ritual ties of brotherhood among the members of a *cosca*. Once initiated each becomes a brother to all other members with whom they share an obligation of mutual aid without limits and without measure. Thanks to the trust and solidarity created by fraternization, it becomes possible to pursue the personal interests of the members through collective action (Paoli 2001). When the *cosca* initiates a novice, he assumes an identity as a "man of honor" and subordinates all previous allegiances, even those based on blood ties (Paoli 2003).

At the center of the cosca are four or five blood relatives (Arlacchi 1986). The *cosca* is devoid of any rigid organization; it is simply *gli amici degli amici*—"friends of friends." The members are *gli uomini qualificati* ("qualified men"). Flexibility prevents the *cosca* from becoming bureaucratic: "The need continually to broaden the scope of the networks of social relationships reinforced the impossibility of creating stable organizational structures" (Catanzaro 1992: 40). The *mafioso* succeeds because he commands a *partito*, a network of relationships whereby he is able to act as an intermediary—a broker—providing services, which include votes and violence for the holders of institutionalized power. All he requests in return is immunity to carry out his activities (Hess 1973). Each village has its own *cosca*, larger ones have more, and collectively they are the Mafia. Barzini (1965) delineates four levels of organization that constitute the Mafia. The first, the *famiglia,* constitutes the nucleus. Some families, he notes, have belonged to the *societá degli amici* for generations, each *padrino* bequeathing the family to his eldest son. The second level consists of a group of several families who come together to form a *cosca;* one family and its *padrino* are recognized as supreme. In the third level, the *cosca* establishes working relationships with other *cosche,* respecting territories and boundaries. The fourth level is achieved when *cosche* join in an alliance called *consorteria,* in which one *cosca* is recognized as supreme and its leader is the leader of the *consorteria—capo di tutti capi,* the boss of all bosses. "This happens spontaneously … when the *cosche* realize that one of them is more powerful, has more men, more friends, more money, more high-ranking protectors…. All the *consorterie* in Sicily … form the *onerata societá,* a solidarity that unites all *mafiosi;* they know they owe all possible support to any *amico degli amici* who needs it … even if they have never heard of him, provided he is introduced by a mutual *amico*" (Barzini 1965: 272).

Capomafioso-turned-informer Tommaso Buscetta describes the *cosca* as hierarchical, with elected leaders[2] and precise decision-making processes. Each *cosca* takes its name from the territory under its control, and is composed of *uomini d'onore* ("men of honor") in numbers varying from ten to one hundred. They are organized into groups of ten (*decina*) headed by a *capodecina.* Above the *capidecina* is the *capofamiglia* who has a deputy and a few advisors. Three or more families with adjoining territories are represented by *capimandamenti* who are members of the *cupola* or commission, whose creation dates back to the 1970s (Scalia 2010). This central directorate of the Mafia is headed by a commission *capo* who oversees the activities of the organization on a provincial level. Some reports (for example, Jamieson 2000) indicate that the Mafia has become less hierarchical and more impermeable with small, tightly structured cells that, like those of Colombian organizations (discussed in Chapter 6), have a membership that is unknown to all but a few persons. There is greater internal secrecy and selectivity in recruitment, an increased tendency to favor family members to reduce the likelihood of informants, a strategy long-favored by the *'Ndrangheta.* The Mafia has downsized and is outsourcing. Downsizing restricts membership to just a few trustworthy members lowering the risk of turncoats. Racketeering is outsourced to young men who while working independently, are under Mafia control–if arrested, they do not know enough about its structure and its business to jeopardize the organization (Scalia 2010).

In Mafia areas the issue is never who is "right" and who is "wrong." Instead, "preference tended to be given to whichever party proved victorious in the end, irrespective of the original conflict" (Arlacchi 1986: 13). Thus, in Mafia areas, at bottom nothing could really be unjust, and honor "was connected less with justice than with domination and physical strength": a Hobbesian world ruled by the credo "might is right." The *mafioso* brought order, albeit in a conservative if not reactionary form, and dispensed primitive justice in a lawless society. *Mafiosi* were frequently not only tolerated by their communities, but "respected to the point where they could parade as standard bearers of a more equitable system of justice than that provided by the state" (Finley, Smith, and Duggan 1987: 157). "The mafia was outlaw, but tolerated, secret but recognizable, criminal but upholding of order. It protected and ripped off

---

2. Catanzaro (1992) discounts the "electoral procedure" because it is not used to decide between two or more contenders, but simply to confirm the single contender for leadership.

the owners of the great estates, protected and ripped off the sharecroppers who worked the estates, and ripped off the peasants who slaved on them" (Robb 1996: 48).

"As there was no effective State policing, the use of private violence in settling disputes was tolerated and accepted, because people understood that there was no other effective body to intervene"(Maran 2008: 44). "Men with commercial or political ambitions in Sicily were faced with two alternatives: either to arm themselves; or more likely, to buy protection from a specialist in violence, a *mafioso*" (Dickie 2004: 59). *Mafiosi* exploited the landowners who were forced to hire them, stealing as much as they could until the property could be purchased for an artificially low price. Or they would terrorize the owners and their employees until the owner had enough and put it up for auction; there would only be one bidder (Maran 2008).

Every *mafioso* demands *rispetto*, indeed, is referred to as a *uomo di rispetto*—a man worthy of respect. American *mafioso* Bill Bonanno (1999: xiii) points out that this "respect has nothing to do with affection or even with a show of good manners. It is an acknowledgement of power" that Cesare Mori notes requires a concrete recognition of the prerogative of immunity belonging to the *mafioso*, not only in his person, but also in everything that he had to do with or that he was pleased to take under his protection. Thus, "evildoers had to leave the *mafioso* severely alone, and all the persons or things to which, explicitly or implicitly, he had given a guarantee of security." As a man of respect, "the *mafioso* is in a position to provide protection where the state is unwilling or unable; to provide arbitration services superior to those available from local judges, especially to the poor person who cannot afford a lawyer, or for those whose justice is of a social, not a legal, nature—the pregnant daughter whose seducer refuses to marry." The *mafioso*, and in particular the *capomafioso*, can put it all right, and his services are speedy and final (Mori 1933: 69).

These "services" are the essence of *mafia*— the *mafioso* is a provider of protection broadly defined. For legitimate entrepreneurs he provides insurance against otherwise untrustworthy suppliers or customers and will limit competition by restricting market entry. In southern Italy an ethos of mistrust and suspicion pervades personal and business relationships—a dilemma the *mafioso* can overcome by offering himself as a guarantor (Putnam 1993). Even if each side must give him 10 percent, they are assured of being satisfied with a deal in which neither side loses face (Maran 2008). He acts as a guarantor so that persons who do not trust one another can transact business with a significant degree of confidence; this refers to legitimate entrepreneurs and, most particularly, the illegitimate, persons who cannot turn to the police or courts to remedy their grievances. The origins of the Mafia in Sicily trace back to "the structural inability of the State to guarantee, on the one hand, social order and, on the other, the proper functioning of economic transactions" (Becucci 2011: 2).

A *mafioso* engaged in a legitimate business enjoys advantages over other businessmen: Potential competitors are likely to be deterred, and criminals will give his enterprise a wide berth (Gambetta 1993).[3]

"The constitutional state and elected parliament that accompanied Sicily's union with Italy provided a crucial step in the rise to power of the Mafia—Sicily's special kind of middle class" (Servadio 1976: 17). "With an electorate of little more than 1 percent, the landlords and their friends and employees [*mafiosi*] were often the only voters. If there were any doubt about the result of an election, intimidation was usually effective" (Finley, Smith, and Duggan 1987: 183). In 1912, universal male suffrage was introduced and because of its ability to control elections, the Mafia was courted by political powers in Rome. The "Mafia became the only electoral force that counted in Sicily and the government was realistic in acceptance of the fact" (Lewis 1964: 41). The situation remained unchanged until the rise of Benito Mussolini and the Fascist state.

---

3. Inspiring fear without a direct threat is a valuable asset, one that was used quite successfully by the Gambino brothers in New York's garment center, discussed in Chapter 13.

MUSSOLINI AND THE MAFIA

Mussolini's rise to power in the 1920s had important implications for both the Sicilian and American Mafia. Although the south resisted fascism, "once it became clear that the Fascists would obtain a major share in national power, the entire south became Fascist almost overnight" (Chubb 1982: 25). "The mafia had always known how to cozy up to those in power" (Robb 1996: 48). The impact of the Mafia can be seen by comparing the elections of 1922, when no Fascist was elected to Parliament from Sicily, with the elections of 1924, when thirty-eight Fascists were elected out of the fifty-seven representatives from Sicily (Servadio 1976).

Mussolini, known as *Il Duce,* visited Sicily in 1924 and was introduced to Ciccio Cuccia, a *capomafioso* who was also a local mayor. Don Ciccio[4] accompanied *Il Duce* on a tour and, after seeing the large number of police officers guarding him, is reputed to have said: "You're with me, so there's nothing to worry about" (Lewis 1964). To Don Ciccio, the large police escort indicated a lack of *rispetto.* When Mussolini declined to discharge the police contingent, the *capomafioso* arranged for the town piazza to be empty when *Il Duce* made his speech: "When Mussolini began his harangue he found himself addressing a group of about 20 village idiots, one-legged beggars, bootblacks, and lottery-ticket sellers specially picked by Don Ciccio to form an audience" (Lewis 1964: 72).

A totalitarian regime does not tolerate pockets of authority that are not under its control, and Mussolini quickly moved to destroy the Mafia. Elections were abolished in 1925, depriving the Mafia of its major instrument of alliance with government and an important basis for its immunity from criminal justice. The other important basis was intimidation. However, "Fascist courts trying criminal cases in which members of the Mafia were implicated found it just as impossible to obtain convictions as it had been for the democratic courts

of old" (Lewis 1964: 68). Mussolini responded by investing Prefect Cesare Mori of Lombardy, a career police officer, with emergency police powers and sending him after the Mafia. (Christopher Duggan [1989] stresses general lawlessness in western Sicily and a request by a delegation of war veterans as the bases for Mussolini's intervention.)

Mori assembled a small army of agents and set about the task of purging the island of *mafiosi.* "Under the jurisdiction of Prefect Mori, repression became savage. Many *mafiosi* were sent to prison, killed or tortured, but also many left-wingers were called '*mafiosi*' for the occasion, and were disposed of…. In many cases the landowners provided Mori with information against the *mafiosi* they had so far employed, who had been their means to safeguard their interests against the peasantry. This was logical because they saw that the regime would provide a better and cheaper substitute" (Servadio 1976: 74). Thus, the Fascists replaced the Mafia as intermediaries and maintainers of Sicilian law and order.

Mori swooped down on villages and with the free application of torture reminiscent of the Inquisition arrested 11,000 persons, not all of them *mafiosi, and* many powerful *capomafiosi* (Dickie 2004). *Gabelloti* were required to swear an oath of allegiance to the government, and in 1928, Mori declared that the Mafia had been destroyed. However, the reality was otherwise, and the Mafia began to reassert itself by 1941.

Many Mafia bosses assumed important positions within the regime, and the Fascists failed to significantly transform social and economic conditions upon which the Mafia depended. When Mori began to investigate the connection between the Mafia and high-level Fascists, he was forced into retirement (Orlando 2001). "It was no surprise that the Mafia rapidly reemerged as soon as fascism fell" (Chubb 1982: 27). Many *mafiosi* awaited "liberation," which came in the form of the Allied landing in 1943. The campaign against the Mafia did succeed in driving some important *mafiosi* out of Sicily. They traveled to the United States at an opportune time, during the Prohibition era, and took up important positions in a newly emerging form of organized crime. The end of World War II

---

4. The appellation *Don* is an honorific title used in Sicily to refer to clergymen, government officials, and important *mafiosi.* It derives from the Latin *dominus,* "lord," and is used with the person's first given name.

led to a Mafia Renaissance out of which the *Nuovo Mafia*—a "new" Mafia—emerged.

THE NEW MAFIA: *NUOVO MAFIA/ COSA NOSTRA*

World War II had negative consequences for southern Italy, blocking the northward migration of excess labor (Catanzaro 1992). The end of the war brought a Mafia renaissance in Sicily as a vacuum in local leadership was filled by former *capomafiosi*: "Not only were they respected local figures, but as victims of Mori's operation against the mafia they were also in a good position to pose as anti-fascists" (Finley, Smith, and Duggan 1987: 214). Many *mafiosi* became town mayors under the Allied military government, and they violently thwarted the efforts of trade unionists, socialists, communists, and land reformers (Catanzaro 1992; Costanzo 2007; Robb 1996). "Anything that would upset the system they had developed over the previous 100 years was to be resisted" (Maran 2008: 145).

A brief flirtation with Separatism—seceding from the mainland in favor of affiliation with the United States—was discarded in 1946 when the government in Rome announced Sicilian autonomy. In return, the most important *capomafioso*, Calògero Vizzini ("Don Calò"), the illiterate son of a peasant father, pledged support for the Christian Democratic Party (CDP) that would hold power in Italy for almost five decades. In return, *capomafiosi* were frequently accorded places of honor in the party, and "it was not uncommon for prominent politicians to appear as honored guests at the christenings, weddings, and funerals of major Mafia figures. In Sicily, being known as a friend of a *mafioso* was not a sign of shame but of power" (Stille 1995a: 20); it advertised the solidarity of the alliance between official power and the informal power of the Mafia (Dickie 2004).

Born in 1877, Don Calò was imprisoned by Mussolini. Vizzini spent only a few days in prison before being released through the intervention of a young Fascist he had befriended. Vizzini was now a *gabelloto* and mayor of Villalba, and he "would hold court each morning in the small plaza of Villalba. People would approach him for favours, such as help with a bank loan or assistance with a court case—indeed anything in which 'authority' could be useful" (Duggan 1989: 67). As an "anti-Fascist," he possessed a special business license from the Allied military government. This allowed him to head up a flourishing black market in olive oil. In this endeavor Vizzini worked with the American Mafia fugitive Vito Genovese (Lewis 1964).

When Don Calò died of natural causes in 1954, he left an estate reputed to be worth several million dollars (Pantaleone 1966). He was the last of the old-style *capomafiosi*, characterized by modesty in both speech and dress: "The old Mafia chief was a rural animal, holding sway over the countryside, dressed in shirt-sleeves and baggy pants: a multimillionaire who chose to look like a peasant" (Servadio 1974: 21). Actually, notes Pino Arlacchi (1986), the behavior of the old *mafioso* had power—*rispetto*—as its primary goal. In contrast, the modern *mafioso* is a materialist for whom power is simply a means to achieve wealth; and he exudes conspicuous consumption. The new *mafioso* is not bound by the traditions of the rural *cosca*. He dresses like a successful businessman, sometimes a bit flashy, like the American gangster whose pattern he seems to have adopted—cross-fertilization. The New Mafia—called *Cosa Nostra* by its members—has a distinctly American tint, the result of American gangsters being deported to Sicily, "where they immediately assumed leading positions in the Mafia hierarchy of the island" (Lewis 1964: 273).

Initially, *Cosa Nostra* resorted to robbery and kidnapping to accumulate the capital necessary to be a player in legal endeavors such as the construction industry and in the illicit heroin and cocaine marketplaces. Construction contracts based on competitive bidding were undermined by restraint-of-trade arrangements and collusive bidding under supervision of the Mafia (Maran 2008). Similar practices in New York are discussed in Chapter 13.

Drug money changed the functioning and mode of organization of the Mafia in which luxury and extravagant consumerism has become the norm

(Siebert 1996). The New Mafia has continued the *pizzu*, protection money extorted from large and small businesses (Onstad 2011). But financial considerations reportedly play a secondary role in this enterprise, being primarily a Mafia way of maintaining territorial domination (Stille 1993): "While managing millions and operating on a grand scale, he [a *mafioso*] does not slacken his hold over the corner butcher's shop. Not so much for the sake of money perhaps, as to demonstrate the permanence of his power" (Siebert 1996: 123). However, Arnold Maran (2008) reports that in desperation *mafiosi* now collect the *pizzu* for income—not symbolism—and its reach extends to persons heretofore off limits such as doctors, lawyers, and pensioners.

Agrarian reform broke up the landed estates and did away with the traditional *capomafioso* who lived off agricultural profits, theft of cattle, control over water supplies, and peasant labor. "The new Mafia was making deals in luxury hotels, in the offices of multinational corporations, and the well-appointed studies of politicians" (Costanzo 2007: 139). They were becoming increasingly urban—by 1987, there were eighteen *cosche* in Palermo (Maran 2008).

The contrast between the "Two Mafias" is evidenced by a conflict between the *capomafiosi* of Corleone ("Lionheart," named after its ninth century Arab conqueror), a town of about 12,000 in western Sicily about 40 miles south of Palermo. In the immediate postwar years. Michele Navarra was a medical doctor and (despite his education) a representative of the Old Mafia. Luciano Leggio (which the police misspelled Liggio), born in 1925, represented the New Mafia. At the age of 19, Leggio became the youngest *gabelloto* in the history of Sicily (his predecessor was murdered). Navarra was the inspector of health for the area, and head of the town's only hospital (his predecessor was also mysteriously murdered). In the tradition of Don Calò, he was a political power who served as chairman of the local branch of the Christian Democratic Party. The doctor also trafficked in stolen beef. Leggio was his most violent assistant. Leggio and an associate hanged a trade unionist who was a threat to Navarra's power, and the murder was witnessed by a shepherd boy. In a state of shock after telling his story, the boy fainted and was taken to the hospital. There, an injection from the "good doctor" ended the boy's life (Servadio 1976). Navarra was convicted of the murder and, although he was sentenced to five years' exile in Calabria, returned home after a few months (Robb 1996).

With his followers, Leggio began to develop activities of his own. However, the Leggio group "had nothing in common with the organization presided over by Don Calò but its iron laws of secrecy and the vendetta" (Lewis 1964: 123). Leggio chose to control the supply of meat to the Palermo market rather than raise livestock. He drove out all of the tenant farmers on the estate under his protection, burning down their houses, and replaced them with day laborers. He recruited gunmen, and anybody who crossed him was summarily shot. From 1953 to 1958 there were 153 recorded Mafia murders in the Corleone area (Servadio 1976). According to one source (Mangione 1985: 147), Leggio was connected to organized crime in the United States and "had been a key contact man working closely with Joseph Profaci [the "Olive Oil King"] of the American Mafia."

The Old Mafia benefited from feudal conditions, living off control of the land, and cheap labor. When a dam was proposed for the town of Corleone to harness the river water flowing to the ocean, Dr. Navarra vetoed it because he made money from the water pumped from artesian wells. *Cosa Nostra*, oriented toward capitalistic change, recognized the profits that could be earned from control over building projects. Navarra and his followers were living in the nineteenth century, but Leggio was a man of the times. With Navarra in control, nothing would change, and the New Mafia recognized this reality (Lewis 1964). In 1958, fifteen of Leggio's men ambushed Dr. Navarra's car; 210 bullets were found in his body. One by one, the remaining followers of Navarra were murdered and Leggio became the undisputed *capomafioso* of the Corleonesi *cosca* (Servadio 1976).

During the 1960s, emerging *cosche* engaged in a bitter struggle for dominance. The struggle between

---

FOR THE SINS OF THE FATHER

His father had turned state's evidence in a case involving the murder of an anti-Mafia prosecutor. The boy was kidnapped and kept prisoner for two years by the killer who, acting on orders from Mafia boss Totò Riina, strangled the 13-year-old and disposed of his body in a vat of acid (Bohlen 1996; Robb 1996).

Mafia clans led to an emigration of *mafiosi* similar to that experienced during the reign of Mussolini. This proved to be quite beneficial as these overseas *mafiosi* provided the links for greater international operations. The Mafia connection to the cocaine trade is largely a result of this Diaspora (Williams 1995a, 1995b).

In 1974, Leggio was convicted of the murder of Dr. Navarra and sentenced to life imprisonment; he died in prison in 1993. Leggio's right-hand man, Salvatore (Totò) Riina, became head of the Corleone *cosca*. A short, stocky man, the son of poor farmers, with an elementary school education, Riina is known as *La Belva*—"The Beast"—for ordering mass killings and personally participating in some of them. "Rather than wage a street war like the previous Mafia conflict of the 1960s, Riina worked to peel away supporters from his rivals' forces, letting them see the inevitability of the Corleonesi" (Orlando 2001: 67). He built a secret army by initiating men without informing other Mafia leaders (Dickie 2004). He formed private alliances with rising members of many *cosche*, planted his own men in others, and then with a reign of terror came to dominate the Mafia—at a cost of nearly one thousand lives (Robb 1996; Stille 1993, 1995a). Victims were stabbed, strangled, or shot in the street, in bars, in pizzerias, and while in police custody. Some were invited to dine with Riina; at the end of a sumptuous meal, they were strangled and their bodies often dissolved in acid (Follain 2008).

After being tried in absentia and sentenced to life imprisonment for murder and drug trafficking, Riina became the most wanted man in Italy. Nevertheless he was able to avoid authorities for more than twenty-three years, partly because photographs of him were out of date. While living as a fugitive, Riina married the sister of a powerful *mafioso* in a ceremony performed by a Mafia priest (who was eventually defrocked), honeymooned in Venice, sired four children, and continued to oversee the activities of his Mafia clan (Robb 1996).

One of the victims of Riina's campaign to centralize and control the Mafia was *capomafioso* Tommaso Buscetta, who lost ten relatives, including a brother and two sons. In 1983, Buscetta, who had escaped to Brazil, was arrested on an international warrant. He attempted to commit suicide with a strychnine pill. When he recovered, Buscetta agreed to cooperate with American and Italian authorities.[5] In 1987, with the help of Buscetta and other informants, the Italian government held the largest mass trial (referred to as the maxitrial) of its kind ever held in Italy (Paoli 2003): 114 were released due to insufficient evidence and 344 were convicted and sentenced to a total of 2,665 years in prison (Maran 2008). Paralleling events in the United States, a breakdown in the Mafia code of silence caused hundreds of *mafiosi* (*pentiti*) to cooperate with the government.

The New Mafia has a membership in excess of 5,000, each with his own network—a circle of dozens of relatives, friends, associates, and employees—divided into about 180 *cosche* (de Gennaro 1995; Jamieson 2000; Stille 1993). Each *cosca* is held together by a core of blood relatives and encompasses a membership of twenty-five to thirty persons (Argentine 1993; Arlacchi 1986). The *cosche* form alliances that are sealed through marriage: "Such is the strategic significance of marriages for the structure of the criminal organization and the arrangement of alliances between the different cells, that by following the trail of weddings,

---

5. Buscetta died of cancer in 2000.

CLIENTELISM

In the *Mezzogiorno*, you need a recommendation or connections, "a protector, someone who can at least get your foot in the door, if not the rest of you. Presenting yourself without a protector is like showing up without arms and legs" (Saviano 2007: 260). This writer heard similar comments about Chicago during his more than two decades in that city.

---

christenings and confirmations, the judges [in the 1986–1987 Mafia maxitrial] managed to gather information about internal changes within the organization" (Siebert 1996: 29).

FROM *UN UOMO DI RISPETTO* TO GANGSTER

It is said that Italy's curse is to be the home of three world powers: the Italian government, the Catholic Church, and the Mafia, of which the government is the feeblest (Bohlen 1995d). Mafia voting strength is based on the circle of family and friends that each *mafioso* can deliver, as many as forty to fifty votes (Arlacchi 1993): In Sicily, at least half a million persons (out of a population of five million) are directly tied to the Mafia (Cowell 1992f). The Mafia is able to control votes because in the environment in which it operates there is always fear of reprisals. Intimidation, surveillance of polling places, and sometimes rigged elections guarantee an outcome favorable to Mafia candidates. But frequently outright intimidation is unnecessary. In the absence of political enthusiasm and voter passion, a cynical view prevails. Instead of signifying a preference among competing political ideas, the vote simply indicates support for a *clientelistic* group. The leveling of political traditions and an absence ideology among the political parties leads voters almost naturally, without any forcing, to respect the "marching orders" given by the Mafia (della Porta and Vannucci 1999). In 2008, the governor of Sicily was sentenced to five years' imprisonment for providing a Mafia boss with confidential information—while being tried he was reelected.

In 1987, angry over the government's maxitrial, Totò Riina ordered a switch in votes: The Christian Democrats increased their strength throughout the rest of Italy, but in Palermo only Mafia-backed candidates won (Robb 1996). In 1992, the Mafia murdered the Sicilian head of the Christian Democratic Party (CDP) in a Palermo suburb; it was his job to keep peace between the party and the Mafia. "This was the Mafia's way of announcing that it was 'renegotiating' its arrangement with the Prime Minister" (Cowell 1992f; Kramer 1992: 112). It appears that Riina was still furious at the Christian Democrats for not intervening in the Mafia maxitrial (della Porta and Vannucci 1999).

Since the end of World War II, the CDP had ruled Italy, and "the party's bedrock ... was the *Mezzogiorno* and especially the *friends* in Sicily" (Robb 1996: 22). By 1993, increasing scandal and the collapse of European communism finally led to the demise of the CDP, which, despite its corruption and ties to the Mafia, had been the only viable alternative to the Communist Party[6] (Stille 1993). The most powerful Christian Democrat in Sicily was Salvo Lima, the former *mafioso* mayor of Palermo who later became a deputy minister in Rome and a member of the European parliament. When Lima entered a restaurant in Palermo, people fell silent and kissed his hand. However, when scandal drove the Christian Democrats from power, Lima was no longer of use to the *amici*—he was gunned down by a man riding on the back of a motorbike (Robb 1996).

As the political role of *mafiosi* changed, so too did their ability to act as brokers between peasant

---

6. In 1991, the Italian Communist Party, the most powerful in Europe, reorganized itself as the Democratic Party of the Left, social democrats seeking mainstream support (Burnett and Mantovani 1998)

and officialdom. The *mafioso* was no longer *un uomo di rispetto* but simply an urban gangster in the American tradition; that is, a predatory criminal without popular roots or popular backing. The New Mafia reflects the emerging *Mezzogiorno*. The south is changing; modernization, fed by government-sponsored public works, is slowly encroaching on feudal ways. Above all, the mark of respect has more to do with one's wealth than with one's name or reputation. It was power, not wealth, that the traditional *mafioso* pursued: "The possession of wealth, regarded by the traditional *mafioso* as one among the proofs and results of a man's capacity to make himself respected, becomes, in the 1960s and 1970s, meritorious in itself." Family wealth, not family honor, is a reason for violence: "Wealth, in a word, becomes intrinsically honourable and confers honour on its possessors" (Arlacchi 1986: 60)

Since 1971, the *Nuovo Mafia* has assassinated investigative, judicial, and political officials, something that was anathema to the old Mafia: "Offenses against symbols of authority were foreign to the methods of a Mafia that, considering itself an authority and surrogate for the state, wanted to preserve and respect certain values" (Kamm 1982b: E3). Indeed, "the *mafioso* customarily collaborated with the justice system. He would "often appear before those who accused him of illicit activities as an honest citizen who helped bring the true outlaws to justice, claiming it was to his credit that order reigned in his community" (Catanzaro 1992: 24). As the Mafia was reduced to a marginal role in society, many *mafiosi* reacted in a manner similar to other marginalized persons. They pursued wealth as the only way back to honor and power, and Mafia violence as a result of economic competition polluted the Sicilian political system (Arlacchi 1986; Catanzaro 1992).

Following the assassinations of government officials, the New Mafia lost the support of important elements of Italian society. In 1982, Salvatore Cardinal Pappalardo, the Sicilian-born archbishop of Palermo, led Sicilian priests "in a vocal campaign against the Mafia, reversing decades of church indifference toward and even tolerance of local dons"[7] (Withers 1982: 5). Later that year, while on a visit to the island of Sicily, Pope John Paul II issued an attack on the Mafia. And since 1983, Palermo has elected and reelected an anti-Mafia mayor. In 1993, the Mafia struck back at its critics in the Church: Pino Puglisi, a 56-year-old priest who spoke out against the Mafia, was shot to death in front of his rectory in a Palermo slum (Orlando 2001). In 2010, Pope Benedict, at a Mass attended by thousands alongside Palermo's waterfront, hailed Father Puglisi as a hero. The Pope denounced the Mafia and encouraged listeners to imitate the priest's example (Associated Press 2010d).

As part of its campaign of terror, the Mafia bombed two of Rome's most venerable churches, in addition to other bombings in Rome, Milan, and Florence that killed ten people and left dozens injured (Bohlen 1996c). In 1993, the Mafia bombed the world-famous Uffizi gallery in Florence, killing five persons and causing extensive damage (Bohlen 1995c).

In 1992, the prosecutor who helped gather evidence for the Mafia maxitrial, Judge Giovanni Falcone, was killed, along with his wife and three bodyguards, when a half-ton of TNT was detonated by remote control on a road near Palermo. The killers obviously had inside information about Falcone's movements. His murder led to an anti-Mafia demonstration by about 40,000 persons in Palermo, a remarkable occurrence for that city (Cowell 1992a). But it did not prevent the Mafia from striking again. Later that year, Paolo Borsellino, Falcone's replacement as Palermo's chief public prosecutor and head of a new anti-Mafia super-agency, was killed along with five police bodyguards; 175 pounds of a Czech-made plastic explosive placed under a car was detonated while Borsellino was walking outside an apartment building where his mother and sister resided (Cowell 1992d).

The government responded by dispatching 7,000 troops to Sicily in a highly publicized anti-Mafia campaign, and Palermo reelected a crusading

---

7. At times the Church-Mafia relationship was symbiotic, and some clergy were *mafiosi* (see, for example, Gambetta 1993: 48–52).

anti-Mafia mayor (Hundley 1998a). The soldiers were withdrawn in 1998: Italy, which had recently been admitted to the European monetary union, wanted to shed the image of a nation that needs a peacekeeping force occupying its own territory (Stanley 1998). The day after troops were withdrawn, the police arrested scores of *mafiosi*, including twenty members of the Corleone *cosca*, whose boss was already in custody (Associated Press 1998a). And there have been dramatic results: Murders in Palermo, which averaged 130 to 140 annually, fell to fewer than ten in 1997 (Hundley 1998a). As a sign of the Mafia's weakness, in 1999, the president of Italy led an anti-Mafia demonstration in Corleone on a day dedicated to victims of the Mafia (Reuters 1999).

The violence that gained Don Totò Riina his nickname also drove *mafiosi* seeking protection from "the Beast" to the authorities (Cowell 1992e, 1993a). In 1992, Italy enacted a witness protection law. The cooperation of *mafiosi* is believed to be behind the capture of the 62-year-old Riina, arrested in his car on a Palermo street at the beginning of 1993. He and his driver were unarmed. Later that year, Riina was ordered imprisoned for life by a Palermo court, and officials confiscated about $300 million worth of his property (Dickie 2004). The government has been transferring land confiscated from *mafiosi* to groups of young people for agriculture and housing; Riina's stables have been converted into a tourist hotel (Onstad 2011). Like Palermo, Corleone elected an anti-Mafia mayor and the city has a plaza named for the murdered prosecutors, *Piazzo Falcone e Borsellino*, and the *Museo Anti-Mafia*.

Despite its weakened condition, the pool of Mafia prospects remains strong, the result of a high rate of unemployment among the young of Sicily. But since the capture of Riina, the Mafia operates with a much lower public profile, and

AP Photo/Alessandro Fucarini

In 2007, a policewoman looks at dozens of photos of alleged members of a Mafia syndicate arrested in an anti-Mafia round-up called "Occidente" (West) in Palermo, the capital city of Sicily, Italy.

new initiates are from families with long-established Mafia histories (Dickie 2004). Vincenzo Scalia (2010: 291) reports that far from declining, the Mafia continues to be "enshrined in a powerful political and financial network whose influence reaches far beyond Sicily."

NEAPOLITAN CAMORRA

Naples, the capital of the Campania region, with a population of about one million, suffered devastation during World War II. While Campania has agriculturally been the most productive of Italy, its peasants remained chronically poor. During the 1950s there was massive migration into Naples, resulting in a flood of unskilled and unemployed persons surviving on the margins of society. Survival meant resort to illegal activities: illegal markets and renewed vigor by violence specialists providing mediation services. At the same time, the city was home to a prosperous class with large apartments and summer homes. Added to this mix was a type of corrupt machine politics reminiscent of that in the United States discussed in Chapter 2, out of which emerged a new Camorra (Allum 2006).

Whereas the Mafia began as more of an idea than an organization and evolved along cultural lines in rural western Sicily, the Camorra was deliberately structured as an urban-based criminal society. The term *Camorra* is believed to have derived from the Castilian *kamora*, meaning "contestation," and said to have been imported into Naples during the years of Spanish domination (Serao 1911a). Ernest Serao reported that the forebears of the Neapolitan Camorra were the Spanish brigands of the Sierras known as the *gamuri* (1911a: 723): "Not a passer-by nor a vehicle escaped their watchful eye and their fierce claws, so that traveling or going from one place to another on business was impossible for anyone without sharing with the ferocious watchers of the Sierras either the money he had with him or the profits of the business that had taken him on his journey."

Although there are several versions of how the term *Camorra* came into being (Walston 1986), it seems clear that the Camorra as an organization developed in Spanish prisons during the Bourbon rule of the Two Sicilies (the *Mezzogiorno*) early in the nineteenth century. The members of this criminal society eventually moved their control of the prisons into Naples proper. They were "rather tightly, centrally, and hierarchically organized" (Hobsbawm 1959: 55). The Camorra "was organized as openly and carefully as a public school system, or an efficient political machine in one of our own cities. Naples was divided into twelve districts, and each of these into a number of sub-districts. Although burglary and other remunerative felonies were not neglected, extortion was the principal industry; and the assassination of an inconvenient person could be purchased by anyone with the price. In the case of a friend in need, a murder could be arranged without any charge—a simple gesture of affection" (McConaughy 1931: 244). An English diplomat in Naples during the 1860s observed:

> There was no class, high or low, that did not have its representatives among the members of the Society that was a vast organized association for the extortion of blackmail in every conceivable shape and form. Officials, officers of the King's Household, the police and others were affiliated with the most desperate of the criminal classes in carrying out the depredations, and none was too high or too low to escape them. If a petition was to be presented to the Sovereign or to a Minister, it had to be paid for; at every gate of the town Camorristi were stationed to exact a toll on each cart or donkey load brought to market by the peasants; and on going into a hackney carrosel [sic] in the street, I have seen one of the band run up and get his fee from the driver. No one thought of refusing to pay, for the consequences of a refusal were too well known, anyone rash enough to demur being apt to be found soon after mysteriously stabbed by some unknown individual, whom the

police were careful never to discover. (quoted in Hibbert 1966: 181–182)

The Camorra was "more efficiently organized than the police, and set up a parallel system of law in the typical southern Italian style" (Ianni 1972: 22; Serao 191la). The Camorra welcomed Garibaldi and his "Red Shirts" in 1860, and after his success its power increased. Upon the proclamation of the constitution in 1860, *camorristi* were freed from the prisons in Naples, and the new prefect used the Camorra to maintain order: The Camorra constituted not only the *de facto* but also the legally constituted police power in Naples (Walston 1986). Devoid of a political ideology, the Camorra continued to act as mercenaries in the various struggles for power (Behan 1996). The introduction of universal suffrage in the 1880s, notes Felia Allum (2006), provided the Camorra with an opportunity to move into the worlds of politics and business. From 1880 until 1900 "if they so decided, there would not be, in some regions, a single vote cast for a candidate for the Chamber of Deputies who was opposed to their man" (Ianni 1974: 246). A 1901 parliamentary inquiry signaled a Camorra decline fostered by an improvement in the standard of living and the emergence of alternative membership organizations, political parties of trade unions. But the Camorra survived, transmuting into an urbanized form of criminal organization and in more rural Campania becoming Mafia-style violent mediators in business transactions with links to politics. The Camorra invaded any space left vacant by the state (F. Allum 2006).

The Camorra welcomed the Fascists as they had Garibaldi; after that there was not a Camorra: "They are all Fascists, and everything they do is legal" (McConaughy 1931: 248). Fascism ended Camorra influence in the city of Naples; the few remaining members were incorporated into the Fascist power structure, and Camorra groups in the countryside were used by the Fascists to intimidate antigovernment peasants (Behan 1996).

Allum (2006: 87) reports that the term "Camorra" was used during the 1950s to refer to criminal organizations, "but it was not the secret society or 'corporate organization' of the late nineteenth century." Vincenzo Ruggiero (1993: 143) reports that the last boss of the traditional Camorra died of natural causes in 1989 "after having acted for years as an informal 'justice of the peace' in one of the most crowded areas of the city. He settled disputes and, it is said, helped the poor." In an interview shortly before his death, "he mourned an end of an era—that of the men of honour who succored the people—and condemned the present, dominated by cruel, greedy and unscrupulous individuals."

Postwar Naples was plagued with violence attributed to these "unscrupulous individuals." Suspected but not convicted, Sicilian *mafiosi* were forced into "internal exile"—*soggiorno obbligato*—obliged to live Naples. In collusion with local criminals, they began to expand illegal opportunity. In the countryside Camorra groups began to emerge as soon as the Allied forces withdrew. They asserted control over agriculture and cattle markets. Slowly, they began to move into the urban areas of Naples to further their control over these markets, dictating prices and acting as brokers between sellers and buyers. These groups subsequently moved into and expanded upon the Naples contraband industry—from cigarettes to drugs. An estimated three-quarters of the cigarettes sold in Naples, where about one-third of the inhabitants are unemployed, originate in the black market—Italy has very high cigarette taxes. In 1994, when the government threatened a crackdown on this practice, hundreds of street vendors for whom the contraband is their only source of income, took to the streets in demonstrations (Tagliabue 1994). In 1997, more than two-dozen murders were blamed on a feud between two Camorra groups (Mazzarella and Contini clans) for control of the contraband cigarette business (Hundley 1997).

By the 1970s, Camorra structure was reminiscent of its nineteenth-century manifestation—formal rules, defined positions, a set of recruitment policies. This was the result of economic success that required a greater degree of organization. Heroin and cocaine trafficking had become a principal Camorra activity and the source of great wealth that they invested,

---

CAMORRA JUSTICE

Less than twenty-four hours after the arrest of Paolo Di Lauro, Camorra boss of the *Secondigliano Alliance*, the body of the man suspected of betraying him was found in a trash dump—only his lips were still intact: "His body was riddled with holes and encrusted with blood. They had tied him up and tortured him with a spiked bat—slowly for hours. Each blow cut new holes, piercing his flesh and breaking his bones as the nails sunk in were then yanked out. They had cut off his ears, cropped his tongue, gouged out his eyes with a screwdriver—all while he was still alive, awake, conscious" (Saviano 2007: 130).

---

thereby becoming a criminal-business enterprise operating internationally. This wealth made them more attractive to politicians looking for financial support (Allum 2006). The earlier versions of Camorra were not directly involved in politics, but during the 1980s the new Camorra began to penetrate the local political scene, and some members hold local elected office. In Campania, dozens of town counsels were dissolved because of Camorra influence (de Gennaro 1995). When government redevelopment programs were initiated in the Campania region, much like their Mafia "brothers" in Sicily, Camorra clans soon found a new source of income, and their ability to provide jobs gained them political influence (Behan 1996).

Redevelopment was a failure—a testament to political patronage and corruption. This was repeated when an earthquake devastated Naples in 1980, claiming almost 3,000 lives and leaving 300,000 homeless. A huge program of reconstruction was effectively hijacked by corrupt politicians, government bureaucrats, and the Camorra, which diversified its wealth from drug trafficking by moving into the construction industry. The Camorra's ability to intimidate workers thwarted union pressures and ensured lower costs, allowing Camorra firms a competitive advantage (Behan 1996).

Camorra clans control apparently legal commercial activities through which they introduce counterfeit goods, creating a significant economic-financial web involving a variety of countries, in particular the United States, Brazil, Canada, Australia, and the nations of Western Europe. This embedded financial network allows for the attainment of capital that, after being "laundered," can be reinvested in a variety legal commercial activities, thereby increasing the operational capacities of the organization.

Chinese immigrants play an important role in this endeavor, organizing themselves into structures with criminal connotations dedicated not only to the production and marketing of counterfeit goods, but also facilitating the illegal immigration of their fellow citizens; "once the latter reach Italy, they are then inserted within these production and distribution structures" (Patrignani 2009: 74).

This process is exemplified by the business activities of the *Secondigliano Alliance* (*Secondigliano* is a Neapolitan suburb), a collection of some of the most ruthless Camorra clans, which controls clothing manufacturing in a business zone on the outskirts of Naples. "Everything that is impossible to do elsewhere because of the inflexibility of contracts, laws, and copyrights is feasible here" where clan factories "produce garments and accessories identical to those of the principal Italian fashion houses" (Saviano 2007: 38—39). They own entire retail chains that dominate the international clothing market while also distributing to outlet stores. Slightly inferior products go to African street vendors and market stalls. The Alliance branched out into electronics, importing high-quality products from China and adding fake labels for international distribution (Saviano 2007). The Camorra has had remarkable business success in the manufacture of counterfeit designer clothing and consumer electronics and influence extends into the United States where members are reportedly trafficking in these products (California Department of Justice 2007).

While trafficking drugs in the United States can result in long prison sentences, trafficking in counterfeit goods is low risk with minimal penalties.

Camorra clans form alliances, often cemented by marriages. Their enterprises mix legitimate business, such as construction, with illegitimate, such as drug and arms trafficking. Profits from one are invested in the other, and vice versa, but even legitimate business often has a criminal dimension. Camorra firms underbid competitors by cutting corners, for example, using cement to hide waste and exposing workers to toxic dust, substandard scaffolding, bogus insurance, and long hours of toil for substandard wages (Saviano 2007). Campania has been turned into a massive illegal trash dumping ground for the Camorra, threatening the buffalo milk mozzarella—an Italian delicacy—industry which has flourished in the Naples area since ancient times (Fisher and Pinto 2008).

A growing population and rampant poverty led to the development of new Camorra groups that operated for many years without direct conflict with their older and more established brethren who often had Sicilian Mafia ties. A "New Camorra Organization," *Nuova Camorra Organizzata* (NCO), was organized by the leader of one of the important Camorra groups, Raffaele Cutolo. Born in 1941, Cutolo had been running his group while serving a twenty-four-year sentence for murder and extortion. Consistent with the Camorra's historical origins, Cutolo did much of his recruiting among the violent young men in Neapolitan prisons. "Cutolo protected these kids in jail, looked after their families outside and guaranteed a job on release. In return he got an oath of loyalty to the Nuova Camorra Organizzata" based on eighteenth-century Camorra rituals (Robb 1996: 165).

Naples was divided into zones by the older established Camorra groups, but Cutolo shattered the arrangement—and the peace—by attempting to bring all Camorra groups under his NCO. In 1980 and 1981, there were 380 murders attributed to the "Camorra war." Cutolo's opponents formed their own *Nuovo Famiglia* and received help from their Sicilian Mafia allies (Robb 1996). In the end, the NCO attempted takeover failed, and Cutolo was moved to a maximum-security prison on an island near Sardinia. With Cutolo and his NCO no longer a threat, both the NCO and the *Nuovo Famiglia* fell apart into competing and often feuding Camorra groups (Argentine 1993; Behan 1996; Robb 1996). By 2002, a pact and uneasy peace was negotiated by the competing Camorra clans.

A nonfiction book on the Camorra published in 2006 became an Italian-language film. The author of *Gomarrah*, journalist Robert Saviano, has been under police protection as the result of death threats from the Casalesi clan that was highlighted in his book. In 2011, Italian authorities seized $156 million in assets belonging to the Casalesi boss, including his 13,000-square-foot villa (United Press International 2011).

In 2011, the Archbishop of Naples ruled out church funerals for Camorra members. His ruling also denies Camorra members the right to be godfathers at baptisms and confirmations or witnesses at church weddings.

Structure of the Camorra

At the center of a typical Camorra group is a boss whose group is known by his surname, such as the *Alfieri* headed by Carmine Alfieri[8] in Nola. A high turnover has resulted in members and leaders who are younger than those of other southern Italian criminal groups, and the modern Camorra is less structured and less family based than is the Mafia. There is a general absence of rituals, although the NCO used a century-old ceremony to initiate members. Estimated Camorra membership is about 7,000. One of the most important Camorra groups headed by the Nuvoletta brothers had important links to the powerful *capomafioso* Luciano Leggio discussed earlier and is the only clan outside of Sicily that sits on the *cupola*, the Mafia's supreme council (Saviano 2007). The family of imprisoned *camorristi* is entitled to a monthly allowance.

---

8. Alfieri was known as first among equals and able to maintain discipline and territorial integrity among the more than 100 Camorra clans. In 1992, he was arrested and subsequently became a government informer. This led to a breakdown of Camorra order and an upsurge in feuds and murders (Hundley 1997).

Territorial control is reportedly essential to Camorra clans. Although extortion from legitimate businesses provides a relatively low return for the effort and risk involved, it is a way of asserting domination over a geographic area; it also provides an opportunity for those on the lower rungs to prove themselves and thereby move up in Camorra ranks. Roberto Saviano (2007: 51) states, however, that it is only the "beggar clans," inept at more lucrative business and desperate to survive, who practice monthly extortions. Camorra groups dominate illegal gambling and usury within their territorial hegemony, although some of their gambling operations reach northern cities such as Rome, Florence, and Milan. Territorial control extends to local politics and is enhanced by the Camorra's ability to provide employment where unemployment rates are consistently high. "Unlike Sicilian Mafia groups, the Camorra clans don't need the politicians; it's the politicians who need the System," its constituents and financial wealth (Saviano 2007: 47).

Despite their business acumen, like the Sicilian Mafia of recent past, Camorra leaders have engaged in violent struggles that have taken the lives of dozens of people (Arie 2004; Fisher 2005). At the end of 2004, a feud between loyalists and secessionists of a major *Secondigliano Alliance* clan claimed more than twenty-five lives in a little more than a month (Fisher 2004; Horowitz 2004; "Naples Police in Huge Mafia Sweep" 2004). The clans maintain military wings comprised of salaried retainers and many of the killings are perpetrated by young men—twelve to seventeen—enlisted by the military branch of the clans; they are often the sons or brothers of clan affiliates or from families without steady income: "A whole army of them" (Saviano 2007: 105). Even clergy are not spared. In 1994, when Father Giuseppe Diana dared speak out publicly against the Camorra, the thirty-six-year-old priest was gunned down in his church on March 19th, on the feast of San Giuseppe. And like Sicilian *mafiosi*, dozens of *camorristi* have become *pentiti*—government informants. By 2008, there were 236 confessing *mafiosi*, 271 *camorristi*, 86 from the *Sacra Corona Unita*, and 100 from the *'Ndrangheta* (Crisanti 2008).

In contrast to the Mafia, the Camorra and *'Ndrangheta* permit women to participate directly in their criminal activities, usually in the absence of their incarcerated husbands or as a result of his death (Allum 2006).

THE 'NDRANGHETA

The province of Calabria is located in the far south of the Italian "boot." It encompasses about 6,000 square miles of which more than 90 percent is hills or mountains. Italy's poorest province, Calabria has a population in excess of two million people; the capital city, Reggio di Calabria, is home to about 200,000. Lacking the charm of historical sites and world-class art, tourism is almost nonexistent. Much of the housing stock was built illegally by criminal groups, the fearsome *Onerate Societá* ("Honored Society") or *'Ndrangheta* ("Brotherhood"), which in the early twentieth century established groups in Canada and Australia (Nicaso and Lamothe 2005; Paoli 2003).

In Calabria, the term *'ndrangheta*, "society of men of honor," is used to indicate a high degree of heroism and virtue as embodied in the *'ndranghetisti*, men who are governed by *omertá* (Arlacchi 1986; Paoli 1994, 2003). The word *'ndrangheta* derives from the Greek *andra gateo*,[9] meaning to behave like an *able* man. There is a Mafia-type hierarchy in each *andrine or 'ndrina*—equivalent to a *cosca*—and members take a blood oath (Argentine 1993). Paoli (2003: 46) reports that *'ndrangheta* families, often called *locali* in Calabria, "have developed a complex system of ranks and power positions that clearly differentiates them from the biological families of their members."

Originally several bands that grew out of government repression, *'Ndrangheta* gained popular support because of its political stance against the central government. "In 1861, the new Italian government sent troops to police Calabria. The old

---

9. The Greek derivation may be from the word *andragaqos*, "brave man" (Paoli 1994).

POWER AND TREACHERY

When confronted with a power equal or superior to their own, southern Italian criminal entrepreneurs will conform to exchange-relationship norms. When they do not have to fear retaliation, expediency is likely to prevail. Thus, two 'ndranghesti made an arrangement with Turkish traffickers to deliver large quantities of heroin. When a large final payment became due, the Turkish couriers were murdered and their bodies disposed of through the use of a car wrecking compactor (Paoli 2003).

"THE WAGES OF SIN"

In 2008, 'Ndrangheta boss Giuseppe Coluccio was arrested in Canada and extradited back to Italy. In addition to jewelry and traveler checks, when he was arrested outside his luxury lakeside apartment building in Toronto, Coluccio possessed $1.5 million in Canadian currency ("Italy: Mafia Boss Returns to Rome Amid Tight Security" 2008).

economic order had collapsed under the strains of national unification, and the number of criminal groups had increased. Because of the government's deliberate policy of favoring the North over the South in its programs of economic development, and because of its ignorant and arrogant insensitivity to the customs of the South, Calabrese grew to hate the new Italian government and turned to the gangs who mixed political insurrection with banditry and were supported and romanticized by the repressed peasantry (Gambino 1974). But 'Ndrangheta had no positive program; its sense of social justice was basically destructive: "In such circumstances to assert power, any power, is itself a triumph. Killing and torture is the most primitive and personal assertion of ultimate power, and the weaker the rebel feels himself to be at bottom, the greater, we may suppose, the temptation to assert it" (Hobsbawm 1959: 56). Antonio Nicaso and Lee Lamothe (2005: 10) state that Calabria was a place where government interest or involvement was minimal and, therefore, "it was only natural that strong men—as in Sicily—emerge to effectively control citizen's activities."

The 'Ndrangheta, sometimes referred to as the "Calabrian Mafia," consists of 85 (Paoli 1994) to 144 (Snedden and Visser 1994) or 160 (de Gennaro 1995) andrine, some exceeding 200 members, with a combined membership of 5,000 to 6,000. Each group—'ndrina—exerts influence over a well-defined geographic area generally corresponding to a town or village, although the 'Ndrangheta now operates in cities of northern Italy and throughout much of Europe, wherever Calabrese have settled. They are particularly strong in Canada and Australia (Nicaso and Lamothe 2005; Paoli 1994). In larger areas such as Reggio, where two or more 'ndrina could be located, criminal functions are divided either by "turf" or by function. For example, one may control extortion while another will control drugs (Snedden and Visser 1994). The 'Ndrangheta, notes Varese (2011: 33) "is ultimately a loose federation of mafia families, most of which (eighty-six) operate in the province of Reggio Calabria in southern Calabria."

The 'Ndrangheta also collaborates with Sicilian and Neapolitan counterparts. Unlike these groups, however, 'Ndrangheta clans are based on blood ties, allowing for a high degree of internal cohesion that protects against informants. A chief with a large number of sons and men linked by direct kinship has more power in the criminal world, and members are less likely to betray one another (Paoli 2003). *Omertá* remains strong, and there are relatively few cooperating witnesses of Calabrian origin. Their violence is reminiscent of the cruel Colombian practice (see Chapter 6) of *no dejar la semilla* (don't leave the seed): Known as *fida*, all members, including women and children, of a victim's family are killed (Snedden and Visser 1994).

In contrast to the Sicilian Mafia and criminal organizations throughout the world, *'Ndrangheta* blood family and crime family membership overlap and a *'ndrine* for the most part is made of men belonging to the same family lineage (Varese 2011). At its core, a *'ndrina* is composed of one or two biological families and their network of artificial kinships. "In order to strengthen the cohesion of the inner nucleus, the practice of intermarriage between first cousins is strongly encouraged and marriages are also used to cement alliances with other groups in the immediate neighborhood" (Paoli 1994: 215). Loyalty is further promoted through the use of initiation ceremonies similar to those of the American Mafia, and *Malavita*, songs performed at important occasions such as the induction of a new member: "For over 100 years members of the Calabrian Mafia have developed and sung Malavita songs among themselves" (Strauss 2002: B1). These songs have now been recorded and are available on CDs throughout Europe (Ali 2002; Strauss 2002). *'Ndrangheta* women frequently play important roles, maintaining family traditions and even running family enterprises.

Like its Sicilian counterparts, *'Ndrangheta* has a commission that recognizes territorial hegemony and mediates disputes in an effort to reduce the high level of violence for which Calabrese are noted. *'Ndrangheta* bosses from as far as Canada and Australia—"the *'Ndrangheta* has had a remarkable ability to establish branches abroad" (Varese 2006: 42)—regularly attend annual meetings at the Calabrian Sanctuary of Our Lady in Polsi, an indication that the *'ndrine* around the world perceive themselves as being part of the same collective entity. In 2007, a feud between two *'Ndrangheta* clans spread to Germany where six Calabrese were murdered with shots to the head outside of a Duisburg pizzeria (Landler and Fisher 2007).

The organization exhibits its criminal skills mainly in kidnapping, vast-scale international arms and drug trafficking, extortion from almost all profit-making activities, and control of public contracts (de Gennaro 1995). Extortion inhibits legitimate investment and plays a significant role in the backwardness of the region. During the 1980s, ransom kidnappings provided capital for entry into large-scale drug trafficking. The most notorious was the 1970s abduction of John Paul Getty III, heir to the Getty oil fortune. Almost $3 million was paid for his return, but only after one of the youngster's ears was severed. The ear and a photo of the victim were sent to the family (Nicaso and Lamothe 2005). Many of these kidnappings were collaborative efforts between *'Ndrangheta*, Camorra, and Mafia groups (Siebert 1996). Ready access to the sea makes drug, as well as arms and cigarette, smuggling, relatively easy. Drug profits led to the purchase of large tracts of land and the opening of legitimate businesses, such as supermarkets, although not necessarily in Calabria (Paoli 1994). The growing of cannabis has become part of their portfolio, and the *'Ndrangheta* has links to Mexico's Gulf Cartel (discussed in Chapter 6) for the importation of cocaine (UNODC 2010b).

Like the Mafia, the *'Ndrangheta* has been active in provincial politics, but unlike the Mafia, until 2005 the *'Ndrangheta* avoided direct confrontations with the Italian state. In that year, they assassinated the vice president of the regional council (Capé 2005).

A mainstay of their criminal portfolio is the offer of protection. This practice is so routine that the competence of a corporate executive is judged by his capacity to obtain protection at the lowest possible price. The *'Ndrangheta* usually offers protection in return for specific benefits. Thus, a representative of a dominant local *'Ndrangheta* Family approached the administrator of a division of a multinational corporation running container port operations. For $2 million annually they would ensure the security of facilities and pleasant relations with port staff and unions; bureaucratic obstacles would be avoided and criminal activity would not be directed against the company (Sciarrone 2010).

In the area of public works, 'Ndrangheta capacity for intimidation ensures there are no bidders competing with their favored company and will organize collusive restraint of trade agreements that the 'Ndrangheta will police. When operating a legitimate business, the 'Ndrangheta reputation for violence provides an advantage over competitors (Sciarrone 2010).

SACRA CORONA UNITA AND THE ALBANIAN CONNECTION

The Puglia (Apulia) region at the heel of the Italian boot forms an elongated peninsula on the Adriatic and Ionian Seas. The *Sacra Corona Unita* (SCU), Sacred United Crown, evolved in the region already noted for Camorra and 'Ndrangheta activities. As the name suggests, the SCU uses a great deal of Roman Catholic imagery as part of its rituals. But despite these religious trappings, the SCU originated as a criminal organization. At the end of the 1970s and early 1980s, local criminal groups began patterning themselves on their elder Mafia and Camorra colleagues, eventually coalescing into the SCU. The origins of the SCU are traced to Giuseppe Rogoli who, while a prisoner serving a life sentence for murder, reportedly established the organization as a ritual brotherhood on Christmas day 1983 at least in part as a response to the expansionist plans of Camorra leader Raffaele Cutolo discussed earlier (Varese 2006; 2011).

The SCU is organized horizontally with a series of about forty-five autonomous clans accountable to the common interests of the organization (Hess et al. 1999). Total membership is estimated at about 2,000, and women often play important roles in its business operations. The SCU has close ties to the Balkans, particularly Albania, located just across the Strait of Otranto from Puglia. During World War II, Albania was occupied by Mussolini's Italy.

The Albanian Connection

Albania is a primarily Muslim nation with a population of about 3.5 million, slightly smaller than Maryland. Albania declared its independence from the Ottoman Empire in 1912. The country was conquered by Italy in 1939, but Communist partisans took over in 1944. Albania allied itself first with the Soviet Union (until 1960), and then with China (to 1978). A mostly mountainous country with small plains along its long coastline on the Adriatic Sea, Albania is distinguished by its strong sense of familial and clan ties; the country's criminal groups (*fis*) have much in common with their southern Italian colleagues, including the concepts of *omertá* and *famiglia*. Albanian tradition includes absolute loyalty to the extended family and clan, known as *fare*, and the notion of *bessa* requires total respect for verbal promises (Nicaso and Lamothe 2005).

The typical Albanian extended family may well have up to 60 core members and 150 surrounding relatives. Many Albanian men can identify relatives of the seventh to tenth degree and expect to be able to rely on them if they need support in either licit or illicit businesses. As in Sicily and Calabria, Albanian groups place family and community interests and values first even at the expense of the interests of the larger society and in defiance of state law. Their willingness to take up arms to defend such interests and their resulting reputation for violence constitute further comparative advantages for Albanian criminals (Paoli and Reuter 2008).

Organized crime has its roots in the traditional clan structure-based familial ties for protection and mutual assistance. Dating back to the fifteenth century, clan relationships operate under the *kanun*, or code, which values loyalty, and *besa*, or secrecy. Each clan is established in specific territories and controls all activities in that territory. Protection of activities and interests often led to violence between the clans. The elements inherent in the structure of the clans provided the perfect backbone for modern-day Balkan organized crime. *Kanun* remains strong, continuing a tradition of blood feuds (Bilefsky 2008). The *kanun* sets up the rules upon which the traditional ethnic Albanian culture is based, primarily focusing on the concept of honor. Until 1913, the *kanun* was an oral tradition when a Franciscan priest from Kosovo started codifying the laws (Arsovska and Kostakos 2008).

Albanian culture places enormous emphasis on the importance of firearms; male honor is closely linked to the possession of firearms and the courage to use them (Arsovska and Verduyn 2008; Arsovska 2007). It is believed that a man who is disarmed is a man who is dishonored—death would be preferable (SEESAC 2006: 7). A Southern Albanian proverb says, "You can kill an Albanian, but you cannot make him give up his gun."

From 1944 to 1985, Albania was ruled by a Stalinist communist regime that supported a powerful, well-equipped army. In 1997, a violent response to a massive pyramid scheme in which many Albanians lost all their savings led to a complete breakdown of law and order. In the midst of this anarchy, one million light weapons and 1.5 billion rounds of ammunition became available on the black market. Many were transferred from Albania to Kosovo and Macedonia where they ended up in the hands of Albanian nationalists, the Kosovo Liberation Army, the Albanian National Army, and the National Liberation Army, participating in the ethnic violence that resulted from the breakup of the former Yugoslavia.

Since 1992, ethnic Albanian organized crime groups have profited greatly from instability and war in the Balkans to become the fastest growing ethnic criminal presence in Europe, with operations reaching as far as Australia and the United States (LaVerle et al. 2003). Albanian influence in the *Mezzogiorno* dates back to the migration of Albanians driven from their country by the Ottoman invasion in the fifteenth century. Known as *arbresheri*, many settled in Calabria and Sicily where they quickly integrated with the existing culture of southern Italy (Bequai 1979).

Once the most isolated country in Europe, Albania became a haven for local and foreign criminal groups after the collapse of its Stalinist regime in the early 1990s. "During the communist years, the Fifteen Families—fifteen *fis*—had controlled organized criminal activities in Albania, primarily through smuggling and corruption. But with the collapse of the communist government and the military, the Fifteen Families were in essence the only groups that didn't descend into anarchy and chaos" (Nicaso and Lamothe 2005: 187). Albanians suffered a classical form of anomie: "A social disorganization of the entire society ensued. Organized social life, as it used to be under communism, was now outdated; yet the new societal behavior was not yet in place" (Gjoni 2004: 2). From the firm hand of Stalinesque communism to unbridled freedom—anarchy—criminal groups quickly filled the power vacuum. Most of these groups are small and flexible—less than a half-dozen members—and the death or incarceration of a leader will often cause the members to disperse and join other groups. A few are larger—fifteen to twenty members—and have a more hierarchical structure resembling that of the Sicilian Mafia. Even when these groups operate on a transnational basis, they prefer to reside in Albania where they benefit from a weak and corrupt justice system (Gjoni 2004).

The opening of the country's borders and political disarray have allowed Albania to become a primary alternative to traditional Balkan smuggling routes through the former Yugoslavia that were disrupted by the breakout of ethnic fighting in the early 1990s. Taking advantage of a weak central government and a great deal of political chaos, SCU clans were quick to establish a presence in Albania, linking up with local criminal groups.

Massive migration of Albanians abroad during the 1990s and the drastic increase of the Albanian Diaspora in the United States, Canada, and Europe provided a perfect cover for Albanian criminals who brought with them a strong sense of extended family. Similar to the culture of the *Mezzogiorno*, "family interests and values are put first and pursued even at the expense of the interests of the larger collectivities and in defiance of state rules" (Paoli and Reuter 2008: 26).

The major source of income for Albanian crime groups is derived from trafficking in economic migrants, women, children, drugs, contraband, weapons, and automobiles. "Albania is an origin and transit country and the criminal elements

---

WE'VE HAD ENOUGH

In 2008, in Bari, capital city of the Puglia region, at a rally of as many as 100,000 persons, politicians and anti-Mafia leaders shouted *"basta!"*—enough (Forte 2008).

---

take advantage of the instability, corruption and lack of organization and resources of the Albanian law enforcement entities. Illicit funds are being laundered back into Albania from abroad to purchase and develop choice properties suspiciously acquired during the privatization program" (Gjoni 2004: 15).

In neighboring Yugoslavia, ethnic Albanian crime Families were looking to widen their drug, prostitution, and weapons smuggling rings. Some dispatched lieutenants to countries such as Italy, Germany, and Slovakia. Their criminal endeavors eventually intersected with activities of the Kosovo Liberation Army (KLA), whose guerrillas since 1998 have fought for independence for Kosovo's 1.8 million ethnic Albanians. In this struggle against Serbian anti-Albanian policies, Kosovo's Albanians developed a strong ethnic conscience, a sense of collective identity that facilitated their ability to engage in organized crime. It also encouraged links between Albanian organized crime, Albanian ideals, politics, military activities, and terrorism. Albanian drug lords established elsewhere in Europe supported the independence cause (LaVerle et al. 2003). In 2008, Kosovo, despite Serbian and Russian opposition, declared its independence from Serbia.

Being a rather recent phenomenon not as strong as the Mafia or Camorra, SCU leaders apparently decided to join forces rather than run the risk of a conflict with Albanian groups who are known to be extremely violent. As a result, in certain areas of Italy, the market for cannabis, prostitution, and the smuggling of illegal immigrants is run mainly by Albanians. The U.S. State Department (2010: 58) reports that "Albania is a source country for men, women, and children subjected to trafficking in persons, specifically forced prostitution and forced

labor, including the forced begging of children. Albanian victims are subjected to conditions of forced labor and sex trafficking within Albania and Greece, Italy, Macedonia, Kosovo, and Western Europe."

"As the Albanian groups continue to proliferate, the SCU has been there to support them in joint venture opportunities such as the trade of weapons and drugs" (Hess et al. 1999: 390). The SCU is behind the smuggling of thousands of Albanians into Italy, including Albanian women sold into prostitution. Macedonia, which borders on Albania, has become a major center of the European sex trade (Gall 2001).

A crackdown in Sicily led hundreds of *mafiosi* to relocate to the Albanian coastal town of Vlorë, and their Albanian counterparts are found throughout Italy (Cilluffo and Salmoiraghi 1999). Albanian criminals frequently reside in Calabria, indicating ties to the 'Ndrangheta. With its strategic position on the Adriatic, the SCU is able to provide smuggling services to the Mafia, Camorra, and 'Ndrangheta. They routinely use Albania's long and now virtually unguarded coastline as a staging area for smuggling drugs—Southwest Asian heroin, hashish, and, to a lesser extent, cocaine—arms, and other contraband across the Adriatic Sea to Italy. There are also ties between the SCU, Colombian cartels, Russian, and Southeast and Southwest Asian criminal groups.

Albanian criminals are also involved in the traffic of illegal immigrants to Western Europe—not only Albanians, but also Kurds, Chinese, and people from the Indian subcontinent. Albanian groups are mainly responsible for the crossing of the Adriatic Sea from the Albanian coast to Italy. From Italy, illegal immigrants are transported by allied criminal groups such as the SCU. Besides being a source of income, immigration is important in creating networks in foreign countries, establishing bridgeheads for the Albanian Mafia abroad. Reports indicate that some of the people admitted into Western Europe or North America as refugees during the Kosovo conflict had been carefully chosen by the Albanian Mafia to stay in the host country and act as a future liaison for the criminal networks (Hess et al. 1999; National Security Council and Interpol information).

A 2011 federal indictment unsealed in Brooklyn, New York, revealed a syndicate comprised several interrelated ethnic Albanian family clans (*fis*) with hundreds of associated members, workers, and customers spanning three continents. In operation for more than a decade, the syndicate had established connections with Mexican and Colombian drug traffickers, allowing them to import and distribute of tens of thousands of kilograms of hydroponic marijuana from Canada and Mexico, substantial quantities of MDMA from the Netherlands and Canada, hundreds of kilograms of cocaine from Mexico, Colombia, Venezuela and Peru, and large quantities of diverted prescription pills, such as oxycodone. The drugs were distributed in various locations in the United States, including New York, California, Georgia, Colorado, and Florida, as well as in Canada and Europe.

Now that we have examined the criminal organizations of Italy and Albania, in the next chapter we will cross the Atlantic to Latin America.

SUMMARY

1. Appreciate the unique history of southern Italy and how it led to the development of four types of criminal organizations:
   - The southern Italian experience led to the development of a culture that stresses the variables necessary for survival in a hostile environment, *omertá and vendetta,* in which the only basis of loyalty is *famiglia.*
   - The family was organized hierarchically, headed by the family patriarch.
   - The *Mezzogiorno,* lags far behind northern Italy in economic development.
   - Unification of Italy was harmful to the south as the new government issued edict after edict that affected the southerners adversely. This history led to the development of different types of criminal organization: Mafia, Camorra, 'Ndrangheta, and more recently, *Sacra Corona Unita.*
2. Understand the role of criminal organizations in southern Italy:
   - These criminal organizations act as brokers between politicians and businessmen and between businessmen and union officials.
   - Evildoers have to leave the *mafioso* alone, along with all the persons or things to which, explicitly or implicitly, he had given a guarantee of security. As a man of respect, he is in a position to provide protection where the state is unwilling or unable.
   - The *mafioso* provides legitimate entrepreneurs with insurance against otherwise untrustworthy suppliers or customers and offers himself as a guarantor for business transactions.
3. Know how Mussolini influenced both the Sicilian and American Mafia:
   - Mussolini used police-state powers to move against the Mafia, and many fled to the United States where Prohibition was in force.
   - The post-World War II *Nuovo Mafia* has adopted the patterns and the dress of the American Mafia and entered the drug market, which was an anathema to the old Mafia.
4. Be able to distinguish between the traditional Mafia and the *Nuovo Mafia:*
   - The *mafioso* is no longer *un uomo di rispetto* but simply an urban gangster in the

American tradition, a predatory criminal without popular roots or popular backing.

- With *mafiosi* lacking popular support in Sicily, the government moved vigorously against them.
- The *Nuovo Mafia* has responded with attacks on public officials.

5. Know the differences between Mafia and Camorra:
   - Whereas the Mafia began as more of an idea than an organization and evolved along cultural lines in rural western Sicily, the Camorra was deliberately structured as an urban-based criminal society.
   - Camorra groups began to emerge as soon as the Allied forces withdrew. They asserted control over agriculture and cattle markets and moved into the urban areas of Naples to further their control over these markets. They moved into and expanded upon the Naples contraband industry, from cigarettes to drugs.
   - A huge program of reconstruction was effectively hijacked by corrupt politicians, government bureaucrats, and the Camorra, which diversified its wealth from drug trafficking by moving into the construction industry.
   - Camorra clans control apparently legal commercial activities through which they introduce counterfeit goods, creating a significant economic-financial web involving a variety of countries. They have had remarkable success in the manufacture of counterfeit designer clothing and consumer electronics.
   - Camorra clans form alliances, often cemented by marriages, their enterprises mixing legitimate business, such as construction, with illegitimate, such as drug and arms trafficking.
   - At the center of a typical Camorra group is a boss whose group is known by his surname, such as the *Alfieri* headed by Carmine Alfieri.
   - Territorial control is essential to Camorra clans as a way of asserting domination over a geographic area and extorting from legitimate businesses; it also provides an opportunity for those on the lower rungs to prove themselves and thereby move up in Camorra ranks.
   - Like the Sicilian Mafia, Camorra leaders have engaged in violent struggles.

6. Appreciate differences between Mafia and *'Ndrangheta*:
   - The province of Calabria is located in the far south of the Italian "boot" and is home to *'Ndrangheta*.
   - *Ndrangheta* clans are based on blood ties, allowing for a high degree of internal cohesion which protects against informants.
   - *Omertá* remains strong, and there are relatively few cooperating witnesses of Calabrian origin.

7. Understand the development of the *Sacra Corona Unita* and its ties to Albania and Albanian criminal organizations:
   - The Puglia region at the heel of the Italian boot is home to the *Sacra Corona Unita* (SCU), Sacred United Crown.
   - Despite the Roman Catholic imagery it uses as part of its rituals, the SCU originated as a criminal organization in 1983 by an inmate serving a life sentence.
   - Albania, a primarily Muslim nation was occupied by Italy in 1939.
   - A mostly mountainous country with small plains along its long coastline, Albania is distinguished by its strong sense of familial and clan ties, and the country's criminal groups have much in common with their southern Italian colleagues with whom they are sometimes allied.
   - Their reputation for violence and obsession with firearms provides comparative advantages for Albanian criminals.
   - Many Albanians settled in Calabria and Sicily where they quickly integrated with the existing culture of southern Italy.
   - Massive migration of Albanians abroad provided a perfect cover for Albanian criminals who brought with them a strong sense of extended family.

REVIEW QUESTIONS

1. How did Italian unification affect the *Mezzogiorno*?
2. What aspects of Southern Italian culture led to the development of the Mafia?
3. How does a *mafioso* act as a broker?
4. What is the guarantor role of a *mafioso*?
5. How did Mussolini's rise to power in the 1920s impact both the Sicilian and American Mafia?
6. How does the *Nuova Mafia* differ from the old Mafia?
7. How do the Mafia and Camorra differ?
8. What are the characteristics of *'Ndrangheta*?
9. What are the similarities between the Camorra and *Sacra Corona Unita* (SCU)?
10. Why does the SCU have close ties to Albania?
11. What aspects of Albanian culture are suited to organized crime?
12. What led to the international expansion of Albanian organized crime?

Arrested Sinaloa cartel gunmen and their weapons cache.   © AP Photo/Gregory Bull/Corbis

Latin American Organized Crime

On July 21, 2011, the U.S. Department of Justice announced that almost 2,000 persons have been arrested by federal agents on narcotics-related charges as part of a twenty-month multi-agency law enforcement investigation known as Project Delirium. The operation targeted the *La Familia Michoacana* drug cartel, an organization noted for its extreme level of violence even as contrasted with other violent Mexican drug organizations.

Through their violent drug trafficking activities, including their hallmark of supplying most of the methamphetamine imported into the United States, *La Familia* is responsible for recklessly and violently destroying countless lives on both sides of the border. Federal agents also seized $770,499,635 pounds of methamphetamine, 118 kilograms of cocaine, and 24 pounds of heroin (FBI press release, July 21, 2011).

La Familia and the other notable Mexican drug cartels will be discussed in this chapter.

CHAPTER 6 WILL ENABLE THE READER TO UNDERSTAND:

- How the history and culture of Colombia influenced the development of drug trafficking organizations
- The role of left- and right-wing organizations in drug trafficking
- The structure of Colombian drug trafficking organizations
- Changes that occurred since the collapse of the Medellín and Cali drug cartels
- Mexican history and the connection between politics, corruption, and drug trafficking
- The structure and business operations of Mexican drug organizations
- What led to the extreme violence that pervades Mexico
- The role of Dominican organizations in the drug business
- The role of MS-13
- The history of the prison-based Mexican Mafia and its expansion beyond the institution

A common element that characterizes criminal organizations examined in this chapter is extensive, if not exclusive, involvement in drug trafficking. "Narcotics and drug traffic have the same pattern of relationship which surrounded alcohol and bootlegging during the Prohibition era" (Ianni 1974: 320). If anything positive can be said for the drug business, it is that trafficking is *an equal opportunity employer* (Durk and Silverman 1976).

As noted in Chapter 1, a criminal organization can exhibit a formal structure while its economic activities may actually involve partnerships among members and nonmember associates. This is often the case with outlaw motorcycle clubs and the American Mafia. In contrast, the income-producing activities of many Latino organized crime groups are integrated into a bureaucratic structure devoid of the substantial subcultural traditions that distinguish the Sicilian Mafia and outlaw motorcycle clubs.

In the United States, most Latino organized crime groups import their criminal organizations along with the drugs they sell. Most prominent among them are groups based in Colombia and Mexico.

COLOMBIA

Colombia, with a mostly urban population of more than 44 million, is noted for the quality of its coffee exports and is the primary supplier of cut flowers for the United States. It also controls most of the world's cocaine industry. Colombia is the only South American country with both Pacific and Caribbean coastlines. The high Andes divide the country into four ranges, with most of Colombia's population concentrated in green valleys and mountain basins that lie between the Andes ranges. Travel between populated areas is difficult (Buckman 2004). Prior to the initiation of "Plan Colombia" in 2000, which provided billions of dollars in U.S. aid, half of Colombia didn't have a government security presence (Roma 2011).

Colombia has been torn by political strife, with three civil wars during the nineteenth century and two in the twentieth (1902 and 1948). The 1948–1958 civil war between wealthy landowners and poor *campesinos* is known as *La Violencia*, and cost the lives of about 300,000 persons (Griswold 2005; Riding 1987a). Most of the deaths were from atrocities and vengeance killings, not the result of conflict between armed forces. It was touched off by the assassination of the popular Liberal mayor of Bogotá in the street before thousands of his supporters. The assassin was immediately lynched, and three days of rioting ensued. The war officially ended when the Liberals and the Conservatives formed the National Front. (The names of the parties do not correlate to the ideological meanings these words have in the U.S. political vernacular [Bruce and Hayes 2010].) Nevertheless, Marxist insurgencies and right-wing paramilitaries continue to threaten the stability of the central government. *La Violencia* "debased the incipient development of judicial and police apparatuses, as well as the moral foundations of political action" (Palacios 2007: 138).

In Colombia, drug traffickers exemplify a lack of belief in the legitimacy of the country's political and economic institutions. When citizens doubt the fairness of their country's political and economic institutions, even if they do not themselves violate the law, they become more accepting of its violation by others (Villarreal 2002). "Breaking the law—any law—is justified, and not just for the usual economic reasons that criminals favor. For traffickers, the law, law-enforcement officials, U.S. drug operatives, and drug-control organizations all represent the traditional elite, international imperialism, or other international competitive economic interests, none of which has any historical moral standing in their eyes. Therefore, moralistic arguments about restraining violent behavior do not capture these people's attention [and] allows traffickers to garner enthusiastic support in some areas" (Tullis 1995: 66).

Murders occur frequently and often with sadistic methods, such as the *corte de corbata*—the infamous "Colombian necktie"—in which the victim's throat is cut longitudinally and the tongue pulled through to hang like a tie. Another practice, *no dejar la semilla* ("don't leave the seed"), includes the castration of male victims and the execution of women and children (Wolfgang and Ferracuti 1967): "In Colombia, it wasn't enough to hurt or even kill your enemy; there was a ritual to be observed." Rape had to be performed before family members. "And before you killed a man, you first made him beg, scream, and gag ... or first you killed those he most loved before his eyes. To amplify fear, victims were horribly mutilated and left on display.... Children were killed not by accident but slowly, with pleasure" (Bowden 2001: 14).

"At the root of Colombia's easy violence is an extraordinary indifference toward death" (Romoli 1941: 37). The homicide rate is eight times higher than that of the United States. Murder is the leading cause of death for Colombian males aged 15 to 44 (Schemo 1997a). The country has the highest child murder rates in the world—street children kill each other, and hundreds are murdered by vigilante groups as part of their campaign of "social cleansing" (Luft 1995a; Palacios 2007).

In this sociopolitical atmosphere, bandits have roamed freely, engaging in a combination of brigandage, terrorism, and revolution. In the northern cities of Barranquilla and Santa Marta and in the La Guajira peninsula, which juts out into the Caribbean, smuggling groups (*contrabandista*) have operated for decades. Bandits, *contrabandistas*, and Guajiran Indians, often backed and financed by businessmen in Bogotá, emerged as crime Families, or a *narcomafia*. Members are often related by blood, marriage, or *compadrazgo* (fictional kinship), and in many important respects the core groups resemble those of the Sicilian Mafia, except that Colombian groups are sometimes headed by women. When President Richard Nixon declared a "war on drugs" in 1972, the United States succeeded in shutting down the flow of marijuana from Mexico. Encouraged by drug entrepreneurs from the United States, four years after Nixon's success on the Mexican border, marijuana was being widely cultivated in Barranquilla, Santa Marta, and La Guajira for the U.S. market (Paternostro 2007).

In a country where drug barons act as a state within a state, dozens of well-armed paramilitary groups "ply their murderous trade in the cities and countryside, sometimes selling themselves to the highest bidder as outmanned and intimidated judges and government officials feel helpless to stop them" (de Lama 1988a: 5; also Duzán 1994). These paramilitaries are sometimes allied with—sometimes fighting against—the drug traffickers, and they receive financial backing from wealthy landowners. Indeed, paramilitary leaders have become wealthy landowners themselves by making the rightful owners an offer that cannot be safely refused. The land is then registered in the names of third parties (Forero 2004f).

Colombian Drug Trafficking

When Fidel Castro overthrew the corrupt dictatorial regime of Fulgencio Batista early in 1959, he expelled American gangsters who operated gambling casinos in Havana. Many of their Cuban associates fled to the United States, along with *narcotraficantes* who had distributed cocaine in Cuba. They settled primarily in the New York, New Jersey, and Miami areas and began to look for new sources of income. Many Cubans who fled with, or soon after, the Batista loyalists were organized and trained by the Central Intelligence Agency (CIA) in an effort to dislodge Castro. After the Bay of Pigs debacle in 1961, members of the CIA-organized Cuban exile army were supposed to disband and go into lawful businesses. However, as Donald Goddard (1978: 44) points out, "They had no lawful business." Elements of these exile groups began to enter the cocaine business. At first they imported only enough cocaine to satisfy members of their own community, but by the mid-1960s the market had expanded way beyond the Cuban community, and so they began to import the substance in greater quantities.

Until the early 1970s, the importation of marijuana and cocaine into the United States was largely a Cuban operation, although the suppliers were Colombians. During the latter half of the 1960s, Colombians began immigrating to the United States in numbers sufficient to establish communities in Miami, Chicago, Los Angeles, and New York. Many were illegal immigrants who entered the

United States through the Bahamas carrying false documents such as phony Puerto Rican birth certificates and forged immigration papers of high quality.

The Colombian traffickers became highly organized both in the United States and at home, and by 1973 independent foreign nationals could no longer "deal drugs" in Colombia. In 1976, the Colombians became dissatisfied with their Cuban agents in the United States, who were reportedly making most of the profits and shortchanging the Colombians. Enforcers, often young men from Colombia's version of the "Wild West," La Guajira, or from Barrio Antioquia, the slums of Medellín, were sent in and systematically executed Cubans

in Miami and New York. By 1978, Cubans remaining in the cocaine business had become subordinate to the Colombians. Then the cocaine wars between rival Colombians began, bringing terror to South Florida.

Colombians have been able to control the cocaine market for a number of reasons. The President's Commission on Organized Crime (1986a: 78–79) notes, "Colombia is well-positioned both to receive coca from Peru and Bolivia and to export the processed drug to the United States by air or by sea" (see Figure 6.1). And "the country's vast central forests effectively conceal clandestine processing laboratories and air strips, which facilitate the traffic." The Colombians "have a momentum by

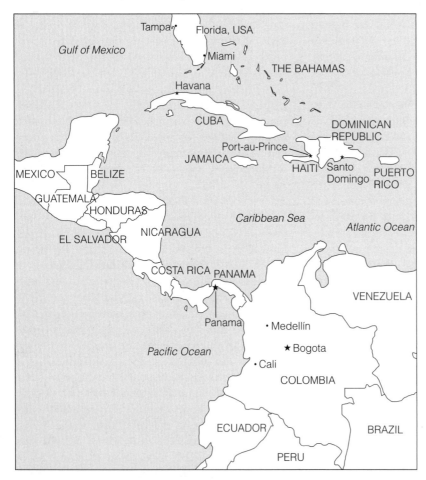

F I G U R E 6.1 Map of Northern Latin America, Colombia

benefit of their early involvement in the cocaine trade. "In 1968, in an attempt to bolster its domestic economic performance, Colombia proudly established the Institute of Advanced Chemical Research in Bogotá, which started to train top-class chemists, who were later to find lucrative work in the employ of the Medellín and Cali cartels" (Glenny 2008: 245).

The Colombian reputation for and propensity to use violence serves to maintain discipline, intimidate would-be competitors, and led to the domination of potential Bolivian and Peruvian rivals in the cocaine business. It permitted Colombian cartels to face down attempts at intimidation by other criminal organizations. On several occasions, the Sicilian Mafia tried to acquire the monopoly of the European cocaine market, unsuccessfully challenging the Colombians. During the 1990s, ties between the Cali cartel and Italian Mafia Families were revealed (Chepesiuk 2003).

The economic modernization of Colombia failed to bring about a corresponding respect for government. Delegitimization of government and *La Violencia* "left legacies which have worked to permit, if not encourage, the development of the cocaine industry" (Thoumi 1995: 84). Delegitimization spurred the development of smuggling, particularly export of products out of Colombia and into Venezuela and Ecuador—cattle, emeralds, coffee—that provided experience in the contraband trade and money laundering. The drug trade "melded with a preexisting illegal trade in emeralds" (Palacios 2007: 197). Aside from their disdain for Colombian institutions and their long criminal records, Colombian traffickers share other characteristics. "They appear to be great believers in fate and providence and seem unmoved by normal considerations of personal danger. It is a perspective unaltered by normal law-enforcement efforts and one that makes dealing with or trying to control them such a dangerous enterprise" (Tullis 1995: 67). Speculative capitalism, focus on very high short-term profits—a feature of Colombia's financial elite—provided the resources for development of a cocaine industry (Thoumi 1995).

Colombia is a relatively large country, and many regions have only a weak federal presence. "While Colombian authorities built suburbs and major highways between cities, they ignored vast sections of the country; much of rural Colombia is isolated by hilly, trackless terrain" (Duzán 1994: 63). During the 1960s, the government encouraged Colombians to move into the remote southern province of Caquetá. There, farmers used slash and burn tactics to clear the land and plant subsistence crops. But an absence of adequate roads delayed marketing until the 1980s when the drug cartels persuaded them to grow coca. In the 1990s, when international pressure caused a reduction in coca planting in Bolivia and Peru, Colombian coca provided a readily available alternative (Villalón 2004) and Colombian coca accounted for about 80 percent of the cocaine reaching the United States (Marquis and Forero 2004).

In the south, three steep Andean ranges run the length of Colombia, dividing impenetrable jungle. Government presence is concentrated in the cities of the Andean mountains and is essentially nonexistent in southern Colombia and marine outlets that provide access to both the Caribbean Sea and the Pacific Ocean. "The government didn't lose control of this half of Colombia; it never had it" (Robinson 1998a: 39). The vacuum left by the central government has proved ideal for coca cultivation and cocaine manufacture because it left areas where only local officials had to be bribed—a cheaper and less risky action (Thoumi 1995). With the collapse of the Medellín and Cali cartels (discussed later), Marxist guerilla forces saw an opportunity.

The Politics of Dope

Drug money entered Colombia freely through the "ask no questions" attitude of the central bank and through unregulated currency exchanges. This movement of money was stimulated by periodic tax amnesties, and money was laundered though the purchase of rural and urban real estate and contraband imports—some of it "ended up in the increasingly costly campaigns of Colombian politicians" (Palacious 2007: 198).

In remote jungle areas where coca is cultivated, Marxist guerilla forces of the Revolutionary Armed

Forces of Colombia (FARC) protect the crops and levy taxes on the drug business. According to the Drug Enforcement Administration (Mulvey 2008), FARC is organized hierarchically with a seven-member secretariat and a twenty-seven-member central general staff, or *Estado Mayor*. At the bottom of the hierarchy are seventy-seven distinct military units—called fronts—organized by their geographical location. Clusters of fronts form seven blocs, each led by a bloc commander. Government successes against and defections from FARC have considerably weakened the organization, whose membership is estimated to be between 8,000 to 10,000 (Nir and Romero 2011).

FARC continues to be effective against Colombia's poorly trained and motivated conscript army. Members of the Colombian military, often those trained by the United States, have been involved in the widespread human rights abuses that generate support for the rebels and drug

FARC commander who was asked to give his towel to a Colombian museum. Colombian peasants traditionally carry a towel to wipe sweat.

traffickers (Schemo and Golden 1998). Attempts to eradicate the coca crop have encountered stiff opposition from the subsistence farmers, for whom coca is an economic lifeline ("Anti-Drug Efforts Encounter Resistance in Colombia" 1995).

At the end of 1998, in an effort to advance peace negotiations with the guerillas, the Colombian government evacuated its security forces from a swath of central Colombia the size of Switzerland. There, FARC acts as a "labor organizer in the coca fields, keeping the price of a bushel up while taking a hefty percentage from the farmers" (Howe 2000: 38). In FARC-controlled areas, the economy is built on coca, and coca paste often serves as the local currency. Paper currency is in short supply, so "it is not unusual for people to be paid for their work in coca. They, in turn, pay for the necessities with the paste, which is soft and powdery like flour" (Forero 2001h: Sec. 4: 12). The traffickers buy the paste, process it into cocaine, and ship it by the ton to the United States, while FARC taxes the trade. "To prevent narcotraffickers from ripping off farmers, the rebels set a minimum price for a kilo of coca paste. They also tax the traffickers for protection of smuggling routes, the use of clandestine runways, the importation of cocaine-processing chemicals, and the export of every kilo of refined cocaine shipped from the region" (Semple 2001a: 61).

By 2002, it became apparent that FARC had no intention of arriving at a negotiated end to the hostilities, and the government demanded that the guerillas vacate the demilitarized zone. When they refused, hostilities resumed. Subsequent military success against FARC reduced its capability and forced a retreat, leaving them and their peasant supporters more vulnerable to right-wing paramilitaries (Bruce and Hayes 2010).

Right-wing paramilitaries who often receive assistance from wealthy landowners, ranchers, and the Colombian military are part of a loose-knit coalition called the United Self-Defense Forces of Colombia (AUC). About 13,000 strong, they are fighting Marxist guerillas for control of poppy- and coca-producing regions. Ranchers who had been under siege from the guerillas helped transform this small group of outlaws into a formidable army (Forero 2001d). The major banana importer, Chiquita Brands, was fined $25 million by the United States for making payments to the AUC. The paramilitaries control several northern states that contain major drug trafficking routes, and they are aligned with one of the country's most notorious drug cartels, the Norte del Valle group (Forero 2004a, 2004b, 2004d, 2004e). One of the paramilitaries consists of about 8,000 uniformed, well-trained, and well-armed men who regularly do battle against leftist guerrillas. Their methods are characterized by their nickname, "The Headcutters." Victims—anyone believed collaborating with leftists—are frequently kidnapped and usually found decapitated.

Operating out of the foothills of the Sierra Nevadas is another paramilitary group, *Los Chamizos* (Charred Trees), who routinely kill suspected leftists, including university professors, student activists, and trade unionists (Forero 2001f). Between 1985 and 2008, more than 2,500 union members were killed because of their involvement in the labor movement—the paramilitaries are believed responsible (Romero 2008a). *Los Chamizos* are reputed to control a drug syndicate that annually exports more than $1 billion worth of cocaine to the United States and Europe, but is not adverse to other means of raising money. In 1995, they kidnapped a wealthy local businessman and demanded a $1 million ransom. After the money was delivered, the victim was shot and his body carved up with chain saws. Three years later, they abducted the victim's widow and demanded a ransom of $5 million. After the money was delivered, she met the same fate as her husband.[1]

The militias have proven more effective against the guerillas than government forces, and this has endeared them to elements of the population at risk. The militias have reinforced this support by building roads and schools in the areas from which they have driven the guerillas (Forero 2001d). "Through its infiltration of Colombian institutions, including the security forces, regional governments and even Congress, the group has a level of power that even the most notorious drug trafficker, the late Pablo Escobar [discussed later], never had" (Forero 2004f).

In exchange for not being prosecuted, beginning in 2003, paramilitary leaders agreed to disarm, and many turned to politics to maintain power. They have elected governors and mayors across northern Colombia by bribing, murdering, or intimidating opposing candidates and boast of having influence over one-third of the Colombian congress (Forero 2005d). In some areas, their candidates succeed by winning more than 90 percent of the votes or run unopposed. The militias are also being reshaped into criminal networks that traffic in cocaine, smuggle cheap subsidized petrol from Venezuela, extort from businesses, and loot local governments (Forero 2006). Some have adopted exotic names—Black Eagles (*Aguilas Negras*) and New Generation Organization (*Organización Nueva Generación*—ONG). While there is no consensus on what the new groups actually are and to what extent they continue the AUC, which is a U.S. State Department-designated foreign terrorist organization, and although all are involved criminal activity, organization and modus operandi vary from region to region. Some are made up of paramilitaries who did not demobilize, while others are commanded by former mid-ranking AUC leaders who took up arms again. Still others are the armed wing of drug-trafficking organizations that have existed for years. Some, such as the ONG, continue the tradition of wearing military-style uniforms, while others, such as the Black Eagles, prefer civilian garb (*Colombia's New Armed Groups* 2007).

A gold rush in Colombia is providing an additional source of revenue for armed groups on the right and the left, who at times work together "illustrating the post-ideological nature of today's conflict" (Romero 2011: 1, 3). With the recent upsurge in the price of gold and the success of coca eradication efforts, former-militias groups and FARC have turned their attention to gold mining. Unlike cocaine, gold is a legal product, and while they have long been involved in mining, it typically involved money laundering and extortion.

---

1. Kidnapping is a major source of funds for both right- and left-wing groups, as well as common criminals in Colombia.

Colombian headquarters: The drug lord oversees operations through designates who are responsible for regional directors. He will also have a staff responsible for Colombian operations including production, transportation, distribution, finances, and enforcement. Each of his employees is given a code number a record of which is kept at headquarters.

Regional director: Responsible for overall operations of the several cells within a region, the regional director reports via cell phone, fax, or email to a designate in Colombia. They have discretion in the day-to-day operations, but ultimate authority rests with the leadership in Colombia.

Cell: Compartmentalization involves cells of ten or more members, each operating independently—members of one cell typically do not know members of other cells. Upper echelon and management levels of these cells are normally comprised of family members or longtime close associates who can be trusted because their family members remain in Colombia as hostages to the cell members' good behavior. Operating within a geographic area, each cell specializes in a particular facet of the drug business, such as transport, storage, wholesale distribution, or money laundering. The head of each cell reports directly to a regional director.

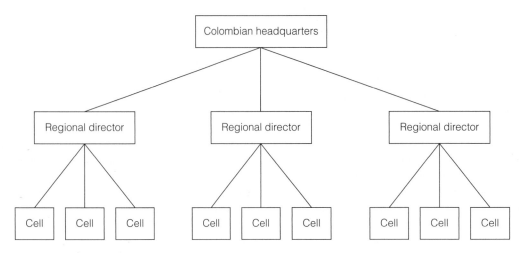

F I G U R E 6.2 Compartmentalized Colombian Drug Organization

Colombian Drug Trafficking Organizations

The term *cartel* identifies a criminal network whose structure resembles that of a holding company: a collection of flexible groups with senior managers responsible for coordinating cartel operations (Glenny 2008). The cartels are compartmentalized (see Figure 6.2) to control each intermediate step required in processing and exporting cocaine. Each cartel contains various sections with a separate function, such as manufacturing, transportation, distribution, finance, and security. This bureaucratic structure not only promotes greater efficiency, but it also protects the organization: "Few members of one section are aware of the others involved, and

the loss of one member or even a whole section does not threaten the stability of the entire organization" (PCOC 1984c: 562). In fact, at the lower levels of organization there are workers who move between one organization and another and are often unaware of which organization they are working for at any given time. At the highest levels, members are insulated from the physical operations of their organizations. "The money generated by the wholesale cocaine transaction is maintained for the organization by financial experts familiar with international banking and investing drug profits, and for assuring that a portion of the drug profit is returned to Colombia for reinvestment in the organization's cocaine enterprise. The cartel's own financial experts are supported by a complement of bankers, lawyers, and other professionals in the United States, who play a crucial role in facilitating these transactions" (PCOC 1986a: 82).

In the United States, cartel representatives act as brokers to coordinate deliveries to the various drug networks, usually a hundred kilos at a time, franchising others, particularly Dominican organizations (discussed later) and, to a lesser extent, Jamaican posses (discused in Chapter 7), to distribute drugs. Colombian distribution networks are informally structured and operate in a fluid, transactional manner. Often, a network will develop solely to distribute a single shipment of cocaine. The network may operate from six months to one year and then dissolve. Although structurally independent of the cartels, these distribution networks are symbiotic and in regular contact with their cartel sources. "While the main organizers are hand-picked by the Colombian traffickers, individual members of the same network seldom know one another and usually deal with one another only on a single occasion. Each drug transaction is conducted separately and each part of the network is compartmentalized. Inventories are stored in hidden locations. After raids or arrests, the cartels conduct internal investigations to assure that their employees were loyal, security measures were followed, and lessons were learned to improve the operation" (Comptroller General 1989: 14).

The sheer volume of cartel transactions makes them vulnerable to sophisticated law enforcement efforts. "While most drug traffickers conduct financial transactions in cash, the volume of business conducted by the Colombian traffickers requires sophisticated record-keeping to track expenses and sales. Modern methods of monitoring inventories and deliveries are used; advanced communication centers arrange for the arrival of smuggled drugs, their distribution, the movement of cash proceeds, and other logistical matters." Distributors maintain accurate records of sales and relay the information to Colombia (Comptroller General 1989: 19).

Infiltrating a Colombian group is near impossible. A prospective wholesale buyer must establish his bona fides at an audience with top management in Colombia. "If he is approved, he is not required to pay cash up front. He will send the cartel payment after he resells the drugs to middlemen. The wholesale buyer must put up collateral, cash, or deeds to real property, as insurance if he is caught. He must also provide human collateral in the form of his family in Colombia, who will pay with their lives if he ever turns informer" (Shannon 1991: 32). The most notorious of the Colombian cartels are those of Medellín and Cali.

Medellín

Medellín, an Andean industrial and tourist city of about three million people in the province of Antioquia, has a culture of violence that "makes its streets among the most dangerous on earth" (Griswold 2005: 82). It is the home of some of Colombia's most notorious drug traffickers. Antioquia and neighboring provinces bore the brunt of the civil war violence of 1948–1958. Long before cocaine emerged as an important commodity, Medellín had a longstanding reputation for smuggling and a school for pickpockets. It is known as a place where assassins are trained in such techniques as the *asesino de la moto*: a passenger on a motorbike uses an automatic weapon—usually a .45 caliber machine pistol. The murder rate in Medellín is nearly nine times that of New York City. The city served as the headquarters for drug trafficking organizations known in Colombia as *Los Grandes Mafiosos* and in the United States as the Medellín Cartel, whose founders include Pablo Escobar, the Ochoa clan, and Carlos Lehder-Rivas.

Lehder-Rivas was indicted in 1981 by a Jacksonville, Florida federal grand jury for drug trafficking and income tax evasion, and in 1983 the United States requested his extradition. Lehder-Rivas went underground, emerging back in Medellín denouncing the United States for imperialism and threatened to join forces with the Marxist revolutionary group known as M-19. In a 1987 shootout, Lehder-Rivas was arrested by Colombian authorities and extradited to the United States. The following year he was convicted of shipping 3.3 tons of cocaine to Florida and Georgia in 1979 and 1980 and sentenced to life without parole. In 1991, he appeared as a U.S.

government witness in the trial of General Manuel Noriega, who, he stated, provided enormous help—and sometimes double-crossed—the cartel. Lehder-Rivas alleged that Noriega had sold the cartel an arsenal of Uzi submachine guns as well as photographs and addresses of DEA agents but had also seized their cocaine and, after being praised by the DEA, sold it back to the traffickers (Rohter 1991).

Ochoa Family

The class and social backgrounds of the Ochoa clan differs from that of their Medellín colleagues. The *paterfamilias* of the Ochoa clan, Fabio Ochoa Restrepo, owns a country estate with herds of cattle and horses, *La Finca de la Loma* ("The Ranch on the Hill") in Medellín. Nearby is a bullring in which he has invested; his family business is inextricably tied to bullfighting. Don Fabio, as he is known locally, heads a wealthy and close-knit clan of old-line cattle breeders and landowners. They claim to have descended from the second wave of settlers to Colombia from the Basque region of Spain who founded Medellín in 1616. These Spaniards enslaved and annihilated the native Indians they found.

During the early 1970s, Fabio Ochoa experienced financial difficulties that forced him to sell off some horses in Venezuela. At the time, his middle son, Jorge Ochoa (Vasquez), lived in Miami, where he headed an import-export firm that imported cocaine for Jorge's uncle, Fabio Restrepo Ochoa. A narrow escape from the DEA caused Jorge to flee to Medellín, where he informed his father, Don Fabio, of the demand for cocaine in the United States (Eddy, Sabogal, and Walden 1988). Fabio Restrepo Ochoa was mysteriously murdered in Miami shortly after his nephew returned to Colombia (Gugliotta and Leen 1989).

Jorge Ochoa, born in 1949, owns large tracts of land in Medellín, where he raises horses for bullfighting. He also owns a horse-breeding farm near Bogotá and a bullfighting arena near Cartagena. He was a frequent traveler to Panama, where his assets are in secret accounts, to Brazil, where he has important investments, and to Spain. In 1984, Jorge Ochoa and his associate Rodriguez Orejuela,

of the Cali cartel, were arrested while living under assumed names in Spain; they were reportedly setting up a Colombian cocaine network in Europe. After two years in a Spanish prison awaiting extradition to the United States, they were instead extradited to Colombia. Meanwhile, Spain emerged as a major consumer and transshipment point for cocaine—as in the United States, cocaine operatives were able to mix with their law-abiding compatriots who in Spain number about one-quarter million persons (Paoli and Reuter 2008).

In Colombia, Jorge Ochoa was convicted of illegally importing bulls—it turned out that they had hoof-and-mouth disease and had to be destroyed. Although serious drug charges and a U.S. extradition request were outstanding, Ochoa was released pending appeal. Even though the judge who released Ochoa lost his job, he remains alive and is rumored to be quite wealthy. The Colombian extradition treaty with the United States was subsequently declared unconstitutional.

In response to the release of Jorge Ochoa, U.S. customs increased inspections of all cargo, passenger luggage, and passengers arriving from Colombia. This stirred strong feelings of nationalism and generated anti-U.S. sentiment that was exploited by Colombian left-wing political groups, who often denounce the United States as "imperialistic." Colombian officials chide the United States for not providing enough material support for Colombian efforts against the *narcotraficantes* and for not doing enough about the demand for cocaine in the United States.

In 1981, Lehder-Rivas was kidnapped. He escaped, but not before being wounded by the Marxist revolutionary group M-19 (Gugliotta and Leen 1989). That same month M-19 kidnapped Jorge Ochoa's 28-year-old sister, Marta Nieves, from the campus of the University of Antioquia in Medellín and demanded a ransom of $1 million. In response, the Ochoa family called a meeting of traffickers—223 attended. Leaflets later announced that each had contributed to a common fund to establish a special enforcement section, *Muertes a Secuestradores* ("Death to the Kidnappers"—MAS), for the "immediate execution of all those involved in kidnappings." The leaflet warned that those who escaped would simply leave their families and friends liable for retribution. Soon afterward, dozens of persons believed connected to M-19 were tortured and murdered (Kerr 1988c): "Ten M-19 guerrillas were kidnapped and tortured, and two of them—who were on the Colombian army's 'most wanted' list—were handed over to the military commanders amidst widespread publicity. In Medellín, MAS invaded homes and shot suspected guerrillas—but also trade unionists, old ladies, young children, horses, pigs, and chickens. Mere sympathizers of M-19 were abducted from the university, tortured, and, if they were lucky, sent home in their underwear." After a few weeks of this Marta Nieves was released unharmed[2] (Eddy, Sabogal, and Walden 1988: 289). MAS surpassed its original purpose and proved capable of protecting trafficker's lands, eventually morphing into a paramilitary.

The Ochoas responded to a government offer of amnesty for major traffickers, surrendered, and confessed. In 1996, after serving five and one-half years, the Ochoa brothers, Jorge, Fabio Ochoa Sanchez, and David, were released from prison for "good behavior." They were whisked away in a bulletproof Mercedes Benz, rich men who own farms and other valuable properties. The United States protested their release, and in 1999, Fabio Ochoa Sanchez was one of thirty-one persons arrested in Colombia for drug trafficking and money laundering. In 2001, Colombia's Supreme Court ordered him extradited to the United States where he was convicted of drug conspiracy in Miami and in 2004 sentenced to thirty years' imprisonment.

Pablo Escobar

The most notorious member of the cartel was born in 1949. His father was a farmer, his mother a schoolteacher. Pablo Escobar (Gaviria) received a high school education but was too poor to attend college. He embarked upon a career in petty crime,

later rising to bodyguard-enforcer for an electronics smuggler. By 1976, Escobar headed a small group of "mules" who transported raw coca paste and base from the south into Colombia, where it was processed into cocaine. In that year he was arrested with five other men and charged with attempted bribery—they had attempted to smuggle a thirty-nine-pound shipment of cocaine inside a spare tire. After three months, the case was dropped on a technicality. The records of the case subsequently disappeared and the two officers who had arrested Escobar were murdered.

As the market for cocaine in the United States increased dramatically, Escobar invested much of his profits in a fleet of planes. He was able to deal directly with source countries (Peru and Bolivia) for his coca paste and coca base and to ship the finished cocaine directly to the United States. As his wealth grew, his lifestyle changed accordingly. Escobar purchased several large ranches, houses, and apartments in and around Medellín, and he invested in legitimate businesses. In 1980, he purchased a Miami Beach mansion and the following year, the King's Harbor Apartments in Plantation, north of Miami, for more than $8 million.

In 1982, Escobar was elected as an alternate Colombian representative in Envigado, a *barrio* outside Medellín. There he cultivated a Robin Hood image, building 500 small houses for slum squatters, which is still known as Barrio Pablo Escobar, and financing the construction of eighty soccer fields for the young men. His newspaper, *Medellín Cívico*, was a public relations piece that promoted Escobar as an up-from-the-slums statesman. As a representative, he enjoyed immunity from arrest, until that was removed by the government. Escobar shared a trait with Al Capone and John Gotti—he enjoyed being in the public spotlight. He even hired publicists to advance his image (Bowden 2001).

Marco Palacios (2007) reports that the Medellín bosses offered to abandon the drug business, deposit all of their funds in Colombian banks, dismantle their drug laboratories, and with official oversight sell the chemical and transportation businesses that supported the cocaine trade. In return, they wanted the elimination of the extradition

---

2. In 1990, M-19 disarmed its fighters and formed a political party whose leader was appointed the Colombian minister of health. A small group of members, however, returned to insurgency.

treaty with the United States. When their offer was rejected, Escobar declared an all-out war. Ron Chepesiuk (2003: 62) notes, Escobar and his cartel colleagues never realized their political ambitions: "When the Colombian state bureaucracy began to breathe down their necks in the mid-1980s, they dropped out of mainstream politics and turned to the terrorist's way of doing business."

In 1984, the minister of justice responsible for a major seizure of Medellín cocaine labs was murdered, sparking a public backlash against the Medellín cartel. This was followed by the murder of more than thirty judges who had been considering extradition requests from the United States for cartel members. In a communiqué from the "Extraditables" printed in Colombian newspapers, Escobar warned anyone who supported extradition to the United States. With his high public profile, Escobar bore the brunt of a campaign to bring cartel members to justice. Escobar's carefully crafted public persona was abandoned for a more instinctive reaction: He orchestrated a campaign of increasing terror. In 1989, his men executed the favored candidate for president of Colombia because he had pledged to bring the *narcotraficantes* to justice. Three months later, in an effort to kill his victim's successor, Escobar had a bomb planted on an Avianca airliner—110 passengers died when the plane was blown out of the sky.

In response to the intensive police campaign to apprehend him, Escobar offered a bounty of $4,200 for each police officer killed. In the following month, forty-two police officers were murdered, and in 1990, some 250 more were murdered (Brooke 1990). The police responded by killing dozens of major traffickers and their enforcers as well as many innocent civilians (Marx 1991). Escobar operatives were tortured with electric shocks and thrown out of police helicopters (Bowden 2001).

In 1990, Escobar began hinting that he would surrender and, in an effort to dictate the terms, went on a bombing campaign that terrified the public. His men kidnapped ten journalists—two were eventually killed. In 1991, ten hours after the constitutional assembly voted to ban extraditions, Pablo Escobar, at 41, surrendered to authorities. He was accompanied by a popular television priest who had helped negotiate the surrender and placed in a specially built jail overlooking his hometown of Envigado. In Envigado, Escobar assisted in the construction of a hospital and sports stadium and endeared himself to the people with jobs and lavish gifts.

The jail was a converted mountaintop ranch with many amenities—jacuzzi, waterbed, bar, wood-burning fireplace, sophisticated electronic equipment that included a computer, 60-inch television set, and cellular telephone. Guards were assigned by Envigado's mayor, and several aides to Escobar also surrendered to provide him with companionship and security while he awaited further legal action. And he also enjoyed female companionship. On July 22, 1992, the Colombian government attempted to transfer Escobar to a more secure prison, a site where he would (in theory, at least) be unable to continue overseeing the drug trade. The result was a furious gunfight during which Escobar and nine of his aides escaped.

After his escape, the police began tracking and killing his men; Escobar responded by killing more police officers. Early in 1993, bombs began destroying property linked to Escobar and the bodies of his associates began turning up in Bogotá and Medellín—the work of two extended families whose members, former Escobar associates, had been killed by the drug lord. They called themselves *Los PEPES*, an acronym in Spanish for "People Persecuted by Pablo Escobar." Information targeting the victims of *Los PEPES* reportedly came from Colombian law enforcement who were privy to the results of high-tech monitoring by American operatives in Colombia—monitoring that eventually led to Escobar himself (Bowden 2001; Brooke 1993). On December 2, 1993, the drug lord was killed in a rooftop shootout with police and soldiers while "attempting to escape"—Escobar probably realized there was no chance he would be taken alive. The fugitive was making a cellular call to his family when his whereabouts were determined by the use of telephone tracking equipment contributed by the United States (Brooke 1992a, 1992b; Christian 1992; Treaster 1991c;). Of course, this being organized crime, the death of Escobar did not end the operations of his organization—a former henchman took over.

Cali Cartel

The drug boom inspired a competing cartel in Cali, a city of 1.5 million persons located about 250 miles south of Medellín. Cali is second only to Spain in the number of Spanish language books it publishes each year, and advanced printing technology has also made the city a center of counterfeiting, mostly of U.S. currency (Brooke 1991b). The Cali cartel refers to a loose alliance of five major trafficking groups with preeminence shared by the kinship/crime families of Gilberto Rodriguez Orejuela ("the Chess Player"), born in 1939, his brother Miguel, born in 1943, and José Santacruz Londono ("Don Chepe") (*Intelligence Bulletin Colombia* 1995). The brothers grew up in a poor Cali barrio. Gilberto never finished high school and his brother reportedly purchased a college degree (Chepesiuk 2003). As teenagers, both were widely feared and became involved in criminal activities with their boyhood friend José Santacruz Londono. In the 1970s, they reportedly used $75,000 from kidnappings to finance entry into the drug business. While Pablo Escobar was a typical gold-chain, fancy-car gangster who enjoyed a flamboyant lifestyle, members of the Cali cartel were low key and manipulative: "Buy Colombia, rather than terrorize it became their guiding philosophy" (Chepesiuk 2003: 68).

The Orejuelas owned banks, supermarkets, television stations, a leading soccer team, and a national chain of drugstores—the latter of which could import cocaine precursor chemicals. Gilberto's seven children have been educated at U.S. and European universities (Moody 1991). Santacruz Londono was trained as an engineer. When he was refused membership in a local club, he had a replica built in an exclusive suburban neighborhood (Brooke 1991a). Members of the Cali cartel favored bribery over violence—cartel members were taped talking about millions of dollars in contributions to the

successful presidential bid of Ernesto Samper.[3] In 1995, Londono was indicted in the United States and subsequently arrested in Colombia, only to slip out of a maximum-security prison in 1996. Two months later he was killed in a shootout with police.

Cartel members took a percentage of the profits from shipments by smaller organizations and, in return, provided transportation, distribution, and enforcement services. Despite their reputation for preferring diplomacy, enforcement services could be quite violent—suspected informants were immersed in barrels of acid or dismembered with chain saws (Brooke 1995a).

Organized in a patriarchal manner, the Cali cartel stressed discipline and loyalty. Leaders operated compartmentalized organizations (see Figure 6.2) so that the loss of any one section did not destroy the enterprise. In Cali, there was a chief executive officer whose subordinates were responsible for acquisition, production, transportation, sales, finance, and enforcement (Shannon 1991). There were also dozens of overseas branches.

Cali operations in the United States were headquartered in the Elmhurst-Jackson Heights section of Queens, New York. Home to more than 30,000 Colombians, this neighborhood is known as "Little Colombia" because of the numerous ethnic restaurants and businesses owned by Colombians. Close to La Guardia Airport and within easy distance of Kennedy Airport, the neighborhood provides cover and financial outlets for the group's activities. A walk through the neighborhood reveals an excess of travel agencies and wire services that facilitate the movement of drug money to Colombia.

In 1991, the Orejuela brothers and forty-two others were indicted in the United States for allegedly laundering $65 million a year in drug profits from Miami, New York, and Los Angeles. In 1995, Gilberto was apprehended in a secret compartment

---

3. In 1996, the Clinton administration revoked Samper's entry visa to visit the United States. Several officials of the Samper campaign team have been sentenced to imprisonment for taking money from the drug traffickers. In 1998, the man who had accused Samper of accepting drug money, Andrés Pastrana, was elected president—he defeated the candidate who had defended Samper.

at a luxurious house in Cali and Miguel was arrested two months later. The brothers confessed to drug trafficking and agreed to turn over $2.1 billion in assets in order to secure leniency; in 1997, Miguel and Gilberto received sentences of nine and ten years, respectively. At the end of 2004, Gilberto Rodriguez Orejuelo was extradited to the United States, followed by his brother Miguel, where in 2006 they were sentenced to thirty years in prison.

Evolution of the Colombian Drug Business

The Medellín and Cali cartels were vertically integrated to maintain control over cocaine through the entire chain from manufacturing to wholesale distribution. While it worked, the profits were astronomical. But as with any vertically integrated organization, a broken link can be devastating. The successors to these major cartels learned this lesson. A multiplicity of smaller organizations—*cartelitos* ("baby cartels")—is filling the vacuum, and they maintain lower profiles in Colombia and the United States than their Medellín and Cali cartel predecessors. Although the fragmentation reduces efficiency, combating this multiplicity requires even more personnel and greater intelligence-gathering efforts (Chepesiuk 2003). Independent traffickers who worked in the shadows of the major cartels have joined forces and the cycle continues. "The proliferation of new drug regimes made the trafficking business more robust than ever"(Bruce and Hayes 2010: 51). As Silvana Paternostra (2011: 17) notes, "If Colombia in the early 1990s had two huge cartels—the Medellín and the Cali cartels—it now has hundreds of *cartelitos*, and thousands of narco-tycoons."

Power has passed to experienced traffickers who have seized opportunities to increase their own share of the drug trade (Romero 2008e). These enterprising traffickers come primarily from the Caribbean North Coast and the Norte Valle del Cauca region, of which Cali is the capital city, located on Colombia's southeast coast. The Norte Valle cartel (NVC) employs hundreds of individuals who work in various "offices," or "crews." "Drug offices" are responsible for the manufacture, transportation, and export of multiton loads of cocaine from Colombia to Mexico, and ultimately to the United States. "Money laundering offices" employ dozens of money launderers, money couriers, accountants, and individuals who operate multimillion-dollar *coletas*, or money stash houses. "Corruption offices" are responsible for bribes to the police and other public officials in exchange for information about law enforcement actions against members of the cartel. The "offices of the *sicarios*" employ dozens of gunmen who carry out murders, tortures, kidnappings, and violent collections of drug debts ("Cocaine Cartel Leader to Face Charges in the United States" 2008). NVC representatives in Mexico arrange for drug shipments to that country's cartels for their ultimate destination, the United States (DEA press release, June 17, 2010).

While Colombia-based organizations remain the dominant players in the international cocaine trade, they have aggressively increased their share of the U.S. heroin market. Colombian entry into heroin is based on demographics. During the 1980s, the popularity of cocaine began to fade among urban professionals, and "cokeheads" tend to burn out after five years. With this dwindling consumer base, the Colombians expanded into Europe but with only limited success—heroin was the hard drug of choice and that market was dominated by Pakistani and Turkish groups. So the Colombians diversified, importing poppy seeds, equipment, and expertise from Southwest Asia (Golden Crescent). By 1999, Colombians had become major heroin wholesalers, often selling cocaine and heroin to wholesalers as part of a package deal. They required their Dominican cells in the United States to take a couple of kilos of heroin for every hundred kilos of cocaine to give out free samples to customers—and the strategy worked, creating an entirely new client base for heroin. The purity level of their heroin permits it to be prepared for smoking,[4] ridding the product of its dirty needles and HIV reputation

---

4. Heroin is either heroin salt or heroin base. Heroin salt dissolves readily in water, so it is easy to inject or sniff. To smoke, heroin base needs to be mixed with an acid like vitamin C in order to dissolve.

(Brzezinski 2002). Smoking is a less efficient way of ingesting than intravenous use because a lot of the drug literally goes up in smoke. Therefore, only when it is relatively cheap and therefore plentiful will smoking heroin predominate.

The dismantling of the Cali cartel created opportunities for their Mexican colleagues, some of whom forged direct links with cocaine sources in Bolivia and Peru. Colombians often have to compete with Mexican organizations for the U.S. market.

MEXICO

Mexico is a nation of about 110 million persons, 75 percent of who live in urban areas; despite an abundance of natural resources, poverty is widespread. The struggle for independence from Spain took eleven years, 1810–1821, and cost the lives of an estimated 300,000 persons. It was followed by a series of revolutions, rigged elections, and general turmoil. There was a war with the United States in 1848 and a French invasion and occupation from 1863 to 1867. In still another violent overthrow, Porfirio Diaz, a hero in Mexico's wars with the United States and France, came to power in 1876 and ruled Mexico for thirty-five years. The revolution that ousted Diaz left turmoil and widespread violence in its wake. In 1929, political stability was achieved by the emergence of a dominant political party known as the *PRI* (rhymes with *free*)—*Partido Revolucionario Institucional*.

In the Mexican culture, "people are not treated alike; strangers, those outside the circle of family and close friends, are not wholly to be trusted. One is much safer giving one's confidence only to friends of long-standing or family members. Thus, as in Southern Italy [see Chapter 5], societal focus is on the interests of the immediate and extended family, not the wider interests of a more impersonal societal good" (Shelley 2001). This effect is visible in Mexican political life where each political leader has his intimate circle of contacts, relatives, and friends from childhood "whom he protects and appoints to key positions as he moves up the career hierarchy. These *camarillas*, or cliques of friends, are

in some ways the basic unit of Mexican politics" (Needler 1995: 51). Patron-client relationships, political patronage, and endemic corruption provide the backdrop against which Mexican organized crime is to be understood.

For decades after its founding, the PRI "was a tool of successive presidents using authoritarian methods to insure one-party rule" (Dillon 1999b: 1). The police forces—federal, state, and local—that evolved out of this atmosphere were deployed not to protect but to control the population. Moreover, police officers have been poorly paid, and it was understood that they could supplement their pittance with bribes as long as they remained loyal to the PRI dominated government (Dillon 1996f). Until the PRI fell from power in 2000, the cartels operated in a country run by a political party that was more or less happy to stay out of their way in exchange for relative peace (Longmire 2011). The police could smack gangsters around if they got too big for their boots. "Police could also bust anyone who wasn't paying his dues, showing that they were fighting the war on drugs and clocking up seizures and arrests. The system ensured that crime was controlled and everyone got paid" (Grillo 2011: 53).

Using tactics reminiscent of the political machines discussed in Chapter 2, the PRI ruled Mexico for more than seventy years without any strong opposition, during which corruption became endemic (Shelley 2001). The PRI governed through the use political bosses known as *caciques* whose power derived from their connection to the national party structure. In return for party loyalty, bosses were able to operate with a great deal of immunity, securing resources for followers and withholding them from and threatening violence against opponents (Villarreal 2002).

Free market reforms and its gradual implementation pushed many ordinary Mexicans to find alternative employment. "As the global economy grew, so did a diversified and innovative network of illicit entrepreneurs, and drug trafficking presented the most lucrative of black market opportunities.... Although Mexico had been a longtime source of marijuana, opium, and synthetic drugs for the U.S.

CORRUPTION IN MEXICO

Due to distrust of Mexican law enforcement, the families of victims of ransom kidnappings often fail to inform the authorities. This lack of trust is abetted by a confirmed fear that it is the police who often carry out the kidnappings. In 2008, the 14-year-old son of a wealthy businessman was kidnapped by men dressed as federal police officers who tortured—all of his teeth were pulled out—and killed his driver and bodyguard. The boy's body was later found despite the family having paid a ransom reportedly in excess of $5 million (Lacey and Betancourt 2008).

In 2010, it was disclosed that inmates in a Mexican prison, armed with weapons issued to prison guards, were allowed out at night to carry out drug trafficking-related executions (Malkin 2010).

Mexico has become one of the most dangerous places to practice journalism. Drug dealers, corrupt police officers, and military personnel regularly kill those who write about them. With the assistance of foreign advisors, many of whom also advised the former Soviet Union in the same process, Mexico embarked on an ambitious program of privatization in the 1990s. As in Russia, this was done in the absence of a free and vigorous press in a system that lacked grounding in the rule of law. The lack of sufficient safeguards accompanying this economic transformation led to the acquisition of valuable assets—banks, communications, food sectors—by families whose source of capital was gambling and drugs, "thereby facilitating the infiltration of organized crime into the larger Mexican economy" (Shelley 2001: 218).

market, its rise as a transit point for cocaine created profitable new employment opportunities for the estimated 450,000 people who rely on drug trafficking as a significant source of income today" (Shirk 2011: 7).

In 1997, an emerging opposition party critical of PRI-inspired corruption won control of the lower house of Mexico's congress. In 1999, in an effort to change its image, the PRI voted to hold a national primary to select its presidential candidates; previously, the sitting president was allowed to choose his successor. In 2000, in a major political upset, the PRI candidate for president was defeated by the National Action Party. However, the pace of political change has not been uniform. Many parts of the country, particularly rural areas, are still governed by PRI bosses, and by 2011, the PRI had made a remarkable political comeback.

As noted in Chapter 3, during the Capone era, the election of a reform mayor in Chicago shattered stable but corrupt relationships between politicians, the police, and the city's Prohibition-era gangs. This led to the onset of the "Chicago Wars" as gang lords struggled for supremacy. Similarly, the defeat of the PRI in Mexico ruptured a longtime implicit arrangement between *narcotraficantes* and the PRI-controlled government. When it ruled

Mexico as an elective dictatorship, the PRI "accommodated but regulated the drug cartels" (Padgett 2009: 39). Richard Snyder and Angelica Duran Martinez (2009) refer to this as a state-sponsored protection racket whereby public officials refrain from enforcing the law or enforce it selectively in exchange for a share of the profits generated by criminal organizations. With the government no longer acting as an arbitrator, an unparalleled level of violence erupted as drug lords struggle for supremacy and politicians in the new multiparty environment eagerly accept funds from the traffickers (Bussey 2008; Finnegan 2010b). State-sponsored protection rackets can have a powerful pacifying effect on illicit markets, be it in Chicago or Mexico, while the unintended consequence of political and administrative reform aimed at reducing corruption is a dramatic upsurge in violence. In the four years following President Felipe Calderón's 2006 declaration of war against Mexican drug cartels, more than 34,000 people died in drug-related killings (Stevenson 2011).

Despite political changes, Mexico remains in an economic crisis, crime has skyrocketed, and the criminal justice system is in an advanced stage of deterioration—more than 95 percent of violent crimes in Mexico go unsolved—the police are

---

BLESSED IS THE FATHER

The padre is at the celebration to christen a child when he notices the boss wearing a large gold crucifix encrusted with diamonds, the ultimate in *narcotraficante* chic. He slips away and notifies the police. Their raid nets a lot of cocaine and $1 million in cash. The priest gets the crucifix and the rest of the loot is turned over to Mexico's chief drug enforcement official, who enforces the law against those who compete with the Gulf cartel that pays him millions for his efforts (Bowden 2009).

---

intimidated, corruption endemic, and human rights violations widespread (Padgett 2011). "Torture by the authorities is so common in Mexico that it seemingly fails to shock anyone to whom it has not happened" (Finnegan 2010: 71). In 2011, Human Rights Watch accused the Mexican military of engaging in torture, forced disappearances, and extra-judicial killings in its war against organized crime. Corruption and intimidation extend into the media: journalists receive payoffs or threats and avoid offending politicians and the military, or probing the drug business (Bowden 2011). Since 2007, almost seventy Mexican journalists have been murdered (Padgett 2011).

The popular culture of Mexico is infused with songs, *corridos* (ballads), and *narco-corridos* glamorizing drug trafficking. Major *narcotraficantes* are celebrated, along with their subculture of violence (Edberg 2001). Many songs contain references to an outlaw code of behavior, and their music videos depict violence including torture and the murder of police officers (Dillon 1999a). In the "if you play with fire" category, more than a dozen performers have been the victims of the violence they extol, often tortured before they are murdered (McKinley 2007c). The cartels and the gang members they employ exalt Al Pacino in his movie role as *Scarface* (Grillo 2011). During raids on the homes of cartel members, officials have discovered movie posters of the machine-gun-wielding Pacino as a vicious drug kingpin (FBI press release, August 12, 2010). Ioan Grillo (2011: 171) notes that a "cult of the outlaw" prevails in the hinterlands of Northern Mexico where the *narco* is revered: "On the streets of Sinaloa, people traditionally refer to gangsters as *los valientes*, 'the brave ones.'"

Mexican Drug Trafficking

Chinese immigrants who entered Mexico at about the time of the U.S. Civil War, secured employment on railroads and in the mines, much as their brethren had done in the north (discussed in Chapter 12). And they brought with them the practice of smoking opium. These immigrants and their descendants recognized the opportunities afforded by growing the poppy and selling the opium to Chinese dealers in the United States. As repeal approached, Mexican bootleggers who had profited from Prohibition in the United States, sought new areas of profit; they eyed the opium trade. Mexican criminals stirred up anti-Chinese sentiments and with a violent and racist campaign took control of the business (Grillo 2011). In Ciudad Juárez, for example, Ignacia Jasso, known as "La Nacha," controlled much of the drug trade, distributing to El Paso and other U.S. cites for over fifty years (Carey 2011).

Mexican drug trafficking organizations "control most of the U.S. drug market and have established varied transportation routes, advanced communications capabilities, and strong affiliations with gangs in the United States," overseeing drug distribution in more than 230 U.S. cities (National Drug Intelligence Center 2009a: 45). They manage "complex smuggling, transportation, and distribution networks that compartmentalize duties; employ advanced security and communication techniques; gather intelligence; and use violence and intimidation to deter law enforcement authorities, control organization members, and secure smuggling territories" (NDIC 2009c: 4). They have moved away from traditional hierarchical structures in favor of decentralized networks of interdependent, task-oriented cells. Cell diversity, a division of labor, provides operational flexibility and reduces the risk of apprehension for organization leaders.

In the early 1990s, Mexican drug trafficking organizations struck a deal with the Colombians whose cocaine they were moving from Mexico into the United States on a contract basis: For every two kilograms of smuggled cocaine, the Mexicans would keep one kilogram as payment in kind (O'Brien and Greenberg 1996; Wren 1996). The deal was brokered by Sandra Ávila Beltrán, a beauty born in 1960 and known as Queen of the Pacific who is part of the Sinaloa cartel (discussed later). She is the niece of Miguel Ángel Félix Gallardo, a major trafficker and former police officer—"the path from policeman to villain is alarmingly common in Mexico" (Grillo 2011: 4)—imprisoned since 1989 for the 1985 torture-murder of a U.S. DEA agent. Married twice,

both of her husbands were police-commanders-turned-traffickers and both were murdered. In 2007, Beltrán was arrested by Mexican authorities along with her lover, Juan Diego Espinoza Ramírez ("El Tigre"), part of the Colombian Norte del Valle cartel (McKinley 2007a).

Mexican traffickers attempted to convert Peruvian coca paste into cocaine, but the product had the odor of kerosene so the effort was abandoned in favor of dealing with Colombians (McMahon 1995). Both sides benefited from the arrangement. Colombians had an abundance of cocaine, and Mexicans had a distribution network in the United States that they had been using for heroin. This arrangement was aided by the North American Free Trade Act (NAFTA), which further opened the already porous borders with Mexico (see Figure 6.3). As a consequence, Mexican traffickers control a substantial

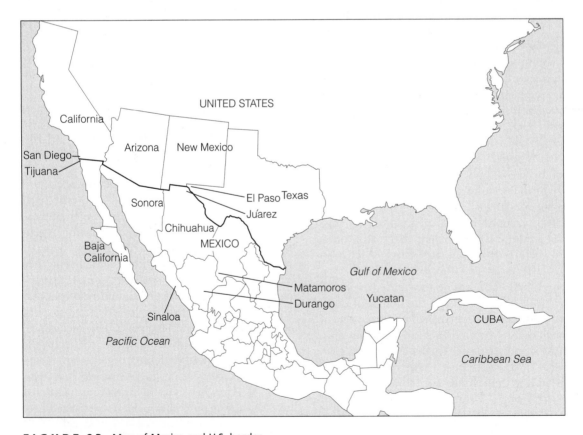

FIGURE 6.3 Map of Mexico and U.S. border

LOSING HEADS OVER DRUGS

Acapulco, Mexico: "Only a week into the new year, fifteen human heads sat outside a gleaming shopping center on the other side of the lush hills that frame this seaside resort's big tourist hotels" (Archibold 2011: 3).

Later in the year, masked gunmen blocked traffic on a busy avenue in the Gulf of Mexico city of Boca del Rio and dumped the bodies of thirty five murder victims. believed to be Zetas punished by rivals for engaging in extortion.

proportion of wholesale cocaine distribution throughout the western and Midwestern United States. They also provide money-laundering services for Colombian clients and direct delivery to wholesale-level customers on behalf of the major Colombian-based cocaine groups (Marshall 2001). Mexican representatives in Colombia arrange for delivery to Mexico or Central America, especially Panama and Honduras. Mexicans then move the cocaine into the United States via light aircraft, ships, even submarines, or overland in cars, trucks, and SUVs (Grillo 2011).

The relationship with the Colombians also led to structural changes, with some Mexican drug groups modeling their organizations along Colombian lines—compartmentalized units operating independently of each other but controlled hierarchically (see Figure 6.2 earlier in this chapter). The leading syndicates "are highly and efficiently organized, often led by family members at the top, involving hundreds of individuals with specialized roles—from security chiefs to hired guns to marketing agents, accountants, financial consultants, and money-laundering specialists. They make regular use of sophisticated technology, counter-surveillance methods, and state-of-the-art communications devices. Financial rewards and intimidation help maintain strong internal discipline. Although they may be big businesses, Mexican drug organizations are family-run operations with a corresponding high degree of personal trust (P. Smith 1999).

Mexican heroin smuggled into the United States is transported to metropolitan areas in the western and southwestern states with sizable Latino populations. Mexican heroin is also transported to primary markets in Chicago, Denver, and St. Louis. Attempts to find markets for black tar heroin[5] in

East Coast cities, such as Boston and Atlanta, failed (Marshall 2001). On the Mexican side of the border across from Laredo, Texas, Nuevo Laredo, a city of more than 300,000, has been turned into a "Little Baghdad" by warring drug organizations—the Gulf cartel versus the Sinaloa cartel (discussed later)—attempting to control this critical distribution center. Victims have included journalists and police officers (G. Thompson 2005a). Assassins are often adolescents, some are U.S. citizens, trained by instructors from the Mexican military in the employ of the cartels. In 2005, hours after being sworn in, a businessman who had volunteered to become Nuevo Laredo's police chief—no one else wanted the job—was assassinated by men firing assault rifles from an SUV. The federal government responded by sending in the military (Jordon and Sullivan 2005). Later that year, federal authorities arrested fifteen Laredo police officers for abducting people on orders from the Gulf cartel (Iliff 2005). In 2008, gunmen killed the head of the federal organized crime division, and two weeks later the chief of the federal police. Mexican authorities subsequently charged six men with links to the Sinaloa cartel including the man who hired the shooter, a federal police officer (McKinley 2008f, 2008g).

Superior organization and an extensive drug portfolio enabled Mexican cartels to diversify, dividing operations into heroin, cocaine, marijuana, and methamphetamine units. Mexican involvement with methamphetamine apparently began when the Hell's Angels turned to them in order to avoid the practical

---

5. As opposed to the white heroin from Southwest and Southeast Asia, the less pure Mexican product has a dark color (discussed in Chapter 12).

BLESSED BE THE TRAFFICKERS

Jesús Malverde, considered a "Robin Hood" by many Mexicans, was reportedly killed by the police in 1909; he is the patron saint of drug traffickers. While historians are unsure if he actually existed or is simply a legend, a shrine has been erected atop Malverde's gravesite in the remote city of Culicán in the state of Sinaloa. There, drug bosses pay homage and ask for his assistance; they often sport tattoos of their venerated saint. Kneeling in front of his statue, they dip flowers in water and wipe them tenderly over his face and leave notes of thanks on the altar and place money in the donation box (Hawley 2010a). His image appears on candles, rosaries, trading cards, and stamps; and the traffickers drink Malverde beer, "holy water," from a nearby Mexican microbrewery (Hawley 2008; K. Murphy 2008).

---

hazards posed by the drug's manufacture: It is explosive, the chemicals are caustic, inhalation can be fatal, and the strong odor can alert law enforcement. Mexican national trafficking organizations now dominate wholesale methamphetamine trafficking, using large-scale laboratories based in Mexico and the western and southwestern United States. Outlaw motorcycle clubs are still active in methamphetamine production, but do not produce the large quantities distributed by Mexican groups. Mexican-based trafficking organizations have ready access to the necessary precursor chemicals on the international market. These chemicals have fewer controls in Mexico than in the United States (Keefe 2001a). And methamphetamine provides an opportunity for profit that does not have to be shared with others, as cocaine does with the Colombians.

As opposed to the instability of the heroin and cocaine markets in the United States, marijuana retains its marketability and profitability. Mexican marijuana is transported to the United States in pickup trucks driven over a ramp that has been placed on border security fences, or though cross-border tunnels. Sometimes they simply throw bales of marijuana over the fence to be retrieved by confederates on the U.S. side. The September 11, 2001, terrorist attacks led to substantial tightening of the U.S.–Mexican border that affected marijuana smuggling routes. To avoid smuggling, cartels harvest on the U.S. side where they lease fertile land such as vineyards or grow and harvest marijuana in national forests (Moore 2009a). In March and April growers are driven to planting sites that were scouted during the winter. In teams of 4 to 10, the growers move into the forest with seedlings and lightweight irrigation systems and live there until autumn, often poaching deer and bear, when the crop is harvested (Verini 2007). Traffickers bring in tons of equipment, plastic irrigation piping, fertilizer, drip timers booby traps, propane tanks, camping equipment, and food stocks (Longmire 2011). Plant growth hormones have been dumped into steams and the growing areas have become polluted with weed and bug sprays banned in the U.S., and rat poison used to keep animals away from the young plants (Cone 2008). Their campfires have been blamed for wildfires including the 90,000-acre Santa Barbara wildfire in 2009 that took several weeks to be fully contained (McKinley 2009c). A large-scale operation targeting marijuana cultivation in three California counties in 2010 found 15.5 tons of trash, 29 miles of irrigation line, and 4,580 pounds of fertilizer. The growers had altered or destroyed 270 acres of land (Longmire 2011).

Mexican drug organizations have diversified into ransom kidnapping and extortion. Extortion has become widespread and, as opposed to most targets of drug violence, extortion victimizes ordinary citizens and generates community anger, so much so that the Sinaloa cartel avoids the practice as bad for business (Malkin 2011). Their theft of oil is projected to lower the profits of Pemex, the national oil company, by some $500 million in 2011. A U.N. estimate places their annual income from human smuggling in the billions. Their involvement in the counterfeit merchandise industry has grown to the point that six out of ten transactions in Mexico involve a pirated good (Corcoran 2011).

Unlike American organized crime Mexican traffickers have at their disposal an army of personnel, an arsenal of weapons, and the finest technology that money can buy. Cartel militarization and the Mexican government's military response—beginning in 2007, thousands of troops sent into border towns—have resulted in fierce gun battles. Gunmen have refused to surrender and have ambushed soldiers and police officers. They have corrupted local police departments and assassinated honest police commanders. In 2008, after a violent gun battle with soldiers and police officers in Rio Bravo, Mexican authorities arrested three U.S. citizens, gunmen working for the Gulf cartel who had been recruited from across the border (McKinley 2008h). A few days later in Tijuana, government forces fought a three-hour battle with gunmen who used heavy machine guns and rocket-propelled grenades (McKinley 2008d, 2008e). The group acquired military-grade weapons, including assault weapons and ammunition, in the United States and smuggled them back into Mexico.

In Mexico, civilians must obtain permission from the military to buy firearms, and they are not permitted to own large caliber rifles or high-powered handguns, which are considered military weapons. Mexican drug dealers purchase such arms in the United States and smuggle them back to Mexico along with their drug profits. They are particularly partial to assault rifles such as the AK-47 (McKinley 2009a). One in eight licensed firearm dealers in the United States is located along the border (Rice 2011).

In 2009, a resident of Houston was sentenced to eight years imprisonment for unlawfully purchasing firearms that were smuggled into Mexico. The firearms included fifteen assault rifles and additional weapons chambered in ammunition known in Mexico as *mata policias* ("police killers") because of their reputed ability to defeat body armor worn by the police. The trafficker recruited "straw buyers" who purchased more than a hundred firearms. Many of these weapons were subsequently recovered at crime scenes involving assaults and murders committed by Mexican drug cartels; victims included police officers (U.S. Department of Justice press release, April 17, 2009). In 2011, a member of Los Zetas (discussed later) was sentenced to thirty years in federal prison for smuggling assault rifles secured by "straw purchasers" in Texas to confederates in Mexico (U.S. Department of Justice press release, August 22, 2011).

Tim Padgett, a *Time* reporter who has covered the Mexican drug scene for more than twenty-two years, points out that traffickers who once killed only one another have morphed "into monsters who routinely slaughter innocents" (2011: 26). At the end of 2009, in a two-hour shootout, Mexican marines killed the wanted drug lord Arturo Beltrán Leyva; six other traffickers and one marine were also killed. Several hours after the dead marine's mother attended his memorial service in Mexico City, where she received the Mexican flag covering her son's coffin, gunmen armed with assault rifles broke into the marine's home, killed his mother, his aunt, and two siblings (Associated Press 2009c). In 2010, gunmen sealed off a highway in Michoacán with buses that they set ablaze, trapping a convoy of federal police trucks. Raining down gunfire from high ground on both sides of the highway, they killed twelve officers (Hawley 2010b). In 2010, Los Zetas executed seventy-two migrant workers because they could not pay extortion money.

In 2011, a U.S. Customs and Enforcement agent was gunned down on a Mexican highway, the first American law enforcement agent to be killed in line of duty in Mexico in more than twenty-five years. Shortly afterward, more than 3,000 U.S. federal, state, and local law enforcement officers arrested more than 450 persons believed to have ties to Mexican trafficking organizations.

The Mexican military has been mobilized to combat the drug cartels, but critics claim the army is a major part of the problem: There is a history of collusion between the armed forces and drug traffickers and the military has been responsible for widespread human rights abuse (Caputo 2009). Amnesty International, Human Rights Watch, Mexican human rights groups, as well as the U.S. Department of State, have accused the Mexican military of widespread human rights violations that include kidnappings and extra-legal killings

(Lacey 2009f; Archibald 2011c). Meanwhile, violence between feuding Mexican drug cartels has spilled over the border. A renegade unit of the Arellano-Félix cartel, *Los Palillos* ("The Toothpicks"), for example, has been responsible for numerous murders and kidnappings in the United States (Moore 2009b).

By 1995, it became apparent that Mexican drug trafficking was dominated by about a half-dozen *padrones* (bosses). These leaders of cartels were sometimes allied, sometimes in competition, and sometimes in violent conflict. They are often referred to by their geographic location, such as the "Gulf cartel." Although they operate out of discrete sites in Mexico, their stature "comes not from controlling territory so much as from the international scope of their contacts and their ability to operate across Mexico with Government protection" (Golden 1995b: 8). Thus, the leader of the infamous Juárez cartel in the state of Chihuahua, Amado Carrillo-Fuentes, resided in Culiacán, in the neighboring state of Sinaloa, which is actually the home of another cartel by that name.

Territorial control typically has as its purpose the ability to tax entrepreneurs, legitimate and/or criminal. Major drug cartels have little or no interest in the relatively high effort/low return from "protection" insofar as it involves the provision of police and adjudicatory services. Rather than territory, major trafficking organizations strive to control transportation routes and hubs known as *plazas*. While a cartel may dominate a *plaza* at any given time, control is often contested resulting in a great deal of the violence plaguing Mexico. The absence of a strong sense of territoriality means the Mexican drug organizations are best described as *enterprise syndicates*. We will examine the most prominent.

Herrera Family

For many years trafficking in Mexican heroin was dominated by the Herrera Family whose operations began shortly after World War II. From their first laboratory in Mexico, the Herreras shipped heroin to relatives who had moved to Chicago. Actually a cartel of six interrelated family groupings, the Herrera Family has been headed by the sometimes-imprisoned Jaime ("Don Jaime") Herrera-Nevarez (born 1924 or 1927), a former Mexican Judicial Police Officer. (The Judicial Police are similar to the Royal Canadian Mounted Police in jurisdiction.) Headquartered in Durango, a city of about 200,000 in the state of Durango (with a population of about one million), the organization is estimated to have around five thousand members, about two thousand of whom are related by blood or marriage.

Because key members are tied by blood, marriage, or fictional kinship (godparenthood), the group has proven to be very difficult to infiltrate on both sides of the border. In the United States the Family operates out of Chicago where Mexican heroin and marijuana are wholesaled to groups in New York, Philadelphia, Boston, Detroit, and Louisville. Organizational management is maintained by some two dozen executive-level directors and a vast array of field representatives in a number of American cities. The network is held together through the Herrera organization's Chicago headquarters and through communications and trips back to the organization's headquarters in Durango. Don Jaime has lived the life of a *padrone*, giving to the poor, befriending the rich, and playing godfather at weddings and baptisms. "In the village of Santiago Papasquiaro, where many of the opium farmers lived, the clan built the water system, installed streetlights, and created a town square. Three hospitals benefited from the clan's philanthropy" (Shannon 1988: 59). The Herreras did not buy off the power structure in Durango—they *are* the power structure.

By the 1980s, the Herrera Family had established cocaine contacts throughout Latin America. In fact, Colombians have now married into the family. In 1985, Judicial Police arrested Don Jaime's son for cocaine trafficking. His case was subsequently transferred from Mexico City to Durango, where he was ordered released by a local judge for lack of evidence. In that same year, 135 persons comprising eight separate Herrera-related distribution rings were indicted in Chicago. By 1987, the Herrera Family was reeling under a continuing federal investigation in the Chicago area that resulted in more than eighty convictions, and dozens more became fugitives. By the end of 1988, however, those who had been convicted and those who were fugitives had been replaced. Herrera Family operations in cocaine surged, and intelligence gathered from two heroin laboratory seizures that occurred in the state of Durango "indicates that the members of the Herrera family continue to be active in the Mexican heroin trade" (Library of Congress 2003: 17). They are considered part of the "Federation," popularly known as the Sinaloa cartel with whom they have maintained a close relationship since the 1960s.

Sinaloa Cartel

Sinaloa is a northwestern Pacific coast agricultural state with four hundred miles of coastline whose dealers are legendary in the state where they are memorialized in *narcocorridos*. In 1989, the entire police department of Culiacán, a city of 700,000 and the capital of Sinaloa, was taken into custody by the Mexican army. Also arrested was the assistant director of the antinarcotics program in Sinaloa, who confessed to receiving $23,000 a month to keep an infamous drug boss informed of police activities against him (Rohter 1989b).

The head of the Sinaloa, cartel was born in 1957. Joaquín Guzmán Loera, known as "El Chapo" or "Shorty,"—he is 5 feet 6 inches—was often beaten by his father, a small-time opium grower, and had to live with his grandfather. He worked as a field hand but as an adolescent found an escape, working for the Guadalajara cartel run by Mexican godfather Miguel Angel Félix Gallardo. After Gallardo was arrested in 1989, his organization split, and Guzmán took over Sinaloa operations, controlling trafficking routes through Arizona and battling the Arellano Félix cartel for the border city of Tijuana. In 1993, Arellano Félix gunmen attempted to assassinate Guzmán at the Guadalajara airport, but instead killed a Roman Catholic Cardinal, outraging Mexicans.

Entrepreneurial acumen and a penchant for violence eventually elevated him to the top of Mexico's drug world. His inner-circle consists of relatives and operatives organized into cells responsible for operations in a designated area—they never meet their boss who conveys directions through trusted insiders. He employs lawyers to represent him in relations with politicians, the police, and the military. When one of "his" politicians was sentenced to thirty-three years for drug trafficking, he told the judge: "I will go free and you will die." Six days later he was released and the judge's body was found riddled with thirty-three bullets. A note explained: one bullet for each year (Beith 2010).

In 1993, Guzmán was arrested in Guatemala and tried in Mexico for murder and cocaine trafficking. He was sentenced to twenty years, but the Sinaloa cartel remained intact and continues to smuggle tons of cocaine each month into the United States. They built a 1,500-foot concrete-reinforced, air-conditioned tunnel between Tijuana and Otay Mesa, a community within the City of San Diego that is one of the busiest commercial land border crossings in the United States. At the end of 2010, U.S. agents discovered another tunnel, two-and-a-half-miles long and equipped with rail tracks connecting Tijuana and San Diego (Cathcart 2010). In 2011, two more Tijuana-to-Otay Mesa tunnels were discovered (DEA press release, November 15, 2011).

Transferred to Mexico's toughest prison—two guards for each inmate, isolated cells, and sophisticated video surveillance—Guzmán continued to receive large sums of money from his cartel confederates and many of the prison staff were in his employ. Those who turned down his largess placed their families in danger. Gradually the prison became his personal playground: women, whiskey, gourmet meals, and mobile phones for conducting cartel business (Beith 2010). In 2001, a day after Mexico's Supreme Court ruled that he could be extradited to the United States, Guzmán escaped. On a Saturday evening in 2005, Mexico's most wanted fugitive entered a fashionable Nuevo Laredo restaurant accompanied by a phalanx of heavily armed men. Shocked diners watched as his men locked the doors and collected cell phones until he had finished eating a steak dinner. Before leaving, Guzmán picked up the tab for the forty customers (Pinkerton and Grillo 2005). His cartel is the source of funding for schools and hospitals, for which locals are indebted (Beith 2010).

In 2011, it was reported that the Sinaloa cartel has brought relative peace to the otherwise violent battleground city of Tijuana. Control over this strategic gateway to United States led to thousands of deaths, but homicides declined notably in 2011 as the Sinaloa cartel emerged an uncontested winner. While the business of drugs continues unabated, nightclubs and restaurants that closed during the peak of violence in 2008 have cautiously begun to reopen their doors and investment is picking up (Díaz 2011).

Gulf Cartel

Juan García Ábrego was born in 1944 into a notorious smuggling family—his uncle is the legendary "godfather" of crime in Matamoros, Mexico (Dillon 1996b). Ábrego eventually emerged as a leader of the Gulf cartel, controlling drug trafficking throughout northeastern Mexico and along the Gulf of Mexico. The chubby, curly-haired drug czar called "the Doll" or "Dollface" by his subordinates, borrowed organizing techniques from the Cali cartel, including compartmentalizing his organization into cells (Dillon 1996d, 1996g). He is reputed to have pioneered the Mexican role in cocaine trafficking and in over a decade built an empire estimated to be worth $15 billion (Eskridge 1998). Rather than pay cash for moving Cali cartel cocaine into the United States, Ábrego decided to take cocaine as payment in kind. "He would guarantee delivery anywhere in the United States for 50 percent of the load. He would assume all risks" (Lupsha 1995: 90). "Instead of being paid $2,000 to move a kilo [2.2 pounds] of cocaine, García Ábrego allegedly would turn it into $16,000 or more by selling the drug in Houston, Dallas, or New York, his three main markets" (McMahon 1996: 4). Ábrego paid millions of dollars in bribes and headed a private army—whose members included law enforcement officers—that slaughtered dozens of people (Dillon 1996e; McMahon 1996). In 1996,

it was disclosed that the deputy attorney general in charge of Mexico's Judicial Police counter-narcotics program had accumulated $9 million by protecting Ábrego's organization (Dillon 1996c). In 2008, the mayor of Matamoros was arrested in California and charged with smuggling cocaine into the United States.

Ábrego was indicted in the United States in 1990, and in 1996 he was arrested in Monterrey by Mexican authorities. He was quickly flown to the United States where a reward of $2 million had been offered for his capture and where he received eleven life terms. Although Mexico refuses to extradite its citizens for drug charges, Ábrego holds U.S. citizenship and was technically *expelled* from Mexico. About sixty members of Ábrego's organization are already serving time in U.S. prisons, which increased the power of competing cartels in the Mexican cities of Juárez and Tijuana (Katel 1996). At the time of his arrest, Abrego's power was waning: His Cali suppliers had cut him off because of the notoriety he had attracted and his most influential government protectors were out of office. He became a victim of Mexico's need to show progress in dealing with drug trafficking (Dillon 1996a). The primary witness against Ábrego was a Mexican-American FBI agent who, by pretending to be corrupt, had infiltrated his organization.

Under new leadership, the Gulf cartel recruited Mexican military special forces veterans to serve as its enforcement arm. Known as *Los Zetas*, they subsequently formed their own criminal organization (McKinley 2010).

Los Zetas

Formerly in the employ of the Gulf cartel this unit originally consisted of former Mexican special forces (*Grupo Aeromovil de Fuerzas Especiales*) trained in the United States and known by the radio call name of their original leader who was killed in 2002. "Their defection from the Mexican military and subsequent break with the Gulf Cartel introduced new militarized tactics to the drug war, brought new forms of extreme violence (such as beheadings), and led other drug trafficking organizations to use similar methods"

MEXICAN JUVENILE DELINQUENCY

In 2011, the 15-year-old was sentenced to three years' imprisonment, the maximum for juveniles in the Mexican state of Morelos where the case was tried. At age fourteen, in the employ of a drug cartel, he killed four men whose decapitated bodies were found hanging from a bridge in a vacation spot near Mexico City (Archibald 2011b).

(Shirk 2011: 10). "The original Zetas are mainly dead, but their style—decapitations, military precision in attacks—spread and they are now the models for killers in many cartels" (Bowden 2011: 25). They also serve as an inspiration for soldiers to desert and join the cartels.

In 2004, the unit's chief was captured after a gunfight with Mexican agents who found a cache of military-grade automatic weapons and grenades (McKinley 2004a). That same year, a well-organized jailbreak freed five suspected cartel gunman who were being held on murder charges (Reuters 2004a). In 2005, it was reported that the Zetas were operating in Texas, both along the border and further north into San Antonio and Houston where they are believed to be responsible for dozens of murders (Associated Press 2005d).

Their leader, Heriberto Lazcano, 38, known as "El Verdugo," The Executioner, "is reported to have fed victims to the lions and tigers he keeps on his ranches. Lazcano was part of an elite special forces unit sent to combat drug trafficking on the eastern border that, instead, began working for Gulf cartel in the late 1990s. In place of their military pay of $700 a month, they are paid $15,000 a month. Their military discipline, training, arsenal, and wiretap capability make them a formidable organization that has expanded into ransom kidnapping and extortion from businesses (Padgett 2005). In 2008, Mexican federal agents arrested six Zetas who were guarding suitcases stuffed with $6 million in cash (McKinley 2008c).

The lethality of the Zetas has been strengthened by their recruitment of Mexican-American teenagers, some as young as 13 years old, who are trained for months in the use of assault rifles and hand-to-hand combat and placed in comfortable houses on both sides of the border. While awaiting assignments, youngsters receive a retainer of $500 a week and from $10,000 to $50,000 per assassination. There are also perks such as parties with attractive women and luxury cars for outstanding work (McKinley 2009b). "Los Zetas has since expanded beyond its enforcement and security services to become fully engaged in trafficking illicit drugs to the United States" (National Drug Intelligence Center 2009b: 9). Along with other trafficking organizations, Los Zetas have extended their portfolios to include a variety of businesses such as spas and day care centers. Zetas wholesale pirated movies and CDs under their own label containing the organization's unicorn logo (McKinley, Jr. and Lacey 2009). Drug traffickers have been major contributors to the impoverished Church in Mexico, helping to build chapels. In one instance, a plaque on a church in Pachuca, Mexico, reveals its benefactor as Heriberto Lazcano, leader of Los Zetas (Cave 2011).

Tijuana Cartel

A city of more than one million persons just across the border from San Diego, Tijuana is the home of the Arellano-Félix family, seven brothers and four sisters. Noted for their level of violence—brother Ramón is a suspect in more than sixty murders—they literally shot their way into control of drug smuggling along the Mexico–California border (Preston and Pyes 1997). But they have not overlooked bribery: In 1998, two members of an elite Mexican drug enforcement unit working undercover were arrested by federal and state police acting on behalf of the Tijuana drug cartel (Dillon 1998d). Mexican police are reputed to have supplied the cartel with a steady flow of stolen vehicles, and members of the military have arranged for the purchase of assault weapons and machine guns. Using brokers, the brothers have provided money to politicians and struggling business people (Golden 2000b).

Like their Colombian counterparts, the Tijuana cartel has intimidated and murdered journalists who have reported on their activities; victims also include law enforcement officers (Dillon 1997; DEA "Fact Sheet" n.d.). In 2000, cartel gunmen tortured and murdered three Mexican drug agents, one of whom was an expert on the Arellanos and their chief pursuer. The three were returning to Tijuana from San Diego, where they were living for security reasons. They were intercepted shortly after crossing the border and before they could retrieve their weapons—there is a dispute between Mexico and the United States about whether agents of one country working in the other can carry weapons (de la Garza 2000; Golden 2000a). On the U.S. side of the border, the cartel employs California street gang members to carry out murders (de la Garza 1997b).

In 1999, ten men believed to be overseeing operations for the Tijuana cartel in southern California were arrested. They were in possession of 1,100 pounds of cocaine and four pounds of heroin; one of those arrested also had $100,000 in cash in his home (A. O'Connor 1999). In addition to heroin and cocaine, the cartel deals in methamphetamine and marijuana. In 2000, DEA agents arrested more than eighty persons in the United States who were involved with selling 117 tons of Tijuana cartel marijuana to Jamaican traffickers. Among those arrested were employees of the FedEx parcel service who arranged to ship the drugs from California to the East Coast (Sniffen 2000).

"The Arellano-Félix family, headed by Benjamin, evolved into one of Mexico's most powerful criminal drug enterprises for smuggling multi-ton quantities of drugs yearly" (Constantine 1999b: 8). While Benjamin managed the multimillion-dollar business, his brother Ramón headed security-related operations. Ramón's functions included recruitment of enforcers and killers

from the streets of San Diego and Tijuana. In 2000, Ramón and Benjamin were indicted by a federal grand jury, and the U.S. Department of State offered a $2 million reward for their capture. In 2002, Ramón Arellano-Félix, 37, carrying a gold-plated handgun and fake federal police identification, was reportedly killed in a shootout with police. Before a positive identification could be made, his body was claimed by two unidentified persons and cremated.

Benjamin was arrested shortly afterward and received a five-year sentence for arms possession. He was subsequently sentenced to twenty-two years for cocaine trafficking. In 2006, one of the remaining brothers, Francisco Javier, was captured by the U.S. Coast Guard while deep-sea fishing off Baja California. The following year, he pled guilty to running a criminal enterprise and received a life sentence. In 2008, one of the Arellano-Félix brothers, Francisco Raphael, 58, was released from a U.S. prison. He had been extradited from Mexico after serving a prison sentence, but was not successfully prosecuted in the United States.

Juárez Cartel

Ciudad Juárez, in the state of Chihuahua, is just across the Rio Grande from El Paso, Texas; it is an easy walk from downtown Juárez to downtown El Paso via a pedestrian bridge over which about 14,000 persons cross daily. With a murder rate of more than 200 per 100,000 residents, Juárez is the most dangerous city in the world (Padgett 2011), while El Paso is one of the safest cities in the United States. The absence of violence in El Paso may be the result of a rational choice by the cartels, "which calculate that creating chaos in the United States would disrupt this fairly free flow of goods" (Rice 2011: 23). Legitimate trade between Juárez and El Paso amounts to more than $70 billion annually.

With a population of 1.5 million, Juárez is racked by poverty and lacks a sewage treatment facility, but is home to one of Mexico's richest drug organizations. The Juárez cartel is the result of a mid-1980s consolidation of various drug rings accomplished by a notoriously corrupt commander of a local unit of the Judicial Police, and his brother. They were succeeded by Amado Carrillo-Fuentes.

Carrillo-Fuentes proved to be gifted with organizational skills. The nephew of one of Mexico's drug trafficking pioneers, he started his career in the early 1980s as a drug mule for his uncle and built his own organization in the late 1980s, developing important ties to the Herrera Family and the Cali cartel. He spent lavishly to gain protection from government at all levels. By 1993, Carrillo-Fuentes and his brothers were in control of the Juárez cartel and the owners of a fleet of Boeing 727s, from which Amado derived his nickname "Lord of the Skies" (Brant 1997b). Estimates of his wealth reached $25 billion, and the head of Mexico's antidrug agency was on his payroll—police and military forces were used on his behalf in efforts against rival drug organizations, in particular, the Tijuana cartel (Dillon and Pyes 1997a; Golden 1998a). Responsible for as many as 400 drug-related murders, Carrillo-Fuentes, nevertheless, contributed heavily to the church (de la Garza 1997a). In 1997, at age 41 or 42—neither his birth date nor his face is known to the police—Amado Carrillo-Fuentes died of heart failure after undergoing eight hours of plastic surgery at a posh maternity hospital in Mexico City (Brant 1997a).

In the employ of the enforcement arm of the cartel is *Barrio Aztecas,* (BA) whose members sport tattoos of Aztec symbols such as snakes and pyramids. Formed in prison in the 1980s, "they carry both American passports and high-caliber weapons" (Lacey 2010: 6). With about 600 active members on the street and in prison, BA is based primarily in West Texas, Juárez, Mexico, and throughout state and federal prisons in the United States and Mexico. They have a militaristic command structure that includes captains, lieutenants, sergeants, and soldiers. A major racketeering case against BA several years ago effectively dismantled its leadership, but the group reorganized, and younger members—dubbed the "Pepsi Generation"—have been promoted to top positions (FBI Press Release, September 21, 2010).

The Juárez cartel maintains drug transportation and distribution cells in U.S. cities such as Los Angeles, Houston, Chicago, and New York from which it distributes cocaine to Nashville, Miami, Detroit, Raleigh, Houston, Newark, Philadelphia, San Antonio, Tulsa, and Los Angeles, where it is sold to domestic organizations. Much of the violence in the city is a result of conflict between the Juárez and Sinaloa cartels for control of the Juárez *plaza* (McKinley 2008b).

La Familia Michoacána

Operating out of the southern Pacific state of Michoacána is the most fearsome of Mexico's drug organizations headed by Nazario Moreno, known as El Más Loco—"The Craziest One"—whose "calling card" is a severed head. In 2009, after the arrest of a ranking member of *La Familia Michoacána*, a series of retaliatory attacks ensued resulting in the killing of three federal officers and two soldiers. Several days later, the bodies of twelve military intelligence officers who were investigating *La Familia* were found bound, blindfolded, and tortured (Malkin 2009; "12 Mexican Intelligence Agents Tortured, Slain" 2009).

The author of his own bible, *Pensamientos* ("Thoughts"), Moreno was influenced by evangelical Christianity, and core leaders of *La Familia*—which is reputedly run by a council—regularly attend church services. Moreno carries a Bible and espouses a pseudoreligious philosophy whose stated goal is to protect Mexicans from the influence of drugs: the group claims it opposes the sale of drugs to Mexicans, but supports its consumption by Americans. Instead of buying off public officials, *La Familia* supports favored candidates with extensive funding and is viewed by many as "Robin Hood" which lavishes food and money on poor residents (Padgett and Grillo 2010). Similar to sophisticated criminal organizations throughout the world, *La Familia* appears to have taken on a quasi-governmental role in Michoacána, working with or instead of the police as guarantors of public safety and providing debt-collection services for businesses. They have built schools and recreation facilities (Finnegan 2010b).

In 2005, United States restrictions on over-the-counter sales of pseudoephedrine, a methamphetamine precursor used in nasal decongestants, caused a decline in clandestine meth labs. *La Familia* quickly filled the vacuum by establishing about a thousand meth labs in Michoacána to convert pseudoephdrine smuggled from Asia into methamphetamine destined for the United States (Padgett and Grillo 2010). The labs are an important source of employment in this poverty-stricken region. *La Familia* recruits members as young as 14 who are inculcated with a religious doctrine that demands loyalty and a commitment to kill rivals as "divine justice." The group has an extensive distribution network in the United States (Booth and Fainaru 2009; McKinley 2009d: 1, 24) and in 2009 more than 300 persons in 19 states were arrested for being part of that network: Officials seized 550 pounds of cocaine, 729 pounds of methamphetamine, 967 pounds of marijuana, and $8 million (Archibald 2009c; FBI press release, October 22, 2009). But it hardly made dent in the organization's distribution network (Finnegan 2010b). In 2010, federal and local law enforcement officials announced the arrest of forty-five persons belonging to *La Familia* cells headquartered in Atlanta, and the seizure of 46 pounds of methamphetamine, a clandestine methamphetamine laboratory, 43 kilograms of cocaine, 4,120 pounds of marijuana, 20 firearms, and $2,349,000 (DEA press release, November 8, 2010). In 2011, the FBI announced the arrest of nearly 2,000 persons connected to *La Familia*, the seizure of 635 pounds of methamphetamine, 118 kilos of cocaine, 24 pounds of heroin, and $770.499 (FBI press release, July 21, 2011).

DOMINICANS

The Dominican Republic, with a population of 8.8 million, occupies about two-thirds of the Caribbean island of Hispaniola, which it shares with Haiti (see Figure 6.4). The Dominican Republic is a major transit country for cocaine moving to the United States and serves drug smugglers as both a command-and-control center and transshipment point. Increasing amounts of designer drugs, especially "ecstasy," are being moved through the Dominican Republic from Europe to the United States and Puerto Rico.

The movement of drugs is aided by the existence of structured and integrated criminal organizations of Dominicans, Puerto Ricans, and Colombians that operate in Santo Domingo as well as in New York, Boston, Providence, and other U.S. cities. Colombians are generally in charge of control and supply in the Caribbean and begin the first phase of the transport. Later, Dominicans become the primary transporters (U.S. Department of State 2001). Dominicans have also imported MDMA ("ecstasy") directly from the Netherlands (Weiser 2002).

Although the Dominican Republic is not as depressed as Haiti, in the mid-1960s political unrest and economic upheavals caused many residents to seek their fortunes by going north. In New York City, there are about 575,000 Dominicans, many of whom have illegally entered the United States. They are among the poorest New Yorkers, with a poverty rate of 32 percent compared with the city total of 19 percent (Archibold 2004). Some of these immigrants, legal and illegal, have entered the drug trade. Known as Dominican-Yorks, the traffickers keep a low profile in the United States, returning their profits to cities in the Dominican Republic such as San Francisco de Macorís, conspicuous for its wealth in a country where the per capita income is less than $1,000 a year.

The center of the Dominican community is the Upper Manhattan neighborhood of Washington Heights. In recent years, some drug traffickers have slipped out of New York and are running operations from their homeland where corruption is endemic among airport officials and law enforcement. Until 1998, the Dominican Republic refused to extradite its citizens for crimes committed in the United States. In that year, two notorious traffickers were sent to New York where they were wanted for drug trafficking and murder.

Dominicans have demonstrated the necessary talent for moving large amounts of heroin and cocaine at the wholesale and street level. They serve as midlevel cocaine and heroin distributors to lower-level distributors, principally smaller

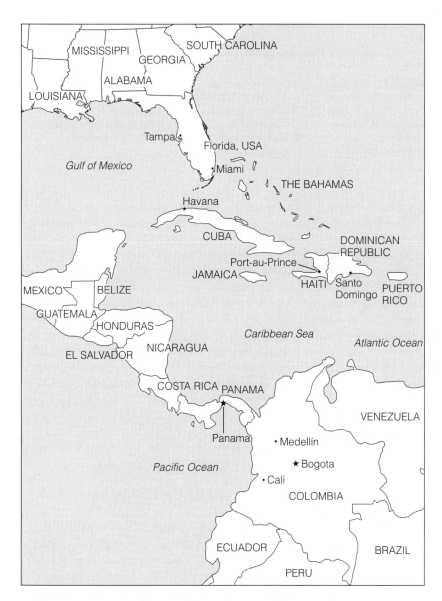

FIGURE 6.4 Map of Hispaniola and the Eastern U.S. coastline

Dominican criminal groups and street gangs (NDIC 2009d: 5). Dominicans purchase directly from Colombian importers, with whom they share a common language and entrepreneurial values. They have applied their well-known skills as tradesmen and merchants to the drug trade. They generally provide top-quality uncut drugs at competitive prices, avoiding the common practice of diluting the product as it passes through the distribution chain. Dominican drug trafficking organizations, either under contract to Colombian cartels or acting independently, transport or distribute cocaine and heroin in the New York/New Jersey area. They routinely smuggle cocaine by private and commercial vehicles

---

ECSTASY

Ecstasy is the common name for MDMA (3, 4-Methyle-neDioxyMethAmphetamine), a synthetic drug possessing stimulant and hallucinogenic properties. Ecstasy proved popular among white professionals—earning its nickname as a "yuppie drug"—and persons who consider themselves part of the New Age spiritual movement. It is reported to be popular on college campuses in the United States and at dance parties or raves. MDMA is usually ingested orally in tablet or capsule form. It is also available as a powder and is sometimes snorted and occasionally smoked (Abadinsky 2011).

---

and aboard maritime vessels from South America and the Caribbean; they smuggle heroin using couriers on commercial aircraft that fly into major airports within the region. Couriers typically conceal the drug underneath clothing, or they ingest the drug in "pellets" after packaging it in rubber items such as condoms, the fingers of surgical gloves, or balloons. A typical "swallower" can ingest between forty and ninety-five pellets, each weighing between 7 and 10 grams.

The structure of Dominican drug trafficking organizations is based on familial or regional loyalties. Organizations are vertically integrated, with the family maintaining control over several consecutive stages of the operation. Activities of the group are directed by the leader through a number of "lieutenants," who may include brothers, sisters, cousins, and friends from home. Although Dominicans developed a reputation as reliable dealers who promptly pay their suppliers and avoid competitive violence, several groups have become noted for their excessive violence, both to maintain internal discipline and to deal with competitors.

Dominicans dominate the middle echelon between the Colombians and the street dealers of cocaine and heroin in the New York City area and into New England. This is due in part to Colombian dissatisfaction with their Mexican counterparts. By 1995, major Colombian organizations had established themselves in the Dominican Republic to coordinate activities with their Dominican partners, and they have made Haiti the fastest growing transit point for cocaine being shipped to the United States. Haiti has proven attractive to the traffickers because it is

the poorest country in the hemisphere, making it relatively cheap to find criminal labor and bribe officials. The police had to be created from scratch after the old force was abolished in the wake of the American troop landing in 1994; they have limited training and resources and have become notoriously corrupt. Light aircraft land with their drug cargoes on Route 9 in Port-au-Prince where Haitian national police block traffic and help with offloading and ground transport. Smugglers then leave Haitian ports in speedboats laden with drugs without interference from the understaffed coast guard (Polgreen and Weiner 2004; Sisk 2004).

MARA SALVATRUCHA
(MS-13 OR *LOS MARA*)

According to some versions, in Salvadoran slang, *mara* means posse, and *salvatrucha* means "street-tough Salvadoran." Some sources (for example, Martel 2006) state that the name derives from a Spanish term for fire ants—*marabunta*. José Cruz (2011: 384n) discounts these explanations. The use of the term *mara*, he notes, is common in Salvadoran jargon, and "was part of the Salvadoran slang long before *Mara Salvatrucha* emerged in the 1980s. In the Salvadoran vernacular, the term refers "to any group of people and is widely used as synonymous with 'folks'."

El Salvador is one of the poorest countries in Latin America with almost half its population living in poverty. A civil war that began in 1980 left more than 70,000 people dead and displaced a fifth of the population. Political unrest caused many Salvadorans to emigrate to the United States where thousands of young men grew up in the streets of Los Angeles. They associated with other Latin Americans, mostly Chicano and Mexican immigrants, who had formed gangs. "At first they joined Mexican and Chicano gangs and later began to form a separate gang with their own identity" (Cruz 2011: 384).

The United States adopted a get-tough policy and began deporting thousands of Central Americans, including members of MS-13 who suddenly found themselves in the wake of a civil war. MS-13 spread among demobilized soldiers from the *Farabundo Marti Front for National Liberation* (FMNL), a leftist guerrilla organization trained in the use of firearms, explosives, and booby traps. In response, El Salvador cracked down on MS-13. While in prison, they began to organize themselves in a more structured fashion. Dozens of MS-13 members from different *clikas* and from different places throughout the country, established contact with each other and created a more structured organization. They set up networks in prison and countrywide structures that expanded beyond prison walls, resembling much of what some members had witnessed while being in U.S. prisons. Following the model of prison gangs such as the Mexican Mafia (discussed later) they established a national leadership. Thus, indiscriminate government repression ended up strengthening *mara* networks and "the quality of their operations consequently became more focused, more structured, and more organised" (Cruz 2011: 396).

After being stranded in a country they did not know, many MS-13 deportees made their way back to the United States accompanied by their battle-hardened brethren from the FMNL. The recycling continues, and there are an estimated 6,000 to 10,000 members in the United States—many of whom have been previously arrested and deported (Campo-Flores 2005; Quirk 2008). They smuggle drugs, primarily powdered cocaine and marijuana, into the United States and transport and distribute them throughout the country. Some members also

are involved in alien smuggling, identity theft, prostitution operations, robbery, and weapons trafficking (National Gang Intelligence Center 2009).

MS-13 members have international connections with members maintaining constant contact with counterparts in El Salvador. To the dismay of U.S. authorities, these alliances provide MS-13 members with access to military arms and the wherewithal to traffic them to this country. Their experience with illegal immigration has led MS-13 to control many of the "coyote services" that bring aliens from Central America into the United States.

In the United States, MS-13 operates in small groups, *cliques* whose members range in age from 11 to 40 and each are led by one or two individuals known as *veteranos*, usually older members who have the overall responsibility for organizing meetings, directing criminal activity, regulating behavior, and maintaining cohesion. *Los Mara* is reputed to be highly organized and disciplined with a vertical command structure in El Salvador, but this is presently absent in the United States (Campos-Flores 2005). While MS-13 operates in at least forty-two states and the District of Columbia, according to the FBI there is no official national leadership structure.

Individuals seeking membership in MS-13 are subject to various forms of initiation including beatings. Some candidates are "jumped in," a ritual that consists of a candidate being beaten by members for a period of thirteen seconds. In some *cliques*, participation in felonious activity may be required. There have also been instances where individuals have been required to assault a police officer in order to gain full membership. To signify allegiance, once accepted into the organization, members are expected to display a tattoo (New Jersey Commission of Investigation 2004). Indeed, most *Los Mara* members and are easily recognized by the tattoos on their heads, necks, and arms bearing the group's symbols: "MS," "13," and "18," in addition to dice, crossbones, and daggers, the colors blue and white, and hand signs: the thumb holding the two middle fingers pressed to the palm (Brzezinski 2004).

Los Mara quickly developed a reputation for being extremely violent, and "members have committed violent offenses at appalling levels—dismembering bodies, terrifying drive-by shootings in broad daylight, and, in a few cases, hacking entire families to death" (Vaquera and Bailey 2004: 6). Rounding out their criminal repertoire is large-scale theft, chop shops, and extortion. They have developed important ties to Mexican and Colombian drug cartels. Because many are illegal immigrants to the United States, the U.S. Bureau of Immigration and Customs Enforcement (ICE) has been a leading agency in efforts against the MS-13 (LeDuff 2005). Other law enforcement agencies have been critical of ICE for arresting and deporting *Los Mara* members who had been under intense investigation before they can be charged with new crimes because deported members often return to the United States, and the recycling continues. In response to the threat posed by the group, the FBI has created an MS-13 National Gang Task Force.

THE MEXICAN MAFIA

Prison-based gangs have gained prominence as organized criminal groups, most notably the Mexican Mafia. Found in at least nine state prison systems and reputed to be the most powerful of the prison crime groups, the Mexican Mafia (also known as *la M*—pronounced *la em-aay*) is comprised primarily Mexican-American convicts and ex-convicts from the barrios of East Los Angeles. Like many other prison gangs, as well as their street counterparts, the Mexican Mafia has a "blood-in-blood-out" credo: Murder or the drawing of blood is a prerequisite for membership, and those seeking to resign will be killed.

Its origins are traced to the Deuel Vocational Institute in Tracy, California, where, in 1957, thirteen young Mexican Americans from the Maravilla area of East Los Angeles began the Mexican Mafia as a self-protection group. The number 13 has additional significance for *la M,* since *M* is the thirteenth letter of the alphabet. They soon "began to control

such illicit activities as homosexual prostitution, gambling, and narcotics. They called themselves the Mexican Mafia out of admiration for *La Cosa Nostra*" (PCOC 1986: 73). Attempts by the Department of Corrections to diminish gang power by transferring members to other institutions only helped spread their influence. Vigorous recruiting occurs among the most violent Mexican-American inmates, particularly those housed in adjustment centers for the most dangerous and incorrigible. In 1967, Mexican Mafia reliance on wholesale violence increased, and in that year members attacked the first Mexican American outside their group. This attack on an inmate from rural northern California led to the formation of a second Mexican–American gang, *La Nuestra Familia,* with whom the Mexican Mafia has been feuding ever since. The Mexican Mafia is anti-black and has aligned itself with the Aryan Brotherhood, an extremely violent prison-based white supremacist gang.

By the mid-1960s the Mexican Mafia had assumed control over prison heroin trafficking and numerous other inmate activities. In 1966, it started to move its operations outside the prison, and organized Hispanic gangs into a confederation to confront black Los Angeles gangs for control of the drug trade (Mydans 1995). A 2011 federal indictment revealed Mexican Mafia control over street gangs in Orange County who are expected to pay *la M* a portion of their drug proceeds. In return, they are permitted to exert influence over their neighborhoods and territories and seek protection or assistance from the Orange County branch of the Mexican Mafia.

The formidable presence of the Mexican Mafia in California prisons allows them to exert control on the street since criminals realize they will need protection in the event of their own incarceration. A similar pattern is found in Russia where *vory v zakone* control in the prison system enhances their influence among criminals on the street.

In the next chapter, we will examine domestic African American and black foreign-based criminal organizations.

SUMMARY

1. Know how the history, culture, and geography of Colombia influenced the development of drug trafficking organizations:
   - Colombia is the only South American country with both Pacific and Caribbean coastlines.
   - Colombia is a relatively large country, and many regions have only a weak federal presence.
   - Colombia has been torn by political strife, with three civil wars during the nineteenth century, and two in the twentieth—in 1902 and 1948.
   - The war officially ended when the Liberals and the Conservatives formed the National Front, but Marxist insurgencies and right-wing paramilitaries continue to threaten the stability of the central government.
   - Until the early 1970s, the importation of marijuana and cocaine into the United States was largely a Cuban operation. When Colombian traffickers became highly organized both in the United States, Cubans became subordinate.
   - Colombians have been able to control the cocaine market because Colombia is well-positioned both to receive coca from Peru and Bolivia and to export the processed drug to the United States by air or by sea and the country's vast central forests effectively conceal clandestine processing laboratories and air strips. The Colombian reputation for violence serves to maintain discipline and intimidate would-be competitors.

2. Recognize the role of left- and right-wing organizations in drug trafficking:
   - Marxist guerilla forces of the Revolutionary Armed Forces of Colombia (FARC) protect the crops and levy taxes on the drug business.
   - Paramilitaries are sometimes allied with—sometimes fighting against—the drug traffickers and receive financial backing from wealthy landowners.

3. Understand the structure and vulnerabilities of Colombian drug organizations:
   - Colombian drug trafficking organizations are compartmentalized and individual members of the same network seldom know one another.
   - The sheer volume of Colombian drug transactions makes them vulnerable to sophisticated law enforcement efforts because the volume of their business requires sophisticated record-keeping to track expenses and sales.
   - The Medellín and Cali cartels were vertically integrated to maintain control over cocaine through the entire chain from manufacturing to wholesale distribution. But as with any vertically integrated organization, a broken link can be devastating.

4. Understand the changes that have occurred with the collapse of the Medellín and Cali cartels:
   - In the absence of powerful drug lords, the drug trade has become more decentralized
   - The dismantling of the Cali cartel created opportunities for their Mexican colleagues.

5. Be knowledgeable about Mexican history and the connection between politics, corruption, and drug trafficking:
   - In Mexico, societal focus is on the interests of the immediate and extended family, not the wider interests of a more impersonal societal good.
   - Mexico has a history of one-party domination intertwined with corruption, particularly in the underpaid law enforcement sector.
   - Drug groups are bureaucratically organized, but in a Mexican fashion built around familial relationships.

6. Know what led to the extreme violence that pervades Mexico:
   - The defeat of the PRI in Mexico ruptured a longtime implicit arrangement between

narcotrafficantes and the PRI-controlled government and led to an unparalleled level of competitive violence.

- The popular culture of Mexico is infused with songs glamorizing drug trafficking, and major *narcotraficantes* are celebrated, along with their subculture of violence.

7. Be familiar with the structure and business operations of Mexican drug organizations:
   - Mexican drug trafficking organizations control most of the U.S. drug market and have affiliations with gangs in the United States.
   - They have moved away from traditional hierarchical structures in favor of decentralized networks of interdependent, task-oriented cells.
   - Mexican drug organizations are family-run operations with a corresponding high degree of personal trust.
   - Unlike American organized crime, organized crime figures in Mexico have at their disposal an army of personnel, an arsenal of weapons and the finest technology that money can buy.
   - Rather than controlling territory, Mexican drug organizations seek to control *plazas*, transportation routes, and hubs.
   - Mexican drug trafficking is dominated by about a half-dozen cartels: Herrera Family, Sinloa, Gulf, Los Zetas, Tijuana, Juárez, *La Familia Michoacána*.

8. Know the role of Dominican organizations in drug trafficking:
   - The Dominican Republic serves as a transshipment point for drugs, and Dominican criminals in the United States purchase directly from Asian and Colombian importers, sharing a common language and entrepreneurial values with the latter.
   - Dominicans serve as midlevel cocaine and heroin distributors to lower-level distributors.

9. Know the role of MS-13:
   - In the late 1980s, a small number of the roughly 300,000 Salvadorans living in Los Angeles formed *mara salvatrucha* or MS-13.
   - Estimated to have 30,000 to 50,000 members, 8,000 to 10,000 of who reside in the United States, MS-13 smuggles powdered cocaine and marijuana, into the United States and transport and distribute the drugs throughout the country.

10. Understand the history of the prison-based Mexican Mafia and its expansion beyond the institution:
   - Prison-based gangs have been gaining prominence as organized criminal groups, most notably the Mexican Mafia whose members, when released from prison, traffic in drugs and extort money from weaker dealers.

REVIEW QUESTIONS

1. What aspects of Colombian history and culture help promote drug trafficking?
2. What was the relationship between Cuban exiles, Colombians, and cocaine trafficking?
3. Why did the relationship end?
4. What variables account for the Colombian success in the cocaine business?
5. What is the role of Marxist FARC guerillas in the cocaine business?
6. How does their structure serve to protect Colombian trafficking organizations?
7. Why are Colombian drug trafficking organizations vulnerable to law enforcement?
8. How did the Medellín cartel differ from the Cali cartel?
9. How did the business structure of the Medellín and Cali cartels make them both highly profitable and vulnerable?

10. How did the Colombian drug business change since the demise of the Medellín and Cali cartels?

11. What led to the Colombian entry into the heroin business?

12. How has the political climate of Mexico aided in the development of criminal organizations?

13. How did the dismantling of the Cali cartel affect Mexican traffickers?

14. What aspects of Mexican history and culture help promote drug trafficking?

15. Why did the election of a reform president in Mexico lead to an unparalleled level of competitive violence?

16. With what have Mexican trafficking organizations replaced traditional hierarchical structures?

17. How do organized crime leaders in Mexico differ from those of the American Mafia?

18. What are *plazas* that Mexican drug organizations seek to control?

19. What role is played by Dominicans in drug trafficking?

In custody, "Dudas" Coke, boss of Jamaica's Shower posse.   AP Photo/Louis Lanzano, File

Black Organized Crime

Jamaican crime lord Christopher "Dudus" Coke faces up to twenty-three years in prison after pleading guilty to assault and racketeering charges in a New York federal court. He admitted to using "fear, force and intimidation" to control the notorious "Shower Posse" (Pettitfor 2011).

The fact that Dudus could have flourished in Jamaica from the early 1990s is a graphic illustration of the failure of the Jamaican state. Not only did Jamaica fail to arrest him, it actively supported Coke and his criminal enterprises by rewarding him with lucrative multimillion-dollar contracts.

Even the women who came out to proclaim him lord and savior last year knew what kind of creature he was, but we could not do one damn thing about him. That is until the Americans intervened to force Coke's extradition and liberate us from his criminal tyranny. The action against Christopher Michael Coke demonstrates the value of having a Great Power strong enough to force weak states to respect the rule of law (Boyne 2011).

Dudas Coke and his Shower Posse will be discussed in this chapter.

CHAPTER 7 WILL ENABLE THE READER TO UNDERSTAND:

- The affect of prejudice on domestic black criminal organizations
- The affect of the Vietnam War on black criminals
- The development of the Gangster Disciples and their primary Chicago opponents, the Black P. Stone Nation
- Factors thwarting African Americans from following the historical pattern of neighborhood-gangs-into-organized-crime
- The variables that make West Africa attractive for the development of criminal organizations
- The role of Nigerian criminal organizations in the globalization of organized crime
- The connection between politics and Jamaican criminal organizations

Black is an imprecise term that includes many diverse groups, domestic and international, and "black organized crime" encompasses a variety of criminal groups that may in fact share only their race.[1] But race is an organizing variable much as religious background served as a common denominator for Jewish criminals, and a shared cultural heritage serves the same purpose for the American Mafia. This chapter will examine African American, West African, and Jamaican organized crime.

AFRICAN AMERICAN
ORGANIZED CRIME

African American criminal groups use the drug trade much as their Irish, Jewish, and Italian predecessors did bootlegging. Black criminal groups in the United States, however, lack the incubation provided by the corrupt urban political machines discussed in Chapter 2 and ineffective federal law enforcement of previous centuries.

Important black criminal entrepreneurs were operating in the United States in the early decades of the twentieth century. In Chicago, African American entrepreneurs were successful in controlling extensive gambling operations in the city's "black belt," where they delivered votes and funds to Republican mayor "Big Bill" Thompson. In 1927, after Thompson had been out of office for four years, black voters helped sweep him back into city hall. In the election of 1931, Thompson lost to what became known as the Chicago Democratic machine that dominated the city until almost the end of the twentieth century (discussed in Chapter 3). Like their white counterparts, black political–criminal leadership switched their allegiance and became part of the Democratic machine (Lombardo 2002b).

African American criminals dominated the numbers (illegal lottery) racket in cities such as New York, Philadelphia, and Chicago until they were overpowered by violent white gangsters such as Dutch Schultz (New York) and Sam Giancana (Chicago) who had superior police/political connections (Lombardo 2002b; Schatzberg 1994). Until his death of natural causes in 1968, Ellsworth ("Bumpy") Johnson headed an organization that ruled over the black Harlem underworld in New York in an alliance with the Genovese crime Family. The civil rights/"black power" movements of the 1960s eventually made it impossible for white criminals to operate with the freedom necessary to continue dominating indigenous black criminal organizations.

A variety of black criminal groups exist throughout the United States; some are home-grown, such as Chicago's Gangster Disciples, while others, such as Jamaican posses, are imported. Important black criminal organizations have been active in the heroin business in New York, Detroit, Chicago, Philadelphia, and Washington, DC. Although blacks have traditionally been locked out of many activities associated with organized crime (labor and business racketeering, for example) by prejudice, *dope is an equal opportunity employer.* African American criminal groups made important strides in the heroin business when the Vietnam War exposed many black soldiers to the heroin markets of the Golden Triangle—previously, black groups were dependent on American Mafia Families for their heroin. As a result of their overseas experience, African American criminals were able to bypass the American Mafia and buy directly from suppliers in Thailand. A pioneer in this endeavor was Frank Lucas and his "Country Boys."

Frank Lucas and Leslie ("Ike")
Atkinson

The activities of Frank Lucas were popularized in the 2007 motion picture *American Gangster* starring Denzel Washington and Russell Crowe. Born to a large sharecropper's family who would later become part of his drug ring, in 1946, Lucas arrived in Harlem from North Carolina as a teenager with a serious criminal history. He continued his criminal activities as an armed robber until he found work

---

1. *Race* is also an imprecise term, but discussion of the topic is beyond the scope of this book.

AP Photo/Jim Cooper

Frank Lucas, the man that Denzel Washington portrayed in "American Gangster," is shown in New York in 2007.

with Bumpy Johnson as a collector in the numbers business; he also picked up Mafia heroin packages from "Pleasant Avenue."[2] In 1951, Johnson received a fifteen-year sentence for drug trafficking. Released after four years, in 1968, Bumpy was awaiting trial on another drug charge when he died of a heart attack. Johnson had introduced Lucas to the drug business and after Bumpy's death, he had an inspiration, a way to bypass the Genovese ("French") connection—Lucas decided to go to Southeast Asia.

In the early 1970s, the famed "French Connection" was coming apart, and although he had never been to the Far East, the brazen, streetwise Lucas, traveling alone, quickly made contact with sources of heroin. A former Army sergeant, a North Carolina "homeboy" married to a Lucas cousin, was running a bar in Bangkok; together they organized a "military-homeboy" organization. They brought in a country carpenter from North Carolina who con-

2. Manhattan's Harlem neighborhood is informally divided into black, Latino, and Italian sections. The Italian section, known by its major street, Pleasant Avenue, has been a stronghold of the Genovese crime Family.

structed copies of government coffins, but with false bottoms to hold 6 to 8 kilos of heroin. Military personnel were bribed and the Southeast Asian connection was complete (Jacobson 2000).

Ron Chepesiuk and Anthony Gonzalez report that they interviewed the aforementioned Army sergeant—Leslie ("Ike") Atkinson—in federal prison where he was completing a thirty-one-year sentence and present a different version of the Lucas story: It was Atkinson, familiar with the military, who set up the drug-smuggling operation with a group of partners dubbed the "Black Masonic" club. And it was Atkinson who helped the barely literate Lucas get a visa through the Thai embassy in Washington and who agreed to allow Lucas to run the U.S. end of the enterprise. Atkinson teamed up with a fellow homeboy and paratrooper, Jack Jackson.

Atkinson told Chepesiuk and Gonzalez that drugs were never shipped in coffins. Atkinson-Jackson heroin wholesalers picked up their supplies for distribution through networks that spanned the United States. Ike provided heroin and at times loans for Lucas's Country Boys, who had a penchant for violence—Atkinson claims that as a civilian he never carried a firearm. But he personally sold to buyers he did not know well and inevitably one turned out to be a confidential informant. In 1972, Jackson received a thirty-year federal sentence while Atkinson cooperated in the government's effort to convict two drug agents for corruption and was able to stave off incarceration. Having amassed a considerable fortune, this would have been an ideal time to exit the drug business, but Atkinson would not let go. He was eventually sentenced to thirty-two years and released in 2007 (Chepesiuk 2010).

The stateside Country Boys organization was restricted to blood relatives and friends from rural North Carolina who actively trafficked the Lucas "Blue Magic" brand of heroin on Harlem's 116th Street while two Lucas brothers, Shorty and Larry, operated in northern New Jersey and the Bronx, New York. Lucas also supplied rings in Chicago, North Carolina, and Los Angeles (Langlais 1978). Lucas quickly became a multimillionaire with a Cayman Islands bank account, office buildings in Detroit, apartments in Miami and Los Angeles, a string of gas stations and dry cleaning shops, and a several-thousand acre spread in North Carolina with three hundred head of Black Angus cattle.

Like other major criminals before and after, such as Al Capone and John Gotti, Lucas had a fatal flaw. He enjoyed the public spotlight, and his high-profile drug-kingpin lifestyle—a Rolls Royce, flashy diamond jewelry, a chinchilla coat, retinue of bodyguards, women, and associates—eventually attracted law enforcement scrutiny (and apparently the ire of the Genovese Family). In 1975, a New York Police Department/Drug Enforcement Administration (DEA) task force, acting on a tip from "Pleasant Avenue" sources, staged a surprise raid on Lucas's Teaneck, New Jersey, residence. They recovered more than half a million dollars in small bills and keys to safe deposits in the Cayman Islands. In 1975, Lucas was convicted of drug violations, and although sentenced to a federal forty-year term, he was subsequently released in 1983; he had provided the government with valuable information—the man who fashioned himself "Superfly" had become "Supersnitch" (Chepesiuk and Gonzalez 2007; Jacobson 2000). In 1984, Lucas was convicted again, this time for arranging to sell one ounce of heroin, and sentenced to seven years.

Nicky Barnes

Another high-profile criminal would suffer the same fate as Frank Lucas. Leroy Antonio ("Nicky") Barnes was born in New York's Harlem in 1933. In 1977, he posed for a color photo on the front page of the *New York Times* magazine that declared him "Mister Untouchable" because he had beaten government charges thirteen times—witnesses against Barnes disappeared or were found murdered. An outraged President Jimmy Carter ordered the Justice Department to make Barnes a priority.

Barnes cultivated a public image: He donated turkeys to homeless shelters and toys to children at Christmas and sponsored a Harlem basketball team. In the nightspots he frequented, the superbly dressed heroin trafficker, his business notwithstanding, would enter like a movie star and be treated accordingly by adoring fans (Chepesiuk 2007b).

A street-level drug dealer working for Dominicans, in 1959 Barnes was convicted and sent to New York's Green Haven Correctional Facility, a maximum-security prison located in Stormville. There, Barnes met Matthew Madonna, a drug dealer and member of the Lucchese Family; they discussed how best to run the drug business. Paroled in 1962, three years later, Barnes was back in Green Haven for possessing $500,000 worth of heroin. There he met Joe ("Crazy Joey") Gallo, a member of the Colombo Family who aided him in finding an attorney who succeeded in overturning Barnes's conviction.

From Madonna, Barnes got the idea of establishing a council of major traffickers in Harlem. Failing in his first attempt in 1969, with Madonna's Pleasant Avenue connection providing heroin, Barnes set up a council consisting of seven lieutenants, each of whom controlled a dozen midlevel distributors, who in turn supplied about forty street-level dealers. Like the American Mafia, council members took an oath of brotherhood, pooled their resources, and allocated territories. In a typical operation, a Madonna confederate would park a car whose steel-reinforced trunk was loaded with plastic-wrapped kilos of heroin. The confederate would slip the key to Madonna who would hand it off to Barnes at a prearranged location. Barnes in turn would slip the key and the car's make and location to a confederate. Payments were handled in the same manner—an exchange of keys to a car whose trunk was filled with hundreds of thousands of dollars (Barnes and Folsom 2007). The council eventually distributed heroin throughout New York State, in Pennsylvania and Canada, and as far west as Arizona (Chepesiuk 2007b).

Each kilo of heroin was cut—diluted—by an assembly line of women who worked naked—a precaution against purloining any of the precious powder—throughout the night. With a quarter spoon they scooped the heroin and added mannitol (a colorless, crystalline sugar) and quinine before placing the mix in a glassine envelope, the kind used by stamp collectors; the envelopes were sealed with black tape. In this manner, a kilo of almost pure heroin could be converted into 8 to

10 kilos. From there, sacks of individual packets of heroin would be moved to middlemen. A shipment of 200 kilos of heroin cost the council $5 million and earned them $20 million in 1973 dollars (Barnes and Folsom 2007).

But his career as Mr. Untouchable was relatively brief. In 1976, Madonna was arrested by federal agents during a key handoff, and the following year Mr. Untouchable was convicted and sentenced to life imprisonment by the first federal trial to use an anonymous jury. In 1981, he discovered that while members of the council were not supporting his legal efforts, they were making a very public display of cavorting with both his wife and his girlfriend—the DEA had sent him photographic proof. Barnes became a government informant leading to the conviction of fifty dealers and their associates. He was never offered an early release for his cooperation and languished in prison for fifteen years until released into the Witness Security Program in 1998 (Barnes and Folsom 2007; Chepesiuk 2007b).

Gangster Disciples

Frank Lucas could use his rural North Carolina ties to build a personalistic organization, but other African American criminals resorted to a bureaucratic model. Francis Ianni (1974: 158) noted that for African American criminals, in a pattern similar to that of the early Camorra (discussed in Chapter 5), "prisons and the prison experience form the most important locus for establishing the social relationships that form the basis for partnerships in organized crime." And like the early Camorra, a bureaucratic model was adopted by Chicago's best-known African American crime group, the Gangster Disciples (GDs).

The occupational opportunity structure of the United States has changed dramatically, characterized by a significant reduction in the number of good-paying jobs available to low-skilled workers. As such, the structural sources of mobility available to earlier immigrant groups have narrowed considerably. The deindustrialization of American society means that major cities are different places today

than they were during the times of major European immigration. Advances in transportation and communication, industrial technology, and the global economy have transformed cities from centers of production and distribution to centers of administration, finance, and the exchange of information. In this environment, the blue-collar jobs that once provided a means of social mobility have vanished or moved to the Third World.

The congruent processes of social and spatial mobility that allowed earlier disadvantaged inner-city residents to succeed in society do not apply to large numbers of African Americans today. As a result, we have witnessed the formation of an urban underclass composed of men and women who are excluded from participation in mainstream occupations. This structural entrapment denies people a method of maturing out of crime and has fueled the development of super-gangs such as Chicago's Gangster Disciples (Robert M. Lombardo,[3] personal correspondence).

The GD was the result of a merger of two South Side gangs, one headed by Larry Hoover (Supreme Gangsters) and the other by "King" David Barksdale (Black Disciples). The primary symbol of the GD is a six-pointed "star of David" and crossed pitchforks; more elaborate versions include a heart.

In 1973, Hoover, born in Jackson, Mississippi, in 1950, was convicted of planning and ordering the murder of a man who had held up a GD drug house; he has been incarcerated ever since, serving a 150-year sentence. After Barksdale's death from kidney failure in 1974, and despite his imprisonment, leadership was assumed by Hoover, who was able to merge the Disciples into his organization now called the GDs. With plenty of time on his hands, the incarcerated Larry Hoover developed a corporate-type structure for his organization (Figure 7.1).

While dabbling in community activities and local politics, the GD have remained active in selling cocaine and heroin throughout Chicago, a

3. Loyola University, Chicago.

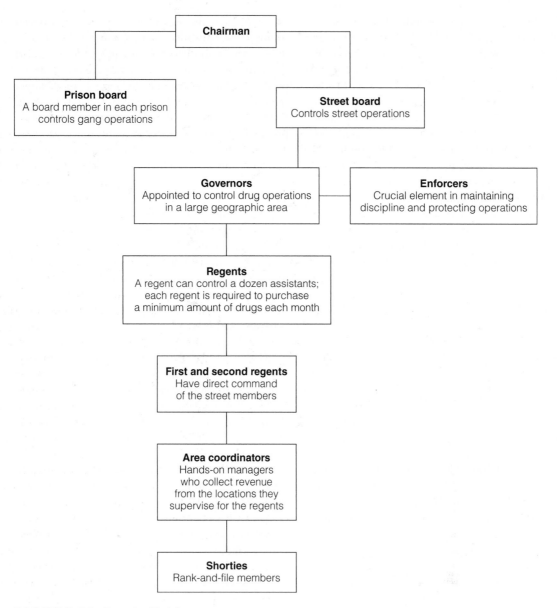

FIGURE 7.1 Gangster Disciples

number of suburban areas, and in several states including Wisconsin, Indiana, Missouri, Oklahoma, and Georgia. They also extort money from other drug dealers for the right to sell in areas in which the GD assert control. Independent dealers who have achieved a level of success are typically approached by GD representatives and told to choose from three alternatives: join the GDs, stop selling drugs, or be killed.

Lower-ranking members who actually sell the drugs at the retail level keep most of the profit they make—they do not necessarily share it with higher-ranking members or the organization as a whole. Instead, the hierarchy makes considerable income from wholesaling drugs to these members. The GD have been able to pool drug profits, street taxes, and membership dues to establish and operate legitimate businesses including apartment buildings, sometimes for the purpose of money laundering and to serve as centers for illegal operations. As noted earlier, a criminal organization can exhibit a formal structure while its economic activities may actually involve small firms or partnerships among members and include nonmember associates—the formal structure is not necessarily the same as the economic structure. However, the Gangster Disciples' size—about 6,000 members—requires a corporate-style structure.

Indeed, the size of the GDs requires a level of bureaucracy rarely seen in organized crime, making the organization vulnerable to prosecution. A list is kept of all persons dealing drugs in GD territory so they can be forced to pay street taxes—one day's profit per week. In a 1995 raid on a GD front group—Save the Children Promotions, Inc.—federal agents found detailed records including an organizational chart, a list of GD officers and their rank, a list of opposing gang leaders, the gang's pledge of allegiance, and its "laws"—sixteen that each member must memorize (Decker, Bynum, and Weisel 1998). Their logo, a pitchfork with the letters "CG," when drawn upside down is a sign of disrespect toward the GDs.

Inside prison, "legal coordinators" and "education ministers" indoctrinate new members with GD propaganda and assist fellow inmates in their appeals. Imprisoned members are instructed to complete their high school education and learn rudimentary principles of law from law books available in prison. They are directed to strengthen their bodies in prison weight rooms.

The GDs are politically active, at least in part to aid in the parole release efforts of their imprisoned leader. Under the name of 21st Century VOTE, GD engaged in voter registration drives and have supported candidates for the city council. Support for Hoover's parole came from a former Chicago mayor and several state and local elected officials interested in the support of 21st Century VOTE. Most of these officials expressed dismay—if not

remorse—when in 1995, Hoover and thirty-eight GDs were named in an indictment charging 149 counts of criminal conduct involving drug trafficking operations. Authorities devised a prison visitor's pass with a hidden transmitter, and Hoover was recorded passing orders to lieutenants who visited him at the Vienna (Illinois) Correctional Center. One of those indicted was a Chicago police officer who had been assigned to the Gang Crimes Unit—she received a twelve-and-one-half-year prison sentence.

During GD trials it was revealed that the offices of 21st Century VOTE served as a drop-off site for street taxes collected by gang members. In 1997, Hoover and the GD street leader were convicted of forty counts of drug trafficking (O'Connor 1997). Hoover was given six additional life sentences. Later that year, the GD who ranked second below Hoover was sentenced to death for his role in the murder of two GD members who were suspected of being informants—he had rewarded the executioners with new cars. In 1999, three GD officers who had vied for gang leadership were sentenced to life imprisonment for supervising a multimillion-dollar cocaine operation (O'Connor 1999). Following his additional convictions, Hoover was transferred to a federal supermax prison in Colorado.

As a result of the imprisonment or indictment of virtually its entire hierarchy and the conviction of about one hundred members and associates, the GDs is experiencing difficulties maintaining discipline and thwarting encroachments by rival groups. Street taxes often go unpaid or uncollected, and since the 1995 indictments, several members have been killed by other GD members or gangs selling drugs where the GDs once claimed hegemony. In 1997, the 19-year old GD who ran a drug territory on the South Side was recorded exhorting his juvenile drug sellers to carry firearms at their drug spots—he received a twenty-four-year federal prison sentence. That same year, the government taped a meeting at which a leading GD board member exhorted members to join in a "war" to retake territory lost to rivals since the federal crackdown, in particular, to deal with the

---

"BLACK POWER"

The Outfit overseer for the black belt of Chicago's Southside had summoned him. Jeff Fort, the high profile leader of the Blackstone Rangers, entered the restaurant and was directed to a table in the back where three heavy-set white men sat. Fort, who usually traveled with a retinue of bodyguards, was alone.

He sat down at the table and remained impassive as one of the men let loose with a barrage of curses and threats—"putting the nigger in his place." Fort stood up and left the restaurant as silently as he had entered. Later that night, the restaurant burned to the ground.

Black P. Stone Nation. The GD have been warring with the Black P. Stone Nation on and off for decades. In 2011, this conflict resulted in the accidental shooting death of a 10-year-old boy who was walking to a candy store with his friend (Meisner 2011).

BLACK P. STONE NATION

Chicago's El Rukns was founded by Jeff Fort who was born in Mississippi in 1947. One of ten children, Fort was brought to Chicago by his mother in 1956, and they eventually settled on South Blackstone Avenue in the poverty-stricken Woodlawn neighborhood. Slightly built, Fort left school after the fourth grade but nevertheless emerged as leader of Woodlawn's notorious Blackstone Rangers, named after the intersection of Sixty-fifth Street and Blackstone Avenue. He would grow into a physically imposing adult—from lifting weights in prison—with a beard and braids, often sporting fur coats and a Chinese coolie-type triangular hat.

The tough-guy reputation of the Blackstone Rangers drew the attention of black adult gangsters in the area, who began to use them as lookouts, numbers runners, drug couriers, collectors of protection money, and occasional executioners. But in the 1960s, federal antipoverty money poured into the area and black gangsters found they could not compete with community organizations who were focusing their efforts on the Rangers—they had already "lost their street muscle to the Italian outfit" (Moore and Williams 2011: 25). The Rangers extorted protection money from area businesses

and taxed pimps and the operators of gambling houses. Social service agencies who received federal antipoverty money protected them. The Rangers split with the Black Power/civil rights movement over the issue of nonviolence.

With Fort at its head, the Blackstone Rangers fought a long and bloody gang war with a rival group. In 1965, the charismatic leader organized a coalition of twenty-one gangs ruled by a commission known as the "main 21," with Fort as the head. From an initial membership of about 200, in three years it was in the thousands. As opposed to the exclusiveness of American Mafia membership, the Blackstone Rangers actively recruited and there are indications of violence being used against those who declined a membership invitation. Under Fort's direction they moved from extorting money from pimps to businesses in Woodlawn that catered to upscale clientele in Hyde Park (Chepesiuk 2007b). In 1968, the Blackstone Rangers became the Black P. Stone Nation (Moore and Williams 2011).

In 1969, referring to the Black P. Stone Nation as a community group, President Richard Nixon invited Fort to his inauguration—he sent a representative. Through the efforts of some white clergymen and community activists who were seeking to channel gang violence into more constructive pursuits, the Black P. Stone Nation was given a federal grant of $1 million from the Office of Economic Opportunity for an elaborate grassroots learning program. Mayor Richard M. Daley was outraged, and in 1968 and 1969 the grant was the subject of a U.S. Senate investigation. In response to a subpoena, Fort appeared before the Senate Permanent Subcommittee on Investigations, introduced himself, and then walked out. In 1972, he was imprisoned for contempt of Congress and embezzlement of $7,500 in federal funds (Glab 1997).

While in prison, Fort had an epiphany and founded the El Rukns, a "Moorish" religious organization, and dubbed himself Prince Malik. El Rukn refers to the cornerstone of the Muslim holy city of Kaaba in Mecca, and the term is Arabic for "The Black Stone"; Fort had discovered that his old street bore the name of the holiest shrine in Islam (Brune and Ylisela, Jr, 1988). After serving two years of a five-year sentence, the 29-year-old Fort was paroled and his organization began to dominate large areas of the black community. As a condition of his release, he could not reside in Chicago. He purchased a home in Milwaukee for his wife and children but spent most of his time in Chicago's South Side riding in a chauffeured limousine with several bodyguards. Fort granted no interviews and rarely spoke to anyone who was not part of his organization, which he had restructured into a corporate-style entity with handpicked generals at the top. He reduced the numbers of rank-and-file members from several thousand to several hundred, for greater control. Many of the older Rangers resisted the conversion to Fort's version of Islam, considering themselves Christians and unwilling to adhere to Muslim rules. Fort was a singular leader who sat on a throne at the El Rukn headquarters, a once-elegant theater at 3949 S. Drexel converted into a heavily fortified headquarters, the Grand Major Temple of America. The El Rukn application for tax-exempt status as a religious organization, however, was denied (Chepesiuk 2007b).

In line with a longstanding Chicago tradition, the El Rukns established the Young Grassroots Independent Voters, and in the 1983 mayoral race, the Cook County Democratic organization paid them $10,000 to campaign in black wards and serve as poll watchers for Mayor Jane Byrne. In 1984, the Reverend Jesse Jackson publicly praised them for their role in a voter registration drive on behalf of his presidential campaign (Shipp 1985).

The El Rukns established their own real estate company and invested in apartment buildings; there were plans for restaurants and construction companies when, in 1983, Fort was indicted for participation in a cocaine conspiracy. Before his trial could begin, Fort pled guilty and was sentenced to thirteen years' imprisonment. In 1987, Fort and four members of the El Rukns were convicted of plotting terrorist acts on behalf of Moammar Gadhafi of Libya; Fort was sentenced to eighty years. In 1988, Fort and three other El Rukns were convicted of the 1981 murder of a rival gang member who had failed to heed the El Rukn warning to share the proceeds of his drug dealing. With Fort in prison, the gang's headquarters were forfeited and destroyed, and a series of indictments and convictions followed. In 1989, sixty-five El Rukns were indicted, and by 1991, nineteen had been convicted of drug- and murder-related offenses. In 1992, numerous El Rukn generals who had held the highest rank under Fort, all in their thirties and forties, received long prison sentences. In 1993, serious charges of prosecutorial misconduct resulted in the convictions of many El Rukn defendants being thrown out and new trials ordered. Many already-convicted members were subsequently resentenced to significantly reduced terms.

Remaining El Rukns assumed their former name and "What is left of the Almighty Black P Stone Nation can be categorized into three groups: older Stones who never converted to El Rukns, El Rukns, and the new generation of Stones" who claim the mantle (Moore and Williams 2011: 257). In 2011, Chicago police arrested fifteen persons for being part of a Black P. Stone Nation drug operation. One of those arrested is Jeff Fort's nephew and when his house was searched in 2010, police found a shrine to the imprisoned founder (Main 2011).

OTHER DOMESTIC AFRICAN AMERICAN CRIMINAL ORGANIZATIONS

Jerome Skolnick and his colleagues (1990) distinguish between two gang types: *Cultural gangs* are strongly grounded in a neighborhood identity, and members may be involved in crime, including drug trafficking; *Entrepreneurial gangs* are organized for the express purpose of distributing drugs. The first type is maintained by loyalty to the gang and the neighborhood; the second is based on continuing economic opportunity. In the cultural gang, involvement in drug use and dealing can serve as membership requirements; stature in the group may be linked to success in the drug trade. Unlike the entrepreneurial gangs, these groups define themselves in terms of brotherhood, are highly protective of their turf, and engage in nonutilitarian violence with other gangs. Although the cultural gang is not organized expressly to sell drugs, "the gang organization facilitates that activity" (1990: 7). The ability of either type to follow in the tradition of late nineteenth/early twentieth century neighborhood-gangs-into-organized-crime is hindered by the low level of cohesiveness, loose organization, high member turnover, and unstable leadership typical of most street gangs (Klein, Maxson, and Cunningham 1991).

In contrast with the American Mafia, African American criminal groups have an inherent weakness: Confinement to the inner city thwarts the development of symbiotic community relationships that promote the survival of indigenous crime organizations. American Mafia Families have traditionally generated "goodwill" by providing certain community services and by keeping the more predatory kinds of crime (such as drugs, prostitution, and robbery) out of their own neighborhoods even while organizing it elsewhere in the city. While African American numbers operators (discussed earlier) cultivated considerable goodwill, drug traffickers prey almost exclusively on their own people and thereby generate organized opposition from within their communities (Pennsylvania Crime Commission 1990). Furthermore, the Racketeer and Corrupt Organizations (RICO) statute (discussed in Chapter 14), and effective federal law enforcement militate against the development and expansion of upstart criminals into self-perpetuating criminal organizations.

The best known of these gangs are the Crips and the Bloods. The Crips, whose membership is reputed to be more than 10,000, have moved from Los Angeles to Seattle and other large cities in the West and Midwest, as well as into smaller cities throughout California. Along with the Bloods, a smaller gang, members of the Crips have been slowly moving east, establishing drug distribution networks in Baltimore and Washington, DC. Bloods and Crips are heavily armed and quick to use violence.

Outside of California, Crips and Bloods are typically splinter groups utilizing the gangs' name as a means of identifying their organization. These subgroups are independent entities, often operating in competition with one another—they are extremely violent. "Neither gang is rigidly hierarchical. Both are broken up into loosely affiliated neighborhood groups called 'sets,' each with 30 to 100 members. Many gang members initially left southern California to evade police. Others simply expanded the reach of crack by setting up branch operations in places where they visited friends or family members and discovered that the market was ripe" (Witkin 1991: 51).

AFRICA

African criminal enterprises developed rapidly since the 1980s due to globalization of the world's economies and the great advances in communications technology. Easier international travel, expanded world trade, and financial transactions that cross national borders have enabled criminal entrepreneurs to branch out of local and regional crime to target international victims and develop criminal networks within more prosperous countries and regions. The political, social, and economic conditions in African countries like Nigeria, have helped some enterprises expand globally (FBI information).

In Africa, in addition to drug trafficking, criminal organizations traffic in human beings, small arms, light weapons, and natural resources; they also illegally dump toxic waste. One of the countries most affected is Guinea-Bissau, which is emerging from decades of conflict. While most people live in poverty, some are tremendously wealthy because cocaine and illegal drugs are swamping the country's tiny export economy.

The value of the cocaine transiting through Guinea-Bissau exceeds the entire national income. Law enforcement is woefully inadequate, and Guinea-Bissau risks becoming a *narcostate*. Even when arrested, international drug traffickers are seldom sentenced—the country does not have a single prison (UNODC 2008a). In 2011, the country's Naval Chief of Staff was reappointed despite being a U.S. Treasury-designated drug kingpin.

West African Organized Crime

Several factors have made West Africa (see Figure 7.2) attractive for the development of criminal organizations, including wide inequalities in wealth, unchecked population growth, and associated rapid and uncontrolled urbanization, differing according to their own ethnic situations, cultural backgrounds and endowments in natural resources. Just as we have seen in the United States during an earlier era, organized crime in West Africa provides an option for individuals seeking to break out of poverty. The region suffers from chronic armed conflict, extremely high rates of poverty, porous border security, governmental inefficiency, and corruption. These conditions promote the growth of armed insurgent groups; extensive narcotics trafficking networks centered in Nigeria; trafficking in women and children originating in many countries of the region; misallocation of natural resources such as timber, precious metals, and diamonds; and an enormous arms trafficking industry that is supplied from Eastern Europe and the former Soviet Union (LaVerle et al. 2003). "The very structure of many West and Central African economies, based on exploitation of natural resources (mining or single-crop, export-oriented agriculture), coupled with a patrimonial conception of the state within which national natural and financial resources belong to the individual(s) in power also contribute to the creation of an environment where a disregard for existing laws and the use of institutional prerogatives for private goals is considered not only justified, but an indicator of power" (Mazzitelli 2007: 1072). This has facilitated the growth of local and transnational criminal networks.

The structure of African criminal organizations is not that of the Sicilian Mafia (discussed in Chapter 5) or the Japanese *yakuza* (discussed in Chapter 8), but more closely akin to that of Russian organized crime in the United States (discussed in Chapter 9): project-based cells organized by kinship along ethnic or clan lines which complete an operation and disperse to regroup at a later date for another transaction. Groups may use religious rituals to further solidarity while each member brings a particular skill to the enterprise.

Criminal organizations in West Africa use techniques similar to those of legitimate traders and business people typical of a lineage-based society. As the volume of business grows, an entrepreneur who succeeds in making money in a particular field invites one or more junior relatives or other dependents to join him in the business. They become apprentices to the original entrepreneur. If further additional personnel are required, they are recruited via personal acquaintances or relatives for a specific task, but not otherwise retained in permanent employment. It is common for junior associates to swear an oath of secrecy on a traditional oracle that implies death for its violation. This mode of operation creates strong associations between specific families, lineages, or ethnic groups, while those taking the greatest risks (such as those actually transporting drugs, for example) have no permanent connection and are typically hired by a person using an alias. Should this person be arrested, he or she can provide little that would endanger the enterprise (United Nations Office on Drugs and Crime 2005; hereafter UNODC).

While trafficking in persons for cheap labor is the work of small networks, employing ships for this purpose requires significant investment and extensive transnational contacts, often involving different organizations in a cooperative venture: a transnational enterprise. Enterprises aimed at the commercial sex market are typically run by well-developed criminal networks. A recruiter and transporter of a woman to Europe spends approximately $2,000 to bribe appropriate officials, procure travel

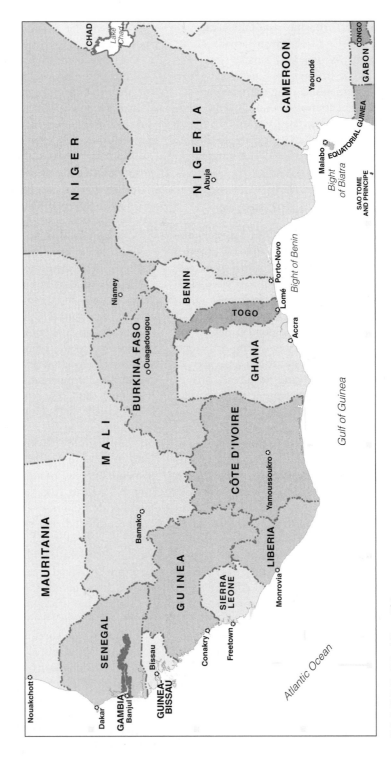

F I G U R E 7.2 West Africa

documents and safe houses, and transport the woman to a madam, who pays approximately $12,000 for the victim (Mazzitelli 2007).

Although drug trafficking remains by far the most lucrative transnational criminal activity, criminal networks have diversified their portfolios in order to reduce risk and to make it more difficult for law enforcement agencies to trace them: trafficking in people and smuggling of migrants, stolen vehicles, natural resources, firearms, counterfeiting and intellectual piracy, and cybercrime. These activities are accompanied by money laundering and corruption.

As a result of stepped-up enforcement against drugs entering Europe through Spain and the Netherlands, West Africa has become more attractive to smugglers. "The geographical position of West Africa, combined with a permissive working environment—corruption and inadequate law enforcement—makes the region an ideal staging post from South America to cocaine markets in Europe" (UNODC 2007: 6). Latin American cocaine moves into West Africa's long Atlantic coast where it is rerouted for European markets by Nigerian and Ghanaian networks who are paid for their logistical services or who purchase the drugs directly. Heroin from the Golden Crescent and Golden Triangle (discussed in Chapter 12) enters West Africa to be re-exported to Europe and, to a lesser extent, the United States. Some of these drugs also enter the domestic market.

Cocaine is usually shipped to West Africa on fishing boats and freighters concealed in areas built especially for that purpose in the frame of the boat, such as a modified oil tank. These concealment areas make it very difficult to detect drugs without specific intelligence as to its location (UNODC 2007a). Larger vessels may be used as mother ships from which small boats bring the drugs ashore. Drug smuggling routes are also used to move counterfeit and pirated items.

Antonio Maria Costa, Executive Director of the UNODC, points out:

> With growing demand for cocaine in Europe, and improved security along traditional trafficking routes, criminals are now using West Africa as a hub for their illicit trade. Countries like Guinea Bissau are off most people's radar screens. They are poor, weak, and yet not so unstable as to attract attention. This makes them a perfect cover for criminal groups. As a result, in the past few years, the amount of cocaine moving from South America via West Africa to Europe has risen dramatically. In some cases, like Guinea Bissau, the value of the cocaine trafficked through the country may be greater than the entire national income.
>
> With their low risk/high return business, drug traffickers can afford satellite phones, move around in fast boats and expensive cars, transfer money and information discreetly and buy protection. The mismatched police, who have low salaries that are seldom paid, lack phones, computers, and even electricity, have almost no ships for patrol. (UNODC 2007b: 1)

Nigerians

Nigerian criminal entrepreneurs are the most significant of African groups and operate in more than eighty countries. They are among the most aggressive and expansionist international criminal groups, and are primarily engaged in drug trafficking and financial frauds.

The most profitable activity of the Nigerian groups is drug trafficking: delivering heroin from Southeast and Southwest Asian into Europe and the United States and cocaine from South America into Europe and South Africa. Large populations of ethnic Nigerians in India, Pakistan, and Thailand have given these enterprises direct access to 90 percent of the world's heroin production. The associated money laundering has helped establish Nigerian criminal enterprises on every populated continent of the world (FBI information).

About twice the size of California, Nigeria is Africa's most populous country: 100 million persons divided into 250 ethnic groups with a labor force employed primarily in agriculture. The country has an Atlantic coastline and a major port in its commercial center, the city of Lagos (Abujain).

This former British colony, where the official language is English, was granted full independence in 1960, but has been marked by civil wars and coups. In 1999, military rule ended and a civilian government was elected. Nevertheless, there has been a great deal of unrest and violence, the result of northern states attempting to enforce Islamic law (*Sharia*) and southern ethnic groups demanding more autonomy and control of natural resources. Through wanton violence, Muslim and Christian militias have created Muslim- or Christian-only enclaves (Sengupta 2004).

Inefficiency and decades of corruption continue to hamper this oil-rich country—Nigeria is the sixth largest oil producer in the world but the per capita income is about $1,000 a year. The military dictator who ruled Nigeria from 1993 to 1998 stole at least $3 billion that he deposited in foreign bank accounts (Polgreen 2005). The Nigerian police are poorly organized and financed, and carry the baggage of British rule during which the police served as an instrument of colonialism. "Corruption touches virtually every aspect of Nigerian life, from the millions of sham email messages sent each year by people claiming to be Nigerian officials seeking help with transferring large sums of money out of the country, to the police officers who routinely set up roadblocks, sometimes every few hundred yards, to extract bribes of about … 15 cents from drivers" (Polgreen 2005: 1).

This climate proved fertile for the creation of crime syndicates that are active in drug trafficking as well as an array of sophisticated economic crimes such as bank, credit card, and insurance fraud. Nigerian criminal syndicates are headquartered in Lagos and many have global networks and operate with virtual impunity in an environment of pervasive corruption. Their organizational structures are flexible and fluid, cell-like syndicates that break apart and re-form in other criminal initiatives with interchangeable members: "A noticeable trait that's fairly consistent is formation of small groups along tribal or family ties" (Nicaso and Lamothe 2005: 239).

An extensive transnational network of narcotics traffickers extends out from Nigeria, which has become the West African center for drugs and money laundering. That network extends into neighboring countries and as far as central Asia and South America. Nigerian groups have established ties with criminal groups in the United States, Europe, South America, Asia, and South Africa. A significant proportion of heroin arriving in the United States from Asia passes through Nigeria, and Nigerian agents in South America move cocaine to points in Europe, North America, and South Africa (LaVerle et al. 2003).

Nigerian drug networks are able to coexist with the more hierarchical, mafia-style operators who may dominate particular aspects of the drug trade, such as the powerful Colombian groups that may deal in very large quantities of cocaine. Nigerian networks generally deal in smaller quantities, thus not posing a major commercial threat to other criminal organizations, while providing valuable smuggling services to major criminal operatives. While successful Nigerian syndicates import smaller quantities, they enjoy an exceptional range of contacts and an impressive flexibility of organization that enable them to exploit market niches that the more powerful organizations cannot always reach. "It is by these means that Nigerian drug traders have managed to gain a major stake in what is, literally, the world's most cutthroat market, yet without themselves using violence" (UNODC 2005: 22).

Nigerian narcotics traffickers also are involved in counterfeiting documents, trafficking in migrants, and financial fraud; and financial fraud sometimes turns violent—more than a dozen foreign businesspeople caught up in Nigerian fraud have been murdered in several countries. Nigerian criminal cells target banks and financial institutions through credit card, check, student loan, and mortgage frauds; insurance companies through fraudulent claims for automobile accidents, personal injuries, and life insurance; and government entitlement programs through false or appropriated identifications. Nigerian criminals infiltrate major companies by applying for employment as security guards and cleaning personnel, positions giving

THE 419 SCAM

The target receives an unsolicited fax, email, or letter often concerning Nigeria or another African nation containing either a money laundering or other illegal proposal or a legitimate business proposal. Common variations include "overinvoiced" or "double invoiced" oil or other supply and service contracts where the solicitor wants to get the overage out of Nigeria (Classic 419); crude oil and other commodity deals (a form of Goods and Services 419); a "bequest" left you in a will (Will Scam 419); "money cleaning" where the solicitor has a lot of currency that needs to be "chemically cleaned" before it can be used and he needs the cost of the chemicals (Black Currency 419, also called Wash-Wash); "spoof banks" where there is supposedly money in your name already on deposit; "paying" for a purchase with a check larger than the amount required and asking for change to be advanced (cashier's check and money order 419); fake lottery 419; chat room and romance 419 (usually coupled with one of the other forms of 419); employment 419 (including secret shopper 419) ; and ordering items and commodities off "trading" and "auction" sites on the web and then cheating the seller.

At some point, the victim is asked to pay an upfront sum of some sort, be it an "Advance Fee," "Transfer Tax," or "Performance Bond," or to extend credit, grant COD privileges, or send back "change" on an overage cashier's check or money order. If the victim pays the fee, there are often many "Complications" which require still more advance payments until the victim either quits, runs out of money, or both.

Source: FBI

them access to records during periods of minimal presence of company employees. Stolen data becomes the basis for securing false documents.

The most notorious of the Nigerian operations is the advance fee scam—referred to as 419s after a section of the Nigerian Criminal Code—in which thousands of unsolicited letters, faxes, and emails based on fraudulent representations are sent to people worldwide with the promise of great profits for an upfront cash investment. Simple investment schemes are set forth with promises of easy money, elaborate assurances, and extraordinarily low risk. They provide detailed instructions for establishing linked bank accounts and exchange of authorization letters and account numbers giving the appearance of legitimacy, and then require various transaction fees before any money can be released. Operators may portray themselves as former heads of state or government ministers with vast fortunes requiring a foreign partner for laundering purposes. Victims of Nigerian fraud schemes may be strung along for months or years paying transactions fees and taxes before realizing they are being conned (*Nigerian Advance Fee Fraud* 1997; UNODC 2005).

Nigeria is located at the historical trading crossroads both on the African continent and along maritime routes between East and West. Accordingly, the international criminal operations of Nigerian syndicates are the legacy of a history of moving capital and commodities on a global scale. Nigerian involvement in international drug trafficking, however, is remarkable, because the country is not contiguous to any major drug producer or consumer state (Williams 1995b). Although Nigeria produces no precursor chemicals or drugs that have a significant impact on the United States, the country is a major trafficking hub and the base for criminal organizations responsible for a significant amount of heroin used in the United States.

Organized along familial and tribal lines, high-level traffickers seldom deal with outsiders. In the capital of Lagos, multimillionaire drug barons rule vast organizations, at the bottom of which are drug couriers who take most of the actual risks. False birth certificates and passports are easy to obtain, and Nigerian couriers based in Lagos travel to Pakistan to obtain heroin or to Brazil to obtain cocaine, and then continue on commercial flights to their final destinations; or they return to Nigeria to repackage the drugs into smaller amounts for smuggling throughout the world. Nigerian students or poor residents of Lagos are used as mules; they receive a few thousand dollars a trip for bringing in a hundred grams, usually by swallowing drug-filled condoms. Some Nigeria-based traffickers conduct "training schools" that teach couriers how to avoid the suspicions of customs officials. Traffickers often place many couriers on the same flight. This tactic, known as "shotgunning," overwhelms customs officials when the flight arrives. Even if most of the couriers on the flight are caught, a number will inevitably get through during the confusion. The markups on heroin trafficking are so high that if only a small percentage of the product gets through, the traffickers will still reap huge profits. But as a result of increasing law enforcement pressure, Nigeria-based traffickers are beginning to switch from courier shipments to the use of express mail packages. In 1997, Nigerian organizations began using express mail services with shipments routed through European countries. Drugs can be mailed anonymously to fictitious persons or mail drops that decrease the risk and cost associated with couriers (DEA information).

Customs officials use X-rays of the digestive tract to discover the drugs. In 1991, a Nigerian-Chicago connection was uncovered that used the Philippines as a transshipment point. Asian women transported heroin from Bangkok to Manila, where Caucasian American women received the drugs for transportation to the United States. This elaborate setup was designed to reduce the suspicion that would accompany Asian women flying from Thailand to the United States. Couriers carried between 4.5 and 6.5 pounds of heroin and were paid $20,000 plus expenses (Schmetzer 1991a).

In 1996, thirty-six persons in three countries were arrested for being part of a Nigerian drug ring that had been in business for fifteen years. The group's leader, known as "the Policeman" for his ability to impose discipline, was living in Bangkok. While members operated out of London, Amsterdam, Pakistan, New York, and Detroit, most of those arrested were in Chicago where the group was headquartered at an African women's boutique in the Edgewater neighborhood on the city's North Side. Orders were placed by telephone and delivered to Chicago by female couriers who usually traveled with children from Bangkok, taking circuitous routes through Europe, Guatemala, and finally Mexico, before reaching the United States (Martin and O'Brien 1996; O'Brien 1996). Nigerians are also involved in human trafficking, especially in women for the sex trade in Europe. (Human trafficking is discussed in Chapter 11.)

In recognition of the problem of Nigerian crime groups, the U.S. Department of Justice established a Nigerian Crime Initiative that coordinates the federal investigations of Nigerian criminal enterprises by using joint task forces in six major U.S. cities.

JAMAICAN ORGANIZED CRIME

Jamaica is a picturesque Caribbean island south of Cuba and slightly smaller than Connecticut, with a population of 2.8 million persons—2 to 3 million more live abroad—and a high murder rate: more than 1,550 murders in 2007. (In comparison, New York City, with two and one-half times the population, had fewer than 500 murders in 2007.) Jamaica is less than 550 miles from Miami and roughly the same distance to Colombia, making it an ideal transshipment point for drugs from South America to the United States. With 638 miles of coastline and over a hundred unmonitored airstrips, Jamaica is a major transit point for cocaine entering the United States and the largest producer and exporter of marijuana in the Caribbean (U.S. Department of State 2005).

Jamaica received its independence from Great Britain in 1962—the official language is English—but the island remained plagued by widespread poverty, particularly problematic in the capital city of Kingston. In the poorest sections of the city, criminals—known as *rankings*—are organized into *posses* that have traditionally been supported and protected by the residents among whom they foster a Robin Hood image.

In a situation reminiscent of ties between big city political machines and gangs in the United States (discussed in Chapter 2), those at the top of the rankings' food chain maintain ties with one of Jamaica's two major parties, the People's National Party (PNP) and the Jamaica Labour Party (JLP). Both use posses to intimidate and attack opponents. In Jamaica, a parliamentary democracy based on the British model, a politician's survival depends entirely on his or her ability to win repeatedly in his local constituency. One sure method of ensuring repeated victories is to create a "garrison constituency": "a pocket of housing erected with public funds, with carefully screened residents who will constitute the unbeatable core of the politician's voters" (Patterson 2001: 21). Public housing projects were built for the partisans of each political party and their affiliated posses.

In addition to the name, posses developed their style and gunslinger ethos from American action movies, particularly the Westerns popular in Kingston. When they lost their favored position with their political party patrons, the posses began trafficking in homegrown marijuana and imported cocaine. Profits from drug trafficking helped to unravel political ties, and party leaders, menaced by an outlaw underworld they could no longer control, turned the Jamaican police loose to imprison or execute their former allies. Like Mussolini's campaign against the Mafia (discussed in Chapter 5), this drove posse members to the United States at an opportune time: Colombians were looking for street-level dealers to sell a new product, crack cocaine. Jamaicans quickly acclimated to the United States where their language skills were an asset—the patois of Jamaica is a distinctly accented English. The posses also "brought with them a killer enthusiasm honed by years of warfare with one another and the police, and when they came onto America's mean streets, they were afraid of no one" (Gunst 1996: xv). The infamous Shower Posse became entrenched in Toronto, Canada, where they brokered the sale of drugs to street gangs.

In the aftermath of the bloody 1980 election for president, more Kingston criminals began leaving the island for the United States, "transforming their island gang alliances into mainland drug posses" (Gunst 1996: xiv). By 1984, the Shower Posse, with close ties to the JLP, had moved its base of operations to south Florida, followed by the rival Spanglers, affiliated with the PNP. Their Jamaica-based antipathy

was transferred to the United States, a rivalry that led to many murders.

In the mid-1980s, Jamaican posses shifted from marijuana to cocaine and became heavily involved in the exploding crack cocaine trade. Jamaica became an important transshipment point for Colombian cocaine bound for the United States (Jones 2002). This was the source of much of the cocaine hydrochloride that the posses used to convert into crack. During the crack cocaine era, the posses gained a reputation as one of the most violent, sadistic group of criminals that ever operated in the United States. The Shower Posse's chief enforcer would hold captive family members of those who owed the group money and repeatedly rape and sodomize the females until the debt was paid (Cardwell 2001). In one six-month period in the late 1980s, posse members were involved in 744 murders. Some of their victims were boiled alive; others were dismembered, with body parts shipped back to their families in Jamaica (DEA information).

Posse members are fascinated with firearms, particularly high-caliber weapons, and prefer to always be armed. Therefore, they avoid the use of commercial airplanes. Their favorite weapons include the Uzi and Mac-11, and a variety of high-quality semiautomatic handguns. The Jamaican's typical method of operations includes multiple shots with multiple weapons in a crowded public place. The 5,000-member Shower Posse reportedly got its name for engaging in frenzied shootouts—*showering* gunfire (Witkin 1991).

Jamaican posses differ from other trafficking groups in that their members are importers, wholesalers, and distributors. They maintain control over the product from acquisition of the cocaine powder close to the source, through cutting, manufacture, and distribution, to street sales. Therefore, their profit margin is higher than that of traffickers who use middlemen. "A posse that controls fifty crack houses in one city can make $9 million a month. Other major importers of illegal narcotics, such as the Colombians and Cubans, are usually only wholesalers. They will turn a profit on only one sale. The Jamaicans, on the other hand, never exchange any money until the narcotics are sold at the street level by members of the organization. The money is then funneled back up to the leaders" (McGuire 1988: 22).

At the national level, posses have one or more top leaders, sometimes called "generals." The first region of the country in which a posse operates may evolve into a "headquarters" or base of operations from which the subsequent expansion of operations is directed. From headquarters, posse leaders may send "captains" or "lieutenants" to establish operations in new regions. They are responsible for recruiting supervisors to manage workers, frequently illegal aliens smuggled from Jamaica into the United States (Pennsylvania Crime Commission 1990).

Street-level operations are carried out by managers, couriers, sellers, lookouts, and steerers who are mostly African Americans (*Crack Cocaine* 1994). In 1990, federal agents arrested seventeen members of the Gulleymen—named after a neighborhood in Kingston, Jamaica—a posse that controlled crack houses in Brooklyn and Dallas and has been linked to at least thirty murders. As part of their business operations, the Gulleymen sold franchises to street-level dealers, providing them with crack and protection (McKinley 1990).

The demise of some major posses was largely a result of their predilection for violence, which helped undermine loyalty: "Loyalty was a scarce commodity within the posse ranks. And when the dons resorted to violence to discipline their troops, some of the soldiers started going to the police with information... . Once the cops were able to flip one or two gang members it was only a matter of time before they could rope the don" (Gunst 1996: 140). By the mid-1990s, posses abandoned many of the brutal practices that were their trademark and began referring to themselves as "crews." Many also dropped out of the crack cocaine trade and returned to marijuana. They reasoned that a conviction for selling crack would mean serious time in prison, whereas a conviction for selling small amounts of marijuana generally results only in the payment of a fine.

The source of supply for some Jamaican groups in the United States has shifted. Instead of acquiring marijuana from their counterparts in Jamaica, some have begun to purchase marijuana from Mexico-based criminal organizations in the Southwest Border area and then transport it back to eastern U.S. cities. The Mexicans also provide them with cocaine and heroin (DEA information). In 2005, authorities arrested nineteen members of the Harlem-based Two Mile Posse (named after an area of Jamaica) for trafficking in marijuana and carrying out at least four murders. The group, which maintained a base in Tucson and a distribution hub in Houston, purchased marijuana from Mexico for about $500 a pound and sold it wholesale for about $1,100 a pound (J. Lee 2005).

Cynics note that when the bullets fly in Jamaica, it means an election is coming. The gangs "have their own source of funds, the sale of drugs, but the parties still provide political cover for gang support at polling time" (Borger 2001: 6).

The Shower Posse has been linked by U.S. authorities to more than a thousand murders. Founded by the Kingston-born Vivian Blake when living in Brooklyn during the 1980s, the group has strong ties to the JLP. In 1988, Blake was indicted in the United States and fled back to Jamaica. Pursuant to a deal with U.S. authorities, in 1999 he returned to the United States where he served eight years of a twenty-eight-year prison sentence. After his release in 2009, he was deported to Jamaica where he died of natural causes the following year (Campbell 2010).

In 2010, more than a thousand police and soldiers entered Tivoli Gardens, a stronghold of the opposition JLP, in an effort to arrest the head of the Shower Posse, sometimes called the Presidential Click, Christopher ("Dudus") Coke, who had been indicted in New York on drug and arms trafficking charges. Battles raged, seventy-six people were killed including several police officers, and Coke eventually walked into a police station and surrendered. After nine months of procrastination, the prime minister acceded to a U.S. request for his extradition (Associated Press 2010a, b, c) and in 2011 Coke, 42, pled guilty to racketeering in a New York federal court. Coke's office in Tivoli Gardens was converted into a facility for security forces (Barrett 2010).

Jamaican criminal groups have proven troublesome in the United Kingdom, where they are referred to as "Yardies." To Jamaicans a Yardie is someone who comes from Jamaica or "Yard"—as in backyard. A crackdown in Jamaica led to an increase in Jamaican emigration and, in England, Yardie activity. The phenomenon was first noted in the late 1980s and linked to crack cocaine. The rise of crack cocaine is mirrored by that of Yardie members who are linked to drug and arms dealing, as well as robbery. Their lifestyle in England has been synonymous with violence—impulse shootings and gangland-style executions are used to sort out internal squabbles. There is no central control or brotherhood structure, so Yardies have few affiliations or loyalties. Yardie gangs are loose-knit and often fall out with each other, sometimes violently.

SUMMARY

1. Appreciate the affect of prejudice on domestic black criminal organizations and how the Vietnam War influenced black criminals:
   - African American criminal groups are using the drug trade much as their Irish, Jewish, and Italian predecessors did bootlegging.
   - Black opportunity in organized crime has roughly paralleled opportunity—and discrimination–in the wider legitimate community.
   - The Vietnam War exposed many black soldiers to the heroin markets of the Golden Triangle, allowing black criminals to bypass the American Mafia and buy directly from suppliers in Thailand.
   - Frank Lucas and Nicky Barnes had a fatal flaw—high public profiles.
   - For African American criminals, the prison experience often forms the basis for partnerships in organized crime.
2. The development of the Gangster Disciples (GDs) and their primary Chicago opponents, the Black P. Stone Nation:
   - The bureaucratic model was adopted by Chicago's Gangster Disciples—their size requires a corporate-style structure.
   - The GDs are active in selling cocaine and heroin throughout Chicago, a number of suburban areas, and in several states and also extort money from other drug dealers.
   - The GDs have been warring with the Black P. Stone Nation on and off for decades.

   - The GD and El Rukns followed a long-standing Chicago tradition of criminals being involvement in politics.
3. Know the factors thwarting African Americans from following the historical pattern of neighborhood-gangs-into-organized-crime:
   - Black criminal groups in the United States lack the incubation provided by the corrupt urban political machines and ineffective federal law enforcement of previous centuries.
   - A low level of cohesiveness, loose organization, high member turnover, and unstable leadership hinders the ability of typical street gangs to become organized crime.
4. The variables that make West Africa attractive for the development of criminal organizations:
   - In West Africa, chronic armed conflict, extremely high rates of poverty, porous border security, governmental inefficiency, and corruption promote the growth of organized crime.
   - African criminals form project-based cells organized by kinship along ethnic or clan lines which complete an operation and disperse to regroup at a later date for another transaction.
   - In addition to drug trafficking, African criminal organizations have diversified portfolios that include trafficking in people, stolen vehicles, natural resources, firearms, counterfeiting and intellectual piracy, and cyber-crime.

5. Appreciate the role of Nigerian criminal organizations in the globalization of organized crime:
    - Nigerian criminal entrepreneurs are among the most aggressive and expansionist international criminal groups are engaged in drug trafficking and financial frauds.
    - Nigerian police are poorly organized and financed, and carry the baggage of British rule during which the police served as an instrument of colonialism.
    - Organizational structures are flexible and fluid, cell-like syndicates that break apart and reform in other criminal initiatives with interchangeable members along tribal or family ties and high-level traffickers seldom deal with outsiders.
    - The most notorious of Nigerian crimes is the "419 Scam."
6. Know the role of island politics in the development of Jamaican organized crime:
    - Jamaica has a high murder rate and, with 638 miles of coastline and over a hundred unmonitored airstrips, is a major transit point for cocaine entering the United States and the largest producer and exporter of marijuana in the Caribbean.
    - Similar to historical ties between big city political machines and gangs in the United States, Jamaican criminal organizations have strong political affiliations with one of Jamaica's two major parties.
    - In a pattern similar to Mussolini's campaign against the Mafia, enforcement activities in Jamaica drove many criminals into the United States where they linked with Colombians looking for street-level distributors.
    - Jamaican criminals bring with them several advantages including the ability to speak English, a reputation for being fearless, and extensive experience with violence.

REVIEW QUESTIONS

1. How did the Vietnam War affect black drug traffickers?
2. How has black opportunity in organized crime differed from that of white criminals?
3. What flaw did Frank Lucas and Nicky Barnes share with Al Capone and John Gotti?
4. How is Chicago's Gangster Disciples similar to the early Camorra?
5. Why do the GD require a bureaucratic style of organization?
6. In what way did the GD and their rivals the El Rukns follow a longstanding Chicago tradition?
7. What hinders the ability of typical street gangs to become organized crime?
8. What are the factors that have fostered the growth of African organized crime?
9. What are the characteristics of African criminal organizations?
10. What activities are part of the business portfolios of African criminal organizations?
11. How are Nigerian criminal organizations structured?
12. What is so extraordinary about the Nigerian success in drug trafficking?
13. What is the Nigerian "419 Scam?"
14. What makes Jamaica a major transit point for cocaine and marijuana entering the United States?
15. What advantages do Jamaican criminals bring with them to the United States?

Japanese *yakuza* display their traditional tattoos. © Michael Rubenstein/Redux

Asian Organized Crime

Shinsuke Shimada, Japan's most popular television comic and host, retired from the entertainment industry after admitting to extensive ties to the yakuza. Shimada, 55, hosted six different TV programs, aired in Osaka and Tokyo. His ties to organized crime were disclosed when a series of emails he sent to a yakuza boss were leaked to the media by another senior yakuza figure who had been the subject of derogatory comments made by the TV host. In America, the scandal would be the equivalent of Jay Leno or David Letterman confessing to having ties to the Sinaloa or Gulf cartels discussed in Chapter 6. The scandal has disclosed yakuza domination of the entertainment industry (Adelstein 2011).

The yakuza will be discussed in this chapter.

CHAPTER 8 WILL ENABLE THE READER TO UNDERSTAND:

- The historical and cultural characteristics of China and overseas Chinese communities that promote entrepreneurship, legal and illegal

- The Triad phenomenon and its role in global organized crime

- How anti-Chinese sentiments led to the establishment of Chinatowns and the role of tongs

- Differences between Triads, tongs, and Asian gangs

- Japanese organized crime: the *yakuza*

Asian is a rather imprecise term that can include many diverse groups. In the United States, for example, Asian communities are made up of thirty-four distinct ethnic groups, including Chinese, which itself has several different groups such as Cantonese and Mandarin (Song 1996). A number of unrelated Asian groups are involved in organized crime. This chapter will examine the most prominent: Chinese and Japanese.

CHINESE ORGANIZED CRIME

Secret societies have a long history in China, with some dating back to the beginning of the Common Era (Chin 1990; Fong 1981). An Chen (2005) notes that criminal organizations in China are generally referred to as "secret societies," and, in contrast with those of a more political or religious nature, they are called "black gangs" or "black societies."

China has experienced radical regime changes over the past hundred years, from feudal dynasty, to warlords, to the Nationalist government of Chiang Kai-shek, to Mao Zedong's repressive totalitarian regime, and finally to neo-authoritarianism. Almost completely wiped out under Mao, Chinese secret societies nevertheless demonstrated an ability to adapt to these changes (Chen 2005; Xia 2008). In the post-Mao era, market reform and more socio-economic freedom led to a flourishing of secret societies that are frequently entwined in local politics and government (Chen 2005).

Before we can understand these groups, we need to explore the unique cultural dynamics of Chinese society in which loyalty to family and friends is a moral imperative (Liu et al. 1998). Any member of the Chinese community is part of a latent organization because of the existence of *guanxi*, a phenomenon that parallels *partito*, discussed in Chapter 5: "Chinese are born into a hierarchically organized society in which they never see themselves or others as free individuals, but as bound to others in an ever expanding web of social relations bearing mutual obligate bonds of varying strength." *Guanxi* "embraces many concepts, some

familiar to Westerners, such as connections, networks, and patron-client relations." They are built upon "a series of dyadic relationships, some that are naturally present and others which must be acquired, cultivated, and maintained" (W. Myers 1995: 3).

The Chinese concept of *qinqing* parallels that of the southern Italian *famiglia*: Family, the primary and most important group to a Chinese individual, "serves as the crucible for formation of the ideals of harmonious social relations and the model for social interaction. It is an association composed of parental and filial bonds carrying the strongest obligations of mutual reciprocity." Family resources "are pooled and shared according to apparent or expressed need. Each member is obligated to contribute to the family as able and the family is obligated to provide each member with the resources for living" (W. Myers 1995: 4). Pooling of familial resources has advanced the business interests of overseas Chinese in the many communities they have settled.

In this cultural setting, notes Willard Myers (1995), law is marginalized, relegated to a position well below mediative mechanisms within a particularistic social order of human relationships. Like *famiglia* and *partito*, these cultural manifestations, although not ipso facto criminal, facilitate criminal organization. Chinese immigrants throughout the world were subjected to pernicious discrimination to which they responded by relying on cultural attributes that provided great advantages in business, both legal and illegal. And *guanxi* is global, providing a dynamic for international business, both legal and illegal. The Triad phenomenon is a natural extension of these cultural attributes.

Triads

Despite its enormous population, China has only about 150 surnames representing different clans that often have their own mutual-aid associations. In times of unrest, many people with different surnames formed brotherhoods for protection, using secret oaths and rituals to substitute for familial ties. These secret societies practiced armed robbery, ransom kidnapping, and piracy. In 1821, the principal of an Anglo-Chinese college wrote the first systematic account of these secret societies that he called "Triads" (Lintner 2002). A political dimension was added when the Qing (or Ch'ing) dynasty, established by the conquering Manchus (from Manchuria) in 1644, attempted to wipe out the Triads (Fong 1981).

The term *Triad* refers to the societies' common mystical symbol: an equilateral triangle representing the three basic Chinese concepts of heaven, earth, and man. Triad members are assigned numbers based on their position. For example, enforcers or "Red Poles" are assigned number 426; an ordinary member is a 49; a leader or "Hill Chief" is 489. Based on ancient occult numerology, assigned numbers always begin with a 4 (Booth 1990). These groups engage in highly ritualized dress and behavior—secret hand signs, passwords, and blood oaths are used in elaborate initiation ceremonies. The initiation ceremony includes the recital of the Triads' thirty-six oaths, each of which ends with the death penalty for its violation. For example: "If I am arrested after committing an offense, I must accept my punishment and not try to place blame on my sworn brothers. If I do so, I will be killed by five thunderbolts" (Carter 1991a). The ceremony may take six or seven hours (Booth 1990).

In contrast, the man who would later emerge as head of the powerful Big Circle (discussed later) recalls his initiation into the Green Gang (Triad) in a Bangkok hotel room in 1969. Instead of an elaborate ceremony, in the presence of his Green Gang mentor, he handed a cup of tea and an envelope with $108 to a ranking member, stating in Shanghai dialect: "If you accept me, I'll be very happy." The man placed the envelope in his jacket and responded: "Never tell secrets. Never betray anyone. If ever your brothers need help, never refuse them." "Thank you master," he responded, and they adjourned to a celebratory meal at a Chinese restaurant. His subsequent admission into another (Red Gang) Triad, however, in addition to the ceremonial $108, was replete with thirty-six oaths, the decapitation of a live chicken, and the drawing of blood from his finger (J. Sack 2001). In any event, membership requires a sponsor who is a ranking official of the Triad.

The Qing dynasty ended in 1911 with the success of Dr. Sun Yat-sen (1866–1925)—the "George Washington" of China. His successor, General Chiang Kai-shek, possibly a Triad member himself, imposed a military regime with help from secret societies, in particular, the Green Gang (*Qing Bang*), a Triad that Bertil Lintner (2002: 54) refers to as China's first modern secret society. During World War II, many criminal Triads aided the Japanese in their occupation of China (Schneider 2009).

In 1949, Communist forces under Mao defeated Chiang's Nationalists who were forced to flee the Mainland for Taiwan. Mao established the People's Republic of China and in 1952 moved to obliterate the secret societies that were seen as competitors to the Communist Party. Among the victims was the Green Gang that had virtually ruled the city of Shanghai. Triad members who fled to Taiwan with Chiang were tightly controlled by the Kuomintang, his Nationalist Party, and unable to expand their criminal operations on the island (Chin 1990). Driven out of the mainland and into British-ruled Hong Kong, the leaderless "Greens" survived in small pockets, their power eclipsed by the 14K.

The 14K was founded in 1947 by a Kuomintang general who fled with hundreds of his followers to Hong Kong after the Communist victory. The Triad has branches throughout the world, but they are not connected to each other through an overarching hierarchy (Lintner 2002). According to Yiu Kong Chu (2005), the 14K is less organized than most other Triads, with subgroups forming separate societies. The 14K is reputed to have as many as 30,000 members in Hong Kong (the former colony has a population of 5.6 million) and about 10,000 in Taiwan. In the nearby former Portuguese colony of Macau (population over 500,000), forty-five-year-old Wan Kuok-koi ("Broken Tooth Koi") headed the local 14K. When the colony was under the Portuguese, he directed a violent conflict to control the lucrative gambling business that accounts for more than 40 percent of the enclave's economy. Wan financed a film on his exploits and in a promotional interview promised to wipe out an opposition group. Less tolerant than their Portuguese predecessors, the

People's Republic imprisoned Wan Kuok-koi in 1999 (Sly 1999).

"After China started its reforms in the late 1970s, the triads then returned to the mainland and emerged as the most systematic and best-organized criminal groups" (Xia 2008: 10). Although most Triad societies are based in Hong Kong, Taiwan, or Macau, their influence spans international boundaries with members located in virtually every country that has a sizable Chinese community. Triads, which have an estimated worldwide membership that exceeds 100,000, are fluid associations of ethnic Chinese criminals and quasi-legitimate businessmen involved in an array of criminal enterprises. Most of the approximately fifty Hong Kong Triads have evolved into loose-knit groups operating and cooperating with each other on the basis of personal introductions and mutual interests. While they are traditional secret societies, Triads are best described as loose cartels made up of independent groups that "adopt a similar organizational structure and ritual to bind their members together" (Chu 2005: 5). Triad leaders do not dictate to members what criminal activities they should pursue, and generally do not receive monetary benefits unless they are directly involved with the actual criminal enterprise. As in American Mafia Families and outlaw motorcycle clubs, Triads have an associational hierarchy that does not exert vertically integrated control over the members' criminal enterprises. Instead, leaders "devote their time to advancing the influence of the organization for the benefit of themselves and their members. When control is exercised, it is to mediate a dispute or ensure the loyalty of a member" (Chu 2005: 5).

Fenton Bresler, testifying before the President's Commission on Organized Crime (PCOC 1984b: 42–43), points out that each Triad has its own triangular flag and territory. "If I want to become a new Triad head, I have to ask the original guy back in Hong Kong or Taiwan to give me a flag which means I can bring it over and that means this is my territory.... It authorizes me to go to the new town and organize my branch." Although each Triad affiliate boss is theoretically independent, that is, has his own flag, he is really only semi-independent. Spiritually he is linked with the old country.

Martin Booth presents the typical structure of a Triad lodge. Each has a hierarchy that determines its activities (1990: 33–35, edited):

The leader is called the Shan Chu, and there is a deputy leader, the Fu Shan Chu. Below them come the Heung Chu, or Incense Master, and the Fin Fung, or Vanguard. These two officers administer the lodge rituals and have the power to invest, initiate, and order retribution against the members. Beneath them are a number of departmental heads responsible for the everyday running of the society and of any sub-branches, each of the latter having an internal structure similar to that of the main lodge except for the Incense Master and Vanguard. These are only found in principal lodges and their presence is a sign that a lodge has reached maturity and achieved power in its own right. Sub-branches are controlled by a leader, the Chu Chi, and his deputy, the Fu Chu Chi. Some lodges also have a treasurer, but this is comparatively rare. All Triad officers are appointed for fixed periods and are elected by lodge members. Initiate members are required to pay an entrance fee. They must also obtain a sponsor, to whom further fee is payable—often far in excess of the entrance fee. This is a private arrangement and is only reached after the initiate's credentials have been thoroughly checked by the Incense Master and the Vanguard. A sponsor must also be found, and paid for, when a member seeks promotion within the lodge. All monies earned by an individual society, from whatever source, are deposited in the central lodge fund. Embezzlement is not uncommon and has caused major rifts in some societies, sometimes leading to violence.

Within each society there are four ranks of officials. The first is the Hung Kwan, or Red Pole, who is a fighter and is responsible for discipline. The Paz Tsz Sin is also known as the White Paper Fan and occupies a position similar to the *consigliere* in the Mafia. The Cho-Hai or Messenger is a liaison officer who acts as a go-between in lodge affairs and as a representative in its dealings with the outside world or with other lodges.

Major Triads like 14K, Sun Yee On, and United Bamboo have autonomous branches extending worldwide that help to facilitate transnational criminal activities. In the 1990s, Hong Kong Triads strengthened their presence and relationships in Western countries by making investments in legitimate businesses as a hedge against the political, economic, and law enforcement uncertainties in the wake of Hong Kong's reversion to China in 1997. The 14K and Sun Yee On have made substantial property investments in Canada, and the 14K is reportedly the fastest-growing Triad in Canada. But, contrary to expectations, there has not been a mass Triad migration to Western countries; instead, they have increasingly entered the booming Chinese market (Chu 2005). Varese (2011: 152) points out that Chinese authorities do not usually pursue fugitives and criminals unless they commit new crimes. In fact, they view their presence as an opportunity to attract foreign investment. As long as criminals bring investments to the mainland, they are welcomed as businessmen by the authorities.

United Bamboo was established in Taiwan in 1956 and maintains strong ties to the Kuomintang Party. Although it was reputed to have only about one hundred members as late as 1970, the organization's size and sophistication have since increased notably (Huston 2001). The reputed leader of the United Bamboo is a wanted man in Taiwan who served several prison terms in the United States for drug trafficking. Nevertheless, he resides in Shenzhen, China, just north of Hong Kong. His activities might be anathema to officials in Taiwan

and even in Beijing and Shenzhen, but his ties to Taiwan and to potential dealmakers and smugglers abroad make him a potential ally to the rich and influential. His politics—reunification of Taiwan with China—make him an attractive ally to Beijing. His presence in China highlights the ties between organized crime figures and the Communist Party (Pomfret 2001). Through the use of Triad members, Communist China "has extended its influence in North America's ethnic Chinese communities," and the "Donorgate" scandal of 1996 revealed that Beijing was using underworld figures to funnel money to a presidential candidate in the United States (Lintner 2002: 369).

At the top of the hierarchy of United Bamboo in Taiwan is an Ultimate Leader, an Ultimate Enforcer, an Ultimate Superintendent who oversees members and their activities, and an Ultimate Executive who operates organization businesses. There are reportedly more than sixty Taiwan branches, each with a Branch Leader, Deputy Branch Leader, and "brothers" or members. Some branches have other positions such as enforcer, communications officer, war officer, and internal regulator. There are neither specific requirements nor initiation ceremonies for membership. One becomes a member after hanging out and being introduced into the branch by a friend. Members of United Bamboo are heavily armed and engage in a plethora of business activities including extortion, debt collection, gambling, prostitution, trafficking in persons, and pirated movies. With a burgeoning of the economy, they branched out into construction and bid rigging (National Central Police University 2005).

It is not unusual for different Triads to work together where there is a specific opportunity for mutual profit. Hong Kong police, however, maintain that there is no international Triad network or centralized control over cross-border activities, such as drug trafficking or alien smuggling, between China and Hong Kong. Police state that most cooperation in such criminal enterprises is more ad hoc. That is, criminal groups from mainland China, typified by the Big Circle (*Dai Huen Jai*) and the Fuk Ching, have cells operating in countries around the world that cooperate with one another on an ad hoc basis to conduct far-reaching criminal schemes. These criminal cells typically operate autonomously with no known central authority controlling them. Cell leaders use their extensive connections to arrange complex criminal operations that require a high degree of organization and planning. Coordinated efforts of members in various countries enable them to carry out international drug trafficking, arms trafficking, alien smuggling operations, as well as a variety of sophisticated financial fraud crimes. Most smuggling organizations such as the Fuk Ching are based in China's southwestern Fukien province whose residents have a history of overseas travel. The province's coast and harbors provide easy access to shipping (Huston 2001).

The Big Circle (Society or Brotherhood) has its origins in Communist China's Red Guard, Mao's personal militia established to enforce the "Great Cultural Revolution." When the Revolution was called off three years later, many of the paramilitary Red Guards fled to Hong Kong, but maintained camaraderie as the Big Circle—from their red armbands—and engaged in well-planned robberies, particularly of jewelry stores. As a result of their relationship with a leading Triad member in Hong Kong, the major bosses of Big Circle were initiated into the Society of Tranquil Happiness (Triad) and, in a short time, became one of the most active Asian criminal organizations in the world. Thus, although Big Circle is not itself a Triad, many of its members belong to Triads "in the typical pattern of overlapping membership among Chinese groups" (Curtis, Gibbs, and Miró 2004: 10).

By the early 1990s, the Big Circle had established criminal cells in Canada, the United States, and Europe that are highly sophisticated in their use of technology to thwart law enforcement. Known primarily for the manufacture and distribution of counterfeit credit cards and other documents, this group has also been involved in drug trafficking, extortion, prostitution, and gaming offenses (Huston 2001; National Security Council and Criminal Intelligence Service of Canada information; Sack 2001).

A report prepared by the U.S. Library of Congress (Federal Research Division 2002) points out that even when they are part of a specific organization, Big Circle members usually operate in small cells or partnerships that are often dissolved at the completion of a particular goal. In other words, Big Circle cells exhibit structural fluidity and flexibility, and it is not unusual for members and associates to conduct "numerous dissimilar criminal activities, often with different groups simultaneously, be they ethnically homogeneous or heterogeneous." Instead of an overarching pyramid, "Asian organized crime groups are organized more as autonomous mini-pyramids, with small cells and mini-bosses dictating the actions of only their particular cell" (Federal Research Division 2002: 4). Cells located in different countries provide important networking capabilities, contacts they can trust and do business with on a transnational level. In a pattern similar to outlaw motorcycle clubs, while they have a distinct subculture and hierarchical structure, "it is the individual members, not the organizations, that run the illicit business" (Lo 2010a: 852).

T. Wing Lo (2010a: 852) notes that since the 1990s, Triad societies have been undergoing a gradual process of disorganization. Incidents of internal conflict have increased and group cohesiveness and member loyalty have diminished. Procedures on promotion, recruitment, and communication have not been followed closely and "headquarters did not have full control over sub-branches. To maximize benefits and expand power and territories, members from different triads joined hands to run both legitimate and illicit activities."

Hong Kong Triads were designated patriotic societies by the People's Republic in an effort to keep out their Taiwan-based counterparts who it was feared would join forces with anti-Beijing liberals. The definitional change allowed the Hong Kong Triads to establish *guanxi* with officials and state enterprises, enabling them to gain access to business status and wealth. It also helped them locate licit and illicit business opportunities on the mainland (Lo 2010a, 2010b).

Triad Business

Drug trafficking Triads expanded their operations during the Vietnam War, when thousands of troops were attracted to the potent heroin of Southeast Asia. When the Americans withdrew from Vietnam, Triads followed the market and internationalized their drug operations. Many soldiers were stationed in Europe, so a major Triad marketplace developed there, with operations headquartered in Amsterdam.

Triads control prostitution in designated areas in Singapore, Hong Kong, and Macau. Prostitutes are brought in by the Triads and their solicitation of customers is confined to Triad-controlled territory where there is a systematic maintenance of law and order by the Triads themselves so as to avoid police intervention. As long as prostitution is confined, running smoothly, and does not pose a risk to the society at large, it is tolerated by the police (Lo 2010b).

Triads bring women in under the guise of being tourists. Members connect with Mainland criminal groups for the selection of women who work more than twelve hours a day in casino hotels or guest houses, first to recoup their travel expenses, food, and accommodation, and then to earn their "wages," of which the Triads take a percentage. When their tourist visa expires, they return home and another group of women arrives to take their place. "Because of the short-term stay and high turnover of prostitutes, both the cost and risk of running such an operation is low" (Lo 2010b: 16).

Hong Kong-based Triads are involved in the manufacture of counterfeit credit cards. They recruit restaurant or entertainment workers who might be in debt to them as skimmers and provide them with a pocketsize skimming device to steal credit card data from customers. The workers pass on the data to repay their debts and the data is used to manufacture counterfeit cards. The cards are sold to professional shoppers for the purchase of luxury goods (Curtis et al., 2003). Banks now issue immediate warnings to customers if their credit cards are used overseas and/or if the amount is large, and this has restricted the criminality.

Macau-based Triads have been absorbed by the gaming industry. Through *guanxi*, Triads have been subcontracted to run VIP rooms inside casinos. "Triad members serve as casino agents and recruit rich businessmen and government officials from Southeast Asia, Taiwan, and China to gamble in the VIP rooms with rebates. Triads provide one-stop service to their clients, such as transport, escort, accommodation, protection, sex service, and loans" (Lo 2010b: 20).

Tongs

Chinese laborers were originally brought into the United States after 1848 to work in the gold fields of California, particularly in those aspects of mining that were most dangerous because few white men were willing to engage in blasting shafts, placing beams, and laying track lines in the gold mines. Chinese immigrants also helped to build the Western railroad lines at pay few whites would accept—known as "coolie wages." After their work was completed, Chinese were often banned from the rural counties; by the 1860s they were clustering in cities on the Pacific coast, where they established Chinatowns. Hostility toward Chinese was codified in 1882 with the passage of the Chinese Exclusionary Act. This law was repealed in 1943, a time when the United States was allied with China in war against Japan.

Chinese became the targets of abuse and random violence and found refuge in urban areas where they established "Chinatowns" and formed mutual aid societies and tongs. "*Tong* is an Anglicization of the Mandarin word *tang*. This in turn translates as 'hall' or 'lodge,' but it usually refers to the organization itself, not the building it might meet in" (Huston 2001: 46). Tongs were first established in San Francisco in the 1850s as benevolent societies (Chin, Kelly, and Fagan 1994). Creations of the expatriate community, tongs provided loans and legal assistance while overseeing vice operations that catered to the primarily male Chinese population (Keefe 2009).

While most tongs were business, fraternal, or political in character, "fighting tongs" licensed illegal businesses and were part of a tight-knit nation-wide alliance. A purely local dispute between fighting tongs, therefore, "could and often did precipitate a fight between affiliates in every U.S. Chinatown" (Light 1977: 472). During the last decade of the nineteenth century and the first two decades of the twentieth, tong wars occurred on the East and West Coasts. In New York in 1909, a tong war between the On Leong ("Peaceful Dragon") and Hip Sing ("Prosperous Union") claimed an estimated 350 lives (Sante 1991).

As the importance of gambling and house prostitution in Chinatowns declined following World War I, vice entrepreneurs discovered the profitability of tourist enterprises, and restaurants replaced the brothels and gambling halls. Nevertheless, the struggle between the On Leong and Hip Sing to control vice operations in New York's Chinatown continued into the 1930s. Contemporary tongs such as the Hip Sing and the On Leong have dropped the term from their names because of its association with "tong wars" (Chin 1990).

Some Chinese immigrants, like Sicilian immigrants who had been *mafiosi*, were Triad members at home. In a pattern similar to that of the *Unione Siciliana* discussed in Chapter 3, many of these men joined tongs that have been able to transcend the worlds of legitimate business and crime. Because tong members' primary loyalty is to each other, if a member is involved in criminal activity, "the others are pledged not to turn him into the police" (Huston 2001: 60). As with almost all organized criminal groups before the onset of Prohibition, Asian criminal organizations have typically exploited only their own countrymen and were therefore able to avoid serious law enforcement efforts due to Chinese antipathy toward the police.

Tongs continue to be associated with illegal gambling. In 1988, for example, federal agents raided the Chicago headquarters of the On Leong, where they found evidence of extensive commercial gambling, including more than $320,000 in cash and records indicating extortion from local Chinese merchants. A 1990 indictment accused the Chicago On Leong and affiliates in New York and Houston of being a key part of a gambling operation that netted $11.5 million annually. Gambling, in particular *Pai Gow*, an ancient Chinese domino game, was available from 9:30 A.M. to 7:00 P.M., seven days a week, at the On Leong Chicago headquarters, which were subsequently forfeited to the government. In 1994, Chicago On Leong officers were found guilty of running gambling operations, making payoffs to the police, and paying street taxes to the Outfit. They also bribed a state judge to fix a murder case involving three members of a New York Chinese gang brought to Chicago to kill a troublemaker (Hayner 1990; O'Connor 1994a, 1994b).

Peter Huston (2001: 62) points out, "Important tong members have a network of social contacts throughout the country that often provide them with considerable help in carrying out complex criminal schemes or avoiding justice."

In addition to gambling, tongs provide loans at usurious interest and are involved in operating prostitution outlets—"massage parlors"—that cater to both Asian and non-Asian customers. Rounding out their activities, often joint efforts with Triad members, is tong involvement with alien smuggling, discussed shortly.

Asian Gangs

Many contemporary tongs are national in scope, particularly the Hip Sing, On Leong, and Tsung Tsin, and some are connected to Chinatown gangs such as the Ghost Shadows and the Flying Dragons in New York, Chicago, Boston, and San Francisco. Dating back to the 1960s, these gangs consist of American-born Chinese (ABCs) whose self-declared mission was to fend off attacks by non-Asian outsiders. At the same time, new immigration laws resulted in a large influx of youths from Hong Kong. Some of these FOBs (fresh off the boat) became alienated from school, found little economic opportunity, were beyond family control, and began to form their own gangs (Kelly, Chin, and Fagan 1993; D. Lee 2003). The result was an upsurge of violent street crime in communities that heretofore had been relatively crime free—"the gangs transformed themselves completely from self-help groups to predatory groups" (Chin, Zhang, and Kelly 1998: 131). "They terrorized the community by demanding food and money from businesses and robbed illegal gambling establishments. When the youth gangs began to 'shake down' merchants and gamblers who were themselves tong members, the tongs decided to hire the gangs as their street soldiers to protect themselves" (Chin, Zhang, and Kelly 1998: 131). "Wherever large sums of money exchanged hands, the gangs sought a slice of the action. Counterfeit handbags did not originate with the gangs, but they soon began getting a cut. Massage parlors and prostitution rings offered another revenue stream. By the mid-80s, 'China White' [heroin] was added to the list" (Lee 2003: CY 16). The gangs served as the final leg of a heroin distribution network that started in the Golden Triangle (discussed in Chapter 12).

Benny Ong, the venerable head of the Hip Sing, much like Tammany Hall leader Charles Murphy (discussed in Chapter 2), decided to distance the tong from its illegal activities. He subcontracted these activities to the tong's enforcement cadre, the Flying Dragons, and reinvented himself as a successful businessman. The rival On Leong did the same, outsourcing illegal activities to the Ghost Shadows (Keefe 2009). If a tong needs help from its affiliated gang, the message will be conveyed to the *Dai Dai Lo* ("Big Brother") by the *Ah Kung* ("Grandpa"). A *Dai Dai Lo* may also be an officer of the affiliated tong. Likewise, the highest leaders of the gangs have served as officers of the affiliated adult organizations (Chin, Kelly, and Fagan 1994).

Established gang leaders are often martial arts masters operating out of their own athletic clubs. Members go through an initiation ceremony that is a simplified version of Triad rituals. "The youth takes his oaths, burns yellow paper, and drinks wine mixed with blood in front of the gang leaders and the altar of General Kwan, a heroic figure of the Triad subculture" (Chin 1990: 124). Members often dress in black outfits and sport exotic tattoos—dragons, serpents, tigers, and eagles. The gang becomes a substitute for the member's family. "They are not youth gangs in the usual sense but, rather, a young form of organized crime" (Dannen 1992b: 77).

A 1995 federal indictment revealed that New York's Chinatown, the largest in the United States, was divided into fiefdoms under the domination of tongs aided by their affiliated gangs. Through this arrangement protection money was collected from virtually every Chinatown business, legal or illegal; the latter included 24/7 gambling dens. In addition to the tong leaders, two Chinese-American police officers were prosecuted for providing information about police investigations and planned raids on gambling houses and brothels; they also engineered raids on competing casinos (English 1995a; Faison 1995a, 1995b; Frantz and Toy 1995; Fried 1995; Kleinfield 1995; Sexton 1995).

Although these gangs draw upon the traditions of the Triads, particularly the ceremonial aspects of initiation, they have many members who are Vietnamese (of Chinese ancestry); the latter are apparently favored because of their reputed ability with firearms. There are also mixed gangs of Vietnamese and Chinese-Vietnamese (*Viet Ching*, ethnic Chinese born in Vietnam), who are usually heavily armed. They operate mainly in California but also reach into Vietnamese and Chinese communities in other locales. One such gang was founded by a member of New York Chinatown's Flying Dragons, David Thai, who was born in Saigon in 1956 and arrived in the United States in 1976.

As a Vietnamese, Thai was consigned to a smaller unit known as the Vietnamese Flying Dragons. Dissatisfied with his lesser status among Chinese criminals, Thai attracted adolescents who were recent immigrants from Vietnam, offering them a place to live and employment, slowly forming his own gang, which became known as the "Canal Boys"—their headquarters was on Chinatown's Canal Street. They asserted their territoriality by extorting money from the local Canal Street merchants. In 1989, Thai formed a confederation of Vietnamese gangs in the New York City metropolitan area and adopted the name Born to Kill (BTK), a slogan that often appeared on the helmets of American GIs in Vietnam. Thai was the leader, *Anh hai*, and constituent gangs were headed by a *dai low*. Each BTK member signed a paper agreeing to abide by the group's rules, which included a vow of secrecy and a requirement to clear all planned criminal activity with his *dai low*. Members were tattooed with the initials BTK, a coffin, and three candles, signifying that they do not fear death (English 1995a; Lorch 1990). The BTK had many non-Vietnamese associates, some of whom were non-Asians, who participated in their robberies. The leadership and core members, however, were all Vietnamese.

Because they were viewed as interlopers and left out of the criminal power structure in Chinatown, there was nothing to restrain the BTK who victimized massage parlors, bars, and tong gambling dens. In broad daylight and in front of numerous witnesses, two Flying Dragons who had insulted David Thai were shot to death. BTK members subsequently killed two Ghost Shadows at their hangout and, on orders from Thai, a BTK member blew up a police van in front of an NYPD precinct house (English 1995a). The ultimate insult, however, was Thai's 1990 refusal to meet with Chinatown's "godfather," Benny Ong,[1] leader of the Hip Sing tong.

This loss of face brought swift retribution— Thai's closest associate was gunned down, and at the funeral gunmen sprayed automatic fire at the mourners. Shortly afterward, three BTK members were slain execution style. This did not stop the BTK from committing a string of armed robberies in New England, the South, Canada, and anywhere else Asian businesses could be victimized. In Georgia they seriously wounded a jewelry storeowner who had resisted. The arrest of a BTK member involved in the Georgia robbery led to an extensive interagency investigation and successful prosecutions of the group's leadership (English 1995a).

Chinese groups—*snakeheads*—are involved in smuggling illegal aliens for employment in garment-manufacturing sweatshops, particularly in New York and California. The aliens are treated as indentured servants—forced to work at below minimum wages to pay back their benefactors for getting them into the United States. Women are sometimes forced into brothels. "People who leave China illegally are often called 'human snakes'; thus those who lead them across the borders are called snakeheads" (*Characteristics of Chinese Human Smugglers* 2004: 1).

One notorious Chinese criminal organization, the Fuk Ching, was employed by snakeheads to hold illegal immigrants hostage until their passage was paid for. Realizing that alien smuggling was lucrative and less risky than heroin trafficking, they became subcontractors to established snakeheads, providing small vessels to offload immigrants from the mother ship (Keefe 2009). The leader of the Fuk Ching, a fugitive from U.S. justice, often relayed orders to New York by telephone from his fortress-like headquarters in China's Fujian province. He was eventually arrested in Hong Kong and returned to the United States in 1994 where he became a government informant (Faison 1993; Keefe 2009; Treaster 1993b). Successful prosecutions of the Fuk Ching eventually decimated the group.

In 1996, in a scenario further reminiscent of betrayals in the American Mafia, four top leaders of the Ghost Shadows became government witnesses, all but demolishing the gang. Racketeer and Corrupt Organizations (RICO) (discussed in Chapter 14) prosecutions eventually decimated every Chinatown gang and the top leadership of the tongs (D. Lee 2003).

Meanwhile, gambling and heroin, the economic lifeblood of the gangs, began to dry up. Atlantic City casinos offered major entertainment and cheap bus rides; the Colombians offered cheaper heroin. In a manner reminiscent of the Irish and the Jews, the once readily available cohort of potential gang members also began to dry up, the result of education and legitimate opportunity (Lee 2003).

---

1. Benny Ong died of natural causes at age 87 in 1994.

YAKUZA RELIEF

In 1995, the city of Kobe, Japan, was hit by a massive earthquake. About 6,500 people lost their lives, thousands of building were destroyed, and the population was without adequate supplies. The government response was slow, but a large number of heavily tattooed men, some with clipped fingers, quickly began distributing provisions, as ordered by their boss, Yoshinori Watanabe, *kumicho* of the Yamaguchi-gumi, the country's largest *yakuza* organization.

Yakuza

Yakuza have been in existence for about 300 years and have their roots in the Tokugawa period (1600–1867) when Japan united under a central system of government. With the end of Japanese feudalism, *samurai* (knights) lost their role in life, and many roamed the countryside as freelance mercenaries (Rome 1975). *Yakuza*—masterless *samurai*, unscrupulous itinerant peddlers, professional gamblers, and common criminals—eventually formed structured groups, *boryokudan* ("violent groups"). They frequently refer themselves as *gokudo*, literally "the ultimate path" (Adelstein 2009).

Under the leadership of their *kumi-cho* (boss), they are able to exert control over sections of Japan's urban areas. The largest *boryokudan*, the 35,000-strong Yamaguchi-gumi (*gumi* means "group") dominates the industrialized, densely populated region extending from Kyoto through Osaka to Kobe, as well as Tokyo and most other major centers in Japan. The group's heavily guarded headquarters takes up a full city block in an upscale neighborhood. Steel doors are illuminated with floodlights and monitored by video cameras; bodyguards are quick to challenge unknown visitors. Each of its subgroups pays monthly dues, but because too many *yakuza* were underreporting their income, during the 1970s payments became a fixed amount (Hill 2003). The money is funneled to the top of the organization: "Every month the Yamaguchi-gumi headquarters takes in (at a conservative estimate) more than $50 million" (Adelstein 2009: 87).

By adhering to rules of conduct that preclude violence against the police and innocent civilians, *yakuza* syndicates have been able to operate openly, with high-profile headquarters. *Yakuza* "crime control" is believed to be at least partly responsible for Japan's low crime rate. In Asia, there has always been a symbiosis between the law and organized crime that "helps the authorities police more unpredictable, disorganised crime to keep the streets safe" (Lintner 2002: 10). *Yakuza* groups that emerged after World War II were used by the government to maintain stability in the absence of competent law enforcement (Fukumi 2010).

The term *yakuza* "is derived from an old card game … whose object was to draw three cards adding up as close as possible to 19 without exceeding it," similar to the game of "21" or blackjack. "*Ya-ku-za* represents the Japanese words for 8, 9, 3, which total 20, a useless number—like 22 in blackjack. Basically, *yakuza* means 'good for nothing'" (Haberman 1985: 6). Like many of their American counterparts, the *yakuza* "were born into poverty and graduated from juvenile delinquency into organized crime" (Kirk 1976: 93). The Al Capone of Japan, Kazuo Taoka, was, like Capone, born into a poor family. He began his criminal career as a bouncer in Kobe, much as Capone filled this capacity in Brooklyn before going to Chicago. Taoka, like Capone, played a major role in the mob conflicts of the day, and both men rose to prominence because of their penchant for violence and talent for organization. When Taoka, 68, died of a heart attack in 1981, his funeral was attended by more than 1,200 *yakuza*. "Taoka's friendships and contacts extended to the highest levels of government, with two former prime ministers … among his friends. That kind of relationship reflected not only Taoka's personal success but also historic ties between gangsters and prominent government figures" (Kirk 1981: 17; Adelstein 2009). *Yakuza* have long-standing links with their country's ruling political parties.

Yakuza Structure

Each *yakuza* group has a pyramidal structure with four or five ranks (Fukumi 2010). Decisions that affect the organization as a whole are made by the boss and his senior executives, while routine day-to-day decision making is decentralized. A senior executive may act as an underboss, and there are executives, soldiers, and trainees. "On occasion when a follower reaches a certain status in the hierarchy [usually a senior executive], he is given permission to train his own followers and become a small boss [while still remaining a senior executive]. He announces the name of his own family and, in accordance with his prestige, he is permitted to call himself either the boss of a 'branch of the family' or boss of a 'whole family'" (Iwai 1986: 216).

Boryokudans distinguish between members and associates who have not been initiated into the secrets of the organization by way of an elaborate *sake* ceremony, and are therefore at the bottom of the *yakuza* world. "Rising in the ranks depends on the amount of money sent up to superiors in the organization, and one's share of profits is in order of rank, with the boss [*kumi-cho*] getting about half" (Iwai 1986: 217).

Initiation into a *boryokudan* involves an elaborate ceremony: At the front of a banquet hall is a simple wooden altar laden with *sake* and food, offerings to the gods of Shinto. Behind the altar are banners with the names of the sun goddess, the patron god of warriors, and another associated with the imperial household. Recruits dressed in kimonos sip *sake* and are given their regalia, a sword, a map of the group's turf, seals, and some swathes of cotton. There is a short address by the boss, and the new members accompany kimono-clad women for some less formal drinking (Lintner 2002).

The *boryokudans* "form closed societies in their individual groups, but the groups are interlinked

through a widespread underworld syndicate" (Takahashi and Becker 1985: 3). *Yakuza* syndicates in a particular area often form a confederation for inter-group conflict resolution (Hill 2003).

Recruitment is accomplished by "talent scouts" who scour hangouts most likely to attract young delinquents, who are given pocket money and employed in various errands as they are drawn into their mentor's circle. Due to increased involvement in white-collar crime, *yakuza* also welcome persons with financial and computer skills. Each recruit has a mentor, and *yakuza* apprenticeships range from six months to three years during which the apprentice lives in the house of the boss or other ranking member, performing housekeeping and other chores while learning *yakuza* protocol; learning includes being hit for committing an error (Hill 2003).

World War II served to delineate *yakuza* groups, a situation that closely parallels that of the "old" and *Nuovo Mafia* in Sicily (Chapter 5). After Japan's defeat, the new *yakuza* that emerged was populated by unemployed returning combat veterans and was far more violent and materialistic than their prewar predecessors. Abandoning many *yakuza* traditions, they emulated American gangsters in dress, often using firearms obtained from American GIs in place of a traditional *samurai* sword. The "new *yakuza*" entered a burgeoning black market that included trafficking in amphetamines, whose use had been promoted by the military and among industrial workers during the war to boost productivity.

Beginning in the 1950s, Japan experienced remarkable economic growth to which these postwar "economic mobsters" responded with expansive international connections that extend to Hong Kong, Southeast Asia, Russian Asia, Australia, and Latin American countries with large numbers of Japanese immigrants (French 2001; Hill 2003; Lintner 2002). Economic growth fostered development of an entertainment industry that included gambling and commercial sex—*yakuza* businesses—and the need for construction and waterfront labor whose supplies are controlled by *yakuza* firms. *Boryokudan* membership burgeoned, reaching a peak in 1963 of more than 180,000 members; so did competitive violence (Hill 2003).

The self-image of the *yakuza* stands in contrast to that of their American counterparts *Yakuza* view themselves as modern *samurai* and have traditionally maintained exotic rituals, including extensive tattooing that often covers their bodies from necks to ankles, and clipped fingers that have been self-amputated with a short sword in a ritual (*yubizume*) that serves as a sign of contrition for mistakes. The amputated top of the smallest digit is placed in a small bottle filled with alcohol with the person's name written on it; it is sent to whomever one is asking for forgiveness, typically a boss. Tattooing was originally used by authorities to make it easier to recognize outlaws and has become a tradition among *yakuza* (Lintner 2002). Though not obligatory, tattooing indicates the ability to withstand pain and commitment to the *yakuza* life—they make it difficult to integrate back into conventional society (Milhaupt and West 2000).

The Yamaguchi-gumi is listed in the telephone book and publishes a membership newsletter and, until 1991, its headquarters were clearly marked for all to see. Group members typically wore lapel pins that designated their *boryokudan*, and its logo. The golden diamond-shaped design of the Yamaguchi-gumi, appeared on their headquarters building in Kobe, on lapel pins, and on members' business cards. Such displays were outlawed in 1991 and the lowered public profile of *yakuza* has coincided with an increasing involvement in legitimate business (Fukumi 2010). Modern day *yakuza*, notes Jake Adelstein (2009: 88), "are innovative entrepreneurs, rather than a bunch of tattooed nine-fingered thugs."

Resignation or expulsion is accomplished with a *homojo* or "red letter" to all members of the *boryokudan*, which signals that the person is no longer a member (PCOC 1984b). Expulsion is considered a more serious punishment than *yubizume*: former *yakuza* are not permitted to practice any illegal trade under penalties that include death; to do so as unaffiliated criminals would make them quite vulnerable. Yet prior *yakuza* membership means they are virtually unemployable in the legitimate

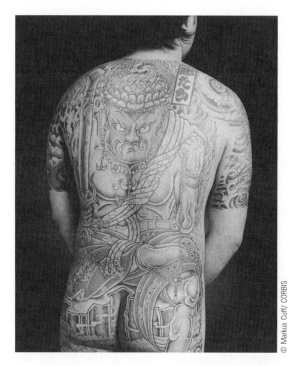

© Markus Cuff / CORBIS

Yakuza view themselves as modern samurai and maintain exotic rituals, including extensive tattooing that often covers their bodies from neck to ankles, and clipped fingers that have been self-amputated with a short sword in a ritual that serves as a sign of contrition for mistakes.

sector. After a period of time, expelled members who have conducted themselves honorably may be given an opportunity to rejoin (Hill 2003; Milhaupt and West 2000).

In 1999, Tokutaro Takayama, then 71, godfather of the Aizu Kotetsu-kai *boryokudan,* was interviewed by reporters at his private office just outside of Kyoto, surrounded by surveillance cameras and bodyguards with missing pinkies. He decried the state of *yakuza* in present-day Japan: "Today, they don't care about obligations, traditions, respect and dignity. There are no rules anymore" (Jordon and Sullivan 1999). Similar sentiments could be uttered by the elders of America's organized crime Families. Takayama's view is supported by the 2007 slaying of the mayor of Nagasaki by a member of a local branch of the Yamaguchi-gumi who confessed to the police. Police were unable to determine a reason for the murder (Fackler 2007).

About 60 percent of the estimated 85,000 *yakuza*[2] are affiliated with one of three groups: the Yamaguchi-Gumi, Sumiyoshi-Kai, and Inagawa-Kai. *Yakuza* share similar backgrounds. In sharp contrast to Russian organized crime and reminiscent of the early days of American organized crime, *yakuza* are typically lower working class, high school dropouts, with one or two parents of Korean or Chinese extraction—marginalized persons with a history of juvenile delinquency (Seymour 1996). An estimated 75 percent of the Yamaguchi-gumi are ethnic Koreans or *burakumin,* descendants of outcasts—Japanese "untouchables"—who have been subjected to generations of discrimination because their families are associated with "dirty" occupations: butchers, tanners, and grave diggers (Kristof 1995a). In Japan, organized crime is an equal opportunity employer.

In contrast to most organized crime groups (see attributes of organized crime in Chapter 1), the *yakuza* have a distinct ideological orientation—ultranationalistic, conservative on matters of foreign policy, and vigorously anticommunist. This has endeared them to many right-wing politicians, and *yakuza* are intimately involved in the politics of Japan. The relatively low rate of street crime in Japan is often ascribed to a symbiotic, love/hate relationship between the *yakuza* and the police (Hill 2003; Kaplan and Dubro 1986). The police share the political views of the *yakuza* and historically have done little against them—police raids are often publicity stunts. The *yakuza* reciprocate by keeping disorganized crime under control. In 1995, when leaders of the Pacific Rim countries met in Osaka, the Yamaguchi-gumi, like others concerned with the city's image, explained through a spokesman: "All members of our group want to do our part for our country. So we agreed to exercise self-control over our businesses" (Kristof 1995b: 6).

Yakuza are concerned about their public image: When famed Japanese film director Juzo

Itami (*Tampopo; A Taxing Woman*) portrayed them in an unflattering manner in film, he became the victim of a knife attack by assailants who slashed his neck and face (Goozner 1992; Sterngold 1992b). In 1995, when a devastating earthquake hit Kobe and killed 5,500 people, the relief efforts established by the Yamaguchi-gumi proved superior to those of the government. This was seen as a way of blunting the high-profile police campaign against the group (Sterngold 1995). The earthquake also provided a vehicle for Yamaguchi-gumi controlled construction firms to increase their wealth; they threatened rivals so that they did not submit lower bids and collected "greetings fees" as insurance against construction site disruptions (Kristof 1995c).

An internal rebellion by the Ichiwa-kai faction against the Yamaguchi-gumi resulted in a great deal of violence. Although loyalists had numerical superiority, the Ichiwa-kai had seized most of the organization's arsenal. By the end of 1988, the war had left twenty-five dead and seventy injured. The Yamaguchi-gumi was eventually able to lure back many defectors, and other Ichiwa-kai members found it difficult to operate without the established reputation of the Yamaguchi-gumi. Hill (2007: 50) points out that this exemplifies the need for an organized crime group to have a "brand image."

Yakuza Business

Yakuza control most organized criminal activity in Japan, including drug trafficking. Japan has a drug problem, particularly the abuse of amphetamines, which the *yakuza* produce in clandestine laboratories in Japan, the Philippines, and Korea. They are at the center of an international trade in sexual slavery: females, often children, bought and sold throughout Third World countries. *Yakuza* helped popularize the Southeast Asian "sex tours" (*Kisaeng* parties) favored by Japanese businessmen. These women and children also serve in the *yakuza*-dominated sex entertainment centers of Tokyo.

They control illegal gambling, practice extortion and white-collar crime through infiltration of legitimate businesses, and loansharking. Yakuza buy databases of heavily indebted persons who are

---

2. This represents a significant drop in members since the peak years.

contacted by phone or email about available loans. They are referred to storefront outlets similar to their legitimate counterparts, save for the usurious interest charged and methods of collection—delinquent borrowers receive *yakuza* visits and threats to life and family. Movies that portray *yakuza* as noble gangsters are popular in Japan, and the *yakuza* are influential in the Japanese movie industry. They finance movies and real *yakuza* often portray themselves in these films (Adelstein 2009). In 2011, a popular Japanese TV host retired after his ties with a senior member of the Yamaguchi-gumi were revealed. Showbiz types involvement with yakuza is frequently the result of asking for a favor, such as collecting unpaid appearance fees (Shimbun 2011).

Yakuza have had close financial ties to the banking industry, which provided funds for them to invest in real estate. When property values deteriorated as a result of a market downturn, financial institutions found themselves holding many bad loans; efforts to collect proved dangerous.

As is the case with their counterparts in Italy, the former Soviet Union, and elsewhere, *yakuza* provide alternatives to official mechanisms for dispute resolution (Fukumi 2010). Japan has relatively few lawyers, and "Japanese courts are notoriously slow and indifferent to the complaints of individuals. Essentially, the *yakuza* have taken on the role of lawyers-cum-negotiators" (Seymour 1996: 202). Rounding out *yakuza* criminal activities are extortion from both legitimate and illegitimate entrepreneurs, intimidation, and the evicting of people from their homes on behalf of real estate developers—Japanese law makes it virtually impossible to legally evict tenants (Milhaupt and West 2000). Automobile accident victims will sometimes hire *yakuza* to retrieve damage payments on a contingency-fee basis (Weisman 1991). Similarly, yakuza-backed adjusters handle most Japanese bankruptcies informally, and the police are reluctant to intervene in what they consider civil matters. Bankers sometimes dispatch *yakuza* to bankrupted businesses to confiscate property ahead of unsecured creditors (Hirsch and Takayama 1997; Kaplan 1998).

Police crackdowns on *yakuza* business interests and a downturn in the Japanese economy affected organized crime. When the easy money was plentiful, *yakuza* "stuck closely to their own turf and honored hierarchy as if it were life itself. Things were so simple, in fact, that using a little muscle often meant little more than, say, depositing a dead cat on the doorstep of a landlord being pressured into selling a coveted property" (French 2001: 4). With business expense accounts slashed, *yakuza*-controlled bars and nightclubs began hurting and members are having a more difficult time paying monthly honorariums to their leaders, and discipline has lapsed.

Following the low-key approach of his predecessor Yoshinori Watanabe, who retired in 2005, the sixth Yamaguchi-gumi *kumicho*—supreme leader—eschewed a high profile role when he assumed office in 2005; Kenichi Shinoda took a train to his induction ceremony rather than the traditional chauffeured limousine.

SUMMARY

1. Know the historical and cultural characteristics of China and overseas Chinese communities that promote entrepreneurship, legal and illegal:
   - A cultural dynamic of Chinese society is loyalty to family and friends as a moral imperative.
   - A member of the Chinese community is part of a latent, hierarchically organized family.

2. Understand the Triad phenomenon:
   - Triads, which have a long history in China, engage in highly ritualized dress and behavior.
   - Triads span international boundaries with members located in virtually every country that has a sizable Chinese community.
   - Triads are fluid associations of ethnic Chinese criminals, loose-knit groups

operating and cooperating with each other on the basis of personal introductions and mutual interests.

- Triads have an associational hierarchy that does not exert vertically integrated control over the members' criminal enterprises.
- Chinese criminal groups have cells operating autonomously with leaders who use their extensive connections to arrange complex criminal operations.
- Triad business includes international heroin trafficking, trafficking in persons for commercial sex, and manufacture of counterfeit credit cards.

3. Appreciate how anti-Chinese sentiments led to the establishment of Chinatowns, the role of tongs, and differences between Triads, tongs, and Asian gangs:
- Chinese were targets of abuse and violence and found refuge in urban areas where they established "Chinatowns" and formed mutual aid societies and tongs.
- Tongs, fraternal benevolent societies, also oversaw Chinatown vice activities.
- Although they have dropped the term tong, members are involved in Chinatown illegal gambling, loansharking, prostitution, and alien smuggling.

- Like the Irish and the Jews, the available cohort of potential Chinatown gang members began to dry up, the result of education and legitimate opportunity.

4. Appreciate the unique qualities of Japanese organized crime:
- *Yakuza* are partly responsible for Japan's low crime rate.
- Each *yakuza* group has a pyramidal structure with four or five ranks. Decisions that affect the organization as a whole are made by the boss and his senior executives, while routine day-to-day decision making is decentralized.
- The self-image of the *yakuza* stands in contrast to that of their American counterparts: *Yakuza* view themselves as modern *samurai*.
- In contrast to most organized crime groups, *yakuza* have a distinct ideological orientation.
- After Japan's defeat, the new *yakuza* emerged that was far more violent and materialistic than their prewar predecessors a situation that closely parallels that of the "old" and *Nuovo Mafia* in Sicily.
- *Yakuza* control most organized criminal activity in Japan, including drug trafficking and international trade in sexual slavery.

REVIEW QUESTIONS

1. What dynamics of Chinese culture provide advantages in both legal and illegal business?
2. How are Triads structured?
3. How is the structure of Triads similar to that of the American Mafia and outlaw motorcycle clubs?
4. How do the cells of Chinese criminal organizations operate?
5. What are the businesses of Triads?
6. How are tongs similar to the *Unione Siciliana* of the 1920s and 1930s?
7. What is the relationship between tongs and Chinatown gangs?

8. What led to the demise of Chinatown gangs?
9. How do *yakuza* differ from most other organized crime groups?
10. What is the relationship between Japan's low crime rate and *yakuza*?
11. How are *yakuza* groups structured?
12. What are the parallels between the old and new *yakuza* and the old Sicilian Mafia and the *Nuova Mafia*?
13. What are the various *yakuza* businesses?

Prospective member questioned by Russian *vor v zakonye* bosses. © Focus Features/Courtesy Everett Collection

Russian Organized Crime

Criminals from the former Soviet Union (FSU) have proven capable of engaging in a virtual smorgasbord of crimes in the United States. Some are relatively pedestrian, such as drug trafficking, while others require the technical skills often possessed by FSU immigrants. For example, the Armenian Power organization (based in southern California, made up of several hundred Armenians and Russian-Armenians), has been involved in drug trafficking, loansharking, and kidnapping, but it has distinguished itself from other crime groups by engaging in bank fraud and cyber-crime.

In one complex scheme, members installed credit card skimming devices at cash registers in "99 Cents Only" stores across southern California and used the stolen information from hundreds of customers to create counterfeit credit and debit cards. In another, they collaborated with a local African American gang to bribe insiders at banks in Orange County to gather information that allowed them to take over bank accounts.

CHAPTER 9 WILL ENABLE THE READER TO UNDERSTAND:

- How the history of Russia and the former Soviet Union paved the way for organized crime

- What Russian organized crime has in common with America's "Robber Barons"

- How the collapse of the Soviet Union fostered pirate capitalism and organized crime

- The overlapping categories of Russian organized crime

- The oft-invisible boundary between Russian criminals and businessmen

- How organized crime in the former Soviet Union differs from Russian organized crime in the United States

Armenian Power is allied with the Mexican Mafia (discussed in Chapter 6) while maintaining ties to Armenia and Russia, dealing directly with high-level Armenian/Russian organized crime figures. Among those high-level crime figures are traditional "Thieves-in-Law," *vory*, who are used to resolve disputes (FBI press release, February 16, 2011; Lovett 2011).

In this chapter we will look at organized crime in the FSU and Russian organized crime in the United States.

Ruled by a succession of czars since 1547, devastating defeats of the Russian army by Japan in 1905 and Germany in World War I led to rioting in major cities and in 1917 the overthrow and execution of the last czar and his family. Communists under Vladimir Lenin seized power and formed the Union of Soviet Socialist Republics (USSR). Following Joseph Stalin's brutal rule (1922–1953) the Soviet economy stagnated until Mikhail Gorbachev introduced *glasnost* (openness) and *perestroika* (restructuring) in an attempt to modernize. His initiatives released forces that by 1991 led to the splintering of the USSR into Russia and fourteen other independent states (see Figure 9.1), most characterized by autocratic rule.

At 6.5 million square miles, Russia is the largest country in the world, with a landmass that stretches from Europe to Asia—approximately 1.8 times the

FIGURE 9.1 Map of Russia

size of the United States. It has a population of more than 140 million. Although they may speak Russian—often a language imposed on conquered non-Russian peoples—and come from regions that have been dominated by Russia, many ethnic groups and nationalities "do not regard themselves nor do Russians regard them as Russians" (Finckenauer and Waring 1999: 132; Serio 2008). The term *Russian* encompasses any ethnic or national group—such as Armenian, Chechen, Estonian, Georgian, Jewish, Latvian, Lithuanian, Tatar, Ukrainian—from the territory of the FSU. Some also include Albanians (discussed in Chapter 5). But "Russian" does not necessarily reflect the ethnicity or nationality of many identified as part of Russian organized crime (ROC); it is being used to identify those whose origins are from the territory of the FSU

ROOTS OF RUSSIAN
ORGANIZED CRIME

Russian organized crime has more in common with the Robber Barons discussed in Chapter 2 than the Sicilian Mafia discussed in Chapter 5. It remains to be seen if the wealth and power of organized crime becomes institutionalized and its leaders and their progeny emerge as Russian equivalents of Astor, Vanderbilt, Drew, Gould, Sage, Rockefeller, and Stanford.

In the Soviet Union, "organized crime" did not imply a Mafia-style organization, but was simply "a basic system of relationships and access among various sectors of society with the [Communist] Party in the dominant role and the traditional criminal world playing a relatively minor part" (Serio 2008: 19). In the successor states of the FSU, where law enforcement resources have been inadequate to deal with the menace, additional elements have elbowed their way into the world of organized crime. Many poorly paid officers are on criminal payrolls, whereas others left the service to work for their erstwhile opponents full time. Parliamentary bodies became riddled with de facto criminal syndicate representatives who diligently

blocked or watered down any significant anticrime legislation (Voronin 1997). And although Chicagoans refer to politics as a "blood sport," it is less of a metaphor in the FSU where elected and appointed officials are frequently the targets of hired killers (Wines 2002).

The breeding and training ground for ROC was established during the Communist era, and it is against this background that we must understand the variety of ROC. Citizens of the FSU were deprived of a work ethic—"We pretend to work, they pretend to pay us"—and schemed to survive. For the average Russian, the consequence of honesty was deprivation (Rosner 1995: vii). An absence of individual economic accountability and creativity "translated into apathy, often cruel indifference, corruption and the ever burgeoning presence of a second economy" (Rawlinson 2010: 5).

"In Russia, governments both under the rule of the Tzars and that of the Communist state represented totalitarianism in one form or another where individual freedom was suppressed. As such, like the invading foreigners of Sicily, the internal government system of Russia has made the Russian, like the Sicilian, distrustful of government" (Albini et al. 1995: 222). And while there is corruption in all countries, "in Russia, corruption is common in all organs of power and establishments" (Gilinsky 2004: 62) and "at every level throughout the society, from garbage removal to school textbook supply" (Cheloukhine and Haberfield 2011: 68), a condition that has roots extending back to at least the sixteenth century (Serio 2008).

ROC "embraces the noxious blend of crime, politics and business that has engulfed Russia since the lifting of Communist control" (Bohlen 1999: WK 6). Post-1987 economic liberalization awoke not only the entrepreneurial spirit of capitalism, but also paved the way for the entry of criminal organizations (Volkov 2002). The connection between the shadow economy (for example, the black market) and criminal organizations was solidified in the scramble for greater power and wealth.

The sudden onset of a market economy gave rise to unrestrained aspirations—the classic condition Émile Durkheim referred to as anomie (discussed in

Chapter 4). Although written in 1897, Durkheim's concept fits the situation of present-day Russia: "The collapse of the previous system brought in fundamental changes in social and political order which shaped the personal lives of individuals in the most profound way. Several years of market reforms which changed the nature of the country's economy also brought with them hyperinflation, a sharp rise in unemployment and an overall drop in the standard of living" (Frisby 1998: 27).

In 1991, when the Soviet Union broke into fifteen independent states, Russia struggled to establish a modern market economy and achieve strong economic growth. The economy initially contracted despite the country's wealth of natural resources, its well-educated population, and its diverse—although increasingly dilapidated—industrial base. Concomitantly, rapid social transformation resulting from market reforms created fantastic wealth for the few *nouveau riche*. Ironically, most of those who had power under Communism not only retained their material status, but frequently improved it considerably. Under Vladimir Putin, a former intelligence agency chief, Russia has experienced the curtailing of civil liberties, and opposition political candidates have not been allowed to compete in national elections (Chivers 2008).

With the collapse of the Soviet Union, the *nomenklatura* (elite Communist bureaucrats) merged with the criminal underworld to take advantage of political and economic opportunity. Expanding illegal business activities to gain maximum profit in minimum time, however, is potentially dangerous, and the new pirate capitalists formed criminal organizations. "Thus, as strange as it might seem, the communist ideology was easily replaced by a criminal one and the former party leaders eagerly entered into cooperation with the criminal world" (Dryomin 2003: 57). While under communism managers of state-owned manufacturing diverted goods for sale outside of government control—a shadow economy—economic reforms enacted before the collapse of the Soviet Union provided managers, in collusion with local officials, unprecedented opportunity to purchase their firms. Among

those to whom they turned to for the necessary capital were criminals (Foglesong and Solomon, Jr. 2001). In Russia, the state has not been hijacked by organized crime but, instead, has mutated into a new entity that incorporates criminal, political, and economic sources of power (Cheloukhine and Haberfield 2011).

Historically, Russia remained estranged from the European Enlightenment ideal of the rule of law, and this did not change with the advent of the Soviet Union (Shelley 2001). People in the FSU do not necessarily equate violating the law with criminality. While people in the West are accustomed to fairly clear standards for judging who is guilty (even if these are not always or evenly applied), in the FSU the standards applied to decide who is criminal are often situational and particularistic: "As under communism, the legal prosecution of an alleged perpetrator may depend on factors in the political-economic domain—such as the accuser's political and economic affiliations and current positioning and economic goals—and the political and economic affiliations and current positioning of the alleged perpetrator." Thus, the law "expresses less a system of shared ideals than a mechanism for exercising power in social relations," a mechanism that "can be used as a weapon by one group against another" (Wedel 2001: 48).

THE EVOLUTION OF RUSSIAN ORGANIZED CRIME

Since the collapse of communism, the legal system has failed to keep pace with dramatic social and economic changes. The sudden transition to a market economy occurred in the absence of a legal structure that could reliably protect property rights, enforce contracts, and settle business disputes. Criminal organizations emerged to fill this vacuum (Varese 2011). Vulnerable businessmen began relying on the suddenly increasing private protection services, a large number of which operate without proper registration or licenses. Many

RUSSIAN TORT ACTION

Traveling way above the village speed limit, the luxury car hit a German shepherd and dragged the dog's body about a hundred feet. The driver, enraged, grabbed the dog's owner and demanded $300 for the damage to his car. After a tussle, the driver left, but not before promising to return. That evening four wheel drive vehicles arrived at the village and stopped in front of the dog owner's house. Men with shotguns emerged and opened fire, terrorizing the villagers. The dog owner sought help from a policeman friend, who arranged for a representative of the gang's boss to come to the village. Driving a BMW and accompanied by men in an Audi, the representative "explained" that the dog owner must pay $300 for the damage to the car—"or else." The dog owner paid (Kalfus 1996).

resorted to taking justice into their own hands, often with assistance from the criminal fraternity. As a result, a kind of "shadow justice" appeared, dominated by criminals (Frisby 1998).

Wars broke out as criminals struggled to claim state enterprises and property, leading to informal agreements that defined territories and functional boundaries. In industries owned or extorted by criminals, the result was higher prices passed on to consumers by industry-wide cartels. Criminals became deeply entrenched in the Russian economy (Tomass 1998). Nascent capitalism, a relaxation of the totalitarian law enforcement apparatus, and liberalization of travel provided a fertile environment for criminals schooled in a system rife with corruption and an underground economy.

Post-Soviet organized crime, notes Louise Shelley (1997: 122–123), represents a new form of non-state-based authoritarianism. "Citizens still live in fear but are now intimidated by non-state actors in the form of organized crime groups…. Traditional authoritarianism is based on total state control. The authoritarianism of organized crime represents abnegation of the state's obligations to its citizenry and reflects its inability to protect them from threats against their life, livelihood, or economic security." Criminal organizations offer *krysha*—literally a "roof" that provides protection—to both legitimate and illegitimate entrepreneurs. They "approach businesses directly, visiting in groups of three or four. One of them speaks in a friendly manner, warning the directors that they must pay"

15 to 20 percent of their company's gross earnings "or suffer violence at the hands of unnamed gangs. If they operate under the guise of a security agency, they may insist that the director sign a contract" (Tayler 2001: 38). Businesses refusing to pay, something rare, are subjected to a campaign that begins with verbal threats and escalates to bullets, bombs, and the torture of family members.

These groups can also provide services such as restraining competition: "If competition with lower prices or better goods appear on the scene, fires, theft, murder, and other bedlam can be arranged" (2001: 38). ROC groups have excelled at restraining trade and controlling pricing in a variety of arenas, including airport taxis and farmers' markets. Businessmen do not necessarily wait for the inevitable "visit." Instead, they may seek out the most effective "roof" able to provide protection from competing ROC groups and predatory criminals (Varese 2001).

In the manner of southern Italy, organized crime bosses provide a viable alternative to a formal justice system that is ineffective, if not corrupt. Instead of hiring lawyers to settle contract disputes, Russians engage crime bosses. Businessmen keep them on retainer to avoid shakedowns or to ensure that they have representation in the event of a business dispute (Gallagher 1995b; Witt 1996). In a country where contract law and a tradition of property rights are weak, the Russian wiseguy, like his Sicilian *mafioso* counterpart, acts as a guarantor so that persons who do not trust one another can transact business with a significant degree of confidence. "The introduction of private property in Russia has led to a demand for protection which the state has been unable to meet—and that organized crime is meeting instead" (Williams 1997: 6). A meeting between *Mafyia* bosses to resolve a business dispute is the *strelka* at which both sides are often accompanied by an armed retinue (Glenny 2008). Criminal organizations provide services to banks experiencing problems collecting debts. Resorting to the courts for such services is time-consuming and runs the risk that the debtor will declare bankruptcy (Varese 2001).

In a scenario that parallels that of American organized crime after the repeal of Prohibition and the onset of the Great Depression, Russian criminals have ready access to investment capital in a society where sources of financing are scarce. "Even apparently legitimate entrepreneurs find it difficult to muster the necessary capital for new enterprises and all too frequently must borrow funds from mobsters at extortionate rates of interest" (Voronin 1997: 56). And many criminals have "displayed a surprising knowledge and expertise in the workings of the market" that is rare in post-Soviet society (Rawlinson 1997: 46).

Rounding out the repertoire of ROC is the production and sale of methadone and similar synthetic narcotics, such as trimethyl phentanyl, often called 3MF. Even when they are not directly involved in trafficking, ROC groups provide protection to drug trafficking networks bringing in Afghan heroin destined primarily for European markets. Transportation is typically split into phases: One group moves the cargo from Afghanistan to Tajikistan where it is sold to a wholesale buyer. The consignment is then loaded on trucks and concealed among legitimate cargo, such as fruits and vegetables. Once the consignment has reached Russian border, it is reloaded onto different trucks and the manifests are altered to disguise the origin of the goods or produce. Guarding the border is a limited number of law enforcement agents and an unlimited opportunity for corruption. "Major heroin trafficking routes from Central Asia lead to Moscow, St. Petersburg, Saratov, Yekaterinburg, as well as the other large cities of Volga Region and Siberia. These locations are not only destination points but also serve as a transshipment point for further shipments to other destinations in Russia and in Europe" (United Nations Office on Drugs and Crime 2008b: 16).

There is also extensive trafficking in military weapons, which frequently wind up in areas of ethnic conflict. It is feared that this could extend to nuclear devices, and the FSU has had more than two-dozen reported nuclear trafficking incidents between 2001 and 2005 (Zaitseva 2007). Although these developments suggest a potential danger, there is an absence of compelling evidence of a solid nexus among trafficking in weapons of mass destruction, terrorism, and organized crime in the FSU (Ouagrham-Gormley 2007).

One of the more nefarious activities associated with ROC is trafficking in women for the sex industry (discussed in Chapter 11). During the Soviet era, borders were tightly controlled and movement limited. "Therefore, human trafficking, or transporting people across borders for financial gain did not occur before 1991" (Glonti 2003: 71). When the Soviet Union collapsed, authorities were completely unprepared for the massive migration that ensued. "New criminal structures created expanding transnational networks for prostitution and exporting young people abroad for various forms of labour exploitation" (Glonti 2003: 71).

Women in the FSU often face chronic unemployment and are forced to look abroad for jobs, making them vulnerable to exploitation. The road to the sex industry typically originates with a newspaper ad or an unexpected meeting on the street, leading to a proposition to work abroad as maid, secretary, showgirl, nanny, or waitress. Victims are often well educated and answer advertisements for positions in service industries for which they are overqualified—such is the state of the Russian economy and job market. Women are usually trafficked in Europe (Belgium, the Netherlands, Poland, and Switzerland) and Asia (China, Japan, and Thailand) (Stocckers 2000).

Criminals can provide their victims with fraudulent travel documents, transportation, guided border crossings, accommodations, and job brokering—for a fee. Upon their arrival in a foreign destination, the women are informed that the job no longer exists, but they are still indebted to the agent for the trip, which usually costs them between $5,000 and $20,000. Women who refuse to cooperate are subjected to physical and sexual abuse; sometimes they are murdered. One victim who refused to have sex with potential customers was taken into a country field, and while other women were forced to watch, her throat was cut. Having lived in a society ruled by an oppressive government, Russian émigrés tend to be inherently distrustful of government and reluctant to speak with or seek assistance from law enforcement (Zalisko 2001).

Out of this environment three overarching and sometimes overlapping categories of ROC appeared: sportsmen and veterans, ethnic-based groups, and the *vory* (Figure 9.2).

Veterans and Sportsmen

Criminal groups having few if any ties to the criminal subculture emerged. Poorly paid, badly housed, and demoralized, Russian military personnel became immersed in criminal activities. As a result of the disintegration of the Soviet military and the breakdown in arms control at weapons plants, high-quality automatic weapons became available throughout the country and military personnel became involved in arms trafficking (Gordon

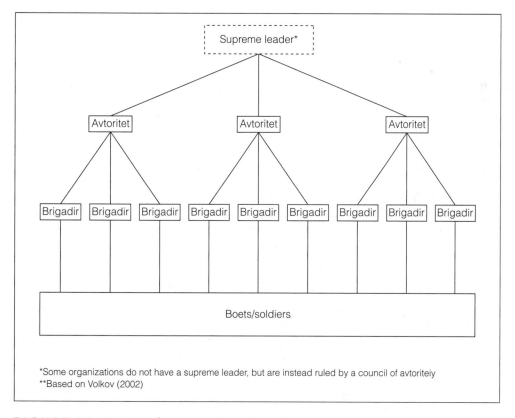

*Some organizations do not have a supreme leader, but are instead ruled by a council of avtoriteiy
**Based on Volkov (2002)

F I G U R E 9.2 Structure of a Russian Criminal Organization**

1996; Hersh 1994; Hockstader 1995; Turbiville 1995).

With their high-level security training and knowledge of advanced military tactics and weapon systems, military officers, especially special-forces personnel, organized private security forces. The line between the private security forces and criminal organizations is often very narrow or nonexistent. Both offer a "roof" that authorizes a businessman to use the name of his protector to thwart attempts at extortion. Without a credible roof, a businessman is vulnerable.

Some ROC groups emerged from the pastime of many Russian young men: participation in sports clubs and fitness centers. In the Soviet Union, sports were a major priority of the state because they expressed its might and socialized its youth. But in different circumstances, sports, especially fighting sports and martial arts, can supply all that is needed to create a racketeer gang: fighting skills, willpower, discipline, and team spirit. When the state withdrew sponsorship, the constraints of a rule-governed nonviolent competition also ended, and this was enough to launch a dangerous process whereby sportsmen started to look for alternative careers.

As Vadim Volkov (2002: 10) notes, the "shared experience of being one sports team, which involves regular training and competition as well as shared victories and defeats, is likely to create strong trust as well and group coherence. Combined with professional fighting skills, this provides a potential social basis for the conversion of teammates into members of a racketeering gang." Powerful gangs emerged from the gyms and sports clubs of the FSU. In Moscow and its suburbs, at the city markets, the first flowering of free trade and private entrepreneurship, the former sportsmen discovered a way for their physical assets to be turned into cash—offering protection for a regular fee. "This capacity," notes Volkov "must be conspicuous." Hence the use of elaborate symbols such as conspicuous jewelry, flattop/military-style haircuts, leather jackets—gangster chic (2002: 59–60).

While they may have lost their original connection to a sports club, the reputation attached to it remains important. The name of criminal organization serves as a "flag" whose members are thus credentialed by affiliation; joining a criminal organization is referred to as "standing up under a flag" (Volkov 2002).

Ethnic-Based Groups

Clans are informal organizations whose members share a set of behaviors and expectations. In many of the former Soviet republics, clans have operated for centuries. Members are united by kinship and friendship ties and conform to unwritten group rules, norms, and practices. Ranging in size from 2,000 to 20,000, clans are governed by an elders' council and/or senior members.

In the absence of Western-style civil society, they "took the situation into their own hands creating a system based more or less on their own strength" (Ceccarelli 2007: 22). Clans may join in an alliance to expand their networks and influence enabling them to effectively compete with state apparatus. They may also compete with each other for influence, a situation that can lead to bloody conflicts. Clans have a close relationship with transnational organized crime groups, not only because they control territory, but also because the main aim of the clan is to provide assets and goods for members in any way possible, legal or illegal. Local criminal groups and drug mafias are also linked to the clans and transnational organized crime (Ceccarelli 2007). And many ex-Soviet states not only fail to take any actions to arrest their citizens who commit crimes in Russia, but also privately support them (Cheloukhine 2008).

James Finckenauer and Yuri Voronin (2001) note the importance of economic deprivation, a shared ethnicity, culture, and language, as the building blocks for the "queer ladder of upward mobility" (discussed in Chapter 4) for ethnic-based organized crime. In the Caucasus (Armenia, Chechnya, Georgia) and Central Asia (Uzbekistan)—organized around feudal clan and tribal relationships, literally "crime families," these groups were well suited to take advantage of dislocations in post-Soviet society.

Chechens. One of these groups originated in the Central Asian region of the Caucasus Mountains due north of the Georgian Republic. Largely Muslim, historically hostile to Moscow, and legendary warriors, Chechens were subjected to massive deportations in 1944 by Stalin, who falsely accused them of collaborating with the Nazis during World War II; they returned to the region in 1957. Known for strong family loyalties and a sense of personal honor, Chechens, like Sicilians, are governed by the concept of *omertá*—*adat* requires vengeance to uphold family honor (Gallagher 1995a; "History of Antagonism" 1994). And the Russian attitude toward Chechens parallels that of northern Italians toward Sicilians.

In 1991, Chechen leaders declared their independence and quickly became locked in violent conflict with the Russian military. Independence leader Dzhokar Dudayev is reported to have turned Chechnya into "Chicago of the twenties." "Chechen mafiosi engaged in some of the most spectacular criminal scams Russia has ever known. With Dudayev's police looking the other way (or, more likely, cooperating at every turn), Grozny [the capital] became a center of illegal trade. The city's airport served as a hub for unsanctioned flights hauling contraband and outlaws.... The flights—from the Middle East, Turkey, central Asia, and elsewhere—brought in huge amounts of narcotics and 'duty free' goods, and a succession of bandits in hiding. Mafiosi were also in the habit of robbing cargo trains traveling through Chechen territory" (Remnick 1995: 53). After two wars, one from 1994 to 1996 and a second that began in 1999, Russian forces were finally successful in thwarting the independence movement and installing a pro-Moscow regime. Fighting continues, but it is sporadic and on a small scale (Kramer 2008a).

Vast supplies of arms were left in Chechnya by the Russian military; arms trafficking and counterfeiting of currency and financial documents are important parts of the Chechen crime portfolio. Chechen crime groups operate in many areas of the FSU, including Moscow. "The group is more structured than most. Most important for them

is the strict hierarchical arrangement of their clan relationships. It is a closed organization, recruiting only from among their own people. Chechens actively recruit juveniles from the Chechen regions where unemployment is high. This ensures a degree of 'purity' in the membership, making it difficult for law enforcement agencies lacking personnel that speak Chechen to infiltrate the group.... Each group has a clear structure: leader, senior advisors, soldiers, and associated members" (Serio 1992b: 5).

Exhibiting the value of a bad reputation, Chechen crime groups guard their reputation for violence; any group claiming a Chechen connection that fails to carry out its threats—devaluing the brand—is likely to be "visited" by the genuine article (Glenny 2008). Protection rackets, enforcement of restraint of trade agreements, and narcotics and weapons trafficking are all part of the Chechen crime repertoire. The Chechen reputation for being both violent and fearless is often sufficient to cow an opponent—but sometimes not: In 1993, a group of well-armed gangsters drove to a building across the Moscow River from the Kremlin to extort money from a local businessman. They were met by the businessman's protectors, Chechens, who opened fire, killing the gangster boss and four of his men (LeVine, McKay, and Lebedeva 1993). Members of Chechen groups have been found throughout eastern and western Europe and have sent members to New York to set up operations. Some have entered the United States for contract crimes—murder, extortion, fraud—after which they return home before authorities can detect and apprehend them.

Chechens are reportedly the only criminal group that does not respect the territoriality of the *vory* (Cheloukhine 2008).

Vory

While the FSU did not have organized crime in the pattern of the American racketeer, it did have an extensive professional underworld with roots that date back to the end of the seventeenth and beginning of the eighteenth century when gangs of itinerant petty criminals began to form a criminal hierarchy called by law enforcement the *vory v zakone*, "thieves with a code of honor." In the tradition of the Neapolitan Camorra (discussed in Chapter 5), the *vory* thrived among hard-core prison camp inmates. With the growth of a revolutionary movement in Russia, the Czar consigned large numbers of educated political dissidents to prison camps where they replaced the older criminal leadership and established a *vory* code that forbade adherence to a conventional lifestyle. The *vory* conspiratorial code forbade any involvement in politics or collaboration with the state. Alexander Yarmysh (2001) considers this an extension of the "peasant commune mentality" according to which involvement with official authorities is forbidden—the state being viewed as hostile and oppressive. However, the *vory* collaborated with prison authorities in order to gain for themselves better conditions in exchange for which they helped maintain order (Rawlinson 2010). Prison domination serves to temper anti-*vory* activity because criminals recognize that they may at some point become incarcerated and subject to *vory* control.

As Stalin's gulags[1] began to fill up with political enemies, an even more rigid *vory* code of behavior evolved, and during World War II the leadership began establishing an interregional corporate-type structure (Cheloukhine 2008). During World War II, the *vory* split into two factions: one (patriots) supported efforts to defeat the invading Nazis, whereas the other (traditionalists) remained aloof. By 1953, the patriots had been driven out of the "thieves' world" for their disloyalty to its traditions (Chalidze 1977; Friedman 2000). Eventually, the *vory* "changed its law to permit the scabs back in and to accept involvement with the authorities" (Schulte-Bockholt 2006: 164).

The code system of the *vory* that developed under the unbearable conditions of the Soviet Gulag includes a long list of behavioral obligations often expressed in the tattoos adorning the bodies of *vory* (Finckenauer and Waring, 1998). Included are the abandonment of family members—father, brothers, sisters, and commitment to life without wife or children—a way of life that ensures absolute loyalty to the world of crime. A *vor* must never insult or raise a hand against another *vor* (unless sanctioned by a *vory* court). Additional commitments include prohibitions against a normative job, even if the person's socioeconomic situation was very difficult, and the obligation to provide moral and material assistance to other *vor*. Mastery of the *vory* code system and their language is required and military service is banned (Cheloukhine and Haberfield 2011; Shoham 2010).

Emblazoned with tattoos, including giant eagles with razor-sharp talons on their chests, the *vory* developed a coded language decipherable only by other members of the criminal fraternity. *Vory* member tattoos often reveal their status in the organization's hierarchy and even their criminal specialty. In fact, within the world of crime in Russia, the tattoo can serve as an identity card. A criminal can go from city to city and be accepted into the criminal world according to his tattoo (Shoham 2010).

Because tattoos are perceived as being an integral, built-in part of *vory* culture, a *vor* lacks the sovereignty to decide regarding the nature and complexity of his tattoo. "The decision is made by the heads of the hierarchy and a tattoo that is 'stolen' and inconsistent with the true reality of the criminal is not permitted, and punishment for this may even be death" (Shoham 2010: 991). The outlaw motorcycle subculture has similar restrictions; a person discovered with an unauthorized Hell's Angels tattoo, for example, could end up having it forcibly removed.

The title *vor* is bestowed at special initiation ceremonies during which the novice (*malyutka*) pledges fealty and is given a new name—a rechristening. *Vory* membership requires three sponsors and a ceremony with an oath of allegiance to abide by eighteen rules, the breaking of which is punishable by death. As does the Sicilian Mafia, *vory* embrace a principle of brotherhood and superiority according to which they have a right to live

---

1. GULAG is an acronym for the Russian prison service and a term used to identify penal colonies (Cheloukhine 2008).

at the expense of others and to confiscate the property of those deemed inferior (Yarmysh 2001).

Vory organizations are conspiratorial and hierarchical. They include representatives of the administration of various enterprises who, during the Soviet era, were often party members with high positions living double lives. Organized into tight networks, "from their cells, crime bosses planned and organized their operations across the country [while] lieutenants, often called *brodyagi* (vagabonds), conducted formal dealings with the outside" (Handelman 1995: 209). The criminal society has a form of insurance: "*obshchak*—derived from members' contributions and fines for violating the thieves' code, that is used to bribe officials inside and outside of prison, to provide amenities to imprisoned members and to help support their families. After leaving prison, members are expected to repay the *obshchak*" (Finckenauer and Waring 1999: 107).

The *vory* is exclusively male; females, even wives, lack status. Indeed, attachment to a spouse is seen as a weakness—undermining loyalty to the *vory*—as is faithfulness. Paternal bonds lack emotional attachment (Varese 2001). While *vory* membership is mostly Russian, Armenians, Chechens, Georgians, Kurds, and other ethnic groups are represented (Cheloukhine and Haberfield 2011).

Under communism, managers of state-owned enterprises became unofficial entrepreneurs. To meet the quotas set by the regime, they established informal networks to ensure the provision of supplies from other state-owned enterprises. There was rationing and price controls and, as a consequence, a divergence between market values and administrative controls. This led to the development of an underground economy whereby commodities were diverted to informal markets where they could be sold at higher prices. Managers reserved their most valuable goods for the *vory* who paid premium prices that the managers did not report and, subsequently, embezzled. Managers were unwilling to provide scarce goods to ordinary citizens, exacerbating existing shortages. The *vory*, taking advantage of the managers' inability to turn to law enforcement for protection, extorted money from their erstwhile partners in the black market. Subsequent privatization and legalization of joint ownership meant that state enterprises were handed over to corrupt managers and their *vory* partners through worker buyouts.

In a pattern that parallels that of the Chicago Outfit (Chapter 3), "the *vory* ritual now marks the entry of powerful crew leaders into the 'governing body' of the biggest criminal groups in Moscow"; that is, being "made" indicates a management position reserved for the leaders, rather than being a requirement for each group member (Varese 2001: 177).

As the name implies, historically *vory* were thieves in the broadest sense, not racketeers. As such, they were denigrated as relics of an earlier era, and conflict between the *vory* and other criminal organizations ensued. *Vory* maintained their domination of the prisons, but elsewhere, after considerable violence, had to make accommodations with their rivals. Eventually, a new generation of *vory* emerged, and *vor* who prize greater violence came to the fore. This is reflected by a wider repertoire of crime that includes debt collection, contract enforcement, contract killings, and providing protection broadly defined to business (Cheloukhine 2008). "By the beginning of the 1960s," Patricia Rawlinson (2010: 60) notes, "the reign of the traditional criminal elite was all but over, the new leaders enticed more by rubles than rules."

In a situation that parallels the split in post–World War II Sicily between the old and new Mafia (discussed in Chapter 5), a *novye* (new) *vory v zakone* appeared in the late 1980s. The traditional *vory*, steeped in ritual and custom with their rigid code of honor, was eclipsed by one whose ideals were profit-oriented (Rawlinson 1997). "Contrary to the old thieves, the new *vory* appeared to organize and operate on a grander scale and took advantage of an opportunity to make a large sum of money quickly even if in violation of the thieves' traditions" (Serio 2008: 166). Contemporary *vory* are less likely to have served a prison term and often forgo the telltale tattooing. They have moved into more risky spheres of criminal behavior, such as bank fraud and drug trafficking. And the new *vory* command wealth beyond the dreams of the old tradition-bound subculture.

Each *vory* group is headed by a *vor v zakonye* who is recognized by all others as the authority in his territory. A *vor v zakonye* is chosen at a meeting of members and requires the recommendation of at least two other bosses—the more recommendations, the more prestige. By 1992, the most powerful bosses had reportedly divided the country into twelve regions where they interact with bureaucrats and industrial managers. Dressed in leather coats and driving flashy cars, they eat openly with government officials in restaurants they often control (Handelman 1995).

Vory members are given special status—*respect*—in the Russian-American underworld. In 1991, Vyacheslav (*Yaponchik*—"Little Jap") Ivankov, a high-ranking *vor v zakonye* with the *Solntsevskaya* (disussed shortly) was released early (political influence/bribery is suspected) from serving a 14-year prison sentence for robbery, aggravated assault, and extortion. After his release, he went on a campaign of extortion, often torturing victims, and was responsible for ordering many killings, including those of journalists and police officers. His murderous campaign against Moscow's powerful Chechen crime groups further raised Ivankov's profile to a liability: The *vor* leadership's "Circle of Brothers" banished him to America (Friedman 2000).

Shortly after his arrival at JFK airport, Ivankov was given a suitcase with $1.5 million by an Armenian *vor*. He established his headquarters in Brighton Beach and recruited Russian combat veterans with a $20,000 a month retainer. They were sent out to extort money from legitimate businesses worldwide and to assassinate rivals. Fear permeated the Russian émigré community, and its major criminal operatives were soon allied with Ivankov—or they were dead (Friedman 2000).

Ivankov's reign as the reputed leading Russian crime boss in the United States did not last long: In 1995, he was arrested for Hobbs Act (see Chapter 14) violations, attempting to extort millions of dollars from two immigrant businessman—both embezzlers—who had been kidnapped at gunpoint from a Manhattan hotel (Dubocq and Garcia 1997;

Vyachelav ("Little Jap") Ivankov, a top-ranking vory, being escorted by FBI agents from the agency's New York headquarters.

L. Myers 1995). Ivankov become personally involved in the plot and was recorded on a wiretap giving instructions on how it was to be carried out; he also threatened the two businessmen who, unbeknown to him, were cooperating with the FBI. While in custody awaiting trial, Ivankov so alienated his codefendants that two of them became cooperating witnesses against him (Friedman 2000). The following year, Ivankov and three codefendants were convicted of extortion; he received a nine-year sentence (Finckenauer and Waring 1999) and was released from the federal prison at Allenwood, Pennsylvania, in 2007. He was immediately taken into custody by U.S. Immigration and Customs agents who placed him on a chartered flight to Russia where he was wanted for the murder of two Turkish men in Moscow. He was subsequently acquitted. In 2009, Ivankov was shot by a sniper and, at age 69, died in a Moscow hospital of complications from his gunshot wounds. His funeral in Moscow was attended by hundreds, "including thick-necked toughs wearing heavy gold chains and cigar-smoking men in pinstriped suits" (Schwirtz 2009: 6).

In 2011, an Armenian *vor* who entered the United States as a refugee with an asylum application that was granted in 1996—it was subsequently discovered that he had lied on his application—pled guilty in federal court in New York to assisting an Armenian-American ring that engaged in an extensive range of criminal offenses including a $100 million Medicare billing fraud. He also acknowledged engaging in extortion on the ring's and his own behalf (FBI press release, July 8, 2011; M. Wilson and Rashbaum 2010).

Criminal or Businessman?

Leaders of criminal organizations invested their considerable capital in the very businesses they were protecting; they became capitalists and their role changed. While they might continue to use violence against competitors, they prefer to contract with licensed security agencies and to hire lawyers rather than relying on their original sportsmen enforcers (Volkov 2002). The transformation of organized crime into legitimate business continues.

When leaders settle abroad—no matter their origins–they do not engage in shooting in the streets; they act legally. Many are cofounders of commercial banks (Cheloukhine 2008).

The oft-invisible line between criminals and businessmen is exemplified by Semion Mogilevich, an entrepreneur whose business organizational chart includes an enforcement section employing special forces veterans who have carried out executions throughout the world. In the Czech Republic, they tortured and murdered businessmen who resisted their extortion efforts. A Ukrainian-born Jew with a college degree in economics, Mogilevich was originally part of a Moscow crime group during the Soviet era, who made his first fortune by defrauding fellow Jews who were fleeing to the United States. Holding Israeli and Hungarian citizenship—his wife is Hungarian—Mogilevich heads an organization of about 250 persons, many of whom are relatives, whose operations transcend national boundaries. In Hungary, Mogilevich owns nightclubs and a major portion of the Hungarian arms industry; and in the United States, his operatives have been involved in money laundering and contract murders—supplying weapons and spiriting the killers out of the country after their assignment is complete (Friedman 2000). According to Friedman (2000), he was business partner of the notorious Vyacheslav Ivankov (discussed above). In 1993, Mogilevich joined forces with the *Solntsevo* crime syndicate.

The Moscow-based *Solntsevo* (or *Solntsevskaya brigada* or *Solntsevskaya Bratva*—"Solntsevo Brotherhood") is reputed to have thousands of members active in several countries. The organization, which takes its name from a run-down working class Moscow suburb, is both hierarchical and flexible. At the top of the hierarchy is a supreme council consisting of about a dozen people, leaders of individual crews (*brigady*) who meet regularly to discuss matters of importance to the organization. The council manages a joint fund (*obshchak*) to which all brigades allocate money on a regular basis (Varese 2001, 2011). In another example of the value of a bad reputation, the *Solntsevo* are said to have "rented out" their notoriety to less formidable criminal groups—for a fee, they could represent themselves as *Solnetsevo* (Serio 2008).

The boss of the *Solntsevskay*, Sergei Mikhailov, has Russian, Israeli, and Costa Rican passports—he has legitimate business interests in these countries, as well as Hungary and Belgium. Now known as an international businessman and patron of the Russian Orthodox Church, decades ago Mikhailov was employed as a waiter in a Moscow hotel. In 1984, he was imprisoned for collecting insurance on his motorcycle that he had fraudulently reported stolen. Prison contacts helped lay the groundwork for a flourishing criminal career, and when he was released he established a sports club and recruited local toughs in preparation for his entry into the Russian underworld (Bohlen 1999; Varese 2011). The level of his success was revealed in 1998 when he was accused of illegally buying property in Switzerland where he lived with his wife and children in a village outside of Geneva. He had Swiss bank accounts totaling $2 million (Kaban 1998). At the end of 1998, Mikhailov was acquitted by a Swiss court: "If he were an Italian being tried in Italy, he might well have been found guilty under a 1982 law that makes 'mafia association' a criminal offense" (Bohlen 1999: WK 5).

In 1999, it was revealed that Mogilevich, an undesirable prohibited from entering the United States, had set up a magnet manufacturing and importing company in suburban Philadelphia. YBM Magnex had a blue-ribbon board of directors and was audited by two prominent American accounting firms. Before YBM pled guilty to securities fraud, Mogilevich and his associates had made millions of dollars from selling inflated shares of the company's stock (Bonner 1999). He was subsequently linked to a major money laundering operation in which billions of dollars were channeled through the Bank of New York. Some of the money from the account reportedly went to pay contract killers and some went to drug barons (Bonner and O'Brien 1999). Wanted by the FBI—he is on the FBI's Top Ten Most Wanted List—in 2008, Mogilevich, at 61, was arrested in Russia on charges of tax evasion and released the following year—pending trial.

Note the transition made by the *Uralmashevskaya*—whose name derives from a district in the industrialized Urals Mountain city of Ekaterinburg—from gang to "financial-industrial enterprise." Formed around young toughs from the local sports clubs, they produced illegal alcohol and provided *krysha* to area businesses. Assets from these activities were invested in businesses experiencing a need for cash. As their enterprises expanded, the *Uralmashevskaya* began to conflict with similarly ambitious *vory*. Violence broke out in 1992 and 1993, and the *vory* were outmatched by their more ruthless opponents who were better disciplined and schooled in the use of force. After eliminating rivals, the *Uralmashevskaya* expanded their business interests and entered the political arena, financing candidates and having members run for elected office. They completed their transition by establishing institutionalized relations with the regional government (Cheloukhine and Haberfield 2011; Volkov 2000).

"The liberalization of the Russian economy and privatization of state enterprises have essentially made organized crime groups legal, and transformed entrepreneurs with illegally gained capital into legitimate businesspersons" (Cheloukhine and Haberfield 2011: 155).

People who had exhibited absolute disrespect for the law, accountability, and public opinion, ultimately hired lawyers, accountants, and public relations professionals to protect and manage their assets. As discussed in Chapter 2, Robber Barons, notables such as Astor, Rockefeller, and Vanderbilt, successfully "laundered" their infamy so their names would no longer be associated with the methods they used to achieve incredible wealth. We can anticipate a similar process in the FSU.

RUSSIAN ORGANIZED CRIME IN THE UNITED STATES

"In the decade since the collapse of the Soviet Union, the world has become the target of a new global crime threat from criminal organizations and criminal activities that have poured forth over the borders of Russia and other former Soviet republics such as Ukraine" (Finckenauer and Voronin 2001: 1). Unlike the farmers and unskilled laborers who comprised the majority of earlier immigrations to the United States, "Russian émigrés are generally urban in origin, well-educated, and industrially and technologically skilled." Despite a language barrier, although many have learned some English in Soviet-era schools, "they have marketable skills and have not been closed off from the legitimate ladders of upward mobility." Thus, "Russian-émigré crime in this country did not grow out of the same cultural alienation and economic disparity experienced by other immigrant groups." Furthermore, "Russian criminals did not begin their criminal careers as members of adolescent street gangs in ethnic ghettos," as did most of the criminals discussed in Chapters 2 and 3 (P. Williams 1997: 9–10). Russia has universal military service, and Russian criminals, therefore, typically possess martial skills.

Many of the criminals in ROC are Jews. Unlike Jewish immigrant groups that made up organized crime in the past (discussed in Chapters 2 and 3), Russians are relatively well educated and adept at exploiting weaknesses in American society. Jewish émigrés—many from the Ukrainian seaport of Odessa, noted for its criminal subculture—have settled in the Brighton Beach section of Brooklyn ("Little Odessa"), and the New York police department has been handicapped in dealing with the protection rackets and loansharking activities in the community by a lack of Russian-speaking officers.

Russian criminal groups flourish in the United States in the absence of the corrupt political machines (discussed in Chapter 2) that provided a protective incubator for the Irish, Jewish, and Italian criminal organizations of an earlier era. A new wave of Russian emigration, business travel, and tourism quickly exported organized crime to other countries (Cheloukhine 2008). Russian criminals enter the United States with backgrounds for excelling in organized criminal activity without moving through the more traditional routes that typically include street gang delinquency and apprenticeship under adult criminals. "Unlike their ethnic predecessors in crime, Russian émigrés do not have to go through any developmental or learning process to break into the criminal world in this country. They are able to begin operating almost immediately upon their arrival" (Tri-State

Joint Soviet-Émigré Organized Crime Project 1997: 185). They typically have military experience and many are college-educated. "Many of today's foremost Russian mobsters have Ph.D.'s in mathematics, engineering, or physics, helping them to acquire an expertise in advanced encryption and computer technology" (Friedman 2000: xviii).

These criminals established themselves in a number of U.S. cities where Russian immigrants have settled—Boston, Chicago, Cleveland, Dallas, Miami, New York, Philadelphia, Portland, San Francisco, and Seattle. Although known by their fellow Russians as the *organizatsiya* (the organization), the actual degree of organization appears limited. What has not been limited is the exploitation of the Russian émigré community. In Brighton Beach, a major Russian émigré community in Brooklyn, Jewish criminals from the FSU, working in small "brigades," systematically extorted money from legitimate businesses (Friedman 2000).

The Tri-State (New York–New Jersey–Pennsylvania) Joint Soviet-Émigré Organized Crime Project (1997; hereafter Tri-State) concluded that Russian criminals in the United States have neither the critical mass nor the criminal sophistication to create a major local or regional threat, much less a national or international one. They appear to be organized on an enterprise basis—opportunity-driven—and not in a hierarchical manner. At the lower end of the criminal organizational continuum are networks created on a temporary basis that are neither structurally formed nor stable and whose leaders exercise control over the network for only brief periods, although certain individuals turn up repeatedly. Some refer to this as the *swarming model* "in which individuals coalesce for a limited period in order to conduct a specifically defined task and, having succeeded, go their separate ways" (Brenner 2002: 50).

Russian crime groups in the United States are typically fluid, and membership is transient, comprising five to twenty persons. Their pattern has been compared with that of the Zips discussed in Chapter 4 (Finckenauer and Waring 1999; Mitchell 1992). Loosely structured, without formal hierarchy, groups are usually formed on the basis of regional backgrounds or built around a particular enterprise.

One group may comprise mainly immigrants from Kiev, whereas another may consist mainly of Georgians. Or a group may organize to extort money from local merchants or to operate a gasoline tax evasion scheme. After their experience of criminal life in the Soviet Union, where police were feared and treatment of lawbreakers harsh, they view the United States as a haven.

However, Russian émigré criminals in the United States typically mistrust each other. There is generally little or no personal loyalty based on common ethnic or cultural backgrounds, even though some of the criminals knew each other in the FSU. And betrayals have been frequent: Russian criminals, despite a background of hardship, have been quick to become informants to avoid the long sentences that are part of the Racketeer Influenced and Corrupt Organizations (RICO) statute, discussed in Chapter 14 (Tri-State 1997) This has reportedly impeded the development of larger, more structured organizations (Berkeley 2002a).

The Russian émigré criminal network structure is usually an ad hoc team of specialists teamed for specific criminal enterprises. They form opportunistic partnerships that are sometimes based on referrals by other Russian criminals. After the criminal objective is attained, the specialists may split up or may move together to other criminal ventures. There are also professional criminals with a propensity for violence who form small criminal groups to commit extortion or engage in drug trafficking. These groups often center around one or more dominant individuals and the composition of the group is subject to frequent changes. Colombo Family captain Michael Franzese, who worked closely with Russian crime groups, states: "I did not find the Russian criminals to be a very structured group in comparison to the Italian La Cosa Nostra. They were very clannish, however, and the most financially successful Russian was looked up to by his comrades as their leader or boss. The boss was given a lot of courtesy and respect and in return provided the members of his group with opportunities to work for him and make money" ("ROC" 1996: 39).

"One way to contrast La Cosa Nostra and Russian-émigré criminal organizations is to view the former as having a structure—a distinct, definable crime family—that is supported by criminal activities. The structure is continuous, and crime is used to carry out its objectives and maintain its strength and vitality. Russians, however, create floating structures on an as-needed basis to enable them to carry out particular crimes. The criminal opportunities come first, and the necessary structure to take advantage of those opportunities follows" (Tri-State 1997: 24). Russian criminals, however, have been forming more stable groups whose core is usually made up of close relatives. They are reminiscent of the Jewish gangs that emerged with Prohibition and disappeared after World War II. It remains to be seen if they will they will evolve into stable, self-perpetuating criminal organizations or become historical footnotes in the manner of Arnold Rothstein (discussed in Chapter 4) and Bugsy Siegel (discussed in Chapter 11).

The Business of Russian Organized Crime

ROC groups have engaged in sophisticated crimes such as insurance fraud, Medicaid scams, securities-related fraud, identity theft, counterfeiting, and tax fraud. One of their projects involved the evasion of taxes on fuel oil. Using a "daisy chain with a vanishing point," gasoline was transferred on paper from one bogus company to another. Taxes are due when the fuel is finally sold to retailers, but the last company receiving the gasoline existed only on paper, as revenue investigators discovered. By the time auditors and investigators would unravel the series of transactions to determine the tax liability, the "burn" company had disappeared without a trace of records or assets. The taxes were skimmed when the fuel was actually sold at discount prices to dealers (Van Duyne and Block 1995).

The wholesalers need to be able to purchase fuel tax free, and this requires an IRS excise tax Certification of Exemption. The certifications were obtained by buying out registered companies or falsifying documents of legitimate companies. In response to these schemes, in 1993, Congress moved the point of taxation on gasoline from the wholesale distributor to the distribution terminal. Unable to divert the excise tax, the Russians moved to a new project. Using numerous dummy firms, they purchased home heating (diesel) oil, which is tax-free. The diesel oil was then transferred through fake companies and sold as diesel fuel, which is subject to federal excise taxes, and they pocketed the tax money, estimated to have cost the government $140 million (Levy 1995). Legislation enacted in 1994 requires that only fuel dyed red—diesel fuel is typically yellow or green—can be tax exempt and can only be used for off-road purposes such as home heating or in tractors. The dyed fuel is easily spotted by IRS inspectors or state tax agents who check truck stops or set up road checkpoints. The Russians responded by purchasing fuel in low tax states and shipping it to high tax states that can produce a 12 percent advantage.

In 2000, an investigation into the ports of Newark and Elizabeth, New Jersey, revealed a massive smuggling operation orchestrated by Russian criminals. At the behest of Russian criminals in the United States, a number of American distilleries were disguising millions of gallons of their product—192-proof grain alcohol—by adding dye and shipping it in giant containers marked windshield wiper fluid, cologne, mouthwash, and cleaning solvent. Once in Russia, using a formula provided by the distillers, the dye was removed, the alcohol diluted with water, and vodka flavoring added. The product was then distributed by Russia-based criminal organizations, evading millions of dollars in import duty and taxes. The smuggling was encouraged by high Russian tariffs designed to protect domestic alcohol production (Rashbaum 2000a).

In 2010, seventy-three members and associates of an Armenian-American crime group, the Mirzoyan-Terdjanian Organization (named after its principal leaders) were indicted for Medicare fraud. Although headquartered in New York City and Los Angeles, the group operates throughout the world. Among those indicted in New York is an Armenian *vor*. They are alleged to have stolen the identities of thousands of Medicare beneficiaries from around the United States, as well as the identities of doctors who were usually licensed to practice in more than one state. Others leased office space and opened phony clinics—or, in some instances, simply rented a post office box. And still others opened bank accounts to receive Medicare funds—often in the name of the doctor whose identity they stole—and submitted applications to Medicare to become Medicare providers. Once becoming approved Medicare providers, the subjects—who had extensive knowledge of the Medicare system, including what codes to use—would start to bill Medicare for services never provided, using the stolen beneficiary information. And as soon as the funds were directly deposited by Medicare into the designated bank accounts set up to receive them, the money was withdrawn and laundered and sometimes sent overseas.

In many instances, even though Medicare would identify and shut down the phony clinics after several months, they would simply open up another fraudulent clinic somewhere else, usually in another state. All told, the investigation uncovered at least 118 phony clinics in twenty-five states (FBI and U.S. Department of Justice press releases).

SUMMARY

1. Understand how the history of Russia and the former Soviet Union (FSU) paved the way for organized crime:
   - In 1991, the USSR splintered into Russia and fourteen other independent states.
   - Russian organized crime (ROC) refers to those whose origins are from the territory of the FSU.
   - Like the invading foreigners of Sicily, the governmental system of Russia made the Russian, like the Sicilian, distrustful of government.

2. Appreciate what ROC has in common with America's "Robber Barons" and how the collapse of the Soviet Union fostered pirate capitalism:
   - Economic liberalization paved the way for the entry of criminal organizations.

- The communist ideology was replaced by a criminal one and the former party leaders entered into cooperation with the criminal world.
- Because of the lack of a reliable legal system, in the FSU, businessmen rely on "shadow justice" provided by criminal groups.
- Criminal organizations offer "protection" to legitimate and illegitimate entrepreneurs and provide arbitration and restraint of trade services.
- In a scenario that parallels that of American organized crime after the repeal of Prohibition and the onset of the Great Depression, Russian criminals have ready access to investment capital in a society where sources of financing are scarce.
- ROC is involved the production and sale of methadone and similar synthetic narcotics, arms trafficking, and trafficking in women for the sex industry.

3. Recognize the overlapping categories of ROC and the oft-invisible boundary between Russian criminals and businessmen:

- There are three overarching and sometimes overlapping categories of ROC: sportsmen and veterans, ethnic-based groups, and the *vory*.
- Leaders of criminal organizations invested capital in the businesses they were protecting and became capitalists.

4. Know how organized crime in the FSU differs from ROC in the United States:

- Russian immigrants are generally urban in origin, well educated, technologically skilled, and typically possess martial skills.
- Russian crime groups in the United States are typically fluid, and membership is transient, loosely structured, and without formal hierarchy.
- The Russian criminal network consists of specialists teamed for specific criminal enterprises after which they split up or move together to other criminal ventures.
- ROC groups have engaged in sophisticated crimes such as insurance fraud, Medicaid scams, securities-related fraud, identity theft, counterfeiting, and tax fraud.

REVIEW QUESTIONS

1. What is the similarity between the Russian view of government and that of Sicilians?

2. How did the collapse of the USSR affect the Russian economy?

3. How did the post-Soviet economy promote organized crime?

4. How does organized crime fill the vacuum created by the lack of a reliable legal system?

5. How do services provided by ROC parallel that of American organized crime after the repeal of Prohibition and the onset of the Great Depression?

6. What the various business activities of ROC?

7. With respect to organized crime, how does the *vory* differ from "sports club" versions?

8. What is the parallel between Camorra and *vory*?

9. How do Russian immigrants differ from earlier immigrants to the United States?

10. Why do Russian criminals come to the United States well prepared for a life in organized crime?

11. How does organized crime in Russia differ from ROC in the United States?

12. How are Russian crime groups in the United States structured?

13. What are the sophisticated crimes that ROC in the United States has been engaged in?

14. How does the structure of ROC in the United States differ from that of the American Mafia?

Alberta, Canada, Hell's Angels at a police roadblock. AP Photo/*The Canadian Press*, Darryl Dyck

Outlaw Motorcycle Clubs[1]

Most legal cases involving the Hells Angels motorcycle club are tried in criminal court with the United States of America as plaintiff. But the club is zealous in protecting copyrights to the Hells Angels name and their skull-and-wings "Death Head" logo. Use of these indicators of club memberships by unauthorized persons—i.e. nonmembers—dilutes the value of the brand.

The club has brought at least fifteen trademark infringement cases in the past decade against a wide range of defendants including Walt Disney and Marvel Comics. Marvel Comics renamed its Hells Angels comic book "Dark Angel." The 2006 suit against the Walt Disney Co. concerned the script for the movie "Wild Hogs," in which the main

CHAPTER 10 WILL ENABLE THE READER TO UNDERSTAND:

- The history and evolution of outlaw motorcycle clubs
- The structure and rules of outlaw motorcycle clubs and how club activities are separated from pecuniary criminal activities
- Similarities between the major outlaw motorcycle clubs
- Violence between outlaw clubs
- The business activities of outlaw motorcycle clubs
- The connection between outlaw motorcycle clubs and the American Mafia

---

1. The source of information not otherwise cited in this chapter is from court documents and related trial discovery materials in the United States and Canada and interviews with law enforcement personnel.

characters were identified as members of the Hells Angels club and wore the Hells Angels trademarked logo. In 2010, club lawyers sued Alexander McQueen, along with Saks Fifth Avenue and Zappos, for selling hand-bags, jewelry, and clothing with a skull-and-wings "Death Head" design. The defendants agreed to withdraw the offending items. In 2011, the club filed copyright infringement suits against a t-shirt manufacturer whose product stated "My boyfriend's a Hells Angel" (Slind-Flor 2011). The offending merchandise was withdrawn.

The Hells Angels and their outlaw club competitors are discussed in this chapter.

The outlaw motorcycle club is a uniquely American derivation, although several have chapters throughout the world. The outlaw club phenomenon dates to the years after World War II, when many combat veterans, particularly those residing in California, sought new outlets for feelings of hostility and alienation. Some found release in riding motorcycles—military surplus motorcycles were plentiful—and in associating with others in motorcycle clubs. These clubs became a means of continued quasi-military camaraderie. At the same time, the motorcycle became a symbol of freedom from social responsibilities and restraints. Soon these new groups became a nuisance, if not a threat, to local communities in southern California.

Shortly after World War II, a group of California veterans formed a motorcycle club and called themselves the POBOBs, an acronym for "Pissed Off Bastards of Bloomington," a small southern California town in San Bernadino County whose current population is about 20,000. By some accounts, the POBOBs were dedicated to mocking social values and conventional society through acts of vandalism and general lawlessness. Over the Independence Day weekend of 1947, following the arrest of a POBOB member for fighting in the small central California town of Hollister, a reported 750 motorcyclists descended on the small community and demanded his release. When local authorities refused, the cyclists tore up the town, a scene later depicted in the 1954 Marlon Brando film *The Wild One*. The movie, based on a *Harper's* magazine story and originally titled *The Cyclists Raid*, also featured Lee Marvin and actual bikers,

helped fuel the outlaw biker phenomenon (Briley 1997).

Hunter Thompson (1966) reported a different version of this incident, which he states grew out of a July Fourth celebration that included motorcycle races sanctioned by the American Motorcycle Association (AMA). About three thousand cyclists participated, some became unruly, and the seven-man police force was unable to handle the ensuing disorder. The cyclists were easily controlled when additional officers arrived, and the actual riot was timid compared with the film version. Daniel Wolf (1991: 4) states that about five hundred unaffiliated bikers disrupted the AMA-sponsored event "by drinking and racing in the streets of the host town of Hollister. The ineffective efforts of a numerically insufficient seven-man police force, in conjunction with the sometimes provocative vigilante tactics of indignant local residents, caused the motorcyclists to coalesce as a mob." Bikers rode motorcycles into bars and broke windows with beer bottles. This unruly behavior ended thirty-six hours later after the arrival of additional police. At the center of much of the mayhem was "Wino" Willie Forkner of the Boozefighters Motorcycle Club. The World War II veteran died of natural causes at age 76 shortly before he could lead a fiftieth anniversary outlaw biker rally in Hollister (Associated Press 1997; Barker 2008; Hayes 2005).

The Hollister incident gave rise to an important outlaw biker tradition—the annual July Fourth run. Another traditional run occurs over the Labor Day weekend. In 1997, Hollister played host to the fiftieth anniversary of the incident that brought the small town—population about 35,000—fame, and it is now the site of an annual Independence Day rally that attracts about 100,000 bikers (Singer 2002). Bikers, outlaw and otherwise, also rally every August in the Black Hills of South Dakota at the "Sturgis Motorcycle Rally." The six-day event, which began in 1938 with less than two-dozen bikers, now draws in excess of a half-million persons to this town of 5,500, and hundreds of venders, including the Hells Angels who have a booth selling shirts and calendars. It provides the outlaw clubs an opportunity to "profile," the biker equivalent of cruising.

The term *outlaw* was first used by the sheriff of Riverside County to distinguish southern California bikers such as the POBOBs from those motorcycle enthusiasts affiliated with the mainstream AMA. The lifestyles and traditions of the outlaw biker—or *bikies*, as they are called in Australia—are promoted by a handful of magazines catering to both the hardcore outlaw subculture and the "wannabe" outlaw. Biker magazines "make it possible for a man to construct a biker identity and develop a sense of loyalty to that image without having met another biker" (Wolf 1991: 37). The FX television show *Sons of Anarchy*—the most-watched program in the channel's history—helps promote the outlaw lifestyle.

"Members of the outlaw motorcycle gangs refer to themselves as 'one percenters' in reference to an estimate advanced some years ago by the American Motorcycle Association that outlaw motorcyclists comprised less than one percent of the motorcycling population. Outlaw gangs immediately seized on the figure as a reflection of their belief that they are rebels, operating outside society's laws and mores" (PCOC 1986c: 61). James Quinn and D. Shane Koch (2003: 286) note, "Much [one percenter] behavior is linked to their desire to uphold this image because it provides them with a 'marketable commodity' in both legal (e.g., concert security, barroom bouncer) and illegal (e.g., loansharking) spheres of economic endeavor."

"Outlaw bikers view themselves as nothing less than frontier heroes, living out the 'freedom ethic' that they feel the rest of society has largely abandoned. They acknowledge that they are antisocial, but only to the extent that they seek to gain their own unique experiences and express their individuality through their motorcycles. Their 'hogs' become personal charms against the regimented world of the 'citizen.' They view their club as collective leverage that they can use against an establishment that threatens to crush those who find conventional society inhibiting and destructive of individual character" (Wolf 1991: 37). "Outlaw motorcycle clubs exist in their own world, cut off from mainstream society through a rigid system of rules and inherent belief system" (Veno 2003: 40). Their subculture features bars that serve both deviant and conventional bikers and is a place of recruitment for outlaw clubs (Barker 2008).

"In many ways all outlaw clubs are pre-adapted as vehicles of organized crime. Paramilitary organization lies at the core of their tight-knit secret society. It is a society capable of enforcing internal discipline, including an ironclad code of silence.... Uncompromising commitments of brotherhood generate cohesion, mutual dependence, and a sense of a shared common fate.... The political structure of the club, the anti-Establishment attitudes and high-risk nature of the individuals involved, and the marginal social environment in which they operate have the potential to produce a clubhouse of crime" (Wolf 1991: 266). As Veno (2003: 166) notes, "Violence is central to club life."

STRUCTURE

Outlaw motorcycle clubs are characterized by having a constitution, a rigid organizational structure, and heavy levels of commitment to ensure their survival. Peter Leeson and David Skarbek (2011: 282) point out that for criminal organizations constitutions "create consensus by generating common knowledge about the organisation's rules." A constitution enumerates the most critical expectations of members' behavior, such as how members join, the rights of membership, and restrictions on members' behavior. "By creating this common knowledge, constitutions greatly reduce the potential for intra-organisational conflicts."

Consistent with their founders' background as military veterans outlaw clubs exhibit a bureaucratic structure (see Figure 10.1). Although there are some minor variations, they have a mother club that serves as the national or international headquarters. Mother club responsibilities include making decisions on problems that the local chapters are unable to resolve. Some, such as the Hells Angels, provide for more chapter autonomy with important decisions made at regional, national, and international meetings (Barker 2008).

Each club chapter has a president, vice president, secretary-treasurer, enforcer, and sergeant-at-arms (see Figure 10.2). The sergeant-at-arms is usually the toughest member and may also serve as an enforcer. There is also the road captain, who fulfills the role of logistician and security chief for club-sponsored "runs" or motorcycle outings. The road captain maps out routes and arranges for refueling, food, and maintenance stops en route. He establishes "strong points" along the route to protect the main body from police harassment or rival motorcycle clubs. Outlaw clubs have several mandatory runs each year, and all members not otherwise incapacitated—hospitalized or imprisoned—must participate with motorcycles and full colors.

"Colors," or the "patch," are the official club insignia. A member typically wears colors on the back of a denim jacket with the sleeves cut off or, in colder climes, a leather jacket. The insignia consists of three separate sections, or "rockers." The top rocker carries the club name, the center rocker displays the club emblem, and the bottom rocker designates the club location or territory. Colors may also be worn as a tattoo—mandatory for Hells Angels. A member is allowed to have only one club patch, the loss of which can bring sanctions, including expulsion from the club. Also sewed or pinned on the jacket are other "authorized" patches, which are usually quite offensive to conventional society—for example, swastikas, 666 (sign of Satan), FTW ("Fuck the World"), and 1%.

The patch is owned by the club, not the member. A nonmember discovered wearing the patch or displaying the club tattoo will encounter life-threatening violence. Club colors and the accompanying club tattoo signal that the wearer is bona fide and, therefore, to be trusted by other members who he has never met and criminals interested in some type of business relationship. Consistent with a military orientation, various offenses

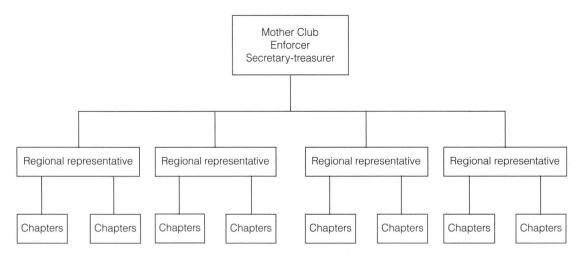

FIGURE 10.1 National Organizational Structure of Outlaw Motorcycle Clubs

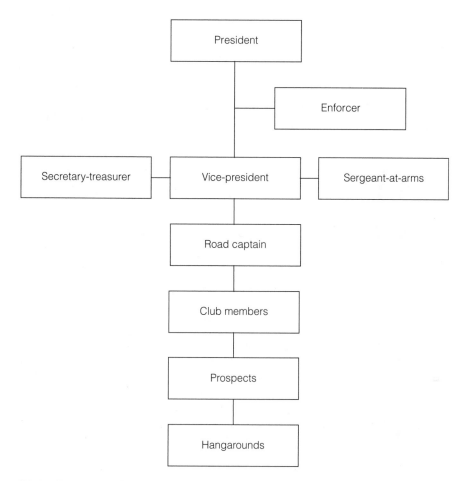

FIGURE 10.2 Chapter Organizational Structure of Outlaw Motorcycle Clubs

can result in the "pulling of patches" and the crossing out of the club tattoo.

The clubs practice precision riding, and club runs are accomplished in a military-style formation (see Figure 10.3).

Outlaw clubs limit chapter membership to about twenty-five, which helps maintain a strong bond between members and facilitates the decision-making process. "Once a club chapter reaches twenty-five, a new chapter will generally be created" (Veno 2003: 89). Each chapter is composed of at least six "full-patch" members, as well as "strikers" or "prospects" who spend from one month to one year (striking period) on probationary status, and "hangarounds," who are permitted to associate with

members, usually in an effort to achieve striker status. Each prospect requires a sponsoring member who is responsible for the probationary member. "Gang members do extensive background checks on prospective members, often using female associates who have been placed in positions with public utilities, government services, and law enforcement agencies to assist them" (PCOC 1986c: 65). The prospect's photo with relevant information will typically be passed around to various chapters giving members an opportunity to object to his becoming a member. This procedure is circumvented in the "patchover" discussed later. In the Hells Angels, having been employed, or even having sought employment, in law enforcement precludes consideration for

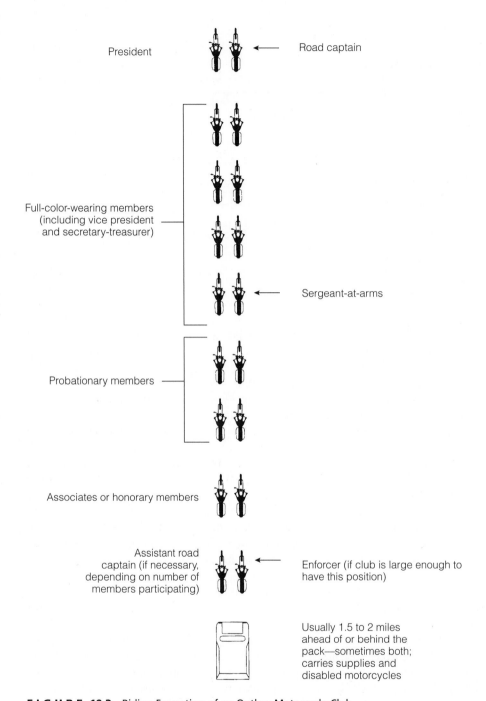

FIGURE 10.3 Riding Formation of an Outlaw Motorcycle Club

membership. If membership slips below six, the chapter may be dissolved, its members moving to become part of another chapter, or other chapters. Or members from nearby chapters may be sent to keep the chapter viable. Club officers are chosen by secret ballot and candidates are usually experienced members. To become a full-patch member of the Hells Angels, a candidate ("prospect") must be at least 21 years of age and have no background in law enforcement. Other outlaw clubs, e.g., Pagans, are less rigid about having law enforcement experience.

Prospects must be nominated by a member and receive a unanimous vote for acceptance into provisional status. They carry out menial jobs at the clubhouse and for other members. Sonny Barger (2000) states that there has never been an initiation rite in the Hells Angels. When a man is admitted to membership, he is allowed to wear the club's colors—the proudest possession of any outlaw club member and clearly parallel to being "made" in the American Mafia. The death's head emblem of the Hells Angels is copyrighted and the club vigorously defends the copyrighted icon and the term *Hells Angels Motorcycle Club*: they are never permitted to be used for pecuniary purposes such as on clothing for sale to the public. Minutes of Hells Angels chapters are filled with discussions of copyright issues. In 2010, club lawyers sued Alexander McQueen, along with Saks Fifth Avenue and Zappos, for selling handbags, jewelry, and clothing with a skull-and-wings "Death Head" design. The defendants agreed to withdraw the offending items.

Club chapters usually meet weekly—"church"—and meetings are conducted as rather formal affairs in accord with *Robert's Rules of Order*: roll call, reading of minutes, motions, discussion, and voting. The failure to attend meetings without justification—imprisoned or hospitalized—results in being fined and can lead to expulsion (Veno 2009). International clubs have monthly executive meetings, annual conventions, and "world runs" attended by members from all countries that have chapters. Major clubs have national meetings to which all chapters are expected to send representatives (Veno 2009).

Major clubs have puppet clubs—a type of farm team—that support their interests and are generally subservient, carrying out orders from the dominant partner. Members of a puppet club who have proven themselves can be elevated to prospect and full-patch members, and there can be a *patchover* by which an entire club becomes a chapter, bypassing the customary waiting period imposed on prospective members. This occurs when a major club wants to establish chapters in certain areas and/or in order to strengthen their position in a struggle with another club.

Outlaw motorcycle clubs usually exhibit racist attitudes, and in the United States no known black males hold membership in any major club. There are predominantly black clubs, such as the Chosen Few, formed in Los Angeles in 1960, with some white members. The Hells Angels has Jewish and Muslim members, and the New Zealand chapter—the first Hells Angels chapter outside of the United State—has Maori members. Arthur Veno (2003), an Australian professor and author, states that he knows of a few black members of the Hells Angels, and they also have Polynesians, Native Americans, and Hispanics. Women associated with a club are treated as nothing more than playthings—objects to be used, traded, and sold. "Old ladies" are the wives or steady girlfriends of club members. Sexual and other demands for their services can be made only by their husbands or boyfriends. "Mamas" and "sheep" belong to the club at large and are expected to consent to the sexual whims of any club member. While women are not permitted to wear club colors, they may wear denim jackets with the inscription "Property of …" with the club's name embroidered on it. Women often carry the club's weapons and engage in prostitution or drug trafficking. Because of the freewheeling image of the outlaw clubs, some teenage girls are attracted to them. The girls may be gang raped, which bikers refer to as "training" or "pulling a train." Girls may also be photographed for blackmail purposes or transported to other states for employment in sex-oriented establishments, such as go-go bars and club-owned massage parlors.

OUTLAW BUSINESS

Outlaw motorcycle clubs "provide a context for individuals with a high propensity for illegal activity to unite long enough to operate enterprises of varying degrees of sophistication" (Quinn and Koch 2003: 281). They are involved in distributing firearms, explosives, stolen motorcycles, and motorcycle parts; providing exotic dancers and prostitutes for various sex-oriented establishments; and trafficking in lysergic acid diethylamide (LSD, a hallucinogen), phencyclidine (PCP, a hallucinogen), cocaine, and methamphetamine. They have been particularly successful in exerting control over the methamphetamine market. George Wethern (with Vincent Colnett 1978), a former ranking member of the Hells Angels in Oakland, states that because of their reputation for violence and antiestablishment attitudes, the Hells Angels are perfect middlemen for drug dealers. The wholesalers sell to the Angels, who then act as distributors for street-level operators. Any number of members may also manufacture methamphetamine. Using violence, they are able to restrict market entry and monopolize the trade in various parts of the United States and Canada (Droban 2007). Other outlaw clubs have done the same.

Although most bikers operate along the lines of short-term hedonism, some profits have been invested in a vast array of legitimate businesses, often for profit and sometimes as fronts for illegal activities. The outlaw clubs have a reliable pipeline of members and chapters for the flow of illicit goods, and the members are highly mobile—they can find support and safety in any city that has a club chapter.

ANALYSIS OF THE STRUCTURE

As we have seen, the outlaw motorcycle club exhibits a number of characteristics that are bureaucratic. Given the military background of the founders and many members of the outlaw biker subculture, this is to be expected. There is a rather elaborate hierarchy, specialization, advancement based on skill, and extensive rules and regulations that are in written form (see Figure 10.4). There is general uniformity in style of dress, colors, and motorcycles—mostly large Harley-Davidsons. The

---

1. All patches will be the same on the back, nothing will show on the back except the HELLS ANGELS patch. City patch is optional for each chapter. 1 patch and 1 membership card per member. Member may keep original patch if made into a banner. Prospects will wear California rocker on back and prospect patch left from where top of pocket is on a Levi jacket.
   FINE: $100 for breaking above by-law.
2. No hypes. No use of Heroin in any form. Anyone using a needle for any reason other than having a doctor use it on you will be considered a hype.
   FINE: Automatic kick-out from club.
3. No explosives of any kind will be thrown into the fire where there is one or more HELLS ANGELS in this area.
   FINE: Ass-whipping and/or subject to California President's decision.
4. Guns on CA runs will not be displayed after 6 PM. They will be fired from dawn until 6 PM in a predetermined area only. Rule does not apply to anyone with a gun in a shoulder holster or belt that is seen by another member if it is not being shot or displayed.
   FINE: $100 for breaking above by-law.
5. Brothers shall not fight with each other with weapons;

when any HELLS ANGELS fights another HELLS ANGELS, it is one on one; prospects same as members. If members are from different chapters, fine goes to CA Treasurer.
   FINE: $100 for breaking above by-law or possible loss of patch.
6. No narcotics burns. When making deals, persons get what they are promised or the deal is called off.
   FINE: Automatic kick-out from club.
7. All HELLS ANGELS fines will be paid within 30 days. Fines will be paid to that chapter's treasurer to be held for the next CA run.
8. One vote per chapter at CA officer's meetings. For CA 2 no votes instead of a majority to kill a new charter and a charter goes below 6 they must freeze or dissolve on the decision of CA Officers' Meeting.
9. If kicked out, must stay out 1 year then back to original chapter. HELLS ANGEL tattoo will have an in-date and out-date when the member quits. If kicked out HELLS ANGELS tattoo will be completely covered with a 1/2 X through the tattoo.
10. Runs are on the holidays; 3 mandatory runs are Memorial Day, July 4th, and Labor Day.
11. No leave period except hospital, medical or jail.

F I G U R E 10.4 Hells Angels California Bylaws

secretary-treasurer records the minutes of meetings and collects and maintains dues. Each member contributes weekly dues to his chapter, and the chapter pays into the national treasury. The Hells Angels also maintain a multimillion-dollar fund to which members and chapters are occasionally asked to contribute. The fund goes for legal expenses and to help support the families of imprisoned members.

As noted in Chapter 1, a criminal organization can exhibit a formal structure even though its economic activities may actually involve small firms or partnerships among members and include nonmember associates. This is often the case with outlaw motorcycle clubs. Each full-patch member of major clubs is reputed to have about ten associates and his own network of friends. For business purposes, each member is at the center of an action group that, although tied to every other member through the structure of the club, operates independently or in partnership. In other words, the formal structure of the motorcycle club is not necessarily the same as its economic structure. Although there is a relatively clear hierarchy within each of the major outlaw clubs, income-generating illegal activities involve several smaller, operationally independent units. But members can call upon the muscle of the club in the event of conflict, making them formidable entrepreneurs. Indeed, it is the club affiliation that enables members to safely conduct illegal business, provides insurance against otherwise untrustworthy suppliers or customers, or criminals who would prey on illegitimate entrepreneurs. Without the affiliation, they would be vulnerable to predatory criminals or rip-offs.

An aura of distrust pervades wholesale drug transactions insofar as they transpire in a Hobbesian world ruled by the credo "might makes right." But "being violent does not make one *generally* credible. If anything it has the opposite effect, as people fear that someone who uses force to protect himself from cheating will also use force when *he* cheats" (Gambetta 2009: 35). Thus, while a violent reputation will scare people, their fear has the potential to undermine otherwise profitable business transactions. However, affiliation with an organization possessing a reputation for *both* violence and "business integrity" allows persons in asymmetrical relationships—who do not have a credible recourse to violence—who cannot turn to the police or courts to remedy a grievance, to transact business with a significant degree of confidence that the "*no drug burns*" rule of the Hells Angels facilitates.

Yves Lavigne (1996: 246) notes that the "Hells Angels are truthful when they say they are not a criminal organization. Rather, they are an organization of criminals. They go out of their way to maintain a barrier between the Hells Angels as a club and the Hells Angels as a business. In response to accusations that they are criminal organizations, outlaw clubs repeat the mantra of Sonny Barger: "Members commit crimes, not the club" (Veno 2009: 62). Criminal matters are discussed among members of many cliques within the gang. Thus, though the outlaw motorcycle club is clearly bureaucratic, its illegal business activities are not, save for directed violence against other outlaw clubs with whom a club is at war.

American Mafia groups are *criminal organizations*—their raison d'être is the business of crime—whereas outlaw motorcycle clubs exist to promote a subcultural biker lifestyle. The American Mafia attracts and selects hardcore criminals. Outlaw biker clubs attract tough, violent young men who were not necessarily in the *business of crime* before joining a club, and the clubs place a firewall between the organization and the criminal activities of its members. This helps to insulate the group as an organization from Racketeer and Corrupt Organizations (RICO) prosecutions (discussed in Chapter 14).

Petter Gottschalk (2009: 70) refers to this structure as a *matrix organization*: "The legal motorcycle club is along the vertical axis, while criminal activities are along the horizontal axis. Criminal activities are not initiated and organized from the top. Instead, an entrepreneurial member initiates a criminal project by identifying opportunity and recruits fellow members for the project."

"Bikers see their personal welfare as contingent upon the club's power and generally assure it some distance from their criminal enterprise" (Quinn and Koch 2003: 300). Each chapter enjoys considerable

---

OUTLAW MOTORCYCLE CLUB CREDO

- Hells Angels: "Three can keep a secret if two are dead."
- Outlaws: "God forgives, Outlaws don't."
- Bandidos: "We are the people our parents warned us about."

- Pagans: "Live Pagan, die Pagan.
- Mongols: "Respect few, fear none."

---

autonomy, and the flexibility this promotes renders it difficult to link members' criminal activities "to the group's formal leadership and keeps the relationship between the club and the actions of its members, chapters, and so forth murky" (Quinn and Koch 2003: 289). Nevertheless, the autonomous local chapters "must live up to the requirements of the club's national charter and maintain the group's power, persona, and reputation" (2003: 291).

Being a member of a major outlaw club provides *credentialing*. The Hells Angels exemplify the "value of a bad reputation" that enables members to operate in a world of criminal anarchy. As portrayed in popular media (for example, Wethern and Colnet 1978; Lavigne 1996) and a book by Sonny Barger, the club is made up of violent and dangerous persons, a "brotherhood of men who will fight and die for each other no matter what the cause" (Barger 2000: 67); men of violence living by the credo "One on all, all on one," which "means that when you fight one Hells Angel, you fight us all" (Barger 2000: 39). While a legitimate organization will fire, expel, or otherwise act against members whose behavior is socially unacceptable if not criminal, in the Hells Angels, "We stick up for our own, right or wrong" (Barger 2000: 40).

In a 1996 ruling (*Lorne Brown et al v. Durham Regional Police*), a judge of the Ontario, Canada, Court of Justice described outlaw motorcycle clubs as:

> close-knit fraternal organizations for which loyalty is paramount and disloyalty may be punishable by death. They are paramilitary in terms of organization with fortified clubhouses and heavy security measures. These

precautions are intended to be defences against the police, the public and rival gangs. Their social activity is marked by the abuse of alcohol and drugs, violence and aggressive behavior and language. They are basically exclusive and antisocial as exemplified by their common use of the slogan, "Fuck the World."

The development of outlaw motorcycle clubs from a subculture of bikers to a criminal organization moved through four stages (Allen ["Rod"] McMillan, personal correspondence):

1. The club shows rebellious and antisocial activity that is random and nonutilitarian.
2. A police response causes less committed members to drop out; members of weaker clubs either disperse or join stronger clubs.
3. The remaining clubs are better able to exercise discipline and control over their membership, particularly control over violence, which now changes from random and nonutilitarian to instrumental. The basic element shared by all members of outlaw motorcycle clubs is a penchant for violence; violence thus pervades the world of outlaw bikers. Rationally used, violence may be for the purpose of maintaining organizational discipline or defending hegemony.
4. The leadership uses organizational skills and intimidation in utilitarian criminal pursuits, and the group becomes a fully committed criminal organization.

From the fun-loving and hell-raising clubs of the immediate post–World War II era, a number of outlaw motorcycle clubs have developed into self-perpetuating, highly structured, disciplined organizations whose major source of income is from criminal activity. But most of the hundreds of outlaw motorcycle clubs are not sophisticated criminal organizations. In this chapter we will look at the most prominent:

Hells Angels, Outlaws, Bandidos, Pagans, and Mongols.

HELLS ANGELS[2]

In 1948, in the Fontana area of San Bernardino County, dedicated outlaws from the POBOBs formed a new group and adopted a name favored by fighter pilots and bomber crews in the world wars—Hells Angels (HA). The club's logo, a grinning, winged death's head wearing a leather aviator's helmet, originally appeared on the fuselage of the 358th Bomber Squadron (Veno 2003). The chapter name was shortened to "Berdoo" to fit on the bottom of the rocker on the back of their jackets (Lavigne 1987). The HA became the first outlaw club to have a formal organizational structure with a constitution and bylaws (Veno 2003), although before the Sonny Barger chapters were independent and operated autonomously (Barker 2008).

In 1957, a 19-year-old former infantry veteran joined the HA. Ralph Hubert ("Sonny") Barger, Jr. dropped out of the tenth grade to join the army; he completed basic training and advanced infantry training before being discharged for being too young. The five-foot, ten-inch, 145-pound novice quickly rose in the biker ranks to become president of the club. He moved its headquarters to Oakland (the "mother club"). In 1967, Barger appeared in a film with Jack Nicholson, *Hells Angels on Wheels,* which did not win an Academy Award but added greatly to the outlaw motorcycle club mystique.

There were three Hells Angels chapters, all in California, and a fourth had been established in (of all places) Auckland, New Zealand (Lavigne 1987). By 1965, police harassment of the HA in California thinned their ranks to fewer than a hundred members; the original Berdoo chapter was reduced to only a handful of diehards (Thompson 1966). Lavigne (1987) reports that police harassment and legal fees left the club on the brink of extinction. However, the HA had been exposed to the drug subculture through a tenuous relationship with the counterculture movement—"hippies" and "flower children." Needing money to survive, they turned to a one-shot deal involving the sale of methamphetamine—"speed." The outlaw bikers eventually broke with the counterculture over the Vietnam War—the former military veterans were rabid hawks. But the easy money they had found in drugs eventually moved the HA beyond the biker subculture and into organized crime.

Until 1965, the HA were virtually unknown outside California. In that year, the state's attorney general unwittingly helped them score a publicity coup. In his annual report, he exaggerated their violent activities, and the California correspondent for the *New York Times* hyped the report for readers of "All the News That's Fit to Print." The result was a spate of articles on the Hells Angels in the national media, including *Time, Newsweek,* and the *Saturday Evening Post.* These articles led to radio and television appearances by club members, whose outrageous dress made for good "visuals." The exposure fueled interest in the HA and the outlaw biker phenomenon, helping to swell their ranks. At the time, Thompson states, most of the Angels were lawfully employed, but the publicity caused many of them to lose their jobs. In 1966, the HA were still confined to California (and New Zealand), but massive publicity and the Vietnam War changed this.

During the late 1960s and early 1970s, interest and membership in outlaw motorcycle clubs swelled because of the return of disgruntled veterans from the Vietnam War (Lavigne 1987). In some instances, entire outlaw motorcycle clubs were issued charters as Hells Angels, a "patchover." The club "expanded

---

2. When it appears on their logo, the possessive is omitted and it is written *Hells.*

The Hells Angels' "tough looks are initially shocking to ordinary people on the street." A "scary appearance and provocative behaviour warn them not to mess with us" (Sonny Barger 2004: 11).

rapidly in the 1980s, patching over motorcycle clubs in countries all over the world" and "systematically set out to eliminate competitors through violence and intimidation" (Lavigne 1996: 50). Sonny Barger explains the patchover process:

> When we award charters in new states, it's always done by national vote. When a prospective club lets us know they want to become Hells Angels, we'll check them out to see if they're standup people. We'll send officers out to meet with them, and in return they'll send guys out to meet with us. We might invite them to a run or two, and likewise we'll send some of our guys to party with them. At some point—time varies—we'll vote on whether they can become prospects. Eventually we'll vote on their membership status. The same process that lets in individuals applies to entire new chapters as well. (2000: 35)

The organization is international in scope, with more than two thousand members in about eighty-five chapters in fifteen countries. They also have "Nomad" chapters whose members have no fixed location, but serve as shock troops reinforcing chapters in conflict with other biker clubs.

In 1973, Barger was convicted and imprisoned for the possession and sale of heroin, marijuana, and other drugs. He was released in 1977, but other indictments against Barger and the HA soon followed. The biker subculture had changed: "Some Hells Angels made big money in the drug business, and suddenly they had something to lose, something to protect. Their bank accounts came first and the brotherhood second. When a member threatened their income, they beat or killed him. The Hells Angels Motorcycle Club was no longer an organization that sheltered social misfits. It became an enclave for some of the underworld's most cunning drug manufacturers and dealers" (Lavigne 1996: 34). But the drug business breeds informants. In 1985, more than a hundred HA across the United States were arrested in a major federal effort against the club's drug trafficking. And dozens more are serving sentences for drug trafficking in the United States and Canada.

In 1997, when HA opened their newest chapter in Stockholm, about three hundred members from several countries gathered to celebrate: They were greeted by three hundred police officers, who put a cordon around their new headquarters, searched all who entered the area, and even arrested one member for failing to wear a helmet (Ibrahim 1997). The authorities in Denmark have passed new laws that bar the bikers from having clubhouses in populated areas, and have asked for assistance from the United States for a problem they see as originating in the states (Associated Press 1996; "Biker Club House" 1997; "Bomb Kills 1 …" 1997; Kinzer 1996a; Moseley 1997; Reuters 1996).

Biker on Biker Violence

While local clubs will be tolerated, major outlaw clubs will not tolerate the establishment of a chapter of a rival club in an area they view as "their territory." In 1994, in Illinois, a local motorcycle club, Hell's Henchmen, was slated to become a chapter of the Hells Angels, a patchover, giving the international club an important presence in the Midwest. The Henchmen are headquartered in Rockford, twenty-five miles away from the Outlaws' headquarters in Janesville, Wisconsin; the Outlaws also have a clubhouse in nearby Chicago. And the Outlaws expressed their outrage: A bomb went off in front of the residence of the Henchmen's president, and six hours later another destroyed the Henchmen's Chicago clubhouse (Thomas 1994a). Later, the Henchmen's president was gunned down at his Rockford residence. In response, three hundred Hells Angels in full colors rode into Rockford for the funeral and a posthumous induction. The Outlaws answered with more bombings and shootings; in 1995, an HA member was shot to death while sitting in his car near the Chicago trucking company for which he worked (Thomas 1994b; Martinez 1995). In 1997, seventeen members of the Outlaws from Wisconsin, Indiana, and Illinois were indicted for these and other acts of violence— listening devices had been planted in several clubhouses and the home of one Outlaw who is said to have orchestrated several murders and bombings. One of those arrested became a government witness and the violence stopped (Starks 1999). In 2000, the former head of the South Side Chicago Outlaw chapter was found guilty of racketeering acts that included the 1995 murder of an HA member (Daley 2000).

The most violent biker conflict involving the HA took place in Canada. The club first displayed its colors in Canada at the end of 1977, when the Popeyes, who had been warring for two years with the Satan's Choice and the Devil's Disciples over drug turf, patched over to become the Angels Montreal, Quebec, chapter. As Hells Angels, they immediately began to fight with the Outlaws Motorcycle Club.

In 1983, the Quebec HA chapter patched over the Thirteenth Tribe club in Halifax, expanded westward into British Columbia, and remained the largest and most powerful outlaw motorcycle club in Canada. During the 1980s, in Montreal, the HA defeated the Outlaws who were driven from the city, and the Angels negotiated affiliations with several local motorcycle clubs—collectively referred to as *Les Hells*. In 1985, five members of the HA Laval chapter were invited to the clubhouse of the Sherbrooke chapter where they were gunned down—their bodies were found in the St. Lawrence River in weighted-down sleeping bags—the HA way of maintaining organizational discipline and a response to the Laval chapter's reckless behavior, which included using cocaine that was intended to be sold.

In 1994, negotiations between the HA and a powerful local club of drug dealers—the Rock Machine—broke down. The Rock Machine refused to adhere to the HA's fixed prices for cocaine and a

Hundreds of bikers head to the cemetery Saturday, May 4, 2002, in Stockton, California, for the burial of Stockton motorcycle shop owner and Hell's Angel member Robert Emmett.

AP Photo/*The Record*, Michael McCollum

violent struggle for control of drug trafficking broke out (Langton 2010). Soon, heretofore independent dealers were told by each camp that they could only buy drugs from that group or its affiliates, a directive enforced by violence (Paradis 2002). In opposition to the HA, a number of independent groups and former Outlaws joined with the Rock Machine and became known as the Alliance (Langton 2006). The conflict with the Rock Machine (the club became a Bandidio chapter) ended in 2001 when Bonanno Family captain Vito Rizzuto[3] reportedly told the notorious Hells Angel president Maurice ("Mom") Boucher that the violence, particularly the indiscriminate use of explosives, was bad for business—but not before it had claimed 160 lives, including that of an 11-year-old killed in an explosion and two randomly selected correction officers murdered by the HA (Lamothe and Humphreys 2006). The murders were ordered by Boucher in an effort to terrorize the criminal justice community in Montreal much as the Medellín cartel had done in Colombia (Langton 2006). In 2004, they resulted in the conviction of Boucher and a life sentence.

The violence in Quebec can be understood by an examination of the profits flowing from control of the drug market. In 2000, police discovered a HA "bank"—apartments with counting machines and computers maintained to receive, record, and disperse funds. The sales for a thirty-nine-day period amounted to more than 18 million Canadian dollars. In raids on three apartments, the police found $5.6 million in Canadian and U.S. currency. The investigation also revealed that each member of the HA Nomads Chapter was receiving a fixed salary of $5,000 a week (Cherry 2005).

Paul Cherry (2005: 21) notes changes in the club fostered by newfound drug wealth: "The new generation of Hells Angels was, for the most part, clean-cut men who took good care of themselves and worked out constantly. Gone was the

Hells Angels Heilbronn Chapter in Germany.

beer gut associated with the image of a debauched biker who rides his Harley-Davidson for hours on end." In fact, Cherry reports, some of the younger members look pretty awkward on their massive machines that they are required to ride in accord with HA international rules.

OUTLAWS

The Outlaws trace their origins to McCook, Illinois, a Chicago suburb that despite its small resident population—less than three hundred—is home to heavy industry. The Outlaws Motorcycle Club was founded in 1935, but the club grew in the postwar years, changing its name to the Chicago Outlaws and moving to that city in 1950. In 1954, the club adopted its skull ("Charlie") and crossed pistons logo, a case of life imitating art: the crossed pistons were

---

3. In 2007, Rizzuto was sentenced to ten years after pleading guilty to participating in the 1981 murder of three Bonanno Family captains—depicted in the movie *Donnie Brasco*—during a struggle for control of that crime Family.

adopted from the colors worn by Marlon Brando in *The Wild One* (Langton 2010).

Outlaw chapters are scattered throughout the Midwest, Northeast, and several southern states; they are particularly strong in Florida. The mother club moved from Chicago to Detroit in 1984 and incorporated as the American Outlaws Association.

The club expanded by patching over other clubs and U.S. law enforcement authorities estimate that the Outlaws have about 94 chapters in 22 states with more than 700 members and chapters in 12 foreign countries. As is the case with the other major outlaw clubs, the Outlaws have been at war with the Hells Angels since 1974. In 2011, the national president of the American Outlaws Association, Jack ("Milwaukee Jack") Rosgawas, was sentenced to twenty years in prison after a jury convicted him of conspiracy to commit racketeering and violent acts. Many of the crimes stemmed from the club's conflict with the Hells Angels.

Colors/patch of the Outlaws in England.

© Nathan King/Alamy

BANDIDOS

In 1965, in the fishing village of San Leon, Texas, a group of military-veteran dock workers got together after work and weekends to party. The next summer, ex-Marine Donald Chambers organized the group into a club and adopted the name Bandidos, from the popular Frito Bandito commercial that used the "Frito Bandito" cartoon character who raises hell to sell potato chips. However, the organization's mascot, known as the "Fat Mexican," was given a machete and a gun. In 1968, the Bandidos moved to Corpus Christi, Texas, and then to Houston, Texas, which is regarded as the mother chapter. Also called the Bandido Nation, the club has about 170 chapters in fourteen countries, including about 90 in the United States, concentrated in Texas, Louisiana, Mississippi, Arkansas, New Mexico, Colorado, South Dakota, and Washington State. United States membership is estimated at 2,400 bikers. As distinct from the Hells Angels, the Bandidos welcomed some nonwhites (Langton 2010)

The Outlaws and the Bandidos are considered affiliated clubs, and they list each other as links on their websites. When the Bandidos wanted to establish a chapter in Oklahoma in the late 1990s, they sought and received permission from the Outlaws who already had Oklahoma chapters (Winterhalder 2005). Both clubs are allied in a struggle against the Hells Angels. This conflict has had international ramifications, such as the war between the Hells Angels and Bandidos in Scandinavia. With support from the California mother club, the Hells Angels organized in Denmark during the 1980s but were challenged by a local group that the Angels almost wiped out—thirteen were shot and stabbed to death before the group disbanded in 1986. Remnants joined a new club that eventually became a chapter of the Bandidos, renewing conflict with the Hells Angels, which in 1994 resulted more killings.

During 1996, the conflict became even more violent with the use of stolen and former Soviet block military weapons—high-caliber machine

National Constitution Outlaws Motorcycle Club of North America

1. ALL MEMBERS MUST BE 21 YEARS OF AGE AND OWN HIS OWN MOTORCYCLE AT ALL TIMES. 30 DAY GRACE PERIOD IS ALLOWED. CHAPTER DECISION.
2. ALL MOTORCYCLES MUST BE AMERICAN MADE 1000 CC OR BIGGER.
3. YOU HAVE TO HAVE 100% VOTE FROM MEMBERSHIP. THE SPONSORING CHAPTER MAY BRING A NEW MEMBER UP FOR VOTE AFTER HE HAS PROBATED FOR A MINIMUM OF SIX MONTHS. HAS ATTENDED AT LEAST ONE NATIONAL. ATTEND ALL FUNERAL BILLS PAID TO DATE. AND 100% VOTE OF SPONSORING CHAPTER. YOU MAY ONLY BRING UP A NEW MEMBER FOR VOTE THREE TIMES.
4. A PROBATE WILL NOT BE TOLD TO DO SOMETHING THAT A MEMBER HIMSELF WOULD NOT DO. PATCH PULLING OFFENSE FOR INSTRUCTING A PROBATE TO COMMIT A FELONY.
5. NO NEEDLE LAW. PATCH PULLING OFFENSE AND EXPULSION IN BAD STANDING FROM CLUB.
6. NO PCP, CRACK, HERON, NO BULLSHIT DEALINGS INVOLVING CLUB. EXPULSION IN BAD STANDINGS FROM CLUB.
7. CLUB HOUSES TO REMAIN CLEAN, AND MEMBERS ARE RESPONSIBLE FOR THEIR GUEST. IF YOU CAN'T EAT IT, DON'T BRING IT.
8. NO PRACTICAL JOKES THAT MAY ALTER THE STATE OF MIND OF YOUR BROTHER OR GUEST. PATCH PULLING OFFENSE.
9. MEMBERS MUST BE IN CLUB FOR ONE YEAR BEFORE BEING ALLOWED TO HAVE A CLUB TATTOO. CLUB TATTOO'S ARE CHARLIE, OUTLAWS, AMERICAN OUTLAW ASSOCIATION, OR ANY ABBREVIATION. MEMBERS MUST HAVE FIVE FULL YEARS IN BEFORE HAVING A BACK PATCH. A MEMBER LEAVING IN GOOD STANDING WILL HAVE HIS TATTOO DATED.
10. WHEN CHANGING CHAPTERS YOU MUST CLEAR THROUGH BOTH PRESIDENTS AND HAVE A 100% VOTE BY NEW CHAPTER. MUST HAVE ONE YEAR IN BEFORE YOU CAN REQUEST A CHANGE.
11. ALL NEW CHAPTERS ARE TO HAVE A 100% VOTE BY ALL PRESIDENTS. NEW CHAPTERS MUST MAKE TWO NATIONALS. ATTEND ALL FUNERALS. ALL PROBATES IN A PROSPECTIVE CLUB WILL WEAR A PROBATIONARY ROCKER ON BACK AND A.O.A. [AMERICAN OUTLAW ASSOCIATION] PROSPECTIVE PATCH ON FRONT.
12. ANY OUTLAW LEAVING CLUB IN GOOD STANDINGS IS TO BE RESPECTED AS SUCH AND ANY BROTHER NOT HONORING THIS WILL IMMEDIATELY HAVE HIS PATCH PULLED. ANY DISRESPECT TO YOUR PATCH OR STEALING FROM BROTHERS IS FORBIDDEN AND IS AN AUTOMATIC PATCH PULLING OFFENSE.
13. WHEN LEAVING CLUB, MEMBERS MUST HAVE AT LEAST TEN YEARS IN BEFORE BEING ALLOWED TO KEEP PATCHES OR ANYTHING WITH CHARLIE OR OUTLAWS ON IT. MAJORITY VOTE OF CHAPTER FOR APPROVAL. MEMBERS IN GOOD STANDING ONLY.
14. LOSS OF PATCH BY NEGLIGENCE WILL RESULT IN A $500.00 FINE, AND TO PROBATE AGAIN. PROPERTY PATCH $100.00 FINE ONLY. FINES PAID TO CHAPTER (1/2) NATIONAL (1/2). STOLEN PATCHES BY LAW ENFORCEMENT WILL BE LEGALLY PURSUED BY PATCH HOLDER.
15. FUCKING UP AT NATIONALS TO FRONT OFF CLUB AND/OR PUTTING YOUR BROTHERS IN YOU WILL PROBATE AGAIN.
16. $100.00 FINE AND A THIRTY DAY PROBATE PERIOD FOR THE FIRST BROTHER THAT PUNCHES ANOTHER BROTHER. FINE PAID TO CHAPTER OF BROTHER PUNCHED.
17. MISS THREE NATIONALS IN A SEASON, YOU PROBATE AGAIN. MAKE ALL FUNERALS UNLESS IN JAIL, HOSPITAL, OR COURT. A $100.00 FINE FOR MISSING THE ABOVE. NATIONAL FINES PAID TO NATIONAL. FUNERAL FINES PAID TO CHAPTER.
18. WHEN IN ANOTHER CHAPTER THEIR BYLAWS AND OFFICERS ARE TO BE HONORED.
19. SECURITY AT NATIONALS SET UP BY REGIONAL OFFICERS WITH HELP OF OTHER CHAPTER OFFICERS BEFORE RUN AND NOT AT THE RUN. NO PROBATE TO STAND GUARD ALONE. ANY MEMBER CAUGHT SLEEPING ON GUARD OR HOUSE DUTY WILL BE DEALT WITH ACCORDINGLY BY CLUB OFFICERS.
20. INVITED GUESTS WILL BE TREATED WITH RESPECT AT ALL RUNS AND EVENTS. ANY PROBLEMS, CHAPTER PRESIDENT FROM CHAPTER THAT BROUGHT THEM WILL BE RESPONSIBLE.
21. A $100.00 FINE FOR PRESIDENT OR VICE PRESIDENT NOT REPRESENTING CHAPTER AT PRESIDENT MEETING. FINES PAID TO NATIONAL. PRESIDENT OR VICE PRESIDENT ONLY TO ATTEND MEETINGS.
22. RETIREMENT: 15 YEARS, ATTEND ONE FUNCTION A YEAR. FINANCIAL SUPPORT TO NATIONAL WHEN POSSIBLE. MEDICAL: TO BE DETERMINED WHEN NECESSARY. ALL RETIRED MEMBERS SHALL BE TREATED WITH RESPECT AND DIGNITY, UNLESS THEIR OWN ACTIONS PROVE OTHERWISE.
23. ALL FINES TO BE PAID WITHIN 30 DAYS.
24. ANY CONSTITUTION CHANGES WILL BE PRESENTED TO MEMBERSHIP AND DECIDED AT PRESIDENTS MEETING BY MAJORITY VOTE.

Bandidos of the Jena, Germany, chapter arrive for a murder trail.

guns, hand grenades, and antitank missiles—in Denmark, Sweden, and Finland. That year, the Copenhagen Hells Angels hosted a party for bikers from the Nordic countries at their headquarters, five buildings surrounded by a ten-foot wooden fence. An antitank grenade fired at the compound from the roof of a nearby building killed two and wounded nineteen, some seriously. Later that year, a jury in Copenhagen found two Hells Angels members guilty of murdering the leader of the Bandidos in an airport ambush. In 1997, the Norwegian headquarters of the Bandidos was obliterated by an explosion, killing a passerby and injuring four people, none of whom were bikers. Later, a rocket-propelled grenade was fired into a Danish jail in a failed attempt to kill an imprisoned Bandido leader. That same year, carloads of Hells Angels drove into a Bandido stronghold in a small resort town near Copenhagen and opened fire with machine pistols, killing one Bandido and wounding three more. More than a dozen people were killed before a truce was called and a very public handshake took place between outlaw club leaders on European TV (Paradis 2002). The peace deal had been brokered by Hells Angels and Bandido leaders in the United States and resulted in the two clubs dividing up territory in Scandinavia (Sher and Marsden 2006).

In 2006, eight members of the Toronto, Canada, Bandido chapter were murdered and their bullet-ridden bodies found inside four vehicles in a farmer's field near London, Ontario. The six killers, one a former police officer, members of the Bandidos Winnipeg chapter, were convicted after a trial in 2009 and sentenced to life imprisonment. The killings were described by police as an internal cleansing, the result of orders from Bandidos leadership in the United States to "pull the patches," remove memberships of the Toronto-based bikers.

In 2011, in a major coup for the HA, between fifty and sixty Bandidos in New South Wales defected and were granted full-patch membership in Sidney, Australia, chapters of the Hells Angels (Welch 20011).

PAGANS

The Pagans were founded in 1959 in Prince George's County, Maryland. Chapters are centered on the East Coast—Pennsylvania, New Jersey, Delaware, Maryland—although there are Pagan chapters in Ohio, the Carolinas, Florida, West Virginia and New Orleans. The mother club, seventeen to twenty members, each of whom is responsible for chapters in a specific geographic area, has no fixed location and often changes whenever a new national president is elected. The mother club has moved from Maryland to Pennsylvania to Suffolk County, New York. It is the only major club that does not have international chapters, although it does have ties to outlaw bikers in Canada. The mother club alternates meetings between Suffolk and Nassau County on Long Island, New York.

The Pagans patch depicts the Norse fire-giant *Surtr* sitting on the sun, wielding a sword, plus the word *Pagans* in red, white and blue. Unlike most outlaw motorcycle clubs, the Pagans do not include on their colors the geographical chapter of the member wearing the club's full patch. Chapter presidents answer to the mother club whose members serve for life (Menginie and Droban 2011).

Their reputation for violence enabled the Pagans to extort $400 a week from topless dance clubs and other adult businesses throughout Long Island, New York. The protection racket was reportedly orchestrated by the president of a Long Island Pagans chapter who is also sergeant-at-arms of the national organization. In a federal indictment, the Pagans were accused of planning to murder a nightclub manager who resisted extortion efforts and who on several occasions beat up Pagan members; once he was stabbed five times while fighting off seven Pagans. They were also accused of plotting to kill members of the Hells Angels operating on Long Island (Draffen 1998; Kessler 1998, 1999). The indictments served to weaken the Pagans on Long Island and apparently encouraged the Hells Angels to claim the area by holding their Hell Raiser Ball in Plainview. The event at a catering hall was attacked by ten vanloads of bat-wielding Pagans, leading to the shooting death of one Pagan and the wounding of several others (Gootman 2002).

Violent conflict arose when the Hells Angels sought to establish a chapter in Philadelphia. In 2005, after a number of skirmishes, the Philadelphia Hells Angels Chapter president was fatally shot and shortly afterward the Hells Angels abandoned Philadelphia ("Motorcycle Diaries" 2005).

MONGOLS

According to the club's former international president, Ruben ("Doc"—he was trained as a medical technician) Cavazos, the Mongols were founded in 1970 in East Los Angeles and almost all of the early members were Mexicans (Cavazos 2008). One of its early members is a former Navy SEAL and ex-governor of Minnesota.

Conflict with the Hells Angels began as a dispute involving the wearing of a "California" rocker on the bottom of their colors that the Hells Angels would not permit any other club to wear. "After seventeen years of war, in which more than two dozen Angels and Mongols were stabbed, machine-gunned, or blown up, the Angels finally backed down" (Queen 2007: 24) and the Mongols agreed not to establish a "Berdoo" chapter in San Bernadino, home of the Hells Angels original chapter.

The club floundered in large part because of how they treated prospective members: "If you came around, they would rough you up. If you came back, they would beat you up again. If you came back after that then you could stay" (Cavazos 2008: 78). A national policy adopted in 1998 prohibits beating prospects (Queen 2005). According to William Queen (2005), a special agent for the U.S. Bureau of Alcohol, Tobacco and Firearms who infiltrated the Mongols, to attain membership a prospect had to prove he owned a firearm and was adept at using it. The Mongols are about 90 percent Latino and members have often been recruited from the street gangs of Los Angeles—violent and aggressive young men who often did not even own motorcycles. According to the club's website, besides the United States, the Mongols have chapters in Mexico, Italy, Germany, and New South Wales. In their conflict with the Hells Angels, they are allied with the Outlaws.

The acrimony between the HA and the Mongols spilled over in Laughlin, Nevada, a town of about 8,000 and the scene of the River Run—third largest annual motorcycle event in the country—that draws as many as 100,000 bikers. In 2002, at Harrah's casino in Laughlin and under the glare of hundreds of security cameras, dozens of Hells Angels and Mongols squared off in a brief battle that left two HA and one Mongol dead and more than a dozen persons injured; police recovered 14 guns and 107 knives and some hammers. Amazingly, no civilians were injured; six Mongols and six Hells Angels accepted plea deals receiving about thirty months each. In 2008, Cavazos and dozens of other Mongols were arrested for racketeering and related charges. Many, including Cavazos

The Mongol's colors/patch.

AP Photo/Ric Francis

pled guilty. In 2011 he received a sentence of fourteen years.

OUTLAW MOTORCYCLE CUBS AND THE AMERICAN MAFIA

Members of outlaw clubs have been involved in activities with the American Mafia, providing muscle, firearms, bombs, or drugs. In 2010, Michael ("Big Mike"—350 pounds) Sarno, a ranking member of the Chicago Outfit, was convicted along with a member of the Chicago chapter of the Outlaws for the bombing of a video gaming device company that was competing with the Outfit. The Outlaw club member used his jewelry store to plan illegal gambling activities with Sarno and to house video gambling devices prior to their distribution to various locations, including Outlaws clubhouses. The store was also a place where Outfit sponsored burglaries and robberies were planned and served to fence stolen merchandise. Two suburban police officers were also convicted in this case and the Outlaw was sentenced to sixty years.

Maurice ("Mom") Boucher, the charismatic president of the Canadian Hells Angels Nomads Chapter, negotiated an alliance with the Montreal-based Bonanno Family crew headed by Vito Rizzuto. Together they centralized the distribution and fixed the wholesale price of cocaine throughout the province (Lamothe and Humprheys 2006). Those who failed to maintain the set price, even if they were Hells Angels, were murdered (Langton 2006).

In Philadelphia, there was a great deal of friction between the Bruno crime Family and the Pagans. On one occasion, a Pagan attempted to shoot Philadelphia *caporegime* Harry ("Hunchback") Riccobene over a drug deal. The biker missed and wounded a former bodyguard for murdered Philadelphia crime boss Phil Testa (Pennsylvania Crime Commission 1989). Afterward, relations between the Philadelphia Family and the Pagans improved, leading to a variety of partnerships in the club's most lucrative activity, the manufacture and distribution of methamphetamine and phencyclidine (PCP, or "angel dust").

There continues to be a close relationship between the Philadelphia Family and the Pagans. The Philadelphia press reported a pact between crime Family boss ("Skinny") Joey Merlino and his childhood friend, former Philadelphia police officer Steven ("Gorilla") Mondevergine,[4] who was at one time president of the local chapter of the Pagans.[5] The Philadelphia crime Family interceded with New York crime bosses to keep the Hells Angels,

who have ties to crime Families in New York, out of the New Jersey–Philadelphia area (Caparella 1999).

As distinct from the American Mafia, as well as Russian, Italian, and Japanese organized crime, outlaw motorcycle clubs have not been known to provide enforcement services for restraint of trade agreements among otherwise legitimate businessmen (discussed in Chapter 13) or representation and arbitration services for legitimate and illegitimate entrepreneurs.

SUMMARY

1. Appreciate the history and development of outlaw motorcycle clubs:
   - The outlaw club phenomenon dates to the years after World War II when some returning veterans found release in riding motorcycles and associating with others in motorcycle clubs.
   - The Hollister incident publicized the outlaw biker phenomenon and gave rise to the traditional July Fourth run.
   - Members of the outlaw motorcycle clubs refer to themselves as "one percenters," a reflection of their belief that they are rebels.
   - Outlaw motorcycle clubs exist in a subculture that features bars that serve both deviant and conventional bikers and is a place of recruitment for outlaw clubs.
2. Know the structure and rules of outlaw motorcycle clubs and how club activities are separated from pecuniary criminal activities:
   - Outlaw clubs are pre-adapted as vehicles of organized crime.
   - Outlaw motorcycle clubs are characterized by having a constitution, a rigid organiza-

   tional structure, and heavy levels of commitment to ensure their survival.
   - Consistent with their founders' background as military veterans outlaw clubs exhibit a bureaucratic structure.
   - Outlaw clubs limit chapter membership to about twenty-five, which helps maintain a strong bond between members.
   - To become a full-patch member of the Hells Angels, a "prospect" must be at least 21 years of age and have no background in law enforcement.
   - When a man is admitted to membership, he is allowed to wear the club's colors, parallel to being "made" in the American Mafia.
3. Recognize similarities between the major outlaw motorcycle clubs:
   - Major clubs have puppet clubs that support their interests and are generally subservient, carrying out orders from the dominant partner.
   - A *patchover* is a process by which an entire club becomes a chapter, bypassing the customary waiting period imposed on prospective members.
4. Know the business activities of outlaw clubs:
   - The primary business of outlaw clubs is drug trafficking, particularly methamphetamine, but they are also involved in distributing firearms, explosives, stolen motorcycles, and motorcycle parts; providing exotic dancers and prostitutes for sex-oriented establishments.

---

4. After three years, Montevergine was dismissed from the police department in 1982 for allegedly accepting bribes to protect a gambling operation. He denied the charges, which were later dropped.

5. In 2011, Mondevergine was sentenced to three to ten years for a shooting and stabbing believed related to a dispute over leadership of the Philadelphia Pagans chapter.

- The formal structure of the club is not the same as its economic structure.
- Being a member of a major outlaw club provides *credentialing* that enables members to safely conduct illegal business.

5. Understand that violence between clubs usually involves the Hells Angels (HA):
   - Of the most prominent outlaw clubs, Hells Angels, Outlaws, Bandidos, Pagans, and Mongols, only the Pagans do not have international chapters.
   - These clubs have been in violent conflict with the Hells Angels and sometimes join together in efforts against the HA.

6. Recognize the danger of outlaw clubs operating with or in cooperation with American Mafia groups:
   - In a number of cities there is a relationship between the American Mafia and outlaw clubs.

REVIEW QUESTIONS

1. What led to the development of the original outlaw motorcycle clubs?
2. What explains the rather bureaucratic structure adopted by outlaw clubs?
3. Why do members of outlaw clubs refer to themselves as one percenters?
4. What are the characteristics of outlaw clubs that makes them vehicles of organized crime?
5. Why do outlaw clubs limit chapter membership to twenty-five?
6. What does wearing the "patch" indicate?
7. What is a "patchover"?
8. What are the various business activities of outlaw clubs?
9. What is the relationship between the formal structure of an outlaw club and members' business activities?
10. How does outlaw club membership provide *credentialing*?

Carmine Persico, imprisoned boss of the Colombo crime Family.   © Yvonne Hemsey/Getty Images

"Goods and Services": Gambling, Loansharking, Theft, Fencing, Sex, Trafficking in Persons, Arms, and Counterfeit Products

At the bottom of the food chain in the distribution of counterfeit products:

On a corner in New York's Chinatown, a woman approached the salesman and he removed a pamphlet from his pocket with photographs of Coach, Gucci, and Louis Vuitton purses. She asked a few questions, pointed to her selection, and handed him cash. He called on a cell phone and soon another man appeared with a plastic bag inside of which was the purse she had paid for—a counterfeit Gucci. As she walked away with her purchase, a woman in a business suit and a tourist family approached the salesman (M. Wilson 2011).

In this chapter we will examine the global market of counterfeit products and the role of organized crime in their manufacture and distribution.

The business of organized crime has been described as providing goods and services that happen to be illegal. According to Task Force on Organized Crime (1967: 1), "the core of organized crime activity is the supplying of illegal goods and services—gambling, loansharking, narcotics, and other forms of vice—to countless numbers of citizen customers." As history has shown, translating morality into a statute backed by legal sanctions does not provide for greater morality; it merely widens the scope of the law and creates both temptation and opportunity for a particular set of social actors (Packer 1968). As in any business, the better organized are usually the more successful, and organized crime is basically a business enterprise. However, the business of organized crime often includes activities that are neither "goods" nor "services" but are clearly parasitic. As will be discussed below, the connection between organized crime and illegal business can take one of three forms:

1. *Parasitic*: members of a criminal organization extort money from illegal entrepreneurs under a threat of violence
2. *Reciprocal*: members of a criminal organization require legitimate or illegal entrepreneurs to pay a fixed or percentage amount but in return provide services such restricting market entry, debt collection, and arbitration
3. *Entrepreneurship*: a member of a criminal organization provides an illegal good such as drugs or a service such as enforcement of restraint of trade agreements

Some organized crime groups such as American, Sicilian, Russian, and Japanese "mafias" provide enforcement services for restraint of trade agreements among otherwise legitimate businessmen (discussed in Chapter 13) and representation and arbitration services for both legitimate and illegitimate entrepreneurs.

"GOODS AND SERVICES" OR EXTORTION?

Thomas Schelling (1971) states that organized crime has a relationship with the purveyors of illegal goods and services that is extortionate: *The business of organized crime is extortion, and those criminals who provide goods and services are its victims.* Thus, Schelling points out, a bookmaker operating in an area dominated by an organized crime unit will be required to pay for the "privilege" of doing business—or suffer from violence (or perhaps a raid by corrupt police). The organized crime unit merely "licenses" the business—in New York known as a "gambling package"—and the bookmaker or other criminal purchases a "license" through the payment of "street taxes" to avoid being beaten or killed (or subjected to police harassment). Edward Hegarty, former special agent in charge of the Chicago office of the FBI, pointed out that although persons in organized crime do not get involved in the theft of automobiles, they extort money from those who do: "Many of the murders which have been committed in the Chicago area in recent years arose from automobile theft and chop shop activity. Generally these murders resulted from a failure, inability, or cheating by lower level organized crime figures on their La Cosa Nostra superiors. They were cheating on the street tax which is imposed on criminal cartels of the lower strength, the lower power base, that you have in and around the Chicago area" (Permanent Subcommittee on Investigations 1983b: 33–34).

During the 1970s, the Outfit began "taking over" (collecting regular street taxes) from the owners of chop shops around Chicago and into Lake County, Indiana. About fourteen of those who resisted were killed (O'Brien 1988). A 1990 federal indictment revealed the Outfit's response when their hegemony over gambling was challenged: Three men from the street crew of Sam Carlisi forced their way into a Chicago apartment at gunpoint, taking money and jewelry from the persons running a high-stakes card game. There were threats of physical harm and a demand for $2,000 from each. The operators agreed to turn over 50 percent of the game's profits to Carlisi, who subsequently became the head of the Outfit. Games in suburban Cicero were similarly raided because the operators had not been paying street taxes. Unaffiliated gambling entrepreneurs in the Chicagoland area were routinely given a choice: "Pay, quit, or die." Attorney Robert Cooley (2004: 14) provides an example involving Harry Aleman, a much-feared Outfit enforcer: "You wouldn't know that Harry was a killer until you looked into his eyes and saw his stone-cold evil stare." At his restaurant, Cooley once watched Harry stare daggers at a Jewish bookmaker because he wasn't paying street taxes. Two weeks later the bookmaker was the victim of a shotgun blast in a pizza parlor.

Aleman's crew, known as "The Wild Bunch," included William ("Butch") Petrocelli, and Gerald Scarpelli—experts at intimidation. Aleman (born in 1939 to a Mexican father and Italian mother), nephew of an Outfit boss, is believed responsible for at least eighteen homicides. His looks—5 feet, 8 inches, and 145 pounds—belie a fearsome reputation, and the mob hit man fancied himself an artist; his canvases usually depict outdoor scenes.[1]

The 5-foot, 9-inch, 220-pound Butch Petrocelli grew up on Taylor Street. An older brother became a Chicago police sergeant, but Butch became a juice loan collector. He was known to sit across the table from a recalcitrant street tax victim, staring intently and in total silence. That was usually sufficient to gain compliance. "Those who somehow missed Butch's silent message became corpses" (Brashler 1981: 152). He traveled all over the country, becoming a prime suspect in many gangland murders. In 1981, when he failed to turn over $100,000 collected for the family of imprisoned Harry Aleman, Petrocelli was found dead in the back seat of his car with his mouth and body bound with duct tape and his eyes and testicles melted away with a blowtorch. He died of asphyxiation (Cooley 2004).

Scarpelli was born in New York in 1938 and raised on Chicago's West Side. Arrested seventeen times since 1960, he served prison sentences for armed robbery and counterfeiting. In 1989, while in federal custody, and after providing information to the FBI, Scarpelli committed suicide (Federal Bureau of Investigation 1988).

A typical ploy used by the trio involved associates who made bets with unaffiliated bookmakers. If the bets were profitable, they would be collected; when a string of losses occurred, they would fail to pay. The bookmakers involved would demand a meeting and usually show up with one or more intimidating colleagues. They would find themselves face-to-face with Chicago's "fearsome threesome." With roles thus reversed, the unfortunate bookmaker would be ordered to pay street taxes—or die.

In Thunder Bay, a city in the western Canadian province of British Columbia, the Hell's Angels Motorcycle Club (HA) required drug traffickers who sold non-HA drugs to pay a tax: $100 an ounce for cocaine, $200 a pound for marijuana. The club would also provide debt collection services for a 50 percent commission.

The boundary between providing a good or a service and being parasitic is not clearly delineated. For example, while professional gamblers may be required to pay street taxes to operate in a particular area, in return the organized crime group may limit

---

1. In 1997, in a historic trial, Aleman was convicted of the 1972 murder of a Teamsters Union steward. Aleman had been tried for the same murder in 1977 and acquitted after a bench trial. It was subsequently revealed that the judge, since deceased, had taken a $10,000 bribe to fix the case. The appellate courts ruled that the special circumstances of this case did not violate the constitutional protection against double jeopardy because there had never been jeopardy in the first trial. Aleman was sentenced to 100–300 years' imprisonment (Cooley 2004; Possley and Kogan 2001).

market entry—competition—and provide collection and/or arbitration services that are vital in such enterprises. Jonathan Rubinstein and Peter Reuter (1978a: 64) note a distinctive service provided by the American Mafia—arbitration: "In an economy without conventional written contracts, there is obviously room for frequent disagreements. These are hard to resolve. Many bookmakers make payments to 'wiseguys' to ensure that when disputes arise they have effective representation." As noted in Chapter 1, organized crime may operate as a shadow government, providing policing and judicial services to a vast underworld, thereby increasing efficiency and coordination in an otherwise anarchic—Hobbesian—environment. The historical effectiveness of the American Mafia is grounded in its power to provide illegal services to its own members and, for a price, to other criminals and legitimate businessmen. "Among the more valuable services are mediation of disputes with other criminals, criminal enterprises, and ventures; allocating turf to Cosa Nostra and other criminal groups; fending off incursions by others into these territories; providing financing, muscle, or a corrupt contact wherever necessary to the success of a criminal venture" (New York State Organized Crime Task Force 1988: 73).

The concept of *rispetto* permits a made guy to act as an arbitrator. If, at the request of an aggrieved party, an *uomo di rispetto* is asked for assistance, he can summon the accused to a "sitdown" or "table," an informal hearing over which he presides. Robin Moore (Moore and Fuca 1977: 64) points out that "anyone in the community, mob-connected or not, who had a legitimate complaint against someone else was entitled to ask for a Table hearing" and "any ranking Mafioso or man of respect could be prevailed upon to preside at a Table." To refuse to appear or to disregard a decision made at a table would indicate disrespect with attendant life-threatening consequences. In Chicago, Outfit boss Joey ("the Clown") Lombardo reveled in his role as an arbitrator for all types of neighborhood disputes. The arbitrator receives a fee for this service when the disputants are criminals (Abadinsky 1983; Reuter 1983).

A successful bookmaker in New York told me that he always kept a wiseguy on the payroll at a cost of several hundred dollars a week. This was insurance—it prevented other criminals from placing bets and then refusing to pay, using their status as made guys to protect them. It also kept other criminals from trying to "shake down" the bookmaker. The wiseguy can also assist in the collecting of debts. The amount he keeps as a "commission" varies, but it can be as high as 50 to 100 percent. In northwestern Indiana, Ken ("Tokyo Joe") Eto, the lottery kingpin, paid thousands of dollars a month in street taxes to the Outfit in order to remain in business. In 2005, thirty-six persons in Queens, New York, were indicted for operating a multimillion-dollar bookmaking ring that paid a monthly tribute to a captain in the Bonanno crime Family in exchange for his "blessing" (Cimino 2005).

The Mafia needs victims who cannot easily hide, states Schelling (1971: 648), or persons with fixed places of business. "Even if one can find and recognize an embezzler or jewel thief, one would have a hard time going shares with him, because the embezzler can fool the extortionist if he can fool the firm he embezzles from, and the jewel thief needn't put his best prizes on display." Schelling underestimates wiseguys who spend a great deal of time on the prowl for information and opportunity. Bartenders, fences, prostitutes, and a host of legitimate and illegitimate persons are often eager to provide the wiseguy with information to be on his "good side." They may owe him favors or money or may simply seek to ingratiate themselves for any number of reasons. Salvatore ("Sally Crash") Panico of the Genovese crime Family found out about upscale brothels operating in Manhattan by perusing sex-oriented publications in which the owners usually advertised. Each location was then visited by Panico and his men. Guns, threats, and robbery soon brought the brothel into line. The scheme ended when Panico appeared on closed-circuit television threatening an FBI agent who was playing the role of bordello manager (Post 1981).

Albert Seedman (1974: 70–74), former chief of detectives in New York City, taped a conversation between "Woody," who had swindled $500,000 from Mays Department Store in Brooklyn, and Carmine ("Jr.," "The Snake") Persico, a capo and subsequently boss of the Profaci/Colombo Family who is currently serving a life sentence for murder. In this edited conversation, Woody wants to know why he is being "asked" to pay a rather large share of the money he had stolen to Persico, who had played no part in the scheme:

PERSICO: When you get a job with the telephone company, or maybe even Mays Department Store, they take something out of every paycheck for taxes, right?

WOODY: Right.

PERSICO: Now why, you may ask, does the government have the right to make you pay taxes? The answer to that question, Woody, is that you pay taxes for the right to live and work and make money at a legit business. Well, it's the exact same situation—you did a crooked job in Brooklyn. You worked hard and earned a lot of money. Now you have to pay your taxes just like in the straight world. Why? Because *we* let you do it. We're the government.

The jewel thief deals in expensive merchandise and needs a fence who can provide large sums of cash on very short notice. Some thieves fence the jewels the same night they are stolen (Abadinsky 1983). A fence connected to organized crime can be relied upon to have, or to be able to raise, large amounts of cash on short notice. Dealing with a "connected" fence also provides insurance for the thief. It guarantees that he will not be "ripped off" by other criminals (because this would indicate a lack of *rispetto* and raise the ire of the crime unit). Thus, dealing with *Cosa Nostra* can provide an umbrella of protection to independent criminals who might otherwise be at risk from other criminals. Marilyn Walsh (1977) notes that although fencing is basically a sideline for the organized crime entrepreneur, the organized crime connection "is particularly helpful to the vulnerable good burglar who needs a somewhat amorphous affiliation with the criminal super-

structure to protect him from some of its less genteel elements" (1977: 132). She provides an example:

> Greg and his three associates had successfully executed a residence burglary, netting a substantial amount of expensive jewelry, one item in particular being an $8,000 bracelet watch. A few days after the theft the following series of events evolved.
>
> A local enforcer in the area decided he wanted the bracelet. Determining who had stolen it, he and two associates proceeded to the apartment of the youngest of the thieves involved and took him "for a ride," explaining that the thieves and the bracelet would be expected to appear the following day at a private club in the city so that he might bargain for the purchase of the bracelet. When the thief returned from his ride, he called Greg and explained the situation. Smelling a shakedown, Greg got in touch with the bodyguard of one of the big syndicate men in the city. He offered to sell the bracelet to the latter individual at an extremely low price and asked for help. It was given.
>
> The next morning only the bodyguard and Greg made the appointment at the private club. On entering it was obvious that Greg's evaluation of the situation had been accurate. There sat the enforcer with nearly ten others waiting for the burglars. The appearance of the bodyguard startled them. This latter individual said only three words, "Joe's getting it," and the whole charade was over. (1977: 108–109)

Because of the extensive network that characterizes the American Mafia, a connection can provide professional criminals, such as Chicago's Frank Hohimer, with invaluable information (1975: xvii–xviii): "The outfit knows them all: Palm Springs, Beverly Hills, Shaker Heights.... You name the state and the Mob will give you not only the names of the millionaires and their addresses, but how many people are in the house, a list of their valuables, and where they keep them and when they wear them.... Their information is precise, there is no guess work. It comes from insurance executives, jewelry salesmen, auctioneers of estates. The same guy who sold you the diamond may be on the corner pay phone before you get home."

Information of value to conventional criminals operating in and around Kennedy Airport in New York comes from cargo handlers and persons holding similar positions. In one instance, a cargo supervisor in debt to organized crime–connected gamblers provided information to a Lucchese Family crew that led to the largest cash robbery in U.S. history—$6 million from Lufthansa Airlines: "He had methodically worked out the details: how many men would be needed, the best time for the heist, how to bypass the elaborate security and alarm system" (Pileggi 1985: 203).

For Vincent Teresa (Teresa and Renner 1973), an associate of the New England crime Family of Raymond Patriarca, what started out as a "service" ended up as an extortion scheme. Joseph Barboza, a vicious ex-fighter, was an unaffiliated criminal operating in Massachusetts with his own band of thugs. One evening they were at the Ebbtide, a legitimate nightclub in the Boston suburb of Revere, where they beat up the owners and threatened to return and kill everybody. The owners went to Teresa for help. Teresa went to Patriarca's underboss, Henry Tameleo, who agreed to help—for a price. Acting on Tameleo's behalf, Teresa found Barboza: "Henry wants to see you." When Barboza hesitated, Teresa explained the alternatives: "You want to come, fine. You don't want to come, you don't have to, but he'll send someone else to see you" (Teresa and Renner 1973: 123). After being "called in," Barboza agreed not to bother the Ebbtide—it was now a "protected" club. This gave Teresa an idea: "We sent Barboza and his animals to more than twenty nightclubs. They would go into these places and tear the joints apart.... These people would come running to us to complain about Barboza, to ask for protection" (1973: 123–124).

Sometimes the approach is less subtle but more lethal: In 1987, Gambino Family member Michael ("Mike Rizzi") Rizzitello, operating out of Los Angeles, decided "to pay a visit to Mustang topless bar owner Bill Carroll. Rizzi had met Carroll while in prison in 1970 and had been attempting to acquire a piece of the club for months. He had warned Carroll repeatedly to come up with part of the $150,000 the Mustang generated each month. Carroll refused. 'This is for not letting us eat,' Rizzitello said as he pumped three bullets into Carroll's head" (J. Smith 1998: 203).

When it comes to "goods and services," then, the picture is mixed. Many of those who provide gambling and other goods and services such as loan-sharking have a relationship with organized crime that is forced upon them. Others find the organized crime connection useful to their enterprise, and sometimes the made guy is a bookmaker, numbers operator, or (more frequently) a loan shark.

To understand the business of organized crime, we need to consider the degree to which a crime group's business activities are integrated into their organizational structure. Outlaw motorcycle clubs (OMC) have a bureaucratic style of organization, but their (illegal) business activities are not under the control and direction of the organizational hierarchy. Instead, members engage in crime in association with other members—persons in whom they have trust—and use their OMC membership for purposes of intimidation and networking. Thus, while an OMC may not be a criminal organization per se, it facilitates the criminal activities of its members. At the other end of this structure–business spectrum are Colombian cocaine cartels whose business structure and organizational structure are one and the same.

Finally, members of an organized crime group may engage in a variety of criminal activities for which membership is neither necessary nor of any particular advantage. For example, they may commit theft or robbery of cash or cybercrime. These crimes can be and are engaged in by persons having no connection to organized crime—a sixteen-year-old with an Internet connection sitting at his computer in Nigeria can be involved in hacking or advance-fees schemes without any organizational affiliation.

With this in mind, we will review the "goods and services" of organized crime. In this chapter we will examine gambling, loansharking, fencing, commercial sex, cyber-crime, and trafficking in persons, arms, and counterfeit products. In Chapter 12, we will look at the business of drugs, and in Chapter 13, we will examine organized crime in labor and business.

GAMBLING

Gambling includes a wide array of games of chance and sporting events on which wagers are made. Some of these are legal, such as state-licensed horse- and dog-racing tracks and casinos. Most states operate lotteries and licensed casino gambling is often operated by Native American tribes; state, county, and municipal governments can earn a great deal of money from these authorized gambling activities. At the same time, there are unauthorized (illegal) gambling operations whose control is the responsibility of these same governments. In such an ambiguous environment, it is easy to understand why gambling enforcement may not generate a great deal of public support or law enforcement interest. The estimated amount of illegal betting increased tenfold between 1983 and 1995, while arrests for illegal gambling declined significantly, particularly in urban centers. In 1960, 123,000 persons were arrested for illegal gambling, but by 1995 that number was down to about 15,000 (McGraw 1997; McMahon 1992).

The low priority given to gambling enforcement adds to its attractiveness. Although profits from drug trafficking are quite substantial, so too are enforcement activities and penalties, whereas sentences for illegal gambling are minimal. Lack of

AP Photo/Mary Altaffer

New York Police Commissioner Raymond Kelly, right, is joined by Queens District Attorney Richard Brown, second from right, as he speaks to reporters during a news conference at New York City Police Department headquarters in 2006. Prosecutors brought charges against twenty-seven people in connection with a billion-dollar-a-year Internet sports gambling ring.

enforcement resources due to competing demands for police services, combined with advanced telephonic communications—the cell phone and the Internet—explain why enforcement has declined. The relatively light sentences for gambling violations is highlighted by the case of the Gambino soldiers Ronnie ("One Arm") Trucchio and his son Alphonse who, at 26, was reputed to be the youngest Mafia member in New York. In 2004, they pled guilty to running a $30 million a year sports betting operation and received sentences of one to three years. That same year, Gambino Family captain Joseph ("Sonny") Juliano received a sentence of one-and-one-half to three years for a sports betting and numbers operation that collected more than $3 million in bets annually. Sentences for wholesale drug convictions are typically decades.

Bookmaking

Bookmakers "book" bets on two types of events— horse and sometimes dog races and sporting events such as football, basketball, baseball, and boxing. In earlier days, "horse parlors" or "wire rooms" were often set up in the back of a legitimate business. Results coming in over the wire service were posted on a large chalkboard for waiting bettors. Today, most bets are placed by telephone directly or through a roving "handbook," "runner," or "sheetwriter" who transmits the bet to the bookmaker. To maintain security, some bookmakers change locations frequently, often monthly, or they may use cell phones. Many use a "call back" system. The bettor calls an answering service or answering machine and leaves his or her number. The bookmaker returns the call from a variety of locations, and the bet is placed.

Bets are written down and may also be recorded by a machine attached to the phone. This helps avoid any discrepancies about what arrangements were actually made over the phone. The larger bookmakers employ clerks, runners, or sheetwriters. The clerks handle the telephone, record the bets, and figure out the daily finances. The runners call the clerks and are given the day's totals for the bets they booked. Based on this information, the clerks either collect or pay off. The runners receive a portion of the winnings, usually half, and they must also share in the losses.

Sports Wagering. The oldest of the major bookmaking activities, illegal horserace wagering, ranks far below sports wagering from a gross dollar volume standpoint. Sports wagering is the king of bookmaking, although the net profit for the bookmaker is typically less than 5 percent. The bookmaker seeks to act as a broker, not a gambler. To achieve balance between teams, one which the bookmaker hopes will attract like sums of money on each contestant, a handicapping process takes place through the use of a *line* or *spread*, which is the expected point difference between the favored team and the underdog. (See Figure 11.1.)

The line theoretically functions as a handicap to balance relative strengths of the opposing teams. It consists of points either added to the underdog teams' final scores or subtracted from the favorite teams' final scores. Then again, theoretically having balanced the relative strengths of the teams, wagers are accepted by bookmakers usually at eleven to ten odds. Thus, for instance, if a bettor desires to bet $500 on the Washington Redskins at −6 (meaning Washington is favored by 6 points and, thus, 6 points are subtracted from Washington's final score to determine the result of the wager), he would actually risk $550 to the bookmaker's $500.

The line is only theoretically a balancing of the strengths of the teams. However, as a practical matter, the line is really a number of points, either added to the underdogs' scores or subtracted from the favorites' scores, which the bookmakers feel will tend to attract relatively even amounts on wagering on both sides of the contest. If the bookmaker achieves an even balance of wagering on a game and he has no gamble or risk, his profit is assured of being 10 percent, the "juice" or "vigorish" of the losing wages. (Harker 1977: 2)

Latest Line
Sports Features Syndicate Inc.

College Basketball Tonight Preseason NIT Quarterfinals		
Favorite	Pts.	Underdog
At Arkansas	1 1/2	Arizona
At Georgia Tech	3	Oklahoma
At Michigan	10 1/2	Weber St.

College Football Tomorrow		
Favorite	Pts.	Underdog
At Baylor	15	Rice
At BYU	5 1/2	Utah
At Brown	7 1/2	Columbia
Cincinnati	4 1/2	at Tulsa
Clemson	4	at S. Carolina
At E. Carolina	13	Memphis
E. Michigan	13 1/2	at Kent
At Florida	42	Vanderbilt
At Illinois	6	Minnesota
Kansas	9 1/2	at Oklahoma St.
At LSU	1 1/2	Arkansas
At Louisiana Tech	3 1/2	N. Illinois
At Louisville	26	N. Texas
At Miami (Fla.)	12	W. Virginia
At Miami (Ohio)	30 1/2	Akron
At Missouri	3 1/2	Iowa St.
At Navy	6 1/2	Tulane
At UNLV	6 1/2	New Mex. St.
New Mexico	13	at UTEP
At N. Carolina	15	Duke
N.C. State	6	at Wake Forest
Northwestern	4 1/2	at Purdue
At Ohio St.	32 1/2	Indiana
At Oregon	16	Oregon St.
At Penn	5	Cornell
Princeton	1 1/2	at Dartmouth
Rutgers	3	at Temple
San Diego St.	8 1/2	at Hawaii

San Jose St.	3	at Nevada
Southern Miss.	6	at SW Louisiana
At Stanford	9	California
Tennessee	25 1/2	at Kentucky
At Texas	17 1/2	TCU
Texas Tech.	19	Ohio
At Utah St.	9 1/2	Pacific
At Virginia	4	Virginia Tech
At Washington	13 1/2	Washington St.
At W. Michigan	8	C. Michigan
At Wisconsin	7	Iowa
At Wyoming	4 1/2	Fresno St.

NBA Tonight		
Favorite	Pts.	Underdog
At Boston	4 1/2	Washington
At Atlanta	3 1/2	Miami
At Chicago	14	New Jersey
Dallas	4 1/2	at LA Clippers
At Denver	1	New York
LA Lakers	7 1/2	At Vancouver
Minnesota	1 1/2	at Toronto
At Philadelphia	3	Cleveland
Phoenix	3	at Sacramento
Seattle	1 1/2	at Charlotte
Utah	4	at Detroit

NHL Tonight		
Favorite	Gls.	Underdog
At Anaheim	1-1 1/2	NY Islanders
Colorado	1-1 1/2	at Calgary
At Dallas	1 1/2-2	San Jose
Detroit	1/2-1	at Edmonton
NY Rangers	E-1/2	at Winnipeg
Pittsburgh	E-1/2	at Washington

E-Even

FIGURE 11.1 Sports Betting Lines

That is because bookmakers build in a profit by requiring a bettor to risk $11 to win $10—the $1 is called vigorish. Thus, to break even, a bettor would have to win 52.38 percent of the time. In the case of the Washington Redskins bet, if bettors won by more than 6 points, the bookmaker would pay out $500. He would receive $550 from someone who bet that amount on the losing team—a profit of $50, or 10 percent.

To make any necessary line changes, major booking operations continuously track changes in the Las Vegas line by computer. Sports betting and the use of the point spread (line) are illegal except in Nevada. Professional gamblers—who bet for income, not fun—also track line changes in an effort to "middle": They shop around for the most advantageous lines and bet opposite sides of a contest, thus ensuring that the only possible loss is vigorish, while possible earnings will be many times that amount. The bookmaker's profits depend on an ability to alter the point spread so that bets keep coming in for both teams. Even though the bookmaker sets the opening line, it shifts largely in response to what bettors do. Too much money one team and the vigorish is endangered and the bookmaker becomes a gambler—unless he can lay off his out-of-balance bets (discussed later).

When there are attempts to fix the outcome of sporting events, the approach is to have key players "shave points." That is, their play will reflect the need to keep the score within the point spread favored by the fixers. The incomes of major league professional athletes make the fix more likely in college sports. If a bookmaker suspects a fix—experiences an influx of bets ("smart money") on a particular underdog, for example—he may "circle" or "scratch" the game. A circle means he will limit the amount any one bettor can wager; a scratch means he will accept no further bets.

How difficult is the bookmaking business? An experienced investigator responds:

> Well you have day games and night games. So you're bookin' from twelve to one during the day, and five-thirty to six-thirty at night—we're talkin' maybe four hours. Then if you use voice mail, you're not even bookin', you're at the golf course. So at night you call up and get all your bets…. Where's the work? There's not much. All you have to worry about is who's winnin' and who's losin'. You pay someone $500 a week to take care of the collecting and payouts. He should set it up where he has a pattern, where he meets the guys at a set time. They usually get retired guys to do this, and these guys don't think they're doing anything wrong. You can't even arrest him—for what, for givin' someone money? (Herion 1998)

Organized Crime and Bookmaking

In an earlier period, bookmaking was an important source of income for organized crime. Organized crime units ran the operation directly, or "licensed" syndicate bookmakers, and the wire service that provided instant race results was an important source of organized crime control over bookmaking.

However, most illegal wagering today involves sports, rather than horse racing, and bets are made by telephone—or over the Internet. Payoffs are made the day after the event, so the prompt results provided by the wire service are no longer relevant. The almost-exclusive use of the telephone provides greater security and has reduced the need for police protection, often an important syndicate service.

Bookmakers (and numbers operators) frequently find their bets sufficiently unbalanced to require that they be laid off (or else the bookmaker becomes a gambler, not a broker). The bookmaker may use legal bookmakers in Las Vegas to accomplish this layoff, or he may contract with a layoff service. The layoff service is actually a bookmaker's bookmaker, accepting bets nationally, and is thereby better able to balance teams from different cities. For example, if a New York team is playing a Chicago team, bookmakers in New York are likely to have too many bets on the home team. The layoff service can balance those bets with excess ones from Chicago, where bookmakers have the same home team problem. Because of its scale, the layoff is typically a service provided by organized crime.

Bookmaking involves many transactions and generates a great deal of paperwork. The wagers are recorded when received, and clerks have to review their receipts to determine winners and losers. In 1995, police raided a major bookmaking operation—estimated gross $65 million, net of 20 percent—where they found all data entries on computers using a custom-made sports betting program. The computers were also linked to an online service from Las Vegas that provided the latest line on sporting events. The operation was connected to the Colombo and Gambino Families (Raab 1995e).

Technical changes have also made it harder to find bookmakers, who have insulated themselves by the routine use of cell phones and call back services. A gambling investigator explains:

> I've been trying to find a guy [bookmaker]. An informant would give me this phone number. I would check it out and it [the address] would be a vacant lot; the bill would go to a Post Office box in some

other county. Suppose you're the bookmaker. You pay me $500 a week. You give me the phone and people call up. I don't know who they are, they all have [ID] numbers. So a guy would call up and say, "Give me $2,000 on the Bulls minus two" … whatever. I write it down, but I don't know them. You're in the background and you're the only one who knows. But you are not involved in bookmaking. You're the bookmaker, but you're not involved in the actual booking itself. You just figure out who won and who lost, and pay or collect. So you meet him [the bettor]. But, if you're real sharp, you have another guy meet him. Now you just meet your guy on a street corner and he hands you an envelope. You meet the guy in a different place all the time. You call him on the phone and give him ten minutes to meet you. Now how am I [as a gambling enforcement officer] supposed to find you? (Herion 1998)

Competition is difficult to control because bookmaking can involve operations outside the United States; cyber-gambling is discussed later.

Lotteries

The American colonies authorized lotteries. "In 1612, King James I authorized a lottery to promote the colony of Virginia. The colonies themselves used lotteries, and such outstanding men as George Washington bought and sold lottery tickets." The lottery was used (unsuccessfully) to help finance the Revolutionary War. Many of America's outstanding institutions of higher learning were supported through the use of lotteries—Rhode Island College (now Brown), Columbia, Harvard, University of North Carolina, William and Mary, and Yale (Chafetz 1960: 20–21).

During the nineteenth century, lotteries under state license or control were found throughout the United States. Because of the negative publicity surrounding problems with the Louisiana lottery, in 1890, the United States enacted legislation prohibiting

lotteries from using the mails and even prohibited newspapers that carried lottery advertisements from using the mails (Chafetz 1960). This prohibition opened the way for the illegal exploitation of the desire to bet on lotteries, often referred to as the *numbers business*.

A variety of elaborate schemes are available for determining the winning numbers, for example, using the amounts for win, place, and show of the first race at a particular racetrack or the last three digits of the racetrack's "handle" (total gross receipts), figures that are available in newspapers. Today, in the more than forty states having a legal lottery, the illegal lottery will often use the same numbers as the state lottery, although the odds in the illegal lottery may be higher than those offered by the state. In the Chicagoland area, the Illinois state lottery pays $500 for each dollar wagered on a three-number bet, but the illegal lottery pays $600; payment for a four-number bet is the same as the state's, but winners are paid cash and no taxes are withheld.

The structure of the illegal lottery requires a great deal of coordination and is labor intensive, providing many jobs for unskilled individuals and thus making it an important source of employment in poor communities. At the bottom of the hierarchy are those who accept wagers directly from the bettors, such as writers, runners, and sellers. These are generally individuals with ready access to the public, such as elevator operators, shoeshine boys, newspaper vendors, bartenders, and waiters. Customarily they are paid a percentage of the wagers they write (unlike sports bookmaking, numbers wagering is done on a cash basis), usually from 15 to 30 percent, and frequently are given a 10 percent tip from winning bettors.

It is essential that wagers reach trusted hands before the winning number or any part of it is known. Sometimes this is done by telephone; other times wager records (commonly known as work, action, or business) are physically forwarded to a higher echelon by a pickup man. In a small operation the wagers may go directly to the central processing office (commonly called the bank, clearinghouse, or counting house). In large enterprises they are often given to management's field representative (known as the field man or controller), who may be responsible for making a quick tally to determine the existence of any heavily played numbers that should be laid off. At such levels of operation one frequently finds charts consisting of 1,000 spaces numbered 000 to 999 where tallies can be made for certain wagers meeting minimum dollar values.

Near the top of the hierarchy is the *bank* where all transactions are handled. During the collection process the bank will be making decisions as to whether or not to lay off certain heavily played numbers. In games using state lottery numbers, the layoff can be accomplished by purchasing large quantities of lottery tickets, although illegal operators may have to absorb some loss on the transaction, because they may pay winners more than the state. After the winning number is known, the bank will meticulously process the paperwork to determine how much action has been written, how many hits are present, and the controllers or writers involved.

Decreasing organized criminal opportunity was one argument for the legalization of certain types of gambling, in particular the state lottery, beginning in New Hampshire in 1964, followed by New York in 1967. The first financially successful lottery, however, was the 50-cent weekly established by New Jersey in 1971 (Gambling Commission 1976). Most lottery states have a variety of games: instant winners, daily drawings, weekly drawings, and multistate lotteries with payoffs in the millions of dollars. This form of gambling was originally offered as a way of reducing the income of the illegal lottery—numbers—and capturing those monies for public use, particularly education. Without doubt, the lottery has added billions of dollars to the public coffers without generating the political heat that raising taxes would: about $12 billion annually (from wagers of about $35 billion). "State sponsorship reflected a lifting of social and moral barriers and initiated an expansion of gambling that continues today" (Wellford 2001: 15).

There is no evidence, however, that the legal lotteries have diminished the revenues of their illegal counterparts. In fact, extensive advertising may have actually increased illegal revenues along with those of state lotteries. The introduction of a legal lottery educates persons who heretofore did not know the intricacies of numbers gambling (Blount and Kaplan 1989). Illegal operators typically provide better odds—and do not report the winnings to tax officials. Furthermore, the daily lottery provides illegal operators with a winning number in which bettors have confidence and offers a free layoff service so that numbers banks can always balance their bets. The illegal lottery, however, does not encourage people to gamble by an unseemly spate of advertising (about $400 million a year). In America's poorest communities, the state lottery "is a dominant force and many poor and modest-income residents are devoted to an endless search for winning numbers in an unswerving belief that a jackpot waits for them" (Pulley 1999: 12).

More than three decades ago, a federal commission warned: "The availability of legal gambling creates new gamblers." Therefore, "a government that wishes merely to legitimize illegal wagering must recognize the clear danger that legalization may lead to unexpected and ungovernable increases in the size of the gambling clientele" (Gambling Commission 1976: 2). In the constant quest for new revenues, states such as New York have introduced new forms of lottery such as Keno, an electronic game in which bettors pick one or more numbers and win if the computer selects their numbers. Instead of a weekly or daily drawing, Keno picks a new number every five minutes—the compulsive gambler's nightmare—and scratch-off tickets selling for as much as $50 each offer instant payouts often to people who can ill-afford to gamble.

Casino Gambling and Related Activities

Casino gambling (with a wide array of games of chance including roulette, chuck-a-luck, blackjack, and dice) requires a great deal of planning, space, personnel, equipment, and financing. In the past, casino gambling was available in "wide-open towns" such as Newport, Kentucky, and Phenix City, Alabama, and along more discreet lines in Saratoga Springs, New York, and Hot Springs, Arkansas. Some cities have a tradition of holding "Las Vegas Nights," events often run under the auspices of, or with the approval and protection of, an organized crime unit, using the legitimate front of a religious or charitable organization. The operators provide gambling devices, personnel, and financing, and they share the profits with the sponsoring organization.

Organized crime operatives may also organize or sponsor high stakes card or dice games, taking a cut out of every pot for their services. These may be in a permanent location such as a social club or veterans' hall, or for security reasons, may "float" from place to place. The games may be operated in the home of a person in debt to a loan shark as a form of paying off the loan. In certain cities, gambling activities not operated under organized crime protection, "outlaw games," run the risk of being raided by the police or being held up by independent criminals or robbery teams sponsored by an organized crime unit. Vincent Siciliano (1970: 50), an armed robber with organized crime connections, reports: "The organization knows there is this game and when some friend in the police needs an arrest, to earn his keep as a protector of the people against the bad gamblers, the organization guy tells the police and off they go with sirens wailing." During the raid, Siciliano notes, the police can also help themselves to much of the game's proceeds. He points out that even the dumbest thief knows which are syndicate games and recognizes the consequences of disregarding the organized crime connection. A career armed robber expressed concern with the possibility of "knocking over" a "connected" operation: "I don't think the Mafia'd read me my rights and let me go consult with an attorney. And I said [to my partners], 'Is this thing connected?' I said, 'Look, if this is the Mafia's money I don't want any part of it. I don't want some guys to come gunnin' for me'" (Greenberg 1981: 93).

Las Vegas

In 1931, the state of Nevada, desperate for tax revenue during the Great Depression, legalized gambling and established licensing procedures for those wanting to operate gambling establishments. Las Vegas "served principally as a comfort station for tourists fleeing the desert heat" (Reid and Demaris 1964: 12). Then came Benjamin ("Bugsy"—a nickname no one ever called him to his face—twice) Siegel, the first important criminal to recognize the potential from legalized gambling in Nevada.

With financing from organized crime leaders throughout the country, Siegel built the Flamingo Hotel, the first of the elaborate Las Vegas gambling establishments. Until then, gambling consisted of a "few ancient one-armed bandits and a couple of homemade crap tables," and most of the action was at the poker table (Reid and Demaris 1964: 12). The former bootleggers were ideally suited to exploit Las Vegas: They had available capital they were used to pooling, expertise in gambling, and business acumen developed during Prohibition. "Without the ex-bootleggers to found and staff the first generation of hotel casinos," argues Mark Haller (1985a: 152), "Las Vegas might not have been possible."

After Siegel's murder in 1947—he had become too independent for the bosses to tolerate—the Flamingo and a number of plush hotels were controlled (through hidden interests) by organized crime units throughout the country. Typically, funds were "skimmed" before being counted for tax purposes, and the money was distributed to organized crime bosses in proportion to their amount of (hidden) ownership. According to federal officials, from 1973 to 1983 at least $14 million was skimmed from just one hotel, the Stardust. In 1983, several Stardust employees were prosecuted and the owners (of record) were forced to sell the hotel. That same year, two Kansas City, Missouri, organized crime figures and an executive of the Tropicana Hotel-Casino were sentenced to long prison terms for skimming operations (Turner 1984). In 1986, the top leaders of organized crime in Chicago, Kansas City, Cleveland, and Milwaukee were sentenced to prison for skimming the profits of Las Vegas casinos (depicted in the book and movie *Casino*).

Las Vegas is no longer a mob-controlled playground. Casinos are major corporate entities, and organized crime has been moved to the fringes of the Las Vegas scene.

Miscellaneous Gambling

In a number of localities, video poker machines are a very popular staple in many bars or taverns. These machines operate like slot machines but are legal because they do not dispense money. Payoffs are provided by the proprietor (or bartender) surreptitiously. In the Chicagoland area, the Outfit provides the machines and splits the profits, which can be several thousand dollars per week per machine. Net profits from the poker machines are typically split fifty-fifty between the distributors of the machine and the proprietor, and each machine can generate $2,000 per week.

In Chicagoland:

They're all over the place. And the poker machines themselves are not illegal....
Mostly snack bars, blue-collar places. Let's say the owner hears about the money you can make. He contacts a guy and the guy explains that they will be partners. He will put a machine in, maybe more. "Whatever you net for the week we'll split down the middle." He can't lose. The machine will take up to $20 at a time; it's got different slots for different denominations. You get so many units for a winning hand. They're not supposed to pay out in cash, but the rule of thumb is every forty units is worth $10. You wave over the clerk or the bartender and he pays $10 for every forty points. The machine adds it up and you can add units by adding more money....
The distributor can set it to pay out whatever he wants. There's no skill, strictly chance. When they first put in the machine, they will maybe set it to pay out up to 80 or 85 percent [of the times]. Then

they get people hooked and the distributor reduces the payout. Some places, like a truck stop I know, they had ten machines and we're making $100,000 a month. Some mom and pop operations couldn't stay open without the machines. They've taken seats out of restaurants so they could make room for more of these machines. (Herion 1998)

A sheriff's investigator reports: "About five months ago our vice unit hit a truck stop somewhere in the Calumet City [just south of Chicago] area, an oasis just off the Calumet Expressway. They brought in ten or twelve machines that had been running for two days, and there was $8,500 registered on them. I think a lot of mom and pop type taverns in the city are probably paying their overhead with the income from the machines" (Scaramella 1998). In 2002, the former mayor of suburban Stone Park was sentenced to eighteen months' imprisonment for taking bribes from the Chicago Outfit to protect video poker machines in the town's taverns.

Cyber-Gambling

There is also online gambling. With an Internet connection, gamblers can access virtual bingo, poker, blackjack, roulette, and other casino games twenty-four hours a day. While federal law prohibits interstate sports betting, the legal status of online games such as blackjack and poker is unclear (Richtel 2011). Although the 1994 Federal Wire Wager Act (18 U.S.C. §1084) makes it a crime to operate a betting or wagering business using telephone lines or other wire communication facility, if the business is legal where it is licensed, the bookmakers are beyond U.S. jurisdiction. "Cyber-bookie" Calvin Ayre is headquartered in Costa Rica where he operates an online casino with 145,000 customers, most of them in the United States. He is not an American citizen, has no physical presence in the United States, and pays no U.S. taxes on a net worth of about $1 billion (Miller 2006). In 2009, members of the Lucchese Family were arrested

---

PROXY SERVER

Fred does not want his online activity to be traced back to his work computer. He starts up the Kazaa program, configures it to use a free proxy server Internet Protocol (IP) address, then searches for the term "Lolita." Fred finds files that match "Lolita" and starts transferring the files to his computer via the proxy server. If an investigator tries to find Fred by tracing Fred's IP address, the investigator will only be able to trace the IP address to the proxy server. If the proxy server maintains logs, the investigator may be able to obtain information to identify Fred's true IP address, unless the proxy server is located in another country, or logs may not be available (National Institute of Justice 2007).

---

for running an offshore sports betting business. Customers were given access codes that enabled them to place bets over the Internet (Zambito 2009).

Online gambling is legal in a number of countries such as Antigua, Costa Rica, and the Isle of Man. Participants can set up an account using a credit or debit card. Money is added or subtracted from the account according to the bettor's success, or lack of it. The Internet Gambling Enforcement Act of 2006 makes it is illegal for American financial institutions to process transactions originating from or directed toward any online gambling operator, prohibiting businesses, including banks and credit card companies from accepting or transferring money to offshore gambling sites. But a variety of schemes are used to get around the law, such as funneling payments through fictitious online businesses or bribing bank officials. A bettor can also open an account by sending a cashier's check, money order, or wire transfer to a licensed bookmaker; a minimum balance of $500 is usually required. Each bettor is given a personal identification number, bets are placed on a special long-distance toll-free number or the Internet, and money is added or subtracted from the account. A bettor can withdraw money, receiving his or her winnings in the mail via check or wire transfer (Dretzka 2001; Financial Crimes Enforcement Network 2000). And while U.S. gamblers are required to declare their winnings on tax returns, cyber-bookies do not file reports with the IRS (Miller 2006).

Cyber-Crime

Transnational organized crime is "increasingly involved in cyber-crime, which costs consumers billions of dollars annually, threatens sensitive corporate and government computer networks, and undermines worldwide confidence in the international financial system. Through cyber-crime, transnational criminal organizations pose a significant threat to financial and trust systems—banking, stock markets, e-currency, and value and credit card services—on which the world economy depends" (*Strategy to Combat Transnational Organized Crime* 2011: 7).

Crime committed with a computer is not necessarily a "cyber-crime." Many crimes that involve the use of a computer are simply traditional crimes that are committed online—unlawful conduct that exists in the physical, "offline" world such as the illegal sale of prescription drugs, gambling, and child pornography. The Internet is used in the furtherance of a broad range of traditional unlawful activities. Criminals use the Internet to trade or share information (e.g., documents, photographs, movies, sound files, text and graphic files, and software programs), identify and gather information on victims, communicate with co-conspirators, coordinate meetings, meeting sites, or parcel drops (National Institute of Justice 2007).

Criminal activity is facilitated by use of encryption to secure both communications over networks and stored data on computers. Encryption makes it difficult or impossible for law enforcement to collect usable evidence using traditional methods,

---

BOTNETS

Botnets are networks of compromised computers controlled remotely. Botnet development and operations use techniques similar to legitimate businesses, including the involvement of personnel with various specialties, feature-based pricing structures, modularization, and software copy protection. The development and sale of kit-based botnets has made it easier for criminals with limited technical expertise to build and maintain effective botnets. Criminals purchase the base kits for a few thousand dollars and can pay for additional features to better target specific web services. Some criminals rent or sell their botnets or operate them as a specialized portion of their criminal organization portfolio.

Botnets that specialize in data infiltration are able to capture the contents of encrypted web pages and modify them in real time. When properly configured, criminals can ask additional questions at login or modify the data displayed on the screen to conceal ongoing criminal activity.

Source: Gordon M. Snow, Assistant Director, FBI Cyber Division, before the Senate Judiciary Committee, Subcommittee on Crime and Terrorism, April 12, 2011.

---

such as court-authorized wiretaps and search warrants. Encryption tools are often built into retail-software and hardware products and requires little skill or effort for users to implement. As a result, criminals can communicate and store information relating to crimes with little fear that law enforcement can discover and use that information.

The profit potential and low risk associated with cyber-crime, however defined, provides organized crime with an extraordinary opportunity to expand their repertoire. While exploiting digital networks for criminal purposes can be accomplished by a single adolescent with an Internet connection, criminal organizations enjoy a capacity to launder dollars, rubles, and yuan. They have the resources to employ quality hackers and their reputation for violence serves to intimidate victims. Moreover, they have the ability to employ and coordinate dozens, if not hundreds, of persons in schemes that exploit "plastic money." In 2008, for example, a Russian criminal organization siphoned nearly $10 million from the U.S. banking system by artificially inflating the balances on prepaid credit or cash cards. The thieves extracted money from the system by distributing the cards to dozens of so-called "money mules," who used them to withdraw millions in cash from ATMs in cities across the country in a coordinated operation that took less than twenty-four hours (Krebs 2009).

The international networks of criminal organizations provide a capacity to quickly convert credit card information into cash. Russian organized crime groups have hired hackers to break into ecommerce computers to steal credit card and bank account numbers. Access to a company's computer system allows them to download proprietary information, such a trade secrets and customer databases. They can then demand payment to avoid disclosure and to patch the compromised system. Criminal organizations will plant agents inside companies they wish to exploit, giving them access to computer codes.

Staying on the cutting edge of crime and technology enabled members of the Gambino Family to direct a scheme that bilked $650 million from consumers by piggybacking bogus charges onto their telephone bills and credit cards. Victims were offered free samples of sex chat lines and pornographic Internet websites. Calling the 800 number trapped the callers' phone numbers on a computer, and they were billed at least $40 a month for unwanted voice mail. Those clicking on the free Internet tours were told credit card information was necessary to keep minors from using the service and that they would not be billed. Instead, they were unknowingly charged as much as $90 a month on their cards.

The principals collected their fees via innocent-sounding titles through a company that consolidated billings for service providers. They also purchased a bank in Missouri to help launder the proceeds (Kilgannon 2005; Marzilli 2005c; Rashbaum 2004). In 2006, the Gambino soldier who mastermind the scheme was sentenced to nine years in federal prison.

In 2007, two Belarusian nationals created an online business to assist identity thieves in exploiting stolen financial information, such as credit card and debit card numbers. The website was designed to counteract security measures put in place by financial institutions to, for example, prevent fraud when account holders try to make transfers or withdrawals from their accounts. Representatives at such financial institutions and businesses are trained to make sure that persons purporting over the telephone to be account holders appear to fit the account holder's profile. So if an account holder is female, the screener is supposed to make sure that the caller does in fact sound like a woman.

Through their website, the two provided the services of English- and German-speaking individuals to persons who had stolen account and biographical information to defeat the security screening processes. They would pose as authorized account holders and place telephone calls to financial institutions and other businesses to conduct or confirm fraudulent withdrawals, transactions, or other account activity on behalf of the website users who were identity thieves. Using information provided by the identity thieves over the website, which was hosted on a computer in Lithuania, the fraudulent callers would, among other things, confirm unauthorized withdrawals or transfers from bank accounts, unblock accounts, or change the address or phone number associated with an account so that it could be accessed by the identity thieves. After the requested call was made, the co-conspirators would report the results to the identity thief, who, if necessary, could issue instructions for further telephone calls.

Both were eventually arrested. One by Czech enforcement authorities who extradited him to the United States where in 2010 he pled guilty to a variety of charges. That same year, Belarusian authorities arrested his partner and Lithuanian law enforcement authorities seized the computers on which the website was hosted. Belarusian authorities also arrested additional co-conspirators for related criminal conduct (FBI press release, February 23, 2011).

In 2011, the federal government announced—with a great deal of fanfare—indictments and arrests of 130 members and associates of the American Mafia. An examination of these indictments revealed that the defendants were involved in crimes typically associated with the American Mafia, for example gambling, loansharking, labor racketeering. There was no mention of technically savvy activities associated with cyber-crime.

LOANSHARKING (USURY)

The generally negative view of money lending is highlighted by the Bible, which cautions against charging interest—*neshek* (to "bite"): "If thou lend money to any of My people, even to the poor with thee, thou shalt not be to him as a creditor; neither shall ye lay upon him interest" (*Exodus* 22: 24); "And if thy brother be waxen poor … thou shalt not give him thy money upon interest nor give him thy victuals for increase" (*Leviticus* 25: 36–37). However, "unto a foreigner thou mayest lend upon interest; but upon thy brother thou shalt not lend upon interest." Thus, the Hebrews could not charge interest on a loan to another Hebrew.[2] Later, the Church adopted a strict interpretation: Christians could not charge interest on loans to other Christians, even for business purposes. This prohibition created problems for commercial enterprises and led to a paradoxical situation.

Within organized Jewish communities, the Hebrew Free Loan Society developed to loan money to Jews without interest—personal loans—and laws and regulations restricting the ability of Jews to purchase land and enter guilds resulted in Jews becoming moneylenders to Christians. William

---

2. According to the Talmud (*Baba Metzia* 5: 4), even though charging interest on personal loans is prohibited, Jews can lend money to other Jews for business purposes and receive an equity stake in the enterprise.

PAYDAY LOANS

The current form of salary lending, frequently known as "payday loans," takes advantage of people who are willing to pay high interest rates to get small, short-term loans, which many banks no longer offer. The payday lender accepts a postdated check that is deposited after a specified period, usually two weeks. In states that do not have caps on interest, rates can be in excess of 500 percent annually. Most borrowers, however, repay the loans in one or two weeks. In Chicago, which has hundreds of payday loan outlets, the common rate is $10 per week for every $100 borrowed—it would be cheaper to borrow from a New York loan shark whose rates are typically 2 to 5 percent a week. Although the payday loan is usually less than $500, some persons become dependent on the loans or take out too many from several outlets at one time (Wahl 1999b, 2000). Some states have caps on interest rates—in New York it is 25 percent a year or 16 percent on person-to-person loans. In 2006, Congress capped rates for payday loans to military personnel at 36 percent (Driehaus 2008).

Shakespeare's character Shylock, in the *Merchant of Venice* (1596), is based on this historical irony. Shakespeare depicted the unsavory Shylock as a money-lending Jew demanding a pound of flesh from a hapless borrower as repayment for a delinquent loan. At the time Shakespeare was writing, there were no Jewish moneylenders in England—Jews had been expelled from that country by Edward I in 1290, and they did not return until the 1650s. And Shakespeare's father had twice been accused of violating usury laws (Greenblatt 2004). The name "Shylock" reportedly became slurred by illiterate criminals into "shark," and the term *loan shark* was born. As noted earlier, the Hebrew term for interest is *neshek*, to bite, something for which sharks are noted.

Between 1880 and 1915 a practice known as "salary lending" thrived in the United States. This quasi-legal business provided loans to salaried workers at usurious rates. The collection of debts was ensured by having the borrower sign a variety of complicated legal documents that subjected him or her to the real possibility of being sued and losing employment. Through the efforts of the Russell Sage Foundation, states began enacting small-loan acts to combat this practice; Massachusetts was the first in 1911. These laws, which licensed small lenders and set ceilings on interest, eventually brought salary lending to an end; credit unions, savings banks, and similar institutions began to offer small loans. However, this also led to the wholesale entry of organized crime into the illicit credit business (Goldstock and Coenen 1978). Loansharking would prove to be a continuing source of profit for the gangsters who emerged out of Prohibition and for those who followed, well into the twenty-first century.

Loansharking embodies two central features: "The assessment of exorbitant interest rates in extending credit and the use of threats and violence in collecting debts" (Goldstock and Coenen 1978: 2). As Prohibition was drawing to a close, and with the onset of the Great Depression, persons in organized crime began searching for new areas of profit. These criminals found themselves in the enviable position of having a great deal of excess cash in a cash-starved economy, which gave them an important source of continued income. "Contemporary loansharking is marked by the dominance of organized crime. This pervasive influence is hardly surprising. Syndicate access to rich stores of capital allows the underworld to pour substantial amounts of cash into the credit market. The strength and reputation of organized operations lends credence to threats of reprisals, thus augmenting the aura of fear critical to success in the loansharking business. Moreover, organized crime's aversion to competition militates strongly against successful independent operations" (Goldstock and Coenen 1978: 4).

Persons in organized crime may insulate themselves from direct involvement in loansharking by using nonmember associates. For example, Gambino

Family soldier Tony Plate (Piatta) employed—actually funded—his associate Charles ("the Bear") Calise. Calise, in turn, employed others as lenders and collectors. The connection with Tony Plate gave the whole operation an umbrella of protection from other criminals and credibility to debtors. Without this connection, a borrower who is a "made guy" or associate of a crime Family could easily avoid paying back the loan, and violence used to collect the debt could bring retaliation from the Family.

Many loan sharks provide loans to other criminals. "There is strong evidence for specialization by loan sharks. Some deal with legitimate businessmen only, some with illegal entrepreneurs. One medium-level loan shark specialized in fur dealers, though he might make loans to other small businessmen. Some specialize in lending to gambling operators" (Rubinstein and Reuter 1978b: Appendix 3–5). Genovese Family soldier Joseph Valachi (Maas 1968) worked as a loan shark and reported that most of his customers were themselves involved in illegal activities such as numbers and bookmaking. Loan sharks "frequently provide capital for a bookmaker who is in financial difficulty" (Rubinstein and Reuter 1978b: 53).

Individual gamblers may also borrow from a loan shark who stays around card and dice games or accepts "referrals" from a bookmaker. In Chicago, the street crew headed by Sam Carlisi "would require that delinquent debtors obtain a juice loan at an interest rate of 5 percent per week to pay off the gambling debt" (*United States v. Carlisi* [1990]). In one New York case, a young gambler borrowed from a loan shark to pay his bookmaker. He continued to gamble and borrow and eventually was unable to pay his loan shark. As a result, he embarked on a series of illegal activities that led to a prison term. He ran high-stakes poker games, at which his wife played hostess, and secured fraudulent loans from numerous banks. On one occasion, he decided to use some of this money to continue gambling and missed his loan shark payment. He was severely beaten in a parking lot, leaving him with two black eyes and a broken nose. The loan shark obviously has methods of collection

not typically employed by other lending institutions. When a debtor fell behind on his juice payments to the brother of Chicago mob boss John DiFronzo, he was given an offer he could not easily refuse: grow marijuana. It became the largest indoor marijuana growing operation ever discovered in Illinois.

The case of Louis Bombacino, a collector for the Chicago Outfit's 26th Street crew, who routinely carried a firearm, vividly reveals the intimidation involved in loansharking. The government intercepted a telephone conversation between Bombacino and a debtor who indicated he could make no further payments. The debtor said he was afraid of the federal government because he had engaged in criminal activity to pay back the loan. Bombacino introduced his associate, "Pete," and the conversation went as follows:

BOMBACINO: Pete can be ten times worse than the "G" [federal government]. The "G" could only put you in jail; Pete could destroy your whole family. [He then put Pete on the phone. Pete made threats of violence against the debtor and his family, and then returned the phone to Bombacino.] I'm glad you talked to this guy, [because] this will be the same guy that'll probably come looking for you…. You know I love you like a brother. You know what? I don't need no more kids to adopt and you got three beautiful daughters. And I really love 'em, that's why I keep protecting you.

DEBTOR: What, what are they gonna do? They gonna kill me for that [paying late]?

BOMBACINO: Yeah, yeah. Ya know why?

DEBTOR: Why?

BOMBACINO: It ain't the money; it's the principle. The money don't mean a fuckin' thing.

In 1997, Bombacino pled guilty to racketeering and received a twelve-year sentence.

Loan sharks, however, are not in the "muscle" business; they are in the credit business, and thus "lend money to customers whom they expect will pay off and eventually return as customers again. The loan shark is not attempting to gain control of the customer's business" (Rubinstein and Reuter 1978b: Appendix 3–4). A loan shark obviously has the money to be in a legitimate business. Loansharking, however, requires very little time and can be engaged in by those with limited intelligence and skills—some persons in organized crime are very bright, but many others would lose an argument with a fire hydrant. Business ineptitude characterizes many a *mafioso*. In the American Mafia, there is even a term for those who have a difficulty making a living; they are derisively referred to as "brokesters."

But sometimes a loan shark finds himself involved with a debtor's business. Joseph Valachi lent money to a legitimate businessman, the owner of a dress and negligee company, and became a partner when the loan could not be repaid. With Valachi's financial backing, however, and his ability to keep labor unions from organizing the factory, the business prospered (Maas 1968). Research into loansharking in New York revealed that collection rarely involves violence or even the threat of violence: "Loan sharks are interested in making credit assessments in the manner of legitimate lenders. Often they secure collateral for the loan, though it may be in an illiquid form. Sometimes a borrower will have to produce a guarantee. In many cases the loan is very short term, less than a month, and collection is simply not an issue. Repeat business is the backbone of those operations we have studied. A good faith effort to make payments will probably guarantee the borrower against harassment, particularly if he has made substantial payment of interest before he starts to have repayment problems" (Rubinstein and Reuter 1978b: Appendix 4).

There are two basic types of usurious loan: the *knockdown* and the *vig*. The knockdown requires a specified schedule of repayment, including both principal and interest. For example, $1,000 might be repaid in fourteen weekly installments of $100. The vig is a "six-for-five" loan: for every $5

borrowed on Monday, $6 is due on the following Monday. The $1 interest is called *vigorish* or *juice*, and loansharking is frequently referred to as the "juice racket." If total repayment of the vig loan, principal plus interest, is not forthcoming on the date it is due, the borrower must pay the interest, and the interest is compounded for the following week. Thus, for example, a loan of $100 requires repayment of $120 seven days later. If this is not possible, the borrower must pay the vig, $20, and this does not count against the principal or the next week's interest. The debt on an original loan of $100 will increase to $120 after one week, to $144 after two weeks, to $172.80 after three weeks, to $207.36 after four weeks, and so on.

The insidious nature of the vig loan is that the borrower must keep paying interest until the principal plus the accumulated interest is repaid at one time. It is quite easy for the original loan to be repaid many times without actually decreasing the principal owed. The loan shark is primarily interested in a steady income and is quite willing to let the principal remain outstanding for an indefinite period.

FENCING

The fence provides a readily available outlet for marketing stolen ("hot") merchandise. He thus provides an incentive for thieves and may also organize, finance, and direct their operations. In her research on fences, Marilyn Walsh (1977: 13) found that about 13 percent of the fences she studied were part of organized crime. "For these individuals fencing appeared to be just another enterprise in a varied and totally illegal business portfolio." In addition to fencing, she notes, these persons were active in loansharking and gambling, and some were enforcers. Genovese Family member Anthony ("Figgy") Ficcorata, for example, forced jewel thieves to deal only with certain fences, from whom Ficcorata would receive a commission (Abadinsky 1983). In Chicago, eight independent burglars "were murdered for refusing to dispose of their loot through syndicate-connected fences" (Nicodemus and Petacque 1981: 5). In

1997, an FBI sting resulted in the videotaping of members and associates of a Gambino Family crew in Canarsie, Brooklyn, disposing of $6 million worth of stolen merchandise, much of it hijacked over a two-year period (Raab 1997b). Because of his connection to a wide variety of criminals and (otherwise) legitimate businessmen, the wiseguy is in a unique position to arrange for the disposition of stolen goods.

COMMERCIAL SEX

Organized crime's involvement in sex as a business has changed with the times. House prostitution (whorehouses or bordellos) was an important social phenomenon during the days of large-scale immigration; immigrants were most often unattached males, single or traveling without their wives (Light 1977). Commercial sex, usually confined to infamous vice ("red light") districts in urban areas, was a target of social and religious reformers. The campaign against this activity became known as the war on the "white slavery" trade, which at the turn of the century was an international problem. In a book entitled *War on the White Slave Trade* (Bell 1909: 48), Edwin W. Sims, U.S. attorney for Chicago, states: "The recent examination of more than two hundred 'white slaves' by the office of the United States district attorney at Chicago has brought to light the fact that literally thousands of innocent girls from the country districts are every year entrapped into a life of hopeless slavery and degradation because parents in the country do not understand conditions as they exist and how to protect their daughters from the 'white slave' traders who have reduced the art of ruining young girls to a national and international system."

In 1904, an international treaty was signed in Paris by all of the governments of Western Europe and Russia. The respective governments, as the treaty preamble states, were "desirous to assure to women who have attained their majority and are subjected to deception or constraint, as well as minor women and girls, an efficacious protection against the criminal traffic known under the name of trade in white women (*Traite des Blanches*)." The U.S. Senate ratified the treaty in 1908. In 1910, the "White Slave Act," called the Mann Act after its sponsor, Congressman James R. Mann of Illinois, prohibited the interstate transportation of women "for the purpose of prostitution, or debauchery or for any other immoral purpose." Nevertheless, the practice flourished. Later we will look at criminal organizations involved in global trade in sex workers, a situation paralleling that which led to the Paris treaty of 1904.

In the United States, there was an elaborate system for procuring and transporting women between New York, Milwaukee, St. Louis, and Chicago (Landesco 1968). The constant transfer of women provided "new faces" and was good for business. The syndicates that dominated the trade included one headed by Big Jim Colosimo and Johnny Torrio in Chicago. Madams opened brothels, attracted prostitutes and customers, and secured protection from the police. The most famous of these establishments was owned and operated by the Everleigh sisters, who left their brutal husbands in Kentucky and traveled to the Windy City at the turn of the century. In 1900, the two sisters opened the lavish Everleigh Club in the downtown area. Despite the high cost of political protection, the establishment netted $10,000 a month, a significant sum in those days. The club was closed in a flush of reform in 1911 (Washburn 1934). The madam also acted as a "housemother," preventing quarrels and providing advice; she was both friend and employer: "Her work made it almost inevitable that she would assume traditionally maternal functions" (Winick and Kinsie 1971: 98).

Organized crime's interest in prostitution waned during Prohibition because money could be made more easily in bootlegging. With Prohibition drawing to a close, and with the advent of the Great Depression, organized crime groups began looking for new areas of income. In many cities they "organized" independent brothels: The madams were forced to pay organized crime middlemen for protection from the police and from violence.

Normalization of the gender ratio and changes in sexual mores led to a reduction in the importance of house prostitution. The brothel industry reached its peak in 1939. During World War II, and more significantly after 1945, the importance of brothels as a source of income for organized crime steadily declined but did not entirely disappear (Winick and Kinsie 1971). Organized crime members may organize or finance or be involved in an extortionate relationship with the proprietors of commercial sex establishments, ranging from brothels to bars that feature sexually explicit entertainment. In some of the Chicago suburbs, such establishments pay "street taxes" to the Outfit for the privilege of operating. And there is also pornography.

The pornography business, like prostitution, suffers from a great deal of "amateur" involvement. Pornography, which at one time was under the almost exclusive control of organized crime, is widely available throughout the United States. Liberal court decisions have virtually legalized the genre and legitimate entrepreneurs have entered the market. In Los Angeles, the entire hierarchy of the Dragna crime Family was convicted of, among other crimes, extorting money from the owners of porn shops. Because they were no longer illegitimate entrepreneurs, porn operators in Los Angeles were able to go to the authorities and complain about the extortion attempt.

TRAFFICKING IN PERSONS, ARMS, AND COUNTERFEIT PRODUCTS

As noted in Chapter 1, the globalization of organized crime has greatly expanded the portfolios of criminal organizations, particularly trafficking in persons, arms, and counterfeit products.

Trafficking in Persons

Trafficking in persons (TIP) "is a form of modern-day slavery" (Women's Bureau 2002: 1). "Traffickers often prey on individuals who are poor, frequently unemployed, or underemployed, and who may lack access to social safety nets. Victims are often lured by traffickers with false promises of good jobs and better lives, and then forced to work under brutal and inhumane conditions" (*Attorney General's Annual Report to Congress and Assessment of U.S. Government Activities to Combat Trafficking in Persons*, 2010: 1). TIP "involves the use of violence, threats or deception to create a pliant and exploitable work force" (UNODC 2010: 39) and includes two broad categories: (1) indenture of undocumented workers who are brought into bonded servitude; and (2) trade in persons for the commercial sex industry. Both often involve the manipulation of persons with promises of legitimate employment. According to U.S. federal law, "human trafficking involves the recruitment, harboring, transportation, provision, or obtaining of a person for the purposes of forced labor or services through means of force, fraud, or coercion. Sex trafficking occurs when a commercial sex act is induced by force, fraud, or coercion, or when the person induced to perform such acts is under the age of 18" (Office for the Victims of Crime n.d. 9).

Trafficking differs from *alien smuggling,* which seeks short-term gain by aiding undocumented persons to gain entry to a country—the relationship with the smuggler ends when the alien reaches his or her destination; human trafficking seeks a continuing exploitive relationship. "In that sense, the smuggling of individuals violates the rights of the state, while human trafficking amounts to the violation of human rights" (Väyrynen 2003: 1).

Organized crime groups facilitate alien smuggling by providing services. Those who can afford it may buy the "full packet solution," in which most or all aspects of their journey are preplanned and coordinated, although local actors may be contracted to provide services within their own domains. Other migrants make use of organized crime assistance piecemeal, engaging with different groups at the various stages of their journey (UNODC 2006). However, what begins as smuggling can become trafficking: women who "begin their trip voluntarily may become victims at the delivery stage, when their illegal status is exploited by those seeking cheap labor. If the smuggling is part of an organized activity, the smuggler may deliver the smuggled individual directly into the sex trade or another form of forced labor. In this case, the individual is both smuggled and trafficked" (Newman 2006: 11).

Trafficking organizations prey on individuals who are poor, often women who are lured with false promises of good jobs and better lives and, instead, are forced to work under brutal conditions. Under federal law, the technical term is "severe forms of trafficking in persons." In the United States, the government estimates that approximately 50,000 women and children are trafficked annually. In Europe, the victims of human trafficking are not only from the most economically deprived and socially and politically unstable areas, but also typically belong to the most disadvantaged social and economic groups in these areas (Lehti and Aromaa 2003).

As Louise Shelley (2010: 3) points out, "For organized crime groups, human beings have one added advantage over drugs: they can be sold repeatedly. In drug trafficking organizations, profits flow to the top of the organization. With the small-scale entrepreneurship that characterizes much of human trafficking, however, more profits go to individual criminals—making this trade more attractive for all involved."

Most trafficking cases follow the same pattern:

People are abducted or recruited in the country of origin, transferred through transit regions, and then exploited in the destination country. People may also be trafficked internally, that is, within the borders of their own country. Trafficking victims include agricultural workers who are brought into the United States, held in crowded unsanitary conditions, threatened with violence if they attempt to leave, and kept under constant surveillance; child camel jockeys in Dubai who are starved to keep their weight down; Indonesian women who may be drawn to a domestic service job in another country, are not paid for their work and are without the

resources to return home; child victims of commercial sexual exploitation in Thailand; and child soldiers in Uganda. (Government Accounting Office 2006: 18)

"Smuggling and trafficking groups have been major beneficiaries of globalization because they have simultaneously exploited advanced technology, the diminution of state control over territory and citizens, and the growing international illicit economy" (Shelley 2010: 138). They are "logistics specialists who can move individuals across vast distances. They often require numerous safe houses along the way where they can lodge their human cargo until it is safe to move them. Frequently the route is not the most direct because traffickers know to avoid policed roads, border checkpoints, and jurisdictions where there is efficient and honest law enforcement" (Shelley 2010: 92). In contrast to drugs, "human cargo must be fed and housed in transit and delivered in 'serviceable' condition" (Shelley 2010: 100). And in contrast to drug trafficking, women frequently play a commanding role in human trafficking (Shelley 2010).

Central to trafficking in persons is the "principle of captivity, applied upon arrival, through seizure of travel documents such as passports and tickets of the trafficked person" (Truong 2003: 62). Wages may be withheld until the employer recovers an advance and the victim is without papers or funds. Trafficking organizations operate through a specialized network of persons—recruitment, passage, documents, workplace—and those at the front end may not even know those at the receiving end (Truong 2003). Violence is frequently used to control victims.

Trafficking in persons has two broad categories, forced labor and sex trafficking. *Forced labor* involves the use of deceit and/or coercion to facilitate an involuntary status akin to slavery. "Trafficking for the purpose of forced labour appears to be limited to labour-intensive enterprises with rigid supply curves: typically, the so called *dirty, dangerous or demeaning* jobs" (UNODC 2010: 41). "It is not the same as situations merely involving low wages or poor working conditions, or lack of choice due to economic necessity. It represents a severe violation of human rights, and restriction of freedom" (F. David 2010: 7).

Because they are out of sight of the authorities (though often in plain view of local communities), sweatshops and other forms of forced labor invariably fail to meet health and safety regulations. Substandard housing and working conditions are associated with increased illness and injury in these populations. In addition to being beaten and starved, women may be made to work long hours without breaks, or forced to work in hazardous or polluted environments. Even in locations where the presence and employment of undocumented immigrants is known, enforcement of health, safety, and labor regulations is at best sporadic. (Newman 2006: 6–7)

In sex trafficking:

[Women] are so isolated from the community that their clients and handlers physically abuse them with impunity, subjecting them to repeated rape and assault. They also deny them prenatal care or medical care in case of pregnancy, infections or injury, and force them to have abortions. Having no recourse, the women are forced to comply with client demands, the majority of whom, research has shown, refuse to use condoms. Thus, the spread of HIV and other sexually transmitted disease is more likely. Furthermore, women are induced into heavy alcohol and drug use as a means of ensuring their continued dependency on their traffickers. (Newman 2006: 6)

Debt is one of the most common means of control. A woman must pay her expenses from future earnings, and the debt is passed from one trafficker to the next until she ends up in the destination country. Inflated housing and living expenses soon leave the victim unable to pay off the debt. Her earnings are taken and the woman becomes totally dependent on her exploiters because she has no financial means to escape. It is also normal to confiscate passports and travel papers. In most European countries, it is almost impossible for the victims to avoid immediate deportation, and that effectively prevents the women from approaching the authorities even in the most aggravated cases of abuse (Lehti and Aromaa 2003).

Alicia Peters (2011: 17) notes, however, that few victims fit the trafficking stereotype most often portrayed as the innocent young girl who has been lured into the sex industry against her will. "Even in cases of forced commercial sex, the majority of women are aware that they will be working in prostitution, but are deceived about the conditions or are later exploited." James Finckenauer and Ko Lin Chin (2011: 149) report that economic factors are the driving force behind whatever choices the women made. Most "made a choice that seemed good enough for them under the circumstances."

Child sex tourism (CST) is a dark side of globalization, with some two million children exploited in the global commercial sex trade. CST involves people who travel from their own country to another to engage in commercial sex acts with children. Tourists typically travel to developing countries looking for anonymity and the availability of children in prostitution. The crime is typically fueled by weak law enforcement, corruption, and poverty in many tourist destinations and, increasingly, technology that facilitates this predatory behavior.

The explosion of the Internet and the growing use of digital cameras and cell phone cameras have given perpetrators additional tools to victimize children. Predators are going online to share stories, trade child pornography, and plan sex tours. Sex tourists use chat rooms, message boards, peer-to-peer file-sharing servers, newsgroups, and specialized websites to obtain information on potential destinations. One disturbing activity is the establishment of "cyber-sex" dens where some children may be sexually abused by a foreign pedophile and the images beamed via a webcam to the Internet. Payment to watch these live "shows" is often made by a credit card via an Internet connection (U.S. Department of State information).

While human trafficking can be accomplished by individual amateurs or small "mom and pop" operations, large-scale international trafficking in women for the sex industry is a characteristic of modern transnational organized crime. Involvement may simply be part of a broad business portfolio for such groups as the Moscow-based *Solntsevo* (discussed in Chapter 9), the Mafia, Camorra, *'Ndrangheta,* and *Sacra Corona Unita* of southern Italy, Albanian clans, and Japan's *yakuza* (Williams 2006). In the Ukraine, for example, the highly organized criminal networks that traffic in women "are also involved in other criminal activities. They traffic drugs, stolen cars, and guns; conduct robberies; and are frequently involved in murders or contract killings" (Hughes and Denisova 2001: 47).

In the states of the former Soviet Union and the volatile Balkans region, women are recruited for lawful foreign employment only to find themselves in the hands of criminals who force them into the sex trade (Hughes and Denisova 2001). As part of a nefarious web that spreads across the Balkans and into Western Europe, "tens of thousands of women have been caught up by the traffickers and have suffered rape, extreme violence and slavery at the hands of criminal groups renowned for their brutality and greed" (Gall 2001: 1). Even traditional enemies such as Albanians and Slavs readily deal with one another in this trade. Women are recruited through ads in newspapers, magazines, and the Internet offering employment as dancers, waitresses, maids, and babysitters in nonspecified Western countries. Russian organized criminal groups engaged in human trafficking are reported to adopt particularly harsh methods of control. Often, before being presented to clients, women are raped by the traffickers themselves in order to initiate the cycle of abuse and degradation. Some women are drugged to prevent them from escaping (UNODC 2010).

Many countries grant "artistic" or "entertainer" visas that facilitate the movement and exploitation of trafficking victims. Women are granted these temporary visas upon presentation of a work contract or offer of engagement by a club owner, proof of financial resources, and/or medical test results. Employment agencies, often licensed under the laws of the origin and destination countries, play a key role in the deception and recruitment of these women. On arrival at their destination, victims are stripped of their passports and travel documents and forced into situations of sexual exploitation or bonded servitude. Having overstayed or otherwise violated the terms of the visa, victims are coerced by their exploiters with threats to turn them over to immigration authorities (U.S. Department of State 2004).

People in the Balkans find it inherently attractive to travel abroad, and although the women in general are aware that the offers for certain types of work abroad in reality means prostitution, a nonspecified number of women are nevertheless misled. The women who are aware that they are going to work as prostitutes consider present living conditions and earning potential as considerably poorer than the prospects held out to them by the sex trade (Task Force on Organized Crime in the Baltic Sea Region 2001). Thus, even in the absence of deception and physical coercion, "trafficking must be seen as part of the world-wide feminization of poverty and of labour migration. When women are structurally denied access to the formal and regulated labour market, they are increasingly pushed into unprotected or criminalized labour markets, such as sexual and exploitive domestic work" (International Organization for Migration 1998: 14).

In Southern and Eastern Europe kidnapping is rare, and traffickers instead exploit the desire to emigrate for well-paying employment: "At recruitment, traffickers generally promise traditionally female service sector jobs, such as waitress, salesperson, domestic worker and au pair/babysitter. However, recruiters also often adapt to the local labour market, promising work similar to that offered by legal agencies, thereby deflecting suspicion." They frequently "use contracts and legal documentation as a means of deflecting concerns about trafficking and masking the intended exploitation" (Surtees 2008: 50, 51). In Albania, women are frequently recruited through promises of marriage that never materializes. Traffickers often use legal travel documents to move victims who do not realize the real purpose of their trips. The documents are subsequently confiscated, making it difficult for the victim to escape (Surtees 2008).

Human trafficking is a serious problem in Myanmar, where transnational criminal organizations and the country's ruling military junta are at the center of the trade. More than one-quarter of Myanmar's population lives below the poverty line, making the country one of the poorest in Southeast Asia. Many victims of transnational crime in Myanmar are the poor, becoming commodities themselves as they are trafficked to be child soldiers for the junta or slaves for sexual exploitation. Junta officials are directly involved in trafficking for forced labor and the unlawful conscription of child soldiers. Women and girls, especially those of ethnic minority groups and those among the thousands of refugees along Myanmar's borders, are trafficked for sexual exploitation in urban centers and commercial centers, truck stops, border towns, and mining and military camps (Wyler 2007).

In West Africa, Nigerians have been at the center of a flourishing trade in prostitutes who are sent to Europe, especially Italy, and the Middle East. Organizers are often women, sometimes former prostitutes themselves, who have succeeded in making money and graduating to the status of madams, although they depend on men for forging travel documents and escorting the girls to their destination. Many girls initiated into prostitution are obliged to undergo quasi-traditional religious rituals that bind them to secrecy before being provided with forged papers and sent abroad, often via other West African countries. They may be initiated into their new trade through rape and other violence.

Nigerian victims report that acquaintances, close friends, or family members play a major role in their recruitment that frequently occurs in the victim's own home. "Nigerian trafficking is characterized by a debt bondage scheme. Victims trafficked into Europe (Italy, the Netherlands, Belgium, Spain, and others) are forced to pay back inflated smuggling fees. Victims mainly travel to Europe by plane from Lagos or other international airports from West Africa. Victims may also have been transported by land and sea across the Mediterranean. The vast majority of West African women and girls are exploited in street prostitution" (UNODC 2010: 46).

Successful madams organize the recruitment of prostitutes in West Africa, often on the pretext that they will find jobs in agriculture or the hotel business in Europe, and procure false or forged travel documents. They bribe immigration officials, both in Nigeria and in transit countries. The madam has a network of operators of hotels or hostels and guides, referred to as "trolleys"; she will use fetish priests, who administer an oath of secrecy on prospective prostitutes, and lawyers who can draft agreements binding a prostitute to a madam. Typically, a madam will claim to have invested $40,000 to $50,000 for the costs of travel to Europe, and the prostitute is required to repay that money (UNODC 2005).

Trafficking can also involve body parts for use in transplant operations. "A criminal who is part of a larger network may pair a poor individual from a developing country with an affluent buyer of his organ. They meet in a country with a loosely regulated hospital system where there is little control over hospital procedures" (Shelley 2010: 16).

Trafficking in Arms

Illicit trafficking in firearms is linked to other forms of organized crime, as well as terrorism. Organized crime groups facilitate the illegal trade of weapons and ammunition to armed groups in conflict and post-conflict areas and urban gangs, especially in Africa and Latin America, where such groups are becoming increasingly militarized. "Further, drug trafficking generates a demand for illegal arms and creates an international infrastructure that can also be used for arms trafficking. Firearms are linked to other global crimes in multiple ways: shared trafficking routes, use of the same distribution networks and money-laundering infrastructure and the exchange of guns for drugs or other commodities" (United Nations 2010: 2).

Trafficking of firearms is unlike many of the other forms of trafficking because firearms are durable goods and a well-maintained AK-47 will last indefinitely. As a result, there is little need for a continuous contraband flow. In addition, the modern pistol or assault rifle represents a mature technology, so current weapons holders do not need to regularly update their stock. There has been very little innovation in small arms design in the last fifty years; there are few ways to make small arms more accurate or more deadly than they are today. For example, the accuracy of the popular .45 caliber semi-automatic pistol known as the "1911," the year it was first offered for sale, is affected only after firing about 30,00 rounds. Consequently, the number of new small arms purchased each year is about 1 percent of those already in circulation. Thus, arms trafficking tends to be episodic, often from an established stockpile to a region descending into crisis (UNODC 2010).

The extent and type of weaponry available to terrorists and other criminals are enormous. These groups exploit and develop local, regional, and global supply channels to traffic in munitions and equipment worldwide. "Their access to weaponry is facilitated through covert transfers by governments and by legal and quasi-legal commercial dealers, outright black-market sales, and the theft or diversion of both state-owned and privately owned arms and weapons stores" (Cragin and Hoffman 2003: iii).

There are two basic explanations for the affinity of organized crime for arms trafficking: They have already established routes for drug and human trafficking, and the obvious need for firearms. Thus, "parallel to, and closely associated with illicit arms trafficking, is increasing trafficking in drugs, people and other contraband, as organized criminal gangs employ the same routes and partnerships to smuggle various illicit commodities across Europe" (Davis, Hirst, and Mariani 2001: 5). The movement of drugs and arms is often connected or overlapping (Curtis and Karacan 2002). The vessels and vehicles that deliver arms can carry drugs on their return,

and vice-versa. While arms smuggling involves institutions and individuals who are not parts of criminal organizations—national defense ministries, national security agencies, banks, legitimate arms dealers—both terrorist and organized crime groups are active participants. Organized crime groups often act as middlemen facilitating the illegal trade in arms.

The dissolution of the Soviet Union and the Warsaw Pact left vast stockpiles of arms. Ineffective inventory monitoring, export controls, and official corruption have made such stockpiles available to arms traffickers, helping to fuel armed conflict in the Caucasus and nearby Balkans. This has served to attract established criminal organizations looking to take advantage of the profits to be made in arms trafficking. Russian and Italian criminal organizations have operated in the midst of the conflicts in the former Yugoslavia, and weapons from the Balkans have been used by terrorist organizations such as the Basque Fatherland and Liberty Organization (ETA) and the Real Irish Republican Army (Curtis and Karacan 2002; Davis, Hirst, and Mariani 2001).

During the Cold War governments on both sides of the Iron Curtain used private arms brokers to facilitate covert arms deals. Vast stockpiles of arms have their origins in the Cold War, supplied by the United States and the Soviet Union to proxy combatants (Cragin and Hoffman 2003). With the end of the Cold War, these brokers remained in the arms business in the void of communist or democratic ideologies. They use their existing networks that also serve to move drugs, diamonds, and other valuable commodities. To facilitate their enterprises, these brokers use legitimate or counterfeit documents and develop corrupt ties with government officials. They often disguise arms shipments as humanitarian aide and use circuitous routes through "friendly" transshipment countries (Stohl 2005).

"Terrorist groups from other parts of the world, especially Asia and Africa, have obtained significant armaments from traffickers based in Western Europe or using Western Europe as part of the delivery route" (Curtis and Karacan 2002: 6). Turkish/ Kurdish groups, criminal and terrorist—there is often overlap—have been part of a drugs-for-arms trade in Europe. Drugs from the Golden Crescent are exchanged for arms that remain part of the group's arsenal or are trafficked again: "Although illegal trafficking in arms frequently coexists with illegal trafficking in narcotics, the two activities do not necessarily have a symbiotic relationship; rather, conditions that promote one type of trafficking very often promote the other. Thus organized crime groups in Italy, Albania, and the former Yugoslavia trade in both types of commodity, taking advantage of available resources as well as favorable conditions. Often, narcotics and arms are items of exchange in a complex deal that involves third and fourth parties," and the exchange may also include diamonds and ivory (Curtis and Karacan 2002: 21).

In Latin America, arms dealers have been attracted to areas of conflict such as Nicaragua, El Salvador, Guatemala, and, of course, Colombia. Arms are stolen from military supplies and production facilities and move into the black market. The triborder area discussed in Chapter 1 is a source of illegal weapons. While the United States and Russia have dominated the small-arms market, this is no longer true. Indeed, most law enforcement officers in the United States are armed with foreign-made handguns, mostly Glock (Austrian), but also Beretta (Italian), and Sig Sauer (Swiss/German). Governments in Africa, Asia, and Latin America frequently manufacture their own small arms for security forces and also sell them to both legitimate merchants and less scrupulous "merchants of death" who can camouflage their enterprises within the network of legitimate arms trading (Cragin and Hoffman 2003).

In 2008, Thai authorities arrested a former Russian air force major who was the inspiration for the 2005 Nicholas Cage motion picture *Lord of War*. Victor Bout, 40, was the successful target of a U.S. Drug Enforcement Administration sting operation during which he offered an enormous supply of arms to undercover agents he believed to be representatives of Colombia's FARC guerillas. With his own airline, Bout supplied arms to, among other groups, the Taliban. This made him a high-priority target for the United States to which he was subsequently extradited.

The problem of illicit arms trafficking is complicated by the ambivalent position of the United States, a prominent supplier of small arms to volatile regions. "In doing so, it has at times bought and transported arms through the same gray networks and dealers that in Europe have been accused of illegal trafficking" (Chivers 2008b: 5).

The primary mechanism of international arms control is the "end user certificate," a document that verifies that the end user of the weaponry sold is a legitimate buyer and not an embargoed state or criminal/terrorist group. But much of the diversion of arms occurs after the delivery to the nominal end users, a practice known as "Post Delivery Onward Diversion." In these cases, corrupt elements within the named destination state are complicit. If all the paperwork is in place, there may be no legal reason for the vending state to refuse the request for export. Another method is "Point of Departure Diversion," where unauthorized or fake end user certificates provide arms traffickers with the documentation necessary to obtain arms export licenses. Rather than being delivered to the specified destination, the weapons are directly diverted to an embargoed state or group. "This technique only works when the exporting state is negligent or corrupt in verifying that the country named in the end user certificate has actually requested the arms—large-scale arms trafficking is dependent on corruption" (UNODC 2010: 144).

Traffickers and their support organizations are a diverse group, with some originating in countries with large arms surpluses, some in regions with stability problems, and some from wealthier nations. "Most are multilingual and hold a number of passports. They operate chains of shell companies and often own small fleets of surplus planes and other vehicles" (UNODC 2010: 144).

Trafficking in Counterfeit Products

A variety of categories are associated with counterfeit products, ranging from intellectual property, such as books, music, videos, and computer software, to brand-name and designer clothing, handbags, and

A FORTUNE, BUT NOT FORTUNE COOKIES

A shopkeeper in Italy placed an order for three thousand pairs of brand-name athletic footwear. The Chinese factory owner received a sample of authentic products from the shopkeeper that he took apart and "designed." One month later, the counterfeits were shipped to Italy. But the factory owner does not make the big money—"that's for the networks running importation and distribution" (Schmidle 2010: 41).

CHINA CONNECTION

In 2011, Chun-Yu Zhao, of Centreville, Virginia, and Donald H. Cone, of Frederick, Maryland, were convicted by a federal jury in Alexandria, Virginia, of importing and trafficking in counterfeit products. Zhao's family members in China operated a large-scale counterfeit computer-networking equipment business. She and her associates used a number of sophisticated schemes to defraud U.S.-based purchasers through a Virginia-based firm that also produced counterfeit Cisco software and created labels and packaging in order to mislead consumers into believing the products it sold were genuine. To evade detection, Zhao used various names and addresses in importation documents and hid millions of dollars of counterfeit proceeds through a web of bank accounts and real estate held in the names of her family members in China (U.S. Department of Justice press release, May 26, 2011).

jewelry, to pharmaceuticals. As Peggy Chaudhry and Alan Zimmerman (2009: 11) point out, "Counterfeiting is a major funding source for organized crime and terrorist organizations." Well-known criminal organizations are involved in the counterfeiting market: Triads, *yakuza*, Camorra, and the Russian Mafia. Product counterfeiting is particularly attractive to criminal organizations because the level of profitability is significant, similar to that found in the drug trafficking, but the level of risk is significantly lower—law enforcement tends to focus on drug trafficking—and penalties are less severe (Patrignani 2009). In 2011, for example, five members of a ring that mass-produced counterfeit music CDs and DVD movies received sentences ranging from probation to five years in prison (FBI Press Release). As the chief of the FBI's Asian/African Criminal Enterprise Unit notes, "the profits are high and the penalties are low" (Schmidle 2010: 41).

This appeal is enhanced by the relative logistical simplicity of the commerce itself: widespread distribution of technologies which allow for a faithful reproduction of name-brand products and the use of trade routes and synergies that were previously created by to manage other types of illegal trade. Pirates avoid the usual costs associated with research and development, quality control, competitive wages, and warranty service. There is also "split runs" by subcontractors who make legitimate products under contract while producing "after-hours" copies. Unfinished counterfeits may also be shipped to a free-trade zone, such as *Ciudad del Este*, for further processing, adding counterfeit trademarks, labels, and/or repackaging (Chaudhry and Zimmerman 2009).

Commerce of this nature, particularly on a large scale, can be efficiently managed only by large organizations that are also involved in other types of illegal trade such as drugs and weapons. The illegal distribution of counterfeit products therefore benefits from the existence of trade routes that have been previously and successfully exploited for other activities (Patrignani 2009).

With the advent of outsourcing, companies in developed countries research, design, and market products, while the actual manufacturing takes place in countries with a cheaper workforce. These manufacturing countries are generally poor with limited capacity for oversight. This is not usually a problem, because the licensing company provides quality control—shoddy workmanship or substandard materials mean loss of contracts and possibly legal action.

However, lack of regulatory oversight promotes unauthorized production. "Products in high demand can be manufactured based on the same or similar designs, often packaged and branded in ways to make them indistinguishable from the original. The counterfeit goods can then be sold through parallel markets, or even introduced into the licit supply chain. Without the overheads of the licit products, these counterfeits can be priced extremely competitively while remaining vastly more profitable" (UNODC 2010: 173). "Major counterfeit operators may set up legitimate businesses, such as clothing manufacturing or sales businesses, as fronts for counterfeit operations and sales. Some may be involved in licit import and export operations as well" (UNODC 2010: 179).

Central to much product counterfeiting is the scale and the nature of Chinese manufacturing which often involves a large number of small firms collaborating to produce a single product, leaving the country vulnerable to counterfeiting. The situation is similar to that found around Naples, where a large number of cottage industries have traditionally produced the world's *haute couture* alongside the world's best counterfeits. As noted in Chapter 5, Camorra clans have been actively trafficking in counterfeit goods. They "control thousands of Chinese factories contracted to manufacture fashion goods, legally and illegally, for distribution around the world" (Treverton et al. 2009: 60).

Human smuggling and product counterfeiting can be integrated by criminal organizations who compel clients to pay off their debts by peddling counterfeit DVDs as street vendors, in bars, flea markets, and similar outlets (Treverton, et al. 2009).

SUMMARY

1. Know the different types of relationship between organized crime and the providers of illegal goods and services:
   - The business of organized crime includes activities that are neither "goods" nor "services" but are parasitic.
   - The connection between organized crime and illegal business can be *Parasitic*, *Reciprocal*, or *Entrepreneurship*.
   - The boundary between providing a good or a service and being parasitic is not clearly delineated.
   - To understand the business of organized crime, we need to consider the degree to which a crime group's business activities are integrated into their organizational structure.

2. Understand the business of bookmaking and numbers/lottery and their relationship to organized crime:
   - The low priority given to gambling enforcement and the relatively light sentences make it attractive to organized crime.
   - To achieve equality between teams, a handicapping process takes place through the use of a *line* or *spread*, the expected point difference between the favored team and the underdog.
   - A layoff service can enable a bookmaker to balance his bets.
   - The legal lottery has benefited the illegal numbers business by promoting gambling and offering a method for laying off bets.

3. Know why organized crime is involved in cyber-crime:
    ■ Criminal organizations enjoy a capacity to launder various currencies, resources to employ quality hackers, the ability to quickly set up and coordinate dozens, if not hundreds, of persons in schemes that exploit "plastic money."

4. Appreciate why organized crime is uniquely suited for loansharking:
    ■ Organized crime success in loansharking is based on access to cash and reputation for violence.

5. Understand the changed role of organized crime in commercial sex:
    ■ The pornography business, like prostitution, suffers from a great deal of "amateur" involvement with little evidence of organized crime.

6. Know the role of organized crime in the global market for trafficked persons, arms, and counterfeit products:
    ■ Trafficking in persons includes two broad categories: (1) indenture of undocumented workers who are brought into bonded servitude; and (2) trade in persons for the commercial sex industry.
    ■ Organized crime involvement in the global trade in sex workers parallels that which led to the Paris treaty of 1904.

■ *Trafficking* differs from *alien smuggling* that seeks short-term gain by aiding undocumented persons to gain entry to a country.
■ Organized crime groups facilitate alien smuggling by providing services.
■ In contrast to drugs, human cargo must be fed and housed in transit.
■ In TIP, debt is one of the most common means of control.
■ Organized crime groups facilitate the illegal trade of weapons and ammunition to armed groups in conflict and post-conflict areas and urban gangs.
■ Trafficking of firearms is unlike many of the other forms of trafficking because firearms are durable goods and will last indefinitely.
■ Organized crime has an affinity for arms trafficking: It has already established routes for drug and human trafficking, and the obvious need for firearms.
■ The movement of drugs and arms is often connected or overlapping.
■ Product counterfeiting is attractive because the level of profitability is significant, but the level of risk is significantly lower as are penalties than are those for drug trafficking.

REVIEW QUESTIONS

1. What are the three forms that the connection between an illegal business and organized crime takes?

2. Why is the boundary between providing a good or a service and being parasitic often not clear?

3. How does the concept of *rispetto* enable a member of organized crime to act as an arbitrator?

4. Why is it often important for a professional criminal to have ties to organized crime?

5. Why is illegal gambling particularly attractive to organized crime?

6. In sports bookmaking, what is the purpose of the "line" or "spread"?

7. When do bookmakers require a layoff service?

8. How has the legal lottery benefited organized crime?

9. What advantages does organized crime have when engaging in cyber-crime?

10. What led to the wholesale entry of organized crime into loansharking?

11. Why is loansharking a logical business for organized crime?

12. Why are American Mafia members well situated to engage in fencing?

13. Why is there little involvement of organized crime in the business of pornography and prostitution?

14. What are the two broad categories of "trafficking in persons" (TIP)?

15. How does TIP differ from alien smuggling?

16. What is the role of organized crime in alien smuggling?

17. How does TIP differ from drug smuggling?

18. In TIP, what is a common means of control?

19. What explains the affinity of organized crime for arms trafficking?

20. How does trafficking of firearms differ from many of the other forms of trafficking?

21. Why is product counterfeiting attractive to organized crime?

Afghan villagers tend to opium poppies in Helmand province, in southern Afghanistan. © STRINGER/AFP/Getty Images

CHAPTER **12**

Organized Crime and Drug Trafficking

In the mist-shrouded mountains along the border between China and Myanmar, where the monsoon washes away roads linking villages without electricity or running water, heroin begins its long journey to North America. By the time it reaches the streets of America's cities, the heroin will have traveled through half a dozen countries, soared at least 5,000-fold in price, and changed hands a hundred times. A kilo that will ultimately sell for more than $200,000 wholesale in New York City costs as little as $2,500 in Myanmar. The real profits in heroin are all downstream, in transportation and distribution. The first fingers to touch it, though, belong to people such as a certain 36-year-old mother of seven. She and her husband begin the harvest by scoring each poppy pod with a needlelike knife. A creamy gum oozes from the cuts, and once it turns black, it is scraped off with a crescent-shaped tool that has been in her family for as long as she can remember. It is painstaking

CHAPTER 12 WILL ENABLE THE READER TO UNDERSTAND:

- Similarities between the drug business and legitimate business
- The history of drugs, drug trafficking, and how it has defied the "war on drugs"
- How nativism and hostility toward minorities influenced drug laws
- The connection between foreign policy and the drug trade
- The business of heroin and major producer regions
- The history and business of cocaine
- The different levels involved in the drug business, ranging from the international to the street
- Methamphetamine and methamphetamine trafficking
- Other trafficked drugs such as oxycodone, marijuana, barbiturates, Phencyclidine, Ecstasy, LSD, and designer drugs

277

work, and for their labor they earn $600 annually—barely enough to feed their children. Brokers come from the valley in early March to purchase the raw opium gum, which sells for about $135 a kilogram (Brzezinski 2002).

At the highest levels, drug trafficking is a global business requiring a great deal of organization—organized crime—that will be examined in this chapter.

International and domestic trafficking in illegal drugs is by any estimate a multibillion-dollar industry with enormous profit-to-cost ratios. Heroin, for example, can be purchased in 700-gram units in Bangkok, Thailand, for between $7,500 and $9,500 and sold in the United States for $60,000 to $70,000. Because the product is illegal but nevertheless in great demand, drug trafficking is characterized by a level of free enterprise that Adam Smith never envisioned: a market totally devoid of legal constraints in which prices and profits are governed only by the law of supply and demand.

Sylvia Longmire (2011: 10) notes that drug "cartels are run like profit-seeking corporations; so when the market makes a move, so do they." She points out that "over the years, they have shown an amazing ability to adjust to changing drug-consumer tastes and increasing law enforcement initiatives." Mexican and Colombia cartels "keep a constant finger on the pulse of U.S. demand for drugs in order to keep their biggest consumer happy."

The business of illegal drugs shares some elements with the business of selling legal products: "It requires lots of working capital, steady supplies of raw materials, sophisticated manufacturing facilities, reliable shipping contractors and wholesale distributors, the all-important marketing arms and access to retail franchises for maximum market penetration" (Brzezinski 2002: 26). As in any major industry there are various functional levels: manufacturers, importers, wholesalers, distributors, retailers, and consumers. Workers in the drug business range from leaders of powerful international cartels to street dealers whose activities support a personal drug habit. At the manufacturing and importation levels, the drug business is concentrated among a relatively small group of people who head major

trafficking organizations; at the retail level, it is filled with a large, fluctuating, and open-ended number of dealers and consumers.

Drugs are smuggled into the United States from both source and transshipment countries. Traffickers may use circuitous routes to avoid the suspicion that is normally generated by shipments from source countries. Cocaine, for example, may be shipped from Colombia to Africa and move from there to Europe and the United States as part of legitimate maritime cargo. Indeed, "traffickers are increasingly using Africa, both east and west, to smuggle cocaine from Latin America into Europe" (Lacey 2006: 4; *Cocaine Trafficking in West Africa* 2007; *World Drug Report* 2008). Pleasure crafts and fishing vessels blend in with normal maritime traffic, and low-profile vessels made of wood or fiberglass and measuring up to forty feet in length are difficult to spot and do not readily appear on radar. Smugglers also use aircraft, landing on isolated runways and even highways or dropping their cargo from the air. "In addition to the forty-three legitimate border crossing points, the Southwest border includes thousands of miles of open desert, rugged mountains, the Rio Grande River, and maritime transit lanes into California and Texas" (Office of National Drug Control Strategy 2009b: 13).

Motor vehicles use land routes across Canada and Mexico and onto Indian reservations bordering the United States. Often with the aid of Native American criminal groups, the traffickers then move the drugs across national borders into the United States for distribution (Kershaw 2006; National Drug Intelligence Center 2008a). The *Tohono O'odham Nation* reservation in Arizona straddles 75 miles of the U.S.–Mexican border and emerged as a major transit point for drug smuggling, particularly marijuana, a bulky product that cannot be safely smuggled through official border checkpoints. The once placid reservation is home to tribal members enticed by the financial rewards or fearful of declining the smuggler's offers (Eckholm 2010).

HISTORICAL BACKGROUND

To fully appreciate the relationship between drug trafficking and organized crime, it is necessary to examine the history of how drug trafficking, like bootlegging during the Prohibition era, became an important criminal enterprise. The earliest "war against drugs" in the United States was in response to opium, an analgesic (pain reliever) and central nervous system depressant that can provide relief from stress; its source is the *Papaver somniferum*, or opium poppy, of which there are many species. There is some dispute about when opium was first used. Wherever the poppy plant is found, the young leaves have been used as potherbs and in salads; its small, oily seeds are high in nutritional value. The seeds can be eaten; they can be pressed to release an edible oil, baked into cakes, and ground into flour, and the oil may be burned in lamps. As a source of vegetal fat, "the seed oil could have been a major factor attracting early human groups to the opium poppy" (Merlin 1984: 89). Wherever it was found, opium was used both medicinally and recreationally.

Explaining the popularity of opium is easy when we realize that the chief end of medicine until the beginning of the nineteenth century was to relieve pain. Therapeutic agents were directed at symptoms rather than causes. Therefore, "it is not difficult to understand the wide popularity of a drug which either singly or combined was so eminently suited to the needs of so many medical situations" (Terry and Pellens 1928: 58). At a time when the practice of medicine was quite primitive, opium became the essential ingredient in innumerable remedies dispensed in Europe and America for the treatment of diarrhea, dysentery, asthma, rheumatism, diabetes, malaria, cholera, fevers,

bronchitis, insomnia, and pain of any kind (Fay 1975).

As the primary ingredient in many "patent" medicines—actually, secret formulas that carried no patent at all—opiates were legal and readily available without prescription in the United States until 1914. Doctors and others provided them for general symptoms as well as for specific diseases. The smoking of opium was popularized by Chinese immigrants who brought the habit with them to California, which became a state in 1848. During the latter part of the nineteenth and early twentieth centuries, Chinese in the United States also operated commercial "opium dens" that often attracted the attention of the police, not because of the use of drugs but because they became gathering places for criminals.

Around the turn of the eighteenth century, a German pharmacist poured liquid ammonia over opium and obtained an alkaloid, a white powder that he found to be many times more powerful than opium. He named the substance *morphium* after Morpheus, the Greek god of sleep and dreams. Ten parts of opium can be refined into one part of morphine (Bresler 1980). It was not until 1817, however, that the publication of articles in scientific journals popularized the new drug, resulting in its widespread use by doctors. Quite incorrectly, as it turned out, the medical profession viewed morphine as an opiate without negative side effects.

By the 1850s, morphine tablets and a variety of morphine products were readily available without prescription. In 1856, the hypodermic method of injecting morphine directly into the bloodstream was introduced to American medicine. The popularity of morphine rose dramatically during the Civil War when it was used intravenously in an indiscriminate manner to treat battlefield casualties (Terry and Pellens 1928). Following the war, the increase in morphine use was so marked among ex-soldiers as to give rise to the term *army disease*. "Medical journals were replete with glowing descriptions of the effectiveness of the drug during wartime and its obvious advantages for peacetime medical practice" (Cloyd 1982: 21). Hypodermic kits became widely available, and the use of unsterile needles by many doctors and laypersons led to abscesses or disease (Morgan 1981).

In the 1870s, morphine was exceedingly cheap—cheaper than alcohol. Pharmacies and general stores carried preparations that appealed to a wide segment of the population. Physicians commonly prescribed morphine for any complaint, from a toothache to consumption and widely abused the substance themselves (Latimer and Goldberg 1981). Until the late 1870s, the concept of addiction was not widely known or understood (Morgan 1981). Although it eventually became associated with the underworld elements of urban America, morphine abuse in the latter part of the nineteenth century was apparently most prevalent in rural areas (Terry and Pellens 1928). In 1900 alone, 628,177 pounds of opiates were imported into the United States (Bonnie and Whitebread 1970).

At the turn of the twentieth century, diacetyl-morphine was synthesized, creating the most powerful of the opiates—*heroin*—marketed as a non-habit-forming analgesic to take the place of morphine (Bresler 1980; Nelson et al. 1982). Morphine, albeit now highly regulated, is available in the United States for the treatment of chronic pain. It is essential for treating traumatic battlefield injuries. Heroin, however, is an illegal substance without accepted medical use in the United States.

China and the Opium Wars

The American response to drugs in the twentieth century is directly related to international affairs and trade with China. Until the sixteenth century, China was a military power whose naval fleet surpassed any that the world had ever known. A power struggle ultimately led to a regime dominated by Confucian scholars. In 1525, they ordered the destruction of all oceangoing ships and set China on a course that would lead to poverty, defeat, and decline (Kristof 1999). In 1626, a British warship appeared off China and its captain bombarded Canton. In response to the danger posed by British ships, the emperor opened the city of Canton to trade.

The British East India Company enjoyed a government-granted monopoly over the China trade. Shipments of tea to England were particularly important. By the 1820s a trade imbalance existed between England and China. Although the British consumer had an insatiable appetite for Chinese tea, the Chinese desired few English goods. The exception was opium (Beeching 1975). Poppy cultivation had been an important source of revenue for the Mughal emperors (Muslim rulers of India, 1526–1857). When the Mughal empire fell apart, the British East India Company salvaged and improved upon the system of state control of opium. In addition to controlling the domestic market, the British supplied Indian opium to China.

Opium was first prohibited by the Chinese government in 1729, a time when only small amounts of the substance were reaching China. Years earlier, tobacco had been similarly banned as a pernicious foreign good. Opium use was strongly condemned in China as a violation of Confucian principles, and for many years the imperial decree against opium was supported by the population (Beeching 1975). In 1782, an attempt by a British merchant ship to sell 1,601 chests of opium resulted in a total loss, for no purchasers could be found. By 1799, however, a growing traffic in opium led to an imperial decree banning the trade.

The ban was not successful—official corruption was endemic in China. As consumption of imported opium increased and the method of ingestion shifted from eating to smoking, official declarations against opium increased, as did smuggling. "When opium left Calcutta, stored in the holds of country ships and consigned to agents in Canton, it was an entirely legitimate article. It remained an entirely legitimate article all the way up to the China Sea. But the instant it reached the coast of China, it became something different. It became contraband" (Fay 1975: 45).

Opium provided the British with silver needed to buy tea. Because opium was illegal in China, however, its importation—smuggling—brought China no tariff revenue. Before 1830, opium was transported to the coast of China, where it was offloaded and smuggled inland by the Chinese themselves. The outlawing of opium by the Chinese government led to the development of an organized underworld and Triads (discussed in Chapter 8) continue to smuggle heroin to destinations all over the world (Latimer and Goldberg 1981). The armed British opium ships were safe from Chinese government intervention, and the British were able to remain aloof from the actual smuggling.

In the 1830s the shippers grew bolder, entering Chinese territorial waters with their opium cargo. The British East India Company, now in competition with other opium merchants, sought to flood China with cheap opium and drive out the competition (Beeching 1975). In 1837, the emperor ordered his officials to move against opium smugglers, but the campaign was a failure and the smugglers grew even bolder. In 1839, in a dramatic move, Chinese authorities laid siege to the port city of Canton, confiscating and destroying all opium waiting offloading from foreign ships. The merchants agreed to stop importing opium into China, and the siege was lifted. The British merchants petitioned the Crown for compensation and retribution. The reigning parliamentary Whig majority, however, was very weak, and compensating opium merchants was not politically or financially feasible. Instead, the cabinet, without Parliament's approval, decided to wage a war that would result in the seizure of Chinese property (Fay 1975).

In 1840, a British expedition attacked the poorly armed and organized Chinese forces. The emperor was forced to pay $6 million for the opium his officials had seized and $12 million as compensation for the war, and Hong Kong became a crown colony. Opium was not mentioned in the peace (surrender) treaty, but the trade resumed with new vigor. By the mid-1840s, in a remarkable reversal of the balance of trade, China had a significant opium debt (Latimer and Goldberg 1981). In the wake of the First Opium War, China was laid open to extensive missionary efforts by Protestant evangelicals, who, although they opposed the opium trade, viewed saving souls as their primary goal. Christianity, they believed, would save China from opium (Fay 1975).

The Second Opium War began in 1856, when the balance of payments once again favored China. A minor incident between the British and Chinese governments was used as an excuse to force China into making further treaty concessions. This time, the foreign powers seeking to exploit a militarily weak China included France, Russia, and the United States. Canton was sacked, and a combined fleet of British and French warships sailed right up the Grand Canal to Peking and proceeded to sack and burn the imperial summer palace. The emperor was forced to indemnify the British in an amount more than enough to offset the balance of trade that had actually caused the war. A commission was appointed to legalize and regulate the opium trade (Latimer and Goldberg 1981). In the 1870s, the British opium monopoly in China was challenged by opium imported from Persia and cultivated in China itself. Because British colonial authorities were heavily dependent on a profitable opium trade, they increased the output of Indian opium. This caused a decline in prices, driving the competition out of business. This oversupply resulted in an increase in the amount of opium entering the United States for the Chinese population.

The "Chinese Problem" and the American Response

Chinese workers were originally encouraged to emigrate to the United States in 1848 to labor in the gold mines, doing dangerous work refused by most white men, such as blasting shafts, putting beams in place, and laying track lines in the mines. Chinese immigrants also helped build the Western railroad lines at "coolie wages"—pay few whites would accept. After their work was completed, Chinese were often banned from the area. By the 1860s they were clustering in Pacific Coast cities, where they established Chinatowns—and smoked opium.

In 1883, Congress raised the tariff on the importation of smoking-grade opium. In 1887, Congress responded to obligations imposed on the

United States by a Chinese–American commercial treaty by banning the importation of smoking opium by Chinese subjects. Americans were still permitted to import the substance, and many did so, selling it to both Chinese and U.S. citizens (PCOC 1986a). The typical American opiate addict during the nineteenth century was a middle-aged white woman of the middle or upper class (Courtwright 1982). Compared with the Chinese, however, this addict did not smoke opium but rather ingested it as medicine. During the nineteenth century, opiates were not associated in the public mind with crime. While opium use may have been frowned upon by some as immoral, employees were not fired for addiction, and children were not taken from their homes and lodged in foster homes or institutions because one or both parents were addicted. "Addicts continued to participate fully in the life of the community. Thus, the nineteenth century avoided one of the most disastrous effects of current narcotic laws and attitudes—the rise of a deviant addict subculture, cut off from respectable society and without a 'road back' to respectability" (Brecher 1972: 6–7).

Domestic anti-Chinese legislation raised the ire of China against the United States. In an effort to increase American influence in China, and thus improve its trade position, the United States supported antiopium efforts of the International Reform Bureau (IRB). A temperance organization representing more than thirty missionary societies in the Far East, the IRB sought a ban on opiates, which was also the position of the Chinese government. In 1901, Congress enacted the Native Races Act, which prohibited the sale of alcohol and opium to "aboriginal tribes and uncivilized races." The provisions of the act were later expanded to include "uncivilized elements" in the United States proper: Indians, Eskimos, and Chinese (Latimer and Goldberg 1981).

In 1898, as a result of the Spanish–American War, the Philippines were ceded to the United States. At the time of Spanish colonialism, opium smoking was widespread among Chinese workers on the islands. The Reverend Charles Henry Brent (1862–1929), a supporter of the IRB, arrived in the Philippines as the Episcopal bishop. His arrival coincided with a cholera epidemic that began in 1902 and that reportedly led to an increase in the use of opium. As a result of his efforts, in 1905 Congress banned the sale of opium to Filipino natives except for medicinal purposes and three years later banned sales to all Philippines residents. "Reformers attributed to drugs much of the appalling poverty, ignorance, and debilitation they encountered in the Orient. Opium was strongly identified with the problems afflicting an apparently moribund China. Eradication of drug abuse was part of America's white man's burden and a way to demonstrate the New World's superiority" (Morgan 1974: 32).

The Reverend Brent proposed the formation of an international opium commission to meet in Shanghai in 1909. This plan was supported by President Theodore Roosevelt, who saw it as a way to assuage Chinese anger over the 1882 Chinese Exclusion Act, a pernicious statute making it difficult if not impossible for Chinese to enter the United States and denying citizenship to those immigrants already in the country (Latimer and Goldberg 1981). The International Opium Commission, chaired by Brent and consisting of representatives from thirteen nations, convened in Shanghai on February 1. Brent successfully rallied the conferees around the American position that opium was evil and had no use outside of medical applications. The commission unanimously adopted a number of vague resolutions (Terry and Pellens 1928).

Only the United States and China, however, were eager for future conferences, and strong antiopium legislative efforts in the United States following the conference were generally unsuccessful. Southerners distrusted federal enforcement, and the drug industry was opposed to any new regulations. Attempts to gain Southern support for antidrug legislation focused on the purported abuse of cocaine by blacks, which reputedly made them "uncontrollable." On February 14, 1914, a *New York Times* headline screamed: "Negro Cocaine 'Fiends' Are a New Southern Menace." This caused many Southern police departments to change from

.32 caliber revolvers to more powerful .38 caliber revolvers (Kinder 1992).

A second conference was held in 1912 in The Hague, with representatives from the United States, China, and ten other nations. A number of problems stood in the way of an international agreement: Germany wanted to protect her burgeoning pharmaceutical industry and insisted on a unanimous vote before any action could be agreed upon; Portugal insisted on retaining the Macao opium trade; the Dutch insisted on maintaining their opium trade in the West Indies; Persia and Russia wanted to continue growing opium poppies. Righteous American appeals to the delegates were rebuffed with allusions to domestic usage and the lack of drug laws in the United States (Latimer and Goldberg 1981). Nevertheless, the conference resulted in a patchwork of agreements known as the International Opium Convention, which was ratified by Congress in 1913. The signatories committed themselves to enacting laws designed to suppress the abuse of opium, morphine, and cocaine, as well as any drugs prepared or derived from these substances (PCOC 1986a). In 1914, the Harrison Act, representing the U.S. attempt to carry out the provisions of The Hague Convention, was signed by President Woodrow Wilson.

Harrison Act

The Harrison Act provided that persons in the business of dealing in drugs covered by the act—opium, cocaine, and their derivatives—were required to register yearly and pay a special annual tax of $1. The statute made it illegal to sell or give away opium or opium derivatives and coca or its derivatives without a written order on a form issued by the Commissioner of Internal Revenue. Persons who were not registered were prohibited from engaging in interstate drug trafficking, and anyone who possessed drugs without first registering and paying the tax faced a penalty of as long as five years' imprisonment and a fine of as much as $2,000. Rules promulgated by the Treasury Department permitted only medical professionals to register, and they had to maintain records of the drugs they

dispensed. Within the first year, more than 200,000 medical professionals registered, and the small staff of Treasury agents could not scrutinize all the prescription records generated (Musto 1973).

Concern over federalism—constitutional limitations on the police powers of the central government—led Congress to use the taxing authority rather than the police authority of the federal government to respond to the problem of drug control. At the turn of the twentieth century, federal authority to regulate narcotics and the prescription practices of physicians was generally thought to be unconstitutional (Musto 1973). In 1919, the use of taxing authority to regulate drugs was upheld by the U.S. Supreme Court (*United States v. Doremus,* 249 U.S. 86).

The Harrison Act was supported by the American Medical Association (AMA), which by that time "was well on its way to consolidation of American medical practitioners" (Musto 1973: 56), and by the American Pharmaceutical Association, which, like the AMA, had grown more powerful and influential in the first two decades of the twentieth century. The medical profession had been granted a monopoly over the dispensing of opiates and cocaine. The Harrison Act also effectively imposed a stamp of illegitimacy on most narcotics use, fostering an image of the degenerate "dope fiend" with immoral proclivities (Bonnie and Whitebread 1970). At this time, there were an estimated 300,000 opiate addicts in the United States (Courtwright 1982).

But the addict population was already changing. The medical profession had, by and large, abandoned its liberal use of opiates. Imports of medicinal opiates declined dramatically during the first decade of the twentieth century. The public mind came to associate heroin with urban vice and crime. Unlike the "respectable" opiate addicts of the nineteenth century (who were often female), opiate users of the twentieth century were increasingly male habitués of pool halls and bowling alleys, denizens of the underworld. As in the case of minority groups, this marginal population was an easy target of drug laws and drug-law enforcement.

The Commissioner of Internal Revenue was in charge of upholding the Harrison Act. In 1915, 162 collectors and agents of the Miscellaneous Division of the Internal Revenue Service were given the responsibility of enforcing drug laws. In 1919, a narcotics division was created within the Bureau of Prohibition, with a staff of 170 agents and an appropriation of $270,000. The narcotics division, however, suffered from its association with the notoriously inept and corrupt Prohibition Bureau and from a corruption scandal of its own: There was "public dissatisfaction with the activities of the Narcotics Division, which was tainted by its association with the country's anti-liquor laws" (PCOC 1986a: 204).

In 1916, the Supreme Court ruled in favor of a physician who had provided maintenance doses of morphine to an addict (*United States v. Jin Fuey Moy,* 241 U.S. 394). But private physicians found it impossible to handle the sudden upsurge in their drug clientele: They could do nothing "more than sign prescriptions" (Duster 1970: 16). Three years later, the Court ruled (*Webb v. United States,* 249 U.S. 96) that a prescription for morphine that was issued to a habitual user who was not under a physician's care and that was intended not to cure but to maintain the habit was not a prescription and thus violated the Harrison Act. In 1922, the Court ruled (*United States v. Behrman,* 258 U.S. 280) that a physician was not entitled to prescribe large doses of proscribed drugs for self-administration *even if* the addict was under the physician's care. The Court stated: "Prescriptions in the regular course of practice did not include the indiscriminate doling out of narcotics in such quantity as charged in the indictments." In 1925, the Court limited the application of *Behrman* when it found that a physician who had prescribed small doses of drugs for the relief of an addict did not violate the Harrison Act (*Linder v. United States,* 268 U.S. 5).

The powers of the narcotics division were clearly limited to the enforcement of registration and record-keeping regulations. "The large number of addicts who secured their drugs from physicians were excluded from the Division's jurisdiction." Furthermore, the public's attitude toward drug use "had not much changed with the passage of the Act—there was some opposition to drug use, some support of it, and a great many who did not care one way or the other. The Harrison Act was actually passed with very little publicity or news coverage" (Dickson 1977: 39). Richard Bonnie and Charles Whitebread (1970: 976) note similarities between the temperance and antinarcotics movements. "Both were first directed against the evils of large scale use and only later against all use. Most of the rhetoric was the same: These euphoriants produced crime, pauperism, and insanity." However, "the temperance movement was a matter of vigorous public debate; the antinarcotics movement was not. Temperance legislation was the product of a highly organized nationwide lobby [discussed in Chapter 2]; narcotics legislation was largely ad hoc. Temperance legislation was designed to eradicate known evils resulting from alcohol abuse; narcotics legislation was largely anticipatory."

Writing in 1916, Pearce Bailey (1974: 173–174) noted that the passage of the act spread dismay among heroin addicts. The price of heroin soared 900 percent and was sold in adulterated form, putting it beyond the easy reach of the majority of users. Beginning in 1918, narcotic clinics opened in almost every major city. Information about them is sketchy and there is a great deal of controversy surrounding their operations (Duster 1970). While they were never very popular with the general public, most clinics were well run and under medical supervision (Morgan 1981).

Following World War I and the Bolshevik Revolution in Russia, xenophobia and prohibitionism began to sweep the nation. The United States severely restricted foreign immigration, and alcohol and drug use were increasingly associated with an alien population. In 1922, federal narcotic agents closed the drug clinics and began to arrest physicians and pharmacists who provided drugs for maintenance. At issue was section eight of the Harrison Act, which permitted the possession of controlled substances if prescribed "in good faith" by a registered physician, dentist, or veterinarian in accord with "professional practice." The law did not define "good faith" or "professional practice." Under a policy developed by the federal narcotics agency, thousands of persons, including many physicians, were charged with violations: "Whether conviction followed or not mattered little as the effects of press publicity dealing with what were supposedly willful violations of a beneficent law were most disastrous to those concerned" (Terry and Pellens 1928: 90). "After this initial burst of arrest activity directed against registrants, the Narcotics Division turned its attention to closing clinics that had been established to conduct research and treat large numbers of addicts who could not afford private care" (PCOC 1986a: 202). They were declared illegal by the drug agency and were closed down (Terry and Pellens 1928).

The medical profession stopped dispensing drugs to addicts, forcing them to look to illicit sources, which gave rise to an enormous black market. Those persons addicted to opium smoking eventually found their favorite drug unavailable—the bulky smoking opium was difficult to smuggle—and they turned to the more readily available heroin, which was prepared for intravenous use (Courtwright 1982). The criminal syndicates that resulted from Prohibition added heroin trafficking to their business portfolios. Heroin took up very little space and was secreted on the whiskey ships of Arnold Rothstein (discussed in Chapter 4) and smuggled into the United States, where it was distributed to criminal organizations in several states. When Prohibition was repealed in 1933, profits from bootlegging disappeared accordingly, leaving drug trafficking as an important source of revenue for organized crime.

THE BUSINESS OF HEROIN

The opium poppy,[1] *Papaver somniferum*, requires a hot, dry climate and very careful cultivation (Wishart 1974). Poppy seeds are scattered across the surface of freshly cultivated fields. Three months later when the poppy is mature, the green stem is topped by a brightly colored flower. Gradually the flower petals fall off, leaving a seedpod about the size of a small egg. Incisions are made in the seedpod just after the petals have fallen but before it is fully ripe. A milky-white fluid oozes out and hardens on the surface into a dark brown gum—raw opium. The raw opium is collected by a labor-intensive process of scraping the pod with a flat, dull knife. The raw opium is dissolved in drums of hot water and lime (calcium oxide). Fertilizer is added, precipitating out organic wastes and leaving morphine suspended near the surface. After residual waste is removed, the morphine is transferred to other drums, where it is heated and mixed with concentrated ammonia. The morphine solidifies and falls to the bottom of the drum where it is filtered out in the form of chunky white kernels. In this form, morphine weighs about one-tenth as much as the original raw opium. To produce 10 kilograms (one kilogram = 2.2046 pounds; hereafter kilo) of almost pure heroin, the chemist mixes 10 kilos of morphine and 10 kilos of acetic anhydride and heats it at exactly 185 degrees for six hours, producing an impure form of heroin. Although this step is not complex, it can be dangerous: "If the proportion of morphine to acetic acid is incorrect or the temperature too high or too low the laboratory may be blown up." Acetic acid is also highly corrosive, attacking both skin and lungs (Lamour and Lamberti 1974: 17).

Next, the solution is treated with water and chloroform until the impurities precipitate out. The heroin is drained off into another container, to which sodium carbonate is added until crude heroin particles begin to solidify and drop to the bottom. The particles are filtered out and purified in a solution of alcohol and activated charcoal. This mixture is heated until the alcohol begins to evaporate, leaving granules of almost pure heroin at the bottom. In the final step, the granules are dissolved in alcohol, and ether and hydrochloric acid are added to the solution. Tiny white flakes begin to form. These flakes are filtered out under pressure and dried in a special process, the result being a

---

1. Sales of poppy seeds for cultivation, not culinary use—they often appear on bagels—have been illegal in the United States since 1970. The plant's pretty red flower looks elegant when dried.

white crystalline powder between 80 and 99 percent pure, known as *No. 4 heroin*. (The Mexican product known as *No. 3 heroin* contains impurities that give it a thick oily "black tar" or a more refined brown powder color.)

For street sale, the white powder is typically diluted ("stepped on" or "cut") with any powdery substance that dissolves when heated, such as lactose, quinine, flour, or cornstarch. Until the 1990s, consumer-available heroin prepared for intravenous use usually had a purity of less than 5 percent. In recent years, purity levels of retail heroin sold in parts of New York City have approached 90 percent, revealing that heroin is being subjected to little if any cutting before it reaches the consumer level. Increased purity makes smoking and sniffing feasible. The increased purity and the concern about AIDS caused a shift from injecting to smoking and sniffing among many heroin users. Heroin can be sniffed like cocaine and even smoked. When smoked—

"chasing the dragon"—heroin is heated and the fumes inhaled, usually through a small tube.

Like any business that is international in scope, heroin trafficking requires extensive transportation networks, but since the commodity is illegal, these operate in the shadows of global trade. Consolidation and vertical integration, cherished buzzwords of multinational corporations, are impossible. Instead, drug barons base their operations in remote safe havens, "the more war-torn and chaotic the better" (Brzezinski 2002: 26). Most heroin smuggled into the United States originates in areas where the opium poppy thrives—parts of Asia known as the Golden Triangle, the Golden Crescent, Mexico, and, more recently, Colombia (Figure 12.1). Afghanistan, part of the Golden Crescent, is the source of about 90 percent of the world's illicit opiates; significant quantities are also produced in Myanmar, part of the Golden Triangle, and Latin America, notably in Mexico and Colombia. Since 2003, Mexico has

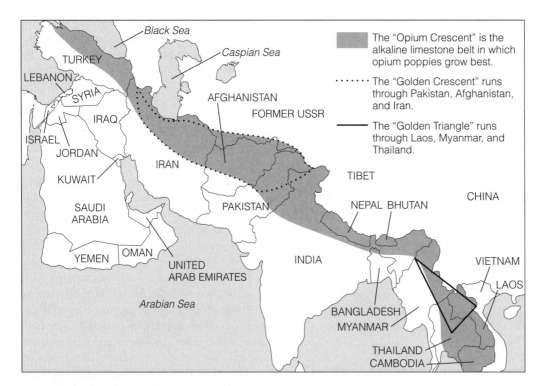

The "Opium Crescent" is the alkaline limestone belt in which opium poppies grow best.

⋯⋯⋯ The "Golden Crescent" runs through Pakistan, Afghanistan, and Iran.

——— The "Golden Triangle" runs through Laos, Myanmar, and Thailand.

FIGURE 12.1 Major Asian Opium Regions

been the world's third largest source of opium with quantities close to that produced in Myanmar (UNODC 2010b).

Golden Triangle

The Golden Triangle of Southeast Asia encompasses approximately 150,000 square miles of forested highlands, including the western fringe of Laos, the four northern provinces of Thailand, and the northeastern parts of Myanmar (known before 1989 as Burma). Myanmar is the world's second largest producer of opium. It is slightly smaller than Texas, with a population of more than 47 million. Since a coup in 1962, this poverty-ridden country has been dominated by a repressive military dictatorship—the world's longest-running military regime (Pepper 2008). A nominally civilian government took office in 2011, but the military remains the dominant power. The regime is marked by brutality against ethnic minorities and collaboration with drug trafficking continued. In 2003, rights organizations and the U.S. State Department accused the Myanmar military of a policy of systematic rape of ethnic minority women (Mydans 2003a).

Transnational organized crime groups in Myanmar operate a multibillion-dollar criminal industry that stretches across Southeast Asia. Humans, drugs, wildlife, gems, timber, and other contraband flow through Myanmar where collusion between traffickers and the country's ruling military junta allows organized crime groups to function with virtual impunity and bolsters a regime that fosters a culture of corruption and disrespect for the rule of law and human rights (Wyler 2007).

In 1826, the British introduced opium use into their colony of Burma. In the strongly Buddhist south, use of the drug was considered a violation of religious principles and was not widespread. In the northern Kachin and Shan tribal areas, opium was valued, particularly as a medicine, and its use was acceptable to the mostly non-Buddhist population. The British managed the different ethnic groups in their colony by dividing them into discrete states that, as a result, began to develop

aspirations of autonomy. When the colonial regimes retreated, these aspirations intensified (Renard 2003).

French colonial officials in Golden Triangle used paramilitary organizations and indigenous tribes against various insurgent groups, particularly those following a Marxist ideology. As support for overseas colonies dwindled at home, French officials in Southeast Asia utilized the drug trade to finance their efforts. The French would buy raw opium from Hmong tribesmen in Vietnam and provide it to criminal organizations that administered red-light districts in Saigon (now Ho Chi Minh City) and aided in the suppression of Communist opposition to French rule (Schulte-Bockholt 2006). Some Golden Triangle opium was also shipped to Marseilles where the Corsican underworld processed it into heroin for distribution in the United States—the "French Connection." The French withdrew from Southeast Asia in 1955 and several years later the United States took up the struggle against Marxist groups—the Vietnam War is part of this legacy. The U.S. Central Intelligence Agency (CIA) waged its own clandestine war and, again, heroin played a role: many of the indigenous tribal groups recruited and armed by the CIA cultivated opium. In Laos and South Vietnam, corrupt governments were heavily involved in heroin trafficking, making the substance easily available to American soldiers (McCoy 1972: 1991). This longstanding tradition of using drugs to help finance military efforts continues in this part of the world.

With the end of colonial rule, countries emerged with relatively weak central governments, their rural areas inhabited by bandits and paramilitary organizations such as the Kuomintang.

Kuomintang

With defeat of the Chinese Nationalist forces in 1949, the Third and Fifth Armies of Chiang Kai-shek stationed in the remote southern province of Yunnan escaped over the mountainous frontier into Burma's Shan States. Although part of this army dispersed and became integrated with the local population, "more than 6,000 of them remained together as a military entity, their numbers being swollen by indigenous tribesmen" (Lamour and Lamberti 1974: 94). By 1952, the Kuomintang (KMT), numbering about 12,000, became the de facto power in the eastern part of the Shan States. In 1951 and 1952, with support from the United States, the KMT was rearmed and resupplied and, with additional troops from Taiwan and recruits from the Hmong hill tribesmen—poppy cultivators—attempted to invade China. When these attempts failed, U.S. interest and support waned, and the KMT settled permanently in Burma. For several years the Burmese military attempted to evict the KMT and finally succeeded in 1954, forcibly escorting them to the Thai border, from which the Nationalist government evacuated about 6,000 troops to Taiwan. Nevertheless, the strength of the KMT grew through secret reinforcements from Taiwan and recruitment among indigenous tribes to about 10,000 troops.

In 1961, a resentful government in Burma, perhaps with assistance from the People's Republic of China, finally drove the KMT into the Thai portion of the Golden Triangle (Lamour and Lamberti 1974), where it sold its military skills to a joint CIA/Thai Army command fighting communist insurgents in the Shan States. The force fought to prevent the Laotian communist Pathet Lao from linking up with local insurgents. In 1961 and 1969, U.S.-backed airlifts of KMT troops to Taiwan were the last official contacts between the KMT remnants on the mainland and Chiang Kai-shek's government, but unofficial ties remained strong (Lamour and Lamberti 1974). The remaining troops became known as the Chinese Irregular Forces (CIF). While the KMT had always dabbled in opium, it now became the sole support of the CIF. Despite this, the CIF was tolerated on the Thai border as a barrier against communist insurgents.

Shan United Army/Mong Tai Army

The Shan States, an area somewhat larger than England, lie on a rugged, hilly plateau in the eastern part of central Burma, flanking the western border of China's Yunnan Province. They contain an array of tribal and linguistic groupings; the largest, the Shans, speak Thai and have more in common with their neighbors in Thailand than those in Myanmar.

The Shans are lowland rice cultivators, but hill tribes on the mountain ridges around them cultivate opium. During British colonial rule (1886–1948), the Shan States were administered independently from Burma, and the Shan princes, or *sawbwas*, enjoyed a great deal of autonomy. When Burma won independence in 1948, the Shans, with great misgivings, agreed to join the Union of Burma in return for statehood and guarantees of a number of ministry posts. As a final incentive, the Shans were given the right to secede after 1957. But the Burmese government's heavy-handed approach to the Shan States set the stage for revolution.

Official Burmese financial policies were devastating to many hill farmers, who turned increasingly to poppy cultivation as a cash crop outside of central government control (Delaney 1977). The *sawbwas* "had been encouraged to introduce the opium poppy to their fiefdoms by the British as far back as 1866 and opium shops had been opened … to retail the narcotics to licensed addicts" (Bresler 1980: 67). In later years, the British made a number of efforts to abolish opium cultivation in the Shan States, although they were never completely successful (McCoy 1972). In any event, many Shans blamed the *sawbwas* for accommodating the central government, and traditional systems of authority deteriorated.

Originally known as the Shan United Army (SUA), the Mong Tai Army (MTA) resorted to opium trafficking in order to purchase arms and support its independence movement (Delaney 1977). The MTA was led by a half-Chinese, half-Shan former KMT soldier named Chang Chifu, better known as *Khun Sa*. He was authorized by the Burmese military to set up militias as a way of fighting groups rebelling against the central government, but he eventually rebelled against Burma and was imprisoned from 1969 to 1974. After his release, he established the SUA (Fuller 2007a).

The SUA/MTA came to dominate the opium trade along the Thai-Burma border where about

400,000 hill tribesmen had no source of income other than heroin (Permanent Subcommittee on Investigations 1981a). In 1965, an opium war broke out between the CIF and the indigenous Shan United Army (SUA), and the CIF drove SUA leader Khun Sa into Laos. Khun Sa returned and in 1981 defeated the CIF. The SUA/MTA was able to control both the shipments of opium and the production of heroin in its laboratories.

In the 1980s, the Thai government succeeded in driving the MTA out of Thailand and back into Burma, but the group continued to dominate opium traffic, taxing drug caravans crossing their territory. In 1990, the Shans suffered significant setbacks: Khun Sa was indicted for drug trafficking by a federal grand jury, and the United States offered a $3 million reward for his capture and conviction in an American court. And his MTA suffered defeats by primitive but ferocious Wa tribesmen (Schmetzer 1990).

In 1994, a joint U.S.–Thai operation ("Tiger Trap") closed the Thai–Myanmar border in areas where the MTA operated. This cut off Khun Sa's ability to move heroin into Thailand and curtailed purchases of supplies for his forces. Later that year, Thai police arrested thirteen major MTA brokers who had been indicted by a federal grand jury in New York. The squeeze was complete when in 1995 the Myanmar army moved against Khun Sa, whose forces were low on food, ammunition, and medical treatment for their wounded. Shortly afterward, ethnic strife broke out: The rank-and-file ethnic Shans mutinied against the MTA, whose top officers are ethnic Chinese (Shenon 1996). Khun Sa began secret negotiations with Myanmar, and in 1996 a deal was made: In front of reporters from Thailand, Khun Sa submitted his resignation (he was retiring to raise chickens, he told them), disbanded the MTA, and closed MTA laboratories. The 15,000-strong MTA disintegrated; many soldiers returned home, while others turned to banditry or joined other rebel groups (Lintner 2002).

As a result, the amount of Southeast Asian heroin entering the United States dropped dramatically (replaced by heroin from Colombia). The Myanmar government refused to extradite Khun Sa, and until his health deteriorated, he regularly golfed with the generals against whom he fought a protracted guerrilla war; he died in 2007 at age 73. The Shan States continue to be a major area for heroin production as well as the production of methamphetamine (UNODC 2010; U.S. State Department 2008; Wyler 2007).

Golden Triangle traffickers began to recognize the value of switching from heroin to methamphetamine. They no longer needed to cultivate vast fields of poppies, and manufacturing could be accomplished in small one-room laboratories. Khun Sa also recognized that, as compared to the rather stable and fixed heroin market, a drug that could be taken orally instead of by injection, which energized its user, would have a greater potential market. Early in the 1990s, opium producers began manufacturing methamphetamine (Renard 2003). The precursor chemical for methamphetamine production, ephedrine, is derived from ephedra, a shrub that grows wild throughout Yunnan, the Chinese province bordering the Golden Triangle (Finckenauer and Chin 2007). "By 2007, the trend of a declining opium market and an increasing ATS [amphetamine-type stimulants] market was apparent in all countries in Southeast Asia" (Kramer, Jelsma, and Blickman 2009: 99).

United Wa State Army

Until 1989, another formidable private army in the Golden Triangle served the Burmese Communist Party (BCP). The BCP force had in the past received support from the People's Republic of China. After Beijing cut off this aid in order to improve relations with Burma, the BCP, following a long-established precedent in the region, went into the opium business. The BCP controlled much of the poppy-producing area and received opium as a form of tax and tribute from local farmers, which it then refined into heroin in its own laboratories.

In 1989, its ethnic rank-and-file Wa tribesmen—fierce warriors whose ancestors were headhunters—rebelled, and the BCP folded as an armed force

(Haley 1990). Most Wa political groups reached an accommodation with the Myanmar ruling junta, but one faction of the Wa reorganized as the United Wa State Army (UWSA). Headquartered on the border of China's Yunnan Province, the UWSA uses heroin and methamphetamine trafficking as a means of funding efforts against Burmese control. Nearly one million Wa straddle the border between Myanmar and China, and the UWSA operates freely along the China and Thailand borders, controlling much of the Shan State with a militia estimated to have about 18,000 members, well armed with ground-to-air missiles and modern communications equipment. Ironically, the Wa routinely executes anyone caught dealing drugs for local use. Since Khun Sa's surrender, the USWA has reigned supreme in drug production in Myanmar (Wyler 2007).

In 2000, Myanmar negotiated a truce with the Wa that gave them autonomy in their state, and the Wa reached an accommodation with China. In return for sophisticated weapons and expertise from China, the Wa moved their people, their army, and their drug laboratories into the Thai–Myanmar border area known as Doi Lang. The Chinese were concerned with their own drug problem and preferred the Wa to be a Thai rather than a Chinese problem. But the situation has grown complex and volatile, with China, Thailand, and Myanmar supporting different rebel groups.

Whether the source is the CIF, MTA, or the UWSA, heroin and methamphetamine are usually brokered in Thailand, which has modern communications and transportation systems—and a serious drug problem. Thailand has a large market of methamphetamine users in the region whose drug source is primarily Myanmar (UNODC 2010c). A nation of 50 million persons, Thailand is almost as large as France. A staunch anti-Communist ally of the United States, Thailand sent troops to fight alongside American soldiers in Korea and Vietnam. In addition to its role in drug trafficking, Thailand, with an estimated 50,000 active brothels, has a reputation of being the "world's biggest whorehouse" with a law enforcement apparatus permeated with corruption (Mydans 2003b). The Thai sex industry, fueled by human trafficking (discussed in Chapter 11),

involves government officials who assume a key role in the trade (Shelley 2010). Thailand enjoys a close relationship with Myanmar's military regime with whom they share important commercial interests (Kaplan 2008).

"Once the sourcing and processing stages are complete, isolated countries like Myanmar or Afghanistan [discussed later] lose their competitive advantage" because they simply do not have the sophistication or international networks to get their product to market. This is what the foreign syndicates, who reap the greatest profits, provide (Brzezinski 2002: 27). At the center of much of Thai drug trafficking are ethnic Chinese organizations such as the Triads, discussed in Chapter 8, who dominate a major part of the world heroin market. "In Southeast Asia, not only did the British and French opium monopolies create massive addict populations, but they also inadvertently formed a smuggling network that was crucial to the post–World War II heroin epidemic. Although the colonial administrations reaped huge profits, they never became involved in the drug's distribution and sale. That work was left to each colony's licensed opium merchant. Invariably they were Chinese" (Posner 1988: 66). According to the U.S. Department of State (2008), ethnic Chinese groups dominate the drug syndicates operating in the Shan area.

Bangkok has a large population of Thai-born Chinese, called *Haw*, who are known by Thai names but maintain close ties with compatriots in Hong Kong, Yunnan province,[2] Amsterdam, and British Columbia. From Bangkok, Chinese criminal organizations have flooded their "China White" into major cities of Europe, Canada, and the United States.

The central role that the Golden Triangle played in the heroin trade has been significantly diminished, in part because of economic pressure

---

2. Because it is located next to the Golden Triangle, China's Yunnan ("south of the clouds") province, with a population that includes 20 of the country's minority groups, has been a center for drug trafficking. High-quality heroin passes easily over borders that were opened for trade decades ago, supported by rampant corruption among the police and other officials.

from China. The UWSA publicly pledged to eliminate opium poppy cultivation, there have been crackdowns on opium farmers, and traffickers have switched from opium cultivation to manufacturing methamphetamine ("Ice") turning the Golden Triangle into a new "Ice Triangle." As a result, Golden Triangle heroin has been largely eclipsed by that from the Golden Crescent (Fuller 2007b).

The Golden Crescent

The Golden Crescent of Southwest Asia includes parts of Iran, Afghanistan, and Pakistan. The region has limestone-rich soil, a climate and altitude ideal for poppy cultivation, and, like the Golden Triangle, a ready abundance of cheap labor for the labor-intensive production of opium. Afghan opium is processed into heroin in local laboratories or shipped to processing plants in Pakistan.

Pakistan has been a producer of opium for export since the earliest time of Muslim rule and the later British Empire. In Pakistan, the typical poppy farmer lives in a semiautonomous northern tribal area outside the direct control of the central government in Islamabad. The Pakistani authorities have little control in these areas and must appeal to tribal leaders to move against the region's dozens of illegal processing laboratories. As a result of eradication efforts in recent years, the amount of opium production has been greatly reduced. Instead, opium products are often processed into morphine base or heroin in Afghanistan and then shipped through Pakistan to world markets by Pakistan-based traffickers.

Unlike Southeast Asia, Afghanistan's rugged terrain and the martial tradition of its tribes kept it free of colonialism. Western interest in this nation of about 27 million was limited until the Soviet invasion. The Pashtuns, a tribal group that founded Afghanistan and ruled it for all but about four years of its history, populates Pakistan's Northwest Frontier Province and compose almost half of the country's inhabitants (Waldman 2003). The border dividing Pashtuns in Pakistan from their tribal brethren in Afghanistan was drawn by the British more than a century ago, and is generally ignored—there are few border patrols in the region (Ahmed-Ullah 2001). Known as exceptional warriors, the Pashtuns are also the major drug traffickers in the region. Along with other Islamic groups, many Pashtuns fought a guerrilla war against the Soviet-backed regime in Kabul. In late 1979, the Soviets rolled their tanks into the opium provinces of Afghanistan. "Suddenly, the tribes which had spent the last decade maneuvering their heavily armed drug caravans past the increasingly troublesome patrols of the U.S. Drug Enforcement Administration's agents found themselves flung into the limelight as the new anti-communist 'crusaders'" (Levins 1980: 20).

United States anti-Soviet efforts in Afghanistan were orchestrated by the CIA, and the agency adopted a benign attitude toward drug trafficking. As the conflict wound down, the United States became increasingly concerned with rebel drug activity. Opium is the cash crop that has traditionally enabled feuding tribes in Afghanistan and in Pakistan's Northwest Frontier Province to purchase weapons and ammunition. In 1991, U.S. officials announced that they would no longer provide military assistance to Afghan rebels. Prior to its disintegration, the Soviet Union also agreed to stop aiding the Afghan government. The following year, *mujahedin* forces entered Kabul without encountering any resistance, and the war officially ended, but warfare between rebel groups continued, supported by heroin. By 1998, the Islamic fundamentalist Taliban movement, made up primarily of Pashtuns, controlled most of the country, and Afghanistan became the world's largest producer of heroin. "Poppy growing is so uncontrolled that despite millions of aid dollars spent to train antidrug forces and to help farmers grow other crops, Afghanistan is showing no signs of leaving its position as the world's biggest producer of opium. It accounts for almost three-quarters of global opium production" (Gall 2006: 4; also United Nations Office on Drugs and Crime 2008b). "What crude oil is to the Middle East, poppies are to Afghanistan" (B. Powell 2007: 31).

Until 2001, Afghanistan was the world's second largest grower of the opium poppy, producing about one-third of the heroin entering the United States and about 80 percent of the heroin consumed in Europe. Despite the severe economic ramifications, in 2001, the Taliban leadership banned the growing of poppies as a sin against the teachings of Islam. Compliance was immediate and thorough (Bearak 2001). In the wake of the September 11, 2001 terrorist attacks and the U.S. military reaction, the Taliban told farmers they were once again free to grow the opium poppy, which became an indispensable crop in parts of Afghanistan. In areas that they dominate, the Taliban levy a tax on the harvest (Anderson 2007).

Antidrug efforts are hampered by a lack of alternative crops for impoverished farmers— poppy prices are ten times those for wheat. The drug trade represents more than half of the country's gross domestic product (GDP). So critical is opium to the Afghan economy that American officials have been reluctant to engage in an antidrug war that could conflict with efforts to deal with the Taliban. Wealth from the drug trade has increased the power of local warlords whose militias are a threat to the central government (Rhode 2007; Schmitt 2004). High-ranking members of the government are reportedly profiting from the drug trade: In one downtown Kabul neighborhood, there are dozens of gaudy "poppy palaces" owned by former warlords and senior Afghan government officials (J. L. Anderson 2007; Moreau and Yousafzai 2006).

Afghan heroin destined for Europe is frequently transported across the forbidding Margo desert. Heavily armed convoys traveling at high speeds move their supplies into Iran where thousands of police officers have been killed battling the trade (Gall 2005). Turkey, which serves as a land bridge to markets in the West for heroin from the Golden Crescent, is fighting a similar battle. Kurdish separatists and Turkish criminal groups (*babas*) have important connections in the Western drug market. They move heroin across the highways of Turkey and into Europe where other criminal organizations, in particular Mafia and Camorra

groups, distribute the drug throughout the European market.

Mexico

Mexico is the source of "black tar" or brown heroin. Its position in the American drug market in the five years after the collapse of the "French Connection" grew until it became the major source of U.S. heroin. "Mexico's rise was logical: the country contains extensive regions suitable for both opium cultivation and refining and shares a lightly guarded 2,000 mile border with the United States. Mexicans could manufacture heroin and smuggle it into the United States with little risk of detection. This simplified trafficking system resulted in increased Mexican heroin availability in the United States" (PCOC 1986a: 107).

Black tar heroin is a less refined but more potent—and very popular—form of the substance. The conversion of opium gum to black tar heroin is more convenient and requires only simple equipment that can be readily dismantled if law enforcement is detected in the area. In addition, almost anyone can be trained to perform the conversion process, making it unnecessary to pay the higher salary that would most certainly be demanded by skilled chemists who would be required to produce the higher purity No. 4, white heroin (DEA 1991b). While heroin from the Golden Triangle and the Golden Crescent can approach 100-percent purity, Mexican heroin purity generally ranges from 65 to 85 percent.

The poppy is not native to Mexico but was brought into the country at the turn of the twentieth century by Chinese laborers who were helping to build the railroad system. Chinese immigrants dominated heroin trafficking until anti-Chinese riots and property confiscations during the 1930s caused the trade to pass into Mexican hands (Lupsha 1991).

Poppy fields are generally small and difficult to detect, although larger fields cultivated by more sophisticated growers have been discovered. The poppies are grown in remote areas of the Sierra Madre states of Durango, Sinaloa, and Chihuahua, as well as Sonora (the Mexican state just south of

Arizona). Opium gum is then transported to nearby villages. *Acaparadores,* or gatherers, travel around the countryside buying large quantities of opium gum, which is flown to secret laboratories owned and operated by major drug organizations.

The conversion process for Mexican heroin takes about three days, although with special equipment and trained personnel it can be accomplished in one. Once the conversion is finished, the heroin is moved to large population centers. From there, Mexican couriers transport the heroin to members of the trafficking organization in the United States.

The drug trade is big business in poverty-wracked Mexico. Large traffickers (discussed in Chapter 6) have traditionally received protection from the highest levels of government and law enforcement. Indeed, some important traffickers have backgrounds in law enforcement. As Peter Lupsha notes, "For some of Mexico's top enforcement officials entrance into drug trafficking has simply been a lateral transfer" (1990: 12). As noted in Chapter 6, Mexican organizations are also transporting cocaine into the United States.

The vast and remote border between Mexico and the United States makes patrolling very difficult and facilitates the transportation of drugs into Texas, California, Arizona, and New Mexico. Private aircraft, flying low to avoid radar detection, use privately owned "soft-surface" runways that dot the U.S.-Mexican border and dozens of larger airstrips on the Yucatán Peninsula to move drugs north. Drugs are secreted in a variety of motor vehicles and smuggled past official border entry points. More than 30 million personal vehicles and 12 million pedestrians cross the U.S.-Mexico border annually. Drug traffickers also transport drug shipments as airfreight or by courier aboard passenger flights (NDIC 2009). And there are "dope tunnels."

Since authorities began keeping records in 1990, dozens of dope tunnels have been found along the Mexican border with the United States. In 2010, DEA agents in San Diego uncovered a sophisticated 600-yard underground cross-border tunnel. Approximately 30 tons of marijuana seized in the United States and Mexico have been linked to the tunnel. A crawlspace-sized passageway, the tunnel connected an Otay Mesa warehouse with a similar building in Tijuana, Mexico. The tunnel was equipped with rail, lighting and ventilation systems (DEA press release, November 3, 2010).

As noted in Chapter 6, since the 1980s Colombia has become a major poppy grower and Colombians have become major heroin wholesalers. At the end of 1991, police raids in Colombia disclosed thousands of acres of poppy plants ("Colombian Heroin May Be Increasing" 1991). By 1998, Colombian heroin accounted for more than 50 percent of the drug smuggled into the United States. It has a high purity level—it passes through fewer hands from "the farm to the arm." This enables ingestion by sniffing and smoking, which are methods far safer than injection, the only way to gain a potent high with weaker versions of the drug.

COCAINE

Cocaine is an alkaloid found in the leaves of two species of coca shrub that grow in parts of Colombia, Bolivia, Ecuador, and Peru. The practice of chewing coca leaves has been carried on by Indians in Peru for at least twenty centuries. The leaves are used as a poultice for wounds and to brew a tea, *mate de coca*, said to cure the headaches of tourists bothered by the 12,000-foot altitude of La Paz. Although cash crops raised on the mountain slopes of Peru require a great deal of care—the nutrient-poor soil needs continuous fertilization—coca is a hardy jungle plant with abundant seeds that needs little or no fertilizer. "Once a coca field is planted, it will yield four to five crops a year for thirty to forty years, needing little in return but seasonal weeding" (Morales 1989: xvi).

Spanish explorers observed indigenous people chewing coca leaves during their colonization of South America, but did not adopt the practice. In the middle of the nineteenth century, scientists began experimenting with the substance, noting that it showed promise as a local anesthetic and had an effect opposite that of morphine. At first cocaine was used to treat morphine addiction, but the result was often a morphine addict who also became dependent on cocaine (van Dyke and Byck 1982). "Throughout the late nineteenth century, both coca itself (that is, an extract from the leaf including all its alkaloids) and the pure chemical cocaine were used as medicines and for pleasure—the distinction was not always made—in an enormous variety of ways" (Grinspoon and Bakalar 1976: 19). By the late 1880s, a feel-good pharmacology based on the coca plant and its derivative cocaine was promoted for everything from headaches to hysteria. The most famous beverage containing coca, however, was first bottled in 1894 (Helmer 1975). Coca-Cola continues to use nonpsychoactive residue from the coca plant for flavoring.

After the first flush of enthusiasm for cocaine in the 1880s, its use declined. Although it continued to be used in a variety of notions and tonics, cocaine did not develop a separate appeal as did morphine and heroin (Morgan 1981). Indeed, cocaine gained a reputation for inducing bizarre and unpredictable behavior. After the turn of the century, cocaine, like heroin, became identified with the urban underworld. From 1930 until the 1960s there was limited demand for cocaine and, accordingly, only limited supply. Cocaine use was associated with deviants—jazz musicians and the denizens of underworld—and supplies were typically diverted from medical sources. Cocaine has limited medical use: It constricts blood vessels when applied topically, the only local anesthetic that has this effect. Because of this quality, cocaine is used in surgery of the mucous membranes of the ear, nose, and throat, and for procedures that require the passage of a tube through the nose or throat (van Dyke and Byck 1982).

During the late 1960s and early 1970s, attitudes toward recreational drug use became more relaxed, a spin-off of the wide acceptance of marijuana. Cocaine was no longer associated with deviants, and the media played a significant role in shaping public attitudes: "By publicizing and glamorizing the lifestyle of affluent, upper-class drug dealers and the use of cocaine by celebrities and athletes, all forms of mass media created an effective advertising campaign for cocaine, and many people were taught to perceive cocaine as chic, exclusive, daring, and nonaddicting. In television specials about cocaine abuse, scientists talked about the intense euphoria produced by cocaine and the compulsive craving that people (and animals) develop for it. Thus, an image of cocaine as being extraordinarily powerful, and a (therefore desirable) euphoriant was promoted" (Wesson and Smith 1985: 193).

Cocaine soon became associated with a privileged elite. The new demand was sufficient to generate new sources, refining, and marketing networks outside of medical channels and the development of the international cocaine organizations discussed in Chapter 6 (Grinspoon and Bakalar 1976). Greater availability of cocaine led to a corresponding increase in use.

The Business of Cocaine

Coca is a flowering bush or shrub that in cultivation stands three to six feet tall. Each shrub yields at most four ounces of waxy, elliptical leaves that are about 1 percent cocaine by weight. Pulverized leaves of the coca bush are soaked and shaken in a mixture of alcohol and benzol (a petroleum derivative). The liquid is then drained, sulfuric acid is added, and the solution is again shaken. Sodium carbonate is added, forming a precipitate, which is washed with kerosene and chilled, leaving behind crystals of crude cocaine known as coca paste. Between 200 and 500 kilos of leaves are made into 1 kilo of paste; 2.5 kilos of coca paste are converted into 1 kilo of cocaine base—a malodorous, grainy, greenish yellow powder of more than 66 percent purity. Cocaine base is converted into cocaine hydrochloride by being treated with ether, acetone, and hydrochloric acid. One kilo of cocaine base is synthesized into 1 kilo of cocaine hydrochloride, a white crystalline powder that is about 95 percent pure.

In the United States cocaine hydrochloride is cut for street sale by adding sugars such as lactose, inositol, or mannitol, or talcum powder, borax, or other neutral substances, and local anesthetics such

Jungle lab in Colombia for processing coca leaves into cocaine.

as procaine hydrochloride (novocaine) or lidocaine hydrochloride. (Novocaine is sometimes mixed with mannitol or lactose and sold as cocaine.) After cutting, the cocaine typically has a consumer sale purity of less than 20 percent. Huge increases in the availability of cocaine results in consumer sale purity levels as high as 50 percent—and a concomitant increase in the number of emergency room admissions for cocaine overdose.

The most common method of using cocaine is "snorting"—inhaling it into the nostrils through a straw or rolled paper or from a "coke spoon." Some abusers take it intravenously, which is the only way to ingest 100 percent of the drug. When the drug is inhaled, its effects peak in 15 to 20 minutes and disappear in 60 to 90 minutes. Intravenous use results in an intense feeling of euphoria that crests in 3 to 5 minutes and wanes in 30 to 40 minutes. Cocaine causes the release of the natural substance adrenaline: "In essence the cocaine-stimulated reactions in the body are mimicking a natural physiological stress response." The body prepares for "fight" or "flight," but the brain sends the message that everything is better than fine (Gold et al.

1986). In small doses, cocaine will bring about a sensation of extreme euphoria and indifference to pain, along with illusions of increased mental and sensory alertness and physical strength. At higher doses, the drug has the potential to produce megalomania and feelings of omnipotence in most individuals (Gold et al. 1986).

For many decades, coca leaf was converted to cocaine base in Bolivia and Peru, and then smuggled by small aircraft or boat into Colombia where it was refined into cocaine in jungle laboratories. Laboratories have relocated to cities far from cultivation sites to be closer to sources of precursor chemicals and also because improved law enforcement methods facilitate the detection of jungle laboratories. Essential precursor chemicals are usually manufactured in the United States and Germany, and Panama and Mexico serve as major transit sources. Colombian cartels, using dummy companies and multiple suppliers, pay as much as ten times the normal prices for these chemicals.

Some Colombian traffickers have set up laboratories in other Latin American countries in response

---

RESIDUAL PROFITS

When cocaine-transporting fast boats run into patrols from the United States or Nicaragua along that country's Mosquito Coast, traffickers throw the bales overboard. Sometimes they run out of fuel or have an accident. In any event, tons of cocaine wash up on the coast of one of the Caribbean's most desolate regions where villagers wait to recover the valuable cargo. Colombian traffickers or Nicaraguan middlemen offer them about $4,000 a kilo, which has allowed many indigenous fishermen to move out of their huts and into multistory homes with satellite dishes (Carroll 2007).

---

to increased law enforcement in Colombia and the increasing cost of ether, sulfuric acid, and acetone in Colombia. Although sulfuric acid and acetone have wide industrial use in Colombia, ether does not, and each kilo of cocaine requires 17 liters of ether. The Cali cartel pioneered setting up coke labs in rural parts of the United States in order to have a ready source of precursor chemicals (Chepesiuk 2003). The cost of these chemicals has increased because of controls imposed by the Colombian government on their importation and sale and because of DEA efforts to disrupt the supply of chemicals essential in the cocaine refinement process. Acetone, sulfuric acid, and ether, however, are widely available for commercial purposes in the United States (Hall 2000).

In the past, because the quality of Colombian coca was significantly less than that grown in Peru and Bolivia, Colombia was not a major coca producer; but success in eradicating coca in Bolivia and Peru led to a major increase in Colombian coca cultivation, and by 1998, Colombia was the world's leading coca producer (Goering 1998; Krauss 2000). Colombian traffickers achieved extraordinary levels of efficiency in extracting cocaine from their coca crops (*International Narcotics Control Strategy Report* 2000). By 2002, however, coca was making a comeback in Peru, driven by a combination of poverty and soaring prices for coca. In Bolivia, coca production shot up in 2005, the result of a backlash against U.S.-financed eradication programs that helped to destabilize the country and topple several governments; and at the end of the year, Bolivia elected a coca-growing socialist president (Forero 2002, 2005b, 2005c).

In Colombia, about three-quarters of the coca is grown in six rural provinces about the size of Kansas, southwest of Bogotá, with a population of about six million. The area is desperately poor and plagued by left- and right-wing paramilitary groups (Forero 2001b). Indeed, Colombia is the only country in Latin America still fighting a major guerilla insurgency (discussed in Chapter 6).

DRUG DISTRIBUTION

The organizers who arrange for the importation and wholesale distribution of heroin and cocaine typically avoid physical possession. "The key figures in the Italian heroin establishment never touched heroin. Guys who were in the business for twenty years and had made millions off it had never seen it. After all, does a commodities trader on Wall Street have to see hog bellies and platinum bars?" (Durk and Silverman 1976: 49). Importation often entails little or no risk of arrest—heroin or cocaine can be secreted in a variety of imported goods, and possession cannot be proven. Furthermore, although a single shipment may be detected and confiscated, smugglers often divide their supplies so that other shipments arrive unimpeded—"shotgunning." Colombian dealers have been known to offer to insure their shipments through a joint arrangement. The cost of insurance is passed on to the import buyer, who is then financially protected in the event of interdiction by American authorities.

CRACK

Although cocaine hydrochloride cannot easily be smoked, freeing the alkaloid from the hydrochloride attachment produces purified crystals of cocaine base that can be crushed and smoked in a special glass pipe or sprinkled on a tobacco or marijuana product. Cocaine hydrochloride powder is easily converted into crack by cooking it in a mixture of sodium bicarbonate (baking soda) and water, and then removing the water. The soap-like substance is then cut into bars or chips, sometimes called "quarter rocks," and smoked. It is generally sold on the street in small glass vials. The nickname "crack" comes from the crackling sound the drug makes when it is smoked in a glass pipe. Smoking crack produces a short but very powerful euphoria that lasts 10 to 15 minutes.

After importation, drugs are typically sold in 10- to 50-kilo quantities to wholesalers—"kilo connections." The substances are then cut or "stepped on," diluted several times. When the cutting is complete, jobbers—"weight dealers"—who have been waiting for a telephone call arrive with the necessary cash, which they exchange for 2 to 5 kilos of the cut drugs. The jobbers move it to wholesalers, who cut it again. From there it moves to street wholesalers, then to retailers, and finally to consumers. At each step of the process, profits increase as the kilo of pure heroin or cocaine increases in bulk, the result of further cutting.

The enormous profits that accrue in the business of drugs are part of a criminal underworld where violence is always an attendant reality. Transactions must be accomplished without recourse to the formal mechanisms of dispute resolution usually available in the world of legitimate business. This reality leads to the creation of private mechanisms of enforcement. The drug world is filled with heavily armed and dangerous persons in the employ of the larger cartels, although even street-level operatives are often armed. These private resources for violence limit market entry, ward off competitors and predatory criminals, and maintain internal discipline and security within an organization.

Below the multi-kilo wholesale level, cocaine or heroin is an easy-entry business, requiring only a source, clientele, and funds. A variety of groups deal heroin and cocaine, including street gangs in many urban areas. In several parts of the country, particularly New York City and Los Angeles, the relatively stable neighborhood criminal organizations who dominated the heroin and cocaine trade found new competitors: youthful crack dealers. Crack cocaine requires only a small investment for entry to the trade. Street gangs or groups of friends and relatives entered the market, often touching off explosive competitive violence that frequently involved the use of high-powered handguns and automatic weapons. The sharp decline in murder in some major cities such as New York is believed related to a stabilizing of the crack market, much as post-Prohibition organized crime–related murder dipped significantly in Chicago in the absence of competition.

The sale of heroin and cocaine/crack is carried out by thousands of small-time operators who dominate particular local markets—a public housing complex, a number of city blocks, or simply a street corner location. Control is exercised through violence. Even though retail dealers typically work long hours and subject themselves to substantial risk of violence and incarceration, their net profits are rather modest. Less successful participants eke out a living that rivals minimum wage. Many are involved to support their own drug habits, to supplement earnings from legitimate employment, or both.

Many retail operators sell more than one drug—they are often "walking drug stores." The lower down on the distribution chain, the more likely the person or organization will be involved in the sale of more than one substance. And the business of drugs includes substances other than heroin and cocaine.

METH LAB HAZARDS

"Due to the chemicals used to make the drugs and the wastes generated during the 'cooking,' clandestine laboratories present significant safety and health risks to law enforcement and to the public. Clandestine drug laboratories also present serious environmental concerns, such as soil and ground water contamination. Many of these wastes are flammable, corrosive, reactive, toxic, or explosive and can harm individuals if inhaled or absorbed through the skin. In addition, drug manufacturers commonly dump the hazardous waste chemicals into bathtubs, sinks, and toilets, as well as on the ground, roads, and creeks surrounding the clandestine drug laboratories. In some cases, surface and groundwater drinking supplies can be contaminated from the waste" (Office of Inspector General 2010: i).

METHAMPHETAMINE

Amphetamines are synthetic drugs, and their effects are similar to those of cocaine. Amphetamines mimic the naturally occurring substance adrenaline and cause a biochemical arousal—being "turned on"—without the presence of sensory input to cause such arousal. The body becomes physiologically activated. Because they ward off sleep, amphetamines have proven popular with college students cramming for exams and long-haul truck drivers.

First synthesized in 1887, amphetamines were introduced into clinical use in the 1930s and were eventually offered as a "cure-all" for just about every ailment (D. E. Smith 1979). Between 1932 and 1946 there were thirty-nine generally accepted medical uses ranging from the treatment of schizophrenia and morphine addiction to low blood pressure and caffeine and tobacco dependence. It was believed that the substance had no abuse potential (*Drug Abuse and Drug Abuse Research* 1987). Because amphetamines appear to act on the hypothalamus to suppress the appetite, they were once widely prescribed to treat obesity. Compared with more natural forms of dieting, however, the appetite returns with greater intensity after withdrawal from the drug. Only as a "last resort" is methamphetamine hydrochloride (Desoxyn) used to treat obesity as one component of a weight-reduction regimen, and even then the treatment is limited to only a few weeks.

Legally produced amphetamine is taken in the form of tablets or capsules. Some abusers crush the substance, dissolve it in water, and ingest it intravenously. Illegally produced amphetamine is available in tablet and powdered form (called "ice") that is sometimes smoked. There are three basic types of amphetamine, but the methylamphetamines have the greatest potential for abuse because they are fast acting and produce a "rush." Methamphetamine hydrochloride, one of the methyl group, is a widely abused drug known on the street simply as "meth"; in liquid form it is often referred to as "speed." As with cocaine, methamphetamine in small doses will bring about a "rush," a sensation or euphoria often described in sexual terms, along with indifference to pain and illusions of increased mental and sensory alertness and physical strength.

The main active ingredient in methamphetamine, phenyl-2-propanone, referred to as P2P, is widely available in Europe, and bulk shipments of P2P from Germany are often the source of illegal methamphetamine produced in the United States. But the dynamics of illicit methamphetamine production and trafficking have been changing with P2P as the primary precursor being replaced by ephedrine. Mexican manufacturers typically produce the drug in three phases, using such precursor chemicals as ephedrine, pseudoephedrine, red phosphorus, and hydriodic acid. Canada has been the source of pseudoephedrine that is imported in powder form, mostly from China, for use as a decongestant (Krauss 2002).

Although most of the chemicals needed are easily obtained or manufactured clandestinely, they present numerous hazards both during the production process and after when they are discarded because of their caustic, flammable, or reactive nature. The danger of chemical fires and explosions extends beyond manufacture. After producing the finished methamphetamine, clandestine lab workers are typically left with 5 to 6 pounds of hazardous waste for each pound of the finished drug produced. Most of this waste consists of corrosive sodium hydroxide. Traces of red phosphorous remain on discarded materials and equipment, presenting a flammable hazard for three to four decades.

The illegal activities associated with methamphetamine production and hazardous waste encompass more than the clandestine lab cooks and workers. Just as legitimate industries generate secondary services, clandestine lab site "brokers," property owners, and "oil barons" support and profit from the manufacture of methamphetamine, with the former two negotiating or allowing the use of property and the latter recycling hazardous waste material.

Even when law enforcement is able to arrest and prosecute the individuals involved, there can be staggering costs associated with removing the containers, contaminated apparatus, and chemical waste. Depending on the extent of the contamination and whether the area affected is a structure, soil, or water, costs can range from thousands of dollars to do the initial cleanup to hundreds of thousands of dollars to cleanse a water supply or make a dwelling habitable again. Undetected contaminated areas continue to do incalculable damage to the environment (Nieves 2001).

In unpopulated desert areas in Southern California, Mexican organizations produce d-methamphetamine, a drug twice as potent as its predecessor (dl-methamphetamine) and with a longer lasting high than cocaine. The substance is distributed using networks previously established for heroin and cocaine.

OXYCODONE

Just as methamphetamine can substitute for cocaine, oxycodone can do the same for heroin. Oxycodone,

a synthetic version of morphine, is a DEA Schedule II drug that was first introduced in 1995 and marketed under the trade name of OxyContin. Prescribed for chronic or long-lasting pain, oxycodone is also found in medications such as Percodan and Tylox. However, OxyContin contains between 10 and 80 milligrams (mg) of oxycodone in a timed-release tablet, while painkillers such as Tylox contain 5 mg and often require repeated doses to bring about pain relief because they lack the timed-release formulation. People who abuse OxyContin either crush the tablet and ingest or snort it or dilute it in water and inject it. Crushing or diluting the tablet disarms the timed-release action of the medication and causes a quick, powerful high ("OxyContin: Prescription Drug Abuse—2008 Revision": 1).

In 2007, several executives of Purdue Pharma of Connecticut, the company that produces OxyContin, pleaded guilty to misleading doctors and patients by claiming that the drug was less likely to be abused than heroin. In fact, experienced drug users and novices alike quickly discovered that crushing the pills and swallowing, inhaling, or injecting the powder produces an immediate and intense reaction (Meier 2007). The popularity of black market OxyContin in Appalachia led to its being dubbed "hillbilly heroin" (Meier 2007).

CANNABIS/MARIJUANA

The source of marijuana, the hemp plant, grows wild throughout most of the tropical and temperate regions of the world, including parts of the United States. Hemp has been cultivated for several useful products: The tough fiber of the stem is used to make rope, the seed as part of feed mixtures, and the oil as an ingredient in paint. The psychoactive part of the plant is a substance called Delta9THC, or simply THC. It is most highly concentrated in the leaves and resinous flowering tops of the plant. The THC level of marijuana cigarettes varies considerably: Domestic marijuana typically has had less than 0.5 percent, because the plants were originally introduced to produce hemp fiber. More recently developed strains, however, exhibit considerably higher levels, the result of careful cross breeding by outlaw horticulturalists. The domestic cultivation of marijuana has spawned a significant market in horticultural equipment. These suppliers advertise in *High Times*, a magazine devoted to marijuana.

Jamaican, Colombian, and Mexican marijuana ranges from 0.5 to 4.0 percent THC. The most select product, sinsemilla (Spanish *sin semilla*, "without seed"), is prepared from the unpollinated female cannabis plant. Sinsemilla has been found to have as much as 8.0 percent THC. Hashish, which is usually imported from the Middle East, contains the drug-rich resinous secretions of the cannabis plant, which are collected, dried, and then compressed into a variety of forms—balls, cakes, or sheets. It is usually mixed with tobacco and smoked in a pipe. Hashish potency can be as high as 10 percent. "Hashish oil" is a dark, viscous liquid, the result of repeated extractions of cannabis plant materials. It has a THC level as high as 20 percent. A drop or two on a cigarette has the effect of a single marijuana cigarette. Marijuana prepared for street sale may be diluted with oregano, catnip, or other ingredients and may contain psychoactive substances such as lysergic acid diethylamide (LSD).

In the United States, marijuana is usually rolled in paper and smoked. The user typically inhales the smoke deeply and holds it in the lungs for as long as possible. This tends to maximize the absorption of the active THC, about one-half of which is lost during smoking. The psychoactive reaction occurs in 1 to 10 minutes and peaks in about 10 to 30 minutes, with a total duration of 3 to 4 hours. The most important variables with respect to the drug's impact are the individual's experiences and expectations and the strength of the marijuana ingested. Thus, the first-time user may not experience any significant reaction. In general, low doses tend to induce restlessness and an increasing sense of well-being and gregariousness, followed by a dreamy state of relaxation; hunger, especially a craving for sweets, frequently accompanies marijuana use. Higher doses may induce changes in sensory perception—heightening the senses of smell, sight, hearing, and taste—which may be accompanied by subtle alterations in thought formation and expression.

In addition to imported marijuana, some areas of the United States have apparently gotten hooked on the business. In Kentucky, most cultivation takes place in the eastern region: the mountainous and inaccessible Appalachia. The region has a high unemployment rate and poverty—and thus incentive—is widespread. Endemic poverty and ideal growing climate fuels the industry and Appalachia's rugged terrain provides a natural camouflage for the marijuana. Much of the domestic cultivation occurs on federal lands to avoid forfeiture laws (discussed in Chapter 14). As noted in Chapter 6, Mexican traffickers have been cultivating marijuana on leased land and national forests in the United States.

The biggest influence on marijuana legislation has been racism. State laws against marijuana were often part of a reaction to Mexican immigration (Bonnie and Whitebread 1970). By 1930, sixteen states with relatively large Mexican populations had enacted antimarijuana legislation. "Chicanos in the Southwest were believed to be incited to violence by smoking it" (Musto 1973: 65). Because of marijuana's association with suspect marginal groups—Mexicans, artists, intellectuals, jazz musicians, bohemians, and petty criminals—it became an easy target for regulation (Morgan 1981). By 1931, twenty-two states had marijuana legislation, often part of a general-purpose statute against narcotics (Bonnie and Whitebread 1970). In 1937, Congress passed the Marijuana Tax Act, which put an end to lawful recreational use of the substance. Despite being outlawed, marijuana was never an important issue in the United States until the 1960s: "It hardly ever made headlines or became the subject of highly publicized hearings and reports. Few persons knew or cared about it, and marijuana laws were passed with minimal attention" (Himmelstein 1983: 38).

BARBITURATES

There are about 2,500 derivatives of barbituric acid and dozens of brand names for these derivatives.

Lawfully produced barbiturates are found in tablet or capsule form. Illegal barbiturates may be found in liquid form for intravenous use because lawfully produced barbiturates are poorly soluble in water. "Barbiturates depress the sensory cortex, decrease motor activity, alter cerebralar function, and produce drowsiness, sedation, and hypnosis" (*Physicians' Desk Reference* 1987: 1163). They inhibit seizure activity and can induce unconsciousness in the form of sleep or surgical anaesthesia. Unlike opiates, barbiturates do not decrease one's sense of pain. They can produce a variety of mood alterations, ranging from mild sedation to hypnosis and deep coma. A high dosage can induce anesthesia, and an overdose can be fatal. Barbiturates are used primarily as sedatives for the treatment of insomnia and as anticonvulsants (Mendelson 1980), although in some persons, they produce excitation (*Physicians' Desk Reference* 1988). The euphoria that follows barbiturate intake makes them appealing as intoxicants (Wesson and Smith 1977).

Barbiturates are classified according to the speed with which they are metabolized (broken down chemically) in the liver and eliminated by the kidneys: slow, intermediate, fast, and ultra fast. The fast-acting forms—the best known is sodium pentothal—are used to induce unconsciousness in a few minutes. At relatively high dosages, they are used as anesthetics for minor surgery and to induce anesthesia before the administration of slow-acting barbiturates. In low dosages, barbiturates may actually increase a person's reaction to painful stimuli. The fast-acting barbiturates, particularly Nembutal (sodium pentobarbital), Amytal (amobarbital sodium), Seconal (secobarbital sodium), and Tuinal (secobarbital sodium and amobarbital sodium combined) are the abuse risks (O'Brien and Cohen 1984).

There is no apparent pattern to the illegal market in barbiturates, and traffickers may sell them as part of their portfolio.

PHENCYCLIDINE (PCP)

Phencyclidine is reported to have received the name PCP—"peace pill"—on the streets of San Francisco.

The drug was reputed to give illusions of everlasting peace. Frequently referred to as "angel dust," PCP was first synthesized in 1956 and found to be an effective surgical anesthetic when tested on monkeys. Experiments on humans were carried out in 1957, and although PCP proved to be an effective surgical anesthetic, it had serious side effects. Some patients experienced agitation, excitement, and disorientation during the recovery period. Some male surgical patients became violent, and some females appeared to experience simple intoxication (Linder, Lerner, and Burns 1981). "When PCP was subsequently given to normal volunteers in smaller doses, it induced a psychotic-like state resembling schizophrenia. Volunteers experienced body image changes, depersonalization, and feelings of loneliness, isolation, and dependency. Their thinking was observed to become progressively disorganized" (Lerner 1980: 14).

There are more than one hundred variations (analogs) of the substance. Unlike other anesthetics, PCP increases respiration, heart rate, and blood pressure, qualities that make it useful for patients endangered by a depressed heart rate or low blood pressure. In the 1960s, PCP became commercially available for use in veterinary medicine as an analgesic and anesthetic, but diversion to street use led the manufacturer to discontinue production in 1978. It is now produced easily and cheaply in clandestine laboratories in tablet, capsule, powder, and liquid form and sometimes sold as LSD. Its color varies, and there is no such thing as a standard dose. As with any drug sold on the street, PCP is often mixed with other psychoactive substances. Most commonly, PCP is applied to a leafy vegetable, including marijuana, and smoked. "Street preparations of phencyclidine have continuously changed in name, physical form and purity" (Lerner 1980: 15).

A moderate amount of PCP produces a sense of detachment, distance, and estrangement from one's surroundings within 30 to 60 minutes of ingestion, and the effects last as long as hours. Numbness, slurred speech, and a loss of coordination also occur. These symptoms are often accompanied by feelings of invulnerability. "A blank stare, rapid and involuntary eye movements, and an exaggerated gait are among the more common observable effects" ("Drugs of Abuse" 1979: 30). Users may also experience mood disorders, acute anxiety, paranoia, and violent behavior. Some reactions are similar to LSD intoxication: auditory hallucinations and image distortion, similar to fun-house mirror images. "PCP is unique among popular drugs of abuse in its power to produce psychoses indistinguishable from schizophrenia" ("Drugs of Abuse" 1979: 30).

ECSTASY

Ecstasy, the common name for 3, 4-*MethyleneDioxy-MethAmphetamine* or MDMA, is a synthetic drug with a chemical structure similar to the stimulant methamphetamine and the hallucinogen mescaline (Grob et al. 1996). Some therapists used it in the 1970s to help patients explore their feelings for each other. In a controlled setting, MDMA was reputed to promote trust between patients and physicians (Karch 1996). In 1985, scheduling hearings on MDMA were conducted and the administrative law judge expressed his view that there was sufficient evidence for safe use under medical supervision and recommended DEA Schedule III status. He was overruled by the director of the Drug Enforcement Administration who placed MDMA in Schedule I—high potential for abuse and no medically accepted use.

MDMA is usually ingested orally in tablet or capsule form. It is also available as a powder and is sometimes snorted and occasionally smoked. Ecstasy did not receive a great deal of attention until its "rediscovery" in the late 1970s because of its purported ability to produce profound pleasurable effects: acute euphoria and long-lasting positive changes in attitude and self-confidence, with some symptoms resembling those caused by LSD but without the severe side effects typically associated with methamphetamine.

"The effects of MDMA usually become apparent twenty to sixty minutes following oral ingestion of an average dose (100–125 milligrams) on an empty stomach. The sudden and intense onset of the high experienced by many users is commonly referred to as the 'rush' (also the 'wave' or 'weird period')." This phase is often (particularly during initial use) experienced with a certain degree of trepidation, tension, stomach tightness, or mild nausea. Discomfort is generally transitory and melts away into a more relaxed state of being. "Although novice users occasionally experienced some apprehension during this initial onset, anxiety levels typically decreased with subsequent use, allowing for increased enjoyment" (Beck and Rosenbaum 1994: 63). The total effects last from three to six hours.

The drug's rewarding effects vary with the individual taking it, the dose and purity, and the environment in which it is taken. In high doses, ecstasy may cause the body's temperature to markedly increase (malignant hyperthermia) leading to muscle breakdown and kidney and cardiovascular system failure, which has proven fatal in some cases. Drinking water does not reduce the effects of ecstasy, but prevents dehydration. Drinking too much water, however, may lead to serious health complications in some people. Ecstasy may also produce a hangover effect: loss of appetite, insomnia, depression, and muscle aches. It can also make concentration difficult, particularly on the day after ecstasy is taken. Higher doses of ecstasy can produce hallucinations, irrational behavior, vomiting, and convulsions. Some evidence suggests that long-term use of ecstasy may cause damage to the brain, heart, and liver.

Although most ecstasy consumed domestically is produced in Europe—primarily the Netherlands and Belgium—a limited number of labs operate in the United States. In recent years, Israeli crime syndicates, some composed of Russian émigrés associated with Russian organized crime, have forged relationships with Western European traffickers and gained control over a significant share of the European market. The Israeli syndicates are reputedly the primary source of U.S. distribution.

Overseas ecstasy trafficking organizations smuggle the drug in shipments of 10,000 or more tablets via express mail services, couriers aboard commercial airline flights, or through air freight shipments from several major European cities to cities in the United States. Ecstasy costs as little as 25 cents per pill to produce, but wholesale prices range from $5 to $20 and retail prices range from $10 to $50 a dose. Ecstasy traffickers use brand names and logos as marketing tools and to distinguish their product from that of competitors. The logos are often produced to coincide with holidays or special events. Among the more popular logos are butterflies, lightning bolts, and four-leaf clovers (*National Synthetic Drugs Action Plan* 2004).

Ecstasy use is associated with dance parties known as *raves*, which usually start late at night and continue into the morning. *Ravers* often wear or carry glow sticks or other brightly lit accessories and eat lollipops and candy necklaces.

LYSERGIC ACID DIETHYLAMIDE (LSD)

In 1949, LSD was introduced into the United States as an experimental drug for treating psychiatric illnesses, but until 1954 it remained relatively rare and expensive, because its ingredients were difficult to cultivate. In that year the Eli Lilly Company announced that it had succeeded in creating a completely synthetic version of LSD (Stevens 1987). LSD ("acid") affects the body in a variety of ways. The visual effects range from blurring to a visual field filled with strange objects; three-dimensional space appears to contract and enlarge, and light appears to fluctuate in intensity. Auditory effects occur but to a lesser degree. All of these changes are episodic throughout the "trip." Temperature sensitivity is altered, and the environment is perceived as being abnormally cold or hot. Body images are altered—out-of-body experiences are common, and body parts appear to float. Perceptions of time are affected: Sometimes time is perceived as running fast-forward or fast-backward.

There are "good acid trips" and "bad acid trips." This appears to be controlled by the attitude, mood, and expectations of the user and often depends on suggestions of others at the time of the trip. Favorable expectations produce "good trips," but excessive apprehension is likely to produce the opposite. The substance appears to intensify feelings, so the user may feel a magnified sense of love, lust, and joy, or anger, terror, and despair: "The extraordinary sensations and feelings may bring on fear of losing control, paranoia, and panic, or they may cause euphoria and even bliss" (Grinspoon 1979: 13). Ingesting LSD unknowingly can result in a highly traumatic experience, since the victim may feel that he or she has suddenly "gone crazy" (Brecher 1972), and it only takes 0.01 milligram to have an effect.

LSD is colorless, odorless, and tasteless, and it is relatively easy to produce. One ounce contains about 300,000 human doses (Ray 1978). Although LSD has been used experimentally to treat a variety of psychological illnesses, it currently has no accepted medical use. It may be taken orally in a pure form as a white powder, mixed with a number of other substances, or absorbed on paper ("blotter acid"), sugar, or gelatin sheets ("window panes"). A trip begins between 30 to 60 minutes after ingestion, peaks after 2 to 6 hours, and fades out after about 12 hours.

LSD was popular for a time during the 1960s, when it became part of the "hippie" culture. Current use appears limited, and distribution patterns are not well known.

ANALOGS AND DESIGNER DRUGS

There are many chemical variations, or analogs (also called "designer drugs"), of the drugs discussed in this chapter. Examples include semisynthetic opiates such as hydromorphine, oxycodone, etorphine, and diprenorphine, as well as synthetic opiates such as pethidine, methadone, and propoxyphene (Darvon). The synthetic drug fentanyl citrate, which is often used intravenously in major surgery, works exactly like opiates: It kills pain, produces euphoria, and leads to addiction if abused. The substance is easily produced by persons skilled in chemistry. Fentanyl compounds are often sold as "China White," the street name for the finest Southeast

Asian heroin, to addicts who cannot tell the difference. Those who know the difference may actually prefer fentanyl because it is usually cheaper than heroin and some users believe it contains less adulterants than heroin (Roberton 1986). In fact, fentanyl compounds are quite potent and difficult for street dealers to cut properly, a situation that can lead to overdose and death. Fentanyl has been used (illegally) to "dope" racehorses, because the substance is very difficult to detect in urine or blood. Since the passage of the Antidrug Abuse Act of 1986, all analogs of controlled substances have themselves become controlled substances.

SUMMARY

1. Know the similarities between the drug business and legitimate business:
   - Drug trafficking has enormous profit-to-cost ratios, a market devoid of legal constraints governed only by the law of supply and demand.
   - The business of illegal drugs shares some elements with the business of selling legal products.
2. Appreciate the history of drugs, drug trafficking, and how nativism and hostility toward minorities influenced drug laws:
   - Prejudice against Chinese and Mexican immigrants resulted in support for drug laws.
   - Issues of foreign policy, not a domestic problem with drugs, led to enactment of the Harrison Act.
   - Opiates were legally available without prescription in the United States until 1914.
3. Understand the business of heroin and major producer regions:
   - Most of the heroin smuggled into the United States originates in areas where the opium poppy thrives: Golden Triangle, Golden Crescent, Mexico, and Colombia.
   - In these regions, politics and drug trafficking are connected.
4. Understand the history and business of cocaine:
   - Coca is a hardy jungle plant with abundant seeds that needs little or no fertilizer, and will yield four to five crops a year for thirty to forty years.
   - Until the 1960s there was limited demand for cocaine.
   - Attitudes toward recreational drug use became more relaxed and cocaine became associated with a privileged elite. The demand generated new sources and the development of the international cocaine organizations.
   - In Colombia, about three-quarters of the coca is grown in six rural provinces, which are desperately poor and plagued by left- and right-wing paramilitary groups.
5. The different levels involved in the drug business, ranging from the international to the street:
   - After importation, drugs are sold in 10- to 50-kilo quantities and then cut or "stepped on," diluted several times until it reaches the consumer.
   - Transactions must be accomplished without recourse to the formal mechanisms of dispute resolution available in the world of legitimate business.
   - As with cocaine, methamphetamine in small doses will bring about a "rush," a sensation or euphoria.
   - Most of the chemicals needed for methamphetamine are easily obtained but present numerous hazards.
   - There is little or no pattern to marijuana trafficking in the United States, although some rural areas have apparently gotten hooked on the business.

- There is no apparent pattern to the illegal market in barbiturates, and traffickers may sell them as part of their portfolio.
- Most ecstasy is produced in the Netherlands and Belgium.

- There are many analogs of the primary drugs of abuse.

REVIEW QUESTIONS

1. What are the elements that drug trafficking shares with the business of selling legal products?
2. What was the real cause of the Opium Wars?
3. Until they were made illegal in the United States, why were opium products so popular?
4. What was the connection between anti-Chinese legislation and the Harrison Act?
5. How did Supreme Court rule with respect to the Harrison Act?
6. How did the federal drug enforcement agency respond to the Harrison Act?
7. What are the similarities and differences between trafficking in alcohol during Prohibition and drug trafficking after the Harrison Act?
8. Why is it difficult, if not impossible, for an organized crime unit to control the drug market?
9. Why does increased heroin purity make smoking and sniffing popular?
10. What are the four areas of the world from which most heroin smuggled into the United States originates?
11. What is the relationship between politics and drug trafficking in these four areas?
12. What led to the widespread popularity of cocaine during the late 1960s and early 1970s?
13. Why is the drug business so filled with violence?
14. What is oxycodone?
15. What is MDMA/Ecstasy and why is it attractive to users?
16. Where is most Ecstasy produced?
17. What are analogs?

Labor racketeer Lepke Buchalter, on right, being sentenced in 1941.

CHAPTER 13

Organized Crime in Labor, Business, and Money Laundering

In 1957, Albert Anastasia, boss of what became known as the Gambino Family and unofficial ruler of the Brooklyn waterfront, was murdered while in a barber's chair at a New York hotel. His brother, ("Tough") Tony Anastasio, a member of the Gambino Family and official ruler of the Brooklyn waterfront, remained head of International Longshoremen's Local 1814 in Red Hook, Brooklyn, until his death from natural causes in 1963. That year, Anthony Scotto, Tony's son-in-law and a *caporegime* in the Gambino Family, took over Local 1814. In 1979, Scotto was convicted of federal bribery and racketeering charges. Anthony ("Todo") Anastasio, a member of the Gambino Family and nephew of the Anastasio/Anastasia brothers, controlled Local 1814 until his 2009 trial for racketeering, extortion, and arson. In 2010, he was sentenced to thirty months, but before he could begin serving his sentence, the 81-year-old committed suicide.

This chapter will discuss the International Longshoremen's Association and three other international unions noted for their connection to organized crime.

More than 15 million persons belong to labor unions in the United States. The unions to which they belong provide representation through collective bargaining that is guaranteed by federal law—the National Labor Relations (Wagner) Act of 1935 (upheld by the Supreme Court in the 1937 case *National Labor Relations Board v. Jones and Laughlin Steel Corporation,* 301 U.S. 1).

Labor racketeering refers to infiltration, domination, and use of a union for personal benefit by illegal, violent, and fraudulent means. Ronald Goldstock points out that the "sometimes bewildering array of labor rackets assume three basic forms: the sale of 'strike insurance' in which the union threatens a walkout and the employer pays to assure a steady supply of labor; the 'sweetheart deal' in which management pays the labor representative for contract terms unobtainable through arm's-length bargaining; and the direct or indirect siphoning of union funds" (PCOC 1985a: 658). An employer may be tempted into a corrupt relationship with labor unions because "he may hope that through a payment to the union officers he can persuade them not to organize his shop, thereby allowing for payment of less than the going union wage. Such an arrangement is particularly beneficial when his competitors are organized." If he cannot stifle organization, "he may at least be able to get a lenient 'sweetheart' agreement with the union." Furthermore, the "union itself can be used for the benefit of the employer through the limitation of competition. Competition can be limited by the union in several ways—either through the refusal to work on goods or by directly enforcing price agreements" (Newell 1961: 79). Although labor and related business racketeering can be conducted by anyone, the history of the labor movement shows that the most substantial corruption of unions is conducted by organized crime.

Labor and business racketeering distinguish the American Mafia and its predecessor groups from later forms of organized crime: Irish, Jewish, and Italian organized crime groups helped shape the economic life of the United States. The rise of organized labor and the subsequent reaction of American business generated a conflict that provided fertile ground for the seeds of racketeering and organized crime. The leaders of organized crime provided mercenary armies to unions that were willing to use violence to organize workers and thwart strikebreakers. In the spirit of ideological neutrality, they also provided private violence to business for use in its efforts against organized labor and dealing with the demanding competition of a capitalistic marketplace.

ORGANIZED LABOR IN AMERICA

The Civil War led to the dramatic industrialization of America. War profiteers accumulated large amounts of capital, enabling them to invest in the trusts: oil, coal, iron, steel, sugar, and railroads. Congress imposed protective tariffs, and industry blossomed during the Gilded Age of the Robber Barons. "Within twenty-five years of the assassination of Abraham Lincoln, America had become the leading manufacturing nation in the world" (Brooks 1971: 39).

At the bottom of this industrial world was labor, often immigrants who spoke English with foreign accents, if they spoke English at all. Children of both sexes often labored twelve hours a day, six days a week, under conditions that threatened life and limb. Labor's struggle for better working conditions and wages resulted in what Sidney Lens calls *The Labor Wars* (1974: 4): "The labor wars were a specific response to a specific set of injustices at a time when industrial and financial capitalism was establishing its predominance over American society. In a sense the battles were not different from the hundreds of other violent clashes against social injustices, as normal as the proverbial apple pie in the nation's annals."

From the first half of the nineteenth century to the Civil War, criminal conspiracy statutes were used against labor's efforts to organize and strike. This approach was replaced by the use of equity—a civil procedure—in the form of injunctions restraining unions from striking. The unions sought relief from Congress, but in 1908 the Supreme Court declared that Congress had no power with respect to union activities (*Adair v. United States,* 208 U.S. 161). It was not until the Great Depression that Congress stripped the federal courts of their power to issue injunctions in labor disputes (1932 Norris-La Guardia Act). In 1935, the Wagner Act gave explicit protection to the rights of workers to organize and engage in collective bargaining.

From the earliest days of the Industrial Era until the passage of the Wagner Act, labor confrontations with employers often took on a particular scenario: Company spies, often from the Pinkerton Private Detective Agency, would identify union leaders, who were then fired by management. The guard force would be increased and strikebreakers secured. Company lawyers would secure injunctions from friendly judges prohibiting a strike. The union would organize "flying squadrons" to guard against the influx of strikebreakers and plan for mass picketing. If the guard force proved inadequate, hired thugs, deputy sheriffs, policemen, National Guard, and even U.S. Army troops would be used to deal with strikers.

LABOR RACKETEERING:

IN THE BEGINNING ...

The first step away from union democracy was a response to power wielded by employers. In order to avoid the problem of company spies reporting to management, some unions employed the "walking delegate" or business agent, who was empowered to call a strike without any formal vote by the union membership. As an employee of the union, he was immune from management intimidation, and his power enabled the union to strike quickly and at the most opportune time, for example, at a construction site during the height of the building season. The men chosen for this position were usually tough, and it was this quality rather than intelligence, integrity, and commitment to labor that characterized business agents. Before long some of these men began abusing their power, calling needless strikes and engaging in extortionate practices (Seidman 1938). In 1928, for example, two racketeers set up the United Lathing Company and hired the Lathers Union walking delegate. He would appear at job sites and issue a strike order. When contractors asked for an explanation, he would refer them to the United Lathing Company, where, for a fee, the strike would be called off (Nelli 1976).

In the early days, labor unions provided "muscle" from the ranks of their membership to deal with Pinkerton agents and strikebreakers. In the first decade of the twentieth century, however, a need arose for a more systematic and professional approach. Enter Benjamin ("Dopey"—an adenoid gave him a sleepy look) Fein, leader of a Lower East Side gang who became an integral part of the Jewish labor movement. Whenever a strike was called under the auspices of the umbrella organization called United Hebrew Trades (UHT), "Dopey and his men were given union cards as pickets and union delegates" (Joselit 1983: 109). They protected fellow pickets against management goons—strong-arm personnel who were employed by licensed detective agencies.

Fein formed alliances with locally powerful New York gangs, assigning territories and working out businesslike arrangements and patterns of operation. He also assisted the union in keeping its members in line. It soon became clear, however, that it was easier to hire gangsters than it was to fire them (Seidman 1938). Two leading members of Fein's organization, Louis ("Lepke") Buchalter and Jacob ("Gurrah") Shapiro, revolutionized labor racketeering, dominating many of the industries into which they had been invited.

Lepke Buchalter

Lepke, short for *Lepkeleh,* an affectionate Yiddish term for "Little Louis," was born on New York's Lower East Side in 1897 into a family of Russian immigrants. He had three brothers: One earned a Ph.D. and became a rabbi and college professor; another became a pharmacist; and a third was a dentist. Lepke took a different route; he was arrested and imprisoned for burglary several times. After being released from Sing Sing Prison in 1922, he teamed up with Russian-born Jacob Shapiro and the two began working as strong-arms for labor-industrial racketeers.

"Instead of using his sluggers and gunmen to terrorize labor unions during strike periods, Lepke worked them directly into the unions. By threat and by violence they controlled one local after another" (Berger 1944: 30). Manufacturers who hired Lepke to deal with the unions "soon found themselves wriggling helplessly in the grip of Lepke's smooth but deadly organization. He moved in on them as he had on the unions" (Berger 1944: 20). Until 1940, Lepke was the head of an organization that extorted wealth from New York's garment, leather, baking, and trucking industries. Not always successful, he was driven out of the fur industry in 1933 by the fierce resistance of industry workers (Kavieff 2006).

Lepke's estimated income was between $5 million and $10 million annually—this was during the Depression (Turkus and Feder 1951). "All through the Prohibition era, when other mobsters were splashing headily in alcoholic wealth and getting their names in headlines with a series of competitive killings that strewed urban and suburban landscapes with untidy corpses, Lepke went his quiet way" (Berger 1940: 30).

That changed in 1937 when, in an effort to eliminate all possible witnesses against him, Lepke ordered a murder rampage—the number of killings at his direction is estimated at between sixty and eighty (Berger 1944). The murder binge backfired as loyal Lepke men became informers seeking police protection (Turkus and Feder 1951). In 1939, according to a prearranged plan, Lepke surrendered to J. Edgar Hoover. He was subsequently turned over to New York authorities and prosecuted for extortion, for which he received a sentence of thirty-years-to-life. Then, in 1941, he was prosecuted for murder in Brooklyn. After a protracted legal battle, in 1944 Buchalter was electrocuted at Sing Sing Prison. But the pattern had been set.

LABOR RACKETEERING AND THE "BIG FOUR"

Labor racketeers "didn't target steel mills and auto factories and foundries, the giant pool of workers who truly needed the protection of a collective bargaining agreement." Instead, they "picked on small, vulnerable mom-and-pop operations such as dry cleaners, taverns, and bakeries." Or they exploited their control over labor to extort money from vulnerable businesses such as those selling wholesale fish. "Because of the perishable nature of the product, seafood wholesalers depend on speed for display and delivery, which makes them vulnerable to threats of delay" (Neff 1989: 20).

Leaders of industrial unions working alongside hundreds or even thousands of other workers in factories or mines proved difficult to intimidate. In contrast, unions whose members worked in geographically dispersed locations for numerous small employers, such as restaurant workers, teamsters, and construction workers, or those representing workers whose employment was sporadic or seasonal, such as construction laborers or longshoremen, proved susceptible to racketeering (Jacobs 2006).

Unions fought not only with management, but also with each other. In 1938, a number of industrial unions led by John L. Lewis broke with the American Federation of Labor (AFL) and formed the Congress of Industrial Organizations (CIO). During struggles over jurisdiction and representation between the AFL and the CIO, both sides resorted to muscle from organized crime. But for whatever reason, whomever utilized organized crime was "playing with the devil." Many locals and some internationals were delivered into the hands of organized crime.

In 1982, a congressional committee concluded: "At least four international unions are completely dominated by men who either have strong ties to or are members of the organized crime syndicate. A majority of the locals in most major cities of the United States in the International Brotherhood of Teamsters (IBT), Hotel and Restaurant Employees Union (HRE), Laborers' International Union of North America (Laborers), and International Longshoremen's Association (ILA) are completely dominated by organized crime" (Permanent Subcommittee on Investigations 1982: 5).

Laborers' International Union of North America (LIUNA)

Formed in 1903, LIUNA is one of fifteen unions belonging to the Building Construction Trades Department of the AFL-CIO. Representing about 800,000 laborers in hundreds of locals in the United States and Canada, LIUNA members perform the dirtiest, most strenuous, and most dangerous work associated with building construction. Control over laborers provides control over many construction sites.

In Chicago, the Laborers' Union has always had close ties to the Outfit. For more than a decade, the 19,000-member Chicago District Council of the Laborers' Union was headed by Ernest Kumerow, who is married to the daughter of the late Outfit boss Tony Accardo. Until his death in 1992, Accardo spent winters in a coach house in the rear of Kumerow's home. Street boss Vincent Solano was president of Local 1 until his death from natural causes in 1992, and his son remained a LIUNA official. Street boss Alfred Pilotta was president of Local 5 until he was convicted in 1982 for his role in a kickback scheme involving the union's welfare benefit fund. In 1992, a veteran LIUNA official and Outfit boss in charge of the southern suburbs was sentenced to thirty-two years for extorting money from bookmakers in northwest Indiana. His codefendant, a Laborers' Union field representative, received thirty-six years. In 1997, the LIUNA secretary-treasurer of Local 5, a top lieutenant for

the South Side Outfit boss, was charged with the 1988 murder of the owner of a pallet company who refused to pay a $100,000 juice loan—he had been shot six times. In 2000, while awaiting trial for murder, the LIUNA official died of natural causes. In 2001, John Serpico, a former international vice president of LIUNA and reputed Outfit associate, was convicted of receiving kickbacks for using his union influence to arrange for millions of dollars in loans from the union.

Surveillance tapes contain conversations involving New Jersey Family boss Sam DeCavalcante, during which he discussed how control of Laborers' Union locals enabled him to "shake down" building contractors who wanted to avoid using expensive union labor. When DeCavalcante retired, the man he chose to replace him, John Riggi, was business agent for LIUNA Local 394 in Elizabeth, New Jersey (G. Smith 2003). For much of his adult life, until he was voted out in 1992, Matthew ("Mikey") Trupiano, head of the St. Louis *Cosa Nostra*, led Laborers' Union Local 110. In 1985, the President's Commission on Organized Crime concluded that in New York, several LIUNA locals are controlled by members of the five crime Families.

In 1995, the U.S. Department of Justice reached a consent agreement with the union under which the federal government would monitor efforts to purge LIUNA officials connected to organized crime. As part of the agreement, LIUNA agreed to hold direct elections for the union's top posts; previously they were chosen by delegates at the annual convention. In only one instance did an opposition candidate ever challenge the union slate, and he was physically beaten on the floor of the 1981 convention (Johnson 1996). Chicago's Bruno Caruso lost the government-monitored election to Arthur Coia.

Coia is the son of a former secretary-treasurer of LIUNA who allegedly had close ties with New England crime boss Raymond Patriarca. A native of Rhode Island, Arthur Coia first headed the Laborers' local in Providence and later throughout New England. He admitted knowing Raymond Patriarca, Jr., who took over the crime Family after his father died of natural causes in 1984. Coia has also admitted that he met with mob figures in Chicago—he denied knowing they were connected to the Outfit. He stated that he was told to meet with them in order to get permission to take the top spot in the union (Greenhouse 1997, 2000c).

Under an arrangement with the Department of Justice, the union conducted an internal investigation led by a former federal organized crime prosecutor. As a result, the Justice Department dropped a 1995 civil complaint that sought to remove Coia and place the union under receivership. One of those suspended in the subsequent union purge was president of the Chicago LIUNA Local 225 who in 1999 was convicted of syndicated gambling—accepting $200,000 in sports wagers over a three-week period—for which he was placed on probation. In 1999, the president of LIUNA Local 2 in Chicago was removed for his alleged role in the Outfit's North Side crew. In 2001, a federal hearing officer removed the business managers of Local 1001 and 1006 in Chicago; according to the government, the brothers Bruno and Leo Caruso, along with Outfit members, rigged union elections (Possley 2001). The Caruso brothers are the sons of Frank ("Skids") Caruso, for many years the Outfit boss of Chinatown who died in 1983, and nephews of a convicted First Ward alderman.

A civil RICO (discussed in Chapter 14) action was taken to rid the Buffalo, New York LIUNA local from organized crime control. In 1996, the government concluded that eleven Buffalo LIUNA officials were made members of the Buffalo crime Family, and they were barred from the union. The Buffalo local was subsequently placed in trusteeship under the provisions of RICO (Office of Inspector General 2000).

In 2000, a hearing officer cleared Coia of associating with members of organized crime but fined him $100,000 for buying a $450,000 Ferrari with help from a supplier to the union. The hearing officer's ruling was criticized by the Department of Justice, union dissidents, and Republican lawmakers (Franklin 1999; Greenhouse 1999; Kaiser 1999). Under Coia, the union was one of the three biggest contributors to President Bill Clinton's 1997 inauguration and the union has also been one of the

biggest contributors to the Democratic Party. On the first day of 2000, after agreeing to plead guilty to defrauding Rhode Island of about $100,000 in taxes, Coia retired as LIUNA president (Greenhouse 2000a). Later that year, the Justice Department agreed to relax its oversight of LIUNA; this, after the union removed 220 corrupt officials from union positions, 127 of them found to be members or associates of organized crime (Office of Inspector General 2000).

Hotel Employees and Restaurant Employees International Union (HEREIU)

HEREIU was established in Chicago in 1891: "At first, only workers from pubs and restaurants were represented. Yet as America's cities began to grow so did the international, and soon hotel workers as well as food and beverage workers were represented. Thwarted only by prohibition in the 1920s, the international became the fastest growing union in the United States in the 1930s. By 1941, the international was the seventh largest union in North America" (Permanent Subcommittee on Investigations 1982: 4). Today the HEREIU is the largest service union in the United States, with about 260,000 members in 235 locals in the United States and Canada.

HEREIU charters often provided the basis for extortion from restaurants in Chicago, as U.S. Senator John L. McClellen explained (1962: 141–142):

> If an owner knew what was good for him,
> he agreed to have his place unionized upon
> the first visit of the organizer. The workers
> were not consulted in this organizing
> drive; they rarely knew it was going on.
> The restaurant owner was told that the
> union wasn't greedy, a compromise figure
> would always be accepted. If the owner had
> forty employees, then twenty memberships
> would be given to the union. The owner
> paid the initiation fees and the dues for
> twenty names that he gave the organizer.

That arrangement usually continued for years. It didn't make any difference to anyone concerned in the deal that, after a period of time, possibly ten or more of the twenty union members may no longer be employees.... Dues continued to be collected for twenty names.

In return, there "were no sudden fires in the middle of the night, no beatings, no sugar poured into gas tanks, no tires slashed, no vandalism" (1962: 142). The restaurant owners did not have to worry about workers' salaries or working conditions—conditions of employment that are the concerns of legitimate unions.

Many HEREIU locals were reputed to be under the domination of organized crime. Chicago Local 450 was chartered in 1935 by Joey ("Doves") Aiuppa, a top leader in the Outfit. For forty years, the Outfit wielded power in Chicago area HEREIU locals and their joint executive board. "Their actions took on national proportions when Edward Hanley [a former bartender from Chicago's West Side], who began his career in Local 450 as a business agent in 1957, was elected to the HEREIU presidency in 1973" (PCOC 1986b: 73). When Hanley, who has never been convicted of any crime, appeared before a U.S. Senate investigating committee, he refused to answer any questions, invoking the Fifth Amendment thirty-six times (Franklin 1995a). In Illinois, the 40,000-member union local has made significant political contributions, and Hanley has been feted by the Cook County Democratic organization.

HEREIU Local 54 in New Jersey has about 22,000 members, most of them employed in the Atlantic City casino business. The local has been controlled by the Philadelphia crime Family once headed by Angelo Bruno. As a result, Bruno Family members were able to force hotels in Atlantic City to buy supplies and provisions from companies they own. In 1980, when the president of the Philadelphia Roofers Union Local 30 attempted to organize bartenders in Atlantic City—even though they belonged to Local 54—he was murdered at his home. Two union officials were convicted of ordering the murder and are serving life sentences. In 1981, the New Jersey Casino Control Commission concluded

that Local 54 was controlled by Philadelphia crime boss Nicky Scarfo, and legal action eventually forced the local's president to resign. In 1991, the local was placed in government receivership, which has since been lifted.

In New York, HEREIU Locals 6 and 100 had long been under the control of organized crime. The locals were used to dictate the way in which restaurants "could do business in New York. In return for payoffs, restaurant owners could pay reduced wages and pension and welfare fund contributions, or buy a lease on a restaurant shut down because it owed money to the union, or hire and fire without regard to grievance procedures, or operate without regard to union work rules" (PCOC 1986b: 83–84). At one point, there appeared to be a jurisdictional dispute between the two locals, something that is not unusual in organized labor. However, intercepted conversations between union officials and important organized crime figures revealed that the split was in fact "a market allocation of New York's entire restaurant business between the Colombo and Gambino crime families" (PCOC 1986b: 84).

In 1995, as the result of a settlement of a civil RICO lawsuit, the U.S. Department of Justice placed the HEREIU under supervision and appointed a monitor with disciplinary and oversight authority (Franklin 1995a). In 1998, faced with another federal investigation, Edward Hanley, who ran the union for twenty-five years, was forced to retire—with a guaranteed $267,000 annual salary for the rest of his life. In 2000, at age 67, Hanley was killed in a traffic accident. The government-appointed monitor expelled seventeen union officials and at the end of 2000, the Justice Department agreed to end five years of intensive monitoring (Greenhouse 2000b).

International Longshoremen's Association (ILA)

New York City's premier position as a commercial capital is due in large part to its deep-water harbor, the finest in North America. The New York waterfront encompasses over 700 miles of wharves and shoreline and 1,900 piers. Combined, the New

York–New Jersey waterfront is an integrated commercial marketplace composed of several separate ports, including the Port of New York and the Port of New Jersey, occupying a common harbor and encompassing some 1,500 square miles and 234 municipalities. The waterfront harbor plays a critical role in the movement of manufactured, agricultural, and other goods throughout the Eastern seaboard and has a major impact on this nation's commerce. With government regulation absent, organized crime was able to assert control over this lucrative piece of geography.

With the able assistance of men such as Antonio Vaccarelli, a professional boxer better known as Paul Kelly, the ILA was organized in the 1890s and gained complete control over the New York waterfront by 1914 (Nelli 1976). Kelly, leader of New York's notorious Five Points Gang—Al Capone and Lucky Luciano were members—became vice president of the union.

Until the twentieth century, about 95 percent of the longshoremen in the New York City area were Irish. By 1912, Italians comprised about 35 percent, and by 1919, they accounted for about 75 percent of the area's longshoremen. The Irish controlled the notoriously violent West Side ("Hell's Kitchen") docks and those in Hoboken and Jersey City, while the Italians dominated the East Side, Brooklyn, and most New Jersey docks except the piers in Hudson County, where the Irish had been entrenched for decades. William Murphy headed Longshoremen's Local 2 in Hoboken until 1973 when two masked gunmen shot him while he was stopped at a traffic light. A few months later, Frank Murray, the head of ILA Local 1247 in Jersey City, vanished while en route to a union-related meeting in Manhattan. The Jersey side of New York harbor came completely under the control of the American Mafia (Stewart 2006).

By the end of World War II, the ILA had 40,000 members in the Port of New York. Today, the union represents nearly 65,000 dockworkers and other waterfront-related employees at three dozen ports from Maine to Texas.

For poorly educated and often illiterate immigrants, the waterfront provided attractive employment opportunities. It was also attractive to racketeers for its lucrative illegal opportunities. The "shape up," vividly portrayed in the Academy Award–winning film *On the Waterfront*, provided corrupt ILA officials with kickbacks from workers eager for a day's wage. Loansharking, large-scale pilfering, smuggling, and deals with employers eager for "labor peace" profited the criminals who dominated the waterfront. The "necessity for speed, plus the lack of rail connections to the piers, gave rise to the coveted 'loading' racket, which involved moving cargo from the pier floor to waiting trucks. Since demand for cargo loading was inelastic and dependent upon immediate need when ships arrived, loading generated extraordinary profits, and was a principal incentive for organized crime to infiltrate the ILA" (PCOC 1986b: 33). Whoever controls waterfront labor controls the waterfront.

While Paul Kelly led an influx of criminals to the waterfront, it was under Joseph P. Ryan that organized crime control of the waterfront became complete (Nelli 1976). As union president, Ryan dispensed union charters to groups of workers to form their own ILA locals. A strident anticommunist—which endeared him to many politicians—Ryan served as ILA president from 1927 to 1953, when he was convicted of embezzling union funds. On the West Coast, where organized crime was weaker, Australian-born Alfred Reuton ("Harry") Bridges withdrew from the ILA and formed the International Longshoremen and Warehousemen's Union (ILWU), which became part of the rival CIO. Bridges, who was born in 1901 and came to the United States as a merchant seaman in 1920, went to work as a longshoreman in San Francisco. He reactivated a dormant ILA local in 1933 and led a successful strike in 1934, a strike opposed by ILA president Joe Ryan. Ryan attacked Bridges for his leftist views and close association with communists (Lens 1974). During the 1940s, the House of Representatives voted to have Bridges deported as an undesirable alien, an order that was overturned by the Supreme Court. In marked contrast to the ILA, always a strongly anticommunist union, the ILWU has been free of organized crime influence. Nevertheless, the ILWU was expelled from the CIO in 1950 for "following the communist line." A variety of unions, including the Teamsters, unsuccessfully attempted to raid the ILWU membership (Kimeldorf 1988). Bridges headed the ILWU until his retirement in 1977; he died in 1990 (Saxon 1990). Today, the ILWU has about 25,000 members employed at twenty-nine West Coast ports and remains remarkably free of organized crime.

Once in control of the union, organized crime found the shipping industry an attractive and easy target for the more traditional types of racketeering (PCOC 1986b: 34–35): "When a ship docks, it must be emptied quickly. The cargo may include perishable foodstuffs, and in any event, the owner gathers no return for his capital investment—the ship—while it is in port. Ship turnaround time is thus a crucial key to profitability." Pier bosses regularly shook down shippers by threatening walkouts. "Time pressures also encouraged owners to maintain an oversupply of labor so that all ships, even on the busiest days, could be unloaded at once. The lucrative and commonly used 'kickback' racket also arose from time pressures. Because the number of ship arrivals fluctuated, the hiring boss (usually a union officer) selected the necessary number of workers from the surplus of men at the daily 'shape up.' The criterion for selection on many piers was the willingness, evidenced by a prearranged signal, such as a toothpick by the ear, to 'kickback' a part of the day's wages to the boss."

Other traditional rackets ran rampant on the ILA-controlled waterfront: gambling, loansharking, and cargo theft. Organized crime–corrupted port employees provided "access to cargo shipments and storage areas, security for the movement of contraband, such as narcotics, falsification of invoices and shipping documents in insurance scams, and collusion in the expropriation of stolen property, such as luxury vehicles and construction equipment" (PCOC 1986b: 35).

In 1953, the AFL convention voted to revoke the ILA charter because of rampant corruption. Shortly afterward, under indictment for misappropriating union funds, Ryan stepped down and

William Bradley was elected president. The AFL attempted to wrest control of longshoremen from the ILA by setting up a rival union, the International Brotherhood of Longshoremen (IBL). In 1955, the AFL and CIO merged into the AFL-CIO, and in 1959, after a series of often bloody physical battles between the rival longshoremen's unions, the IBL and ILA merged. Shortly afterward the ILA was admitted to the AFL-CIO.

Bradley refused to cooperate with organized crime. Taped conversations between leading waterfront racketeers indicate that he "was visited by mob members who told him he'd have to give up his position to Teddy Gleason or he'd be killed" (Permanent Subcommittee on Investigations 1981b: 447). In 1963, after Bradley declined to run for reelection, Thomas W. ("Teddy") Gleason was unanimously elected president of the ILA, a post he held until his retirement in 1987, when he stepped down because of poor health; he died of natural causes in 1992. Without any opposition, the post went to his associate and ILA executive vice president, John Bowers.

In 1953, Michael Clemente, president of ILA Local 856 in Manhattan and a member of the Genovese Family, was convicted of extorting money from waterfront employers and of committing perjury before the New York State Crime Commission (PCOC 1986b). Upon his release from prison, however, Clemente resumed his control of the Manhattan waterfront. Another Genovese Family member, Tino Fiumara, exercised similar control on the New Jersey side. When he died of cancer in 2010, Fiumara was reputed to be on the three-man panel running the Genovese Family (Rashbaum 2011).

As a result of more stringent law enforcement efforts in the ports of New York and New Jersey, notes Donald Goddard (1980: 66), "ILA racketeers moved operations to Florida, where they plundered the booming Port of Miami." The ILA shifted from exploiting its members to "carving up the cargo traffic among the port's stevedores and 'taxing' them on their shares." The ILA used its domination of the port to establish a system whereby competition among stevedoring companies and other waterfront firms was significantly reduced. Goddard

WATERFRONT COMMISSION

In 1952, it was revealed that organized crime, using its control of the ILA, "had for years been levying the equivalent of a 5 percent tax on all general cargo moving in and out of the harbor" (Goddard 1980: 35). The outrage generated led to the 1953 establishment of the New York–New Jersey Waterfront Commission.

The Waterfront Commission has subpoena power and investigative authority in New York and New Jersey. The commission employs investigators who possess full police powers in both states. With a budget of about $7.5 million, financed from a 2 percent assessment on gross wages of port employers, the commission regulates waterfront employees and licenses stevedoring concerns that contract with shipping companies to unload their ships. The stevedoring firms own or rent the heavy equipment needed and hire longshoremen who provide the labor. Companies seeking to hire waterfront workers must submit applicants' names to the commission, which does a background investigation. The commission also limits the number of waterfront employees.

The commission has banned persons with serious criminal records from the docks, and the notorious "shape-up" has been eliminated. Convicted criminals are prohibited from holding office in waterfront unions, and the commission audits the books and records of licensed stevedore firms to guard against illegal payoffs and other violations of law.

As a result of containerization (cargo shipped in large corrugated containers), shipping into the ports of Manhattan and Brooklyn, which have only limited room for such mechanization, has been significantly reduced, as has the number of dockworkers, who now number about 7,000.

points out that ship owners, agents, stevedores, contractors, and service companies were caught up in a web of corrupt practices with the ILA—and few wanted to escape. "They only had to pay their 'rent' in order to enrich themselves with guaranteed profits." Louis J. Freeh of the FBI noted before a congressional committee (Permanent Subcommittee on Investigations 1981b: 183): "You do not have extortion, you do not have threats, you do not have violence. What you have is a businessman who is as corrupt as the ILA official who he pays looking for additional business, looking for an advantage against his competitors and using his organized crime connection to have that union official contact another businessman to extend an economic advantage."

The FBI's UNIRAC investigation (1975–1979) was accomplished with the help of stevedore Joe Teitelbaum, who was approached by ILA officials for a $3,000 payoff as a down payment for continuing to do business in Miami. When he declined to pay, shipping clients began to receive calls from the union officials indicating Teitelbaum was having labor problems and could not guarantee to provide longshoremen when their cargo needed offloading in Miami. Teitelbaum went to the FBI and agreed to serve in an undercover capacity. The investigation revealed that ports along the East Coast from New York to Florida had been divided between the Genovese and Gambino Families into spheres of interest with attendant corrupt practices:

- Payoffs in lieu of employer contributions to ILA pension and welfare plans
- Payoffs to secure "labor peace" and avoid adhering to costly ILA rules that amounted to "featherbedding"
- Payoffs by businessmen to secure union contracts that were necessary to qualify for maritime work in ports under ILA control
- Payoffs to help firms secure new business and to keep the business they had without competitive bidding

UNIRAC resulted in 117 convictions, including that of Tino Fiumara, Michael Clemente, and Anthony Scotto. New York's governor and two former New York City mayors acted as character witnesses at Scotto's trial.

The relationship between racketeers and employers has frequently been mutually beneficial: "Convicted union officers have gone back to the ports working for industries closely associated with the port, thus enabling them to circumvent the provisions of the Landrum-Griffin Act" that bars them from holding union office (PCOC 1986b: 44).

American Mafia activities on the waterfront have continued into the twenty-first century, with the Genovese Family asserting influence in New Jersey and the Gambino Family in Brooklyn and Staten Island (Marzulli 2004b). In 2001, the imprisoned acting boss of the Genovese crime Family was indicted for laundering money he siphoned from the ILA benefit fund (Rashbaum 2001b). The following year, Gambino Family members including Richard Gotti, a captain and one of John Gotti's brothers, and Peter Gotti, acting Family boss, were indicted for controlling the appointment of union officials and extorting money from dockworkers and the union's managed care system (Rashbaum 2002). All were subsequently convicted.

International Brotherhood of Teamsters (IBT)

The IBT is the most important union to come under the domination of organized crime—virtually every consumer product needs to be trucked. The IBT is the largest labor union in the United States, representing more than 1.4 million truckers, delivery drivers, warehouse workers, flight attendants, and other workers. The union has lost considerable membership since the 1970s, when it represented 2.2 million workers. The union once represented about 80 percent of long-haul truck drivers, but now represents only about 8 percent.

In 1899, the Team Drivers International Union, headquartered in Detroit, received a charter from the AFL for its membership of 1,200 drivers. In 1902, Chicago members of the Team Drivers established a rival Teamsters National Union with 18,000 horse handlers. The following year, Samuel Gompers, president of the AFL, arranged for a merger of the two, which became the IBT. The union was marked by violence from its inception. When the Teamsters went on strike, the public suffered and therefore supported efforts against the drivers. Allen Friedman, IBT vice president and former strong-arm for the union,

reports that "[the Teamsters'] answer was to fight back, sending their own men to do battle with baseball bats, knives, guns, blackjacks, and any other weapon they owned or could make. They also teamed up with local gangsters who enjoyed being paid to break heads for either side." Unfortunately, the influx of neighborhood gangsters marked a major change in the Teamsters. "Suddenly there were men involved who had neither loyalty nor ideology. They began changing the face of organized labor in many communities, taking control and becoming extortionists" (Friedman and Schwartz 1989: 9).

Although the Teamsters remained a relatively weak union, by 1933 they had about 125,000 members concentrated in industrial centers such as Detroit and Chicago. In 1907, Dan Tobin became IBT president and served without major scandal until 1952. He was succeeded by Dave Beck of Seattle who controlled the Western Conference of Teamsters. Because of the support he received from Jimmy Hoffa, head of the Teamsters in Detroit, Beck awarded Hoffa with an IBT vice presidency. In 1957, before a U.S. Senate (McClellen) Committee, Beck took the Fifth Amendment 142 times. That year he was convicted of state charges and in 1959 of federal charges—embezzling union funds and income-tax violations—for which he received a five-year prison sentence. Beck died at the end of 1993, at age 99.

At the 1957 IBT convention in Miami, James R. Hoffa, who had been accused of dozens of improper activities by the McClellen Committee (see Chapter 14), was elected president. That same year, the IBT was expelled from the AFL-CIO (Moldea 1978). In 1987, the AFL-CIO readmitted the IBT to its ranks. At the time, the Teamsters were struggling against a Justice Department effort to place them under the control of a court-appointed trustee under provisions of the Racketeer Influenced and Corrupt Organizations (RICO) statute.

Jimmy Hoffa

James Riddle Hoffa was born in Brazil, Indiana, in 1913 and moved to Detroit with his family in 1924. A high school dropout, Hoffa eventually became a warehouse worker and developed a reputation as a tough street fighter who always stood up for his fellow workers against management. Because of this, Hoffa was fired from his warehouse job and hired as an organizer for Local 299 of the IBT, a troubled local—misuse of funds, rigged elections—that had to be taken into receivership by the IBT. He and other IBT organizers battled management goons in their organizing efforts throughout Detroit. Hoffa also used organized crime connections to shake down an association of small grocery stores, leading to his first criminal conviction, for which he paid a fine. After he had risen to a leadership position in Local 299, Hoffa continued to work with organized crime in Detroit, using the threat of labor trouble to force businesses to employ a mob-controlled overalls supply firm (Friedman and Schwarz 1989).

In 1941, Hoffa found himself in a battle with the CIO that began a "raid" to represent Detroit's teamsters. The CIO action was backed by a small army of goons, and the AFL-affiliated IBT was literally being beaten in the streets of Detroit. Hoffa turned to his friends in the Detroit underworld and secured the assistance of the powerful Meli Family. "The CIO raiders were defeated by the end of the year. And considering the new players on Hoffa's team, it was a miracle that the CIO survived at all in Detroit" (Moldea 1978: 38). The victory was not without cost: "The CIO's defeat, brought about by Hoffa's ringers, became the major factor in his rapid plunge from union reformer to labor racketeer. His pact with the underworld, no matter how tenuous at the time, took him out of the running as a potentially great leader of the Teamsters' rank and file" (1978: 38).

Hoffa's road to power and the presidency of the IBT was strewn with scandal. For example, his alliance with Anthony Provenzano "was typical of the bargains Hoffa struck with gangsters around the country; they helped push him to the top, and he helped them use their union posts for a series of money-making schemes: extortion from employers, loan-sharking, pension-fund frauds" (Brill 1978: 125). Pension fraud schemes involving union officials have some common elements. Typically,

a corrupt union official will approve the investment of pension monies through investment service providers associated with organized crime, who in turn may be exerting influence over the pension plan. In exchange for transferring money, service providers offer kickbacks from fees generated from servicing the plan.

Tony Provenzano and Local 560

Born in 1917, Anthony ("Tony Pro") Provenzano was one of six sons of a Sicilian immigrant couple living on the Lower East Side of New York. He dropped out of school at age 15 to become a truck helper and later a driver. He had aspirations of becoming a professional boxer and his reputation for violence brought him to the attention of a next-door neighbor, Anthony Strollo ("Tony Bender"), a *caporegime* in the Genovese Family and a powerful waterfront racketeer. As a result of Bender's patronage, Provenzano became a member of the Genovese Family and an organizer for IBT Local 560 in New Jersey. By 1941, Provenzano was a shop steward and in 1959, with the help of Jimmy Hoffa, was elected president of the local. In 1960, Hoffa appointed Provenzano to fill a vacancy among IBT vice presidents. He also rose in the ranks of the Genovese Family, reportedly becoming a *caporegime* (McFadden 1988).

Union opponents of Provenzano found themselves subjected to threats, beatings, or (in at least two instances) murder. In 1961, a rival was beaten and garroted by mob executioners led by the infamous ex-fighter Harold ("Kayo") Konigsberg (Konigsberg 2001). In 1963, another Provenzano rival was shot to death in Hoboken, New Jersey. By 1963, Provenzano's union salaries totaled $113,000—at the time he was the highest-paid union official in the world. That same year, he was convicted of extorting $17,000 from a trucking company to end a discipline problem the firm was having with its union employees. During the four and one-half years he was in prison and the five years he was disqualified from holding union office (as per the 1959 Landrum-Griffin Act discussed in Chapter 14), his brothers Salvatore ("Sammy") and

Nunzio headed the local while Tony ran its affairs. In 1978, Tony Pro was convicted of the 1961 murder and sentenced to life imprisonment.

In 1981, Nunzio Provenzano, president of Local 560, was sentenced to ten years' imprisonment for accepting $187,000 from four interstate trucking companies to ensure "labor peace" and permitting them to avoid contract rules for hiring Local 560 drivers. Brother "Sammy Pro" became president of Local 560. In 1984, Sammy Pro went to prison, and a close Provenzano aide, Michael Sciarra, became interim president; Tony Pro's daughter became the secretary-treasurer. That same year, the federal government invoked the civil racketeering provision of the RICO statute and a federal judge in New Jersey removed Local 560's executive board and put the local into trusteeship "until such time as the membership can freely nominate and elect new officers" (PCOC 1986b: 123).

After more than two years under government trusteeship, the members of Local 560 voted in the local's first contested election in twenty-five years. Sciarra was barred from seeking his former position as the local's president after a federal judge released tapes indicating that Matthew ("Matty the Horse") Ianiello, a *caporegime* in the Genovese Family, wanted Sciarra to head the local. In 1988, when mailed ballots were counted by government monitors, Danny Sciarra—running as a surrogate for his brother Michael—won by a vote of 2,842 to 1,535 (Sullivan 1988). Four days later, at age 71, Anthony Provenzano died of a heart attack in a California hospital near the federal prison where he was incarcerated. At the end of 1998, a former truck driver running on a reform platform was elected president of the 4,400-member local, and the following year the local was released from a court-ordered federal trusteeship (McFadden 1999).

John Dioguardi and Anthony Corallo

Elections were scheduled to be held in 1956 to choose officers for the IBT's Joint Council 16 in New York City. If Jimmy Hoffa could affect the outcome of the Joint Council 16 elections, it would enable him to win control of the IBT national presidency. Accordingly, in 1955 Hoffa had seven new Teamster charters issued to his friend John ("Johnny Dio") Dioguardi.

Born on the Lower East Side in 1914, Dioguardi was the nephew of a *caporegime* in the Lucchese Family and he became a member of that crime Family. In 1956, Dioguardi was convicted for extorting money from the trucking industry and indicted for ordering the acid-throwing attack that blinded labor reporter Victor Reisel—Reisel had been critical of union racketeering. The charges were dropped when a witness refused to testify. In 1967, Dioguardi received a five-year sentence for bankruptcy fraud ("scam") discussed later. When he finished that term he was convicted of stock fraud involving a car-leasing company and died in prison in 1979 (Kihss 1979).

Along with Anthony ("Tony Ducks") Corallo, also a member of the Lucchese Family, Dioguardi filled IBT locals for which he had charters from Hoffa with a number of gangsters who could then vote in the 1956 union election. Five of the seven locals did not have a single legitimate member—they were "paper locals." Corallo had already gained control of five other Teamster locals, although he held office in only one. Dioguardi and Corallo brought into the newly chartered locals 40 men with an aggregate record of 178 arrests and 70 convictions. Corallo was subsequently described by Robert F. Kennedy (1960: 84) as "an underworld figure of great influence whose unusual nickname stems from his reputation for 'ducking' convictions in court cases in which he is arrested. Tony Ducks, whose police record includes drug and robbery charges and who is on the Treasury Department's narcotic list, lost only one bout with the law." In 1941, Corallo was sentenced to six months for unlawful possession of narcotics. In 1962, he received a two-year sentence for bribing a judge in a fraudulent bankruptcy case. In 1968, Corallo was convicted for his part in a kickback scheme that involved a New York City water commissioner and received a three-year sentence. He subsequently became boss of the Lucchese Family.

While Hoffa was interested in winning over the locals and their votes in his quest for the IBT presidency, Dioguardi and Corallo were interested in the financial rewards that control of the locals promised. The newly "elected" officers would approach various nonunion employers with an offer they could not easily refuse: pay the union initiation fees and membership dues for your employees (who would not even know they were members of a union) and you keep your business free of all labor problems, including demands by legitimate unions; fail to pay, and labor problems, or worse, will result. By the time Hoffa gained control of the IBT in New York, twenty-five of the men Dio and Ducks brought into their locals had already been convicted of crimes, including bribery, extortion, perjury, and forgery (Brill 1978; Sheridan 1972). According to the federal government, Lucchese Family control over IBT Local 295 continued into the 1990s. In 1992, a special trustee was appointed by a federal judge to monitor the local's activities (Fried 1992).

An important part of Hoffa's Teamster legacy involves his connection to Allen Dorfman and the looting of the IBT pension fund.

Allen Dorfman

Born in 1923, Allen Dorfman was awarded the Silver Star during his World War II service with the Marine Corps. In 1948 he was a physical education teacher at the University of Illinois, earning $4,000 a year; five years later he was a millionaire. Allen's stepfather, Paul ("Red") Dorfman, was a professional boxer and a close friend of Chicago crime boss Tony Accardo. In 1928, Red Dorfman was indicted for rigging election ballots and employing terrorist tactics in a local election, although there is no record of the disposition. In 1940, the founder and secretary-treasurer of the Chicago Waste Handlers Union was murdered. Red Dorfman, who had never been a member of the union or a waste handler, showed up at a union meeting, paid his dues, and on the same night became the new secretary-treasurer. In 1942, he was arrested as the result of a dispute with the chairman of the waste handlers

employers' association—the two disagreed over wages to be paid to men in Dorfman's union. Using brass knuckles concealed in a glove, Dorfman severely beat the man in his office. The charges were dropped when the victim refused to prosecute. In 1949, Red Dorfman assisted Jimmy Hoffa by introducing him to important people in the Outfit and gaining their help in Hoffa's organizing drive for the Teamsters (Brill 1978).

Allen Dorfman established an insurance agency and in 1950 and 1951, Hoffa successfully maneuvered the insurance business of the Teamsters health and welfare funds to Red and Allan Dorfman. Subsequently, the Dorfmans, with absolutely no experience in the insurance field, "received more than $3 million in commissions and service fees on Teamsters insurance over an eight year period" (Permanent Subcommittee on Investigations 1983: 83).

In 1955, Jimmy Hoffa negotiated the IBT's first pension plan, into which each employer was to contribute $2 per week per Teamster employee: the Central States, Southeast and Southwest Areas Pension Fund and Health and Welfare Fund (usually referred to simply as the Central States Pension Fund). Allen Dorfman was appointed as a consultant to the fund's board of trustees and turned it into "a bank for the underworld and their cronies in the 1960s and early 1970s" (Frantz and Neubauer 1983: 1). Dorfman had the trustees lend millions of dollars to Las Vegas casinos, organized crime–connected resorts, and speculative hotel and land ventures, projects that conventional lending institutions would not finance. Investments in Las Vegas casinos were directed by organized crime bosses in Chicago, Kansas City, Milwaukee, and Cleveland, who were then able to skim casino profits.

In 1972, as a result of the FBI's PENDORF investigation, Dorfman was convicted of taking $55,000 in kickbacks to secure a $1.5 million loan from the pension fund, and he served ten months in federal prison. In 1974, he was indicted along with Irwin Weiner, and Outfit members Joey Lombardo and Anthony Spilotro, on charges of fraud in connection with another pension fund loan. They were acquitted after the chief government witness was gunned down outside his business establishment. In 1977, the federal government forced the trustees of the Central States Pension Fund to relinquish financial control to an independent management firm (Frantz and Neubauer 1983).

On December 15, 1982, Dorfman, Lombardo, and Teamster president Roy L. Williams were found guilty of attempting to bribe U.S. Senator Howard Cannon of Nevada in return for his help in delaying legislation that would substantially deregulate the trucking industry. Dorfman, Lombardo, and Williams were scheduled for sentencing on February 10, 1983.[1] On January 20, 1983, Dorfman was walking with Weiner in a motel parking lot in suburban Lincolnwood, just outside Chicago. Two men approached from behind. One carried a sawed-off shotgun under his coat, and the other drew a .22 caliber semiautomatic with a silencer attached and fired five shots, point blank, into Dorfman's head. Weiner ducked down between two cars and the gunmen made no effort to harm him. The two men then pulled on ski masks and fled in a car driven by a third person. The murder remains (officially) unsolved.

Hoffa versus Kennedy

During the 1950s, the activities of the Teamsters Union gained the attention of the U.S. Senate, in particular, the Permanent Subcommittee on Investigations, which for many years was chaired by John L. McClellen of Arkansas. IBT officials, however, refused to cooperate with the committee. They "would not produce records; they repeatedly challenged the jurisdiction of the Permanent Subcommittee to probe the inner workings of the union; they exerted considerable and constant pressure upon members of Congress in both houses to have Teamster activities rest in the traditionally gentle hands of the Senate's Labor Committee" (McClellen 1962: 14).

"The response of the Senate," notes Senator McClellen (1962: 19), "was prompt and decisive." With a unanimous vote, on January 30, 1957, an eight-member bipartisan Senate Select Committee on Improper Activities in the Labor or Management Field was established. The senator wrote of his experiences with the IBT in a 1962 book, *Crime Without Punishment*. Robert Kennedy, who was chief counsel to the committee, also authored a book on his experiences with the committee, *The Enemy Within* (1960). The first IBT target of the committee was its president, Dave Beck. The committee spotlight shone very brightly on Beck, and within months of his appearance he was convicted of embezzling union funds and of income-tax violations. The spotlight then turned to James R. Hoffa.

Subpoenaed to appear before the Select Committee, Jimmy Hoffa was sometimes blunt, sometimes evasive, in his testimony (McClellen 1962). At times the Teamster leader referred to Kennedy as "Bob" or "Bobby" and as "nothing but a rich man's kid." Law professor Monroe Freedman states: "From the day that James Hoffa told Robert Kennedy that he was nothing but a rich man's kid who never had to earn a nickel in his life, Hoffa was a marked man" (quoted in Navasky 1977: 395).

In 1957, FBI surveillance cameras recorded Hoffa giving $2,000 in exchange for confidential McClellen Committee documents to a New York attorney who was cooperating with the government. Hoffa had recruited the attorney to serve as a plant on the committee. When FBI agents arrested Hoffa the following day, he had confidential committee reports on him. Nevertheless, Hoffa was acquitted in a jury trial. The following year, Hoffa was tried for illegally wiretapping the phones of some Teamster officials. The first trial resulted in a hung jury, the second in an acquittal.

In 1960, John F. Kennedy was elected president of the United States and appointed his brother Robert attorney general. Robert Kennedy made the Labor Racketeering Unit of the Criminal Division his personal "Get Hoffa Squad." The unit was headed by former FBI special agent Walter

---

1. In 1982, Senator Cannon was defeated in his bid for a fifth term; Williams received a ten-year sentence and was paroled in 1989.

Sheridan, who was actually on the attorney general's payroll as a "confidential assistant" (Navasky 1977). Sheridan subsequently wrote a book on the IBT and the government's efforts to prosecute Hoffa, *The Fall and Rise of Jimmy Hoffa* (1972).

Soon federal grand juries across the country were investigating the IBT and several important convictions were secured, including that of Anthony Provenzano. In 1962, Hoffa was charged with a conflict-of-interest violation of the Taft-Hartley Act—a misdemeanor. Victor Navasky (1977: 417) comments: "Never in history had the government devoted so much money, manpower, and top-level brainpower to a misdemeanor case." The trial lasted two months and ended in a hung jury—7 to 5 for acquittal. Hoffa was subsequently accused of trying to bribe jurors and in 1964 was convicted of jury tampering and sentenced to eight years' imprisonment.

In 1971, President Richard Nixon approved his application for executive clemency—the IBT had supported Nixon for president—and Hoffa was released from prison. Despite a condition added to the pardon that Hoffa abstain from union affairs for ten years, by 1975, he was actively seeking the Teamster presidency, and IBT officials loyal to him were holding fund-raising dinners to prepare for the campaign. Hoffa began attacking Frank Fitzsimmons, the man who had replaced him as IBT president. Ironically, Hoffa criticized Fitzsimmons as a tool of organized crime.

On July 30, 1975, Hoffa arrived at a suburban Detroit restaurant to meet with several persons, including his friend Anthony ("Tony Jack") Giacalone, a *caporegime* in the Detroit crime Family, and Anthony Provenzano. Giacalone had arranged the meeting ostensibly to mediate differences between Provenzano and Hoffa over Hoffa's quest for the IBT presidency.[2] None of the principals were at the restaurant and Hoffa has not been seen since. Fitzsimmons died of natural causes in 1981. In a biography published after his death,

Frank Sheeran, an associate of the crime Family in Pittson, Pennsylvania, and long-time confidant of the ex-Teamster president, admitted to killing Hoffa on orders from the Family boss Russell Bufalino (Brant 2004).

Organized crime Families maneuvered behind the scenes to ensure that Roy L. Williams of Kansas City, Missouri would become the new IBT president. At the same time, "the Senate Permanent Subcommittee on Investigations rushed out a report spotlighting William's LCN [*La Cosa Nostra*] ties. The senators revealed a portion of the Justice Department's evidence that Williams was getting kickbacks of cash skimmed from Las Vegas casinos bought with Teamster pension loans, and kickbacks funneled through Nick Civella's Kansas City Mafia family" (PCOC 1985a: 42)

Nevertheless, the IBT executive board chose Williams to fill the unexpired term of Frank Fitzsimmons, and the Teamster convention subsequently elected him to a full term. After his 1982 conviction, Williams testified before the President's Commission on Organized Crime that his election had been engineered by organized crime bosses and that he himself was under the control of the Kansas City boss. When Williams resigned, Jackie Presser of Cleveland was chosen to head the IBT, despite (or because of) his close ties to organized crime.

Jackie Presser

Born in Cleveland in 1926, Jackie Presser learned about organized labor at an early age from his father, Bill Presser, a Teamster Union official and close associate of the Cleveland crime Family. Large for his age, Jackie was an unruly, brawling student who dropped out of school at 16 and joined the Navy. He was honorably discharged in 1947. As expected, Jackie went into the union business, securing a position with the Teamsters. He was joined by his uncle, Allen Friedman, an ex-convict and juice loan collector. Jackie soon showed that he lacked the tact necessary for successful labor racketeering: His threats, shakedowns, and embezzlements attracted so much attention that he had to temporarily bow out of union activities. Using IBT pension fund

---

2. At the time of his death in 2001, Giacalone, 82, was awaiting trial for racketeering and extortion.

loans, Jackie opened up several bowling alleys, but they failed due to mismanagement, and the Teamster money was lost.

Nevertheless, Bill Presser had a new IBT local chartered for his son, and Jackie teamed up with two relatives, Allen Friedman and his brother Harry—both stalwart union organizers and ex-convicts—to organize warehouse workers for the IBT. With Bill Presser's help, they raided other IBT locals, and Jackie's local prospered, moving beyond warehousemen and adding other workers to Local 507's membership. Part of the local's success was due to the sweetheart contract: Employers fearful of other (legitimate) unions organizing their workers agreed to recognize the local and sign a contract with Jackie.

When Jimmy Hoffa went to prison and Frank Fitzsimmons became acting president of the IBT, Bill Presser filled a vacancy on the executive board, becoming a union vice president. Bill organized a political action committee called DRIVE to raise money and support political candidates, and Jackie was given a major role in DRIVE efforts. Jackie Presser was astute enough to recognize the value of good public relations. He began a major effort to clean up the image of the IBT, hiring a public relations firm and personal publicist. However, he continued to cheat his union members.

When Bill Presser fell seriously ill, Jackie replaced him as an IBT vice president. When IBT president Fitzsimmons became terminally ill, Roy Williams became acting president. Williams's conviction in the PENDORF case (discussed earlier) cleared the way for Jackie Presser to become IBT president. Jackie was supported by leaders of Cleveland's organized crime Family who lobbied organized crime chieftains in Chicago and New York on Presser's behalf (Neff 1989).

With Jackie's backing, DRIVE and the IBT supported Ronald Reagan's successful candidacy for president. After the election, Allen Friedman reports: "[My brother-in-law, Bill Presser,] handed me a briefcase he said was filled with cash and told me to take it to [Attorney General] Edwin Meese in Washington. This was back in late November or early December after Ronald Reagan

became president. I don't know how much was in that case; Bill knew I would never open it. But after Reagan got in, he named Bill's son, Jackie Presser, to his transition cabinet. Then he wanted to make Jackie undersecretary of labor, though I guess cooler heads prevailed. Jackie's presence would have been just one more scandal for the administration. After all, though Jackie never did time in jail as Bill and I did, that was only because his father and I covered his ass, not because he was ever an honest man" (Friedman and Schwarz 1989: 3).

Jackie Presser died of cancer in 1988. In 1989, as part of a RICO case against the IBT, court disclosures revealed that he had been providing information to the FBI for nine years (Serrin 1989). The Chicago Outfit had informed Anthony ("Fat Tony") Salerno, boss of the Genovese Family, that Presser was an informant, but Salerno refused to believe them.

In 1988, Rudy Giuliani, then U.S. attorney for the Southern District of New York, filed a RICO complaint against the IBT, the first time it had been used against an entire union. In addition to union officers, named as defendants were the heads of New York's five Families, as well as those in Chicago and Milwaukee. That same year, William J. McCarthy became IBT president, and the following year he reached an agreement with the Department of Justice to a settle a RICO suit against the union. McCarthy became the last Teamster president chosen at a national convention by delegates from the various locals; he died of natural causes in 1998. In 1991, for the first time, the union's international officials were elected by the rank-and-file in a secret ballot supervised by the government. Ronald R. Carey was elected president.

Carey, a longtime IBT dissident, headed the United Parcel Service local in Long Island City, New York. Despite his reform credentials, Carey was criticized in 1992 by a federal judge overseeing the consent decree that helped elect him: the judge accused the IBT of dragging its feet on reform. Fifteen months after taking office, Carey suspended six of the top officers of the 14,000-member IBT Local 705 in Chicago, long-linked to organized crime, and appointed trustees to run the local. In 1995, he brought a lawsuit against the former officers, alleging that they had defrauded the local (Franklin 1993, 1995b). He also placed more than two dozen locals in the New York City area under trusteeship control.

Carey's enemies in the union alleged that he had ties to organized crime and had engaged in improper financial deals. These accusations were supported by a former acting boss of the Lucchese crime Family ("Gaspipe" Casso) when he became a government witness. A three-member panel created by a federal court order, however, found no evidence to support the allegations (Raab 1994c).[3] Carey's most serious challenge, however, came from Jimmy Hoffa, Jr., son of the missing Teamster leader and five years younger than Carey. Hoffa, Jr., a labor lawyer with backing from much of the union's "old guard," challenged Carey for the union's presidency in 1996, but lost. Carey was reelected to a second five-year term with about 52 percent of the vote.

The following year, the election was declared invalid because Carey had received more than $220,000 in illegal contributions. He was subsequently barred from running in the new election—a rematch against Jimmy Hoffa, Jr.—because it was discovered that he had backed a plan to divert union funds for his campaign. A court-appointed review board subsequently expelled Carey from the Teamsters Union, and a new election in 1998 pitted Hoffa against a leader of the reformist wing of the IBT. Hoffa, who has never been a truck driver or laborer, easily beat the reform candidate. In 2011, Hoffa, 70, was re-elected president of the IBT, the only union under federal supervision, the result of lawsuit settled in 1989 (Associated Press 2011).

BUSINESS RACKETEERING

As we have seen with respect to the waterfront, there is no hard-and-fast rule separating labor racketeering from business racketeering—one is often

an integral part of the other. In many schemes involving corrupt union officials, "legitimate" businessmen have willingly cooperated in order to derive benefits such as decreased labor costs, inflated prices, or increased business in the market (PCOC 1986b). Jonathan Kwitny (1979) describes the machinations of racketeer-extraordinaire Moses ("Moe") Steinman, who dominated the wholesale meat industry in New York City. Because of his connections with important organized crime figures such as John Dioguardi and Paul Castellano, Steinman was able to deal with racketeer-controlled unions and thus affect labor relations in the meat industry. This ability secured him a position as a supermarket chain executive who led industry-wide negotiations with meat industry unions. Utilizing under-the-table payments to the union leaders, Steinman determined from whom the supermarkets purchased their meat. Supermarket officials bought from firms recommended by Steinman, overpaying for their beef; they were rewarded with kickbacks, and Steinman was paid handsome commission fees by the beef companies for these sales.

Steinman's greatest achievement was his relationship with the founder of Iowa Beef, the largest meat-processing firm in the world. The patrician Midwestern businessman and the hard-drinking, inarticulate New York racketeer had something in common—greed. In return for opening up New York markets for Iowa Beef and assisting the company with "labor relations," Iowa Beef gave millions of dollars to Steinman and his friends and relatives (Kwitny 1979). Two former FBI agents (O'Brien and Kurins 1991) allege a similar relationship between Gambino Family boss Paul Castellano and chicken tycoon Frank Perdue.

Certain industries and their associated businesses are more attractive, and thus more vulnerable to organized crime. These are relatively easy businesses to enter, do not require a large cash investment, and are highly competitive. Other characteristics include an intense need for timely action, for example, businesses dealing with perishable foods and industries where any disruption of work or deliveries can be quite costly, such as the

---

3. Jeffrey Goldberg (1995) presents a less flattering portrait of Carey and the report that cleared him.

construction industry. Organized crime is drawn to labor-intensive industries that provide an opportunity to control related component businesses through a "choke point strategy." For example, domination of the concrete business provides influence over widely divergent construction activities dependent on a steady and predictable delivery of concrete supplies. Or control over the supply of labor—through control of a union local—enables domination of an industry dependent on a predictable supply of workers (Edelhertz and Overcast n.d.). The role of trucking in New York's garment center provides an example.

The Garment Center

Extensive business racketeering in New York's garment industry dates back to the days of Lepke Buchalter, discussed earlier, who, in addition to his influence over key unions, controlled interstate garment center trucking (Kavieff 2006). Its more contemporary manifestation has centered on the ability of racketeers to control local trucking: Whoever controls trucking controls the industry. The fast-paced nature of the fashion industry cannot countenance even short delays in shipping garments. "In New York City, garment manufacturers do not, as a rule, actually cut cloth and sew it into a dress, shirt, or other garment. They design clothes, order cloth, and arrange for the cutting and sewing to be done in smaller shops, called contractors. As a result, cloth is constantly being shipped by truck from manufacturer to contractor, from contractor to contractor, and from contractor back to manufacturer" (Mass 1991: 38–39).

Until 1992, control over garment center trucking was exercised by the multimillionaire sons of Carlo Gambino, Thomas and Joseph. Crime Family boss Gaetano Lucchese had been introduced to the garment center by Lepke Buchalter himself, and Thomas Gambino is Lucchese's son-in-law. Residing in an 1881 mansion in the exclusive Lenox Hill neighborhood, Thomas Gambino, a graduate of Manhattan College, is known for his charitable contributions; he is also known as a *caporegime* in the crime Family that bears his father's name.

The Gambino brothers owned Consolidated Carriers, the major garment-center cartage firm. Together with a trucking firm owned by a Lucchese Family member, they divided manufacturers and contractors among a limited number of truckers and assigned one to each shop: "None of these truckers will carry garments for a shop not assigned to him. If a shop uses a gypsy trucker and is caught, it is required to pay its regular trucker for the goods shipped, just as if the assigned trucker had carried them. Elaborate rules govern the trading of shops among the cartel members and the allocation of a trucker to a company leasing space that was formerly occupied by another company serviced by a cartel member" (Mass 1991: 39). Manufacturers and contractors knew who they were dealing with, which was usually enough to ensure compliance with the allocation scheme.

Because there was an absence of competition, trucking prices remained high, while service remained poor. Some companies fled the garment center, and others refused to move in. The number of people employed in the industry declined substantially, and this impacted negatively on the New York City economy.

Evidence against the Gambinos was compiled through an elaborate sting operation orchestrated by investigators from the office of Manhattan District Attorney Robert M. Morgenthau. First, an undercover state police officer drove around Chinatown posing as a gypsy trucker soliciting business from companies that had been serviced by the Gambino cartel. He quickly found that no matter how competitive his prices, he could not secure any accounts. One manufacturer whispered the reason: "the Mafia." Another undercover officer succeeded in being hired by Consolidated Carriers.

On Halloween night 1989, investigators disguised as Consolidated Edison workers broke into the Gambino trucking company headquarters and planted a court-authorized "bug." State police investigators opened up their own garment manufacturing firm which was the ultimate weapon in the Gambino sting. In 1992, in exchange for not being imprisoned, the Gambino brothers pled guilty to restraint of trade violations and agreed to quit New York City's garment center and pay a fine of $12 million (Blumenthal 1992; Mass 1991). After three years without the Gambino brothers, shipping costs in the garment center fell dramatically, taking about 7 percent off the price of a finished garment. The fine paid by the Gambinos financed a government-appointed monitor for the garment center, as well as providing funds for the district attorney's office and the state police and compensation to several overcharged companies (Raab 1995b). In 1993, Thomas Gambino, at 64, was found guilty of racketeering charges stemming from his control of a Connecticut gambling operation and sentenced to five years' imprisonment. He entered a federal prison in 1996 and was released in 2000.

The end of Gambino brothers' operations did not end racketeering in the garment center. In 1998, the acting boss of the Lucchese Family and eleven others, including members of the Gambino and Genovese Families, were indicted for an extortion scheme that netted $30,000 to $40,000 a month. In return for payments, garment makers (sewing, cutting, and dying plants) were given "protection" and guaranteed labor peace; if they were not unionized, they were allowed to remain so (Weiser 1998b). Most of the defendants subsequently pleaded guilty.

Robert Stewart (2006: 65) points out that organized crime can bring stability to the potentially chaotic world of *laissez-faire* capitalism, and it is stability that the employer craves because it almost always results in a decent profit. The employer makes a cost-benefit evaluation: "The Mafia racketeer is always there for the employer, with a sympathetic ear, ready to intervene in any problem as an expediter. As long as the unionized employer pays, he can expect the trucks to operate on schedule, production will never be disrupted, and potential competitors will be discouraged for a moderate surcharge."

Restraint of Trade

Bid rigging and customer allocation are restraint of trade violations of the Sherman Act (discussed in Chapter 14) and carry a maximum sentence of ten years' imprisonment and a maximum fine of $1 million for individuals and $100 million for corporations. The policing of restraint of trade agreements is a service provided by organized crime, but in some cases, organized crime involvement is a matter of "muscling in," something relatively easy to accomplish because the participants are operating outside of the law and cannot easily complain to the authorities. In New Jersey, for example, the organizer of a waste haulers association that had effectively restrained competition found himself being pushed out by an emissary from Jerry Catena, who ran New Jersey operations for the Genovese Family. The head of the association described his response: "I had a feeling, fear, that if I did not just put my tail between my legs and allow myself to be pushed out, they would find another way to get me out" (Abadinsky 1981a: 30).

Following a pattern set in Chicago, in Detroit during the 1920s cutthroat competition among the owners of dry cleaning plants led to the formation of the Wholesale Cleaners and Dyers Association. Soon afterward, the association ruled that retail cleaning shops could not switch from one plant to another. Wholesalers were now free to increase prices without worrying about losing customers. The Purple Gang, a group of notorious Jewish gangsters, was employed to police this restraint of trade. Independent wholesalers and retailers who balked were terrorized: "Bricks destroyed plant windows at night and shops were stench bombed—a practice that ruined thousands of dollars worth of clothing" (Kavieff 2000: 58). If more were required, there would be arson and bombs. Eventually, Purple Gang leader Abe Bernstein declared himself the head of the retail cleaners association and his gunmen would attend meetings until all member dues were collected. A representative of the association sided with a decision to take Bernstein off the payroll—a subsequent coroner's examination revealed he had been beaten to death.

Organized crime is not necessarily a crucial element in restraint of trade schemes as these press releases from the U.S. Department of Justice reveal:

- Northwest Airlines LLC agrees to plead guilty to fixing prices on air cargo shipments and pay a criminal fine of $38 million (July 30, 2010)

- Panasonic and Whirlpool agree to plead guilty for their role in a price-fixing conspiracy involving refrigerant compressors and to pay a total of $140.9 million in criminal fines (September 30, 2010)

- Samsung agrees to plead guilty in a color display tube price-fixing conspiracy and to pay a $32 million criminal fine (March 18, 2011)

- JPMorgan Chase admits to rigging bids on municipal bonds and agrees to pay $228 million in restitution and penalties (July 7, 2011)

As discussed at the beginning of Chapter 11, organized crime is sometimes a provider of illegal goods and services—helping to arrange and enforce collusive bidding arrangements, for example—while at other times it is simply a predator imposing itself on those involved in such activities. With this in mind, we will examine business racketeering in the construction and private waste hauling industries.

Construction Industry

Construction is both a lucrative and highly competitive industry. While competition is advantageous to the builder, it reduces the profits of construction firms. Organized crime can play a crucial role in limiting competition by enforcing a system of collusive bidding. The President's Commission reports: "Participating construction contractors, with the guidance of union officials and LCN family members, allocate construction jobs among themselves and exclude noncartel contractors whose entry into the New York market might threaten the stability, predictability and control of construction work that the cartels offer their members. Under such a system, the participant companies are beneficiaries, not victims, since the benefits of the cartel may totally offset the increased costs it imposes" (PCOC 1986b: 219).

In New York City, the construction industry is huge and fragmented, "with over one hundred thousand workers, many hundreds of specialty subcontractors, hundreds of general contractors, and dozens of major developers. There are also a large number of one-time or infrequent builders ranging from large corporations to small entrepreneurs" (New York State Organized Crime Task Force 1988: 3; hereafter NYSOCTF). Construction businesses range from those building private single-family dwellings to those putting up shopping centers and high-rise buildings. Construction workers are organized into approximately one hundred local unions for the building trades, who engage in collective bargaining with the approximately fifty employer associations formed by contractors in the same type of construction work.

"Traditionally, unions have had a great deal of leverage in high-rise construction because they have had a monopoly over the skilled workers needed to carry out this highly complex type of building" (NYSOCTF 1988: 44). Through collective bargaining agreements, construction unions typically control access to skilled labor: "Some pre-hire contracts contain clauses requiring contractors to hire all or part of their employees from union hiring halls. Even where there is no hiring hall provision, the union's designation as exclusive bargaining agent gives its elected officials control over who works for that contractor" (NYSOCTF 1988: 45–46). Through control over labor unions, racketeers are able to offer benefits to or impose prohibitive costs on contractors. The ability to assign (or not assign) workers to jobs is a powerful tool that can be used against union members who might wish to challenge racketeer leadership. There is also the very real threat of violence.

The industry's structure creates fragmentation and fragility: "An organized crime syndicate can use its network of relationships throughout the construction industry to reduce uncertainties and promote needed stability. For example, if more than one union has a jurisdictional claim over a particular construction task, an organized crime syndicate in return for a payoff can work out a reasonable arrangement between the contractor and the affected unions. In this role, the syndicate serves the same functions, albeit by criminal means, as a highly effective, legitimate labor consultant" (NYSOCTF 1988: 66).

More than two decades ago, the President's Commission reported that in "New York City organized crime controls all construction contracts of a half-million dollars or more extending up to amounts of approximately $100 million…. The prime source of influence and the prime point of contact for organized crime are the twenty or so largest contractors in New York City who from time to time, through collusive bidding, decide among themselves who will get a particular project." After winning the rigged bid, an emissary of organized crime or a union official approaches the general contractor and informs him "who his suppliers will be, who his subcontractors will be, from whom he will purchase materials, and at what price those materials will be purchased, and, on occasion, designating to the general contractor which unions he will use during the course of the construction of the building and other construction jobs in the New York City area" (PCOC 1985a: 71–72).

Bidding on concrete-contracting work, for example, was rigged so that big jobs were rotated among a small group of contractors and suppliers. For this service there was a "tax" of 1 or 2 percent. Jobs under $2 million required "1 point"; "2 points" were required for jobs over $2 million. In return, construction firms got guaranteed contracts and good workers who did not have to be paid according to the full union contract. Failure to pay meant the company was out of business (Owen 2003).

The agreement was policed by Ralph Scopo, a member of the Colombo Family and president of the Cement and Concrete Workers District Council of the Laborer's Union. He would "go to a building site, and the owner of the construction company would come out and sit with him in his car, and Scopo would talk about how 'the family' needs this money, and how you want to be sure that your wife and kids are OK" (Owen 2003: 72). The rigged bidding inflated costs and drove up the price of everything from raw materials to finished office space.

In 1987, Scopo and a *caporegime* in the Colombo Family were convicted of racketeering. (Scopo died in 1993 while serving a one-hundred-year sentence.) In 1988, ten union officials and

contractors were convicted in Brooklyn federal court for accepting or extorting payoffs from contractors in return for labor peace and rigging bids on projects to reward companies that paid bribes and to punish those that did not (Rangel 1988). In 1991, a federal jury convicted the *consiglieri* of the Genovese and Colombo Families for heading a twelve-year bid-rigging scheme involving contracts for installing windows in New York City Housing Authority projects (Lubasch 1991b). Likewise, in Sicily, the *mafiosi* serve as guarantors for price rigging and collusive bidding on building projects, and "any businessman who defects from the collusive agreement or refuses to take part in it, exposes himself to violent retaliation from a Mafia protector" (della Porta and Vannucci 1999: 229).

In 1996, a major New York City contractor who had designed and helped build scores of Manhattan skyscrapers, in addition to working on the Javits Convention Center and a new federal courthouse, admitted to being a *caporegime* in the Colombo crime Family. In the courthouse he helped build, the 62-year-old contractor pled guilty to being the Colombo Family representative on the mob council that oversaw activities in the construction industry ("Contractor Admits Double Life" 1996). In 2005, labor racketeering expert and New York University law professor James Jacobs and Kristin Stohner reported that a key construction union, the New York City District Council of Carpenters, was still being influenced by organized crime. That view was reinforced by a federal judge who in 2008 ordered an extension of government oversight of the union that had already spent fourteen years under supervision (Greenhouse and Rashbaum 2008). In 2011, the court-appointed monitor reported that the Carpenters Union was still under the influence of organized crime (Rashbaum 2011b).

Payments to organized crime may be direct, or by making a racketeer (or one of his relatives) a business partner, or by employing "ghost employees," persons on a construction payroll who receive salaries but do no work. When two union construction workers began complaining about ghost employees on the payroll of a contractor helping to build the World Trade Center in New York, one of the "ghosts," the boss of the Genovese Family, referred the problem to his private "police force," headed by Anthony ("Figgy") Ficarotta, a former professional boxer:

> Figgy, Joey, Louie and me went over to the Twin Towers construction site. The building was up about eleven stories and there were no walls, just the frames and concrete floors. The elevator was in an open shaft, and that's how the workers got up and down. We went up to the top floor and Figgy sees these two guys working. "Follow me," he says and we start walking around the floor. Figgy is telling the other workers: "Why don't youse go to lunch, go ahead." One of the workers says: "Who are you? We take our orders from Phillie." "Well I'm over Phillie," Figgy says, "so just go down and when you see him tell him who sent you—a short guy with the funny nose."
>
> We walked around telling guys to go downstairs until we got to the two guys and they start to walk toward the elevator shaft. "You guys goin' to lunch?" Figgy asks. They are standing by the shaft for the lift to come back and Figgy picks up a two-by-four and pushes it under the chin of this guy. The guy grabs onto the shaft to keep from fallin' in: "So you want a fuckin' check too, huh? Well it's waitin' for you on the ground. I'm gonna see that you get it—in a hurry." The guy is hanging on for his life and Figgy keeps pushing him further into the shaft. The second guy doesn't know what to do—there's nowhere to run. Joe and Louie start backing him up—and there's nowhere to go except down eleven stories.
>
> The guy with Figgy is yelling: "No, no, please, I don't want no check." "Why? You been bitchin' about some checks and I'm gonna send you down to get one." "Please no. I don't want no check." Joey

and Louie back the other guy up to the edge and he yells out: "I don't want no check either." "Then just do your fuckin' work and shut the fuck up. Or we'll be back." Figgy threw the piece of wood down and we went onto the lift. There was no further trouble. (Abadinsky 1983: 131)

In New Jersey, firms owned by Philadelphia crime boss Nicky Scarfo and his underboss were able to gain lucrative construction contracts because of their influence over a few key labor unions, particularly Concrete Workers Local 33 and Ironworkers Local 350. Contractors subcontracting work to the Scarfo firms were guaranteed labor peace and were able to underbid rivals by violating the union contract with respect to pension and other benefits (New Jersey Commission of Investigation 1987). In fact, the construction industry is quite inefficient, characterized by various unions having overlapping jurisdictions and a great deal of featherbedding. "The existence of so much inefficiency provides a strong incentive to pay off union officials not to press their jurisdictional claims or to reach out to racketeers who can dictate accommodations between competing unions" (NYSOCTF 1988: 50).

Private Solid Waste Carting

If there is a legitimate business activity that conjures up an image of organized crime, it is the private collection of solid waste—it is "Tony Soprano's" business. Back in 1931, columnist Walter Lippman (1962: 61) noted that "racketeering in many of its most important forms tends to develop where an industry is subjected to exceedingly competitive conditions." Companies "faced with the constant threat of cutthroat competition are subject to easy temptation to pay gangsters for protection against competitors." Peter Reuter (1987) offers additional insight into an industry's attractiveness to organized crime. When the entrepreneurs have a low-status (for example, limited education) background, and the enterprises are small, local, and family-based,

---

POLICING ILLEGAL CONTRACTS, INTERNATIONAL

"Whether in the United States, Italy, Russia, or Japan, trust is not always sufficient to enforce illegal agreements and to avoid individuals exiting from the covert exchanges. Coercion provided by organized crime may be needed as an additional resource to punish 'lemons,' 'free riders,' or those who threaten to denounce the corrupt system" (della Porta and Vannucci 1999: 22).

---

the industry is vulnerable to organized crime infiltration.

The solid waste collection industry meets these criteria. It is characterized by numerous, relatively small competing firms that are often family-based. It is an easy-entry enterprise, requiring only some trucks and a willingness to work hard. Competition for a customer's business drives down profits until, at some point, with or without help from organized crime, an association is formed. Association members divide up the industry, usually allocating geographic areas (territories) or specific customers ("property rights"). The members (illegally) agree not to compete for another member's business. Each is thereby free to charge whatever the market will bear for its services (State Commission of Investigation 1989). Based on a study by Solomon Smith Barney, the New York [Manhattan] District Attorney's Office estimated that because of organized crime, customers paid an overcharge of 30 to 40 percent or more; $500 million a year more than they should have (Gerlat 2002).

Organized crime may become involved if there is a need to police the (illegal) agreement. In 1956, New York City began requiring all commercial enterprises to arrange for their own garbage collection services. Prior to that, businesses operating in residential blocks had their garbage hauled for free by the Department of Sanitation. "Overnight, more than 50,000 businesses were up for grabs" (Cowan and Century 2002: 14). Within months, restraint of trade cartels were in place, formed around waste hauling trade associations (Behar 1996). A made guy would sit on the grievance committees that settle disputes between members of the associations "using the basic rule that whoever serviced the site first has continuing rights to any customer that occupies the site.

While there is little evidence of either threats or actual violence,[4] it seems reasonable to infer that the racketeers provide a credible continuing threat of violence that ensures compliance with the ruling of the committee" (Reuter et al. 1983: 11; also Fried 2005). James ("Jimmy Brown"—partial to brown clothes) Failla, a *caporegime* in the Gambino Family, headed the Association of Trade Waste Removers of Greater New York for thirty years, organizing and facilitating restraint of trade agreements (Fried 1993b). In 1999, Failla, 80, died while serving a seven-year sentence for his role in the 1985 murder of Gambino Family boss Paul Castellano.

In New York City, about 300 trash haulers served 250,000 businesses. In 1995, four waste hauling associations (as well as individual firms and their owners) affiliated with the Gambino and Genovese Families were accused of having carved out a system of *property rights*:

> A carter "owns" the building where his customer is located. If the customer leaves or goes out of business, the carter has the right to service the new customer. If the carter loses a stop to another carter, the "owner" of the stop has the right to be compensated for his loss either by receiving a stop of comparable value or through the payment of a multiple of the monthly charges the "owner" had charged. The multiple is frequently "40 to 1" or more, meaning 40 times the monthly fee charged by the "owner." Disputes

---

4. But there has been violence: In 1989, two owners of a family-run private waste hauling business on Long Island, brothers-in-law Robert Kubecka and Donald Barstow, were murdered for refusing to participate in an organized crime price-fixing cartel (Carlo 2008; Fried 2005).

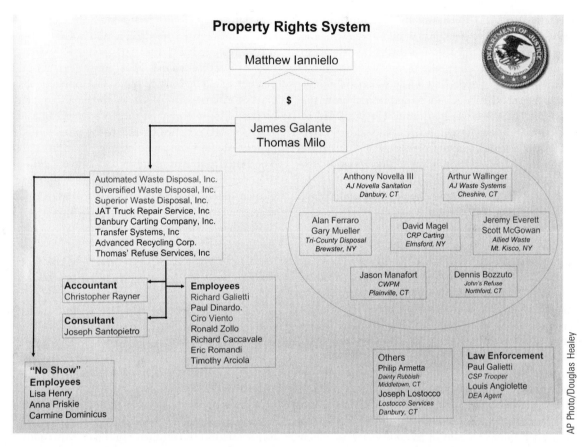

Property Rights System

This government graphic shows the organization and individuals involved in an investigation in which trash haulers used the Mafia as a silent partner for more than a decade. In New Haven, Connecticut, in 2006, twenty-nine people, including a reputed mob boss, a former Waterbury mayor, and the region's largest garbage hauler, were indicted by federal prosecutors.

AP Photo/Douglas Healey

over which carter has the "right" to service a particular stop are mediated by the associations. (District Attorney of New York County and the New York City Police Department 1995: 2)

Carters not belonging to the associations—"outlaws"—faced economic and physical intimidation if they attempted to compete with association members.

The investigation that broke this cartel began when the Manhattan district attorney received a complaint from the second-largest waste hauling company in the country, Browning-Ferris Industries (BFI) of Houston.[5] The company was attempting to compete in the New York market but found it virtually impossible to win and maintain customers despite submitting lower bids. Company officials were subjected to intimidation—one received the freshly severed head of a German shepherd with a note that read: "Welcome to New York." In the ensuing investigation, a detective worked three years undercover as an executive for an "outlaw" firm—one that refused to join the cartel. His role began inadvertently.

---

5. BFI has been accused of price fixing in several markets and has paid millions of dollars in fines for such activities (Myerson 1995).

Detective Richard Cowan was investigating the arson of an empty garbage truck. As he was interviewing the owner, two thugs burst in and threatened the trash firm's owner, who said the detective was his cousin. As the "cousin," Detective Cowan successfully infiltrated the trash hauling industry and helped break the organized crime–dominated cartel. His work led to the conviction of fourteen persons, including its two leaders, a *caporegime* in the Genovese Family and a soldier in the Gambino Family—both headed trash collecting trade associations (Raab 1997a, 1997d). Detective Cowan authored a book on his undercover activities that provides an insider's view of the process (Cowan and Century 2002).

As a result of these efforts, cartel customers who (often with great trepidation) switched to BFI saved as much as 60 percent on their trash hauling contracts (Behar 1996). With the cartel broken, members scrambled to keep customers, lowering their fees to become more competitive. One of the largest privately owned buildings in Manhattan had been paying $1.2 million for garbage pickup; Browning-Ferris bid $120,000. In 1996, New York put a cap on what businesses could be charged for waste hauling and created a Trade Waste Commission, which can deny a license to any firm with ties to organized crime (Goozner 1996). Dozens of persons were convicted of restraint-of-trade–related charges, and dozens of small firms were driven out of business.

In 2001, New York City created the Organized Crime Commission to, among other responsibilities, regulate the private solid waste hauling industry. Renamed the Business Integrity Commission (BIC), in addition to solid waste hauling, the agency has both regulatory and law enforcement authority over seafood distribution areas, public wholesale markets, and shipboard gambling. The agency has more than sixty employees who are supported by city police officers. As a condition of granting a license or registration, BIC can impose a monitor to oversee the activities and affairs of the applicant business. BIC has investigative, audit, and subpoena powers at its disposal, allowing the commission to secure search warrants and affect arrests for criminal activities. BIC enforces laws and regulations governing regulated businesses and industries.

But BIC has no jurisdiction in Connecticut where in 2003 the head of a solid waste company was threatened by the "trash czar," owner of twenty-five companies who controlled about 80 percent of the carting industry in Connecticut and parts of eastern New York. With the assistance of a high-ranking member of the Genovese Family and aided by several corrupt law enforcement officers, James Galente maintained a property rights system. The FBI was able to insert an undercover agent into the operation, ending Galente's reign with a guilty plea in federal court. Thirty-two others were also charged in the case and pled guilty (FBI press release, November 4, 2008).

CRIMINALS IN A LEGITIMATE BUSINESS

In addition to their illegal business activities, persons involved in organized crime often own or invest in legitimate enterprises. One popular activity of government officials has been to decry the "infiltration" of organized crime into legitimate business. Michael Maltz (1975: 83) states that the "alternative to penetration of legitimate business is the reinvestment of the ill-gotten gains into some criminal enterprises, which may cause greater social harm." Annelise Anderson (1979: 77) points out, however, that funds from illegal business activities cannot easily "be profitably reinvested in illegal market enterprises without aggressive expansion of the territory controlled by the group." Thus, organized crime members may have an oversupply of illegally derived funds that cannot be profitably used to expand their illegal activities. Maltz (1975) concludes that the penetration of organized crime into legitimate business can be viewed as the equivalent of the legitimation of family fortunes by the Robber Barons discussed in Chapter 2.

However, Mark Moore (1987: 51) points out that the features of the organized crime group, rather than the substantive offenses committed, make it a societal menace. "What is bad about organized crime is that the criminal groups seem resistant to law enforcement measures, that they seem to become rich as a result of their crimes, that they coolly calculate how best to make money without worrying about whether a planned enterprise is illegal and violent, and that they threaten additional criminal activity in the future even if their current conduct is tolerable." In other words, organized crime groups would pose a threat to society "even if they were engaged largely in legitimate activities and even if their criminal activities produced relatively insignificant levels and kinds of victimization" (1987: 52). Moore suggests that organized crime groups be viewed as a business firms pursuing profit with a portfolio that encompasses illicit as well as licit enterprises and that poses a serious societal threat. Activities of a Genovese Family crew in New Jersey provide an example of Moore's observations. In addition to more traditional activities—gambling, loansharking, and labor racketeering—the Hoboken-based crew controlled a firm that arranged managed group health care for employers and locals of the Teamsters, Laborers, and Hotel Workers unions. According to the New Jersey attorney general, the firm increased its profit margin by coercing plan administrators into approving inflated fees for service (Raab 1996d).

Anderson (1979) provides six reasons for organized criminal involvement in legitimate business:

1. *Profit.* For persons in organized crime, profit provides motivation; not all members of organized crime are able to make a "respectable" income from illicit activities. In an intercepted conversation, New Jersey underboss Anthony Russo complained to boss Sam de Cavalcante that *amici nostri* could not even support themselves. In another incident, de Cavalcante arranged for the removal of a local union official, who was also a *caporegime* in his crime Family, because the official was not providing *legitimate* employment to the *amici nostri* as construction laborers. Jimmy Fratianno's biography, *The Last Mafioso* (Demaris 1981), contains very little discussion of his business activities. Indeed, it appears that Fratianno's most successful enterprise was a legitimate trucking firm he owned in California.

2. *Diversification.* A legitimate business provides the organized crime member with security of income. While it may be subject to market and other business conditions, a legitimate enterprise is usually not a target of law enforcement efforts. (As will be discussed in Chapter 14, since Anderson wrote her book in the late 1970s, federal and local governments have become increasingly active in the civil seizure of the assets of members of criminal organizations, including those derived from legitimate businesses.)

3. *Transfer.* Illegitimate enterprises are difficult, if not impossible, to transfer to dependents (particularly if they are female). Investing in legitimate enterprises such as a business or real estate ensures that an estate can be legally inherited.

4. *Services.* An organized crime member with a legitimate business is in a position to act as a patron for a person in need of legitimate employment—for example, persons on probation or parole or relatives he wants to shield from the stigma and risks associated with criminal enterprises.

5. *Front.* A legitimate business can provide a front or a base of operations for a host of illegal activities such as loansharking, gambling, fencing, and drug trafficking.

6. *Taxes.* A legitimate business can provide a tax cover, thereby reducing the risk of being charged with income-tax evasion. Funds from illegitimate enterprises can be mixed with those from the legitimate business, particularly if it is a "cash" business.

Obviously, these categories are not mutually exclusive. It is quite likely that organized crime involvement in legitimate business involves a combination of these six reasons. Persons in organized crime may also use a legitimate business as part of a scam.

The Scam/"Bust Out"

The scam, sometimes referred to as a "bust out," is a bankruptcy fraud that victimizes wholesale providers of various goods and sometimes insurance companies. The business used as the basis for a scam may be set up with that scheme as its purpose, or it may be an established business that has fallen into organized crime control as a result of gambling or loan shark debt. Scam operations are popular in industries with merchandise that has a high turnover potential, is readily transportable, and is not easy to trace. There are several basic variations and we will look at one (De Franco 1973).

A successful business with good credit references is purchased or falls into the hands of a loan shark, or a new corporation is formed and managed by a front man, or "pencil" who has no prior criminal or bankruptcy record. This person may owe money to a loan shark and may participate in the scam to help pay off the debt. A large bank deposit, known as the "nut," is made to establish credit. This money, plus other money subsequently deposited, is later withdrawn. A large store is rented, and orders for merchandise are placed with as many companies as possible. The size of these orders appears to indicate a successful operation to the suppliers. The owners then proceed with the three steps:

1. Smaller orders are placed during the first month, and such orders are paid for in full. During the second month, larger orders are placed, and about a quarter of the balance due on such orders is paid.
2. During the third month, using credit established as a result of the payments made for the previous orders, very large orders are placed. Items easily converted into cash, such as jewelry and appliances, usually constitute a large proportion of these orders. Thereafter, merchandise is converted into cash through a fence or a surplus-property operator, normally one with a sufficiently large legitimate inventory to easily intermix the scam merchandise into the normal inventory.
3. The company is then forced into bankruptcy by creditors because, according to plan, all cash has been appropriated by the scam operators.

A common time for the scam operator is just before a seasonal increase in the popularity of particular merchandise, when rush deliveries are commonplace and thorough credit checks are often overlooked. In some scams, arson is the final step: The business is "torched" for the insurance instead of declaring bankruptcy.

Stock Fraud

Entry of organized crime into the stock market is not new. It was noted earlier that John Dioguardi, who died in prison in 1979, was convicted of stock fraud involving a car-leasing company. The securities industry employs a great many persons—clerks, runners—whose pay is relatively low. Employees with gambling or loan shark debts or those merely seeking to supplement their incomes can find a ready market for such "paper." All that is needed is an organized crime connection. Although many people may have access to valuable securities, few can put stolen securities to immediate use. Organized crime groups serve as the intermediate link in the criminal enterprise. Bookmakers and loan sharks who may have exerted the pressure that induced the thief to take the securities frequently serve as the conduit by which the stolen securities get into the hands of other organized crime figures. Passing through the network of organized crime, the stolen securities eventually reach the hands of someone who does have the expertise, the capital, and the personnel to effect a profitable disposition.

Stolen securities can be transferred to a country with strict bank secrecy laws regarding such transactions, such as Panama. The securities are deposited in a bank, which issues a letter of credit that is used to secure loans that are eventually defaulted. They can be used as collateral for bank loans from "cooperative" loan officials or "rented" to legitimate businessmen in need of collateral for instant credit. Panama's strategic location between the Atlantic and Pacific Oceans, North and South America, its dollar-based economy, and its modern international trade and financial sectors, makes the country magnet for such schemes.

More recently, the organized crime foray into the stock market has added elements—intimidation and violence—to widely known scams. With the entry of organized crime, "boiler room" and "pump and dump" schemes, in addition to financial dangers, unsuspecting customers can now face physical dangers. In 2000, the federal government accused 120 persons throughout the United States, including members of the Colombo and Bonanno Families, of involvement in a Manhattan brokerage and investment bank that bilked investors of at least $50 million. The indictment alleged that brokers who refused to cooperate were assaulted. Some of the principals in the case were part of a defunct brokerage, one of whose officers was found dead in his New Jersey mansion in 1999. His body was found with that of another broker—both had been shot execution style.

Brokers for the firm used traditional high-pressure "boiler room" tactics to sell worthless stocks, created phony stock trades, and bribed brokers from other firms to push the stock in an effort to inflate the price. The wiseguy stock would then be sold off at enormous profits. Brokers who had a change of heart or refused further cooperation in the scheme were threatened with violence and assaulted (Roane 2000; Sullivan and Berenson 2000).

In 2001, another indictment alleged that twenty persons working with members of the Gambino Family bilked thousands of investors of more than $50 million; two victims lost at least $12 million. Investors identified from lists of retirees and business-persons would receive a "cold call" from a broker promoting shares in several companies. After the purchase, the brokers would drive up the price—the "pump"—and demand that the victims hold on to their stocks, refusing to execute sell orders, and threatening some with violence if they did anything that could drive the price down. The brokers would then sell off their shares of the stocks—the "dump"—at huge profits (Christian 2001).

MONEY LAUNDERING

Cash-rich criminals have a problem: purchasing luxury cars, yachts, planes, homes, and jewelry cannot be easily accomplished using cash, particularly if income taxes have not been paid. Ever since Al Capone was imprisoned for income-tax evasion, financially

successful criminals have sought ways to "launder" their illegally secured "dirty" money so that it can be used safely. The practice has developed its own lexicon: "Getting currency into the bank, around the reporting system, at home or abroad, is called *placement*. Once the money is in the form of a bank entry, the launderer hides its criminal origins through a series of complex transactions. Police call it *layering*. The launderer then makes the proceeds available to the criminals in an apparently legitimate form. The term for this is *integration*" (Blum 1999: 59).

Modern financial systems permit criminals to instantly transfer millions of dollars through personal computers and satellite dishes. Money is laundered through currency exchange houses, stock brokerage houses, gold dealers, casinos, automobile dealerships, insurance companies, and trading companies. "The use of private banking facilities, off-shore banking, free trade zones, wire systems, shell corporations, and trade financing all have the ability to mask illegal activities. The criminal's choice of money laundering vehicles is limited only by his or her creativity" (U.S. Department of State 1999: 3).

Money laundering has been greatly facilitated by advances in banking technology. A customer can instruct his or her personal computer to direct a bank's computer to transfer money from a U.S. account to one in a foreign bank. The bank's computer then tells a banking clearinghouse that assists in the transfer—no person talks to another. While depositing more than $10,000 in cash into an account requires the filing of a Currency Transaction Report (CTR), the government receives more than 16 million such reports annually and is hopelessly behind in reviewing them. A CTR is required for each deposit, withdrawal, or exchange of currency or monetary instrument in excess of $10,000. It must be submitted to the IRS within fifteen days of the transaction. In 1984, tax amendments extended the reporting requirements to anyone who receives more than $10,000 in cash in the course of a trade or business. A CMIR (Currency and Monetary Instrument Report) must be filed for cash or certain monetary instruments exceeding $10,000 in value that enter or leave the United States. Federal Reserve regulations require banks to file a suspicious activity report

(SAR) when they suspect possible criminal wrong-doing in transactions (CTR, CMIR, and SAR forms appear in Chapter 14).

The Internet facilitates money laundering. A launderer establishes a company—the Abadinsky Computer Co.—offering high-end products over the Internet. The launderer purchases products from the Abadinsky Computer Co. over the Internet using credit cards. The Abadinsky Computer Co. invoices the credit card company that, in turn, forwards payment for the purchases. "The credit card company, the Internet service provider, the Internet invoicing service, and even the bank from which the illegal proceeds begin this process would likely have no reason to believe there was anything suspicious about the activity, since they each only see one part of it" (Financial Action Task Force on Money Laundering 2001: 4).

A cash business, such as a vending machine firm, can be used to mingle cash from illegitimate sources with legally earned money. Some criminals use casinos for the same purpose or to convert cash from small denominations to $100 bills. Casinos were made subject to the Bank Secrecy Act in 1985 (discussed in Chapter 14), so purchasing large amounts of chips while engaging in minimal gambling attracts unwanted casino attention. In response, collusive pairs began betting large amounts on both "red and black" or "odd and even" on roulette, or both with and against the bank in baccarat, or both the "pass line" or "come line" and the "don't pass line" or "don't come line" in craps. The "winning partner" then cashes in his or her chips and gets a casino check. Some will cash out chips multiple times a day at different times or at different windows/cages keeping the amount of each transaction below $10,000 to avoid the filing of a CTR.

In some schemes, money launderers use dozens of persons (called "smurfs") to convert cash into money orders and cashier's checks that do not specify payees or are made out to fictitious persons. Each transaction is held to less than $10,000 (called "structuring") to avoid the need for a CTR. "Smurfing" has now been made a

federal crime, and increased bank scrutiny has made tellers suspicious of cash transactions just under $10,000.

Transactions involving the proceeds of drug trafficking often consist of large amounts of cash in small denominations. In such instances, the first step is to convert the small bills into hundreds—$1 million in $20 bills weighs 110 pounds; in $100 bills, it weighs only 22 pounds. To avoid IRS reporting requirements under the Bank Secrecy Act, transfers of cash to cashier's checks or $100 bills must take place in amounts under $10,000 or through banking officials who agree not to fill out a CTR. The cash can then be bulk-shipped over the U.S.–Mexican border where outgoing vehicles do not encounter the same scrutiny of those entering the United States. (GAO 2010).

The use of prepaid cash cards offer a compact, easily transportable way of moving money. Profits from crime are used to buy cards that can be used to connect to ATMs or for debit purposes. Cash is loaded onto the cards and then moved out of the country. The cards can be re-loaded over the Internet. Launderers typically use open system cards since they can be used at a myriad of stores, merchants, or automated teller machines within and outside the United States. These cards can be purchased on-line or in person. Open system cards may not require a bank account or face-to-face verification of the cardholder's identity. While anyone leaving the country with $10,000 or more in cash must submit a CMIR, cash cards are exempt. Some cards can process tens of thousands of dollars a month; load them in Texas with the proceeds of cocaine sales and collect the cash in local currency from an ATM in Colombia.

Money laundering is facilitated by a variety of private banking operations, formal and informal. In the United States, commercial banks and securities firms may offer special banking services to wealthy persons who deposit $1 million or more. The bank assigns a private banker or broker-dealer in securities who facilitates complex wire transfers throughout the world and creates offshore accounts. An investment manager for a major securities firm in New York pleaded guilty in 2005 to laundering $15 million in drug proceeds generated by Mexico's Gulf cartel. Using a system known as layering, she coordinated the establishment of offshore corporations as well as offshore accounts in the names of third parties with the funds ultimately winding up back in the firm's accounts under the names of fictitious persons (Berkeley 2002a; Preston 2005c).

As part of an overseas laundering scheme, a lawyer acting on behalf of a client creates a "paper" (or "boilerplate") company in any one of a number of countries that have strict privacy statutes, such as Panama, which has about 400,000 registered offshore banks and companies. The tiny Western and Pacific islands of Cook, the Marshalls, Nauru, Niue, Samoa, and Vanuatu have more than 18,000 registered banks and companies; Naura, with a population of about 12,000, has 450 banks registered to a single post office box. The British-administered Cayman Islands, located south of Cuba, an easy flight from either Florida or Colombia, is 100 miles square and has a population of only 23,400. Yet there are about 600 banks and 20,000 registered companies on the Cayman Islands. The island's Georgetown financial district has the highest density of banks and fax machines in the world. Most banks are simply "plaques" or box offices—no vaults, tellers, or security guards—with transactions recorded by Cayman booking centers. Virtually anyone can "establish his or her own shell company for a few thousand dollars in legal fees, open a local bank account and, because the required disclosure is minimal and business operates behind a wall of strict secrecy, no one need know about the company or what funds are stashed there.

The funds to be laundered are transferred physically or wired to the company's account in a local bank. The company then transfers the money to the local branch of a large international bank. The paper company is then able to borrow money from the United States (or any other) branch of this bank, using the overseas deposit as security. Or an employment contract is set up between the launderer and his or her "paper" company for an imaginary service

for which payments are made to the launderer. In some cases, the lawyer may also establish a "boiler-plate bank"—like the company, this is a shell. Not only does the criminal get his money laundered, but he also earns a tax write-off for the interest on the loan. Under the Bank Secrecy Act, wiring or physically transporting cash or other financial instruments out of the country in excess of $10,000 must be reported to the Customs Service. Once the money is out of the United States, however, it may be impossible for the IRS to trace it. In some schemes, the money is returned to the United States or other destination via the purchase of life insurance policies from the British Isle of Man, a center for international insurance firms. The policies frequently taken out in the name of relatives are then cashed out prematurely, the 25 percent penalty being part of the cost of the operation.

Taking advantage of bank secrecy laws to avoid disclosure of ownership has drawbacks: It may be difficult, if not impossible, to pass on these assets to one's heirs.

Trade-based money laundering (TBML) involves use of the international trade system to disguise illicit proceeds to make it appear as legitimate. TBML can be accomplished through the use of informal banking systems such as the *Black Market Peso Exchange* ("BMPE"), in which one or more "peso brokers" serve as middlemen between, on one hand, drug traffickers who control massive quantities of drug cash in the United States, and, on the other, companies and individuals in Colombia who wish to purchase U.S. dollars outside the legitimate Colombian banking system so that they can, among other things, avoid the payment of taxes, import duties, and transaction fees owed to the Colombian government. Transactions are verbal, without any paper trail, and the disconnection between the peso transactions (which generally all occur in Colombia) and the dollar transactions (which generally all occur outside Colombia) make discovery of the money laundering by international law enforcement extremely difficult. Because of these inherent advantages, the BMPE system has become one of the primary methods by which Colombian traffickers launder their illicit funds (DEA press release, May 4, 2004).

More stringent federal laws against money laundering, along with anti–money-laundering measures adopted by traditional financial institutions, have forced criminal organizations to shift the movement of their illicit proceeds outside of the established financial industry. To avoid scrutiny of law enforcement, criminals smuggle bulk cash into, out of, and through the United States.

Criminal organizations are increasingly employing nontraditional methods to move funds, such as the *chop* and *hawala*.

Chop. Chinese criminals are aided by an underground banking system operating through gold shops, trading companies, commodity houses, travel agencies, and money changers, managed in many countries by the same extended Chinese family. "The method of moving money is the *chop*, which is in effect a negotiable instrument. A *chop* can be cashed in Chinese gold shops or trading houses in many countries. The value and identity of the holder of the chop is a secret between the parties. The form of chop varies from transaction to transaction and is difficult to identify. In effect, the chop system allows money to be transferred from country to country instantaneously and anonymously" (Chaiken 1991: 495). For example, $100,000 in cash is deposited in a San Francisco Chinatown gold shop in return for a *chop*. The chop is sent by courier to Hong Kong where the gold shop's associate, usually a relative, gives $100,000 minus a transaction fee to the possessor of chop.

A similar system, the *hawala*, is used in South Asia, where the size of the underground economies is estimated to be 50 to 100 percent the size of documented economies. Similar to the modern practice of "wiring money," the ancient system of *hawala* was the primary money transfer mechanism used in South Asia prior to the introduction of Western banking. "Hawala operates on trust and connections ('trust' is one of the several meanings associated with the word 'hawala'). Customers trust hawala 'bankers' (known as hawaladars) who use their connections to facilitate money movement worldwide. Hawala transfers take place with little, if any, paper trail, and, when records are kept, they are usually kept in code" (U.S. Department of State 1999: 22). In Pakistan, for example, $100,000 (plus a transaction fee) is given to a hawaladar who provides a code term. Via the Internet, the hawaladar informs his broker in the Cayman Islands, where someone who provides the code term is given $100,000 to deposit in an island account.

In both systems, money is never actually moved, and periodically brokers balance their respective transactions, usually by wire transfers using goods and invoices as a cover. In the United States, there are an estimated 20,000 informal remittance businesses working out of a variety of convenience stores, restaurants, and small shops whose owners speak languages unfamiliar to Westerners such as Arabic, Urdu, Hindu, and a variety of Chinese dialects (Freedman 2005).

Money laundering is facilitated through the use of *digital currency*, privately owned online payment systems that allow international payments denominated in the standard weights for gold and other precious metals. While digital currency transactions can be traced back to an individuals computer, proxy servers and anonymity networks protect a person's identity by obscuring the unique IP (Internet Protocol) address as well as the individuals' true location. And mobile payments conducted from anonymous prepaid cellular devices may be impossible to trace to an individual. After a single transaction, the device can be destroyed to prevent forensic analysis. Digital currency account holders also may use public Internet terminals or even "hijacked" wireless Internet connections to access their digital currency accounts, causing transactions to appear to originate with the unsuspecting Internet subscriber. Users of digital currency may encrypt their transmissions to conceal communications between individuals, making law enforcement scrutiny more difficult (NDIC 2008b).

SUMMARY

1. Know the various forms that labor racketeering can take:
   - Labor and business racketeering distinguish the American Mafia from other criminal organizations.
   - Labor racketeering assumes three basic forms: strike insurance, the sweetheart deal, and siphoning of union funds.
   - Until the passage of the Wagner Act in 1935, a particular pattern took place in labor confrontations with employers.

2. Know the history of labor unions and how some were vulnerable to organized crime and the role of Lepke Buchalter in revolutionizing labor racketeering:
   - The first step away from union democracy was a response to power wielded by employers. In order to avoid the problem of company spies reporting to management, some unions employed the "walking delegate" or business agent.
   - In the first decade of the twentieth century a systematic and professional approach to using violence was provided by "Dopey" Benny Fein.
   - Louis Buchalter and Jacob Shapiro dominated many of the industries into which they had been invited.
   - Instead of using his sluggers and gunmen to terrorize labor unions during strike periods, Lepke worked them directly into the unions.
   - Unions whose members worked in geographically dispersed locations for numerous small employers, or those representing workers whose employment was sporadic or seasonal, proved susceptible to racketeering.

3. Understand the connection between four international unions and organized crime:
   - Four international unions have historically been dominated by organized crime.
   - The International Longshoreman's Association shifted from exploiting its

members to restraining competition among stevedoring companies.
   - The International Brotherhood of Teamsters is the most important union to come under the domination of organized crime and is the largest labor union in the United States.
   - The struggle between the CIO and AFL to represent teamsters in Detroit provided an opening for organized crime.
   - Paper locals" were used by Anthony Corallo and John Dioguardi for their financial benefit and they aided Jimmy Hoffa in his quest for the IBT presidency.

4. Recognize how labor racketeering is often the flipside of business racketeering:
   - There is no hard-and-fast line separating labor racketeering from business racketeering—one is often an integral part of the other.
   - Businesses vulnerable to organized crime are relatively easy businesses to enter and highly competitive or have an intense need for timely action.
   - The policing of restraint of trade agreements is a service provided by organized crime.

5. Appreciate why members of organized crime choose to operate a legitimate business:
   - Funds from illegal business activities cannot easily be profitably reinvested in illegal market enterprises.
   - Organized criminal involvement in legitimate business may be based on: profit, diversification, transfer, services, front, taxes.

6. Know the role of organized crime in scam/ "bust out" schemes:
   - A scam is a bankruptcy fraud that victimizes wholesale providers of various goods and sometimes insurance companies.

7. Know the "why" and "how" of money laundering
   - Money is laundered through an array of businesses and informal financial transfers such as the *chop* and *hawala*.

REVIEW QUESTIONS

1. What are the three basic forms of labor racketeering?

2. Why does labor and business racketeering distinguish the American Mafia from other criminal organizations?

3. Until the passage of the Wagner Act in 1935, what was the typical scenario that took place in labor confrontations with employers?

4. What was the reason for unions using a "walking delegate"?

5. What was the role played by "Dopey" Benny Fine in union–management relations?

6. How did Lepke Buchalter and Jacob Shapiro revolutionize labor racketeering?

7. What were the characteristics of unions that made them susceptible to racketeering?

8. What are the four international unions that have historically been dominated by organized crime?

9. How did the International Longshoremen's Union shift from labor racketeering to business racketeering?

10. Why is the International Brotherhood of Teamsters the most important union to come under the domination of organized crime?

11. How did the struggle between the CIO and AFL to represent teamsters in Detroit provide an opening for organized crime?

12. How were "paper locals" used by Anthony Corallo and John Dioguardi?

13. How did the "paper locals" benefit Jimmy Hoffa?

14. With respect to labor racketeering and business racketeering, how can one be an integral part of the other?

15. What are the characteristics of an industry/business that make it vulnerable to organized crime?

16. What is the typical role of organized crime in restraint trade agreements?

17. Why would organized crime groups pose a threat to society if they were engaged largely in legitimate activities?

18. What are the six reasons for organized criminal involvement in legitimate business?

19. What is a *scam*?

20. How do informal financial transfers such as the *chop* and *hawala* facilitate money laundering?

Edward G. Robinson as "Rico" in *Little Caesar*.   © Mary Evans/Ronald Grant/Everett

Organized Crime: Statutes

In 2011, the Racketeer Influenced and Corrupt Organizations Act (RICO) enabled the indictment of 70 defendants alleged to be members and associates of *Armenian Power*, an organized crime group operating out of Southern California (see Chapter 9). Under RICO, the 134 counts in the indictment apply to every defendant insofar as they comprise a *criminal enterprise*. Collectively, they are accused of 450 overt acts that include kidnapping, extortion, bank fraud, aggravated identity theft, credit card fraud, marijuana distribution, and conducting an illegal gambling business. As per RICO, each of the 70 indicted members of Armenian Power—the criminal enterprise—is responsible for the crimes committed by the other members even if they were not direct participants or had no knowledge of the substantive crime. RICO provides a penalty of 20 years imprisonment for each count (FBI press release, February 16, 2011).

RICO and other statutes used in response to organized crime will be examined in this chapter.

CHAPTER 14 WILL ENABLE THE READER TO UNDERSTAND:

- How the Internal Revenue Code is used against organized crime
- The statutes that deal with controlled substances
- The Hobbs Act, the earliest statute designed to deal with racketeering
- How the Sherman Antitrust Act is used against restraint-of-trade agreements
- Become familiar with the connection between the "Apalachin Crime Conference" and the Landrum-Griffin Act and how the act deals with labor racketeering
- The various types of conspiracy and their value in prosecuting organized crime

The business of organized crime involves the violation of numerous laws. Many are routinely enforced by municipal police departments, including laws against gambling, drugs, prostitution, extortion, assault, and murder. The investigation and prosecution of organized crime per se, however, has largely been a responsibility of the federal government, which has a number of specialized statutes to carry out this purpose. We will begin with the Internal Revenue Code.

INTERNAL REVENUE CODE

The Internal Revenue Code is organized into volumes covering a variety of taxes, in particular, U.S. income tax. The code requires residents and citizens (who may reside outside the country) to file a tax return that reveals the source and amount of all income from whatever source it is derived.

In 1927, the U.S. Supreme Court decided the case of *United States v. Sullivan* (274 U.S. 259), which denied the claim of self-incrimination (Fifth Amendment) as an excuse for failure to file income tax on illegally gained earnings. It reasoned that it would be ridiculous if legitimate persons had to file income tax returns but criminals did not. This decision enabled the federal government to successfully prosecute Al Capone and members of his organization. Because persons in organized crime have

obligations as taxpayers, they can be prosecuted for several acts:

1. Failing to make required returns or maintain required business records
2. Filing a false return or making a false statement about taxes
3. Willful failure to pay federal income tax or concealment of assets with intent to defraud
4. Helping others evade income taxes
5. In gambling operations, failing to file a "Special Tax Return and Application for Registry-Wagering"

"Acts which do not comprise a violation or attempt to violate any of these substantive sections may be punishable as part of a conspiracy 'to impair, defeat, and obstruct the functions of the Commissioner of Internal Revenue' by concealing matters relevant to collection of federal taxes" (Johnson 1963: 17). An employer can be prosecuted for not complying with Social Security withholding requirements relative to employees. Thus, the manager of an illegal enterprise, such as a gambling operation, could be prosecuted for such evasions.

In Chapter 15, we will examine the techniques used by the Treasury Department in response to violations of the Internal Revenue Code.

CONTROLLED SUBSTANCES
STATUTES

In 1914, the Harrison Act made it illegal to sell or give away opium or opium derivatives and coca or its derivatives without a written order on a form issued by the Commissioner of Revenue. Persons who were not registered were prohibited from engaging in interstate traffic in the drugs. No one could possess any of the drugs who had not registered and paid the special tax under a penalty of up to five years' imprisonment and a fine of no more than $2,000.

By 1970, the issue of federal police authority had been largely resolved, and the Comprehensive

Drug Abuse Prevention and Control Act of 1970 represented a new legal approach to federal drug policy—it was predicated not on the constitutional power to tax but on federal authority over interstate commerce. This shift had enormous implications for the way in which the federal government would approach drug enforcement in the future. The act "set the stage for an innovation in federal drug law enforcement techniques. That innovation was the assigning of large numbers of federal narcotic agents to work in local communities. No longer was it necessary to demonstrate interstate traffic to justify Federal participation in combating illegal drug use" (PCOC 1986a: 28). The new approach was sustained by decisions of the Supreme Court. The 1970 legislation established five schedules into which all controlled substances could be placed according to their potential for abuse (see Figure 14.1).

Following the federal model, most states have adopted the five-schedule system, but many "have chosen to reclassify particular substances within those five schedules. Variation also exists in the number of schedules employed by the states [North Carolina, for example, uses six] and in the purpose of these schedules" (*Illicit Drug Policies* 2002: 8). Massachusetts categorizes drugs on the basis of the penalty rather than using the federal scheme of potential for abuse and medical use. Like federal law, state statutes refer to the drug involved (e.g., cocaine or heroin), the action involved (e.g., simple possession, possession with the intent to sell, sale, distribution, or trafficking), and the number of prior offenses. Across states

SCHEDULE I

A. The drug or other substance has a high potential for abuse.
B. The drug or other substance has no currently accepted medical use in treatment in the United States.
C. There is a lack of accepted safety for use of the drug or other substance under medical supervision.

SCHEDULE II

A. The drug or other substance has a high potential for abuse.
B. The drug or other substance has a currently accepted medical use in treatment in the United States or a currently accepted medical use with severe restrictions.
C. Abuse of the drug or other substances may lead to severe psychological or physical dependence.

SCHEDULE III

A. The drug or other substance has a potential for abuse less than the drugs or other substances in Schedules I and II.
B. The drug or other substance has a currently accepted medical use in treatment in the United States.
C. Abuse of the drug or other substance may lead to moderate or low physical dependence or high psychological dependence.

SCHEDULE IV

A. The drug or other substance has a low potential for abuse relative to the drugs or other substances in Schedule III.
B. The drug or other substance has a currently accepted medical use in treatment in the United States.
C. Abuse of the drug or other substance may lead to limited physical dependence or psychological dependence relative to the drugs or other substances in Schedule III.

SCHEDULE V

A. The drug or other substance has a low potential for abuse relative to the drugs or other substances in Schedule IV.
B. The drug or other substance has a currently accepted medical use in treatment in the United States.
C. Abuse of the drug or other substances may lead to limited physical dependence or psychological dependence relative to the drugs or other substances in Schedule IV.

FIGURE 14.1 DEA Schedules of Controlled Substances

there is significant variation in the penalties for cocaine-, marijuana-, methamphetamine-, and ecstasy-related offenses (*Illicit Drug Policies* 2002).

The Comprehensive Crime Control Act of 1984 supplemented the 1970 drug statute by authorizing the doubling of a sentence for drug offenders with prior domestic or foreign felony drug convictions. The Anti–Drug Abuse Act of 1986 imposes mandatory prison sentences for certain drug offenses and a mandatory doubling of the minimum penalties for offenders with prior felony drug convictions. In 1988, the military's role in drug-law enforcement was substantially increased and Congress passed a statute to better control the diversion of precursor and essential chemicals for the manufacture of drugs. The Chemical Diversion and Trafficking Act, Subtitle A of the Anti–Drug Abuse Amendments of 1988, established record-keeping requirements and enforcement standards for more than two dozen precursor and essential chemicals. State and federal statutes make the unauthorized trade in any of the listed substances equivalent to trafficking in the actual illegal drugs.

The 1988 statute also created a complex and extensive body of civil penalties aimed at casual users. These include withdrawal of federal benefits, such as mortgage guarantees, and loss of a pilot's license or stockbroker's license at the discretion of a federal judge. Fines of up to $10,000 can be imposed for illegal possession of even small amounts of controlled substances. There are special penalties for the sale of drugs to minors. The statute permits imposition of capital punishment for murders committed as part of a continuing criminal enterprise or for the murder of a law enforcement officer during an arrest for a drug-related felony. The statute also established an Office of National Drug Control Policy headed by a director appointed by the president. The director is charged with coordinating federal drug supply reduction efforts, including international control, intelligence, interdiction, domestic law enforcement, treatment, education, and research.

In response to the Ecstasy [MDMA] Anti-Proliferation Act of 2000, the U.S. Sentencing Commission raised the guideline for judges' sentences for trafficking MDMA. For 800 pills, about 200

grams, the sentence increased from fifteen months to five years; for 8,000 pills, the sentence increased from forty-one months to ten years.

Enacted in 2003, the Illicit Drug Anti-Proliferation Act (sometimes known as the "Rave Act") prohibits "knowingly opening, maintaining, managing, controlling, renting, leasing, making available for use, or profiting from any place for the purpose of manufacturing, distributing or using any controlled substance." Penalties include imprisonment for up to twenty years, criminal fines of $500,000, and civil penalties of $250,000.

People involved in the illegal drug business can be arrested and prosecuted for a number of different offenses: manufacture, importation, distribution, possession, or sale; conspiracy to manufacture, import, distribute, possess, or sell; or failure to pay the required income taxes on illegal income. Possession of drugs may be *actual*—for example, on the person, in pockets, or in a package that the person is holding; or *constructive*—not on the person but under his or her control, directly or through other people. Possession must be proven by a legal search, which usually requires a search warrant as per the Fourth Amendment (an important exception is at ports of entry, discussed in Chapter 15).

THE HOBBS ACT

The earliest statutes designed to deal with "racketeering" are collectively known as the Hobbs Act (18 U.S.C. §§ 1951–1955). Since 1946 they have been amended several times. The Hobbs Act makes it a federal crime to engage in criminal behavior that interferes with interstate commerce:

> Whosoever in any way or degree obstructs, delays, or affects commerce or the movement of any articles or commodity in commerce, by robbery or extortion or attempts or conspires to do so, or commits or threatens physical violence to any person or property in furtherance of a plan or purpose to do anything in violation of this section shall be fined not more than

$10,000 or imprisonment for not more than twenty years or both.

The statute has been broadly interpreted so as to permit the successful prosecution of more than sixty Chicago police officers for extorting payoffs from the owners of saloons. The six-year investigation (1970–1976) by the U.S. Department of Justice was based on the part of the Hobbs Act that makes extortion that in any way affects interstate commerce a federal crime: Federal attorneys "reasoned that because taverns sold beer and liquor, much of which was either delivered from or manufactured in states other than Illinois, extortion of a tavern owner would be a violation of the Hobbs Act" (Biegel and Biegel 1977: 7).

The Hobbs Act also prohibits foreign or interstate travel or the use of interstate facilities, such as the mails or telephones, to advance illegal activities such as gambling, drug trafficking, extortion, and bribery. This permitted the federal government to prosecute corrupt officials and lawyers in Cook County, Illinois—"Operation Greylord"—in the late 1980s and early 1990s.

Section 1954 defines as criminal a union official who misuses an employee benefit plan.

An official who receives or agrees to or solicits any fee, kickback, commission, gift, loan, money, or thing of value because of or with intent to be influenced with respect to, any of the actions, decisions, or other duties relating to any question or matter concerning such plan or any persons who directly or indirectly gives or offers, or promises to give or offer, any fee, kickback, commission, gift, loan, money, or thing of value prohibited by this section, shall be fined not more than $10,000 or imprisoned for not more than three years, or both.

SHERMAN ANTITRUST ACT

Enacted in 1890, the Sherman Antitrust Act prohibits any agreement among competitors to fix prices, rig bids, or engage in other anticompetitive activity: "Every person who shall monopolize, or attempt to monopolize, or combine or conspire with any person or persons to monopolize any part of the trade or commerce among the several States, or with foreign nations, shall be deemed guilty of a misdemeanor." The act does not define key terms such as "attempt to monopolize," leaving interpretation to the courts. And early on the Supreme Court interpreted the act in a manner that favored business (*United States v. E.C. Knight & Co.,* 156 U.S. 1, 1895) and weakened organized labor (*In Re Debs,* 154 U.S. 564, 1895).

Title 15 of the United States Code raises restraint of trade violations to a felony:

Every contract, combination in the form of trust or otherwise, or conspiracy, in restraint of trade or commerce among the several States, or with foreign nations, is declared to be illegal. Every person who shall make any contract or engage in any combination or conspiracy hereby declared to be illegal shall be deemed guilty of a felony, and, on conviction thereof, shall be punished by fine not exceeding $100,000,000 if a corporation, or, if any other person, $1,000,000, or by imprisonment not exceeding 10 years, or by both said punishments, in the discretion of the court.

Under some circumstances, the fine may be increased to twice the gain or loss involved. Collusion among competitors may also violate mail or wire fraud statutes, false statements statute, or other federal felony statutes. Victims of bid rigging and price-fixing may seek civil recovery of up to three times the amount of damages suffered.

Anticompetitive practices can fit five general categories (U.S. Department of Justice information):

Price fixing is an agreement among competitors to raise, fix, or otherwise maintain the price at which their goods or services are sold. It is not necessary that the competitors agree to charge exactly the same price or that every competitor in a given industry join the conspiracy.

Bid rigging is the way that competitors effectively raise prices where purchasers acquire goods or services by soliciting competing bids. Competitors agree in advance who will submit the winning bid on a contract being let through the competitive bidding process.

Complementary bidding (also known as "cover" or "courtesy" bidding) occurs when competitors agree to submit bids that either are too high to be accepted or contain special terms that will not be acceptable to the buyer. Such bids are not intended to secure the buyer's acceptance, but are merely designed to give the appearance of genuine competitive bidding.

Bid rotation involves conspirators who submit bids but take turns being the low bidder. The terms of the rotation may vary; for example, competitors may take turns on contracts according to the size of the contract, allocating equal amounts to each conspirator or allocating volumes that correspond to the size of each conspirator company.

Market division or allocation schemes are agreements in which competitors divide markets among themselves. In such schemes, competing firms allocate specific customers or types of customers, products, or territories among themselves. Competitors agree, for example, to sell only to customers in certain geographic areas and refuse to sell to, or quote intentionally high prices to, customers in geographic areas allocated to conspirator companies.

Proving price fixing, bid rigging, market division, or allocation schemes does not require proof that the conspirators entered into a formal written or express agreement. Instead, proof can be established by direct evidence, such as the testimony of a participant, or by circumstantial evidence, such as suspicious bid patterns, travel and expense reports, telephone records, and business diary entries.

LANDRUM-GRIFFIN ACT

The Labor Management Reporting and Disclosure Act, generally known as the Landrum-Griffin Act, is an outgrowth of several significant events in the history of the American Mafia.

In 1956, the Senate Permanent Subcommittee on Investigations began an inquiry into the Teamsters Union that was greeted with union recalcitrance (see Chapter 13). The following year, Frank Costello, boss of the Luciano Family, who routinely traveled without bodyguards, was rushing to catch the elevator in his luxury apartment building, when a large man wearing a fedora yelled, "This is for you, Frank." As Costello turned, the man fired a revolver at Costello's face from a distance of six to ten feet. The bullet hit Costello in the head but caused only superficial damage. When questioned by authorities, Costello insisted he did not recognize his assailant, the easily recognizable Vincenzo ("Chin") Gigante.[1] Several months later, in what is believed to have been a related incident, Albert Anastasia ("The Executioner" who issued the "contract hits" for Murder, Inc.), Costello's close ally and boss of the Mineo crime Family, was shot to death while in a chair at the Park Sheraton Hotel barbershop in midtown Manhattan. Costello retired, leaving Vito Genovese as boss of the crime Family that now bears his name. In 1959, Genovese, along with fourteen others, was convicted of conspiracy to violate narcotic laws. In 1969, while serving his fifteen-year sentence, Genovese died of a heart ailment. Like the case against Lucky Luciano, the one against Genovese raises many questions: The main witness against him was a Puerto Rican drug dealer who claimed to have discussed drug trafficking with Genovese, an assertion that strains credibility.

The attack on Costello and murder of Anastasia led to a 1957 meeting of leading Mafia bosses at the estate of Joseph M. Barbara, Sr., boss of the Northeastern Pennsylvania crime Family, in upstate Apalachin, New York. A New York state police sergeant became suspicious of the activities at Barbara's estate where a number of expensive automobiles with out-of-state license plates were parked. He conducted a raid on Barbara's house: "Within minutes dozens of well-dressed men ran out of the house and across the fields in all directions" (Salerno

---

1. In 1985, Gigante became boss of the crime Family; he died in prison in 2005.

and Tompkins 1969: 298). Using roadblocks and reinforcements, the police reportedly took sixty-three men into custody—this figure is disputed.

The men were summoned to the sergeant's office where they "gave their names and addresses, took off their shoes, emptied their pockets as troopers searched and watched" (Sondern 1959: 36). More than two dozen leading Mafia figures, after refusing to answer questions as to the purpose of the meeting, were indicted for conspiracy and obstruction of justice. After a three-week trial, a jury found twenty defendants guilty of conspiracy. The verdict was overturned in 1960 by the U.S. Court of Appeals, which concluded that the people at the Barbara estate had been taken into custody, detained, and searched without probable cause that a crime had or was being committed: "In America we still respect the dignity of the individual, and even an unsavory character is not to be imprisoned except on definite proof of specific crime" (*United States v. Bufalino et al.,* 285 F.2d 408, 1960).

The raid at Apalachin generated news headlines throughout the country, and many of the men who were arrested claimed to be labor-management consultants. The Senate responded by establishing the Select Committee on Improper Activities in the Labor or Management Field, chaired by Senator John McClellan of Arkansas. Committee hearings led to the passage of the Landrum-Griffin Act in 1959.

Landrum-Griffin established a Bill of Rights for union members:

1. Every member of a labor organization shall have equal rights and privileges within such organization to nominate candidates, to vote in elections or referendums of the labor organization, to attend membership meetings and to participate in the deliberations and voting upon the business of such meetings.
2. Every member of any labor organization shall have the right to meet and assemble freely with other members; and to express any views, arguments, or opinions; and to express at meetings of the labor organization his views, upon candidates in an election of the labor organization or upon any business properly before the meeting.

3. No member of any labor organization may be fined, suspended, expelled, or otherwise disciplined except for nonpayment of dues by such organization or by any officer thereof unless such member has been (A) served with written specific charges; (B) given a reasonable time to prepare his defense; (C) afforded a full and fair hearing.

The Act provides penalties for violations ranging from one to twenty years imprisonment. For example:

- Any person who makes a false statement or representation of a material fact, knowing it to be false, or who knowingly fails to disclose a material fact, in any report required under the provisions of this section or willfully makes any false entry in or willfully withholds, conceals, or destroys any documents, books, records, reports, or statements upon which such report is based, shall be fined not more than $10,000 or imprisoned for not more than one year, or both.

- Any person who embezzles, steals, or unlawfully and willfully abstracts or converts to his own use, or the use of another, any of the moneys, funds, securities, property, or other assets of a labor organization of which he is an officer, or by which he is employed, directly or indirectly, shall be fined not more than $10,000 or imprisoned for not more than five years, or both.

- It shall be unlawful to carry on picketing on or about the premises of any employer for the purpose of, or as part of any conspiracy or in furtherance of any plan or purpose for, the personal profit or enrichment of any individual (except a bona fide increase in wages or other employee benefits) by taking or obtaining any money or other thing of value from such employer against his will or with his consent. Any person who willfully violates this section shall be fined not more than $10,000 or imprisoned not more than twenty years, or both.

Persons convicted of a variety of felonies, such as murder, extortion, assault, misuse of a position in a labor organization or employee benefit plan, are not permitted to hold any union office or serve as a consultant or adviser in the labor-management field for the period of thirteen years after their conviction.

The Act provides that "Whenever it shall appear that any person has violated or is about to violate any of the provisions of this title, the Secretary [of Labor] may bring a civil action for such relief (including injunctions) as may be appropriate."

CONSPIRACY

The United States does not criminalize participation in a criminal organization, as such, since to do so might implicate constitutional prohibitions against measures inhibiting freedom of association. However, at both the federal and state level, conspiracies to commit offenses are punishable.

Conspiracy is an agreement between two or more persons to commit a criminal act; *the agreement is the corpus* (body) of the crime. To prove a conspiracy, it is not necessary to show that the offense was actually committed. Indeed, in 2003, the Supreme Court, in a unanimous decision (*United States v. Recio*, 537 U.S. 270), ruled that even when the object of the conspiracy (drug distribution) had been frustrated by the police, who turned it into a sting operation, the conspiracy charge is still valid.

Federal conspiracy statutes generally require the government to prove that two or more persons agreed to commit an offense and that one or more of these persons did at least one act to carry out the agreement, such as surveillance of a victim's home or purchasing rope to restrain him. In some cases, like money laundering, it is not necessary to prove that conspirators did anything concrete to carry out the scheme (*Whitfield v. United States*, 543 U.S. 209, 2005). In 1994, the Supreme Court (*United States v. Shabani*, 513 U.S. 10) ruled that conspiring to violate federal drug laws can be a crime even in the absence of overt acts. Withdrawing from a conspiracy requires

the defendant to show *actual* withdrawal—merely ceasing to participate does not meet the burden of proof (Diener and T. Johnson 2005).

Conspiracy statutes provide valuable tools for prosecuting persons in organized crime because:

- Intervention can occur prior to the commission of a substantive offense.

- A conspirator cannot shield him- or herself from prosecution because of a lack of knowledge of the details of the conspiracy or the identity of coconspirators and their contributions.

- An act or declaration by one conspirator committed in furtherance of the conspiracy is admissible against each coconspirator (an exception to the hearsay rule).

- Each conspirator is responsible for the substantive crimes of his or her coconspirators (vicarious liability); even late joiners can be held liable for prior acts of coconspirators if the agreement by the latecomer is made with full knowledge of the conspiracy's objective.

The charge of conspiracy, which federal prosecutors generally include whenever a case involves multiple defendants (Campane 1981a), is particularly effective against upper-echelon organized crime figures: "The fundamental essence of a conspiracy obviates the necessity of establishing that the organization leader committed a physical act amounting to a crime or that he even committed an overt act in furtherance of the object of the conspiracy. It is sufficient if he can be shown to have been a party to the conspiratorial agreement" (Johnson 1963: 2). Its usefulness can be seen in the following incident:

> Two young men entered an Italian restaurant and approached the table of an elderly gentleman who was sipping anisette with a large, burly individual. After he acknowledged them, the two sat down at the table. They were members of the Genovese crime Family; he was the boss. The young men explained that they had

just discovered a large-scale gambling operation that was not tied to organized crime—an "outlaw" game. They wanted to "license" the operation and asked for his approval. The boss said nothing, but gestured approval with his hands and face. The young men excused themselves and left. With several other men they proceeded to assault and threaten to kill the owner of the gambling operation, extorting several thousand dollars from him. They returned and shared the money with their boss, who knew nothing of the details of what had occurred—and never asked.

There are three basic types of conspiracy:

1. *Wheel conspiracies.* One person at the "hub" conspires individually with two or more persons who make up the "spokes" of the wheel. For the conspiracy to be (legally) complete, the wheel needs a "rim": each of the spokes must be aware of and agree with each other in pursuit of at least one objective.
2. *Chain conspiracies.* Like the lights on a Christmas tree, each conspirator is dependent on the successful participation of every other member. Each member is a "link" who understands that the success of the scheme depends upon everyone in the chain.
3. *Enterprise conspiracies.* The RICO enterprise conspiracy avoids the practical limitations inherent in proving wheel and chain conspiracies. The statute makes it a separate crime to conspire to violate state or federal law as the result of an agreement to participate in an *enterprise* by engaging in a *pattern of racketeering activity*. The enterprise must be an ongoing organization, legitimate or illegitimate, formal or informal, whose associates operate as a continuous unit and they need not be economically motivated. Members of the conspiracy need not know each other or even be aware of each other's criminal activities. All that needs to be shown is each member's agreement to participate in the organization— the *enterprise*—by committing two or more acts

of racketeering such as gambling or drug violations within a ten-year period (a pattern of racketeering). The enterprise conspiracy facilitates mass trials with each member of the enterprise subject to the significant penalties— twenty years' imprisonment on each count— that can result from a conviction.

Prosecuting criminal conspiracy cases can be problematic. In a 1974 case (*United States v. Sperling*, 506 F.2d 1323, 1341, 2d Cir.), the court noted that "it has become too common for the government to bring indictments against a dozen or more defendants and endeavor to force as many of them as possible to trial in the same proceeding on the claim of a single conspiracy when the criminal acts could more reasonably be regarded as two or more conspiracies, perhaps with a link at the top. This creates the risk of 'guilt by association,' wherein a jury, confronted by a large number of defendants and a great volume of evidence, is unable to give each defendant the individual consideration that due process requires. In such situations, a finding of guilty brings with it the risk of being reversed on appeal." Constitutional guarantees of a fair trial "make it imperative to determine whether the evidence establishes one large conspiracy as opposed to multiple smaller ones" (Campane 1981b: 30).

Another considerable problem is that conspiracy cases usually require direct testimony of eyewitnesses; these are often participants in the conspiracy who agree to testify ("flip") against their coconspirators in exchange for leniency or immunity from prosecution. "An investigator should therefore be prepared to locate witnesses (often immunized coconspirators) who are willing to testify and are able to explain the complicated or intricate nature of the unlawful activity, and as a consequence, the stake in the venture or mutual dependence each participant has with each other" (Campane 1981b: 29).

RICO

In 1964, Lyndon B. Johnson was serving the remainder of John F. Kennedy's term and seeking election as president. The Republicans nominated

Senator Barry M. Goldwater of Arizona, who launched what has come to be known as a "law-and-order" campaign: The Republicans attacked the Democratic administration for being "soft on crime." Johnson won a landslide victory, but the issue of crime lingered on. In order to blunt criticism (and, Richard Quinney [1974] argues, to divert attention from the Vietnam conflict), Johnson launched his own "war on crime."

On March 8, 1965, in a message to Congress called "Crime, Its Prevalence and Measures of Prevention," the President announced: "I am establishing the President's Commission on Law Enforcement and Administration of Justice. The commission will be composed of men and women of distinction who share my belief that we need to know far more about the prevention and control of crime." Nine different task forces were established, including the Task Force on Organized Crime, headed by Charles H. Rogovin, with Donald R. Cressey, a noted criminologist, and Ralph Salerno, a former NYPD detective, serving as consultants. Cressey (1969) and Salerno (with Tompkins 1969) extended the influence of the President's Commission by writing books on organized crime. In its report to the commission, the Task Force on Organized Crime stated:

> Today the core of organized crime in the United States consists of twenty-four groups operating as criminal cartels in large cities across the Nation. Their membership is exclusively men of Italian descent, they are in frequent communications with each other, and their smooth functioning is insured by a national body of overseers. To date, only the Federal Bureau of Investigation has been able to document fully the national scope of these groups, and the FBI intelligence indicates that the organization as a whole has changed its name from the Mafia to Cosa Nostra. (1967: 6)

The last statement was obviously based on the revelations of Joseph Valachi.

JOSEPH VALACHI

In 1963, Senator John L. McClellan (D-AR), chair of the Permanent Subcommittee on Investigations (PSI), held televised hearings on organized crime and introduced the public to his star witness, Joseph Valachi. Peter Maas (1968: 40) states that Senator McClellan visited Valachi privately at the District of Columbia jail just before the hearings began: "According to Valachi, the senator requested he skip any mention of Hot Springs, in McClellan's home state," which was notorious for its wide-open gambling operations.

In 1962, Joseph Valachi was a 60-year-old convicted drug trafficker and member of the Genovese Family serving a federal sentence for drug trafficking. A fellow inmate accused him of being an informer for the Federal Bureau of Narcotics; because his accuser was also a "made guy," the accusation was life threatening. Valachi was subsequently approached by an inmate he thought was an enforcer for the Genovese Family. He attacked the inmate with a lead pipe—the wrong man, as it turned out—and beat him to death. In 1963, the gravel-voiced Valachi was in Washington, DC, appearing before the McClellan (PSI) Committee.

Valachi was inducted into the faction headed by Salvatore Maranzano during the "Castellammarese War" (discussed in Chapter 3), and had been a soldier for more than 30 years. The career criminal told of a secret society that insiders referred to as *Cosa Nostra*, replete with blood oaths and murders. He discussed the Castellammarese War, Luciano's murder of Joe "the boss" Masseria, Salvatore Maranzano, and the assassination of some forty other Mafia bosses (that never happened). Valachi outlined the structure of each crime Family and explained how they were linked together through a national commission—the "Supreme Court of Organized Crime." Once the television lights were turned on, notes Maas (1968: 41), senators bombarded Valachi with questions designed to score points with the voters back home. Nebraska Senator Carl Curtis, for example, asked about organized crime in Omaha: "After a moment's reflection, the

---

"MOTHER OF MERCY, IS THIS THE END OF RICO?"

The closing line uttered by Edward G. Robinson as mobster Caesar "Rico" Bandello who is dying from gunshot wounds in the 1931 Warner Brothers classic *Little Caesar*. Attorney G. Robert Blakey drafted the

Racketeer Influenced and Corrupt Organizations—RICO—statute, the clumsy title but memorable acronym a tribute to the movie classic.

---

barely literate Valachi carefully cupped his hand over his mouth, turned to a Justice Department official sitting next to him, and whispered something. Those viewing the scene could be forgiven for supposing that Senator Curtis had hit on a matter of some import that Valachi wanted to check before answering. He was in fact asking, 'Where the hell is Omaha?'"

Valachi was a low-echelon soldier whose first-hand knowledge of organized crime was limited to street-level experiences. Much of the information attributed to him is obviously well beyond his personal experience. Virgil Peterson notes that some of Valachi's testimony was extremely vague, confusing, and inconsistent. "Not infrequently, it would appear, he either withheld facts that should have been known to him or deliberately lied" (1983: 425). Nevertheless, this did not prevent his disclosures from becoming the core of a chapter on organized crime in the final report of the President's Commission on Law Enforcement and Administration of Justice.

The Task Force continued what the Kefauver Committee (discussed in Chapter 2) had begun, equating organized crime with Italians. The only new wrinkle was a name change (Messick 1973: 8): "La Cosa Nostra was created [by the FBI via Valachi] as a public image. This simple device of giving the Mafia a new name worked wonders. Hoover was taken off the limb where he had perched for so long, and citizens had a new menace to talk about with tales of blood oaths, contracts for murder, secret societies." Hank Messick (1967) argues that this picture was thirty years out of date. More important, however, were the policy implications.

The Task Force recommended a witness protection program, special federal grand juries, and legislation permitting electronic surveillance—recommendations that were enacted into law. The Task Force noted the inadequacy of budgetary allocations devoted to dealing with organized crime and the lack of coordination among agencies charged with combating organized crime activity. Accordingly, budgetary allocations were increased to deal with the "new" menace, and in 1967 federal organized crime strike forces were established in each city with a *Cosa Nostra* Family. In 1968, the Omnibus Crime Control and Safe Streets Act was enacted, providing law enforcement agencies with legal guidelines for electronic surveillance (discussed later). In 1970, Congress passed the Organized Crime Control Act, which contains the RICO provisions.

The *Racketeer Influenced and Corrupt Organizations* statute, usually referred to as RICO, is the most important single piece of legislation ever enacted against organized crime. "RICO's criminal enterprise model represented a new approach in the government's prosecution of organized crime groups." Existing criminal laws "did not punish individual's for their conduct in connection with criminal enterprises per se, and the elaborate structure of certain organized crime entities could insulate high-level members, such as bosses, and assets, from prosecution and forfeiture." These groups could sustain the loss of easily replaced low-level members and continue operations with new recruits (Wheatley 2010: 86).

RICO (Title IX of the Organized Crime Control Act of 1970) defines *racketeering* in an extremely broad manner, and includes many offenses that do not ordinarily violate any federal statute: "[A]ny act or threat involving murder, kidnapping, gambling, arson, robbery, bribery, extortion, or dealing in narcotic or other dangerous drugs, which is chargeable under State law and punishable by imprisonment for more than one year." Since 1970, RICO has been used to prosecute offenses not usually associated with organized crime, including political corruption and white-collar crimes.

RICO provides the federal government with jurisdiction that heretofore had been exclusively that of state and local law enforcement, which are often ineffective in dealing with organized crime because, in contrast to "street crime," it is a low priority. As a result, the FBI became the lead agency in organized crime law enforcement.

Under traditional conspiracy statutes, prosecution for engaging in organized crime requires agreement among the participants about the specific crime(s). Given the diverse and often unrelated crimes committed by members of organized crime, use of conspiracy statutes proved difficult. The thrust of RICO is to prove a pattern of crimes conducted through an organization—an *enterprise:* "any individual, partnership, corporation, association, or other legal entity, and any union or group of individuals associated in fact, although not a legal entity." In place of having to prove a series of separate conspiracies, under RICO it is a crime to belong to an enterprise, for example, a Mafia Family or outlaw motorcycle club, that is involved in a "pattern of racketeering," even if the racketeering was committed by other members. "It shall be unlawful for any person employed by or associated with any enterprise engaged in, or the activities of which affect, interstate or foreign commerce, to conduct or participate, directly or indirectly, in the conduct of such enterprise's affairs through a pattern of racketeering activity or collection of an unlawful debt." The enterprise must contain some structure distinct from the "pattern of racketeering" (J. Bourgeois et al. 2000).

In order for racketeering to be a RICO violation, there must be a "pattern," which requires the commission of at least two of the specified crimes within a ten-year period, although, in ruling against antiabortion activists, the Supreme Court has determined that RICO does not require defendants to have an economic motive. Isolated criminal acts, however, do not constitute a "pattern." Instead, there must be a relationship between the two (or more) predicate crimes over a substantial period of time (J. Moore and Tschupp 2000). However, section 904(a) of RICO states that "the provisions of this title shall be liberally construed to effectuate its remedial purposes."

The criminal penalties for violating RICO are substantial: Whoever violates any provision "shall be fined not more than $25,000 or imprisoned not more than twenty years, or both." In addition to the criminal penalties, there are civil forfeiture provisions, requiring the violator to forfeit to the government any business or property he or she has acquired in violation of RICO. The government can freeze a defendant's assets before trial.

Under the provisions of RICO, the government can file a petition in federal district court seeking to have a branch (local) of a labor union, or even the leadership of the union itself, removed and the entity placed in receivership. Since this is a proceeding in equity (see Abadinsky 2008), there is no right to a trial by jury. As noted in Chapter 13, this was done with Local 560 of the International Brotherhood of Teamsters (the "Tony Pro local") and Local 54 of the Hotel and Restaurant Employees Union. By 2006, there were twenty successful RICO suits resulting in court-appointed trustees responsible for eliminating the influence of organized crime and establishing union democracy (Jacobs 2006).

Under the provisions of RICO, a federal prosecutor names as defendants union officers and organized crime figures. They are charged with having violated RICO by acquiring or aiding and abetting the acquiring of influence in the union through a pattern of racketeering activity, typically by means of violence and intimidation; and conducting union affairs through a pattern of racketeering activity, typically extortion, theft, and fraud. The government asks that the union defendants be removed from their positions and for the organized crime figures to sever all contacts with the union. Finally, the judge is asked to appoint a trustee empowered to initiate disciplinary charges against union officials who violate the decree, the union constitution, or bylaws. The trustee is also empowered to administer union affairs and to organize and monitor a fair election (Jacobs 2006).

While RICO has as its stated purpose "the eradication of organized crime in the United States," the statute provides no definition of organized crime, and the "broad wording of the statute has allowed it to be used in a vast array of situations totally unrelated to organized crime. For example, RICO's authorization for civil suits is invoked in commercial and business litigation, particularly when there is a claim of fraud (Chemerinsky 2000). RICO has provisions by which private citizens can sue for damages: "Any person injured in his business or property by reason of a violation of section 1962 of this chapter may sue therefore in any appropriate United States district court and shall recover threefold damages he sustains and the cost of the suit, including a reasonable attorney's fee." In *NOW v. Scheidler* (510 U.S. 249, 1994), the Supreme Court ruled unanimously that abortion clinics can invoke RICO to sue violent anti-abortion protest groups for damages. In 1998, a federal jury in Chicago found three leading anti-abortion activists liable under RICO and awarded $85,000 to two abortion clinics, an amount tripled by the judge as per the statute (Pallasch and Peres 1998). In an editorial, the *New York Times* noted: "The use of RICO has raised legitimate concern that this precedent could be expanded to obstruct free speech and political protest" ("Abortion Harassers as Racketeers" 1998).

While it took nearly a decade for federal prosecutors to fully understand and incorporate RICO into their array of prosecutorial tools, it has become clear that the use of the statute has been quite effective. By 1990, more than a thousand major and minor organized crime figures had been convicted and given lengthy prison sentences. "The hierarchies of the five New York LCN Families have been prosecuted, and similar prosecutions have dented the LCN hierarchies in Boston, Cleveland, Denver, Kansas City, Milwaukee, New Jersey,

Philadelphia, Pittsburgh and St. Louis" (Pennsylvania Crime Commission 1990: 18). In fact, the threat of lengthy imprisonment under RICO provides a "stick" that has been used to gain the cooperation of defendants.

> The federal prosecutor derives a variety of benefits from the RICO statute's definitions of enterprise and racketeering activity. For example, it is the only criminal statute that enables the Government to present a jury with the whole picture of how an enterprise, such as an organized crime family, operates. Rather than pursuing the leader of a small group of subordinates for a single crime or scheme, the Government is able to indict the entire hierarchy of an organized crime family for the diverse criminal activities in which that "enterprise" engages. Instead of merely proving one criminal act in a defendant's life, it permits proof of a defendant's whole life in crime. (Giuliani 1987: 106)

Rudolph W. Giuliani, former U.S. attorney for the Southern District of New York, used RICO in successfully prosecuting organized crime cases, including the Colombo Family. Fourteen defendants were indicted as either leaders, members, or associates of the Colombo Family. In setting forth the "enterprise," the indictment identified the boss, underboss, and *consigliere*, of the Family, and five captains, all of who were charged with supervising and protecting the criminal activities of the Family. The leadership as well as the lower-ranking members were included within the Family "enterprise" as a group of individuals associated in fact. The ongoing nature of the enterprise was demonstrated by the fact that the Family selected an acting boss to direct its criminal activities while the boss was incarcerated. Reliance entirely upon traditional conspiracy law without RICO would not have enabled the government to include all of these individuals within a single prosecution or to identify each of their specific roles within the *enterprise*.

In addition, RICO's requirement of proving a "pattern of racketeering activity" and its broad definition of "racketeering activity" allowed the prosecution to join in a single indictment the widely diverse state and federal crimes the Colombo Family had engaged in over the past fifteen years. Thus, the indictment included charges that the Family had engaged in extortion, labor racketeering, drug trafficking, gambling, loansharking, and both state and federal bribery violations. The prosecution was also able to include as predicate acts of racketeering prior federal bribery convictions of three of the defendants.

Venue in RICO cases permits the prosecution of a continuing offense in any district in which such offense was begun, continued, or completed. Thus, the prosecution was able to include crimes committed in the Southern and Eastern Districts of New York, as well as in Florida and New Jersey.

Finally, because of RICO's broad definition of a pattern of racketeering activity, it was possible for the prosecutors to include predicate offenses in which the criminal conduct occurred at a time beyond the reach of the general federal five-year statute of limitations. In this regard, all that RICO requires is that one act of racketeering occurred after the effective date of the statute (October 15, 1970), and that the last or most recent predicate act occurred within ten years of a prior act of racketeering. Given these provisions, the prosecution was permitted to charge a 1970 heroin transaction as well as extortions that took place in 1975.

CRITICISM OF RICO

Five basic criticisms of RICO have been raised:

1. RICO is overreaching, leading to the prosecution of persons who, although they may have been involved in criminal behavior, are not by any stretch of the imagination connected to organized crime.
2. In contrast with sentences typically imposed for corporate crime (when it is subjected to prosecution) leading to death or injury, or significant financial loss, to hundreds, thousands, or even millions, RICO penalties are excessive—twenty years on each count.
3. Invoking RICO can result in assets being frozen even before a trial begins, an action that can effectively put a company out of business. The threat of freezing assets can induce corporate defendants to plead guilty even when they believe themselves to be innocent.
4. A RICO action brings with it the stigma of being labeled a "racketeer," which may be inappropriate given the circumstances at issue.
5. RICO permits lawsuits for triple damages when ordinary business transactions, not organized crime or racketeering, are at issue.

The Organized Crime Act of 1970 (of which RICO is a part) fails to define *organized crime*, and RICO fails to define *racketeer*. This lack of precision coupled with the substantial penalties makes RICO a tempting tool for federal prosecutors to use against persons not connected to organized crime, no matter how widely that term is defined. In Chicago, for example, a deputy sheriff and clerk in traffic court were convicted under RICO for helping to fix parking tickets.

In New York, the U.S. attorney used RICO against a small commodities firm for a transaction so commonplace that on some days such transactions account for a third of the volume on the New York Stock Exchange (Epstein 1988b). In 1988, the government brought a RICO indictment against a securities firm for $500,000 in illegal profits. Prosecutors insisted, however, on a bond of $24 million, forcing the company to liquidate before a trial even began (Nocera 1988). Similar criticism has been leveled at the USA PATRIOT Act enacted in the wake of 9/11 to deal with terrorism. The law has frequently been used in cases having little or nothing to do with terrorism (Lichtblau 2003c).

Supporters argue that RICO has been very effective in combating corporate crime that has traditionally proven difficult to prosecute successfully (Waldman and Gilbert 1989). Illegal business practices—crime—can certainly be defined as organized if they are sufficiently large in scale and are continuously performed by specialists, even in the absence of violence and/or corruption. For example, securities violations involving prestigious brokerage firms have been successfully prosecuted using RICO.

USA PATRIOT ACT

The Uniting and Strengthening America by Providing Appropriate Tools Required to Intercept and Obstruct Terrorism Act (USA PATRIOT Act) of 2001 (Public Law 107-56) increased the ability of law enforcement agencies to search telephone and email communications, as well as medical and financial records. Under the act, the FBI is able to bypass the judicial scrutiny required for obtaining certain categories of records from third parties, such as telephone billing records, electronic communication transactional records, financial records, credit information, and business records, through the use of National Security Letters (NSLs).

The NSL demand contains a gag order, preventing the recipient from disclosing that the letter was ever issued.

The act eases restrictions on foreign intelligence gathering within the United States and expanded the Secretary of the Treasury's authority to regulate financial transactions, particularly those involving foreign individuals and entities. The act expands the definition of *terrorism* to include "domestic terrorism," and the Department of Justice has used many of these powers to pursue defendants for crimes unrelated to terrorism, including drug violations, credit card fraud, and bank theft.

About a thousand civil racketeering suits are filed each year by private plaintiffs seeking to recover triple their damages from a variety of defendants—business competitors, swindlers, securities brokers, and unions, or, as noted earlier, antiabortion activists. In contrast, the government averages about one hundred a year. There are so many cases that the practice has its own publication: *RICO Law Reporter* (annual subscription about $2,800).

While private cases have generally proven hard to win, critics argue that the threat of triple damages—and of being referred to as a "racketeer"—causes many defendants to settle. Furthermore, the triple-damage provision encourages contingency lawyers to sue when under ordinary circumstances the potential reward would not be worth the commitment of time. The courts, however, have fined lawyers for bringing frivolous racketeering claims (Diamond 1988). One critic (O'Brien 1986) argues that in contract disputes attorneys routinely add RICO violations, thereby removing their cases from state court and overloading federal courts. Law professor Robert Blakey (1986) argues that the civil sections provide a powerful tool for persons victimized by swindlers to recover their losses and also serves as a deterrent. To avoid the problem of inappropriate labeling, some recommend that the term *racketeer* be removed from the civil aspects of the statute (Waldman and Gilbert 1989). In 2008, Blakey represented a major hog processing company using a RICO suit against an employee union critical of the company for labor, environmental, and safety issues. What Mr. Blakey calls "racketeering," notes *New York Times* legal reporter Adam Liptak (2008: 14), "sounds quite a bit like free speech."

Some states have laws patterned after RICO. In the first case to limit the scope of a state RICO law, the Supreme Court ruled that the inventory of a Fort Wayne, Indiana, adult bookstore could not be subjected to seizure in advance of an obscenity conviction. In a unanimous decision, the Court referred to prohibitions against "prior restraint" of publications that have not been judged to be obscene. In a 6–3 vote, however, the Court rejected a claim that the First Amendment prohibits the use of RICO to prosecute obscenity cases and left open the possibility that the materials could be confiscated after obscenity is proven at trial (*Fort Wayne Books, Inc. v. Indiana, et al.*, 488 U.S. 445, 1989). That same year, the Supreme Court unanimously refused to limit the scope of RICO with respect to private suits (*H.J., Inc. v. Northwestern Bell Telephone Co.*, 492 U.S. 229).

CONTINUING CRIMINAL ENTERPRISE

The Continuing Criminal Enterprise (CCE) statute is similar in purpose to RICO but targets only illegal drug activity. The statute makes it a crime

COMMISSION CASE

Use of the RICO statute resulted in one of the most important prosecutions ever brought against the American Mafia. A task force of personnel from federal, state, and local law enforcement agencies targeted the commission of Mafia Families in New York. Electronic surveillance was used on an unprecedented scale—bugs were planted in cars, homes, and social clubs. In addition, the Bonanno Family was penetrated by an FBI agent to the point of his being proposed for membership (see Pistone 1987). "The theory of the government's case was that the Cosa Nostra commission constituted a criminal enterprise, that each defendant had committed two or more racketeering acts in furtherance of the commission's goals. According to the prosecution, the defendant's predicate racketeering acts fell into three categories: first, management of a multifamily bid-rigging and

extortion scheme in the New York concrete industry; second, conspiracy to organize loansharking territories in Staten Island; and, third, the murders of Bonanno family boss Carmine Galente and two of his associates in furtherance of the commission's effort to resolve a Bonanno family leadership dispute" (Jacobs 1994: 81).

During the course of the trial, the defense attorneys admitted the existence of *Cosa Nostra* and the commission. They denied, however, the commission's involvement in criminal activity, but to no avail: In 1986 all of the defendants, including Carmine Persico, boss of the Colombo Family, Anthony Salerno, boss of the Genovese Family, and Anthony Corallo, boss of the Lucchese Family, were found guilty. Charges against Paul Castellano, boss of the Gambino Family, were dropped after his murder (*United States v. Salerno,* 85 Cr. 139, SDNY 1985).

to commit or conspire to commit a continuing series of felony violations of the 1970 Drug Abuse Prevention and Control Act when the violations are undertaken in concert with five or more persons. The courts have ruled that *series* requires three or more violations. "For conviction under this statute, the offender must have been an organizer, manager, or supervisor of the continuing operation and have obtained substantial income or resources from the drug violations" (Carlson and Finn 1993: 2). In 1999, the Supreme Court ruled (*Richardson v. United States*, 526 U.S. 813) that juries must agree on which specific illegal acts were committed by a defendant, rather than simply finding that he or she committed a series of drug violations without specifying which ones. The 6–3 decision makes it harder to convict persons for violating the CCE.

CONSUMER CREDIT PROTECTION ACT (CCPA)

The 1968 Consumer Credit Protection Act was designed to combat loansharking. It provides a definition of a *loan shark debt* as any extension of

credit with respect to which it is the *understanding* of the creditor and the debtor at the time the loan is made that delay in making repayment or failure to make repayment could result in the use of violence or other criminal means to cause harm to the person, reputation, or property of any person. The statute chose the term *understanding*, note Ronald Goldstock and Dan Coenen (1978: 65), "in an obvious effort to catch the many loansharks who operate purely on the basis of implication and veiled suggestion." The critical element of the offense is the understanding that violence *could* result if repayment is not timely. The statute even provides an alternative to direct evidence—an implied threat can be assumed: "The state must show the debtor's reasonable belief that the creditor had used, or had a reputation for using, 'extortionate means' to collect or punish nonpayment. Second, if direct evidence of this sort is unavailable (as when the victim is dead or too frightened to testify) and certain other prerequisites are met, the court may allow evidence tending to show the creditor's reputation as to collection practices to show the 'understanding' element" (Goldstock and Coenen 1978: 110–11).

The CCPA also contains a provision intended to make it possible to prosecute upper levels of the organized crime hierarchy who, although they may not make the loans themselves, are often the original source of funding for extortionate credit transactions made directly by underlings: "Whoever willfully advances money or property, whether as a gift, as a loan, as an investment, pursuant to a partnership or profit-sharing agreement, or otherwise, to any person, with the reasonable grounds to believe that it is the intention of that person of making extortionate extensions of credit, shall be fined not more than $10,000 or an amount not to exceed twice the value of the money or property so advanced, whichever is greater, or shall be imprisoned not more than 20 years, or both." The same penalties hold for both the loan shark actually making the loan and those who assist in attempting to collect an extortionate extension of credit.

FORFEITURE

For obvious reasons, governments find forfeiture to be very attractive—they're funds without taxation. In 1972, Hawaii enacted civil RICO legislation with the seizure and forfeiture provision, and by 1989, twenty-five other states had enacted similar legislation. Interest in forfeiture has generated several periodicals. The Treasury Department's Assets Forfeiture Fund was created by the Comprehensive Crime Control Act of 1984 to receive the proceeds of forfeiture. A portion of the money from the fund is given to state and local law enforcement agencies that contributed directly to the seizure or forfeiture.

There are three forfeiture categories:

Criminal forfeiture is an action brought as a part of the criminal prosecution of a defendant. It is an *in personam* (against the person) action and requires that the government charge the property used or derived from the crime along with the defendant. If the jury finds the property forfeitable, the court issues an order of forfeiture.

For forfeitures pursuant to the Controlled Substances Act (CSA), RICO, and money

laundering and obscenity statutes, there are hearings at which third parties can assert their interests in the properties. A defendant who asserts his or her interest in the property is subject to cross-examination without Fifth Amendment protection against self-incrimination. Once the interests of third parties are addressed, the court issues a final forfeiture order.

Civil forfeiture is an *in rem* (against the property) action brought in court against the property. The property is the defendant and no criminal charge against the owner is necessary (see Figure 14.2). Because the action is against property, not a person, an acquittal on criminal charges does not preclude civil forfeiture. In 1996, the Supreme Court ruled (*United States v. Ursery*, 518 U.S. 267) that a criminal prosecution and civil forfeiture in the same case does not violate the constitutional prohibition against double jeopardy:[2] Ordinary forfeiture is not punishment but a device for denying someone the fruits of their criminal behavior.

Statutes permit forfeiture of all profits from drug trafficking and all assets purchased with such proceeds or traded in exchange for controlled substances. It authorizes the forfeiture of all real property used in any manner to facilitate violations of drug statutes, including entire tracts of land and all improvements regardless of what portion of the property facilitated the illegal activities. Currency, buildings, land, motor vehicles, and airplanes have all been confiscated (Stahl 1992). The government also has the right to seize untainted assets as a substitute for tainted property disposed of or otherwise made unavailable for forfeiture (Greenhouse 1994).

Administrative forfeiture is an *in rem* action that permits seizure and forfeiture of property without judicial involvement. Property that can be administratively forfeited includes

---

2. The Supreme Court has long interpreted the Fifth Amendment as prohibiting multiple punishments as well as multiple prosecutions for the same offense (Greenhouse 1996).

IN THE UNITED STATES DISTRICT COURT
NORTHERN DISTRICT OF ILLINOIS
EASTERN DIVISION

UNITED STATES OF AMERICA Plaintiff v. A 1987 ROLLS-ROYCE CORNICHE VIN SCAZDO2A4HCX20937, $152,645.00 in UNITED STATES CURRENCY seized from SAFE DEPOSIT BOX 6265 at CLYDE FEDERAL $30,040 in UNITED STATES CURRENCY seized from SAFE DEPOSIT BOX 5660 at WESTERN NATIONAL BANK $22,400 in UNITED STATES CURRENCY seized from SAFE DEPOSIT BOX 8805–N AT OAK PARK TRUST AND SAVINGS BANK, and UNITED STATES CURRENCY in THE AMOUNT OF $120,023.00 Defendants	NO. **89C1250** FEB 16 1989 JUDGE JUDGE NORGLE MAGISTRATE LEFKOW

VERIFIED COMPLAINT FOR FORFEITURE

The United States of America, by its attorney, Anton R. Valukas, United States Attorney for the Northern District of Illinois for its complaint states:

1.) This is a forfeiture action under Title 21, United States Code, Section 881 (a) (6) and this Court has jurisdiction under Title 28, United States Code, Sections 1345 and 1355.

2.) The defendants named in the caption were seized on land within the Northern District of Illinois and will remain within this Court's jurisdiction throughout the pendency of this action.

3.) On February 7, 1989, a search warrant arising from a narcotics investigation of an individual known as Rufus Sims was executed at a residence at 2606 South Boeger in Westchester, Illinois. The search resulted in the seizure of a large quantity of weapons and twenty-three (23) bags containing cocaine repackaged for sale commingled with United States Currency in the amount of $4,301.00.

4.) During the execution of the warrant at the residence, the police discovered title to the defendant 1987 Rolls Royce Convertible, VIN SCAZDO2A4HCX20937. Review of records at Steve Foley Cadillac revealed that the purchase price of the car was $176,681, of which $129,461 was paid in currency and the remainder of the purchase price came from Sims' trade-in of another Rolls-Royce owned by him.

FIGURE 14.2 Verified Complaint for Forfeiture

merchandise the importation of which is prohibited; a conveyance used to import, transport, or store a controlled substance; a monetary instrument; or other property that does not exceed $500,000 in value.

A seizure can be made incident to an arrest or customs inspection or upon receipt of a seizure order. To obtain a seizure order (actually a warrant), the government must provide sworn testimony in an affidavit spelling out the property to be seized and why there is reason to believe that it is being used to commit crimes or was acquired with money from criminal activity—the same process used in securing a search warrant. The filing of criminal charges against the owner is not required. The owner of the property has a right to contest the seizure only after it has occurred; he or she must prove that the money or property was earned through legal enterprise. In 1993, the Supreme Court (*United States v. Good Real Property*, 510 U.S. 43) ruled that the government cannot seize real estate without providing the owner with a notice and opportunity to contest the proposed seizure. This decision applies only to real estate and not portable possessions.

Although forfeiture laws vary, two legal theories have evolved: *facilitation* and *proceeds*:

The *facilitation* theory allows the government to seize property when it facilitates certain criminal conduct. For example, in drug investigations, any property involved in the manufacture, delivery, and sale of controlled substances can be subjected to seizure. This includes real estate used to store drugs, automobiles and boats used to transport drugs, and other facilitating property, such as cash and firearms. The *proceeds* theory allows the government to seize property that represents the proceeds of certain specified unlawful activities. This can be quite complex because before seizure can occur, the government must identify property and prove ownership. The government also must trace the asset

to the criminal activity, and each time the subject converts the proceeds from one form to another, the more complicated this becomes. (Hartman 2001: 1)

Under federal statutes, before an order to seize property can be issued, the government must show there is a substantial connection between the property and the crime by *a preponderance of the evidence*, the legal standard of proof for civil cases. This is done without notice to the defendant at an *ex parte* (defendant not present) hearing. After seizure, if forfeiture is contested, there is a shift in the burden of proof that diminishes the Fifth Amendment privilege against self-incrimination because the defendant cannot pursue the claim to seized property without explaining its ownership. The Supreme Court has refused to apply the Fifth Amendment's double jeopardy clause or the Sixth Amendment's guarantee of the right to confront witnesses to *in rem* forfeiture (Stahl 1992). Since the process is quasi-criminal, however, the exclusionary rule is applicable, and evidence seized in violation of the Constitution cannot be considered (*One 1958 Plymouth Sedan v. Pennsylvania*, 380 U.S. 691, 701, 1965).

There is a provision for an innocent owner's defense: that the violation occurred without the owner's knowledge. The government can overcome claims of innocence by showing that it would be reasonable to believe that the owner was aware. In addition, some courts have required the owner to prove that he or she took all reasonable steps to prevent the violation (Stahl 1992). There is also a remission procedure—the claimant can file a petition with the attorney general, who can order the return of property if there are mitigating circumstances. However, remission is discretionary. In 1996, the Supreme Court determined that property can be seized even when the owner is innocent of any wrongdoing. In this case, *Bennis v. Michigan* (517 U.S. 1163), a couple's jointly owned car was impounded after the husband used it to solicit a prostitute.

In 1988, the Supreme Court, in a 5–4 decision, ruled that under the Comprehensive Forfeiture Act, the government can freeze the assets of criminal defendants *before* trial (*Caplin and Drysdale, Chartered v. United States,* 491 U.S. 617; *United States v. Monsanto,* 491 U.S. 600). Legislation enacted in 2000 allows federal judges to release property to the owner pending trial if confiscation causes him or her substantial hardship.

Criticism of Forfeiture

A great deal of criticism has been leveled at forfeiture. The normally conservative *Chicago Tribune,* for example, in an editorial (April 1, 1993), stated that while forfeiture, when used appropriately, can be an effective punishment for crime, "a growing number of innocent parties and two-bit players are being swept up in the net. And those who are unfairly trapped find that forfeiture laws turn due process on its head." In 1993, the Supreme Court ruled unanimously that the Eighth Amendment's protection against "excessive fines" requires that there be a relationship between the gravity of the offense and the value of the property seized (*Austin v. United States,* 506 U.S. 602). In 1998, the Court extended *Austin,* ruling 5–4 against the forfeiture of $357,144 in cash that was not the proceeds of crime. The money had been seized from someone who attempted to take cash out of the country to pay debts without filing a Currency Transaction Report (*United States v. Bajakajian,* 524 U.S. 321) discussed later.

Some critics of forfeiture argue that it distorts the purpose of drug law enforcement. For example, police may delay raids until drug caches are depleted and cash is maximized (Worrall and Kovandzic 2008). Or it can result in a "get out of jail free" card, a plea-bargaining device for drug kingpins who can negotiate lighter sentences by promising to reveal hidden assets and not put up court challenges to their seizure. Law enforcement agencies eager for additional funds allegedly promote leniency for those at the top of the drug trafficking ladder, while those down below, without significant hidden assets, face significant penalties (Navarro 1996).

Until 1988, the government was able to prosecute attorneys and seize fees from tainted sources. Defense attorneys argued that this created a situa-

tion "in which a defendant cannot retain an attorney because of the government's threat of criminal and civil sanctions against any attorney who takes the case" (Weinstein 1988: 381). The defendant is left without a free choice of attorneys and dependent upon a public defender, who is not always able to defend against the often-complex nature of RICO prosecutions. Supporters of this legislation argued that criminals who have grown wealthy from crime are not entitled to any greater consideration with respect to legal representation than their less successful criminal colleagues, who are often represented by a public defender. In 1988, President Ronald Reagan signed an anti–drug abuse bill that contained an amendment excluding defense attorneys' fees from criminal money laundering provisions. Thus, while criminal defense fees could still be subject to forfeiture, attorneys who accept tainted fees are exempt from criminal prosecution.

Forfeiture statutes of some states permit all seized assets to be returned to the initiating agency; others provide for distribution to all law enforcement agencies involved and the prosecutor's office; still others permit no proceeds to be returned to law enforcement and, instead, require that they be placed in an education fund. Law enforcement agencies in these states are able to bypass the requirement by having the case "adopted" by a federal agency such as the DEA or FBI, which then passes it off to the U.S. Attorney. The adoption procedure can result in up to 80 percent of the proceeds being returned to the initiating department (Worrall and Kovandzic 2008). Increased police assets via forfeiture provide an incentive for local governments to reduce their allocations for policing (Skolnick 2008).

BANK SECRECY ACT

In 1970, in response to increasing reports of people bringing bags full of cash into banks for deposit, Congress enacted the statute commonly referred to as the Bank Secrecy Act (BSA). (Technically, the BSA is Titles I and II of Public Law 91-508, as amended. Title II is also called the Currency and

Foreign Transactions Reporting Act.) The BSA contains two basic sets of authorizing provisions that are put into effect by implementing regulations. The first set authorizes the Secretary of the Treasury (and in some instances, the Secretary and the Federal Reserve Board jointly) to require banks and other financial institutions to retain records ensuring that details of financial transactions can be traced if investigators need to do so.

Hundreds of thousands of financial institutions are subject to Bank Secrecy Act reporting and recordkeeping requirements. These include depository institutions (e.g., banks, credit unions, and thrifts); brokers or dealers in securities; insurance companies that issue or underwrite certain products; money services businesses, e.g., money transmitters; issuers, redeemers and sellers of money orders and travelers' checks; check cashers and currency exchangers; and casinos and dealers in precious metals, stones, or jewels.

The USA PATRIOT Act of 2001 broadened the scope of the Bank Secrecy Act to focus on terrorist financing as well as money laundering. The Act gives the Financial Crimes Enforcement Network, known as FinCEN, additional responsibilities and authority in both areas.

FinCEN is a government-wide multisource financial intelligence and analysis network. In 1994, FinCEN's responsibilities were broadened to include regulatory responsibilities for administering the Bank Secrecy Act. FinCEN has more than 300 full-time employees, but relies on other agencies to conduct examinations to determine compliance with the BSA and its implementing regulations. The second set of provisions authorizes the Secretary of the Treasury to require financial institutions, and in some cases other businesses and private citizens, to report financial transactions in currency in excess of $10,000 using the Currency Transaction Report (CTR) (see Figure 14.4) and the transportation of currency and bearer instruments in amounts initially in excess of $10,000 (originally $5,000) into or out of the United States using the Report of International Transportation of Currency or Monetary Instruments (CMIR). A specific prohibition was added to the BSA against "structuring" transactions, breaking larger transactions into smaller exchanges, to avoid the impact of the BSA's reporting thresholds. This system generates more than 14 million CTRs annually and more than one million "Suspicious Activity Reports."

The act authorizes the IRS to issue regulations requiring banks and other financial institutions to take a number of precautions against financial crime, including setting up anti–money laundering programs and filing reports determined to have a high degree of usefulness in criminal, tax, regulatory investigations and proceedings, and certain intelligence and counterterrorism matters.

The constitutionality of the BSA was challenged on a number of grounds. In *California Bankers Association v. Shultz*, 416 U.S. 21 (1974), the U.S. Supreme Court rejected claims that various parts of the BSA violated constitutional due process requirements, the Fourth Amendment protection against unreasonable searches and seizures, and the Fifth Amendment privilege against self-incrimination. The Court emphasized information sought from the reporting banks concerned transactions to which the banks themselves had been parties. A later Supreme Court decision (*United States v. Miller*, 425 U.S. 435, 1976) found that bank customers possess no privacy interests protected by the Fourth Amendment in records of their affairs maintained by the banks with which they deal.

MONEY LAUNDERING

Money Laundering is "to knowingly engage in a financial transaction with the proceeds of some unlawful activity with the intent of promoting or carrying on that unlawful activity or to conceal or disguise the nature, location, source, ownership, or control of these proceeds" (Genzman 1988: 1). According to the Treasury Department, money laundering is "the process by which criminals or criminal organizations seek to disguise the illicit nature of their proceeds by introducing them into the stream of legitimate commerce and finance" (Motivans 2003: 1). A person is guilty of money laundering if he or she knows that the property involved represents the proceeds of some illegal activity; attempts to conceal or disguise the nature, the location, the source, the ownership, or the control of the proceeds; or attempts to avoid a transaction-reporting requirement. Furthermore, a person is guilty of money laundering if he or she transports or attempts to transport a monetary instrument or funds out of the United States with the intent to carry out an unlawful activity. If a person knows that the monetary instrument or funds involved represent the proceeds of some form of unlawful activity or attempts to conceal or disguise the nature, location, source, ownership, or control of the proceeds or to avoid a transaction-reporting requirement, he or she is guilty of money laundering.

Prior to passage of the Money Laundering Control Act of 1986, money laundering per se was not a federal crime, although the Department of Justice had used a variety of federal statutes to successfully prosecute money-laundering cases. The 1986 act consolidated these statutes with the goal of increasing prosecutions for this offense. Money laundering was made a separate federal offense punishable by a fine of $500,000 or twice the value of the property involved, whichever is greater, and twenty years' imprisonment (Weinstein 1988). The law provides for the civil confiscation of any property related to a money-laundering scheme. Legislation enacted in 1988 allows the government to file a suit claiming ownership of all cash funneled through operations intended to disguise their illegal source. The courts can issue an order freezing all contested funds until the case is adjudicated. An amendment to the Drug Abuse Act of 1988 requires offshore banks to record any U.S. cash transactions in excess of $10,000 and to permit U.S. officials to have access to the records. Offshore banks that fail to comply can be banned from holding accounts in U.S. banks and denied access to U.S.–dollar clearing and money-transfer systems.

The Annunzio-Wylie Money Laundering Act of 1992 and the Money Laundering Suppression Act of 1994 (the "MLSA") gave the Treasury Department a wide variety of regulatory tools to combat money laundering. Annunzio-Wylie amended the BSA in several respects. Most important, it authorizes the Secretary of the Treasury to require financial institutions and gambling casinos to submit a "Suspicious Activity Report" (SAR) relevant to a possible violation of law or regulation (see Figure 14.3). The statutory SAR authorization includes a "safe-harbor" provision to protect financial institutions from civil liability to their clients and third parties that might otherwise be claimed to have arisen from the designation of transactions as suspicious by reporting institutions.

Annunzio-Wylie authorizes the Treasury Secretary to require financial institutions to carry out anti–money laundering programs and authorize special record keeping. Finally, Annunzio-Wylie made operation of an illegal money-transmitting business a crime (information from the U.S. Department of the Treasury). Because this statute requires proof of "willfulness," in 1994 the Supreme Court ruled that persons who structured their transactions to avoid the CTR, by keeping transactions at $9,500, for example, did not violate the law unless they *knew* such action was illegal (*Ratzlaf v. United States,* 510 U.S. 135). In 1985, Arizona became the first state to enact an anti–money-laundering statute, and since that time at least thirty-five more states have done the same (Motivans 2003).

In the wake of 9/11, statutes were enacted permitting the Department of Justice to seize accounts in foreign banks that do business in the United States. Typically, when suspect source accounts are discovered, federal authorities work through international law enforcement treaties to request that the home country of a foreign bank freeze the money and turn it over to the United States. Some countries, however, do not have treaties with the United States, although most foreign banks maintain "correspondent accounts" in American banks enabling them to exchange U.S. currency and manage other financial transactions in this country. The law permits prosecutors to seize such accounts without the need to trace the money back to the target of the investigation (Lichtblau 2003b). Since the imposition of the first civil penalty in 2002, the Justice Department has undertaken a series of investigations of financial institutions, resulting either in the criminal conviction or

ANTI–MONEY LAUNDERING LAWS

Bank Secrecy Act (1970)

- Established requirements for recordkeeping and reporting by private individuals, banks and other financial institutions

- Requires banks to (1) report cash transactions over $10,000 using the Currency Transaction Report; (2) properly identify persons conducting transactions; and (3) maintain a paper trail by keeping appropriate records of financial transactions

Money Laundering Control Act (1986)

- Established money laundering as a federal crime
- Prohibited structuring transactions to evade CTR filings
- Introduced civil and criminal forfeiture for BSA violations
- Directed banks to establish and maintain procedures to ensure and monitor compliance with the reporting and recordkeeping requirements of the BSA

Anti–Drug Abuse Act of 1988

- Expands the definition of financial institution to include businesses such as car dealers and real estate closing personnel and requires them to file reports on large currency transactions
- Requires the verification of identity of purchasers of monetary instruments over $3,000

Annunzio-Wylie Anti–Money Laundering Act (1992)

- Strengthens the sanctions for BSA violations
- Requires Suspicious Activity Reports
- Requires verification and recordkeeping for wire transfers

Money Laundering Suppression Act (1994)

- Requires banking agencies to review and enhance training, and develop anti–money laundering examination procedures
- Streamlines CTR exemption process
- Requires each Money Services Business (MSB) to be registered by an owner or controlling person of the MSB

- Requires every MSB to maintain a list of businesses authorized to act as agents in connection with the financial services offered by the MSB
- Make operating an unregistered MSB a federal crime

Money Laundering and Financial Crimes Strategy Act (1998)

- Requires banking agencies to develop anti–money laundering training for examiners
- Created the High Intensity Money Laundering and Related Financial Crime Area (HIFCA) Task Forces to concentrate law enforcement efforts at the federal, state, and local levels in zones where money laundering is prevalent. HIFCAs may be defined geographically or they can also be created to address money laundering in an industry sector, a financial institution, or group of financial institutions

Title III of the USA PATRIOT Act of 2001

- Criminalizes the financing of terrorism and augments the existing BSA framework by strengthening customer identification procedures
- Prohibits financial institutions from engaging in business with foreign shell banks
- Requires financial institutions to have due diligence procedures
- Expands the anti–money laundering program requirements to all financial institutions
- Increases civil and criminal penalties for money laundering
- Provides the Secretary of the Treasury with the authority to impose "special measures" on jurisdictions, institutions, or transactions that are of "primary money laundering concern"

Intelligence Reform & Terrorism Prevention Act of 2004

Amended the BSA to require the Secretary of the Treasury to prescribe regulations requiring certain financial institutions to report cross-border electronic transmittals of funds, if the Secretary determines that such reporting is "reasonably necessary" to aid in the fight against money laundering and terrorist financing

Source: U.S. Department of the Treasury

Suspicious Activity Report

July 2003
Previous editions will not be accepted after December 31, 2003

FRB:	FR 2230	OMB No. 7100-0212
FDIC:	6710/06	OMB No. 3064-0077
OCC:	8010-9,8010-1	OMB No. 1557-0180
OTS:	1601	OMB No. 1550-0003
NCUA:	2362	OMB No. 3133-0094
TREASURY:	TD F 90-22.47	OMB No. 1506-0001

ALWAYS COMPLETE ENTIRE REPORT
(see instructions)

1 Check box below only if correcting a prior report.
☐ Corrects Prior Report (see instruction #3 under "How to Make a Report")

Part I Reporting Financial Institution Information

2 Name of Financial Institution

3 EIN

4 Address of Financial Institution

5 Primary Federal Regulator
a ☐ Federal Reserve   d ☐ OCC
b ☐ FDIC   e ☐ OTS
c ☐ NCUA

6 City

7 State

8 Zip Code

9 Address of Branch Office(s) where activity occurred   ☐ Multiple Branches (include information in narrative, Part V)

10 City

11 State

12 Zip Code

13 If institution closed, date closed
___ / ___ / ___
MM   DD   YYYY

14 Account number(s) affected, if any   Closed?
a _____   ☐ Yes ☐ No   c _____   ☐ Yes ☐ No
b _____   ☐ Yes ☐ No   d _____   ☐ Yes ☐ No

Part II Suspect Information   ☐ Suspect Information Unavailable

15 Last Name or Name of Entity

16 First Name

17 Middle

18 Address

19 SSN, EIN or TIN

20 City

21 State

22 Zip Code

23 Country (Enter 2 digit code)

24 Phone Number - Residence (include area code)
( )

25 Phone Number - Work (include area code)
( )

26 Occupation/Type of Business

27 Date of Birth
___ / ___ / ___
MM DD YYYY

28 Admission/Confession?
a ☐ Yes   b ☐ No

29 Forms of Identification for Suspect:
a ☐ Driver's License/State ID   b ☐ Passport   c ☐ Alien Registration   d ☐ Other _____
Number _____   Issuing Authority _____

30 Relationship to Financial Institution:
a ☐ Accountant   d ☐ Attorney   g ☐ Customer   j ☐ Officer
b ☐ Agent   e ☐ Borrower   h ☐ Director   k ☐ Shareholder
c ☐ Appraiser   f ☐ Broker   i ☐ Employee   l ☐ Other _____

31 Is the relationship an insider relationship?   a ☐ Yes   b ☐ No
If Yes specify: c ☐ Still employed at financial institution   e ☐ Terminated
d ☐ Suspended   f ☐ Resigned

32 Date of Suspension, Termination, Resignation
___ / ___ / ___
MM DD YYYY

IRS Cat. No. 22285L

FIGURE 14.3 Suspicious Activity Report

deferred prosecution of at least fifteen different banks, among them Lloyds, Credit Suisse, Wachovia, and Barclays.

Under the Currency and Foreign Transactions Reporting Act the United States can compel other countries to maintain certain financial records similar to those required under the Bank Secrecy Act. The Treasury Department's Financial Crimes Enforcement Network works with bank regulators to ensure compliance with the act. If a country fails to negotiate an acceptable records system, its financial institutions can be denied access to the U.S. banking system. There are problems implementing this legislation: Apart from developed countries with exchange control laws, few countries have legislation requiring their banks and other financial institutions to collect and report such information to their government. Antiterrorism legislation enacted in 2001 permits the Treasury Department to impose sanctions on countries that refuse to provide information on depositors. The legislation also bars American banks from doing business with offshore ("shell") banks having no connection to any regulated banking industry.

The International Emergency Economic Powers Act allows the president to take extraordinary actions in the case of an "unusual threat to national security." In 1995, President Bill Clinton issued a directive under the act, requiring financial institutions to search for and freeze accounts held in the name of persons or companies determined by the government to assist or play a significant role in international drug trafficking. The order also forbids American businesses and officials to trade with those individuals and their front companies (Mitchell 1995).

Casinos are of particular interest with respect to money laundering, and have a CTR-specific form (see Figure 14.5).

TRAFFICKING IN PERSONS (TIP)
STATUTES

Trafficking in persons (discussed in Chapter 11) is prohibited by the Thirteenth Amendment, which outlaws slavery and involuntary servitude—holding persons for service/labor through force or the threat of force.

Statutes that enforce the Thirteenth Amendment have been supplemented by the Trafficking Victims Protection Act (TVPA) of 2000 and the Prosecutorial Remedies and Other Tools to End the Exploitation of Children Today (PROTECT) Act of 2003.

Under TVPA, slavery, peonage, sex trafficking in children and adults, and the confiscation of a victim's documents are felonies. Prior to TVPA statutes were already in place outlawing human smuggling, kidnapping, transportation for prostitution or any criminal sexual activity, and importation of aliens for unlawful activities. The act was passed virtually unanimously by both houses of Congress and addresses issues of worker exploitation resulting from trafficking in persons. The law expands the definition of *forced labor* to reach forms of coercion occurring in contemporary times. Alicia Peters (2011: iii) states that the TVPA "contains an especially complicated and layered definition of trafficking, reflecting the diverse constituencies (anti-prostitution feminists, evangelical Christians, and human rights advocates) that lobbied for radically different versions of anti-trafficking bills. This complexity in the law," she argues, "invites considerable flexibility in interpretation and application."

The statute:

1. Creates new laws that criminalize trafficking with respect to slavery, involuntary servitude, peonage, or forced labor
2. Permits prosecution where nonviolent coercion is used to force victims to work in the belief they would be subject to serious harm
3. Permits prosecution where the victim's service was compelled by confiscation of documents such as passports or birth certificates
4. Increases prison terms for all slavery violations from ten years to twenty years and adds life imprisonment where the violation involves the death, kidnapping, or sexual abuse of the victim
5. Requires courts to order restitution and forfeiture of assets upon conviction
6. Enables victims to seek witness protection and other types of assistance

FINCEN Form 104

(March 2011)
Department of the Treasury
FinCEN

Currency Transaction Report

▶ Previous editions will not be accepted after September, 2011.

▶ Please type or print.

(Complete all parts that apply--See Instructions)

OMB No. 1506-0004

---

1 Check all box(es) that apply: **a** ☐ Amends prior report   **b** ☐ Multiple persons   **c** ☐ Multiple transactions

Part I   Person(s) Involved in Transaction(s)

Section A--Person(s) on Whose Behalf Transaction(s) Is Conducted

2 Individual's last name or entity's name   **3** First name   **4** Middle initial

5 Doing business as (DBA)   **6** SSN or EIN

7 Address (number, street, and apt. or suite no.)   **8** Date of birth ___/___/___ MM DD YYYY

9 City   **10** State   **11** ZIP code   **12** Country code (if not U.S.)   **13** Occupation, profession, or business

14 If an individual, describe method used to verify identity: **a** ☐ Driver's license/State I.D.   **b** ☐ Passport   **c** ☐ Alien registration

   d ☐ Other _____   **e** Issued by: _____   **f** Number: _____

Section B--Individual(s) Conducting Transaction(s) (if other than above).

If Section B is left blank or incomplete, check the box(es) below to indicate the reason(s)

a ☐ Armored Car Service   **b** ☐ Mail Deposit or Shipment   **c** ☐ Night Deposit or Automated Teller Machine   **d** ☐ Multiple Transactions   **e** ☐ Conducted On Own Behalf

15 Individual's last name   **16** First name   **17** Middle initial

18 Address (number, street, and apt. or suite no.)   **19** SSN

20 City   **21** State   **22** ZIP code   **23** Country code (If not U.S.)   **24** Date of birth ___/___/___ MM DD YYYY

25 If an individual, describe method used to verify identity: **a** ☐ Driver's license/State I.D.   **b** ☐ Passport   **c** ☐ Alien registration

   d ☐ Other _____   **e** Issued by: _____   **f** Number: _____

Part II   Amount and Type of Transaction(s).   Check all boxes that apply.

28 Date of transaction ___/___/___ MM DD YYYY

26 Total cash in $_____.00   **27** Total cash out $_____.00

26a Foreign cash in_____.00 *(see instructions, page 4)*   **27a** Foreign cash out _____.00 *(see instructions, page 4)*

29 ☐ Foreign Country_____   **30** ☐ Wire Transfer(s)   **31** ☐ Negotiable Instrument(s) Purchased

32 ☐ Negotiable Instrument(s) Cashed   **33** ☐ Currency Exchange(s)   **34** ☐ Deposit(s)/Withdrawal(s)

35 ☐ Account Number(s) Affected (if any):   **36** ☐ Other (specify)

Part III   Financial Institution Where Transaction(s) Takes Place

37 Name of financial institution   Enter Regulator or BSA Examiner code number ▶ (see instructions)

38 Address (number, street, and apt. or suite no.)   **39** EIN or SSN

40 City   **41** State   **42** ZIP code   **43** Routing (MICR) number

Sign Here ▶

44 Title of approving official   **45** Signature of approving official   **46** Date of signature ___/___/___ MM DD YYYY

47 Type or print preparer's name   **48** Type or print name of person to contact   **49** Telephone number ( )

▶ For Paperwork Reduction Act Notice, see page 4.   Cat. No. 37683N   FinCEN Form **104** (Rev. 03-2011)

FIGURE 14.4 Currency Transaction Report

FINCEN Form **103**

(March 2011)

Department of the Treasury
FINCEN

Currency Transaction Report by Casinos

▶ Previous editions will not be accepted after September 2011.
▶ Please type or print. Items marked with an asterisk* are considered critical. (See instructions.)

(Complete all applicable parts--See instructions)

OMB No. 1506-0005

1 If this is an **amended report** check here: ☐ and attach a copy of the original CTRC to this form.

Part I Person(s) Involved in Transaction(s)

Section A--Person(s) on Whose Behalf Transaction(s) Is Conducted (Customer)

2 ☐ Multiple persons

*3 Individual's last name or Organization's name

*4 First name

5 M.I.

6 Doing business as (DBA)

*7 Permanent address (number, street, and apt. or suite no.)

*8 SSN or EIN

*9 City

*10 State

*11 ZIP code

*12 Country code (if not U.S.)

*13 Date of birth ___ / ___ / ___ MM DD YYYY

*14 Method used to verify identity: **a** ☐ Examined identification credential/document **b** ☐ Known Customer - information on file **c** ☐ Organization

*15 Describe identification credential: **a** ☐ Driver's license/State ID **b** ☐ Passport **c** ☐ Alien registration **z** ☐ Other
Issued by: _____ Number: _____

16 Customer's Account Number

Section B--Individual(s) Conducting Transaction(s) - If other than above (Agent)

17 ☐ Multiple agents

18 Individual's last name

19 First name

20 M.I.

21 Address (number, street, and apt. or suite no.)

22 SSN

23 City

24 State

25 ZIP code

26 Country code (if not U.S.)

27 Date of birth ___ / ___ / ___ MM DD YYYY

28 Method used to verify identity: **a** ☐ Examined identification credential/document **b** ☐ Known Customer - information on file

29 Describe identification credential: **a** ☐ Driver's license/State ID **b** ☐ Passport **c** ☐ Alien registration **z** ☐ Other
Issued by: _____ Number: _____

Part II Amount and Type of Transaction(s). Complete all items that apply.

30 ☐ Multiple transactions

*31 CASH IN: (in U.S. dollar equivalent)
a Purchase(s) of casino chips, tokens, and other gaming instruments $ _____ .00
b Deposit(s) (front money or safekeeping) _____ .00
c Payment(s) on credit (including markers) _____ .00
d Currency wager(s) including money plays _____ .00
e Currency received from wire transfer(s) out _____ .00
f Purchase(s) of casino check(s) _____ .00
g Currency exchange(s) _____ .00
h Bills inserted into gaming devices _____ .00
z Other (specify): _____ _____ .00
Enter total of CASH IN transaction(s) $ _____ .00

*32 CASH OUT: (in U.S. dollar equivalent)
a Redemption(s) of casino chips, tokens, TITO tickets, and other gaming instruments $ _____ .00
b Withdrawal(s) of deposit (front money or safekeeping) _____ .00
c Advance(s) on credit (including markers) _____ .00
d Payment(s) on wager(s) (Including race book and OTB or sports pool) _____ .00
e Currency paid from wire transfer(s) in _____ .00
f Negotiable instrument(s) cashed (including checks) _____ .00
g Currency exchange(s) _____ .00
h Travel and complimentary expenses and gaming incentives _____ .00
i Payment for tournament, contest or other promotions _____ .00
z Other (specify): _____ _____ .00
Enter total of CASH OUT transaction(s) $ _____ .00

*33 Date of transaction (see instructions) ___ / ___ / ___ MM DD YYYY

34 Foreign currency used: _____ (Country)

Part III Casino Reporting Transactions

*35 Casino's trade name

*36 Casino's legal name

*37 Employer Identification Number (EIN)

*38 Address where transaction occurred (See instructions)

*39 City

*40 State

*41 ZIP code

*42 Type of gaming Institution (Check only one) **a** ☐ State licensed casino **b** ☐ Card club **c** ☐ Tribal authorized casino **z** ☐ Other (specify) _____

Sign Here ▶

43 Title of approving official

44 Signature of approving official

45 Date of signature ___ / ___ / ___ MM DD YYYY

46 Type or print preparer's name

47 Type or print name of person to contact

48 Contact telephone number (___) ___ - ___

For Paperwork Reduction Act Notice, see page 4.

Cat. No. 37041B

(03-11)

F I G U R E 14.5 Casino Currency Transaction Report

FORCED LABOR

United States Code, Title 18, Part 1, Chapter 77, section 1589:

Whoever knowingly provides or obtains the labor or services of a person by:

(1) threats of serious harm to, or physical restraint against, that person or another person;

(2) means of any scheme, plan, or pattern intended to cause the person to believe that, if the person did not perform such labor or services, that person or another person would suffer serious harm or physical restraint; or

(3) means of the abuse or threatened abuse of law or the legal process, shall be fined under this title or imprisoned not more than twenty years, or both. If death results from the violation of this section, or if the violation includes kidnapping or an attempt to kidnap, aggravated sexual abuse or the attempt to commit aggravated sexual abuse, or an attempt to kill, the defendant shall be fined under this title or imprisoned for any term of years or life, or both.

TRAFFICKING VICTIMS PROTECTION ACT OF 2000 (TVPA)

Under the TVPA, human trafficking is defined as the recruitment, harboring, transportation, provision, or obtaining of a person for one of three purposes:

1.   Labor or services, through the use of force, fraud, or coercion for the purposes of subjection to involuntary servitude, peonage, debt bondage, or slavery.

2.   A commercial sex act through the use of force, fraud, or coercion.

3.   Any commercial sex act, if the person is under eighteen years of age, regardless of whether any form of coercion is involved.

---

7.   Gives prosecutors and agents new tools to get legal immigration status for victims of trafficking during investigation and prosecution (U.S. Department of Justice information)

TVPA allows foreign TIP victims who are otherwise ineligible for government assistance to receive federally funded or administered health and other benefits and services and protects those who cooperate with law enforcement from deportation.

The Human Trafficking Prosecution Unit (HTPU) in the Civil Rights Division of the Justice Department shares responsibility with the Child Exploitation and Obscenity Section (CEOS) in prosecuting human trafficking crimes. The HTPU is responsible for human trafficking crimes while CEOS oversees prosecution of cases involving sex trafficking of minors. The FBI and Immigration and Customs Enforcement have human trafficking programs at headquarters in Washington, DC, as well as regional investigative units (Peters 2011).

The William Wilberforce Trafficking Victims Protection Reauthorization Act of 2008:

1.   Created new crimes imposing severe penalties on those who obstruct or attempt to obstruct the investigations and prosecutions of trafficking crimes;

2.   Changed the standard of proof for the crime of sex trafficking by force, fraud, or coercion by requiring that the government merely prove that the defendant acted in reckless disregard of the fact that such means would be used;

3.   Broadened the reach of the crime of sex trafficking of minors by eliminating the requirement to show that the defendant knew that the person engaged in commercial sex was a minor

in cases where the defendant had a reasonable opportunity to observe the minor;

4. Expanded the crime of forced labor by providing that "force" is a means of violating the law;
5. Imposed criminal liability on those who, knowingly and with intent to defraud, recruit workers from outside the U.S. for employment within the United States by making materially false or fraudulent representations;
6. Enhanced the penalty for conspiring to commit trafficking-related crimes; and
7. Penalized those who knowingly benefit financially from participating in a venture that engaged in trafficking crimes. (Attorney General 2010: 3).

PROTECT authorizes the prosecution of Americans whose behavior involves the commercial sexual exploitation of children (CSEC) anywhere in the world. The Sex Tourism Prohibition Improvement Act of 2002 removed the intent requirement for individuals and criminalized the actions of sex tour operators. CSEC traffickers who exploit children under age fourteen using force or fraud are subject to life imprisonment. If the crimes do not involve force or fraud and the victim is between ages fourteen and eighteen, the maximum sentence is twenty years.

In 2000, the United Nations General Assembly adopted "The Protocol to Prevent, Suppress and Punish Trafficking in Persons." The protocol includes a range of cases where human beings are exploited by organized crime groups and where there is an element of duress involved and a transnational aspect, such as the movement of people across borders or their exploitation within a country by a transnational organized crime group such as the Mafia, Triads, or *yakuza*. It is designed to facilitate international cooperation against such trafficking. The protocol provides for criminal sanctions, control and cooperation measures against traffickers, and provides measures to protect and assist the victims. The United States has not ratified this protocol.

Local law enforcement agencies generally believe that human trafficking is a rare or nonexistent problem in their community, and relatively few have taken proactive steps such as developing training or protocols or assigning specialized personnel to investigate cases of human trafficking. However, a surprisingly large portion of local law enforcement agencies report having investigated one or more cases of human trafficking since 2000 (Farrell, McDevitt, and Fahy 2008).

IDENTITY THEFT

There are four types of identity theft (Cheney 2005: 22):

1. *Fictitious identity*. Pieces of real data, from one or more consumers, are combined with made-up information to fabricate an identity that does not belong to any real person. In most cases a completely new credit record is established and linked to the fabricated identity.
2. *Payment card*. Stolen payment cards or the account numbers (i.e., credit or debit card account numbers) of existing financial accounts are used to purchase goods and services.
3. *Account takeover*. Control over an existing financial account is established without authority of the legitimate account holder. Thieves attempt to steal the entire balance in a consumer's demand deposit account or to access the full credit line associated with a consumer's credit account.
4. *True name*. The wholesale assumption of another person's identity in an effort to gain access to new credit. Thieves steal personal information, such as name, address, and Social Security number, that allows them to use the victim's credit record when applying for new loans.

A National Institute of Justice report (Newman and McNally 2007: 6) notes the stages involved in identity theft:

Stage 1. Acquisition of the identity through theft, computer hacking, fraud, trickery, force, redirecting or intercepting mail, or purchasing identifying information on the Internet.

Stage 2. Use of the identity for financial gain (the most common motivation) or to avoid arrest or otherwise hide one's identity from law enforcement or other authorities (such as bill collectors). Crimes in this stage may include:

- account takeover
- opening new accounts
- extensive use of the victim's debit or credit card
- sale of the identity information on the street or black market
- acquisition ("breeding") of additional identity-related documents such as driver's licenses, passports, visas, and health insurance cards
- filing fraudulent tax returns for large refunds
- insurance fraud
- stealing rental cars

A number of federal laws apply to identity theft. Some may be used to prosecute identity theft offenses, and some exist to assist victims in repairing their credit history. The primary identity theft statute was enacted in 1998 as part of the Identity Theft and Assumption Deterrence Act (Identity Theft Act). The Identity Theft Act criminalizes fraud in connection with the unlawful theft and misuse of personal identifying information, regardless of whether the information appears or is used in documents. A person violates this statute if he or she "knowingly transfers or uses, without lawful authority, a *means of identification* of another person with the intent to commit, or to aid or abet, any unlawful activity that constitutes a violation of Federal law, or that constitutes a felony under any applicable State or local law."

Means of identification include any name or number that may be used, alone or in conjunction with any other information, to identify a specific individual. It covers several specific examples, such as name, social security number, date of birth, government issued driver's license and other numbers; unique biometric data, such as fingerprints, voice print, retina or iris image, or other physical representation; unique electronic identification number; and telecommunication identifying information or access device. The definition of "document-making implement" includes computers and software specifically configured or primarily used for making identity documents.

The Identity Theft Act provides for a term of imprisonment of not more than fifteen years when an individual commits an offense that involves the transfer or use of one or more means of identification if, as a result of the offense, anything of value aggregating $1,000 or more during any one-year period is obtained. Attempts or conspiracies to violate the act are subject to the same penalties as those prescribed for substantive offenses. If the offense is committed to facilitate drug trafficking, or in connection with a crime of violence, or is committed by a person previously convicted of identity theft, the individual is subject to a term of imprisonment of not more than twenty years. The Act provides for the forfeiture of any personal property used or intended to be used to commit the offense (Hoar 2001).

Most states have identity theft statues but they differ in wording, the types of identity theft that are criminalized, and treatment of the crime as either a felony or a misdemeanor (Newman and McNally 2007).

ELECTRONIC SURVEILLANCE

In 1928, the first wiretap case that confronted the U.S. Supreme Court, *Olmstead v. United States* (277 U.S. 438), concerned telephone wiretaps that were used to prosecute persons involved in large-scale Prohibition violations. The interception of Olmstead's telephone line was accomplished without trespass. Chief Justice William Howard Taft, writing for the majority, determined that since telephone conversations are not tangible items, they cannot be the subject of an illegal seizure, and thus wiretapping is not prohibited by the Fourth Amendment. Shortly after the *Olmstead* decision, Congress prohibited interception of telephonic communication without judicial authorization.

The first case to reach the Supreme Court under congressional restrictions was *Goldman v. United States* (316 U.S. 129) in 1942. The Court, consistent with *Olmstead*, ruled that a dictaphone placed against an office wall did not violate the Fourth Amendment because there was no trespass. In *Silverman v. United States* (365 U.S. 505, 1961), a foot-long spike with a microphone attached was inserted under a faceboard and into the wall until it made contact with a heating duct that ran through Silverman's house. The Court found this activity unconstitutional, not because of trespass but because of actual intrusion into "a constitutionally protected area."

In 1967, the Supreme Court ruled (*Berger v. New York,* 388 U.S. 41) that a New York State law authorizing "eavesdropping" was unconstitutional. The case involved a Chicago public relations man who was convicted of conspiracy to bribe the chairman of the New York State Liquor Authority. The evidence consisted of conversations intercepted by bugs and wiretaps pursuant to a court order. According to the Court, the statute failed to require warrants to state the specific crime being committed and the place or the persons to be surveilled. Also, no time limits were placed on the order once incriminating conversation was secured.

Later in 1967, the case of *Katz v. United States* (389 U.S. 347) came before the Supreme Court. In violation of the Hobbs Act, Katz transmitted wagering information on the telephone (McGuinness 1981: 27):

> In *Katz*, the Government, acting without a warrant or other judicial authorization, intercepted defendant's end of telephone conversations by means of two microphones attached by tape to the top of two adjoining public telephone booths from which Katz regularly made calls. Katz was subsequently prosecuted for the interstate transportation of wagering information by telephone in violation of a Federal statute, and tape recordings of the intercepted telephone calls were introduced in evidence over his objection. The Government argued that since no physical intrusion was made into

the booth and since it was not a "constitutionally protected area" (the defendant having no possessory interest as such in the booth), a search for Fourth Amendment purposes did not occur. In holding that there was a search, the Court stated that it was erroneous to resolve questions of Fourth Amendment law on the basis of whether a constitutionally protected area is involved, "[f]or the Fourth Amendment protects people, not places." This being the case, the reach of the "Amendment [also] cannot turn upon the presence or absence of a physical intrusion into any given enclosure." The Court thus concluded that the Government's activities "violated the privacy upon which [the defendant] justifiably relied while using the telephone," and hence a search within the meaning of the Fourth Amendment had taken place.

The key to understanding *Katz* and subsequent decisions concerning surveillance and the Fourth Amendment are the phrases "reasonable expectation of privacy" or "legitimate expectation of privacy" and "justifiable expectation of privacy" (McGuinness 1981). As Kimberly Kingston (1988: 22–23) notes, the Supreme Court "redefined the term 'search' to include any governmental action which intrudes into an area where there is a reasonable expectation of privacy." However, she points out (1988: 24), it is not the subjective expectation of privacy that is protected but rather "only those that society as a whole is willing to recognize and protect." Thus, while a drug trafficking defendant may have had a subjective expectation that his trash was private, it was not an expectation of privacy that society was willing to recognize and protect—the defendant had exposed his garbage to the public and that included the police (*California v. Greenwood*, 486 U.S. 35, 1988). Supreme Court decisions protect privacy, not *stupidity*. Thus, for example, a criminal conversation over a cell phone in a public place overheard by law enforcement officers is admissible as evidence in court.

During the 1960s, the FBI used electronic surveillance extensively, often without the benefit of judicial authorization. "Numerous Congressional committees and criminal court judges in the 1960s found that the FBI and local police had for decades used illegal electronic surveillance to supplement their investigations. And, worse, they had used taps and bugs to spy on and disrupt the activities of law-abiding citizens and organizations. Civil rights leader Martin Luther King, Jr., for one, was the subject of extensive electronic surveillance in the 1960s" (Krajick 1983: 30). Furthermore, private wiretapping was receiving wide coverage in the press: "The publicity continued to grow, and by the mid-1960s there were regular exposures of industrial espionage and of electronic surveillance operations by private detectives" (National Commission for the Review of Federal and State Laws Relating to Wiretapping and Electronic Surveillance 1976: 39; hereafter National Wiretap Commission).

TITLE III

In order to bring some uniformity into the use of electronic surveillance, Congress enacted Title III of the Omnibus Crime Control and Safe Streets Act in 1968. It was the first time in history that Congress had sanctioned electronic surveillance (Lapidus 1974). "Pressures had been mounting on Congress to enact legislation regulating electronic surveillance, but the scope of the controls could not be agreed to. *Berger* and *Katz* not only forced some legislative action by ruling out law enforcement use of electronic microphones without judicial warrant, but also outlined the scope of the privacy which was protected by the Fourth Amendment and sketched the guidelines for adequate warrant protection" (National Wiretap Commission 1976: 38).

Title III bans all private eavesdropping and authorizes federal officials and prosecutors in states whose laws conform to the federal statute to petition for court authorization to intercept wire or oral communications provided that:

1. There is probable cause for belief that an individual is committing, has committed, or is about to commit a particular offense that is enumerated in Title III.
2. There is probable cause for belief that particular communications concerning that offense will be obtained through such interception.
3. Normal investigative procedures have been tried and have failed, or reasonably appear unlikely to succeed if tried, or are too dangerous.
4. There is probable cause for belief that the facilities in which, or the place where, the oral communications are to be intercepted is being used, or is about to be used, in conjunction with the commission of such offense, or is leased to, listed in the name of, or commonly used by persons believed to commit such offenses.

The *enterprise* dynamic of RICO enables Title III authorization targeting a leader of a criminal organization in the absence of information about his involvement in a specific crime. All that is necessary is probable cause (based on material provided by a confidential informant, for example) indicating he is an active member of the enterprise and electronic surveillance is likely to uncover evidence of his criminality.

The Title III judicial order terminates in thirty days or less, unless extended by the issuing judge:

> No order entered under this section may authorize or approve the interception of any wire or oral communication for any period longer than necessary to achieve the objective of the authorization, nor in any event longer than thirty days. Extensions of an order may be granted, but only upon the application for an extension made in accordance with subsection (1) of this section [essentially the four points listed earlier].... The period of extension shall be no longer than the authorizing judge deems necessary to achieve the purposes for which it was granted and in no event for longer than thirty days. Every order and extension thereof shall contain a provision that the authorization to intercept

shall be executed as soon as practicable, shall be conducted in such a way as to *minimize the interception of communications not otherwise subject to interception under this chapter,* and must terminate upon attainment of the authorization objective, or in any event in thirty days.

The *minimization* noted above requires that great care be taken to avoid intercepting conversations that are not relevant to the judicial order or that are privileged, e.g., between attorney and client, clergy and parishioner, or doctor and patient. In order to ensure that an unauthorized interception does not occur, the eavesdropping equipment must be monitored at all times. Each time a conversation is intercepted, the agent is permitted to listen only briefly, long enough to establish whether the nature of the conversation is within the scope of the judicial order. If the monitoring agent should hear a privileged conversation or a personal conversation between husband and wife unrelated to the judicial order, he or she must discontinue the interception—hit the DNR, Dialed Numbered Recorder button. The recorder stops and an audible tone starts; the DNR prints out the time and date the minimization occurred and whether the monitor went back to the conversation or the conversation ended in the minimization mode. A monitoring agent who allows the recording of a privileged conversation jeopardizes the results of the investigation. Title III requires that the target(s) of the judicial order be notified that their conversations have been intercepted within ninety days after termination of the order.

Judges and prosecutors are required to file reports on their use of Title IIIs with the Administrative Office of the United States Courts (AOUSC) in Washington, DC, and the AOUSC must submit an annual report on Title III to Congress. Although Title III regulates the interception of wire and oral communications, Congress did not explicitly provide any authority for the surreptitious placement of a listening device ("bug") to intercept oral communication—a "black bag job." Federal courts remained in conflict over the issue until *Dalia v. United States* (441 U.S. 238, 1979). FBI agents pried

open a window in the New Jersey office of Lawrence Dalia in order to install a bug in his ceiling. As a result of the intercepted conversations, Dalia was convicted of violating the Hobbs Act by receiving property stolen from an interstate shipment. The Supreme Court concluded that a Title III warrant for eavesdropping implicitly grants authority for covert entry. Amendments to Title III in 1986 authorize "roving surveillance" of suspects using a number of different telephones or sites.

Title III is sometimes criticized by law enforcement officials because of the extensive investigation and documentation required to secure a warrant, although there are emergency exceptions built into the statute:

> Any investigative or law enforcement officer, specially designated by the Attorney General, or by the principal prosecuting attorney of any State or subdivision thereof acting pursuant to a statute of that State, who reasonably determines that (a) an emergency situation exists with respect to conspiratorial activities threatening the national security interests or to conspiratorial activities characteristic of organized crime that requires a wire or oral communication to be intercepted before an order authorizing such interception can with due diligence be obtained, and (b) there are grounds which an order could be entered under this chapter to authorize such interception may intercept such wire or oral communication if an application for an order approving the interception is made in accordance with this section within forty-eight hours after the interception has occurred, or begins to occur.

Any wire or oral communication may be intercepted legally by federal agents (while some states, such as Illinois, have local restrictions) without a court order if one of the parties to the communication gives prior consent. Thus, law enforcement officers and informants may be "wired" to secure incriminating conversation without a court order. In 1979, the Supreme Court (by a 5–3 vote) ruled that the police do not need a search warrant to record the numbers dialed from a particular telephone—there is an absence of a "reasonable expectation of privacy" because the telephone company routinely maintains such information for billing purposes. In *Smith v. Maryland* (442 U.S. 735), the Court affirmed the robbery conviction of a man linked to the crime by a pen register, which, when installed at a telephone company switching station, can record the numbers dialed from a particular phone.

Since Title III was enacted in 1968, more than thirty states have passed statutes permitting electronic surveillance, although some place restrictions beyond those contained in the federal statutes. Some states rarely make use of the law, and cost is a major reason. In addition to the investigative costs of securing the order, monitoring ties up at least two law enforcement officers over three shifts for thirty days or more on a continuous basis. There are cases in which the cost exceeded $2 million—and less than 20 percent of all electronic surveillance actually produces incriminating evidence. Persons in organized crime frequently limit conversations that could be subjected to interception to code phrases. John Gotti, boss of the Gambino Family, was recorded as advising a young associate about telephone conversations: "Don't ever say anything you don't want played back to you some day"—advice he frequently disregarded (Mustain and Capeci 1988: 115). Conversations may be in a foreign language, so monitors have to be fluent in that language, or the conversation may be in a dialect or contain colloquial expressions that are difficult for outsiders to translate.

Material from electronic surveillance must often be enhanced by specialists to reduce background noise from radios or televisions. The conversations then need to be transcribed. Usually only the monitoring agents are familiar enough with the subjects' manner of speech to be able to accomplish this tedious task, which can take months of effort.

In addition to the wire and oral communications covered in Title III, the Electronic Communications Privacy Act (ECPA) of 1987 created a third category, "electronic communications," governing conversations over a broader array of technology including cellular (but not cordless) telephones and email. The ECPA also regulates the use of pen registers, devices that can record the phone numbers of outgoing calls, and trap-and-trace devices that can record the numbers of incoming calls—they are usually used in tandem. A simplified court order is required to install these devices (Colbridge 2000).

While the 1994 Communications Assistance for Law Enforcement Act requires phone companies to install devices that make it easier for the government to intercept cellular calls, the statute does not cover Internet providers.

In the next chapter we will examine how these statutes are enforced.

SUMMARY

1. Know how the Internal Revenue Code is used against organized crime:
   - In 1927, the U.S. Supreme Court denied the claim of self-incrimination as an excuse for failure to file income tax on illegally gained earnings.

2. Know the statutes that deal with controlled substances:
   - The Comprehensive Drug Abuse Prevention and Control Act of 1970 represented a new legal approach to federal drug policy predicated not on the constitutional power to tax but on federal authority over interstate commerce.
   - Legislation in 1970 established five schedules into which all controlled substances could be placed according to their potential for abuse.
   - People involved in the illegal drug business can be arrested and prosecuted for a number of different offenses.

3. Understand the Hobbs Act, the Sherman Antitrust Act, and the connection between the

"Apalachin Crime Conference" and the Landrum-Griffin Act:

- The Hobbs Act makes it a federal crime to engage in criminal behavior that interferes with interstate commerce.
- The Sherman Antitrust Act prohibits any agreement among competitors to fix prices, rig bids, or engage in other anticompetitive activity.
- The Landrum-Griffin Act dealing with labor racketeering was enacted in the wake of the "Apalachin Crime Conference."
- There are five categories of anticompetitive practices.

4. Understand the various types of conspiracy and their value in prosecuting organized crime:
   - At both the federal and state level, a conspiracy—an agreement between two or more persons to commit a criminal act—is a crime.
   - Conspiracy statutes provide valuable tools for prosecuting persons in organized crime.
   - There are three basic types of conspiracy.

5. Know the history and importance of RICO and criticism of the statute:
   - Based on the questionable testimony of Joseph Valchi, the Task Force on Organized Crime concluded that organized crime in the United States consists of twenty-four groups operating in large cities whose membership is Italian.
   - The recommendations of the Task Force led to significant legislation to deal with organized crime.
   - The *Racketeer Influenced and Corrupt Organizations* (RICO) *Act* is the most important single piece of legislation ever enacted against organized crime.
   - There are five basic criticisms of RICO.

6. Understand the unique qualities of the Consumer Credit Protection Act:
   - The Consumer Credit Protection Act does not require proof of threats for a successful loansharking prosecution.

7. Know the various types of forfeiture, how forfeiture statutes are used against organized crime, and criticism of forfeiture:
   - There are three categories of forfeiture.
   - A great deal of criticism has been leveled at forfeiture.

8. Understand the Bank Secrecy Act and other applicable statutes in efforts against money laundering:
   - The Bank Secrecy Act is a response to money laundering.
   - The Money Laundering Control Act makes money laundering a separate federal offense.

9. Be familiar with statutes designed to respond to "Trafficking in Persons":
   - There are a number of statutes dealing with trafficking in persons, some of which enforce the Thirteenth Amendment.

10. Know the variety of identity offenses and statutes to deal with it:
    - There are four types of identity theft.
    - The Identity Theft and Assumption Deterrence Act criminalizes fraud in connection with the unlawful theft and misuse of personal identifying information.

11. Understand electronic surveillance and statutes for carrying it out:
    - Title III bans all private eavesdropping and provides for court authorization to intercept wire or oral communication.
    - Electronic surveillance is expensive in terms of personnel.

REVIEW QUESTIONS

1. What did the U.S. Supreme Court rule in 1927 with respect to the claim of self-incrimination as an excuse for failure to file income tax on illegally gained earnings?

2. What was the new approach to drug policy represented by the Comprehensive Drug Abuse Prevention and Control Act of 1970?

3. What are the different offenses for which people involved in the illegal drug business can be arrested and prosecuted?

4. What does the Hobbs Act criminalize?

5. What is the purpose of the Sherman Antitrust Act?

6. What are the five restraints of trade categories outlawed by federal statutes?

7. What is a conspiracy?

8. Why do conspiracy statutes provide valuable tools for prosecuting persons in organized crime?

9. What are the three basic types of conspiracy?

10. How can "guilt by association" become a problem in a conspiracy prosecution?

11. Why does a conspiracy prosecution usually require an informant to testify?

12. What did the Task Force on Organized Crime conclude?

13. What role did Joseph Valachi play in the conclusions made by the Task Force on Organized Crime?

14. What legislation resulted from the recommendations of the Task Force on Organized Crime?

15. Why is the *Racketeer Influenced and Corrupt Organizations* (RICO) *Act* the most important single piece of legislation ever enacted against organized crime?

16. In what way did the criminal enterprise model of RICO represent a new approach in the prosecution of organized crime?

17. What does the government have to prove in a RICO prosecution?

18. What are the civil provisions contained in RICO?

19. What are the five basic criticisms of RICO?

20. What is unique about the Consumer Credit Protection Act?

21. What are the three categories of forfeiture?

22. What are the levels of evidence applicable in a forfeiture proceeding?

23. What are the criticisms of forfeiture?

24. What is the purpose of the Bank Secrecy Act?

25. What are the provisions of statutes used to combat trafficking in persons?

26. What are the legal requirements for electronic surveillance?

27. In electronic surveillance, what is *minimization*?

28. Why is electronic surveillance expensive in terms of personnel?

29. What led to the enactment of the Landrum-Griffin Act?

30. What is the purpose of the Landrum-Griffin Act?

Captured: Boston gangster and federal informant "Whitey" Bulger.   AP Photo/Reed Saxon/Corbis

Organized Crime: Law Enforcement

CHAPTER 15 WILL ENABLE
THE READER TO
UNDERSTAND:

- Restraints on organized crime law enforcement

- Problems inherent in covert operations and the use of informants in organized crime law enforcement

- The role of the various federal agencies in organized crime law enforcement

- The controversial role of the military in law enforcement

- Various techniques used in organized crime law enforcement

On June 22, 2011, legendary Boston crime boss James ("Whitey") Bulger, eighty-one, was arrested by federal agents in Santa Monica, California. His capture ended a sixteen-year international manhunt.

The Bulger case was an embarrassment to the FBI. Recruited as an informant in the mid-1970s, Bulger was given a virtual "get out of jail free" card by FBI agents in exchange for information on the New England Patriarca Mafia Family. He disappeared early in 1995 after an agent alerted him to an imminent indictment. He was subsequently indicted for 19 murders—most occurring while he was an FBI informant.

While an informant, Bulger lived openly in South Boston while his Mafia rivals were prosecuted and imprisoned. He even collected a share of a $14.3 million state lottery jackpot. A Congressional investigation concluded that FBI agents in Boston were corrupted by their relationship with underworld informers in their war on the Mafia. Bulger and his deputy, Steven Flemmi, regularly entertained their FBI handlers or gave them gifts, while continuing to commit crimes with the agents' knowledge. The agents also provided them with confidential information about government investigations against them and names of mobsters informing on them.

Bulger was arrested without incident at a private residence along with Catherine Greig, who fled with him in 1995. The arrest came after the FBI doubled the reward for information leading to the arrest of Ms. Greig, to $100,000, and began broadcasting public service television advertise-ments on shows catering to a female audience as part of an effort to find Mr. Bulger through Ms. Greig ("James 'Whitey' Bulger" 2011; Nagourney, Adam and Abby Goodnough 2011; Nagourney and Lovett 2011). He was the inspiration for Jack Nicholson's mob boss character in the movie *The Departed*. A former Miss Iceland who had gotten to know the couple in Santa Monica, California, recognized Bulger from a newspaper photo and notified the FBI; she was awarded $2 million.

The need for criminal informants in organized crime investigations and the dangers inherent in using them will be discussed in this chapter.

In this chapter we will look at the various agencies responsible for responding to organized crime and the techniques they use. But first we need to consider three restraints on law enforcement efforts in general, and on organized crime law enforcement in particular: constitutional restraints, jurisdictional limitations, and the intertwining problems of corruption and informants.

CONSTITUTIONAL RESTRAINTS

Law enforcement in the United States operates under significant constitutional restraints. Important protections against government, while they protect individual liberty, also benefit the criminal population: the right to remain silent (Fifth Amendment); the right to counsel (Sixth Amendment); the right to be tried speedily by an impartial jury (Sixth Amendment); and the right to confront witnesses (Sixth Amendment). Particularly important for organized crime law enforcement is the Fourth Amendment and the exclusionary rule. The Fourth

Amendment provides that "the right of the people to be secure in their persons, houses, papers and effects, against unreasonable searches and seizures shall not be violated, and no Warrants shall issue, but upon probable cause, supported by Oath or affirmation, and particularly describing the place to be searched, and the persons or things to be seized." In practice, information sufficient to justify a search warrant in organized crime cases is difficult to obtain because unlike conventional crimes such as robbery and burglary, there are often no innocent victims to report the crime. The exclusionary rule provides that evidence obtained in violation of the Fourth Amendment cannot be entered as evidence in a criminal trial (*Weeks v. United States*, 232 U.S. 383, 1914; *Mapp v. Ohio*, 357 U.S. 643, 1961), although there are a number of exceptions that are beyond the scope of this book.

Intercepting confidential information is a prerequisite for moving against organized crime. However, the Fourth Amendment and Title III of the Omnibus Crime Control and Safe Streets Act of 1968 place restrictions on the way the government can secure this information. In order to surreptitiously intercept conversations by wiretapping telephones or using electronic ("bugging") devices, a court order must be secured. As discussed in Chapter 14, like a search warrant, it must be based upon information sufficient to prove the legal standard of probable cause. When an order to intercept electronic communications is secured (generally referred to as a Title III), it is quite limited, requires extensive documentation, and the persons monitored must be notified after the order expires. These requirements make electronic surveillance quite expensive (in terms of personnel hours expended) and difficult to accomplish.

Jurisdictional Limitations

The Constitution provides for a form of government in which powers are diffused horizontally and vertically. There are three branches—legislative, judicial, and executive—and four levels of government—federal, state, county, and municipal. Although each level has responsibilities for responding to organized criminal activities, there is little or no coordination between them—each level of government responds to the problem largely independent of the others. Federalism was part of a deliberate design to help protect us against tyranny; it also provides us with a level of inefficiency that significantly handicaps efforts to deal with organized criminal activity.

On the federal level, a host of executive branch agencies, ranging from the military to the Federal Bureau of Investigation, have responsibility for combating organized crime. There is also a separate federal judicial system responsible for trying organized crime cases and a legislative branch responsible for enacting organized crime legislation and allocating funds for federal enforcement efforts. The jurisdictions of many federal enforcement agencies overlap, and efforts are often more competitive rather than cooperative. At the municipal level, there are about 20,000 police agencies. Each state has state-level enforcement agents (state police or similar agency), and the state is responsible for operating prisons and the parole system (if one

exists). County government usually has responsibility for prosecuting defendants, and a county-level agency, typically the sheriff, is usually responsible for operating jails. The county may also have a department with general policing responsibilities, independent of or as part of the sheriff's office. Almost every municipality has a police department whose officers enforce laws involving organized criminal activity. Each of these levels of government has taxing authority and allocates resources with little or no consultation with other levels of government. The result is a degree of inefficiency that surpasses that of most democratic nations.

American efforts against drug trafficking are limited by national boundaries: Cocaine and heroin originate where U.S. law enforcement has no jurisdiction. The Bureau of International Narcotics Matters, within the U.S. Department of State, is the primary agency responsible for coordinating international programs and gaining the cooperation of foreign governments in antidrug efforts. But the bureau has no authority to force governments to act in a manner most beneficial to U.S. efforts in dealing with cocaine or heroin. The State Department collects intelligence on policy-level international drug developments, while the Central Intelligence Agency (CIA) collects strategic narcotics intelligence and is responsible for coordinating foreign intelligence on narcotics. The CIA, however, has shielded drug traffickers who have provided foreign intelligence information useful to that agency. Federal efforts against drug trafficking are often sacrificed to foreign policy (Golden 1995a; Sciolino and Engelberg 1988). For example, the U.S.-backed contras in Nicaragua trafficked in cocaine, allegedly with the knowledge if not the assistance of the CIA (Harmon 1993). Similar relationships in Southeast Asia were discussed in Chapter 12.

Ironically, jurisdictional limitations can sometimes overcome constitutional restrictions. Because the Bill of Rights applies only to actions of the U.S. government, the Fourth Amendment and exclusionary rule do not govern seizures in foreign countries by those nations' police. This holds even when the evidence seized is from U.S. citizens—it would be admissible in a U.S. court. Furthermore, the

Supreme Court has held that constitutional protections do not obtain in U.S. government actions against foreign nationals on foreign soil. In *United States v. Verdugo Urquidez* (110 S.Ct. 1056, 1990) a Mexican national who was suspected in the 1985 torture-murder of a DEA agent was apprehended by Mexican police on a U.S. warrant and turned over to U.S. marshals at the California border. At the request of the DEA, Mexican police, without a warrant, searched the fugitive's two residences and seized incriminating documents, which were turned over to the DEA. The evidence was ruled admissible.

In 1992, in another case involving the murder of a DEA agent, the Supreme Court ruled that kidnapping a suspect on foreign soil does not prevent the suspect from being tried in the United States. In this case (*United States v. Alvarez Machain*, 504 U.S. 665) Mexican bounty hunters kidnapped a medical doctor and took him to El Paso; they were paid $20,000 and given the right to settle with their families in the United States. The Mexican government reacted with outrage to the decision.

CORRUPTION

Two basic strategies are available to law enforcement agencies—reactive and proactive—and many use a combination of both. *Reactive law enforcement* has its parallel in firefighting: Firefighters remain in their stations, equipment at the ready, until a call for service is received. Reactive law enforcement encourages citizens to report crimes; the agency then responds. This type of law enforcement is used for dealing with conventional crimes such as murder, rape, assault, robbery, burglary, and theft—crimes that are likely to be discovered by or reported to the police. (With the exception of murder and auto theft, however, studies indicate that most of these crimes do not come to the attention of the police.) *Proactive law enforcement* requires officers/agents to seek out indications of criminal behavior, a necessity when the nature of the criminal violation includes victim participation such as in gambling, prostitution, and drugs. These crimes are often referred to as "victimless" because victims are unlikely to report the crime to the police.

In order to seek out criminal activity in the most efficient manner possible, proactive law enforcement officers must often conceal their identities and otherwise deceive the criminals they are stalking. James Q. Wilson (1978: 59) points out that both reactive and proactive law enforcement officers are exposed to opportunities for graft, but the latter are more severely tested: The reactive law enforcement officer, "were he to accept money or favors to act other than as his duty required, would have to conceal or alter information about a crime already known to his organization." The proactive enforcement agent, however, "can easily agree to overlook offenses known to him but to no one else or to participate in illegal transactions (buying or selling drugs) for his own rather than for the organization's advantage." Undercover officers pretending to be criminals are difficult to supervise; the agency for which they work often knows about their activities only to the extent that the agents inform it. And if they are able to fool wary criminals....

In 1996, prosecutors in New York City had to throw out cases against ninety-eight drug defendants because the police officers involved in their cases were from the Uptown Manhattan 30th Precinct where thirty-three officers had been convicted of drug corruption charges (Kocieniewski 1997). The following year, prosecutors in Chicago had to drop charges in 120 drug cases because police officers involved in the cases had been indicted for taking payoffs and extorting money from drug dealers (Warnick 1997).

Probably the most egregious episode of the nexus between organized crime and corruption was revealed in 2005: two NYPD detectives (retired and currently imprisoned) had been on the payroll of Lucchese Family underboss Anthony ("Gaspipe") Casso. The detectives received $4,000 a month each for confidential information and additional money for specific acts; $65,000, for example, for murdering a Gambino soldier. Information provided by the two also led to the death of an innocent telephone installer who happened

---

TWO HATS

In 2010, the leader of a drug trafficking organization operating out of Ciudad Juárez, Mexico, was sentenced to twenty-seven years imprisonment in a U.S. federal court. The trafficker, was a Juárez police officer assigned to a special counter-narcotics unit (U.S. Drug Enforcement press release, January 19, 2010).

---

to share the same name as the intended victim. One of the detectives was assigned to the Organized Crime Homicide Unit, giving him access to confidential intelligence; the other had a father who was a member of the Gambino Family (DeVecchio and Brandt 2011; Dades, Vecchione, and Fisher 2009; Feuer and Rashaum 2005; Lawson and Oldham 2007; Marzulli 2005b; Marzulli and O'Shaughnessy 2005).

There is also the problem of corruption in foreign countries that grow, process, or serve as transshipment stations for illegal substances. "The corrupt official," notes the President's Commission on Organized Crime (1986a: 178), "is the *sine qua non* of drug trafficking." The commission concluded that "corruption linked to drug trafficking is a widespread phenomenon among political and military leaders, police and other authorities in virtually every country touched by the drug trade. The easily available and enormous amounts of money generated through drug transactions present a temptation too great for many in positions of authority to resist."

A problem related to proactive law enforcement and corruption involves the use of informants.

INFORMANTS[1]

The "snitch" or confidential informant (CI) comes in two basic forms: the "good citizen" and the "criminal." The former is so rare, particularly in organized crime law enforcement, that we will deal only with the criminal informant, an individual who provides help to law enforcement in order to further his or her own ends. These include financial rewards, vengeance, an effort to drive competition out of business, and, most frequently, "working off a beef"—securing leniency for criminal activities that have become known to the authorities.

The more involved the informant is in criminal activity, the more useful his or her assistance. This raises serious ethical and policy questions. Should the informant be given immunity from lawful punishment in exchange for cooperation? If so, who is to make that determination: the agent who becomes aware of the informant's activities, his or her supervisor, the prosecutor who is informed of the situation, or a trial judge? Should a murderer be permitted to remain free because he or she is of value to organized crime law enforcement efforts?

Los Angeles intelligence detective Mike Rothmiller (1992: 89–90) points to a problem with using informants. He was sharing an informant with a DEA agent. On one occasion he arranged to meet the DEA agent at the informant's home. When the detective walked in, he found the informant in the living room with at least a pound of cocaine on a glass table, dividing it up into sale packages—as the DEA agent looked on. Rothmiller motioned the agent into another room.

"What's going on here?" he said. The federal agent explained that his informant was helping him take down some other dealers and that he also claimed to have information on a major hydroponic marijuana-growing operation in Colorado. "You gotta do what you gotta do." The agent shrugged apologetically.

There are other dangers: "Given the number of law enforcement agencies and given their heavy dependence on intelligence, it is inevitable that there are informants who inform on other informants,

---

1. For a discussion of legal issues involving informants, see Schreiber (2002).

DEPARTMENT OF JUSTICE CONFIDENTIAL INFORMANT INSTRUCTIONS

1. You must provide truthful information to the Justice Law Enforcement Agency [JLEA] at all times;

2. Your assistance and the statements you make to the JLEA are entirely voluntary;

3. The United States Government will strive to protect your identity, but cannot promise or guarantee either that your identity will not be divulged as a result of legal or other compelling considerations, or that you will not be called to testify in a proceeding as a witness.

4. The JLEA on his or her own cannot promise or agree to any consideration by a Federal Prosecutor's Office or a Court in exchange for your cooperation, since the decision to confer any such benefit lies within the exclusive discretion of the Federal Prosecutor's Office and the Court. However, the JLEA will consider (but not necessarily act upon) a request by you to advise the appropriate Federal Prosecutor's Office or Court of the nature and extent of your assistance.

5. You have no immunity or protection from investigation, arrest or prosecution for anything you say or do, and the JLEA cannot promise or agree to such immunity or protection, unless and until you have been granted such immunity or protection in writing by a United States Attorney or his or her designee.

6. You have not been authorized to engage in any criminal activity and could be prosecuted for any unauthorized criminal activity in which you have engaged or engage in the future.

who are probably informing on them. A consequence of that is selective prosecution: arbitrary decisions made by police officers and agents as to who will go to jail and who will be allowed to remain on the street. Given the vast amounts of money at stake in the drug business, selective prosecution raises the specter of corruption" (Eddy, Sabogal, and Walden 1988: 85). In 2008, several New York City police officers assigned to drug enforcement were charged with paying informants with confiscated drugs.

This raises the problem of informant veracity. With strong incentives to produce information, how reliable is an informant? Journalist Jack Newfield (1979) quotes an FBI agent who specialized in organized crime cases: "I once had an informant who told me all sorts of stories. Later on I found out the guy was simultaneously an informant to the New York City Police Department, only I didn't know. What he was telling the police was completely different than what he was telling the bureau. And we were both paying him for his bullshit." In Chicago, the FBI paid an informant $10,000 a month for his work in ferreting out corrupt union officials. Unfortunately, the money was wasted and, in at least one case, an innocent union official was framed by the informant. In 1999, the informant was convicted of lying to a grand jury and sentenced to two and a half years in prison (M. O'Connor 1999b).

In 1989, an informant in Los Angeles admitted he had committed perjury in several cases and suggested that some men may have gone to death row based, at least in part, on his false testimony. The informant said he received prison furloughs, a recommendation for parole, a reduction of bail, and $2,700 for his efforts ("Jail Informer's Admissions Spur Inquiry" 1989; Reinhold 1989). One high school dropout began working as a paid informant for the DEA in 1984, after a hitch in the Marines. Despite the fact that the DEA was aware that he had compromised dozens of prosecutions by falsely testifying under oath and concealing his own arrest record, the agency continued to use—and pay—him until 2000, by which time he had earned $1.8 million (Thompson 2001). "Useful CIs," notes Evan Ratliff (2011: 58), "are often paid thousands of dollars, sometimes hundreds of thousands, in retainers. For certain crimes, such as those related to drug trafficking, and money laundering, informants can make as much as 25 percent of the confiscated proceeds."

Working closely with informants is a potentially corrupting influence. The informant helps the agent enter an underworld filled with danger—and great financial rewards. Under such circumstances, there is always concern that the law enforcement agent may become something else to the informer—a friend, an employee, an employer, or a partner. The rewards can be considerable: The agent can confiscate money and drugs or receive payment for not arresting gamblers or traffickers and at the same time improve his or her work record by arresting competing or unaffiliated criminals. It is often only a small step from using criminals as informants to entering into business with them.

FBI special agent Daniel A. Mitrione, an eleven-year veteran of the bureau, was assigned to an undercover operation involving drug trafficking. In his undercover role the agent began working with an informant. Arnold Trebach (1987: 343) reports: "In a familiar scenario that sometimes seems to flow naturally from the dynamics of the situation, one day the informer asked for the privilege of being a real dealer on the side while he was acting like one for the government. Agent Mitrione allowed the man to take a small load of cocaine to Miami and simply failed to tell his FBI supervisors about it. For this small initial courtesy, the appreciative informant-trafficker gave him $3,500 and a $9,000 Rolex watch. Over the next few years, the agent received more than $850,000 and eventually a ten-year prison term."

Criminal informants who testify against former colleagues present problems for any prosecutor. These persons typically have serious criminal histories that may equal or surpass those of the defendants. They are almost invariably provided with significant incentives for their testimony. Acquittals occur in such cases when the informant is key to successful prosecution and juries do not accept his or her credibility. In the 2005 trial of John Gotti, Jr., the government's two most important witnesses admitted a total of six murders, crimes more serious than the charges for which the son of the Gambino Family boss was being tried (Preston 2005b). And there is case of Gregory Scarpa who, because of his penchant for violence, was known as the "Grim Reaper."

Scarpa was a member of the Colombo Family, a wealthy man who ran an important Colombo crew out of his social club in Bensenhurst, Brooklyn. Although arrested ten times from 1950 to 1985, his only jail time was thirty days for attempting to bribe a police officer. His ability to avoid prosecution was the result of being an FBI informant.

After a six-week jury trial in 1995, two Colombo captains and five soldiers were acquitted of murder and firearms charges. Their defense centered on the relationship between Scarpa and his FBI handler. Defense attorneys argued that the FBI agent used Scarpa to foment the war between rival factions of the Family that led to ten dead and fourteen wounded. The defendants claimed that their actions were an effort to avoid being killed (Raab 1994a, 1995f). Before he died of AIDS (from a blood transfusion) in 1994, Scarpa had committed at least four murders while an informant for the FBI. (For a discussion of the relationship between Scarpa and the FBI by his agency handler, see DeVecchio and Brandt 2011.)

The potential dangers of involvement with criminal informants are exemplified by the actions of the FBI in Boston.

Boston

Until the 1930s, organized crime in Boston was dominated by the Irish Gustin Gang, named after a street in South Boston. When they attempted to move into territory in the Italian North End, three of the gang were gunned down. The Irish eventually made their peace with the Italians, whose leader, Raymond Patriarca, operated out of Providence, Rhode Island. Despite the power of the Italians, local Irish-led gangs continued to have a presence in the Boston area and one, the Winter Hill gang—Winter Hill is a neighborhood in the Boston suburb of Somerville—maintained a close working relationship with the Patriarca Family.

From "Southie," as the insular Irish neighborhood of South Boston is known, emerged the Bulger brothers, who grew up in a public housing project. William M. Bulger was president of the state senate for longer than anyone in history until he stepped down to assume the presidency of the University of Massachusetts. Brother James

---

INVESTIGATIVE SHORTCUT

Because of his murderous reputation, fellow members of the Mafia referred to him as the "Grim Reaper"—had they known, they would have called him a "rat." In 1964, J. Edgar Hoover had an assignment for the FBI's Confidential Informant: three civil rights workers were missing in Mississippi and the White House was pressuring the director to do something. The bureau did not have local informants to provide information on the disappearance, but they did have Gregory Scarpa. As confirmed by his FBI handler (DeVecchio and Charles Brandt 2011), Scarpa traveled to Philadelphia, Mississippi, where an FBI agent pointed out a local member of the Ku Klux Klan. The Brooklyn wiseguy quickly got to the bottom of the case. He kidnapped the KKK member at gunpoint and convinced him that a failure to provide relevant information would result in an inability to father children. Shortly afterward, the FBI found the bodies of Michael Schwerner, James Chaney, and Andrew Goodman.

("Whitey") Bulger (b. 1929) was the vicious and widely feared crime boss of Southie. A delinquent in his youth, at 27 Whitey was serving federal time for bank robbery. When he returned home in 1965, to satisfy the conditions of his parole, he took a political job as a courthouse custodian. His parole completed, Bulger became an enforcer and debt collector for a local bookmaker. When his boss became embroiled in a dispute with Howie Winter, head of the Winter Hill gang, Bulger abandoned him and allied himself with the predominantly Irish gang. With the backing of Howie Winter, Whitey became the leading gangster in Southie (Lehr and O'Neil 2000). "Like a neighborhood godfather from long ago, Bulger doled out turkeys to the needy on Thanksgiving and Christmas, lent money to school kids, did favors for his 'constituents,' and settled disputes" (English 2005: 2).

In 1976, Whitey Bulger became a government informant. Unbeknownst to Whitey at the time, his partner, Steve ("The Rifleman")[2] Flemmi, who had declined an invitation to become a made guy in the Patriarca Family, had already been providing information to the FBI. According to Sean Flynn (1998), this arrangement resulted from an attempt by Jerry Angiulo, Patriarca Family underboss in charge of Boston, to use law enforcement authorities to take out the Winter Hill group; they were too dangerous for a more violent approach. Bulger and Flemmi succeeded in turning the tables—aiding the FBI to take out Angiulo. But, for the government, it was a bargain with the devil. Starting in 1965, more than twenty people were murdered by FBI informants, often with the aid of FBI agents (Butterfield 2003).

FBI field offices were under pressure to wage an effective war against the American Mafia, known in New England as the "Office." So, in return for informing on the Patriarca Family, Bulger and Flemmi were given virtually unbridled freedom to conduct their criminal business safe in the knowledge that they were protected by the FBI. If Bulger's victims complained to the FBI, his case agent would see to it that nothing happened, as when vending machine executives complained that Bulger and Flemmi were shaking them down. When the husband and wife owners of a liquor store complained that Bulger and Flemmi had threatened to kill them if they would not sell it to the pair at a "bargain" price, the FBI asked the frightened couple to wear a wire—and tipped off Bulger. Other victims who insisted on action were told of the need to testify and enter the Witness Security Program. When the Massachusetts State Police conducted their own investigation, which included electronic surveillance, Bulger and Flemmi were tipped off by the FBI. They were also tipped off about DEA and local police attempts at electronic surveillance. Despite being told that they could not be involved in murder, Bulger and Flemmi were responsible for at least nineteen, including those of two women with whom the pair were romantically involved (English 2005).

---

2. Flemmi served as a paratrooper during the Korean War.

Massachusetts state police wanted poster of James J. ("Whitey") Bulger, a fugitive Boston gangster who was at the center of a scandal in which the FBI was found to have protected Bulger in return for his providing information about the New England Mafia.

Emboldened by their FBI protection, Bulger and Flemmi engaged in a systematic shakedown of independent bookmakers and loan sharks in the south Boston area. When Howie Winter was imprisoned in 1978, Bulger took over the Winter Hill gang. When cocaine became popular in the 1980s, Bulger and Flemmi extended their shakedowns to include drug dealers. And then there were murders. In 1981, to protect an embezzling accountant, Bulger had the notorious Winter Hill hit man John Martorano kill a business executive in Tulsa, Oklahoma. Martorano was then sent to Florida, and the accountant was found stuffed into the trunk of a car at the Miami airport. In 1982, Bulger was the executioner of a Winter Hill member who had turned informant (Butterfield 2003; Lehr and O'Neil 2000).

Raymond Patriarca was indicted in 1980 for labor racketeering, and in 1981 for ordering a double execution. In 1984, while charges were still pending, he died of natural causes. His son, Raymond Patriarca, Jr., claimed the position and, with the approval of the New York Families, became boss of the Office. By 1989, Junior's reign was in trouble. Information being provided by Bulger and Flemmi and electronic bugs led to the convictions of almost every member of the Boston branch of the Office. Replacements chosen by Junior irritated the Providence branch, and a war broke out.

In an effort to restore peace, in 1989, an initiation ceremony was staged to allow four new members, three from Boston and one from Providence, to be made. The ceremony was recorded by two electronic eavesdropping devices placed in the basement ceiling of a house in a Boston suburb. It was the first time that the FBI had been able to record a Mafia initiation. In 1991, Junior pleaded guilty to racketeering and was sentenced to eight years. Another two years were added as the result of a government appeal of the original sentence. He was released on parole in 1998. Further prosecutions decimated the New England crime Family.

In 1994, Bulger was tipped off by his FBI case agent, John Connelly, that he and Flemmi were about to be indicted for racketeering and extortion. In 1995, Flemmi was arrested and Whitey became a fugitive. In 2002, Connelly received a ten-year sentence for racketeering—for essentially becoming part of Whitey Bulger's organization (Carr 2006). In 2008, he was convicted of second degree murder for warning Bulger that someone was going to implicate him in a murder—"someone's" body was subsequently found in the trunk of a car parked at Miami International Airport. Connelly's FBI supervisor admitted to taking bribes from Bulger and Flemmi but was granted immunity in exchange for cooperating with the government (Cooper and Oppel, Jr. 2011). While an informant, Bulger reputedly murdered eleven people. In 2011, he was apprehended by the FBI in Los Angeles.

During his trial in 1999, Flemmi's attorney argued that the federal government cannot prosecute crimes it effectively authorizes informers to commit (C. Goldberg 1999; especially *United States of America v. Stephen J. Flemmi*, U.S. Court of Appeals for the First Circuit, No. 99-2292, 2000). The chief witness against Flemmi, John Martorano, admitted to twenty murders in return for a sentence of ten to twelve and a half years. Because Bulger and Flemmi were informants, it is believed that Maratorano felt he had no obligation to be loyal to them. In 2001, in exchange for a plea of guilty, Flemmi was sentenced to ten years for extortion and money laundering, and in 2003, he pleaded guilty to ten murders in exchange for a life sentence.

The success of the FBI in prosecuting the Patriarca Family was marred by revelations concerning the activities of some of its agents. As a result of disclosures from this case, it was revealed that in order to protect their informants, the FBI allowed three men to be convicted and imprisoned for a murder they did not commit. Furthermore, the FBI knew of the murder plan and did not intervene. One of the three falsely convicted men died in prison; another had his sentence commuted and was released from prison in 1997; and the third had his conviction vacated and was released from prison in 2001 after serving more than thirty-three years, four of them on death row (Butterfield 2003; C. Goldberg 2001). In the wake of the Boston disclosures, the attorney general toughened the requirements on the use of informants, but a 2005 report by the Justice Department's inspector general revealed that they were routinely violated by FBI agents (Lictblau 2005a).

LAW ENFORCEMENT AGENCIES

Before we examine the law enforcement agencies responding to organized crime and the techniques they use to enforce the statutes reviewed in Chapter 14, certain issues must be noted. General police responsibility is the function of a "full-service" municipal department—there is no national police force in the United States—while the primary responsibility of state police forces is highway traffic enforcement. Most of the resources of a municipal police department go to uniformed services such as patrol; only a small portion goes into plainclothes or detective units. In larger cities, such units include specialties such as "vice" (gambling and prostitution) and drug enforcement. In this function, local police do apprehend some of the participants in organized criminal activity. Organized crime, however, is rarely a priority item for a municipal department. Resources devoted to organized crime detract from the department's ability to respond to citizen demands for police services:

> Few local departments have the luxury of developing a sophisticated organized crime control program. Obviously, the daily realities of police work at the grassroots level militate against a well-developed execution of an organized crime control strategy. Since

---

FEDERAL ORGANIZED CRIME LAW ENFORCEMENT

Department of Justice

- Bureau of Alcohol, Tobacco and Firearms and Explosives
- Drug Enforcement Administration
- Federal Bureau of Investigation
- U.S. Marshals Service

Department of the Treasury

- Internal Revenue Service

Department of Homeland Security

- Coast Guard

- Customs Service and Border Protection
- Immigration and Customs Enforcement
- Secret Service

Department of Labor

- Office of Inspector General

United States Postal Service

- Postal Inspection Service

Department of Health and Human Services

- Office of Inspector General

---

organized crime is often synonymous with vice enforcement—gambling, prostitution, narcotics, and loansharking—there are few incentives for a police administrator to allocate limited and valuable resources toward this particular form of criminality. Often the investment of personnel to enforce laws which govern "consensual relationships" between customer and supplier are met with judicial indifference and public apathy; and as demonstrated through numerous studies and investigations, it is highly questionable from a purely cost-benefit analysis whether the benefits outweigh the costs incurred. Accordingly, most investigative and law-enforcement efforts against organized crime are found at the federal level. (Dintino and Martens 1980: 67)

Because the police are the most visible agents of governmental power, and because Americans have historically distrusted government in general and the federal government in particular, there has never been serious consideration of a federal police force. Over the decades, however, necessity has led to the creation of a number of specialized federal enforcement agencies in an unplanned and uncoordinated manner. Thus, while they all have the same nominal boss—the president—federal law enforcement is

fragmented. The result is a confusing number of agencies in several departments—Justice, Treasury, Labor, Health and Human Services, Postal Service, Defense, and, since 9/11, Homeland Security—whose responsibility for organized crime law enforcement lacks systematic coordination.

DEPARTMENT OF JUSTICE (DOJ)

The Judiciary Act of 1789 created the Office of the Attorney General that evolved over the years into the head of the Department of Justice and chief law enforcement officer of the Federal Government Each of the ninety-four federal judicial districts has a U.S. attorney appointed by the president for a period of four years. U.S. attorneys and about two thousand assistant U.S. attorneys prosecute cases for all federal enforcement agencies. Within the DOJ is the Organized Crime and Racketeering Section (OCRS) responsible for coordinating and developing nationwide programs for responding to organized crime.

Federal Bureau of Investigation (FBI)

With about 14,000 special agents, the FBI is the closest thing to a federal police force in the United

States. Its origins date back to the establishment of the Department of Justice in 1870. Until 1908, the department used private detectives or borrowed men from the Secret Service. In that year, President Theodore Roosevelt directed the attorney general to develop an investigative unit within the Justice Department; it was named the Bureau of Investigation. In 1935, Congress renamed it the Federal Bureau of Investigation. Special agents were given authority to carry weapons and make arrests in response to the "Kansas City Massacre of 1933," when unarmed bureau agents were gunned down.

After World War I, the bureau was involved in a great deal of "antiradical" activity at the direction of Attorney General A. Mitchell Palmer. The agency conducted raids and arrested thousands of people in what became known as the "Red Scare of 1919." The "Palmer Raids" were the subject of a congressional investigation and were strongly defended by the bureau's assistant director, John Edgar Hoover, who was appointed director in 1924 and remained head of the FBI until his death in 1972.

Over the years, the bureau was given responsibility for investigating the interstate shipment of stolen vehicles, kidnapping, bank robbery, interstate fugitives, espionage, and sabotage. After World War II, FBI resources were directed toward the perceived threat posed by domestic communism, while the problem of organized crime was left unattended—in 1956, there were four agents assigned to the New York office to investigate "Crime, Organized" (Volkman 1998). Stanford Ungar (1975: 391) argues that "the Director was simply clever enough to steer clear of the toughest problems—the ones less likely to produce prompt and stunning results, that might test conflicts of loyalty among agents, or that would require them to be exposed to the seamier side of life (and, as with many policemen, tempt them into corruption)."[3] This changed when Robert Kennedy was appointed attorney general.

The FBI is the major law enforcement agency combating organized criminal activity and the lead

agency in using the RICO statute discussed in Chapter 14. In 1982, its broad investigative mandate was expanded when the FBI was given concurrent jurisdiction with the Drug Enforcement Administration for drug-law enforcement and investigation. While the FBI usually does not initiate a drug investigation, if one is uncovered in the course of an investigation, the agency may follow up without having to involve the DEA.

Since 9/11, there is concern that the increased focus on terrorism could detract from FBI efforts to respond to organized crime. A study by a research organization associated with Syracuse University (http://www.trac.syr.edu) revealed that prosecutions in organized crime cases brought by the FBI dropped from 498 in fiscal year 2001 to 163 in fiscal year 2006, and they have continued to drop. In 2011, the Department of Justice announced, with a great deal of fanfare and media attention, the arrest and indictment of nearly 130 members and associates of the American Mafia. Shortly afterward, the FBI downsized its organized crime squads, merging the Bonanno and Colombo squads while combining the Luccese squad with the unit investigating Eastern European organizations; the total number of agents dedicated to organized crime dropped to 45 (Marzulli 2011). Elyssa Pachico (2011) notes that during the 1990s, the best and brightest agents looked to make their careers fighting organized crime. After 9/11, counter-terrorism became far more career-enhancing than work on organized crime.

Drug Enforcement Administration (DEA)

In 1919, a Narcotics Division was created within the Bureau of Prohibition with a staff of 170 agents and an appropriation of $270,000. The Narcotics Division was tainted by its association with the country's antiliquor laws. "Public dissatisfaction intensified because of a scandal involving falsification of arrest records and charges relating to payoffs by, and collusion with, drug dealers" (PCOC 1986a: 204). Responding in 1930,

---

3. Anthony Summers (1993) presents more explanations for Hoover's lack of activity against organized crime.

DRUG ENFORCEMENT ADMINISTRATION

Investigation and preparation for the prosecution of major violators of controlled substances laws operating at interstate and international levels.

Management of a national drug intelligence network in cooperation with federal, state, local, and foreign officials to collect, analyze, and disseminate strategic, investigative, and tactical intelligence information to U.S. law enforcement and intelligence agencies, and, when appropriate, to foreign counterparts.

Seizure and forfeiture of assets derived from, traceable to, or intended to be used for illicit drug trafficking.

Enforcement of the provisions of the Controlled Substances Act as they pertain to the manufacture, distribution, and dispensing of legally produced controlled substances.

Coordination and cooperation with federal, state, local, and foreign law enforcement officials on mutual drug enforcement efforts.

Congress removed drug enforcement from the Bureau of Prohibition and established the Federal Bureau of Narcotics (FBN) as a separate agency within the Department of the Treasury: concern with federalism, constitutional limitation on the police powers of the central government, led Congress to use the taxing authority of the federal government to control drugs. While few people today would question the DEA's right to register physicians and pharmacists and control what drugs they can prescribe and dispense, at the beginning of the twentieth century federal authority to regulate narcotics and the prescription practices of physicians was generally thought to be unconstitutional (Musto 1998). In 1973, responsibility for enforcing federal drug statutes was given to the DEA, which was placed in the Department of Justice.

The DEA is a single-mission agency responsible for enforcing federal statutes dealing with controlled substances by investigating alleged or suspected major drug traffickers. The DEA is also responsible for regulating the legal trade in controlled substances such as morphine, methadone, and oxycodone. Diversion agents conduct accountability investigations of drug wholesalers, suppliers, and manufacturers. They inspect the records and facilities of major drug manufacturers and distributors, and special agents investigate instances where drugs have been illegally diverted from legitimate sources. DEA special agents are also stationed in other countries, where their mission is to gain cooperation in international efforts against drug trafficking and help train foreign enforcement officials.

The basic approach to DEA drug-law enforcement is the "buy and bust" or the "controlled buy." Typically, a drug agent is introduced to a seller by an informant. The agent arranges to buy a relatively small amount of the substance and then attempts to move further up the organizational ladder by increasing the amount of drugs purchased. "The agent prefers to defer an arrest until he can seize a large amount of drugs or can implicate higher-ups in the distribution system or both" (Wilson 1978: 43). When arrests are made, DEA agents attempt the "flip"—convince a defendant to become an informant, particularly if the person has knowledge about the entire operation so that a conspiracy case can be effected. As discussed earlier, the use of informants is problematic. The DEA, usually with the aid of customs agents and state and local enforcement agencies, monitors airports in an effort to interdict drugs being smuggled by "mules," persons who carry contraband on or inside their bodies.

The DEA has five military-trained squads (Foreign-deployed Advisory Support Teams: FAST) of ten agents each that since 2005 have been deployed to fight drug trafficking organizations in countries as far flung as Honduras and Afghanistan, blurring the lines between the "war on drugs" and the "war on terrorism." Working with specially vetted local law enforcement officers, FAST usually operates with a low profile to avoid the potential of a nationalist backlash (Savage 2011).

Through the use of informants the DEA has been able to infiltrate powerful Mexican drug cartels, thereby aiding Mexican authorities to capture or kill about two dozen high-ranking and midlevel traffickers. Because of concern over official corruption and laws prohibiting U.S. forces from operating in Mexico, Mexican officials are typically not informed of DEA-informant operatives (Thompson 2011).

Marshals Service

The Marshals Service is the oldest federal law enforcement agency, dating back to 1789. During the period of westward expansion, the U.S. marshal played a significant role in the "Wild West," where he was often the only symbol of law and order. In the past marshals have also been used in civil disturbances as an alternative to military intervention. Today, they provide security for federal court facilities and the safety of federal judges; transport federal prisoners; apprehend fugitives; serve civil writs issued by federal courts, which can include the seizure of property under provisions of RICO and provide for the custody, management, and disposal of forfeited assets. Their most important task relative to organized crime, however, is responsibility for administering the *Witness Security Program*.

Witness Security Program[4]

Because of the potentially undesirable consequences for a witness who testifies in an organized crime case, efforts have been made to protect such witnesses from retribution. The Witness Security Program was authorized by the Organized Crime Control Act of 1970:

> The Attorney General of the United States is authorized to rent, purchase, modify or

remodel protected housing facilities and to otherwise offer to provide for the health, safety, and welfare of witnesses and persons intended to be called as Government witnesses, and the families of witnesses and persons intended to be called as Government witnesses, in legal proceedings instituted against any person alleged to have participated in an organized criminal activity whenever, in his judgment, testimony from, or a willingness to testify by, such a witness would place his life or person, or the life or person of a member of his family or household, in jeopardy. Any person availing himself of such an offer by the Attorney General to use such facilities may continue to use such facilities for as long as the Attorney General determines the jeopardy to his life or person continues.

The Marshals Service provides full-time security to witnesses while they are in a high-threat environment, including pretrial conferences, trial testimonials, and other court appearances. Witnesses and their families typically get new identities with authentic documentation and financial assistance for housing, subsistence for basic living expenses, and medical care. Job training and employment assistance may also be provided. No Witness Security Program participant following program guidelines has been harmed while under the active protection of the U.S. Marshals Service.

The program was given over to the U.S. Marshals Service to administer, an arrangement designed to enhance the value of witness testimony: "Law enforcement officers wanted the protecting and relocating agency to be in the criminal justice system but to be as far removed as possible from both investigating agents and prosecution. That way the Government could more readily counter the charge that cooperating witnesses were being paid or otherwise unjustifiably compensated in return for their testimony" (Permanent Subcommittee on Investigations, hereafter PSI, 1981c: 54).

The Marshals Service was not prepared for these new responsibilities—its typical duties were related

---

4. For an examination of the program by its founder, see Earley and Shur (2002).

GOOMBA'S

The owner of Goomba's Pizza in Florida became irate when two customers demanded a refund because he had screwed up their calzone order. He responded by vaulting over the counter and pistol-whipping the two, an attack caught on a store video camera. Goomba's owner, a member of the Bonanno Family who had been convicted of two murders, was in the Witness Security Program, the result of his testimony against other Family members (Marzulli 2011c),

---

to support of the judicial system, and moreover, the educational requirements and training of deputy U.S. marshals were not rigorous. This has changed, and the new position of "inspector" was created specifically for the Witness Security Program. Officials had not anticipated the sheer numbers of persons entering the program: They had expected about two dozen annually, not the more than five hundred principals brought into the program each year. By 2005, the program was protecting more than 17,000 witnesses and their dependents.

Some critics of the program have charged that the Marshals Service shields criminals not only from would-be assassins but also from debts and lawsuits. In an attempt to remedy this, an amendment to the 1984 Comprehensive Crime Control Act directs the Justice Department to stop hiding witnesses who are sued for civil damages and to drop from the program participants linked to new crimes. But the program still provides career criminals with "clean" backgrounds they can use to prey on or endanger an unsuspecting public.

The problem is obvious: "The marshals are often dealing with men and women who have never done an honest day's work in their lives. Many of them were skilled criminals—burglars, embezzlers, arsonists, physical enforcers—accustomed to lucrative financial rewards and a high standard of living" (PSI 1981c: 53–54), a standard that is not going to be duplicated by the program. Once the immediate physical danger has passed, some of these protected witnesses begin to yearn for the excitement and, for some, the status and financial rewards that crime brought to their lives. Government witness Sammy Gravano, former underboss of the Gambino Family, was relocated to Arizona. He soon grew bored with his new life and, while keeping his new name, told neighbors his real identity and signed autographs for people who stopped him on the street. In 2000, Gravano was arrested for involvement in an ecstasy drug ring that also included his son, who apparently introduced his father to the trade (Murr 2000). Having few if any noncriminal skills, it is not surprising that some of these protected witnesses return to criminal activity even if it places both their freedom and their lives, and the lives of their families, at risk. While about three-dozen witnesses who left the program have been murdered, none following program guidelines have been harmed.

In some cases, estranged spouses have been unable to visit their own children. This was dramatically portrayed in the 1980 movie *Hide in Plain Sight*, starring James Caan. In 1984, Congress amended the law to provide greater rights to parents in such cases.

Bureau of Alcohol, Tobacco, and Firearms and Explosives

In 2003, the Bureau of Alcohol, Tobacco, and Firearms (ATF) was transferred from the Treasury Department to the Department of Justice. The tax and trade functions of ATF remain in the Treasury Department with the new Alcohol and Tobacco Tax and Trade Bureau. In addition, the agency's name was changed to the Bureau of Alcohol, Tobacco, Firearms and Explosives to reflect its mission in the Department of Justice.

ATF regulates the firearms and explosives industries from manufacture and/or importation through

ATF NATIONAL TRACING CENTER (NTC)

NTC establishes the "paper trail" that allows ATF to "trace" each firearm from its point of manufacture or importation to the point of its first retail sale. The NTC traces crime-connected firearms for federal, state, local, and international law enforcement. By tracing firearms recovered by law enforcement authorities, ATF is able to discern patterns of names, locations, and weapon types. This information provides invaluable leads that aid in identifying persons engaged in the diversion of firearms into illegal commerce, links suspects to firearms in criminal investigations, identifies potential traffickers, and can detect intrastate, interstate, and international patterns in sources.

retail sale. The agency screens and licenses firms engaging in commerce in these commodities and in the case of explosives, there are ATF standards for the safe storage of materials.

ATF traces its origins to 1791, when a tax was placed on alcoholic spirits. Eventually, the Prohibition Bureau evolved. With repeal of Prohibition, the agency became known as the Alcohol Tax Unit. In 1942, the bureau was given jurisdiction over federal firearms statutes and, in 1970, over arson and explosives. ATF agents are empowered to seize and destroy contraband and illegal liquor production facilities, and they are responsible for combating contraband cigarette smuggling from a low-tax state to a high-tax state—North Carolina to New York, for example—and the bootlegging of untaxed tobacco products, activities often engaged in by persons in organized crime who, through their extensive networks, have readily available outlets for such products. Through enforcement of federal firearms and explosives statutes and regulations, ATF has been involved in the investigation of outlaw motorcycle clubs. The Anti-Arson Act of 1982 increased the bureau's jurisdiction over arson. (The FBI has jurisdiction in arson or bombings that occur at federal buildings or other institutions that receive federal funds and in incidents that fit the Department of Justice's definition of terrorism.) ATF's National Response Teams investigate cases of arson and bombings in conjunction with state and local agencies. Each team is composed of special agents, a forensic chemist, and an explosives specialist, and is equipped with sophisticated, state-of-the-art equipment.

DEPARTMENT OF THE TREASURY

The primary responsibility of the Department of the Treasury is the collection of revenues due the federal government. In carrying out these responsibilities, the Treasury Department employs law enforcement personnel in the Internal Revenue Service who have an important role in dealing with organized crime. The mission of the IRS is to encourage and achieve the highest possible degree of voluntary compliance with tax laws and regulations. When such compliance is not forthcoming or not feasible, as in the case of persons involved in organized criminal activity, the Criminal Investigation division (CI) receives the case. Agents examine bank records, canceled checks, brokerage accounts, property transactions, and purchases, compiling a financial biography of the subject's lifestyle in order to prove that proper taxes have not been paid according to the net worth theory discussed shortly.

The Internal Revenue Service of the Department of the Treasury employs about 2,800 special agents in the Criminal Investigation division. While the primary role of the IRS is collection of revenue and compliance with tax codes, CI seeks evidence of criminal violations for prosecution by the Department of Justice. In particular, agents seek out information relative to income that has not been reported: "Additional income for criminal purposes is established by both direct and indirect methods. The direct method consists of the identification of specific items of unreported taxable receipts, overstated costs and expenses (such as personal expenses charged to business, diversion of corporate income to office-stockholders, allocation of income or expense to incorrect year in order to lower tax, etc.), and improper claims for credit or exemption" (Committee on the Office of Attorney General 1974: 49–50).

Persons in organized crime have devised methods for successful evasion of taxes—dealing in cash, keeping minimal records, setting up fronts, and using a *zapper*: an automated sales suppression software program often on a flash drive that is attached to a cash register to facilitate removing cash without leaving a record for tax audit purposes. A dollar amount or percentage is entered and the program calculates which receipts to erase to get close to the cash the person wants to remove. The device then suggests how much cash to remove and erases enough entries so the register balances (Furchgott 2008).

These evasion schemes are countered by the indirect method known as the *net worth theory*: "The government establishes a taxpayer's net worth at the commencement of the taxing period [which requires substantial accuracy], deducts that from his or her net worth at the end of the period, and proves that the net gain in net worth exceeds the income reported by the taxpayer" (Johnson 1963: 17–19). In effect, the Internal Revenue Service reconstructs a person's total expenditures by examining the person's actual standard of living and comparing it with reported income. The government can then maintain that the taxpayer did not report his or her entire income. The government does not have to show a probable source of the excess unreported gain in net worth. Earl Johnson (1963: 18) points out that the Capone case taught many criminals a lesson: "management-level persons in organized crime scrupulously report their income—at least the part of it that they spend."

In 2002, a federal judge ruled that money paid to organized crime—$1.7 million a year to a captain in the Gambino Family—for protection of coin-operated video pornographic booths was not a deductible business expense. The judge found that although such payments might qualify as "ordinary and necessary" payments in this industry, the defen-dant had attempted to hide the payments from the IRS, and the judge ruled that this disqualified the deductions (Johnston 2002).

Financial investigations are by their nature very document intensive. They involve records, such as bank account information and real estate files, which point to the movement of money. Any record that pertains to, or shows the paper trail of events involving money is important. The major goal in a financial investigation is to identify and document the movement of money during the course of a crime. The link between where the money comes from, who gets it, when it is received and where it is stored or deposited, can provide proof of criminal activity.

As a result of the excesses revealed in the wake of the Watergate scandal during the presidency of Richard Nixon, Congress enacted the Tax Reform Act of 1976. The act reduced the law enforcement role of the IRS and made it quite difficult for law enforcement agencies other than the IRS to gain access to income tax returns. Amendments in 1982 reduced the requirements and permit the IRS to better cooperate with the efforts of other federal agencies investigating organized crime, particularly drug traffickers.

In addition to investigating criminal violations of the Internal Revenue Code, IRS jurisdiction includes the Bank Secrecy Act and money laundering statutes. Only the IRS can investigate criminal violations of the IRS code. Due to increased use of automation for financial records, CI special agents are trained to recover computer evidence and use specialized forensic technology to recover financial data that may have been encrypted, password protected, or hidden by other electronic means. The CI division's conviction rate is one of the highest in federal law enforcement and in addition to the substantial sentences handed down by the courts, those convicted must also pay fines, civil taxes, and penalties. The IRS pays money to *whistleblowers*—people who inform on persons who fail to pay the tax they owe. If the IRS uses information provided by the whistleblower, it can provide a reward of up to 30 percent of the additional tax, penalty, and other amounts collected.

The *Financial Crimes Enforcement Network* (FinCEN) was established in 1990 in the Treasury's Office of Terrorism and Financial Intelligence. FinCEN administers the Bank Secrecy Act and relevant parts of the USA PATRIOT Act. FinCEN is a key component of the U.S. international strategy to combat terrorism and organized crime using counter–money laundering laws (discussed in Chapter 14), and provides intelligence and analytical case support to federal, state, local, and international investigators and regulators. Its 300 employees include intelligence analysts and criminal investigators as well as specialists in the financial industry and computer field. In addition, approximately forty long-term detailees are assigned to FinCEN from twenty-one different regulatory and law enforcement agencies. FinCEN maintains a database in Detroit that documents every suspicious-activity report filed since they were initiated in 1996.

DEPARTMENT OF HOMELAND SECURITY

As a result of the Homeland Security Act of 2002, several former Treasury responsibilities, such as customs, have been transferred to the Department of Homeland Security (DHS).

Customs Service and Border Protection (CBP)

CBP has authority to search outbound and inbound shipments. It has more than 21,000 officers screening passengers (more than 300 million persons annually) and cargo at 330 points of entry into United States. CBP Border Patrol Agents are assigned to U.S. borders with Canada and Mexico to prevent illegal entry of persons and contraband. CBP is at the forefront of efforts against human and counterfeit product trafficking, working with commercial carriers, often signing cooperative agreements, to enhance the carriers' ability to prevent their equipment from being used to smuggle drugs and other contraband. CBP's Office of Air

and Marine is the world's largest aviation and maritime law enforcement organization. The agency collects over $30 billion annually in tariffs, and its agricultural specialists are responsible for preventing the entry of harmful pests, and plant and animal diseases that may threaten U.S. agriculture and the food supply.

CBP is not bound by the Fourth Amendment protections that typically restrain domestic law enforcement. Agents do not need probable cause or warrants to engage in search and seizure at ports of entry; certain degrees of suspicion will suffice. The typical case is a "cold border bust," the result of an entry checkpoint search. Because it is impractical if not impossible to thoroughly search most vehicles and individuals entering the United States, agents have developed certain techniques for minimizing inconvenience to legitimate travelers and shippers while targeting those most likely to be involved in smuggling. Besides being alert to various cues that act as tip-offs, the officials at border-crossing points have computers containing information such as license plate numbers and names of known or suspected smugglers. People arrested become targets for offers of plea bargaining in efforts to gain their cooperation in follow-up enforcement efforts.

CBP is hampered by the scope of its task: the need to patrol more than 12,000 miles of international boundary. The frontiers of the United States, to the north and the south, "are the longest undisputed, undefended borders on earth" (F. Weiner 2002: 14). About half the drugs entering the United States come through commercial ports, where they are secreted in tightly sealed steel containers, 20 or 40 feet long, 12 feet high, and 8 feet wide, millions of which enter the country every year. Officials can inspect only a small number (about 10 percent) of these containers, and without advance information, the drugs typically pass right through the ports. Drugs that are intercepted are easily replaced.

CBP has been plagued by charges of corruption on the U.S.–Mexico border. In part, the result of dramatic increases in the number of agents and tougher enforcement that has driven smugglers to engage in greater efforts at compromising security.

There is concern that smugglers are sending operatives to take jobs in border enforcement (Archibald and Becker 2008). In 2011, a CBP inspector pled guilty to being a member of a drug trafficking organization and facilitating the smuggling of drugs and aliens into the United States; he received a seventeen-year sentence (FBI press release, July 6, 2011).

Immigration and Customs Enforcement (ICE)

ICE is charged with the investigation and enforcement of over 400 federal statutes within the United States, and maintains attachés at major U.S. embassies overseas. ICE has more than 20,000 employees assigned to offices in every state and in forty-seven countries as well; more than 7,000 are special agents responsible for investigating a wide range of domestic and international activities arising from the illegal movement of people and goods into and out of the United States. ICE investigates immigration crime, human, drug, and weapons smuggling, financial crimes, export matters, and cyber-crime.

The Cyber Crimes Section (CCS) is responsible for developing and coordinating investigations of immigration and customs violations where the Internet is used to facilitate the criminal act. CCS investigative responsibilities include fraud, theft of intellectual property rights, money laundering, identity and benefit fraud, the sale and distribution of narcotics and other controlled substances, illegal arms trafficking, and the illegal export of strategic/controlled commodities, and the smuggling and sale of other prohibited items such as art and cultural property. The Child Exploitation Section investigates the trans-border dimension of large-scale producers and distributors of images of child abuse, as well as individuals who travel in foreign commerce for the purpose of engaging in sex with minors.

Coast Guard

The Coast Guard is responsible for contraband interdiction on the seas. Its vessels conduct continuous surface patrols and frequent surveillance flights over waters of interest, and its personnel board and inspect suspect vessels at sea. Coast Guard personnel are law enforcement officers who do not have to establish probable cause prior to boarding a vessel. "The Coast Guard conducts both continuous surface patrols and frequent surveillance flights over waters of interest, and boards and inspects vessels at sea. In the past major Coast Guard resources have been concentrated in the 'choke points' traditionally transversed by traffickers" (PCOC 1986a: 313). Cutters patrol the Bahamas, the eastern passes of the Caribbean, and the Gulf, Atlantic and Pacific coastal areas.

A typical seizure begins with the sighting of a suspect plane by a Coast Guard radar plane 250 miles away. The radar plane informs an intelligence center where the suspect plane's flight track is compared with flight plans submitted to the Federal Aviation Administration. If a flight plan has not been filed, a two-engine Coast Guard tracking plane is dispatched. The tracking plane picks up the suspect plane on radar and then turns the radar off to avoid being detected by a "fuzz-buster." The tracker follows behind and above the suspect aircraft, maintaining surveillance with an infrared device that senses heat but does not send out an electronic beam. When the suspect plane prepares to land, the tracker notifies officers aboard a waiting helicopter and they move in to make arrests. If the plane makes a drop at sea for pickup by boat, a Coast Guard helicopter or patrol boat makes the seizure. Coast Guard personnel are sometimes detailed to U.S. Navy ships assigned to drug interdiction because the Posse Comitatus Act prohibits military personnel from making arrests of civilians.

The Coast Guard has been deploying 150 mph Stingray helicopters to intercept "cigarette boats," also known as "go fasts," used to transport drugs from South America or northern Mexico. These slim 30- to 40-foot vessels propelled by 800-horsepower engines can reach speeds of 50 mph on open seas and carry a cargo of up to three tons. The helicopters are equipped with machine guns and high-impact .50 caliber sniper rifles whose rounds are as thick and long as a hot dog

---

"A FISHY HAUL"

In 2004, Naval frigates with Coast Guard officers aboard intercepted two ships from Colombia 300 miles west of the Galapagos Islands. The first had 30,000 pounds of cocaine hidden in a sealed ballast tank; the second contained 26,000 pounds of cocaine hidden under fish and ice in the cargo hold ("A Fishy Haul" 2004).

A RECORD HAUL

The Coast Guard captured thirteen tons of cocaine aboard a fishing boat 1,500 miles south of San Diego. The 152-foot vessel with a crew of ten—eight Ukrainians and two Russians—aroused suspicion because it lacked operable fishing equipment. The cocaine was apparently destined for the Tijuana Cartel/Arellano-Felix drug trafficking organization whose territory is close to where the ship was operating (Fox 2001).

---

and can disable a boat engine, at which time a high-speed Coast Guard cutter effects a seizure (Kilian 2002). This tactic has been so successful that traffickers have resorted to using crude submarine-like vessels to move cocaine from Colombia to Mexico (Franklin and Logan 2008).

Department of Labor Office of Inspector General

The Office of Inspector General (OIG), an independent agency within the Department of Labor, is responsible for conducting audits, investigations, and evaluations of departmental programs and operations; identifying potential problems or abuses; developing and making recommendations for corrective action; and referring cases for prosecution. While federal agencies usually have an inspector general with similar responsibilities, the OIG at Labor is unique insofar as it is also responsible for carrying out a criminal investigations program to combat the influence of organized crime and labor racketeering in the workplace.

OIG special agents of the Division of Labor Racketeering conduct investigations in three general areas: employee benefit plans, labor-management relations, and internal union affairs. Within these broad investigative areas, top priority is given to American Mafia domination of labor unions and/or employee benefit plans.

In 2011, agents from the Department of Labor, FBI, ICE, and federal prosecutors were organized into Antirafficking Coordination Teams (ACTeams) based in Atlanta, El Paso, Kansas City, MO, Los Angeles, Memphis, and Miami. ACTeams focus on developing federal criminal human trafficking investigations and prosecutions to protect the rights of human trafficking victims.

Secret Service

The Secret Service was established as a law enforcement agency in 1865. While most people associate the Secret Service with presidential protection, its original mandate was to investigate the counterfeiting of U.S. currency, a mission the Secret Service is still mandated to carry out.

Today the agency's investigative mission is to safeguard the payment and financial systems of the United States. This has historically been accomplished through the enforcement of counterfeiting statutes to preserve the integrity of United States currency, coin, and financial obligations.

The Secret Service's investigative responsibilities have expanded to include crimes that involve financial institution fraud, computer and telecommunications fraud, false identification documents, access device

---

MEDICARE FRAUD: AN EXAMPLE

In 2010, the U.S. district court in Miami sentenced the founder of a fraudulent Miami-area HIV/AIDS infusion clinic to ten years in prison and the clinic's owner and operator to seventy months after their convictions for a $5.8 million Medicare fraud scheme. The defendants defrauded Medicare by submitting claims for injection and infusion treatments that were medically unnecessary and, in most instances, not provided. They conspired to pay kickbacks to induce Medicare beneficiaries to provide their Medicare numbers and their signatures, which the clinic used to submit fraudulent claims to Medicare for injection and infusion services. Two other codefendants pleaded guilty to the conspiracy charge and were sentenced to prison terms of eighty-four months and thirty-three months, respectively. The court also ordered the four defendants to pay a total of $2.7 million in restitution.

---

fraud, advance fee fraud, electronic funds transfers and money laundering. In 2001, President George W. Bush signed the USA PATRIOT Act and the Secret Service was mandated to establish a nationwide network of Electronic Crimes Task Forces to handle *identity crimes*: the misuse of personal or financial identifiers in order to gain something of value and/or facilitate other criminal activity. The Secret Service is the primary federal agency tasked with investigating identity theft/fraud.

The Secret Service is also the primary federal agency tasked with investigating access device fraud and its related activities. This includes debit cards, automated teller machine (ATM) cards, computer passwords, personal identification numbers, credit card or debit card account numbers, long-distance access codes, and the Subscriber Identity Module (SIM) contained within cellular telephones that assign billing.

The Secret Service investigates computer crimes including unauthorized access to protected computers, theft of data such as personal identification used to commit identity theft, denial of service attacks used for extortion or disruption of ecommerce, and malware (malicious software) distribution of viruses intended for financial gain.

Postal Inspection Service

The Postal Inspection Service, with about 1,400 criminal investigators, is responsible for protecting the integrity and security of U.S. mail and postal facilities. Postal inspectors investigate the use of the mail to conduct fraud, the mailing of contraband, such as drugs, child pornography, and hazardous materials such as mail bombs and biological and chemical weapons.

Department of Health and Human Services Office of Inspector General (HHSOIG)

HHSOIG is the largest inspector general's office in the federal government, with more than 1,700 employees dedicated to combating fraud, waste, and abuse and to improving the efficiency of HHS programs. A majority of the OIG's resources goes toward the oversight of Medicare and Medicaid. The Office of Investigations (OI) conducts criminal, civil, and administrative investigations of fraud and misconduct related to HHS programs, operations and beneficiaries. In cooperation with the FBI, OI responds to the threat posed by international organized crime groups targeting Medicare and Medicaid.

The Health Insurance Portability and Accountability Act of 1996 established a national Health Care Fraud and Abuse Control Program under the joint direction of the Attorney General and the Secretary of the Department of Health and Human Services acting through the Inspector General, designed to coordinate federal, state, and local law enforcement activities with respect to health care fraud and abuse.

Department of Defense (DOD)

The primary role of the Department of Defense is obviously to protect the security of the United States from hostile military activities of foreign powers. Prior to U.S. military involvement in Afghanistan and Iraq, the DOD had been drawn into the fight against drug trafficking, and this role is quite controversial. In the wake of the Reconstruction era, when the Union Army occupied the states of the Confederacy, Congress enacted the 1878 Posse Comitatus Act prohibiting the U.S. Army from performing civilian law enforcement. In 1956, Congress added the Air Force to the Posse Comitatus Act, while the Navy and Marines promulgated administrative restrictions.

The prohibition on military involvement in domestic law enforcement, particularly drug enforcement, is based on fear that DOD involvement could:

- compromise American security by exposing military personnel to the potentially corrupting environment of drug trafficking
- impair the strategic role of the military
- present a threat to civil liberties: "The very nature of military training precludes any considerations of due process or civil rights" (Marsh 1991: 63)

Until 1981, the DOD limited its involvement in law enforcement to lending equipment and training civilian enforcement personnel in its use. In that year, as part of a new "War on Drugs," Congress amended the Posse Comitatus Act, authorizing a greater level of military involvement in civilian drug enforcement, particularly the tracking of suspect ships and planes and the use of military pilots and naval ships to transport civilian enforcement personnel. As a result of this legislation, the DOD provides surveillance and support services, using aircraft to search for smugglers and U.S. Navy ships to tow or escort vessels seized by the Coast Guard to the nearest U.S. port. The 1981 legislation authorized the military services to share information collected during routine military operations with law enforcement officials and to make facilities and equipment available to law enforcement agencies.

Further amendments to the 1981 legislation led to the use of military equipment and personnel in interdiction efforts against cocaine laboratories in Bolivia. These amendments permit the use of such personnel and equipment if the secretary of state or the secretary of defense and the attorney general jointly determine that emergency circumstances exist—the scope of specific criminal activity poses a serious threat to the interests of the United States. Combined operations involving U.S. Army Special Forces, DEA agents, U.S. Border Patrol officers, and Bolivian police and military officers were successful in destroying hundreds of coca-paste laboratories in the coca-growing Champare region. The U.S. Department of State uses former military pilots to fly helicopter gunships, transport planes, and cropdusters used by U.S. and foreign drug agents in countries where U.S. military operations are barred.

Until 1988, the Customs Service and the Coast Guard, with the DOD using radar to help detect smugglers, coordinated federal efforts against airborne drug smuggling. The following year, Congress designated the DOD as the lead agency in these efforts, but a report by the General Accounting Office stated that the equipment used was costly, operated poorly in bad weather, and required frequent maintenance. Furthermore, airborne smugglers responded to the DOD activities by switching airports and finding other ways of entering the country (Berke 1989). In 1999, the United States negotiated a ten-year agreement with Ecuador to allow the basing of Air Force radar surveillance aircraft in Manta to monitor Colombian drug shipments on the Pacific Ocean. In response, the traffickers started to rely less on speedboats and instead began using low-tech submarines built for $1 million in Colombia's jungles. In 2008, Ecuador's president, whose father had been imprisoned in the United States for smuggling, demanded a closing of the base (Romero 2008b).

DOD support roles include air and ground observation and reconnaissance, environmental assessments, intelligence analysts and linguists, transportation, and engineering support. Mobile training teams teach civilian law enforcers such skills as combat lifesaving, advanced marksmanship, and tactical police operations that can be used in counterdrug operations.

Using night-vision gear and thermal-imaging equipment, U.S. service members operate observation posts and patrol the rugged terrain along the two-thousand-mile border between the United States and Mexico. Their job is to watch and listen; if they spot suspicious activity, they radio for the Border Patrol or local law enforcement. Since November 1989, U.S. forces have helped law enforcement agencies in their counterdrug activities in Texas, New Mexico, Arizona, and California, an area covering about 580,000 square miles. By the end of 1995, the mission expanded to provide support throughout the continental United States, Puerto Rico, and the U.S. Virgin Islands (American Armed Forces Information Service information).

United States military officials have traditionally opposed involvement of the armed forces in law enforcement: It is viewed as inappropriate because the goal of military operations is to kill and destroy and civilian casualties ("collateral damage") are often a by-product of military operations. A law enforcement role for the military could potentially undermine its primary mission. Other fears include a threat to civil liberties and the potentially corrupting influence of drug traffickers on the military.

INTERPOL

The International Police Organization, known by its radio designation INTERPOL, assists law enforcement agencies with investigative activities that transcend national boundaries. Founded in 1923 through the efforts of the police chief of Vienna, the organization became dormant during World War II, but was reorganized at a conference in Brussels in 1946. A stormy relationship existed between the director of the FBI and leaders of

INTERPOL, and in 1950 the FBI withdrew from participation. The Treasury Department, anxious to maintain international contacts to help with its drug enforcement responsibilities, continued an informal liaison with INTERPOL.

Until 1968, "INTERPOL meant very little to the United States law enforcement community and was virtually unknown" (Fooner 1985: 19). In that year, Iran announced that it was going to end its ban on opium production. At the same time, there appeared to be an epidemic of drug use in the United States. A U.S. National Central Bureau (NCB) with a connection to INTERPOL was quickly activated in Washington, and by 1970 the NCB was handling about three hundred cases a year. In the mid-1970s, a turf battle ensued between the Treasury Department and the Justice Department: The attorney general, after decades of neglect, decided he wanted the United States to be part of INTERPOL, but the Treasury Department resisted. An agreement—memorandum of understanding—was effected between the two departments in 1977: they would share the responsibility of representing the United States to INTERPOL and operating the NCB. The NCB is now comanaged by the U.S. Department of Justice and the U.S. Department of Homeland Security, and staffed with sworn law enforcement personnel detailed from federal, state, and local law enforcement agencies who work side by side with full-time justice department employees serving as analysts, translators, technicians, and administrators.

There are 188 INTERPOL members. To become a member, a country announces its intention to join. In each country, there is an NCB that acts as a point of contact and coordination with the General Secretariat in Lyon, France. The president of INTERPOL is chosen for a four-year term at its General Assembly, although the organization is under the day-to-day direction of a secretary general. The General Assembly, INTERPOL's supreme governing body, meets once a year to make major decisions affecting general policy. It is composed of delegates appointed by the governments of member countries. Each member country represented has one vote, and all votes have equal standing.

INTERPOL is a coordinating body. It has no investigators or law enforcement agents of its own. The General Secretariat has a staff of about 650 people, 200 of who are law enforcement personnel on loan from member nations. At headquarters are databases containing records of people linked to international crime (Imhoff and Cutler 1998). The number of messages exchanged through the INTERPOL global police communication exceeded three million for the first time in 2003. In that year, INTERPOL began its high-security Internet-based communications infra-structure known as I-24/7. The system provides for swift and efficient cooperation to combat all forms of serious international crime. INTERPOL's communication system links the General Secretariat, National Central Bureaus, and police officials in member countries so that they can send and receive police information, including images, throughout the world on a secure, real-time basis, 24/7. I-24/7 also provides access to INTERPOL's secure web pages that enable the organization to share crime-related information more easily. The system gives immediate interactive access to crime data held at the General Secretariat. This means that real-time checks can be made of any suspect's fingerprints, passports, or vehicles, anywhere in the world, by any police force linked to the system (*INTERPOL at Work* 2003).

INTERPOL acts as a central repository for professional and technical expertise on transnational organized crime and as a clearinghouse for the collection, collation, analysis, and dissemination of information relating to organized crime and criminal organizations. It also monitors the organized crime situation on a global basis and coordinates international investigations.

Requests for assistance from federal, state, and local law enforcement are checked and coded by technical staff and entered into the INTERPOL Case Tracking System (ICTS), a computer-controlled index of persons, organizations, and other crime information items. The ICTS conducts automatic searches of new entries, retrieving those that correlate with international crime. The requests are forwarded to senior staff members who serve as INTERPOL case investigators, usually veteran agents from a national agency whose experience includes work with foreign police forces. Each investigator is on loan from his or her principal agency, and each state, the District of Columbia, Puerto Rico, territories, and New York City, has a designated liaison office through which state and local agencies can connect to NCBs throughout the world (Imhoff and Cutler 1998).

Requests for investigative assistance range "from murder, robbery, narcotics violations, illicit firearms traffic, and large frauds, to counterfeiting, stolen works of art, bank swindles, and locating fugitives for arrest and extradition. The bureau also receives investigative requests for criminal histories, license checks, and other ID verifications. Sometimes locations of persons lost or missing in a foreign country are also requested" (Fooner 1985: 6). The Financial and Economic Crime Unit at INTERPOL headquarters facilitates exchange of information stemming from credit card fraud, airline ticket counterfeiting, computer crime, offshore banking, commodity futures, and money laundering schemes. The monitoring of this activity can sometimes lead to the identification of suspects involved in drug trafficking or other types of organized crime who had previously escaped detection.

INVESTIGATIVE TOOLS IN ORGANIZED CRIME LAW ENFORCEMENT

Enforcing the law against organized criminal activity requires highly trained agents and prosecutors using sophisticated investigative and enforcement tools. In this section we will examine these tools—their advantages, disadvantages, and limitations.

Intelligence

The collection of information about organized crime, its evaluation, collation, analysis, reporting, and dissemination, is referred to as "intelligence" (Dintino and Martens 1983). The *American Heritage Dictionary* (2000) defines *intelligence* as the work of gathering secret information about an actual or potential enemy. "In the purest sense, intelligence is the product of an analytic process that evaluates information collected from diverse sources, integrates the relevant information into a cohesive package, and produces a conclusion or estimate about a criminal phenomenon by using the scientific approach to problem solving (i.e., analysis)" (D. Carter 2004: 7). *Raw intelligence* is information that has been obtained from generally reliable sources, although not necessarily corroborated. It is deemed valid not only because of the sources but also because it coincides with other known information. *Finished intelligence* is when raw information is fully analyzed, corroborated, and made into a report—the product of an intelligence unit (Carter 2005).

Intelligence analysis is laborious and usually unexciting work that requires a great deal of expertise. Justin Dintino and Frederick Martens (1983: 9) conceive of intelligence as "(1) a process through which information is managed which (2) will hopefully increase our knowledge of a particular problem (3) resulting in preventive and/or informed public policy."

Drexel Godfrey and Don Harris (1971) refer to analysis as the "heart" of the intelligence system. An analyst uses the methods of social science research, and central to this approach is the hypothesis. The analyst develops a hypothesis, an "educated guess," about the relevance of the information that has already been collected, collated, and stored. The investigators are then told to seek data that will permit "hypothesis testing." If the hypothesis does not withstand an adequate test, alternative hypotheses must be developed and tested. A hypothesis that has been supported by the data after rigorous testing becomes the basis for an intelligence report. The report guides tactical and/or strategic law enforcement efforts.

Intelligence data are collected for two main purposes—tactical and strategic. At times, these two categories overlap (Godfrey and Harris 1971).

- *Tactical intelligence* is information that contributes directly to the achievement of an immediate law enforcement objective, such as arrest and prosecution.

- *Strategic intelligence* is information that contributes to producing sound judgment with respect to long-range law enforcement objectives and goals. The information is collected over time and put together by an intelligence analyst to reveal new (or newly discovered) patterns of organized crime activity. The information may be unsubstantiated ("raw") data requiring further investigation for confirmation—to become "hard" data.

Robert Stewart (1980: 54) notes the common sources of intelligence data:

- court records
- other public agency documents such as real estate, tax, and incorporation records
- business records
- investigative and intelligence files of other law enforcement agencies
- newspapers, periodicals, books
- utility company records
- documents and items recovered during searches or subpoenaed by the grand jury, administrative agencies, and legislative committees
- electronic surveillance
- information and material produced voluntarily by citizens
- statements and/or testimony obtained from accomplices, informants, victims, and law enforcement personnel

This material can be collected overtly or covertly. Covert collection involves the accumulation of information from subjects who are unaware they are being observed or overheard. Since this type of collection is usually expensive in terms of the personnel required, it is usually tied directly to the goal of securing evidence that can be used in prosecution; that is, it is more tactical than strategic.

Intelligence gathering lacks many of the exciting aspects of law enforcement—there are no television series based on the adventures of intelligence analysts. The results produced by strategic intelligence are never immediate and seldom dramatic.

CAREER PATHS FOR FBI INTELLIGENCE ANALYSTS

Since 9/11, the FBI has worked to establish career paths for intelligence analysts and senior positions to which they can be promoted. After an intensive ten-week basic training course, intelligence analysts (IAs) specialize in one of three analytic areas—tactical, strategic, or collection/reporting. They may work at FBI Headquarters, in one of fifty-six field offices, or internationally in one of the legal attaché offices. As they gain experience and subject matter expertise, IAs can move up the career ladder to intermediate and advanced positions such as supervisory intelligence analysts and senior intelligence officers.

They fail to impress those who allocate funds for law enforcement agencies, and intelligence personnel often have little status in agencies such as the DEA. There have been abuses as well: "A basic principle in collecting information for a criminal intelligence file is that such information should be restricted to what an agency needs to know in order to fulfill its responsibility to detect and combat organized crime in its jurisdiction." Therefore, "the ethnic origin or the political or religious beliefs of any individual, group, or organization should never be the reason for collecting information on them. Criminal activities or associations must be the key factors. If associations are found not to be criminal in nature, the data collected on them should be dropped from the files" (Task Force on Organized Crime 1976: 122).

For several decades this was not the practice. In many urban police departments and the FBI, extensive intelligence efforts were directed against political groups and personalities. In Los Angeles, this type of activity was accomplished under the cover of the Organized Crime Intelligence Division, which "maintained secret Stalinesque dossiers, some of them kept in privately rented units; there were files on virtually every mover and shaker in Southern California" (Rothmiller and Goldman 1992: 9). "Red squads" and similar units would sometimes "leak" raw data whose source was untrustworthy. However, when such data move through a respected law enforcement agency, there is a "cleansing" effect, and the now "laundered" information takes on new importance, particularly when reported by the news media. Law enforcement intelligence files frequently contain news clips whose source is the agency itself—known as "circular sourcing."

During the late 1960s and early 1970s, lawsuits were brought against law enforcement intelligence units who were maintaining files on people absent evidence of criminality. As a result, the courts ordered intelligence files to be purged from police records, and in many cases police agencies had to pay damage awards. Restrictions on what information may be kept in intelligence files and "Freedom of Information" statutes have resulted to correct such abuses (Carter 2005).

Regional Information Sharing System (RISS)

Established in 1974 and supported by the U.S. Department of Justice, RISS consists of six regional centers and a technology support center that provide locally-based services to law enforcement and criminal justice agencies in all fifty states, the District of Columbia, U.S. territories, Australia, Canada, England, and New Zealand. The goal is to enhance the ability of criminal justice agencies to identify, target, and remove criminal conspiracies and activities that span jurisdictional boundaries. While each regional center decides on a choice of multi-jurisdictional crimes to target, for example, gangs, terrorism, drug trafficking, cybercrime, human trafficking, and identity theft, all six target organized crime. Intelligence and analytical personnel, field representatives, and technical systems personnel with law enforcement backgrounds staff the regional centers. They provide controlled input and dissemination, rapid retrieval, and systematic updating of criminal justice information, as well as data analysis.

RISS links thousands of criminal justice agencies through secure communications and provides member agencies with an information-sharing, analysis, and communications network to support investigative and prosecutorial efforts that address multi-jurisdictional offenses and conspiracies The website of each regional center provides region-specific information and offers users easy access to criminal intelligence databases. Centers also provide training and the loan of specialized equipment.

By facilitating the communications and collaboration process, law enforcement personnel can exchange information on similar investigations and work together to solve cases. Member agencies are able to submit large volumes of data for inclusion in the databases. Often, agencies have a need to maintain their own intelligence database but wish to share that information with RISS-affiliated agencies and thereby discover mutual investigative interests.

While RISS is federally funded, it is locally managed. The executive director and policy board chairperson of each of the six regional centers compose the RISS Directors National Policy Group, which has direct control over policies and operations.

Electronic Surveillance

Law enforcement officials believe that evidence necessary to bring criminals from the higher echelons of organized crime to justice will not be obtained without the aid of electronic surveillance. The Task Force on Organized Crime (1976: 148) points out that "because of their organization and methods of organization, organized criminal activities require sophisticated means of evidence gathering. Often witnesses will not come forward, and members are bound by either an oath of silence or threats of violence. Often the use of informants is of limited value, and many organizations are difficult, if not impossible, for undercover agents to penetrate to the point where they can obtain useful evidence." One way to break through these conspiratorial

safeguards is through the use of electronic surveillance that includes:

- *Telephone tap*: An extension hooked into a line at a telephone switching station.

- *Transmitter*: A minute microphone that can be turned on and off from a remote location using a microwave signal.

- *Telephone transmitter*: A microphone wired inside a telephone, from which it draws its power. Some devices are activated by an outside telephone call and can transmit voices as well as telephone conversations.

- *Laser interceptors*: These devices can be pointed at a window to record vibrations on the glass caused by indoor conversations. A computer converts the vibrations into conversations.

- *Satellite relays*: Microphones transmit by way of a space satellite to a ground receiver.

- *Fiber optics*: Microsized fiber optic filaments embedded into walls draw power from a building's electrical system and can be used to intercept conversations.

Electronic surveillance has been complicated by technological advances in communications. Conversations via high-capacity digital lines (human voices translated into numbers) and fiber optic lines (using pulses of light), for example, cannot be intercepted using conventional wiretap equipment. Advances in encryption technology allow for communication virtually impossible for eavesdroppers to decipher; they would need access to the code (or an impossible expenditure of time—years). Inexpensive computer programs and hardware can now scramble telephone calls and computer email.

Additional methods for avoiding electronic surveillance have grown in sophistication, such as the use of anonymous remailers. Messages sent over the Internet are received by the remailer, which automatically strips off all traces of the sender's identity and forwards the message to an electronic mailbox (or to other remailers to further bury the identity of the source). Because messages are remailed in random sequence different from the order in which they arrive, anyone monitoring the remailer cannot

---

TYPO TECHNOLOGY

In 1999, federal agents seized a computer from Nicodemo S. Scarfo, Jr., son of the imprisoned Philadelphia crime boss, who was running a $5 million-a-year bookmaking operation under auspices of the Gambino Family in the Newark, New Jersey, area. However, they were unable to access information because it was stored in an encrypted file. The agents subsequently requested another search warrant (but not a Title IIII wiretap order) to break in and install a "key logger" or "keystroke recorder," a device the size of a sugar cube that conveys the keys pressed on a computer keyboard to a remote location. This device, which heretofore had been used only in national security cases, enabled the FBI to figure out the password and, thereby, decrypt Scarfo's files, which contained records of gambling and loansharking operations (Anastasia 2002; Salkowski 2001; Schwartz 2001). In 2001, after courts ruled against suppressing the computer evidence, Scarfo pled guilty to bookmaking.

---

match outgoing messages with incoming messages to identify who sent which message (Lohr 1999).

Grand Jury

In the federal system, a grand jury is a body of twenty-three citizens empowered to operate with a quorum of sixteen and requiring twelve votes for an indictment. In the state system, the minimum number of jurors varies considerably, although nowhere does the maximum number of grand jurors exceed twenty-three. While some states adhere to the federal rule of twelve for an indictment, in others the range is anywhere from four to nine. Like those serving on a petit or trial jury, grand jurors are selected from the voting rolls; however, they meet in secret to consider evidence presented by the prosecutor.

Because members of a grand jury are not agents of the government—they act as direct representatives of the citizenry—the extensive due process rights typically enjoyed by a criminal defendant are not necessarily relevant to grand jury proceedings. Their activities are secret, and only sixteen states permit the subject of a grand jury inquiry to have an attorney present, and then only to give advice. In the remaining states and the federal system, an attorney is not even permitted to accompany his or her client at a grand jury hearing. There is no right to present evidence or to cross-examine adverse witnesses. While the subject can refuse to answer any questions whose answers may be incriminating, he or she can be granted immunity and required to testify under the threat of being jailed for contempt.

The grand jury can receive virtually any type of information, even that which would not be admissible at a trial, such as certain types of hearsay and evidence that was secured in violation of the Fourth Amendment—the exclusionary rule does not apply to the grand jury (*United States v. Calandra*, 414 U.S. 338, 1974). In every state and the federal system, the grand jury may be utilized for investigative purposes, and when so used has broad investigative authority, including the power to subpoena persons and documents. In those states where statutes permit and in the federal system, the grand jury is used to investigate the operations of law enforcement and other government agencies, particularly when corruption is suspected, and to investigate the activities of organized crime.

The Organized Crime Control Act of 1970 requires that a special grand jury be convened at least every eighteen months in federal judicial districts of more than one million persons. It can also be convened at the request of a federal prosecutor. Its typical life, eighteen months, may be extended to thirty-six months. The special grand jury and grand juries of several states have the power to publish reports at the completion of their terms on misconduct by public officials. While such reports cannot command any particular action, the widespread publicity they typically enjoy usually encourages action by government officials.

According to Robert Stewart (1980: 124), the investigative grand jury is the single most useful tool by which to attack the traditional forms of organized crime:

> For example, convicted drug pushers, bookmakers, numbers writers and runners, prostitutes, weapons offenders and petty thieves can be summoned before the grand jury, immunized and questioned about the higher-ups in a particular enterprise or activity. If the witness is not already under charges, there is little likelihood that the grant of immunity will jeopardize any prosecution. If the witness testifies truthfully, that witness will be ostracized from the criminal community and thereby neutralized as an organized crime operative. Moreover, the defection of one member of an organization may serve as a catalyst forcing others within the organization to defect and cooperate with the state. Whenever any appreciable number of lower-level offenders are summoned before an investigative grand jury, the higher-ups in the organized crime structure can never be sure what, if anything, is being said. This alone is sufficient to generate severe tensions within the organized crime structure. The grand jury can also request a grant of immunity for witnesses who refuse to testify on Fifth Amendment grounds.

Immunity

The Fifth Amendment to the U.S. Constitution provides that no person "shall be compelled in any criminal case to be a witness against himself." This is an important protection for the individual against the coercive powers of the state, and it can be partially neutralized by a grant of immunity. There are two types of immunity:

1. *Transactional immunity* provides blanket protection against prosecution for crimes about which a person is compelled to testify.
2. *Use immunity* prohibits the information provided by a person from being used against him or her, but the person can still be prosecuted using evidence obtained independently of his or her compelled testimony.

In many states and the federal system, the court or the prosecutor may grant immunity to reluctant witnesses. Legislative or administrative bodies investigating criminal activity can also request a grant of immunity. A witness who, after being granted immunity, refuses to testify can be subjected to civil or criminal contempt.

> The *civil contempt* proceeding is summary in nature and relatively simple. First the witness is immunized. Upon refusing to answer in the grand jury [or other authorized body] the witness appears before the court. The prosecutor makes an oral application and the court instructs the witness to testify. The witness returns to the grand jury room; and, if recalcitrant, is directed to reappear before the court. The prosecutor then makes an oral application for the court to enforce its previous order, which the witness has disobeyed. The prosecutor explains what has occurred before the grand jury, and the foreperson or reporter testifies about these facts. The witness is given an opportunity to be heard; and thereafter the court decides whether the witness is in contempt and should be remanded.... The remand order normally specifies that the witness shall remain confined until he offers to purge himself of the contempt by agreeing to testify or for the life of the grand jury, whichever is shorter. (Stewart 1980: 239–240)

The term of a grand jury is usually eighteen months. Legislative committees and administrative bodies have indefinite terms. In 1970, as a result of his refusal to testify before a New Jersey investigating committee after being immunized, Jerry Catena (then acting boss of the Genovese Family) was imprisoned for contempt and remained imprisoned for five years, never testifying.

The *criminal contempt* proceeding is quite different, since it requires a formal trial, and the witness is entitled to the full array of due process rights enjoyed by any criminal defendant. Being found guilty of criminal contempt, however, can result in a substantial sentence of imprisonment: "The purpose of the remand is coercive [to compel testimony], while the purpose of the criminal contempt sentence is punitive and deterrent" (Stewart 1980: 246). Of course, a witness, whether immunized or not, is subject to the laws against perjury.

In 1972, the Supreme Court decided the case of *Kastigar v. United States* (406 U.S. 441), which involved several persons who in 1971 had been subpoenaed to appear before a federal grand jury in California. The assistant U.S. attorney, believing that the petitioners in *Kastigar* were likely to assert their Fifth Amendment privilege, secured from the federal district court an order directing them to answer all questions and produce evidence before the grand jury under a grant of immunity. Nevertheless, the persons involved refused to answer questions, arguing that the "scope of the immunity provided by the statute was not coextensive with the scope of the privilege against self-incrimination, and therefore was not sufficient to supplant the privilege and compel their testimony."

The Supreme Court, in upholding the immunity order, quoted from the federal immunity statute: "The witness may not refuse to comply with the order on the basis of his privilege against self-incrimination; but no testimony or other information compelled under the order (or any information directly or indirectly derived from such testimony or other information) may be used against the witness in any criminal case, except a prosecution for perjury, giving a false statement, or otherwise failing to comply with the order." The Court concluded that since the statute prohibited the prosecutorial authorities from using the compelled testimony in any respect,

it therefore ensured that the testimony could not lead to the infliction of criminal penalties on the witness. In a dissenting opinion, Justice Thurgood Marshall pointed to the possibility of using the testimonial information for investigative leads designed to secure evidence against the witness. The Court majority agreed that the statute barred such use of the testimony.

Civil action against a criminally immunized witness is possible, and a grant of immunity does not protect the witness from a loss of social status, employment, and, most important, revenge from those against whom he or she is forced to testify. Rufus King (1963: 651) raises additional issues:

> The immunity bargain is a somewhat unsavory device per se, inaccurate and potentially very unfair; it should be used only sparingly and where it is absolutely required. Immunity grants are always exchanges, a pardon for crimes that would otherwise be punishable, given in return for testimony that could otherwise be withheld. In every case the interrogating authority must enter into a special "deal" with a wrongdoer to buy his testimony at the price of exoneration for something [for which] he would otherwise deserve punishment.
>
> Such bargains are always somewhat blind. Ordinarily the witness will be hostile, so that his examiners cannot be sure in advance exactly what value the withheld testimony will have. And at the same time, especially in broad legislative or administrative inquiries, it is impossible to tell beforehand just what crimes are likely to be exonerated. Conceivably, the witness may have a surprise ready for his questioners at every turn of the proceedings.

Because of the potentially undesirable repercussions, some prosecutors have developed guidelines for consideration when making an immunity decision. The following guidelines are from the New Jersey Division of Criminal Justice (quoted in Committee on the Office of Attorney General 1978: 27):

- Can the information be obtained from any source other than a witness who wants to negotiate immunity?
- How useful is the information for the purposes of criminal prosecution?
- What is the likelihood that the witness can successfully be prosecuted?
- What is the relative significance of the witness as a potential defendant?
- What is the relative significance of the potential defendant against whom the witness offers to testify? In other words, is the witness requesting immunity more culpable than those against whom she or he is agreeing to testify? Are they in a position to provide evidence against the witness or superior evidence against others?

- What is the value of the testimony of the witness to the case (is it the core evidence upon which the prosecution is based)?
- What impact will immunity have on the credibility of the witness at trial? Are the terms of the immunity agreement so favorable to the witness that the jury will not accept the testimony?
- What impact will immunity have on the prosecutor's personal credibility and that of his or her office?

Robert Rhodes notes, however, "that a grant of immunity has a favorable impact on a jury. It makes a defendant's testimony more credible. A prosecutor can point to the witness with a sordid record and say to the jury, 'What reason does Mr. X have to lie? His immunity is assured and if he lies he will be prosecuted for perjury!'" (1984: 193).

SUMMARY

1. Know the restraints on organized crime law enforcement:
   - Law enforcement in the United States operates under significant constitutional restraints. Important protections against government, while they protect individual liberty, also benefit the criminal population.
   - Electronic surveillance is quite expensive in terms of personnel hours expended.

2. Understand problems inherent in covert operations and the use of informants in organized crime law enforcement:
   - In order to seek out criminal activity in the most efficient manner possible, proactive law enforcement officers must conceal their identities and otherwise deceive the criminals they are stalking.
   - The more involved is the criminal informant in criminal activity, the more useful is his or her assistance.
   - Working closely with informants is a potentially corrupting influence.

3. Know the role of federal agencies in organized crime law enforcement:
   - Federal agencies with responsibility for organized crime are found primarily in the Department of Justice, but also the Department of the Treasury, Department of Homeland Security, and the Department of Labor.
   - The FBI is the major law enforcement agency combating organized criminal activity and the lead agency in using the RICO statute.
   - Since 9/11, there is concern that the increased focus on terrorism could detract from FBI efforts to respond to organized crime and there has been a dramatic decrease in the number of agents dedicated to organized crime.
   - In 1930, Congress established the Federal Bureau of Narcotics as a separate agency within the Department of the Treasury.
   - The Witness Security Program was given over to the U.S. Marshals Service to

administer in order to enhance the value of witness testimony.

- The Bureau of Alcohol, Tobacco, Firearms and Explosives (ATF) regulates the firearms and explosives industries and investigates cases of arson and bombings not related to terrorism.
- ATF ensures that federal taxes are paid on alcoholic beverages and tobacco products, and combats cigarette smuggling from low-tax states to high-tax states.
- Tax evasion schemes are countered by the indirect method known as the *net worth theory*.
- Customs Service and Border Protection agents do not need probable cause or warrants to engage in search and seizure at ports of entry.
- Immigration and Customs Enforcement is responsible for investigating the illegal movement of people and goods into and out of the United States.
- The Coast Guard is responsible for contraband interdiction on the seas. Agents do not have to establish probable cause prior to boarding a vessel.
- The primary investigative mission of the Secret Service is to safeguard the payment and financial systems of the United States. The agency also handles identity crimes.

4. Understand the controversial role of the military in law enforcement:
   - The Posse Comitatus Act prohibits military personnel from making arrests of civilians.
   - The DOD shares information collected during routine military operations with law enforcement officials and makes facilities and equipment available to law enforcement agencies.

5. Know the techniques used in organized crime law enforcement:
   - INTERPOL is a coordinating body linking law enforcement officials in member countries.
   - Intelligence is the product of an analytic process that evaluates information collected from diverse sources.
   - The extensive due process rights typically enjoyed by a criminal defendant are not necessarily relevant to grand jury proceedings.
   - A grant of immunity provides protection against prosecution for crimes about which a person is compelled to testify.

REVIEW QUESTIONS

1. Why is electronic surveillance expensive in terms of personnel hours expended?

2. How do jurisdictional limitations hamper law enforcement efforts against organized crime?

3. Why is proactive law enforcement susceptible to corruption?

4. Why is working closely with criminal informants a potentially corrupting influence?

5. Why has there been a dramatic decrease in the number of FBI agents assigned to deal with organized crime?

6. Why was the Federal Bureau of Narcotics placed in the Treasury Department?

7. What are the primary responsibilities of the Drug Enforcement Administration?

8. What are the responsibilities of the Bureau of Alcohol, Tobacco, Firearms and Explosives?

9. Why was responsibility for the Witness Security Program given to the U.S. Marshals Service instead of the FBI?

10. What is the *net worth theory* used by the IRS for investigating tax evasion?

11. What unusual powers are enjoyed by Customs Service and Border Protection agents?

12. What are the responsibilities of Immigration and Customs Enforcement?

13. What are the responsibilities and special powers of the Coast Guard?

14. Why is the use of military personnel to fight drug trafficking controversial?

15. What is the role of INTERPOL?

16. How does tactical intelligence differ from strategic intelligence?

17. What are the advantages of using the grand jury to investigate organized crime?

18. Why aren't the extensive due process rights of a criminal defendant relevant to grand jury proceedings?

19. What are the advantages and disadvantages of using immunity in organized crime cases?

Conclusion

Organized crime in America can be understood as one stage along a continuum. Our colonial forebears exhibited many of the activities currently associated with organized crime: bribery, usury, and monopoly, not to mention seizure of land by force, indentured servitude, and slavery. Early American adventurers cheated and killed Native Americans, and chartered pirates—privateers—plundered the high seas. During the War of 1812, and later during the Civil War, profiteers accumulated fortunes while the less fortunate suffered and died. The range wars in the West and the frauds, bribery, violence, and monopolistic practices of the "Robber Barons" are part of the context with which we must understand modern forms of organized crime. The cost of organized crime must be measured against the cost of corporate crime, which has the potential to harm far more persons, both financially and physically.

Organized crime has provided economic opportunity for certain groups, allowing them to move into legitimate society on a level that otherwise would not be readily available. There are, of course, ethical and moral objections to "blasting" or "thieving" into the middle or upper strata, even though this has been a feature of U.S. history from the earliest days.

Very few management-level members of organized crime have been able to escape either assassination or significant prison terms. Indeed, law enforcement efforts against organized crime are impressive, retrained as they are by the requirements of a democratic system that provides a great deal of legal protection to even its criminal citizens.

Organized crime evolved out of moralistic laws that created opportunity for certain innovative actors. As circumstances changed, so did available opportunity, and organized crime exhibited great flexibility. Beginning as essentially a provider of "goods and services," it entered racketeering and legitimate business, adapting to changing laws and social and economic conditions. Economic globalization provides unparalleled opportunity, legitimate and criminal, and the line between them is not necessarily apparent. Globalization has promoted cooperative efforts between criminal organizations, based primarily on pecuniary interests but, at times, extends to criminal organizations with a political agenda—terrorism.

We can expect that in the Darwinian world of organized crime, weaker components will die either literally or figuratively, while the survivors will improve on their style of organization and the sophistication of their operations. Impacting on this process will be government, helping to "trim the herd" while occasionally dealing shattering blows to criminal organizations. We can expect that the American Mafia will continue limping along, while others, such as Russian organized crime, will become more structured—and more threatening. Organized crime differs in many significant ways from the nonorganized variety: Organization permits a scope of activities unavailable to conventional criminals, while providing a vehicle for criminal interaction and coordination on a regional, national, and international level. For these reasons, organized crime, like threatening diseases, will always be part of the global community, requiring vigilance and international cooperation to limit its destructive potential.

References

Abadinsky, Howard

2011 *Drug Abuse: An Introduction*, 5th ed. Belmont, CA: Wadsworth.

1987 "The McDonald's-ization of the Mafia." Pages 43–54 in *Organized Crime in America Concepts and Controversies*, edited by Timothy S. Bynum. Monsey, NY: Criminal Justice Press.

1983 *The Criminal Elite: Professional and Organized Crime*. Westport, CT: Greenwood.

1981a *The Mafia in America: An Oral History*. New York: Praeger.

1981b *Organized Crime*. Boston: Allyn and Bacon.

"Abortion Harassers as Racketeers"

1998 *New York Times* (April 23): 20.

Abrahamson, Mark

1996 *Urban Enclaves: Identity and Place in America*. New York: St. Martin's Press.

Ackerman, Kenneth D.

1988 *The Gold Ring: Jim Fisk, Jay Gould, and Black Friday, 1869*. New York: Harper & Row.

Adelstein, Jake

2011 "Ties to Yakuza Are No Laughing Matter." *The Atlantic Wire* (August 26): Internet.

2009 *Tokyo Vice*. New York: Vintage Books.

Agence France-Press

1997 "Japan Fears Reprisals After Mob Boss Is Slain." *New York Times* (August 29): 5.

Ahmed-Ullah, Noreen S.

2001 "Pashtun Identity Defies Colonial Line." *Chicago Tribune* (November 6): 15.

Aichhorn, August

1963 *Wayward Youth*. New York: Viking Press.

Albanese, Jay

2011 *Transnational Crime and the 21st Century*. New York: Oxford University Press.

Albini, Joseph L.

1971 *The American Mafia: Genesis of a Legend*. New York: Appleton-Century-Crofts.

Albini, Joseph L., R. E. Rogers, Victor Shabalin, Valery Kutushev, and Vladmir Moiseev

1995 "Russian Organized Crime: Its History, Structure and Function." *Journal of Contemporary Criminal Justice* 11 (December): 213–43.

Alexander, Herbert E. and Gerald E. Caiden

1985 *The Politics and Economics of Organized Crime*. Lexington, MA: D. C. Heath.

Alexander, Shana

1988 *The Pizza Connection: Lawyers, Money, Drugs, Mafia*. New York: Weidenfeld and Nicolson.

Ali, Lorraine

2002 "The Tunes You Can't Refuse." *Newsweek* (August 26): 54–55.

Allen, Frederick

1998 "American Spirit." *American Heritage* (May/June): 82–92.

Allsop, Kenneth

1968 *The Bootleggers: The Story of Prohibition*. New Rochelle, NY: Arlington House.

Allum, P. A.

1973 *Politics and Society in Post-War Naples*. Cambridge: Cambridge University Press.

American Heritage Dictionary, 4th ed.

2000 Boston: Houghton Mifflin.

Anastasia, George

2002 "Big Brother and the Bookie." *Mother Jones* (January/
February): 63–67.

1998 *The Goodfella Tapes.* New York: Avon.

1991 *Blood and Honor: Inside the Scarfo Mob—The Mafia's Most
Violent Family.* New York: William Morrow.

Anbinder, Tyler

2001 *Five Points: The 19th-Century Neighborhood That Invented Tap
Dance, Stole Elections, and Became the World's Most Notorious
Slum.* New York: Free Press.

1992 *Nativism and Slavery: The Northern Know-Nothings and the Politics
of the 1850s.* New York: Oxford University Press.

Anderson, Annelise Graebner

1979 *The Business of Organized Crime: A Cosa Nostra Family.*
Stanford, CA: Hoover Institution Press.

Anderson, John Lee

2007 "The Taliban's Opium War." *New Yorker* (July 9 and 16):
60–71.

Anderson, Robert T.

1965 "From Mafia to Cosa Nostra." *American Journal of Sociology* 71
(November): 302–10.

Andrews, Edmund L.

1995 "The Mob's Truly Sorry: Killing Upsets the Police."
New York Times (September 6): 4.

Andrews, Wayne

1941 *The Vanderbilt Legend.* New York: Harcourt, Brace.

"Anti-Drug Efforts Encounter Resistance in Colombia"

1995 *New York Times* (December 12): 4.

Arax, Mark and Tom Gorman

1995 "The State's Illicit Farm Belt Export." *Los Angeles Times*
(March 13): 1, 16, 17.

Archibold, Randal C. and Andrew Becker

2011 "From Mexico Drug War, Massacres, But Claims of
Progress." *New York Times* (February 2): 3.

2011b "Killer, 15, is Sentenced in Drug Case in Mexico."
New York Times (July 27): 4.

2011c "Rights Groups Contend Mexican Military Has
Heavy Hand in Drug Cases." *New York Times*
(August 3): 10.

2008 "Border Agents Lured by the Other Side." *New York Times*
(May 27): 1, 18.

2007 "Along the Border, Smugglers Build a World Below
Ground." *New York Times* (December 7): 18.

2006 "Officials Find Surprise Tunnel with Surprising Amenities."
New York Times (January 27): 14.

2004 "Writing a Field Guide to Dominican New York." *New York
Times* (December 28): B2.

Argentine, Adolfo Beria di

1993 "The Mafias in Italy." Pages 19–30 in *Mafia Issues*, edited by
Ernesto U. Savona. Milan, Italy: United Nations.

Arie, Sophie

2004 "Neapolitans Take Stand Against Mafia Turf War." *Christian
Science Monitor* (December 22): 7.

Arlacchi, Pino

1993 *Men of Dishonor: Inside the Sicilian Mafia.* New York: William
Morrow.

1986 *Mafia Business: The Mafia Ethic and the Spirit of Capitalism.*
London: Verso.

Aronson, Harvey

1978 *Deal.* New York: Ballantine Books.

1973 *The Killing of Joey Gallo.* New York: Putnam's.

Arsovska, Jana and Panos A. Kostakos

2008 "Illicit Arms Trafficking and the Limits of Rational Choice
Theory: The Case of the Balkans." *Trends in Organized Crime*
22 (October): 352-78.

Asbury, Herbert

1950 *The Great Illusion: An Informal History of Prohibition.* Garden
City, NY: Doubleday.

1942 *Gem of the Prairie: An Informal History of the Chicago Underworld.*
Garden City, NY: Knopf.

1928 *Gangs of New York.* New York: Knopf.

Associated Press

2011 "Hoffa Leads in Teamsters' Vote." *New York Times*
(November 21): 16.

2010a "Reports: Fugitive Drug Lord Surrenders in Jamaica." *USA
Today* (June 22): Internet.

2010b "Jamaica: Gunfire, Firebombs in Barricaded Slum." *USA
Today* (May 23): Internet.

2010c "Jamaican Police Battle to Arrest Man Facing Drug
Charges." *New York Times* (May 25): Internet.

2010d "Pope Praises Priest Slain for Battling Mob." *New York Daily
News* (October 4): 4.

2008a "Afghan Tribal Leader Convicted on NY Drug Charges."
USA Today (September 23): Internet.

2008b "Miami Jury Convicts Ex-FBI Agent in 1982 Killing." *USA
Today* (November 7): Internet.

2007 "Feds Seize Candy Bars Filled with 5M in Heroin." *New York
Daily News* (February 24): 10.

2006 "Gift Cards Are Increasingly Used to Launder Money,
Report Says." *New York Times* (January 12): 19.

2005a "Dutch Police Arrest 45 Hell's Angels." *Seattle Post
Intelligencer* (October 12): Internet.

2005b "8 From Marsh Are Indicted in Bidding Case." *New York
Times* (September 16): C5.

2005c "Imprisoned F.B.I. Agent Indicted in Killing of Gambling Executive." *New York Times* (May 5): 32.

2005d "Texas Killings Bring New Fear in Drug War." *New York Times* (February 21): 15.

2004a "'Amphetamine King' Gets 50-Year Sentence." *USA Today* (September 22): Internet.

2004b "Bayer Unit Plea-Bargains in Price Fixing." *New York Times* (October 1): C1.

1998a "Italy Arrests Scores of Mafia Suspects." *New York Times* (June 27): 4.

1998b "12 Convicted in Prison Plot to Control Drug Gangs." *New York Times* (May 31): 8.

1997 "'Wino Willie' Forkner; Inspired 'The Wild One.'" *Chicago Tribune* (June 26): Sec. 2: 10.

1996 "Hell's Angels Center Explodes in Denmark." *New York Times* (October 7): 4.

Attorney General. *See Attorney General's Annual Report to Congress and Assessment of U.S. Government Activities to Combat Trafficking in Persons*

2010 Washington, DC: Office of the U.S. Attorney General.

Attorney General's Commission on Pornography

1986 *Final Report*. Washington, DC: U.S. Government Printing Office.

Audett, James Henry

1954 *Rap Sheet: My Life Story*. New York: William Sloane.

Bailey, Pearce

1974 "The Heroin Habit." Pages 171–76 in *Yesterday's Addicts: American Society and Drug Abuse, 1865–1920*, edited by Howard Wayne Morgan. Norman: University of Oklahoma Press.

Baker, Russell

1996 "Taking the Saps." *New York Times* (June 15): 11.

"Bank Officer Is Convicted of Laundering"

1994 *Chicago Tribune* (June 3): 10.

Barboza, David

1999 "$1.1 Billion to Settle Suit on Vitamins." *New York Times* (November 4): C1.

Barboza, Joe and Hank Messick

1976 *Barboza*. New York: Dell.

Barger, Ralph "Sonny" with Keith and Kent Zimmerman

2000 *Hell's Angels*. New York: William Morrow.

Barger, Sonny

2004 "Foreword" to *Hells Angels Motorcycle Club*. Photographs by Andrew Shaylor. London: Marrell.

Barker, Tom

2007 *Biker Gangs and Organized Crime*. Newark, NJ: Matthew Bender and Co.

2005 "One Percent Bikers Clubs: A Description." *Trends in Organized Crime* 9 (Fall): 101–12.

Barnes, Leroy and Tom Folsom

2007 *Mr. Untouchable: The Rise, Fall, and Resurrection of Heroin's Teflon Don*. New York: Rugged Land.

Barrett, Livern

2010 "Coke's West Kingston Office Turns, Regimental." *The Gleaner* (June 208): Internet.

Barzini, Luigi

1977 "Italians in New York: The Way We Were in 1929." *New York* (April 4): 34–38.

1972 *The Italians*. (Paperback ed.) New York: Bantam.

1965 *The Italians*. New York: Atheneum.

Basler, Barbara

1988 "Hong Kong Gangs Wield Vast Power." *New York Times* (December 12): 4.

Bearak, Barry

2001 "At Heroin's Source, Taliban Do What 'Just Say No' Could Not." *New York Times* (May 24): 1, 12.

Beck, Jerome and Marsha Rosenbaum

1994 *Pursuit of Ecstasy: The MDMA Experience*. Albany, NY: State University of New York Press.

Becker, Andrew

2008 "Border Inspector Is Accused in Big Cocaine Case." *New York Times* (November 10): 17.

Becker, Maki and Thomas Zambito

2004 "Corral Coke Kingpin." *New York Daily News* (December 5): 6.

Becucci, Stefano

2011 "Criminal Infiltration and Social Mobilisation Against the Mafia: Gela: A City between Tradition and Modernity." *Global Crime* 12 (February): 1–8

Beeching, Jack

1975 *The Chinese Opium Wars*. New York: Harcourt Brace Jovanovich.

Beers, Rand and Francis X. Taylor

2002 "The Worldwide Connection Between Drugs and Terror." Testimony Before Senate Committee on the Judiciary Subcommittee on Technology, Terrorism and Government Information, March 13: Internet.

Behan, Tom

1996 *The Camorra*. London: Routledge.

Behar, Richard

1996 "How Bill Ruckelshaus Is Taking on the New York Mob." *Fortune* (January 15): 91–100.

Beith, Malcolm

1010 *The Last Narco: Inside the Hunt for El Chapo, the World's Most Wanted Drug Lord*. New York: Grove Press.

Bell, Daniel

1964 *The End of Ideology*. Glencoe, IL: Free Press.

1963 "The Myth of the Cosa Nostra." *The New Leader* 46 (December): 12–15.

Bell, Ernest A., ed.

1909 *War on the White Slave Trade*. Chicago: Thompson.

Belluck, Pam

1998 "44 Officers Are Charged After Ohio Sting Operation." *New York Times* (January 22): 14.

Belsamo, William and George Carpozi

1995 *Under the Clock: The Mafia's First Hundred Years*. Far Hills, NJ: New Horizon Press.

Belson, Kem

2004 "The Call Is Cheap—The Wiretap Is Extra." *New York Times* (August 23): C1, 3.

Bendavid, Naftali

1999 "Vitamin Price-Fixing Draws a Record $755 Million in Fines." *Chicago Tribune* (May 21): 3.

Bennett, David H.

1988 *The Party of Fear: From Nativist Movements to the New Right in American History*. Chapel Hill: University of North Carolina Press.

Bequai, August

1979 *Organized Crime: The Fifth Estate*. Lexington, MA: D. C. Heath.

Berger, Meyer

1957 "Anastasia Slain in a Hotel Here: Led Murder, Inc." *New York Times* (October 26): 1, 12.

1944 "Lepke's Reign of Crime Lasted Over 12 Murder-Strewn Years." *New York Times* (September 21): 1, 20.

1940 "Gang Patterns: 1940." *New York Times Magazine* (August 4): 5, 15.

1935 "Schultz Reigned on Discreet Lines." *New York Times* (October 25): 17.

Bergreen, Laurence

1994 *Capone: The Man and His Era*. New York: Simon and Schuster.

Berke, Richard L.

1989 "U.S. Attack on Airborne Drug Smuggling Called Ineffective." *New York Times* (June 9): 10.

Berkeley, Bill

2002a "Code of Betrayal, Not Silence, Shines Light on Russian Mob." *New York Times* (August 19): 1, 14.

2002b "A Glimpse into a Recess of International Finance." *New York Times* (November 12): C1, 14.

Betts, Kate

2004 "The Purse-Party Blues." *Time* (August 2): 68–70.

Bey, Lee

1995 "Police Don't Buy Hoover's Reform." *Chicago Sun-Times* (September 1): 23.

Biegel, Herbert and Allan Biegel

1977 *Beneath the Badge: A Story of Police Corruption*. New York: Harper & Row.

"Biker Club House Blasted in Norway"

1997 *New York Times* (June 5): 5.

Bilefsky, Dan

2008 "In Feuds, Isolation Engulfs Families." *New York Times* (July 10): 6, 8.

Bishop, Jim

1971 *The Days of Martin Luther King, Jr.* New York: Putnam's.

Black, Donald W. with C. Lindon Larson

1999 *Confronting Antisocial Personality Disorder*. New York: Oxford University Press.

Blakey, G. Robert

1986 "RICO's Triple Damage Threat: The Public's Secret Weapon vs. Boesky." *New York Times* (December 7): F3.

Blakey, G. Robert, Ronald Goldstock, and Charles H. Rogovin

1978 *Rackets Bureau: Investigation and Prosecution of Organized Crime*. Washington, DC: U.S. Government Printing Office.

Blau, Peter M.

1964 *Exchange and Power in Social Life*. New York: Wiley.

Bloch, Max with Ron Kenner

1982 *Max the Butcher*. Secaucas, NJ: Lyle Stuart.

Block, Alan A.

1979 *East Side–West Side: Organizing Crime in New York, 1930–1950*. Swansea, Wales: Christopher Davis.

Block, Alan A. and Frank R. Scarpitti

1985 *Poisoning for Profit: The Mafia and Toxic Waste*. New York: William Morrow.

Blok, Anton

1974 *The Mafia of a Sicilian Village, 1860–1960: A Study of Violent Peasant Entrepreneurs*. New York: Harper & Row.

Blount, William E. and H. Roy Kaplan

1989 "The Impact of the Daily Lottery on the Numbers Game: Does Legalization Make a Difference?" Paper presented at the Annual Meeting of the Academy of Criminal Justice Sciences, March 29, Washington, DC.

Blum, Howard

1993 *Gangland: How the FBI Broke the Mob*. New York: Pocket Books.

Blum Jack A.

1999 "Offshore Money." Pages 57–84 in *Transnational Crime in the Americas*, edited by Tom Farer. New York: Routledge.

Blumenthal, Ralph

1992 "When the Mob Delivered the Goods." *New York Times Magazine* (July 26): 22–23, 31–34.

1988 *Last Days of the Sicilians: At War with the Mafia; the FBI Assault on the Pizza Connection.* New York: Times Books.

Bohlen, Celestine

1999 "To Sicilians, Russia Has No Mafia. It's Too Wild." *New York Times* (January 19): WK 5.

1998 "Russian Lawmaker's Killing Stirs Anger." *New York Times* (November 22): 14.

1997 "Officially, Sicily Is Desperately Short of Jobs, But Sub Rosa, Things Are Rosier." *New York Times* (June 17): 6.

1996a "Italian Police Arrest a Top Mafia Boss in Sicily." *New York Times* (May 22): 1, 6.

1996b "Italy's North-South Gap Widens, Posing Problem for Europe Too." *New York Times* (November 15): 1, 8.

1996c "Italy Treats a Mafia Leader's Repentance with Caution." *New York Times* (August 24): 5.

1995a "Killings in Sicily Raise Fears of Mafia Campaign." *New York Times* (March 9): 4.

1995b "As Omerta Crumbles, the Mafia Changes the Rules." *New York Times* (October 11): 3.

1995c "Uffizi Blast 2 Years Ago Laid to Mafia." *New York Times* (August 7): 2.

1995d "Vatican Draws Criticism for Embrace of Andriotti." *New York Times* (December 20): 7.

1994 "Graft and Gangsterism in Russia Blight the Entrepreneurial Spirit." *New York Times* (January 30): 1, 6.

1993 "Russia [sic] Mobsters Grow More Violent and Pervasive." *New York Times* (August 16): 1, 4.

Boissevain, Jeremy

1974 *Friends of Friends: Networks, Manipulators and Coalitions.* Oxford: Basil Blackwell.

"Bomb Kills 1 at Biker Gang Headquarters"

1997 *Chicago Tribune* (June 6): 14.

Bonanno, Bill

1999 *Bound by Honor: A Mafioso's Story.* New York: St. Martin's Press.

Bonanno, Joseph with Segio Lalli

1983 *A Man of Honor: The Autobiography of Joseph Bonanno.* New York: Simon and Schuster.

Bonavolonta, Jules and Brian Duffy

1996 *The Good Guys: How We Turned the FBI 'Round—And Finally Broke the Mob.* New York: Simon and Schuster.

Bonner, Raymond

1999 "Russian Gangsters Exploit Capitalism to Increase Profits." *New York Times* (July 25): 1, 4.

Bonner, Raymond and Christopher Drew

1997 "Cigarette Makers Are Seen as Aiding Rise in Smuggling." *New York Times* (August 25): 1, C12.

Bonner, Raymond and Timothy L. O'Brien

1999 "Activity at Bank Raises Suspicions of Russia Mob Tie." *New York Times* (August 19): 1, 6.

Bonnie, Richard J. and Charles H. Whitebread II

1970 "The Forbidden Fruit and the Tree of Knowledge: An Inquiry into the Legal History of American Marijuana Prohibition." *Virginia Law Review* 56 (October): 971–1203.

Booth, Martin

1990 *The Triads: The Growing Global Threat from the Chinese Criminal Societies.* New York: St. Martin's Press.

Booth, William and Steve Fainaru

2009 "Mexican Cartels Recruiting Youths." *Philadelphia Inquirer* (November 8): 15.

Bopp, William J.

1977 *O. W. Wilson and the Search for a Police Profession.* Port Washington, NY: Kennikat Press.

Borger, Julian

2001 "Bodies Pave the Way to Jamaican Polls." *Guardian* (July 12): 6.

Bourgeois, Richard L., Jr., S. P. Hennessey, Jon Moore, and Michael E. Tschupp

2000 "Racketeer Influenced and Corrupt Organizations." *American Criminal Law Review* 37 (Spring): 879–91.

Bourne, Peter

1990 "Our Dubious Crusade in Colombia." *Chicago Tribune* (July 2): 11.

Bovenkerkn, Frank

2011 "On Leaving Criminal Organizations." *Crime, Law and Social Change* 55: 261–276.

Bovenkerk, Frank and Bashir Abou Chakra

2004 "Terrorism and Organized Crime." *Forum on Crime and Society* 4 (December) 3–13.

Bowden, Charles

2009 "We Bring Fear." *Mother Jones* (July/August): 29–43.

1991 "La Virgen and the Drug Lord" *Phoenix* (March): 96-103.

Bowden, Mark

2011 *Murder City.* New York: Nation Books.

2001 *Killing Pablo: The Hunt for the World's Greatest Outlaw* New York: Atlantic Monthly Press.

Boyd, Kier T.

1977 *Gambling Technology.* Washington, DC: U.S. Government Printing Office.

Boyne, Ian

2011 "Dudas' Plea: A Bargain for Jamaica." *The Gleaner* (September 4): Internet.

Brant, Charles

2004 *"I Heard You Paint Houses."* Hanover, NH: Steerforth Press.

Brant, Martha

1997a "Liposuctioned to Death." *Newsweek* (July 21): 43.

1997b "Most Wanted Kingpin?" *Newsweek* (March 10): 36.

Brashler, William

1981 "Two Brothers from Taylor Street." *Chicago* (September): 150–56, 194.

1977 *The Don: The Life and Death of Sam Giancana.* New York: Harper & Row.

Brecher, Edward M. and the Editor of *Consumer Reports*

1972 *Licit and Illicit Drugs.* Boston: Little, Brown.

Brenner, Marie

1990 "Prime Time Godfather." *Vanity Fair* (May): 109–15, 176–81.

Brenner, Susan W.

2002 "Organized Cybercrime? How Cyberspace May Affect the Structure of Criminal Relationships." *North Carolina Journal of Law and Technology* 4 (May): 1–50.

Bresler, Fenton

1980 *The Chinese Mafia.* New York: Stein and Day.

Briley, Ron

1997 "Hollywood and the Rebel Image in the 1950s." *Social Education* (October): 352–58.

Brill, Steven

1978 *The Teamsters.* New York: Simon and Schuster.

Bristow, Edward J.

1982 *Prostitution and Prejudice: The Jewish Fight Against White Slavery 1870–1939.* New York: Schocken Books.

Briquet, Jean-Louis and Gilles Favarel-Garrigues, eds.

2010 *Organized Crime and States: The Hidden Face of Politics.* New York: Palgrave Macmillan.

Broder, Jonathan

1984 "As a Tradeoff, Soviets Let Afghan Heroin Flow." *Chicago Tribune* (September 2): 12.

Brodt, Bonita

1981a "'Royal Family' Are Kings of Killing." *Chicago Tribune* (September 6): 5.

1981b "'Royal Family Boss Gets Death Sentence for Killing." *Chicago Tribune* (September 10): 14.

Brooke, James

1995 "Colombia Marvels at Drug Kingpin: A Chain-Saw Killer, Too?" *New York Times* (June 21): 7.

1993 "In a 'Dirty War,' Former Drug Allies Are Terrorizing Escobar." *New York Times* (March 4): 4.

1992a "How Escobar, a Rare Jailbird, Lined His Nest." *New York Times* (August 5): 1, 2.

1992b "Trafficker Is Still Feared in Colombia." *New York Times* (January 21): 5.

1991a "Cali, the 'Quiet Cocaine Cartel,' Profits Through Accommodation." *New York Times* (July 14): 1, 6.

1991b "Colombia's Rising Export: Fake U.S. Money." *New York Times* (April 21): 4.

1990 "In the Capital of Cocaine, Savagery Is the Habit." *New York Times* (June 7): 4.

Brooks, Thomas R.

1971 *Toil and Trouble: A History of American Labor.* New York: Dell.

Bruce, Victoria and Karin Hayes, with Jorge Enrique Botero

2010 *Hostage Nation: Colombia's Guerrilla Army and the Failed War on Drugs.* New York: Knoff.

Brune, Tom and James Ylisela, Jr.

1988 "The Making of Jeff Fort." *Chicago Magazine* (November): Internet.

Brunner, H. G., M. Nelson, X. D. Breakefield, H. H. Ropes, and A. van Oost.

1994 "Abnormal behavior associated with a point mutation in the structural gene for monamine oxidase" *Science* 262: 578–80.

Brzezinski, Matthew

2004 "Hillbangers." *New York Times Magazine* (August 15): 38–43.

2002 "Re-engineering the Drug Business." *New York Times Magazine* (June 23): 24–46, 54–55.

Buckman, Robert T.

2004 *Latin America.* Harpers Ferry, WV: Sryker-Post Publications.

Buenker, John D.

1973 *Urban Liberalism and Progressive Reform.* New York: Scribner's.

"Bugs Moran Dies in Federal Prison"

1957 *New York Times* (February 26): 59.

Bullough, Vern L.

1965 *The History of Prohibition.* New Hyde Park, NY: University Books.

Burnett, Stanton H. and Luca Mantovani

1998 *The Italian Guillotine.* Lanham, MA: Rowman and Littlefield.

Burnstein, Scott M.

2006 *Motor City Mafia: A Century of Organized Crime in Detroit.* Charleston, SC: Arcadia Publishing.

Buse, Renee

1965 *The Deadly Silence.* Garden City, NY: Doubleday.

Bussey, Jane

2008 "Drug Lords Rose to Power When Mexicans Ousted Old Government." *Kansas City Star* (September 17): Internet.

Butterfield, Fox

2003 "Committee Details F.B.I.'s Reliance on Killers." *New York Times* (November 21): 22.

"By Order of the Mafia"

1888 *New York Times* (October 22): 8.

California Department of Justice

2007 "Organized Crime in California." *Trends in Organized Crime* 10 (September): Internet.

Campane, Jerome O.

1981a "Chains, Wheels, and the Single Conspiracy: Part 1." *FBI Law Enforcement Bulletin* (August): 24–31.

1981b "Chains, Wheels, and the Single Conspiracy: Conclusion." *FBI Law Enforcement Bulletin* (September): 24–31.

Campbell, Howard

2010 "Former Posse Boss Dead." *The Gleaner* (March 23): Internet.

Campbell, Rodney

1977 *The Luciano Project.* New York: McGraw-Hill.

Campo-Flores, Arian

2005 "The Most Violent Gang in America." *Newsweek* (March 28): 22–25.

Cantalupo, Joseph and Thomas C. Renner

1990 *Body Mike.* New York: Saint Martin's Press.

Capé, Kevin

2005 "Where Organized Crime Still Thrives." *The* [Eugene, OR] *Register-Guard* (November 23): Internet.

Capeci, Jerry

2003 *Gangland.* New York: Alpha.

Capeci, Jerry and Gene Mustain

1996 *Gotti: Rise and Fall.* New York: Onyx.

"Capone Dead at 48; Dry Era Gang Chief."1947 *New York Times* (January 26): 7.

Caputo, David A.

1976 *Organized Crime and American Politics.* Morristown, NJ: General Learning Press.

Cardwell, Diane

2001 "Fugitive Gang Enforcer Arrested in Push-In Robberies." *New York Times* (March 2): Internet.

Carey, Elaine

2011 *Selling is More of a Habit: Women and Drug Trafficking in North America, 1900 to 1970.* Albuquerque, NM: University of New Mexico.

Carlo, Philip

2008 *Gaspipe: Confessions of a Mafia Boss.* New York: William Morrow.

Carlson, Kenneth and Peter Finn

1993 *Prosecuting Criminal Enterprises.* Washington, DC: Bureau of Justice Statistics.

Carr, Howie

2006 *The Brothers Bulger: How They Terrorized and Corrupted Boston for a Quarter Century.* New York: Warner Books.

Carroll, Brian

1991 "Combating Racketeering in the Fulton Fish Market." Pages 183–98 in *Organized Crime and Its Containment: A Transatlantic Initiative*, edited by Cyrelle Fijnaut and James Jacobs. Deventer, Netherlands: Kluwer.

Carroll, Rory

2007 "Villagers Seek High Life." *Globe and Mail* (October 9): 2.

"Cartel Leader Captured"

2005 *New York Times* (November 22): 14.

Carter, David L.

2005 "Brief History of Law Enforcement Intelligence: Past Practice and Recommendations for Change." *Trends in Organized Crime* 8 (Spring): 51–62.

2004 *Law Enforcement Intelligence: A Guide for State, Local, and Tribal Law Enforcement Agencies.* Washington, DC: Office of Community Oriented Policing Services.

Cathcart, Rebecca

2010 "Second Rail-Equipped Drug Tunnel Is Found at Border." *New York Times* (November 27): 12.

Casey, James

2007 "Dealing with Hawala: Informal Financial Centers in the Ethnic Community." *FBI Bulletin* (February) 10–14.

Cashman, Sean Dennis

1981 *Prohibition.* New York: Free Press.

Catanzaro, Raimondo

1992 *Men of Respect: A Social History of the Sicilian Mafia.* New York: Free Press. Translated by Raymond Rosenthal.

Cavazos, Ruben

2008 *Honor Few, Fear None. The Life and Times of a Mongol.* New York: Harper.

Cave, Damien

2011 "Mexican Church Takes a Closer Look at Donors." *New York Times* (March 7): 1, 5.

Ceccarelli, Alessandra

2007 "Clans, Politics and Organized Crime in Central Asia." *Trends in Organized Crime* 10: 19–36.

Center for Strategic and International Studies (CSIS)

1997 *CSIS Task Force Report: Russian Organized Crime.* Internet.

Cerruti, Giovanni

2011 "Alleged Mobster Nabbed Through Girlfriend's Facebook Post." *Time World* (September 1): Internet.

Chafetz, Henry

1960 *Play the Devil: A History of Gambling in the United States from 1492 to 1955.* New York: Clarkson Potter.

Chaiken, David A.

1991 "Money Laundering: An Investigatory Perspective." *Criminal Law Forum* 2 (Spring): 467–510.

Chalidze, Vallery

1977 *Criminal Russia: Crime in the Soviet Union.* New York: Random House.

Chambliss, William

1975 "On the Paucity of Original Research on Organized Crime: A Footnote to Galliher and Cain." *American Sociologist* 10 (August): 36–39.

1973 *Functional and Conflict Theories of Crime*. New York: MSS Modular Publications.

Chapman, Stephen

1991 "Prohibition—From Alcohol to Drugs—Is a Costly Failure." *Chicago Tribune* (September 1): Sec. 4: 3.

Chaudhry, Peggy and Alan Zimmerman

2009 *The Economics of Counterfeit Trade: Governments, Consumers, Pirates, and Intellectual Property Rights*. Berlin: Springer.

Cheloukhine, Serguei

2008 "The Roots of Russian Organized Crime: From Old-Fashioned Professionals to the Organized Criminal Groups of Today." *Crime, Law and Social Change* 50 (June): 353–374.

Cheloukhine, Serguei and M. R, Haberfield

2011 *Russian Organized Corruption Networks and Their International Trajectories*. New York: Springer.

Chemerinsky, Erwin

2000 "Plaintiff's Use of Rico Limited." *Trial* 36: 123–125.

Chen, An

2005 "Secret Societies and Organized Crime in Contemporary China." *Modern Asian Studies* 39 (February): 77-107.

Cheney, Julia S.

2005 "Identity Theft: Do Definitions Still Matter?" Discussion paper prepared for the Payment Cards Center of the Federal Reserve Bank of Philadelphia.

Chepesiuk, Ron

2010 *Sergeant Smack: The Legendary Lives and Times of Ike*

Atkinson, Kingpin, and His Band of Brothers. Rock Hill, SC: Strategic Media.

2007a "Dangerous Alliance: Terrorism and Organized Crime." *Global Politician* (September 11): Internet.

2007b *Gangsters of Harlem*. Fort Lee, NJ: Barricade Books.

2003 *The Bullet or Bribe: Taking Down Colombia's Cali Drug Cartel*. Westport, CT: Praeger.

Chepesiuk, Ron and Anthony Gonzalez

2007 *Superfly: The True-Untold Story of Frank Lucas*. New York: Street Certified Entertainment.

Cherry, Paul

2005 *The Biker Trials: Bringing Down the Hells Angels*. Toronto, Canada: ECW Press.

Chin, Ko-lin

1990 *Chinese Subculture and Criminality: Non-Traditional Crime Groups in America*. Westport, CT: Greenwood.

Chin, Ko-lin, Robert J. Kelly, and Jeffrey Fagan

1994 "Chinese Organized Crime in America." Pages 213–43 in *Handbook of Organized Crime in the United States*, edited by Robert J. Kelly, Ko-lin Chin, and Rufus Schatzberg. Westport, CT: Greenwood.

Chin, Ko-lin, Sheldon Zhang, and Robert J. Kelly

1998 "Transnational Chinese Organized Crime Activities: Patterns and Emerging Trends." *Transnational Organized Crime* 4 (Autumn/Winter): 127–154.

"Chinatown's New Enforcer"

1995 *New Yorker* (April 3): 36.

Chivers, C. J.

2008a "Medvedev Takes Oath in Russia, but Putin Dominates Much of the Day." *New York Times* (May 8): 16.

2008b "U.S. Position Complicates Global Effort to Curb Illicit Arms." *New York Times* (July 19): 5.

Chrisafis, Angelique

2005 "Spotlight Turns to Slick IRA Money-Making Machine." *Guardian* (February 19): Internet.

Christian, Nichole M.

2001 "Officials Say Stock Scheme Raised Money for the Mob." *New York Times* (March 9): 19.

Christian, Shirley

1992 "Why Indulge Drug Lord? Colombia Pressed to Tell." *New York Times* (July 29): 3.

Chu, Yiu Kong

2005 "Hong Kong Triads After 1997." *Trends in Organized Crime* 8 (Spring): 1–12.

Chubb, Judith

1982 *Patronage, Power, and Poverty in Southern Italy*. Cambridge: Cambridge University Press.

Cilluffo, Frank

2000 "The Threat Posed from the Convergence of Organized Crime, Drug Trafficking, and Terrorism." Testimony before the U.S. House Committee on the Judiciary Subcommittee on Crime, December 13. Internet.

Cilluffo, Frank J. and George Salmoiraghi

1999 "And the Winner Is ... the Albanian Mafia." *The Washington Quarterly*, 22 (Autumn): 21–25.

Cimino, Tonia N.

2005 "Illegal Gambling Ring Busted." *Queens Courier* (May 25): 12.

Clarke, Donald Henderson

1929 *In the Reign of Rothstein*. New York: Grosset and Dunlap.

Clinard, Marshall B., Peter C. Yeager, Jeanne Brissette, David Petrashek, and Elizabeth Harries

1979 *Illegal Corporate Behavior*. Washington, DC: Government Printing Office.

Cloninger, Susan C.

2004 *Theories of Personality: Understanding Persons*, 4th ed. Upper Saddle River, NJ: Prentice-Hall.

Cloward, Richard A. and Lloyd E. Ohlin

1960 *Delinquency and Opportunity*. New York: Free Press.

Cloyd, Jerald W.

1982 *Drugs and Information Control: The Role of Men and Manipulation in the Control of Drug Trafficking*. Westport, CT: Greenwood.

"Cocaine Cartel Leader to Face Charges in the United States"

2008 U.S. Department of Justice press release (August 22): Internet.

Coen, Jeff

2009 *Family Secrets: The Case That Crippled the Chicago Mob*. Chicago: Chicago Review Press.

Coffey, Joseph and Jerry Schmetterer

1991 *The Coffey Files: One Cop's War Against the Mob*. New York: St. Martin's Press.

Coffey, Thomas A.

1975 *The Long Thirst: Prohibition in America: 1920–1933*. New York: Norton.

Cohen, Mickey

1975 *Mickey Cohen: In My Own Words*. Englewood Cliffs, NJ: Prentice-Hall.

Cohen, Stanley

1977 *The Game They Played*. New York: Farrar, Straus and Giroux.

Colbridge, Thomas D.

2000 "Electronic Surveillance: A Matter of Necessity." *FBI Law Enforcement Bulletin* (February): 25–32.

Collins, Randall

1975 *Conflict Sociology*. New York: Academic Press.

"Colombian Heroin May Be Increasing"

1991 *New York Times* (October 27): 10.

Colombia's New Armed Groups

2007 Bogotá, Colombia: International Crisis Group.

Combs, Cindy C.

2003 *Terrorism in the Twenty-First Century*, 3rd ed. Saddle River, NJ: Prentice-Hall.

Commission on the Review of the National Policy Toward Gambling

1976 *Gambling in America*. Washington, DC: U.S. Government Printing Office.

Committee on the Office of Attorney General

1978 *Witness Immunity*. Raleigh, NC: National Association of Attorneys General (NAAG).

1974 *Prosecuting Organized Crime*. Raleigh, NC: NAAG.

Comptroller General

1989 *Nontraditional Organized Crime: Law Enforcement Officials' Perspectives on Five Criminal Groups*. Washington, DC: U.S. Government Printing Office.

Cone, Tracie

2008 "Mexican Marijuana Cartels Sully US Forests, Parks." Associated Press (October 11): Internet.

Connable, Alfred and Edward Silberfarb

1967 *Tigers of Tammany: Nine Men Who Ruled New York*. New York: Holt, Rinehart and Winston.

Connolly, John

1996 "Who Handled Who?" *New York* (December 2): 46–49.

Constantine, Thomas A.

1999a "Statement Before the Subcommittee on Criminal Justice, Drug Policy and Human Resources." March 4.

1999b "Statement Before the U.S. Senate Drug Caucus." February 24.

"Contractor Admits Double Life"

1996 *New York Times* (May 2): 13.

Cook, Fred J.

1973 *Mafia!* New York: Fawcett.

1972 "Purge of the Greasers." Pages 89–109 in *Mafia, U.S.A.*, edited by Nicholas Gage. New York: Dell.

Cooley, Robert with Hillel Levin

2004 *When Corruption Was King*. New York: Carroll and Graf Publishers.

Cooper, Michael and Richard A. Oppel, Jr.

2011 "Mob Figure May Unearth Corruption of Lawmen." *New York Times* (July 1): 1, 15.

Corbitt, Michael with Sam Giancana

2003 *Double Deal*. New York: William Morrow.

Corcoran, Patrick

2011 "Why Lowering US Drug Demand is No Panacea for Mexico Violence." *In Sight* (August 30): Internet.

Costanzo, Ezio

2007 *The Mafia and the Allies: Sicily 1943 and the Return of the Mafia*. New York: Enigma Books.

Courtwright, David T.

1982 *Dark Paradise: Opiate Addiction in America Before 1940*. Cambridge, MA: Harvard University Press.

Cowan, Rick and Douglas Century

2002 *Takedown: The Fall of the Last Mafia Empire*. New York: Putnam.

Cowell, Alan

1994 "Gunmen Linked to the Mafia Kill a Priest in Italy." *New York Times* (March 20): 3.

1993 "Busting the Mafia: Italy Advances in War on Crime." *New York Times* (June 27): 3.

1992a "Inquiry into Sicilian Slaying Looks for Mafia Link to Colombia Drug Cartel." *New York Times* (June 21): 3.

1992b "Italians Defying Shakedowns Pays with Lives." *New York Times* (November 12): 5.

1992c "Italy Arrests 75 in Mafia Roundup." *New York Times* (November 18): 3.

1992d "Mafia Throws the Gauntlet in Italy's Face." *New York Times* (July 21): 5.

1992e "Sicilian Symbolizes Mob's Survival." *New York Times* (August 2): 8.

1992f "A Top Sicilian Politician Is Slain; Pre-Election Mafia Warning Seen." *New York Times* (March 12): 2.

Crack Cocaine

1994 Washington, DC: Drug Enforcement Administration.

Cragin, Kim and Bruce Hoffman

2003 *Arms Trafficking in Colombia*. Santa Monica, CA: RAND.

Cressey, Donald R.

1972 *Criminal Organization: Its Elementary Forms*. New York: Harper & Row.

1969 *Theft of the Nation*. New York: Harper & Row.

Criminal Intelligence Service Canada (CISC)

2004 *Annual Report on Organized Crime in Canada*. Ottawa: CISC.

Crisanti, Layla

2008 "A Battle Against the Mob." *Tandem* [Canada] (June 15–June 22): Internet.

Crouse, Russel

1947 "The Murder of Arnold Rothstein: 1928." Pages 184–200 in *Sins of New York*, edited by Milton Crane. New York: Grosset and Dunlap.

Cruz, José Miguel

2011 "Central American *Maras*: From Youth Street Gangs to Transnational Protection Rackets." *Global Crime* 11 (4): 379–98.

Curtis, Glenn E., John N. Gibbs, and Ramón Miró

2004 "Nations Hospitable to Organized Crime and Terrorism." *Transnational Organized Crime* 8 (Fall): 5–23.

Curtis, Glenn E. and Tara Karacan

2002 *The Nexus Among Terrorists, Narcotics Traffickers, Weapons Proliferators, and Organised Crime Networks in Western Europe*. Washington, DC: Library of Congress.

Dades, Tommy, Mike Vecchione, and David Fisher

2009 *Friends of the Family*. New York: William Morrow.

Daley, Dave

2000 "Biker Is Convicted of '93 Killings of Richmond Couple." *Chicago Tribune* (June 16): Sec. 2: 3.

Daley, Robert A.

1978 *Prince of the City*. Boston: Houghton Mifflin.

Dannen, Federic

1996 "The G-Man and the Hit Man." *New Yorker* (December 16): 68–81.

1995 "Hong Kong Babylon." *New Yorker* (August 7): 30–38.

1992a "The Untouchable? How the FBI Sabotaged Competing Prosecution Teams in the Race to Nail Alleged Mob King John Gotti." *Vanity Fair* (January): 27–44.

1992b "Revenge of the Green Dragons." *New Yorker* (November): 76–99.

Danner, Mark

2005 "Taking Stock of the Forever War." *New York Times Magazine* (September 11): 45–68, 86–87.

David, Fiona

2010 *Labour Trafficking*. Canberra: Australian Institute of Criminology.

David, John J.

1988 "Outlaw Motorcycle Gangs: A Transnational Problem." Paper presented at the Conference on International Terrorism and Transnational Crime, Chicago, August.

Davis, Ian, Chrissie Hirst, and Bernardo Mariani

2001 *Organised Crime, Corruption and Illicit Arms Trafficking in an Enlarged EU*. London, UK: Saferworld.

Davis, John H.

1993 *Mafia Dynasty: The Rise and Fall of the Gambino Crime Family*. New York: HarperCollins.

DEA. See Drug Enforcement Administration

Decker, Scott, Tim Bynum, and Deborah Weisel

1998 "A Tale of Two Cities: Gangs as Organized Crime Groups." *Justice Quarterly* 15 (September): 395–425.

De Franco, Edward J.

1973 *Anatomy of a Scam: A Case Study of a Planned Bankruptcy by Organized Crime*. Washington, DC: U.S. Government Printing Office.

Defus, R. L.

1928 "The Gunman Has an Intercity Murder Trade." *New York Times* (July): XX 3.

de Gennaro, G.

1995 The Influences of Mafia Type Organizations on Government, Business and Industry." *Trends in Organized Crime* 1 (Winter): 36–42.

Deitche, Scott M.

2004 *Cigar City Mafia: A Complete History of the Tampa Underworld*. Fort Lee, NJ: Barricade Books.

de la Garza, Paul

2000 "Mexico Striking Back at Top Drug Cartel." *Chicago Tribune* (June 1): 4.

1998 "With Drug War, Anarchy Reigns in Mexican City." *Chicago Tribune* (October 31): 4.

1997a "The Scent of Scandal Has Church Scrambling." *Chicago Tribune* (October 6): 8.

1997b "In Tijuana, War on Drugs Is Lost." *Chicago Tribune* (March 31): 1, 13.

de Lama, George

1988 "Besieged Colombia Becoming the Lebanon of Latin America." *Chicago Tribune* (November 20): 5.

Delaney, William P.

1977 "On Capturing an Opium King: The Politics of Law Sik Han's Arrest." Pages 67–88 in *Drugs and Politics*, edited by Paul E. Rock. New Brunswick, NJ: Transaction Books.

della Porta, Donatella and Alberto Vannucci

1999 *Corrupt Exchanges: Actors, Resources, and Mechanisms of Political Corruption.* New York: Walter de Gruyter.

Dellios, Hugh

1998 "Once Just a Supplier, Nigeria Develops Heroin Woes." *Chicago Tribune* (July 29): 4.

Demaris, Ovid

1981 *The Last Mafioso: The Treacherous World of Jimmy Fratianno.* New York: Bantam.

1969 *Captive City: Chicago in Chains.* New York: Lyle Stuart.

DeStefano, Anthony M.

2006 *King of the Godfathers: "Big Joey" Massino and the Fall of the Bonanno Crime Family.* New York: Pinnacle Books.

de Tocqueville, Alexis

1966 *Democracy in America.* New York: Harper & Row. Translated by George Lawrence.

DeVecchio, Lin and Charles Brandt

2011 *We're Going to Win This Thing.* New York: Berkley Books.

Diamond, Stuart

1988 "Steep Rise Seen in Private Use of Federal Racketeering Law." *New York Times* (August 1): 1, 15.

Diapoulos, Peter and Steven Linakis

1976 *The Sixth Family.* New York: Dutton.

Díaz, Lizabeth

2011 "Tijuana Violence Slows As One Cartel Takes Control." *Reuters* (September 5): Internet.

Dickie, John

2004 *Cosa Nostra: A History of the Sicilian Mafia.* New York: Palgrave Macmillan.

Dickson, Donald T.

1977 "Bureaucracy and Morality: An Organizational Perspective on a Moral Crusade." Pages 31–52 in *Drugs and Politics*, edited by Paul E. Rock. New Brunswick, NJ: Transaction Books.

Diener, Kathy and Teisha C. Johnson

2005 "Federal Criminal Conspiracy." *American Criminal Law Review* (Spring): 463–99.

Dillon, Sam

1999a "Mexico's Troubadours Turn From Amor to Drugs." *New York Times* (February 19): 4.

1999b "Ruling Party, at 70, Tries Hard to Cling to Power in Mexico." *New York Times* (March 4): 1, 12.

1998a "Gunmen Kill 3 Families in Mexico Over Drugs." *New York Times* (September 18): 6.

1998b "Mexico Arrests Two Accused of Flooding the U.S. with 'Speed.'" *New York Times* (June 3): 7

1998c "Mexico Drug Trafficker Slain; Major Figure Near U.S. Border." *New York Times* (September 12): 3.

1998d "Mexico Jails 2 Drug Agents and U.S. Sees Graft." *New York Times* (September 25): 12.

1998e "Mexico Says Rivalry Between Gangs Led to Mass Murders." *New York Times* (November 11): 10.

1997 "Mexico Editor Hurt in Ambush; His Bodyguard and Gunman Die." *New York Times* (November 28): 5.

1996a "Bribes and Publicity Mark Fall of Mexican Drug Lord." *New York Times* (May 12): 1, 6.

1996b "Canaries Are Singing, But Uncle Juan Won't." *New York Times* (February 9): 4.

1996c "Mexican Aide's Millions; U.S. Charges Drug Link." *New York Times* (November 12): 5.

1996d "Mexico Arrests a Top Suspect in Drug Trade." *New York Times* (January 16): 1, 2.

1996e "Mexican Drug Gang's Reign of Terror." *New York Times* (February 4): 24.

1996f "Mexicans Tire of Police Graft as Drug Lords Raise Stakes." *New York Times* (March 21): 3.

1996g "Mexican Trafficker Plans to Cooperate in FBI's Inquiries." *New York Times* (January 20): 1, 5.

Dillon, Sam and Craig Pyes

1997a "Court Files Say Drug Baron Used Mexican Military." *New York Times* (May 24): 1, 4.

1997b "Drug Ties Taint 2 Mexican Governors." *New York Times* (February 23): 1, 4.

DiManno, Rosie

2011 "Trashy Odour in Naples? It's the Smell of Corruption." *Toronto Star* (May 6): Internet.

Dintino, Justin J, and Frederick T. Martens

1983 *Police Intelligence Systems and Crime Control.* Springfield, IL: Charles C. Thomas.

1980 "Organized Crime Control in the Eighties." *Police Chief* (August): 66–70.

Dishman, Chris

2005 "The Leaderless Nexus: When Crime and Terror Converge." *Studies in Conflict and Terrorism* 28: 237–52.

District Attorney of New York County and the New York City Police Department

1995 "Press Release, June 22." New York: Photocopied.

Dobyns, Fletcher

1932 *The Underworld of American Politics*. New York: Fletcher Dobyns.

Dorsett, Lyle W.

1968 *The Pendergast Machine*. New York: Oxford University Press.

Douglas, Paul H.

1974 "Introduction." *Bosses in Lusty Chicago*, by Lloyd Wendt and Herman Kogan. Bloomington: Indiana University Press.

Downey, Patrick

2004 *Gangster City: The History of the New York Underworld 1900–1935*. Fort Lee, NJ: Barricade Books.

Dretzka, Gary

2001 "Rolling the Dice on Internet Gambling." *Chicago Tribune* (June 15): Sec. 5: 1, 3.

Drew, Christopher

1998 "RJR Subsidiary Pleads Guilty to Smuggling." *New York Times* (December 23): 1, 25.

Driehaus, Bob

2008 "Some States Set Caps to Control Payday Loans." *New York Times* (September 8): 17.

Droban, Kerrie

2007 *Running with the Devil: The True Story of the ATF's Infiltration of the Hells Angels*. Guilford, CT: Lyons Press.

Drug Abuse and Drug Abuse Research

1987 Rockville, MD: National Institute on Drug Abuse.

Drug Enforcement Administration (DEA)

1995a *Illegal Drug Price/Purity*. Washington, DC: DEA.

1995b *LSD in the United States*. Washington, DC: DEA.

1991a *Worldwide Cocaine Situation*. Washington, DC: DEA.

1991b *Worldwide Heroin Situation*. Washington, DC: DEA.

1988 *Crack Cocaine Availability and Trafficking in the United States*. Washington, DC: DEA.

"Drugs of Abuse"

1979 *Drug Enforcement* (July), entire issue.

Dryomin, Viktor

2003 "Organised Crime and Corruption in Ukraine as a System Phenomenon." Pages 49–59 in *Organised Crime, Trafficking, Drugs: Selected Papers Presented at the Annual Conference of the European Society of Criminology*, Helsinki, edited by Sami Nevala and Kauko Armomaa.

Dubocq, Tom and Manny Garcia

1997 "'Redfellas': Cops Say Strip Club Was Hangout for Russian Mob." *Miami Herald* (February 8): 1, 6.

Duggan, Christopher

1989 *Fascism and the Mafia*. New Haven, CT: Yale University.

Durk, David and Ira Silverman

1976 *The Pleasant Avenue Connection*. New York: Harper & Row.

Durkheim, Émile

1951 *Suicide*. New York: Free Press.

Duster, Troy

1970 *The Legislation of Morality: Law, Drugs, and Moral Judgment*. New York: Free Press.

Duzán, Maria Jimena

1994 *Death Beat: A Colombian Journalist's Life Inside the Cocaine Wars*. New York: HarperCollins.

Eagleman, David

2011 "The Brain on Trial." *The Atlantic* (July/August): 112–123.

Early, Pete and Geral Shur

2002 *Inside the Federal Witness Protection Program*. New York: Bantam.

Eaton, Leslie

1997 "Russian Émigrés Run Afoul of Stock Regulators." *New York Times* (January 14): C1, 7.

Edberg, Mark C.

2001 "Drug Traffickers as Social Bandits." *Journal of Contemporary Criminal Justice* 17 (August): 259–77.

Eddy, Paul, Hugo Sabogal, and Sara Walden

1988 *The Cocaine Wars*. New York: Norton.

Edelhertz, Herbert and Thomas D. Overcast

n.d. *The Business of Organized Crime*. Loomis, CA: Palmer Press.

"Editorial"

1995 *Chicago Tribune* (January 2): 12.

Edwards, Peter and Michel Auger

2004 The *Encyclopedia of Canadian Organized Crime*. Toronto: McClelland and Stewart.

Eichenwald, Kurt

2002 "White-Collar Defense Stance: The Criminal-less Crime." *New York Times* (March 3): WK 3.

Elliott, Delbert S., David Huizinga, and Suzanne S. Ageton

1985 *Explaining Delinquency and Drug Use*. Beverly Hills, CA: Sage.

Elliott, Dorinda

1992 "Russia's Goodfellas: The Mafia on the Neva." *Newsweek* (October 12): 50, 52.

Ellis, Lee

1991 "Monoamine Oxidase and Criminality: Identifying an Apparent Biological Marker for Antisocial Behavior." *Journal of Research in Crime and Delinquency* 28: 227–51.

1990 "Universal Behavioral and Demographic Correlates of Criminal Behavior: Toward Common Ground in the Assessment of Criminological Theories." Pages 36–49 in *Crime in Biological, Social, and Moral Contexts*, edited by Lee Ellis and Harry Hoffman. Westport, CT: Praeger.

Engelmann, Larry

1979 *Intemperance: The Lost War Against Liquor.* New York: Free Press.

English, T. J.

2005 *Paddy Whacked: The Untold Story of the Irish American Gangster.* New York: HarperCollins.

1995a *Born to Kill.* New York: William Morrow.

1995b "Where Crime Rules." *New York Times* (June 26): 11.

1990 *The Westies: Inside the Hell's Kitchen Irish Mob.* New York: Putnam's.

Epstein, Edward Jay

1988a "The Dope Business." *Manhattan, Inc.* (July): 25–27.

1988b "Marrying the Mob to Wall Street." *Manhattan, Inc.* (October): 43–47.

1977 *Agency of Fear: Opiates and Political Power in America.* New York: Putnam's.

Epstein, Leon D.

1986 *Political Parties in the American Mold.* Madison: University of Wisconsin Press.

Erie, Steven P.

1988 *Rainbow's End: Irish-Americans and the Dilemmas of Urban Machine Politics, 1840–1985.* Berkeley: University of California Press.

Eskridge, Chris

1998 "The Mexican Cartels: A Challenge for the 21st Century." *Criminal Organizations* 12 (1 & 2): 5–15.

Fackler, Martin

2007 "Mayor's Death Forces Japan's Crime Rings Into the Light." *New York Times* (April 21): 3.

Fahim, Kareem

2006 "Albanian Groups Are Muscling Into Mob Land, Officials Say." *New York Times* (January 3): B1, 3.

Faison, Seth

1995a "Charges Against President Threaten Chinatown Tong." *New York Times* (June 1): 16.

1995b "U.S. Indicts 2 Businessmen as Gang Lords in Chinatown." *New York Times* (September 10): 11.

1993 "How Betrayal Snagged a Chinatown Gang Leader." *New York Times* (August 31): 12.

Farrell, Amy, Jack McDevitt, and Stephanie Fahy

2008 "Understanding and Improving Law Enforcement Responses to Human Trafficking." Boston: Northwestern University Institute on Race and Justice.

Farrell, Ronald A. and Carole Case

1995 *The Black Book and the Mob.* Madison: University of Wisconsin Press.

Fay, Peter Ward

1975 *The Opium War: 1840–1842.* Chapel Hill: University of North Carolina Press.

"FBI Says Los Angeles Gang Has Drug Cartel Ties"

1992 *New York Times* (January 10): 8.

Federal Bureau of Investigation

1988 "Debriefing of Gerald H. Scarpelli." Investigative File # CG183B-2272.

Federal Research Division

2002 "Asian Organized Crime and Terrorist Activity in Canada, 1999–2002." *Trends in Organized Crime* 7 (Spring): 3–18.

Feiden, Douglas

2004 "The Fat Cats on the Waterfront." *New York Daily News* (January 4): 6–7.

Feinberg, Alexander

1959 "Genovese Is Given 15 Years in Prison in Narcotics Case." *New York Times* (April 18): 1, 15.

1944 "Lepke Is Put to Death, Denies Guilt to Last; Makes No Revelation." *New York Times* (March 5): 1, 30.

Ferkenhoff, Eric and Heather Vogell

2001 "Cops Seize $2 Million in Goods." *Chicago Tribune* (February 24): 5.

Fernandez, Manny

2010 "On Pleasant Avenue, a Grisly Past Fades, and a Target Moves In." *New York Times* (July 25): Internet.

2007 "Onetime Mob Stronghold Hears Echo of the Old Days." *New York Times* (June 11): B3.

Feuer, Alan

2001a "Reporter's Notebook: Violent Testimony in Staccato Language." *New York Times* (May 13): Internet.

2001b "7 Are Charged in Running Bank That Was Front for Mob Crimes." *New York Times* (November 7): 19.

Feuer, Alan and William K. Rashbaum

2005 "Blood Ties: 2 Officers' Path to Mob Indictments." *New York Times* (March 12): 1, B4.

Fijnaut, Cyrelle and James Jacobs, eds.

1991 *Organized Crime and Its Containment: A Transatlantic Initiative.* Deventer, Netherlands: Kluwer.

Financial Action Task Force on Money Laundering (FATF)

2001 *Report on Money Laundering Typologies, 2000–2001.* Paris: FATF.

Financial Crimes Enforcement Network

2000 A *Survey of Electronic Banking, and Internet Gambling.* U.S. Department of the Treasury: Internet.

Finckenauer, James O. and Ko-lin Chin

2011 *Researching and Rethinking Sex Trafficking: The Movement of Chinese Women to Asia and the United States for Commercial Sex.* Washington, DC: National Institute of Justice.

2007 *Asian Transnational Organized Crime.* Washington, DC: National Institute of Justice.

Finckenauer, James O. and Yuri A. Voronin

2001 *The Threat of Russian Organized Crime.* Washington, DC: National Institute of Justice.

Finckenauer, James O. and Elin J. Waring

2001 "Challenging the Russian Mafia Mystique." *NIJ Journal* (April): 2–7.

1999 *Russian Mafia in America: Immigration, Culture, and Crime.* Boston, MA: Northeastern University Press (advance page proofs).

Finkelstein, Katherine Eban

1998 "The Brighton Beach Swindle." *New York* (February 2): 39–43, 78.

Finley, M. I., Denis Mack Smith, and Christopher Duggan

1987 *A History of Sicily.* New York: Viking.

Finnegen, William

2010a "In the Name of the Law: A Colonel Cracks Down on Corruption." *New Yorker.* (October 18): 62–72.

2010b "Silver or Lead." *New Yorker* (May 31): 37–51.

Fiorentini, Gianluca and Sam Peltzman, eds.

1995 *The Economics of Organized Crime.* Cambridge: Cambridge University Press.

Fisher, Ian

2007 "Breaking All the Rules, With a Shrug and a Sigh." *New York Times* (February 14): 3.

2005 "Italian Police Arrest Fugitive Crime Leader in Naples Gang War." *New York Times* (September 17): 5.

2004 "New Blood on Naples Streets Brings Back Old Fears." *New York Times* (December 13): 3.

Fisher, Ian and Danielle Pinto

2008 "Italy's Trash Crisis Taints Reputation of Prized Cheese." *New York Times* (March 26): 7.

"Fishy Haul, A"

2004 *New York Daily News* (September 28): 5.

Flinn, John J.

1973 *History of the Chicago Police.* New York: AMS Press. Originally published in 1887.

Flynn, Sean

1998 "Good Guy, Bad Guy." *Boston Magazine* (Internet).

Fogelson, Robert M.

1977 *Big City Police.* Cambridge, MA: Harvard University Press.

Foglesong, Todd S. and Peter H. Solomon, Jr.

2001 *Crime, Criminal Justice, and Criminology in Post-Soviet Ukraine.* Washington, DC: National Institute of Justice.

Follain, John

2008 *The Last Godfathers: Inside the Mafia's Most Infamous Family.* New York: St. Martin's Press.

Fong, Mak Lau

1981 *The Sociology of Secret Societies: A Study of Chinese Secret Societies in Singapore and Peninsular Malaysia.* Oxford, England: Oxford University Press.

Fooner, Michael

1985 *A Guide to Interpol.* Washington, DC: U.S. Government Printing Office.

Forero, Juan

2006 "Commanders Recast Old Militias of Colombia as Syndicates for Drugs and Extortion." *New York Times* (March 5): 4.

2005a "Ammo Seized in Colombia; 2 G.I. Suspects Are Arrested." *New York Times* (May 5): 10.

2005b "Bolivia's Newly Elected Leader Maps His Socialist Agenda." *New York Times* (December 20): 8.

2005c "Turbulent Bolivia Is Producing More Cocaine, the U.N. Reports." *New York Times* (June 15): 5.

2005d "U.S. Voicing Fears of Tampered Elections, Is Rebuked by Colombia." *New York Times* (December 18): 25.

2004a "Attack by Colombia Rebels Threatens Fragile Talks." *New York Times* (June 17): 3.

2004b "With Chief Missing, Colombia Militias Gain Leverage." *New York Times* (May 19): 16.

2004c "Colombia's Landed Gentry: Coca Lords and Other Bullies." *New York Times* (January 21): 4.

2004d "Paramilitary Chief Tied to Drug Trade Gains Power in Colombia." *New York Times* (April 25): 15.

2004e "Rightist Militias Are a Force in Colombia's Congress." *New York Times* (November 10): 3.

2004f "Rightist Militias in Colombia Offer to Disarm 3,000 of Their Fighters." *New York Times* (October 9): 5.

2002 "Farmers in Peru Are Turning Again to Coca Crop." *New York Times* (February 14): 3.

2001a "Europe Expands as Market for Colombian Cocaine." *New York Times* (May 29): 1, 9.

2001b "New Challenge to the Bogotá Leadership." *New York Times* (May 6): 8.

2001c "No Crops Spared in Colombia's Coca War." *New York Times* (January 31): 1, 8.

2001d "Ranchers in Colombia Bankroll Their Own Militia." *New York Times* (August 8): 1, 6.

2001e "Rightist Chief in Colombia Shifts Focus to Politics." *New York Times* (June 7): Internet.

2001f "Union Says Coca-Cola in Colombia Uses Thugs." *New York Times* (July 26): 6.

2001g "In the War on Coca, Colombian Growers Simply Move Along." *New York Times* (March 17): 1, 5.

2001h "Where a Little Coca Is as Good as Gold." *New York Times* (July 8): Sec. 4: 12.

Forte, Elisa

2008 "Thousands in Italy Rally Against the Mafia." Reuters, Internet.

"$4,000,000 in Narcotics Seized Here Tied to Rothstein Ring."

1928 *New York Times* (December 19): 1.

Fox, Ben

2001 "Record Cocaine Cache Seized." *Chicago Tribune* (May 15): 9.

Fox, Stephen

1989 *Blood and Power: Organized Crime in the Twentieth Century.* New York: William Morrow.

"Frank Costello Dies of Coronary at 82; Underworld Leader."

1972 *New York Times* (February 19): 1, 21.

Franklin, Jonathan and Samuel Logan

2008 "Birds of Prey." *Men's Vogue* (June/July): 31–34.

Franklin, Stephen

1999 "Laborers' President Cleared by Union." *Chicago Tribune* (March 10): Sec. 3: 1, 3.

1995a "Hotel Workers' Union, U.S. Reach Oversight Accord." *Chicago Tribune* (August 20): Sec. 3: 1, 4.

1995b "Teamsters Aim at Corruption." *Chicago Tribune* (February 10): Sec. 3: 1, 3.

1993 "Teamsters Move on Local." *Chicago Tribune* (June 17): Sec. 2: 1, 2.

Franks, Lucinda

1977 "An Obscure Gangster Is Emerging as the New Mafia Chief in New York." *New York Times* (March 17): 1, 34.

Frantz, Douglas and Chuck Neubauer

1983 "Teamster Pension Fund Just Fine After Surgery." *Chicago Tribune* (May 29): 1, 10.

Frantz, Douglas with Vivian S. Toy

1995 "Portrait of Man as Mobster Stirs Community's Disbelief." *New York Times* (July 11): 1, B15.

Franzese, Michael and Dary Matera

1992 *Quitting the Mob.* New York: Harper Paperbacks.

Freedman, Michael

2005 "The Invisible Bankers." *Forbes* (October 17): 94–104.

Freeman, Ira Henry

1957 "Anastasia Rose in Stormy Ranks." *New York Times* (October 26): 12.

French, Howard W.

2001 "Even in Ginza, Honor Among Thieves Crumbles." *New York Times* (October 10): 4.

Fried, Albert

1980 *The Rise and Fall of the Jewish Gangster in America.* New York: Holt, Rinehart and Winston.

Fried, Joseph P.

2005 "Family of 2 Victims Finds Satisfaction." *New York Times* (February 13): 42.

1995 "Civic Pillar Pleads Guilty in Slaying Plot." *New York Times* (October 31): B15.

1993a "Government Sues to Seize Gotti's Remaining Assets." *New York Times* (January 15): 16.

1993b "Indictment Links the Mafia to Trash-Hauling Industry." *New York Times* (April 20): B16.

1992 "Inside Man for U.S. Oversees Union at Kennedy in War on Airport Rackets." *New York Times* (May 17): 21.

Friedman, Allen and Ted Schwarz

1989 *Power and Greed: Inside the Teamsters Empire of Corruption.* New York: Watts.

Friedman, Robert I.

2000 *Red Mafia: How the Russian Mob Has Invaded America.* Boston: Little, Brown.

1996 "The Money Plane." *New York* (January 22): 25–33.

Friel, Frank and John Gunther

1990 *Breaking the Mob.* New York: Warner Books.

Frisby, Tanya

1998 "The Rise of Organised Crime in Russia: Its Roots and Social Significance." *Europe-Asia Studies* 50 (January): 27–50.

Fuumi, Sayaka

2010 "The Yakuza and Its Perceived Threat." Pages 99–112 in *Defining and Defying Organized Crime.* Edited by Felia Allum, Francesco Longo, Daniela Irrera, and Panos A. Kostakos. London: Routledge.

Fuller, Thomas

2007a "Khun Sa, Golden Triangle Drug King, Dies at 73." *New York Times* (November 5): B7.

2007b "No Blowing Smoke: Poppies Fade in Southeast Asia." *New York Times* (November 16): WK 3.

Furchgott, Roy

2008 "With Software, Till Tampering Is Hard to Find." *New York Times* (August 30): C6.

Gage, Nicholas

1975 "Carlo Gambino Dies in His Long Island Home at 75." *New York Times* (October 16): 26.

1974 "Questions Are Raised on Lucky Luciano Book." *New York Times* (December 17): 28.

1971a *The Mafia Is Not an Equal Opportunity Employer.* New York: McGraw-Hill.

1971b "Gallo-Colombo Feud Said to Have Been Renewed." *New York Times* (June 29): 21.

Gage, Nicholas, ed.

1972 *Mafia, U.S.A.* New York: Dell.

Gall, Carlotta

2008a "Afghanistan's Opium Harvest Shrinks After Record Crop, U.N. Says." *New York Times* (August 27): 10.

2008b "Bush Ex-Official Says Corrupt Afghan and a Hesitant Military Hinder Drug Fight." *New York Times* (July 24): 12.

2006 "Another Year of Drug War, and the Poppy Crop Flourishes." *New York Times* (February 17): 4.

2005 "Armed and Elusive, Afghan Drug Dealers Roam Free." *New York Times* (January 2): 3.

2001 "Macedonia Village Is Center of Europe Web in Sex Trade." *New York Times* (July 28): 1, 6.

Gallagher, James P.

1995a "In Chechnya, Vendetta Is a Way of Life, Death." *Chicago Tribune* (March 5): 1, 12.

1995b "Corruption Touches Many Lives in Russia." *Chicago Tribune* (August 13): 15, 18.

1994 "Russian Gangs Send the Dead Out in Style." *Chicago Tribune* (November 20): 29.

1992a "Chechens Stir Bloody Cauldron in Caucasus." *Chicago Tribune* (January 10): 20.

1992b "As Law Enforcement Crumbles, Russian Crime, Gangs Proliferate." *Chicago Tribune* (September 2): 6.

Galliher, John F. and James A. Cain

1974 "Citation Support for the Mafia Myth in Criminology Textbooks." *American Sociologist* 9 (May): 68–74.

Gallo, Patrick J.

1981 *Old Bread, New Wine: A Portrait of the Italian-American.* Chicago: Nelson-Hall.

Galvan, Manuel

1982 "Capone's Yacht Sails Calmer Seas Today." *Chicago Tribune* (February 16): Sec. 2: 1.

Gambetta, Diego

2009 *Codes of the Underworld: How Criminals Communicate.* Princeton, NJ: Princeton University Press.

1993 *The Sicilian Mafia: The Business of Private Protection.* Cambridge, MA: Harvard University Press.

Gambino, Richard

1977 *Vendetta.* Garden City, NY: Doubleday.

1974 *Blood of My Blood: The Dilemma of the Italian-American.* Garden City: Doubleday.

"Gamblers Hunted in Rothstein Attack"

1928 *New York Times* (November 6): 1.

Gambling Commission. See Commission on the Review of the National Policy Toward Gambling

"Gang Kills Suspect in Alien Smuggling"

1931 *New York Times* (September 11): 1.

"Gang Linked to Union Charged at Trial"

1934 *New York Times* (January 31): 8.

"Gangster Shot in Daylight Attack"

1928 *New York Times* (July 2): 1.

GAO. See Government Accounting Office

Gardiner, John A.

1970 *The Politics of Corruption: Organized Crime in an American City.* New York: Russell Sage Foundation.

Gately, William and Yvette Fernandez

1994 *Dead Ringer.* New York: Donald I. Fine.

Gender, Alison

2005 "Feds Hook King of Coke." *New York Daily News* (August 20): 5.

Genzman, Robert W.

1988 "Press Release." October 11.

Gerlat, Allan

2002 "Mob Mentality—NYC Breaks Longtime Grip." *Waste News* 7 (April 15): 12.

Giancana, Antoinette and Thomas C. Renner

1985 *Mafia Princess: Growing Up in Sam Giancana's Family.* New York: Avon.

Giancana, Sam and Chuck Giancana

1992 *Double Cross: Inside Story of the Mobster Who Controlled America.* New York: Warner Books.

Gilinsky, Yakov

2004 "Contemporary Russian Corruption." Pages 60–69 in *Organized Crime, Trafficking, Drugs: Selected Papers Presented at the Annual Conference of the European Society of Criminology, Helsinki.* Helsinki, Finland: European Institute for Criminal Prevention and Control.

Giuliani, Rudolph W.

1987 "Legal Remedies for Attacking Organized Crime." Pages 103–30 in *Major Issues in Organized Crime Control*, edited by Herbert Edelhertz. Washington, DC: U.S. Government Printing Office.

Gjoni, Ilir

2004 "Organized Crime and National Security: The Albanian Case." Master's Thesis. Monterey, CA: Naval Postgraduate School.

Glab, Michael G.

1997 "Gang Green." *Chicago Reader* (November 14): 1, 16–34.

Glaberson, William

1989 "U.S. Loses Round in Bid to Curb Mob at Fish Market." *New York Times* (January 25): 12.

Glenny, Misha

2008 *McMafia: A Journey Through the Global Criminal Underworld.* New York: Knopf.

Glonti, Georgi

2003 "Human Trafficking: Concept, Classification, and Questions of Legislative Regulation." Pages 70–80 in *Organised Crime, Trafficking, Drugs: Selected Papers Presented at the Annual Conference of the European Society of Criminology*, Helsinki, edited by Sami Nevala and Kauko Armomaa.

Goddard, Donald

1988 *Undercover: The Secret Lives of a Federal Agent*. New York: Times Books.

1980 *All Fall Down*. New York: Times Books.

1978 *Easy Money*. New York: Farrar, Straus and Giroux.

1974 *Joey*. New York: Harper & Row.

Godfrey, E. Drexel, Jr. and Don R. Harris

1971 *Basic Elements of Intelligence*. Washington, DC: U.S. Government Printing Office.

Godson, Roy and William J. Olson

1995 "International Organized Crime." *Society* (January/February): 18–29.

Goering, Laurie

2001 "Colombia Caught in a Struggle for Power." *Chicago Tribune* (May 27): 1, 12.

1998 "In Peru, Battle Against Flow of Drugs Moves to Amazon River Maze." *Chicago Tribune* (June 30): 6.

Gold, Mark S., Charles A. Dackis, A. L. C. Pottash, Irl Extein, and Arnold Washton

1986 "Cocaine Update: From Bench to Bedside." *Advances in Alcohol and Substance Abuse* 5 (Fall/Winter): 35–60.

Goldberg, Carey

2001 "An Innocent Man Goes Free 33 Years After Conviction." *New York Times* (February 2): 12.

1999 "At Stake in a Messy Boston Trial: How to Handle Informers' Crimes." *New York Times* (March 13): 1, 7.

Goldberg, Jeffrey

1999 "The Don is Done." *New York Times Magazine* (January 31): 24–31, 62–66, 71.

1995 "Hoffa Lives!" *New York* (July 31): 27–35.

Golden, Tim

2001 "The Citibank Connection: Real Money, Shadow Banks." *New York Times* (February 27): 6.

2000a "Killing Raises Doubts on Mexico's War on Drugs." *New York Times* (June 5): 3.

2000b "Mexican Gang Still on Loose Despite Search." *New York Times* (January 10): 1, 9.

1999a "Top Mexican Off-Limits to U.S. Drug Agents." *New York Times* (March 16): 1, 10.

1999b "2 Mexican Banks to Plead Guilty in Laundering Case." *New York Times* (March 30): 3.

1998a "In Breakthrough, Mexican Official Testifies in Texas." *New York Times* (July 15): 1, 6.

1998b "Elite Mexican Drug Officers Said To Be Tied to Traffickers." *New York Times* (September 16): 1, 10.

1998c "Salinas Brother Is Tied by Swiss to Drug Trade." *New York Times* (September 19): 1, 6.

1998d "Saying Salinas Aided Traffickers, Swiss Seize $90 Million." *New York Times* (October 21): 3.

1997a "Mexico and Drugs: Was the U.S. Napping?" *New York Times* (July 11): 1, 10.

1997b "Pakistan's Jailing of a Drug Agent Sours U.S. Ties." *New York Times* (November 17): 1, 10.

1995a "To Help Keep Mexico Stable, U.S. Soft-Pedaled Drug War." *New York Times* (July 31): 1, 4.

1995b "Mexican Connection Grows as Cocaine Supplier to U.S." *New York Times* (July 30): 1, 8.

Goldstein, Joseph

1982 "Police Discretion Not to Invoke the Criminal Process." Pages 33–42 in *The Invisible Justice System: Discretion and the Law*, 2d ed., edited by Burton Atkins and Mark Pogrebin. Cincinnati, OH: Anderson.

Goldstock, Ronald and Dan T. Coenen

1978 *Extortionate and Usurious Credit Transactions: Background Materials*. Ithaca, NY: Cornell Institute on Organized Crime.

Goozner, Merrill

1996 "New York Trying to Trash Mob Hold on Waste-Hauling." *Chicago Tribune* (December 6): 1, 16.

1992 "Thugs Avenge a Movie's Insults." *Chicago Tribune* (June 4): 4.

Gordon, Michael R.

1996 "Key Russian Legislator Accuses Leading Military Officers of Graft." *New York Times* (July 10): 1, 4.

Gosch, Martin and Richard Hammer

1974 *The Last Testament of Lucky Luciano*. Boston: Little, Brown.

Gosnell, Harold

1977 *Machine Politics: The Chicago Model*. Chicago: University of Chicago. Originally published in 1937.

Gottschalk, Marie

2006 *The Prison and the Gallows: The Politics of Incarceration in America*. New York: Cambridge University Press.

Gottschalk, Petter

2009 *Entrepreneurship and Organised Crime: Entrepreneurs in Illegal Business*. Chltenham, United Kingdom: Edward Elgar.

Gottfried, Alex

1962 *Boss Cermak of Chicago*. Seattle: University of Washington Press.

Government Accountability Office (GAO)

2010 *Moving Illegal Proceeds*. Washington, DC: GAO.

2009 *Bank Secrecy Act*. Washington, DC: GAO.

2006 "Human Trafficking: Better Data, Strategy, and Reporting Needed to Enhance U.S. Anti-Trafficking Efforts Abroad." *Trends in Organized Crime* 10 (Fall): 16–38.

Graham, Fred

1977 *The Atlas Program.* Boston: Little, Brown.

Graham, Hugh Davis and Ted Robert Gurr, eds.

1969 *The History of Violence in America: A Report to the National Commission on the Causes and Prevention of Violence.* New York: Bantam.

Grann, David

2004 "The Brand." *New Yorker* (February 16 & 23): 157–71.

Greenberg, Norman

1981 *The Man with a Steel Guitar: Portrait of Desperation, and Crime.* Hanover, NH: University Press of New England.

Greenblatt, Stephen

2004 "Shakespeare's Leap." *New York Times Magazine* (September 12): 50–55.

Greenhouse, Steven

2000a "Ex-Union Leader to Admit Ferrari Fraud." *New York Times* (January 28): 10.

2000b "U.S. Is Easing Close Scrutiny of Hotel Union." *New York Times* (December 3): 31.

2000c "Union Cleanup Praised; U.S. Oversight Is Eased." *New York Times* (January 21): 20.

1999 "Laborers' Union President Is Cleared of Links to Mob." *New York Times* (March 10): 9.

1997 "An Overseer Bars Teamster Leader from Re-election." *New York Times* (November 18): 1, 16.

Greenhouse, Steven and William K. Rashbaum

2008 "Judge Continues Oversight of the Carpenter's Union." *New York Times* (August 13): B3.

Griffin, Dennis and Frank Cullotta

2007 *Cullotta: The Life of a Chicago Criminal, Las Vegas Mobster, and Government Witness.* Las Vegas: Huntington Press.

Griffin, Sean Patrick

2003 *Philadelphia's Black Mafia: A Social and Political History.* Dordrecht, Netherlands: Kluwer.

Grillo, Ioan

2011 *El Narco: Inside Mexico's Criminal Insurgency.* New York: Bloomsbury Press.

Grinspoon, Lester

1979 *Psychedelic Drugs Reconsidered.* New York: Basic Books.

Grinspoon, Lester and James B. Bakalar

1985 *Cocaine: A Drug and Its Social Evolution,* Revised ed. New York: Basic Books.

1976 *Cocaine: A Drug and Its Social Evolution.* New York: Basic Books.

Griswold, Eliza

2005 "Medellín: Stories From an Urban War." *National Geographic* (March): 72–91.

Grob, Charles S., Russell E. Poland, Linda Chang, and Thomas Ernst

1996 "Psychobiologic Effects of 3,4-methylenedioxymethamphetamine in Humans: Methodological Considerations and Preliminary Observations." *Behavioral Brain Research* 73: 103–107.

Grutzner, Charles

1969 "Genovese Dies in Prison at 71; 'Boss of Bosses' of Mafia Here." *New York Times* (February 15): 1, 29.

Gugliotta, Guy and Jeff Leen

1989 *Kings of Cocaine: Inside the Medellín Cartel—An Astonishing True Story of Murder, Money, and International Corruption.* New York: Simon and Schuster.

Gunst, Laurie

1996 *Born Fi' Dead: A Journey Through the Jamaican Posse Underworld.* New York: Henry Holt and Company.

Haberman, Clyde

1985 "TV Funeral for Japan's Slain Godfather." *New York Times* (February 1): 6.

Hagan, Frank

2006 "'Organized Crime' and 'Organized Crime': Indeterminate Problems of Definition." *Trends in Organized Crime* 9 (June): 127–37.

Haley, Bruce

1990 "Burma's Hidden Wars." *U.S. News and World Report* (December 10): 44–47.

Hall, Kevin G.

2000 "Drug Chemicals Difficult to Target." *Chicago Tribune* (November 23): 36.

Haller, Mark H.

1991 *Life under Bruno: The Economics of an Organized Crime Family.* Conshohocken, PA: Pennsylvania Crime Commission.

1990a "Illegal Enterprise: A Theoretical and Historic Interpretation." *Criminology* 28 (May): 207–35.

1990b "Policy Gambling, Entertainment, and the Emergence of Black Politics: Chicago from 1900 to 1940." *Journal of Social History* 24: 719–38.

1985a "Bootleggers as Businessmen: From City Slums to City Builders." Pages 139–57 in *Law, Alcohol, and Order: Perspectives on National Prohibition,* edited by David E. Kyvig. Westport, CT: Greenwood.

1985b "Philadelphia Bootlegging and the Report of the Special Grand Jury." *Pennsylvania Magazine of History and Biography* 109 (April): 215–33.

1974 "Bootlegging in Chicago: The Structure of an Illegal Enterprise." Paper presented at the annual meeting of the American Historical Association, Chicago, December 28.

1971–72 "Organized Crime in Urban Society: Chicago in the Twentieth Century." *Journal of Social History* 5: 210–34.

Hamilton, Don

1998 "For Motorcyclists, It's the Black Hills or Bust." *Chicago Tribune* (July 26): Sec. 12: 1, 7.

Hamm, Richard F.

1995 *Shaping the 18th Amendment*. Chapel Hill: University of North Carolina Press.

Handelman, Stephen

1995 *Comrade Criminal: Russia's New Mafiya*. New Haven, CT: Yale University Press.

Hapgood, Norman and Henry Moskowitz

1927 *Up from the Streets: Alfred E. Smith*. New York: Harcourt, Brace.

Harker, R. Phillip

1978 "Sports Bookmaking Operations." *FBI Law Enforcement Bulletin* (September): FBI reprint.

1977 "Sports Wagering and the 'Line.'" *FBI Law Enforcement Bulletin* (November): FBI reprint.

Harmon, Dave

1993 "Ex-Agent: Drug Sales Aided Contras." *Chicago Tribune* (January 26): 3.

Hartman, Victor E.

2001 "Implementing an Asset Forfeiture Program." *FBI Law Enforcement Bulletin* (January): 1–7.

Hartocollis, Anemona

2006 "Enforcer Paints Picture of Gotti as Powerful Don." *New York Times* (February 23): B6.

2005 "Albanian Gang Portrayed as Aspiring Mafiosi." *New York Times* (December 20): B3.

Hawley, Chris

2010a "Chapel to Patron Saint of Drug War." *USA Today* (March 17): Internet.

2010b "Drug Cartels Outmatch, Outgun Mexico's Police." *USA Today* (June 16): Internet.

2008 "Beer's Outlaw Image Leaves Bad Taste in Critic's Mouths." *USA Today* (September 3): Internet.

Hayde, Frank R.

2008 *The Mafia and the Machine: The Story of the Kansas City Mob*. Fort Lee, NJ: Barricade Books.

Hayes, Bill

2005 *The Original Wild Ones: Tales of the Boozefighters Motorcycle Club*. St. Paul, MN: MBI Publishing Co.

Hayner, Don

1990 "Chinatown Gambling: Inside Story." *Chicago Sun-Times* (September 2): 1, 20–21.

Healey, James R. and Barbara Hagenbaugh

2005 "Online Bettors Furiously Ante Up for March Madness." *USA Today* (March 18): B1, 2.

Healy, Patrick

2003 "Investigators Say Fraud Ring Staged Thousands of Crashes." *New York Times* (August 13): 1, B5.

Heber, Anita

2009 "Networks of Organized Black Market Labour in the Building Trade." *Trends in Organized Crime* 13 (January): 122–44.

Hefling, Kimberly

2000 "Pot Crop Thrives in Appalachia." Associated Press (May 14): Internet.

Helmer, John

1975 *Drugs and Minority Oppression*. New York: Seabury Press.

Henriques, Diana B. with Dean Baquet

1993 "Investigators Say Bid-Rigging Is Common in Milk Industry." *New York Times* (May 23): 1, 12.

Herguth, Robert

2004 "Sons of the Mob Step Up in Family Business—Unions." *Chicago Sun-Times* (July 4): 18.

Herion, Don

2008 *Pay, Quit, Die*. Bloomington, IN: Xlibris Corp.

1998 Director of the Vice Enforcement Unit of the Cook County (IL) Sheriff's Police Department. Personal interviews.

Hersh, Seymour M.

1994 "The Wild East." *Atlantic Monthly* (June): 61–85.

Hess, David, Kenneth Meyers, Michele Gideon, Sal E. Gomez, and John Daly

1999 "Italian Organized Crime and Money Laundering." Pages 345–405 in *Organized Crime: Uncertainties and Dilemmas*, edited by Stanley Einstein and Menachem Amir. Chicago: Office of International Criminal Justice of the University of Illinois at Chicago.

Hess, Henner

1973 *Mafia and Mafiosi: The Structure of Power*. Lexington, MA: D. C. Heath.

Hibbert, Christopher

1966 *Garibaldi and His Enemies*. Boston: Little, Brown.

Hill, Henry, with Douglas S. Looney

1981 "How I Put the Fix In." *Sports Illustrated* (February 16): 14–21.

Hill, Peter B. E.

2003 *The Japanese Mafia: Yakuza, Law, and the State*. Oxford, England: Oxford University Press.

Himmelstein, Jerome L.

1983 *The Strange Career of Marijuana: Politics and Ideology of Drug Control in America*. Westport, CT: Greenwood.

Hirsch, Michael and Hideo Takayama

1997 "Big Bang or Bust?" *Newsweek* (September 1): 44–45.

Hirschi, Travis

1969 *Causes of Delinquency*. Berkeley: University of California Press.

"History of Antagonism, A"

1994 *New York Times* (December 13): 3.

Hoar, Sean B.

2001 "Identity Theft: The Crime of the New Millennium." *USA Bulletin* (March 2001): Internet.

Hobsbawm, Eric J.

1976 "Mafia." Pages 90–98 in *The Crime Society*, edited by Francis A. J. Ianni and Elizabeth Reuss-Ianni. New York: New American Library.

1971 *Bandits*. New York: Dell.

1969 "The American Mafia." *The Listener* 82 (November): 685–88.

1959 *Social Bandits and Primitive Rebels*. Glencoe, IL: Free Press.

Hockstader, Lee

1995 "Crime Atop Chaos: In Post Communist Russia, the Strong Arm of the Mafiya is Everywhere." *Washington Post*, National Weekly Edition (March 20–26): 6–9.

Hoffman, Paul

1976 *To Drop a Dime*. New York: Putnam's.

Hofstadter, Richard

1956 *The Age of Reform: From Bryan to F.D.R.* New York: Knopf.

Hofstadter, Richard and Michael Wallace, eds.

1971 *American Violence: A Documentary History*. New York: Vintage.

Hohimer, Frank

1975 *The Home Invaders*. Chicago: Chicago Review Press.

Homans, George C.

1961 *Social Behavior: Its Elementary Forms*. New York: Harcourt, Brace and World.

Homer, Frederic D.

1974 *Guns and Garlic*. West Lafayette, IN: Purdue University Press.

Hopton, Isobel

1996 "On the Triad Trail." *CJ International* 12 (July–August): 5–6.

Horne, Louther

1932 "Capone's Trip to Jail Ends a Long Battle." *New York Times* (May 8): IX 1.

Horowtiz, Jason

2005 "Italy: 46 Held in Mafia Raids." *New York Times* (January 26): 6.

2004 "Italy's Worrisome South Erupts as Mob Killings Rise in Naples." *New York Times* (November 26): 5.

Howe, Benjamin Ryder

2000 "Out of the Jungle." *Atlantic Monthly* (May): 32–38.

Hudson, Rex

2010 *Terrorist and Organized Crime Groups in the Tri-Border Area of South America*, revised edition. Washington, DC: Library of Congress.

Hughes, Donna M. and Tatyana Denisova

2001 "The Transnational Political Criminal Nexus of Trafficking in Women from Ukraine." *Trends in Organized Crime* 6 (Spring/September): 43–67.

Humphries, Drew and David F. Greenberg

1981 "The Dialectics of Crime Control." Pages 209–54 in *Crime and Capitalism*, edited by David F. Greenberg. Palo Alto, CA: Mayfield.

Hundley, Tom

1998a "Anti-Mafia Sweep Helps Sicilian Capital Clean Up Its Act." *Chicago Tribune* (April 22): 7.

1998b "Euro Conversion Could Be Mafia's Big Chance." *Chicago Tribune* (November 8): 4.

1998c "Sicilian Women Lift Past Veil to Take Charge." *Chicago Tribune* (September 20): 5.

1997 "Violence Tempers Naples' Return to Glory." *Chicago Tribune* (March 1): 7.

Huston, Peter

2001 *Tongs, Gangs, and Triads: Chinese Crime Groups in North America*. San Jose, CA: Authors Choice Press.

Ianni, Francis A. J.

1974 *The Black Mafia: Ethnic Succession in Organized Crime*. New York: Simon and Schuster.

1972 *A Family Business: Kinship and Social Control in Organized Crime*. New York: Russell Sage Foundation.

Iannuzzi, Joseph

1993 *Joe Dogs: The Life and Crimes of a Mobster*. New York: Simon and Schuster.

Ibrahim, Youssef M.

1997 "Sweden's Courteous Police Spoil a Hell's Angels Party." *New York Times* (March 3): 1, 6.

Illicit Drug Policies: Selected Laws from the 50 States

2002 Chicago, IL: Robert Wood Johnson Foundation.

Iliff, Laurence

2005 "Nuevo Laredo Officers Charged With Organized-Crime Activities." *Dallas Morning News* (September 6): Internet.

Imhoff, John J. and Stephen P. Cutler

1998 "INTERPOL: Extending Law Enforcement's Reach Around the World." *FBI Law Enforcement Bulletin* (December): 10–16.

Inciardi, James A.

1986 *The War on Drugs: Heroin, Cocaine, Crime, and Public Policy*. Palo Alto, CA: Mayfield.

1975 *Careers in Crime*. Chicago: Rand McNally.

Intelligence Bulletin Colombia

1995 Washington, DC: Drug Enforcement Administration.

International Narcotics Control Strategy Report, 1999

2000 Bureau for International Narcotics and Law Enforcement Affairs, U.S. Department of State. Washington, DC, March 2000.

International Organization for Migration (IOM)

1998 *Information Campaign Against Trafficking in Women from Ukraine.* IOM.

INTERPOL at Work

2003 Lyon, France: Interpol General Secretariat.

Irey, Elmer L. and William T. Slocum

1948 *The Tax Dodgers.* Garden City, NY: Doubleday.

Israely, Jeff

2004 "Sicily's Invisible Man." *Time International* (September 6): 50.

"Italy: Mafia Boss Returns to Rome Amid Tight Security"

2008 *Adnkronos International* (August 20): Internet.

Iwai, Hiroaki

1986 "Organized Crime in Japan." Pages 208–33 in *Organized Crime: A Global Perspective,* edited by Robert J. Kelly. Totowa, NJ: Rowman and Littlefield.

Jackson, David

1990 "Bad Company." *Chicago* (February): 91–95, 109–10.

Jacobs, D. Lea

2002 *Friend of the Family.* Washington, DC: Compass Press.

Jacobs, James B.

2006 *Mobsters, Unions, and Feds: The Mafia and the American Labor Movement.* New York: New York University Press.

Jacobs, James B. and R. P. Alford

2005 "The Teamsters Rocky Road to Recovery—The Demise of Project RISE." *Trends in Organized Crime* 9 (Fall): 5–23.

Jacobs, James B. with Colleen Friel and Robert Raddick

1999 *Gotham Unbound: How New York City Was Liberated From the Clutches of Cosa Nostra.* New York: New York University Press.

Jacobs, James B. and Elizabeth A. Mullin

2003 "Congress' Role in the Defeat of Organized Crime." *Criminal Law Bulletin* (May–June): 269–312.

Jacobs, James B. with Christopher Panarella and Jay Worthington

1994 *Busting the Mob: United States v. Cosa Nostra.* New York: New York University Press.

Jacobs, James B. and Kristin Stohner

2005 "Ten Years of Court-Supervised Reform: A Chronicle and Assessment." *California Criminal Law Review* 3 (Vol. 6): Internet.

Jacobson, Mark

2000 "The Return of Superfly." *New York* (August 14): 36–45.

"Jail Informer's Admissions Spur Inquiry"

1989 *New York Times* (January 3): 10.

"Jamaican Murders Hit an All-Time High"

2005 *New York Daily News* (November 26): 6.

James, Frank

2011 "James (Whitey) Bulger." *New York Times* (September 7): Internet.

2001 "Tax Havens an Evasive Issue." *Chicago Tribune* (July 22): Sec. 5: 1, 6.

Jamieson, Alison

2000 *The Antimafia: Italy's Fight Against Organized Crime.* New York: St. Martin's.

Jenkins, Philip and Gary W. Potter

1985 *The City and the Syndicate: Organizing Crime in Philadelphia.* Lexington, MA: Ginn Custom Publishing.

Jennings, Dean

1967 *We Only Kill Each Other.* Englewood Cliffs, NJ: Prentice-Hall.

Joe, Karen

1992 "Chinese Gangs and Tongs: An Exploratory Look at the Connection on the West Coast." Paper presented at the annual meeting of the American Society of Criminology, New Orleans, November 4–7.

"Johnny Torrio, Ex-Public Enemy 1, Dies; Made Al Capone Boss of the Underworld"

1957 *New York Times* (May 8): 32.

Johnson, Earl, Jr.

1963 "Organized Crime: Challenge to the American Legal System." *Criminal Law, Criminology, and Police Science* 54 (March): 1–29.

Johnson, Kirk

1996 "Laborers' Union Agrees to Open Up Elections." *New York Times* (February 2): 12.

1986 "Manhattan Gang Is Tied to 30 Unsolved Killings." *New York Times* (December 17): 19.

Johnson, Malcolm

1972 "In Hollywood." Pages 325–38 in *Mafia, U.S.A.,* edited by Nicholas Gage. New York: Dell.

Johnston, David Cay

2002 "Loophole Is Too Small for an Ex-Convict." *New York Times* (March 17): 8.

Johnston, Michael

1982 *Political Corruption and Public Policy in America.* Monterey, CA: Brooks/Cole.

Jones, Marilyn

2002 "Policy Paradox: Implications of U.S. Drug Control Policy for Jamaica." *Annals* 582 (July): 117–47.

Jordon, Mary and Kevin Sullivan

1999 "Exploiting Weakness, Japanese Mobsters Go Mainstream." *Philadelphia Inquirer* (April 25): 17.

Joselit, Jenna Weissman

1983 *Our Gang: Jewish Crime and the New York Jewish Community, 1900–1940.* Bloomington: Indiana University Press.

Josephson, Matthew

1962 *The Robber Barons.* New York: Harcourt, Brace and World. Originally published in 1934.

Kaban, Elif

1998 "Russian Mafia Suspect Goes on Swiss Trial." *Reuters* (November 30): Internet.

Kaiser, Rob D.

1999 "Laborers Union Ousts Local Chief." *Chicago Tribune* (May 18): Sec. 3: 1, 2.

Kalfus, Ken

1996 "Far From Normal: Scenes from the New Moscow." *Harper's* (December): 53–62.

Kaplan, David E.

1998 "Yakuza, Inc." *U.S. News and World Report* (April 13): 40–47.

Kaplan, David E. and Alec Dubro

1986 *Yakuza: The Explosive Account of Japan's Criminal Underworld.* Reading, MA: Addison-Wesley.

Kaplan, Robert D.

2008 "Lifting the Bamboo Curtain." *The Atlantic* (September): 84–95.

Karch, Steven B.

1996 *The Pathology of Drug Abuse*, 2nd ed. Boca Raton, FL: CRC Press.

Katcher, Leo

1959 *The Big Bankroll: The Life and Times of Arnold Rothstein.* New York: Harper & Brothers.

Katel, Peter

1996 "Handing Off a Hot Case." *Newsweek* (January 29): 41.

Katz, Leonard

1973 *Uncle Frank: The Biography of Frank Costello.* New York: Drake Publishers.

Kavieff, Paul R.

2006 *The Life and Times of Lepke Buchalter.* Fort Lee, NJ: Barricade Books.

2000 *The Purple Gang: Organized Crime in Detroit, 1910–1945.* Fort Lee, NJ: Barricade Books.

Keefe, Joseph D.

2001 "Testimony Before the U.S. House of Representatives Committee on Government Reform Subcommittee on Criminal Justice, Drug Policy and Human Resources," July 12.

Keefe, Patrick Radden

2009 *The Snakehead.* New York: Anchor Books.

Kefauver, Estes (Special Committee to Investigate Organized Crime in Interstate Commerce)

1951a *Third Interim Report.* Washington, DC: U.S. Government Printing Office.

1951b *Crime in America.* Garden City, NY: Doubleday.

Kelly, Robert J.

1999 *The Upperworld and the Underworld: Case Studies of Racketeering and Business Infiltrations in the United States.* Hingham, MA: Kluwer.

1986 *Organized Crime: An International Perspective.* Totowa, NJ: Rowman and Littlefield.

Kelly Robert J., Ko-lin Chin, and Jeffrey A. Fagan

1993 "The Dragon Breathes Fire: Chinese Organized Crime in New York City. *Crime, Law and Social Change* 19: 245–69.

Kelly, Robert J., Ko-lin Chin, and Rufus Schatzberg, eds.

1994 *Handbook of Organized Crime in the United States.* Westport, CT: Greenwood.

Kennedy, David M.

1999 "Victory at Sea." *Atlantic Monthly* (March): 51–76.

Kennedy, Randy

1996 "Drugs Stir Neighborhood Worries." *New York Times* (October 3): B12.

Kennedy, Robert F.

1960 *The Enemy Within.* New York: Popular Library.

Kerr, Peter

1988a "Chinese Criminals Move to Broaden Role in U.S." *New York Times* (January 4): 1, 12.

1988b "Cocaine Glut Puts New York in Drug Rings' Tug-of-War." *New York Times* (August 24): 14.

1988c "Cocaine Ring Holding Fast in Colombia." *New York Times* (May 21): 1, 5.

Kershaw, Sarah

2006 "Through Indian Lands, Drugs' Shadowy Trail." *New York Times* (February 19): 1, 26–27.

Kidner, John

1976 *Crimaldi: Contract Killer.* Washington, DC: Acropolis Books.

Kihss, Peter

1979 "John Dioguardi (Johnny Dio), 64, a Leader in Organized Crime, Dies." *New York Times* (January 16): B6.

Kilgannon, Corey

2005 "Phone Executive Admits Conspiracy in Mob Fraud." *New York Times* (January 9): 28.

Kilian, Michael

2002 "Seizure of Drugs at Sea Soaring." *Chicago Tribune* (March 18): 9.

Kilian, Michael, Connie Fletcher, and Richard P. Ciccone

1979 *Who Runs Chicago?* New York: St. Martin's Press.

Kimeldorf, Howard

1988 *Reds or Rackets? The Making of Radical and Conservative Unions on the Waterfront*. Berkeley: University of California Press.

Kinder, Douglas Clark

1992 "Shutting Out the Evil: Nativism and Narcotics Control in the United States." Pages 117–42 in *Drug Control Policy: Essays in Historical and Comparative Perspective*, edited by William O. Walker. University Park: Pennsylvania State University.

King, Rufus

1969 *Gambling and Organized Crime*. Washington, DC: Public Affairs Press.

1963 "The Fifth Amendment Privilege and Immunity Legislation." *Notre Dame Lawyer* 38 (September): 641–54.

Kingston, Kimberly A.

1988 "Reasonable Expectation of Privacy Cases Revive Traditional Investigative Techniques." *FBI Law Enforcement Bulletin* (November): 22–29.

Kinzer, Stephan

1996a "Biker Wars in the Land of Vikings." *New York Times* (May 6): 5.

1996b "In Germany, Vietnamese Terrorize Vietnamese." *New York Times* (May 23): 4.

Kirk, Donald

1981 "Death of Japan Crime Boss Breeds Fear." *Miami Herald* (July 27): 17.

1976 "Crime, Politics and Finger Chopping." *New York Times Magazine* (December 12): 60–61, 91–97.

Kleemans, Edward R. and Christianne J. de Poot

2008 "Criminal Careers in Organized Crime and Social Opportunity Structure." *European Journal of Criminology* 5 (1): 69–98.

Klein, Malcolm, Cheryl L. Maxson, and Lea C. Cunningham

1991 "'Crack,' Street Gangs, and Violence." *Criminology* 29 (November): 623–50.

Klein, Maury

1986 *Life and Times of Jay Gould*. Baltimore, MD: Johns Hopkins University Press.

Kleinfield, N. R.

1995 "Chinatown Officers Said to Forge a Partnership of Vice and Greed." *New York Times* (June 19): 1, B12.

Kleinknecht, William

1996 *The New Ethnic Mobs: The Changing Face of Organized Crime in America*. New York: Free Press.

Klepper, Michael, Robert Gunther, Jeanette Baik, Linda Barth, and Christine Gibson

1998 "The American Heritage 40." *American Heritage* (October): 56–60.

Kobler, John

1971 *Capone: The Life and World of Al Capone*. Greenwich, CT: Fawcett.

Kobrin, Solomon

1966 "The Conflict of Values in Delinquency Areas." Pages 151–60 in *Juvenile Delinquency: A Book of Readings,* edited by Rose Giallombardo. New York: Wiley.

Kocieniewski, David

1997 "New York Pays a High Price for Police Lies." *New York Times* (January 5): 1, 16.

Koerber, Brendan I.

1997 "Extreme." *U.S. Press and World Report* (July 30): 50–60.

Kolliarakis, Georgios

2010 "Networks and the Study of Criminal and Terrorist Organizations." Pages 81–97 in *Transnational Terrorism, Organized Crime and Peace-Building*. Edited by Wolfgang Benedek Christopher Daase, Vojin Dimitrijevic' and Petrus van Duyne. New York: Palgrave Macmillan.

Konigsberg, Eric

2001 "Blood Relation." *New Yorker* (August 6): 46–59.

Koziol, Ronald and Edward Baumann

1987 "How Frank Nitti Met His Fate." *Chicago Tribune* (June 29): Sec. 5: 1, 7.

Koziol Ronald and George Estep

1983 "Fresh Insight into February 14 Killings." *Chicago Tribune* (February 14): 13.

Krajicek, David J.

2007 "Rhode Island Rumrunner." *New York Daily News* (August 5): 38.

Krajick, Kevin

2010 "Wrong Guy Whacked." *New York Daily News* (July 25): 45.

2004 "Officer Billy Club." *New York Daily News* (January 18): 47.

1983 "Should Police Wiretap?" *Police Magazine* (May): 29–32, 36–41.

Kramer, Andrew

2008a "Chechnya's Capital Rises from the Ashes, Atop Hidden Horrors." *New York Times* (April 30): 9.

2008b "Russian Police Arrest a Suspected Racketeer." *New York Times* (January 26): C4.

Kramer, Jane

1992 "Letter from Europe." *New Yorker* (September 21): 108–24.

Kramer, Tom, Martin Jelsma, and Tom Blickman

2010 "Withdrawal Symptoms in the Golden Triangle: A Drugs Market in Disarray." *Trends in Organized Crime* 13: 87–108.

Krauss, Clifford

2002 "U.S. Moves to Close Canadian Drug Route for Illegal Stimulant." *New York Times* (March 5): 5.

2000 "Bolivia Wiping Out Coca, at a Price." *New York Times* (October 23): 10.

Krauss, Clifford and Douglas Frantz

1995 "Cali Drug Cartel Using U.S. Business to Launder Cash." *New York Times* (October 30): 1, 13.

Krebs, Brian

2009 "Organized Crime Behind a Majority of Data Breaches." *Washington Post* (April 15): Internet.

Kreck, Dick

2009 *Smaldone: The Untold Story an American Crime Family*. Golden, CO: Fulcrum Publishing.

Kristof, Nicholas D.

1999 "A Sexy Economic Feud of No Interest to the I.M.F." *New York Times* (June 17): 4.

1995a "Japanese Outcasts Better Off Than in Past But Still Outcast." *New York Times* (November 30): 1, 8.

1995b "Mob Takes a Holiday as V.I.P.'s Tour Osaka." *New York Times* (November 19): 6.

1995c "The Quake That Hurt Kobe Helps Its Gangs Get Richer." *New York Times* (June 6): 1, 4.

Kurtis, Bill

1976 "The Caviar Connection." *New York Times Magazine* (October 26): 132–33, 136–37, 141.

Kwitny, Jonathan

1979 *Vicious Circles: The Mafia in the Marketplace*. New York: Norton.

Labaton, Stephen

2001 "The World Gets Tough on Price Fixers." *New York Times* (June 3): Sec. 3: 1, 7.

1997 "100 Are Arrested as Drug Ring with 'Speed' Is Broken Up." *New York Times* (December 6): 7.

1989a "Banking's Technology Helps Drug Dealers Export Cash." *New York Times* (August 14): 1, 10.

1989b "Bank to Plead Guilty to Laundering Drug Money." *New York Times* (August 11): 1, 10.

Labaton, Stephen and David Barboza

1999 "U.S. Outlines How Makers of Vitamins Fixed Global Prices." *New York Times* (May 21): 1, C6.

Lacey, Mark

2010 "In Search for Killers of 3 in Mexico, Focus Tightens on Cross-Border Gang." *New York Times* (March 19): 6.

2008a "Tijuana's New Police Chief Touts an Achievement: Survival." *New York Times* (August 23): A8.

2008b "In Mexico, Sorting Out Good Guys From Bad." *New York Times* (November 2): 6.

2008c "Officials Say Drug Cartels Infiltrated Mexican Law Unit." *New York Times* (October 28): 10.

Lacey, Mark and Antonio Betancourt

2008 "A Boy's Killing Prods a City to Stand Up to Kidnappers." *New York Times* (August 14): Internet.

Lacey, Robert

1991 *Little Man: Meyer Lansky and the Gangster Life*. Boston: Little, Brown.

Lambert, Bruce

2006 "Law Enforcement Agencies Break 2 Major Drug Rings." *New York Times* (March 31): B3.

Lamothe, Lee and Adrian Humphreys

2006 *The Sixth Family: The Collapse of the New York Mafia and the Rise of Vito Rizzuto*. Mississauga, Ontario, Canada: John Wiley and Sons.

Lamour, Catherine and Michael R. Lamberti

1974 *The International Connection: Opium from Growers to Pushers*. New York: Pantheon.

Landesco, John

1968 *Organized Crime in Chicago*. Chicago: University of Chicago Press. Originally published in 1929.

1933 "The Life History of a Member of the '42' Gang." *Journal of Criminal Law, Criminology, and Police Science* 23: 964–998.

Landler, Mark and Ian Fisher

2007 "German Police Link 6 Dead Men to an Italian Mob Feud." *New York Times* (August 16): 8.

Langlais, Rudy

1978 "Inside the Heroin Trade: How a Star Double Agent Ended Up Dead." *Village Voice* (March 13): 13–15.

Langton, Jerry

2006 *Fallen Angel: The Unlikely Rise of Walter Stadnick in the Canadian Hells Angels*. Mississauga, Ontario, Canada: Wiley.

Lapidus, Edith J.

1974 *Eavesdropping on Trial*. Rochelle Park, NJ: Hayden Book Co.

Lardner, James and Thomas Reppetto

2000 *NYPD: A City and Its Police*. New York: Henry Holt.

Lawson, Guy and William Oldham

2007 *The Brotherhoods: The True Story of Two Cops who Murdered for the Mafia*. New York: Pocket Books.

Lasswell, Harold D. and Jerimiah B. McKenna

1972 *The Impact of Organized Crime on an Inner-City Community*. New York: Policy Sciences Center.

Latimer, Dean and Jeff Goldberg

1981 *Flowers in the Blood: The Story of Opium*. New York: Franklin Watts.

LaVerle, Berry, Glenn E. Curtis, John N. Gibbs, Rex A. Hudson, Tara Karacan, Nina Kollars, and Ramón Miró

2003 *Nations Hospitable to Organized Crime and Terrorism*. Washington, DC: Library of Congress.

Lavigne, Yves

1996 *Hells Angels: Into the Abyss*. New York: HarperCollins.

1987 *Hells Angels: Taking Care of Business*. Toronto, Canada: Deneua and Wayne.

LeDuff, Charlie

2005 "100 Members of Immigrant Gang Are Held." *New York Times* (March 15): 18.

Ledwith, William E.

2000 "Testimony Before the House of Representatives Subcommittee on Criminal Justice, Drug Policy, and Human Resources," February 15.

Lee, Denny

2003 "Years of the Dragon." *New York Times* (May 11): CY 1, 16.

Lee, Henry

1963 *How Dry We Were: Prohibition Revisited*. Englewood Cliffs, NJ: Prentice-Hall.

Lee, Jennifer

2005 "Crime Ring Is Crushed Police Say." *New York Times* (April 28): B6.

Leeson Peter T. and David B. Skarbek

2011 "Criminal Constitutions." *Global Crime* 11 (3): 279–297.

Lehmann, Daniel J. and Tom McNamee

1995 "Gang Busted." *Chicago Sun-Times* (September 1): 1, 22.

Lehmann, Nicholas

2010 "Terrorism Studies: Social Scientists Do Counterinsurgency." *New Yorker* (April 26): 73–77.

Lehr, Dick and Gerard O'Neil

2000 *Black Mass: The Irish Mob, the FBI, and a Devil's Deal*. New York: Public Affairs.

Lehti, Martil and Kauko Aromaa

2003 "Trafficking in Women and Children in Europe." Pages 114–28 in *Organised Crime, Trafficking, Drugs: Selected Papers Presented at the Annual Conference of the European Society of Criminology*, Helsinki, edited by Sami Nevala and Kauko Armomaa.

Lens, Sidney

1974 *The Labor Wars*. Garden City, NY: Doubleday.

Leonard, John

1996 "Bandit King." *New York* (August 19): 55–56.

Leonhardt, David with Barbara Whitaker

2000 "U.S. Companies Tangled in Web of Drug Dollars." *New York Times* (October 10): 1, 20.

Lerner, Steven E.

1980 "Phencyclidine Abuse in Perspective." Pages 13–23 in *Phencyclidine Abuse Manual*, edited by Mary Tuma McAdams, Ronald L. Linder, Steven E. Lerner, and Richard Stanley Burns. Los Angeles: University of California Extension.

Lev, Michael A.

1997 "Meeting Protection Racket Snares Mitsubishi." *Chicago Tribune* (October 24): Sec. 3: 1, 2.

Levine, Edward M.

1966 *The Irish and Irish Politicians*. Notre Dame, IN: University of Notre Dame Press.

Levine, Gary

1995 *Jack "Legs" Diamond: Anatomy of a Gangster*. Fleishmanns, NY: Purple Mountain Press.

Levine, Michael

1990 *Deep Cover*. New York: Delacorte.

LeVine, Steve, Betsy McKay, and Natasha Lebedeva

1993 "A Long Bloody Summer." *Newsweek* (August 30): 38–39.

Levins, Hoag

1980 "The Kabul Connection." *Philadelphia* (August): 114–20.

Levy, Clifford J.

1995 "Russian Émigrés Are Among 25 Named in Tax Fraud in Newark." *New York Times* (August 8): 1, 8.

Lewis, Norman

1964 *The Honoured Society*. New York: Putnam's.

Library of Congress (LC)

2003 *Organized Crime and Terrorist Activity in Mexico, 1999–2002*. Washington, DC: LC.

Lichtblau, Erie

2005a "F.B.I. Found to Violate Its Informant Rules." *New York Times* (September 13): 14.

2005b "Justice Dept. Defends Patriot Act Before Senate Hearings." *New York Times* (April 5): 19.

2003a "Mexico and U.S. Hold 240 and Seize 13 Tons of Cocaine." *New York Times* (August 1): 12.

2003b "U.S. Cautiously Begins to Seize Millions in Foreign Banks." *New York Times* (May 30): 16.

2003c "U.S. Uses Terror Law to Pursue Crimes From Drugs to Swindling." *New York Times* (September 28): 1, 32.

Liddick, Don

1998 *The Mob's Daily Number: Organized Crime and the Number's Gambling Industry*. Lanham, MD: University Press of America.

Lieven, Anatol

1998 *Chechyna: Tombstone of Russian Power*. New Haven, CT: Yale University Press.

Light, Ivan

1977 "The Ethnic Vice Industry, 1880–1944." *American Journal of Sociology* 42 (June): 464–79.

Lindberg, Richard C.

1991 *To Serve and Collect: Chicago Politics and Police Corruption from the Lager Beer Riot to the Summerdale Scandal.* New York: Praeger.

Linder, Ronald L., Steven E. Lerner, and R. Stanley Burns

1981 *PCP: The Devil's Dust.* Belmont, CA: Wadsworth.

Lintner, Bertil

2002 *Blood Brothers: The Criminal Underworld of Asia.* New York: Palgrave Macmillan.

Lippman, Walter

1962 "The Underworld as Servant." In *Organized Crime in America*, edited by Gus Tyler. Ann Arbor: University of Michigan Press. Article originally published in 1931.

Liptik, Adam

2008 "A Corporate View of Mafia Tactics: Protesting, Lobbying and Citing Upton Sinclair." *New York Times* (February 5): 14.

Liu, Jainhong, Dengke Zhou, Allen E. Liska, Steven F. Messner, Marvin D. Krohn, Lening Zhang, and Zhou Lu

1998 "Status, Power, and Sentencing in China." *Justice Quarterly* 15 (June): 289–300.

Lloyd, Henry Demerest

1963 *Wealth Against Commonwealth*, edited by Thomas C. Cochran. Englewood Cliffs, NJ: Prentice-Hall.

Lo, T. Wing

2010 "Beyond Social Capital: Triad Organized Crime in Hong Kong and China." *British Journal of Criminology* 50: 851–72.

2010b "Current and Expected Developments in China." Paper presented at the International Peace Institute Seminar on Transnational Organized Crime and the Palermo Convention: A Reality Check. New York, October 6.

Logan, Andy

1970 *Against the Evidence: The Becker-Rosenthal Affair.* New York: McGraw-Hill.

Lohr, Steve

1999 "Privacy on Internet Poses Legal Puzzle." *New York Times* (April 19): C4.

1992 "Where the Money Washes Up: Offshore Banking in the Cayman Islands." *New York Times Magazine* (March 29): 26–29, 32, 46, 52.

Lombardo, Robert M.

2004 "The Black Hand: A Study in Moral Panic." *Global Crime* 6 (November): 267–84.

2002a "The Black Hand." *Journal of Contemporary Criminal Justice* 18 (November): 393–408.

2002b "The Black Mafia: African-American Organized Crime in Chicago, 1890–1960." *Crime, Law and Social Change* 38: 33–65.

1994 "The Organized Crime Neighborhoods of Chicago." Pages 169–87 in *Handbook of Organized Crime in the United States*, edited by Robert J. Kelly, Ko-lin Chin, and Rufus Schatzberg. Westport, CT: Greenwood.

1979 "Organized Crime and the Concept of Community." Unpublished paper, Department of Sociology, University of Illinois at Chicago.

Longmire, Sylvia

2011 *Cartel.* New York: Palgrave Macmillan.

Longstreet, Stephen

1973 *Chicago 1860–1919.* New York: McKay.

Lorch, Donatella

1990 "Mourners Shot Back at Funeral." *New York Times* (July 30): 9.

Loree, Don

2002 "Organized Crime: Changing Concepts and Realities for the Police." *Trends in Organized Crime* 7 (Summer): 73–78.

Loth, David

1938 *Public Plunder: A History of Graft in America.* New York: Carrick and Evans.

Lovett, Ian

2011 "U.S. Cracks Down on Armenian Crime Syndicate." *New York Times* (February 16): Internet.

Lubasch, Arnold H.

1992a "Death Penalty Sought at a Trial in Brooklyn." *New York Times* (April 14): 16.

1992b "U.S. Moves to Break Up Trash Cartel." *New York Times* (August 18): B12.

1992c "U.S. Prosecutors Say That Gotti Is Still a Functioning Crime Boss." *New York Times* (September 16): 18.

1992d "Mobster Testifies of Bribing Juror." *New York Times* (November 5): 13.

1991 "Ex-Mob Leader Tells Court of Killings." *New York Times* (April 26): 16.

Luft, Kerry

1995 "For Bogotá's Street Children, Death Is Just Around the Corner." *Chicago Tribune* (January 15): 12.

Lupsha, Peter A.

1995 "Transnational Narco-Corruption and Narco Investment: A Focus on Mexico." *Transnational Organized Crime* 1 (Spring): 84–101.

1991 "Drug Lords and Narco-Corruption: The Players Change But the Game Continues." *Crime, Law and Social Change* 16: 41–58.

1990 "The Geopolitics of Organized Crime: Some Comparative Models from Latin American Drug Trafficking Organizations." Paper presented at the annual meeting of the American Society of Criminology, Baltimore, MD, November.

1983 "Networks Versus Networking: Analysis of an Organized Crime Group." Pages 59–87 in *Career Criminals*, edited by Gordon P. Waldo. Beverly Hills, CA: Sage.

1981 "Individual Choice, Material Culture, and Organized Crime." *Criminology* 19: 3–24.

Lupsha, Peter A. and Kip Schlegel

1980 "The Political Economy of Drug Trafficking: The Herrera Organization (Mexico and the United States)." Unpublished paper, Department of Political Science, University of New Mexico at Albuquerque.

Maas, Peter

1997 *Underboss: Sammy the Bull Gravano's Story of Life in the Mafia.* New York: HarperCollins.

1968 *The Valachi Papers.* New York: Putnam's.

MacDougall, Ernest D., ed.

1933 *Crime for Profit: A Symposium on Mercenary Crime.* Boston: Stratford.

Maffei, Stefano and Isabella Merzagora Betsos

2007 "Crime and Criminal Policy in Italy: Tradition and Modernity in a Troubled Country." *European Journal of Criminology* 4(4): 461–82.

Malkin, Elisabeth

2011 "As Gangs Move In on Schools, Teachers say 'Enough.'" *New York Times* (September 26): 4.

2010 "Prisoners Said to Act as Hit Men." *New York Times* ((July 26): 7.

Main, Frank

2011 "Shrine to Gangster Jeff Fort Found in Home of 'Terror Town' Gang Leader." *Chicago Sun-Times* (June 2): Internet.

Maltz, Michael D.

1990 *Measuring the Effectiveness of Organized Crime Control Efforts.* Chicago: Office of International Criminal Justice, University of Illinois.

1976 "On Defining 'Organized Crime.'" *Crime and Delinquency* 22 (July): 338–46.

1975 "Policy Issues in Organized and White Collar Crime." Pages 73–95 in *Crime and Criminal Justice*, edited by John A. Gardiner and Michael A. Mulkey. Lexington, MA: D. C. Heath.

Manca, John and Vincent Cosgrove

1991 *Tin for Sale: My Career in Organized Crime and the NYPD.* New York: William Morrow.

Mangione, Jerre

1985 *A Passion for Sicilians: The World Around Danilo Dolci.* New Brunswick, NJ: Transaction Books.

Mangione, Jerre and Ben Morreale

1992 *La Storia: Five Centuries of the Italian American Experience.* New York: HarperCollins.

"Man Loses Federal Appeal in Internet Gambling Case"

2001 *New York Times* (August 1): 16.

Mann, Arthur

1965 *La Guardia Comes to Power: 1933.* Philadelphia: Lippincott.

Maran, Arnold

2008 *Mafia: Inside the Dark Heart.* New York: St. Martin's Press.

Márquez, Gabriel García

1997 *News of a Kidnapping.* New York: Knopf.

Marquis, Christopher and Juan Forero

2004 "U.S. Government Gains in Eradicating Andean Coca." *New York Times* (March 23): 3.

Marsh, Harry L.

1991 "Law Enforcement, the Military, and the War on Drugs: Is the Military Involvement in the War on Drugs Ethical?" *American Journal of Police* 10: 61–75.

Marshall, Claire

2005 "'Durgaon' Escapes from Mexico Jail." Internet.

Marshall, Donnie

2001 "Testimony Before the U.S. House of Representatives Committee on the Judiciary Subcommittee on Crime," March 29.

1999 "Testimony Before the U.S. House of Representatives Committee International Relations Subcommittee on the Western Hemisphere," March 3: 1–11.

Marshall, Eliot

1978 "State Lottery." *New Republic* (June 24): 20–21.

Martel, Ned

2006 "Taking a Long Look at a Latino Gang Named for Fire Ants." *New York Times* (February 11): B18.

Martin, Andrew

1996 "Even with Leaders in Jail, Gang's Drug Business Is Flourishing." *Chicago Tribune* (January 29): 1, 13.

Martin, Andrew and John O'Brien

1996 "Alleged Drug Hub Didn't Fit the Area." *Chicago Tribune* (October 13): 1, 21.

Martin, Andrew and Matt O'Connor

1996a "Jeff Fort's Son Faces Drug Charges." *Chicago Tribune* (September 4): Sec. 2: 1, 2.

1996b "Gang 'Prince' Stakes Claim to the Throne." *Chicago Tribune* (September 21): 1, 12.

Martin, Raymond V.

1963 *Revolt in the Mafia.* New York: Duell, Sloan, and Pearce.

Martinez, Michael

1995 "Hells Angels Pay Their Last Respects to Slaying Victim." *Chicago Tribune* (March 8): Sec. 2: 1, 4.

Marx, Gary

2011 "FBI Cuts Mob-Fighting Squads." *Daily News* (March 4): 4.

2011b "Wseguy Sicilian the Capo of the Gambinos." *New York Daily News* (July 29): 6.

1991 "Drug Lord, or Ghost, Stalks Colombian Town." *Chicago Tribune* (July 28): 4.

Marzulli, John

2011c "Former Mafia Hitman Joey Calco Likely to Get More Jail Time for Calzone Attack." *New York Daly News* (November 17): Internet.

2006 "The Baby Godfather." *New York Daily News* (November 15): 5.

2005a "Feds Hunt Real-Life 'Luca Brasi.'" *New York Daily News* (February 10): 4.

2005b "Name Got a Good Guy Whacked." *New York Daily News* (March 11): 7.

2005c "$650M Porn Scam." *New York Daily News* (February 15): 5.

2003 "Son Is in Like Chin." *New York Daily News* (July 26): Internet.

Marzulli, John and Jonathan Lemire

2005 "Mobster on Run Nabbed Upstate." *New York Daily News* (March 20): 24.

Marzulli, John and Patrice O'Shaughnessy

2005 "Muscle and Brains Behind Mob Cops." *New York Daily News* (March 13): 4–5.

Mass, Robert

1991 "Law Enforcement Approaches to Organized Crime Infiltration of Legitimate Industry." Pages 37–47 in *Organized Crime and Its Containment: A Transatlantic Initiative*, edited by Cyrelle Fijnaut and James Jacobs. Deventer, Netherlands: Kluwer.

Massing, Michael

1990 "In the Cocaine War, the Jungle Is Winning." *New York Times Magazine* (March 4): 26, 88, 90, 92.

Mazzitelli, Antonio

2007 "Transnational Organized Crime in West Africa: The Additional Challenge." *International Affairs* 83(6): 1071–1090.

McAlary, Mike

1998 "Breaking the Code." *New York* (April 13): 31–35, 74.

McCaffrey, Lawrence J.

1976 *The Irish Diaspora in America*. Bloomington: Indiana University Press.

McClellan, John L.

1962 *Crime Without Punishment*. New York: Duell, Sloan, and Pearce.

McConaughy, John

1931 *From Cain to Capone: Racketeering Down the Ages*. New York: Brentano's.

McCormick, John

1999 "Winning a Gang War." *Newsweek* (November 1): 46–49.

McCoy, Alfred W.

1991 *The Politics of Heroin: CIA Complicity in the Global Drug Trade*. Brooklyn, NY: Lawrence Hill.

1972 *The Politics of Heroin in Southeast Asia*. New York: Harper & Row.

McFadden, Robert D.

2005 "Drug Suspect in Afghan Ring Is Sent to U.S." *New York Times* (October 25): B1, 2.

1999 "Teamsters' Unit Regains Control." *New York Times* (February 26): 19.

1997 "Limits on Cash Transactions Cut Drug-Money Laundering." *New York Times* (March 11): 1, 11.

1988 "Anthony Provanzano, 71, Ex-Teamster Chief, Dies." *New York Times* (December 13): 22.

1983 "Meyer Lansky Is Dead at 81; Financial Wizard of Organized Crime." *New York Times* (January 16): 21.

McGraw, Dan

1997 "The National Bet." *U.S. News and World Report* (April 7): 50–55.

McGuinness, Robert L.

1981 "In the Katz Eye: Use of Binoculars and Telescopes." *FBI Law Enforcement Bulletin* (June): 26–31.

McGuire, Michael

1993 "Airborne Police Wage Losing Battle in Colombia Poppy Fields." *Chicago Tribune* (April 4): 6.

McGuire, Phillip C.

1988 "Jamaican Posses: A Call for Cooperation among Law Enforcement Agencies." *Police Chief* (January): 20–27.

McKinley, James C., Jr.

2010 "Mexican Drug Kingpin Sentenced to 25 Years in Secret Hearing." *New York Times* (February 26): 12).

2009a "U.S. is a Vast Arms Bazaar for Mexican Cartels." *New York Times* (February 26): 1, 18.

2009b "Drug Cartels in Mexico Lure American Teenagers as Killers." *New York Times* (June 23): 1, 18.

2009c "Deep in California Forests, An Illicit Business Thrives." *New York Times* (August 22): 9.

2009d "Vast Drug Case Tries to Disrupt Cultlike Cartel." *New York Times* (October 23): 1, 24).

2008a "After Massacre, a Mexican Town Is Left in Terror of Drug Violence." *New York Times* (May 31): 1, 8.

2008b "Drug War Causes Wild West Blood Bath, Killing 210 in a Mexican Town." *New York Times* (April 16): 10.

2008c "Mexican Federal Agents Seize Millions and Arrest 6." *New York Times* (April 4): 8.

2008d "Mexican Forces Clash with Drug Cartel Gunmen in Tijuana." *New York Times* (January 18): 5.

2008e "Mexico Hits Drug Gangs with Full Fury of War." *New York Times* (January 22): 1, 9.

2008f "Mexico's War Against Drugs Kills Its Police." *New York Times* (May 26): 1, 9.

2008g "6 Charged in Shooting Death of a Police Chief in Mexico." *New York Times* (May 13): 8.

2008h "3 Americans Arrested in Gang Battle with Mexican Police." *New York Times* (January 9): 5.

2007a "In Mexico, a Fugitive's Arrest Captivates the Cameras." *New York Times* (October 12): 3.

2007b "Mexico Tries to Show Resolve with Big Drug Seizure." *New York Times* (November 29): 10.

2007c "Songs of Love and Murder, Silenced by Murder." *New York Times* (December 18): 1, 20.

2006a "A War in Mexico: Drug Runners Gun Down Journalists." *New York Times* (February 10): 6.

2006b "With Beheadings and Attacks, Drug Gangs Terrorize Mexico." *New York Times* (October 26): 1, 12.

2005a "Drug Lord, Ruthless and Elusive, Reaches High in Mexico." *New York Times* (February 9): 3.

2005b "Mexican Troops Seize Prison After Drug Lord Violence." *New York Times* (January 15): 3.

2005c "Mexico: 12 Found Dead in Drug Shootouts." *New York Times* (February 17): 8.

2005d "Scandals Shake Mexico's Confidence in Elite Police Unit." *New York Times* (December 28): 3.

2004a "Mexico Arrests Man Suspected of Leading Drug Cartel's Assassins." *New York Times* (October 30): 6.

2004b "7 in Family Slain in Mexico in Mix-Up Laid to Police Renegades." *New York Times* (November 9): 5.

1990 "17 Charged in Raids of Brooklyn 'Posse' Linked to Deaths." *New York Times* (December 8): 1, 7.

McKinley, James C., Jr., and Marc Lacey

2000 "Torrent of Cash Flows Where the U.S. and Mexico Meet." *New York Times* (December 26): 1, 12.

McKinley, James C., Jr., and Elisabeth Malkin

2010 "From U.S. High School to Mexican Drug Wars." *New York Times* (September 9): 21.

McKinley, James C., Jr., and Elisabeth Malkin

McMahon, Colin

1996 "Top Drug Suspect Seized in Mexico." *Chicago Tribune* (January 16): 4.

1995 "Mexicans Make Their Mark in Drug Game as Middlemen." *Chicago Tribune* (September 18): 1, 14.

1992 "Illegal Wagers Now Are Safer Than Ever." *Chicago Tribune* (November 15): 1, 17.

McPhaul, Jack

1970 *Johnny Torrio: First of the Gang Lords.* New Rochelle, NY: Arlington House.

McPhee, Michele

2003 "Capo, His Young Guns Face New Murder Rap." *New York Daily News* (December 5): 16.

Meisner, Jason

2011 "Gang Member Gets 60 Years in Boy's Murder." *Chicago Tribune* (May 5): Internet.

Mendelson, Wallace B.

1980 *The Use and Misuse of Sleeping Pills: A Clinical Guide.* New York: Plenum.

Menginie, Anthony and Kerrie Dobran

2011 *Prodigal Father, Pagan Son.* New York: St. Martin's Press.

Merlin, Mark David

1984 *On the Trail of the Ancient Opium Poppy.* Rutherford, NJ: Farleigh Dickinson University Press.

Merriam, Charles Edward

1929 *Chicago: A More Intimate View of Urban Politics.* New York: Macmillan.

Merton, Robert

1967 *On Theoretical Sociology.* New York: Free Press.

1964 "Anomie, Anomia, and Social Interaction." Pages 213–42 in *Anomie and Deviant Behavior,* edited by Marshall B. Clinard. New York: Free Press.

1938 "Social Structure and Anomie." *American Sociological Review* 3: 672–82.

Meskil, Paul

1977 "Meet the New Godfather." *New York* (February 28): 28–32.

1973 *Don Carlo: Boss of Bosses.* New York: Popular Library.

Messick, Hank

1973 *Lansky.* New York: Berkley.

1967 *The Silent Syndicate.* New York: Macmillan.

"Mexico Seizes Top Drugs Suspect"

2008 Internet: news.bbc.co.uk.

Mieczkowski, Thomas

1986 "Geeking Up and Throwing Down: Heroin Street Life in Detroit." *Criminology* 24 (November): 645–66.

Milhaupt, Curtis J. and Mark D. West

2000 "The Dark Side of Private Ordering: An Institutional and Empirical Analysis of Organized Crime." *University of Chicago Law Review* 67: 41–98.

Miller, Matthew

2006 "Catch Me If You Can." *Forbes* (March 27): 112–16, 125.

Millman, Nancy

1996 "$100 Million Fine in ADM Guilty Plea." *Chicago Tribune* (October 16): 1, 27.

Mitchell, Alison

1995 "U.S. Freezes Assets of Cartel in New Effort Against Drugs." *New York Times* (October 23): 5.

1992 "Russian Emigres Importing Thugs to Commit Contract Crimes in U.S." *New York Times* (April 11): 1, 18.

Mokhiber, Russell

1988 *Corporate Crime and Violence: Big Business Power and the Abuse of the Public Trust.* San Francisco: Sierra Club Books.

Moldea, Dan E.

1978 *The Hoffa Wars.* New York: Charter Books.

Moody, John

1991 "A Day with the Chess Player." *Time* (July 1): 34–36.

Moore, Mark H.

1987 "Organized Crime as a Business Enterprise." Pages 51–64 in *Major Issues in Organized Crime Control*, edited by Herbert Edelhertz. Washington, DC: U.S. Government Printing Office.

Moore, Natalie Y. and Lance Williams

2011 *The Almighty Black P. Stone Nation.* Chicago: Lawrence Hill Books.

Moore, Robin with Barbara Fuca

1977 *Mafia Wife.* New York: Macmillan.

Moore, Solomon

2009 "Border Proves No Obstacle for Mexican Cartels." *New York Times* (February 2): 1, 10.

Moore, William Howard

1974 *The Kefauver Committee and the Politics of Crime.* Columbia: University of Missouri Press.

Morales, Edmundo

1989 *Cocaine: White Gold Rush in Peru.* Tucson: University of Arizona Press.

Moreau, Ron and Sami Yousafzai

2006 "A Harvest of Treachery." *Newsweek* (January 9): 32–35.

Morgan, Howard Wayne

1981 *Drugs in America: A Social History, 1800–1980.* Syracuse, NY: Syracuse University Press.

Morgan, Howard Wayne, ed.

1974 *Yesterday's Addicts: American Society and Drug Abuse, 1865–1920.* Norman: University of Oklahoma Press.

Morgan, John

1985 *Prince of Crime.* New York: Stein and Day.

Morgan, Thomas

1989 "16 Charged in Scheme to Launder Millions." *New York Times* (May 14): 24.

Mori, Cesare

1933 *The Last Struggle with the Mafia.* London: Putnam's.

Moriarity, Tom

1998 Special Agent, Criminal Investigation Division, Internal Revenue Service. Personal interview.

Moseley, Ray

1997 "Biker War Revving Up in Denmark." *Chicago Tribune* (July 3): 1, 14.

Motivans, Mark

2003 *Money-Laundering Offenders, 1994–2001.* Washington, DC: Bureau of Justice Statistics.

Mueller, Robert S., III

2011 "The Evolving Organized Crime Threat." Speech before the Citizen's Crime Commission, *New York City*, January 27.

Mulvey, Erin

2008 "Associate of Colombian Narco-Terrorist Group Extradited to United States on Cocaine Importation Charges." Drug Enforcement Administration press release, April 22.

Murphy, Kate

2008 "Mexican Robin Hood Figure Gains a Kind of Notoriety in the U.S." *New York Times* (February 8): 12.

Murr, Andrew

2000 "Corralling Sammy 'The Bull.'" *Newsweek* (March 6): 36–37.

Murray, George

1975 *The Legacy of Al Capone.* New York: Putnam's.

Mustain, Gene and Jerry Capeci

1992 *Murder Machine: A True Story of Murder, Madness, and the Mafia.* New York: Dutton.

1988 *Mob Star: The Story of John Gotti, the Most Powerful Criminal in America.* New York: Franklin Watts.

Musto, David

1973 *The American Disease: Origins of Narcotic Control.* New Haven, CT: Yale University Press.

Mydans, Seth

2008 "In Thai Protests, a Divide Between Urban and Rural." *New York Times* (October 13): 6.

2003a "Burmese Women Are Reporting Systematic Rapes by Military." *New York Times* (May 12): 12.

2003b "Thai Vice-King's Lament: Police Don't Stay Bought." *New York Times* (July 30): 8.

2003c "A Wave of Drug Killings Is Linked to Thai Police." *New York Times* (April 8): 3.

1995 "Racial Tensions on the Rise in Los Angeles Jail System." *New York Times* (February 6): 8.

Myers, Gustavus

1936 *History of Great American Fortunes.* New York: Modern Library.

Myers, Willard H., III

1995 "Orb Weavers—The Global Webs: The Structure and Activities of Transnational Ethnic Chinese Groups." *Transnational Organized Crime* 1 (Winter): 1–36.

Myerson, Allen R.

1995 "The Garbage Wars: Cracking the Cartel." *New York Times* (July 30): F1, 11.

1994 "American Express Bank Unit Settles U.S. Laundering Case." *New York Times* (November 22): 1, C8.

Nagourney, Adam and Abby Goodnough

2011 "Long Elusive, Irish Mob Legend Ended Up a California Recluse." *New York Times* (June 24): Internet.

Nagourney, Adam and Ian Lovett

2011 "Whitey Bulger is Arrested in California." *New York Times* (June 23): Internet.

"Naples Police in Huge Mafia Sweep"

2004 *BBC News* (December 7): Internet.

Napoli, Antonio

2004 *The Mob's Guys.* College Station, TX: Virtualbookworm.com Publishing.

Naravane, Vaiju

2008 "Berlusconi Sparks Outrage." *The Hindu* (April 17): Internet.

National Advisory Commission on the Causes and Prevention of Violence

1969 *Staff Report: Crimes of Violence.* Washington, DC: U.S. Government Printing Office.

National Association of Attorneys General

1977 *Organized Crime Control Units.* Raleigh, NC: Committee on the Office of Attorneys General.

National Central Police University, Taipei, Taiwan

2005 "Organized Crime Gangs in Taiwan." *Trends in Organized Crime* 8 (Spring): 13–23.

National Commission on Law Observance and Enforcement

1931 *Report on Police.* Washington, DC: U.S. Government Printing Office.

National Commission for the Review of Federal and State Laws Relating to Wiretapping and Electronic Surveillance

1976 *Electronic Surveillance.* Washington, DC: U.S. Government Printing Office.

National Drug Intelligence Center (NDIC)

2009a *National Drug Threat Assessment.* Johnstown, PA: NDIC.

2009b *North Texas High Intensity Drug Trafficking* Area. Johnstown, PA: NDIC.

2009c *California Border Alliance Group: Drug Market Analysis,* 2009. Johnstown, PA: NDIC.

2009d *New York/New Jersey High Intensity Drug Trafficking Area.* Johnstown, PA: NDIC.

2008a *Indian Country: Drug Threat Assessment.* Washington, DC: U.S. Department of Justice.

2008b *Money Laundering in Digital Currencies.* Johnstown, PA: NDIC.

National Gang Intelligence Center (NGIC)

2009 National Gang Threat Assessment, 2009. Washington, DC: NGIC.

National Institute of Justice

2007 *Investigations Involving the Internet and Computer Networks,* Washington, DC: U.S. Department of Justice.

National Police Agency of Japan

1996 "Promotion of Measures Against Organized Crime Groups." Excerpted in *Trends in Organized Crime* 1 (Spring): 49–57.

National Security Council

2011 *Strategy to Combat Transnational Organized Crime* Washington, DC: Office of the President of the United States.

National Synthetic Drugs Action Plan

2004 Washington, DC: Office of National Drug Control Policy.

Navarro, Mireya

1998 "Upgraded Drug Traffic Flourishes on Old Route." *New York Times* (May 31): 14.

1997 "Russian Submarine Surfaces as Player in the Drug World." *New York Times* (March 7): 1, 9.

1996 "When Drug Kingpins Fall, Illicit Assets Buy a Cushion." *New York Times* (March 19): 1, C19.

Navasky, Victor S.

1977 *Kennedy Justice.* New York: Atheneum.

NDIC. See National Drug Intelligence Center.

Needler, Martin C.

1995 *Mexican Politics: The Containment of Conflict,* 3d ed. Westport, CT: Praeger.

Neff, James

1989 *Mobbed Up: Jackie Presser's High Wire Life in the Teamsters, the Mafia, and the F.B.I.* New York: Atlantic Monthly Press.

Nelli, Humbert S.

1976 *The Business of Crime.* New York: Oxford University Press.

1969 "Italians and Crime in Chicago: The Formative Years: 1890–1920." *American Journal of Sociology* 74 (January): 373–91.

Nelson, Jack E., Helen Wallenstein Pearson, Mollie Sawyers, and Thomas J. Glynn

1982 *Guide to Drug Abuse Research Terminology.* Rockville, MD: National Institute on Drug Abuse.

Neumeister, Larry

2000 "Landmark Conviction in Web Gambling." Associated Press (February 28): Internet.

Newell, Barbara Warne

1961 *Chicago and the Labor Movement: Metropolitan Unionism in the 1930s.* Urbana: University of Illinois Press.

Newfield, Jack

1979 "The Myth of Godfather Journalism." *Village Voice* (July 23): 1, 11–13.

"New Gang Methods Replace Those of Eastman's Days"

1923 *New York Times* (September 9): Sec. 9: 3.

New Jersey Commission of Investigation (NJCI)

2004 The Changing Face of Organized Crime in New Jersey. Trenton, NJ: NJCI.

1987 *Report and Recommendations on Organized Crime-Affiliated Subcontractors at Casino and Public Construction Sites.* Trenton, NJ: NJCI.

Newman, Graeme R.

2006 *The Exploitation of Trafficked Women.* Washington, DC: Office of Community Oriented Policing Services.

Newman, Graeme R. and Megan M. McNally

2007 *Identity Theft: A Research Review.* Washington, DC: National Institute of Justice.

New York State Organized Crime Task Force (NYSOCTF)

1988 *Corruption and Racketeering in the New York City Construction Industry.* Ithaca, NY: Cornell University School of Labor and Industrial Relations.

Nicaso, Antonio and Lee Lamothe

2005 *Angels, Mobsters and Narco-Terorists.* Ontario, Canada: John Wiley.

Nichols, Dave

2007 *One Percenter: The Legend of the Outlaw Biker.* St. Paul, MN: MBI Publishing Co.

Nicodemus, Charles and Art Petacque

1981 "Mob Jewel Fencing Investigated." *Chicago Sun-Times* (November 29): 5, 76.

Nietzel, Michael T., Douglas A. Bernstein, Geoffrey P. Kramer, and Richard Milich

2003 *Introduction to Clinical Psychology,* 6th ed. Upper Saddle River, NJ: Prentice-Hall.

Nieves, Evelyn

2001 "Drug Labs in Valley Feed Nation's Habit." *New York Times* (May 13): 1, 18.

Nigerian Advance Fee Fraud

1997 U.S. Department of State publication.

Nir, Sarah Maslin and Simon Romero

2011 "Leader of FARC Guerilla Movement Killed in Combat, Colombian Officials Say." *New York Times* (November 5): 8.

NNICC

1998 *The Supply of Illicit Drugs to the United States.* Washington, DC: National Narcotics Intelligence Consumers Committee (NNICC).

Nocera, Joseph

1988 "Drexel: Hanged Without a Trial." *New York Times* (December 30): 19.

O'Brien, Edward I.

1986 "RICO's Assault on Legitimate Business." *New York Times* (January 5): F2.

O'Brien, John

1996 "Chicago at Heart of Heroin Case." *Chicago Tribune* (October 12): 1, 9.

1993 "James J. D'Antonio, 65, Mob Driver." *Chicago Tribune* (December 15): Sec. 2: 11.

1988 "Car-Theft Figure Slain at His Home." *Chicago Tribune* (August 16): Sec. 2: 3.

O'Brien, John and Jan Crawford Greenburg

1996 "Raids Reveal How Little Guys Climb the Drug Ladder." *Chicago Tribune* (May 3): 1, 21.

O'Brien, John, Matt O'Connor, and George Papajohn

1995 "U.S. Goes Behind Bars to Indict 39 Gang Leaders." *Chicago Tribune* (September 1): 1, 12.

O'Brien, Joseph F. and Andris Kurins

1991 *Boss of Bosses: The FBI and Paul Castellano.* New York: Dell.

O'Brien, Robert and Sidney Cohen

1984 *Encyclopedia of Drug Abuse.* New York: Facts on File.

O'Connor, Anne-Marie

1999 "10 Alleged Leaders of Drug Ring Arrested." *Los Angeles Times* (February 2): Internet.

O'Connor, Len

1984 "Give Me That Old-Time Politics." *Chicago Magazine* (February): 114–19.

O'Connor, Matt

2000 "Gang Member Is Sentenced to 100 Years." *Chicago Tribune* (December 14): Sec. 2: 5.

1999 "When a Bribe Isn't a Bribe: FBI Mole Lands Prison Term." *Chicago Tribune* (October 15): 1, 14.

1998 "Raiders Net Millions, Ton of Cocaine." *Chicago Tribune* (May 28): Sec. 2: 7.

1997 "Hoover, 6 Others Convicted; Seen as Blow to Gang." *Chicago Tribune* (May 10): 1, 12.

1996 "Gambling Manager for Mob Pleads Guilty to Racketeering." *Chicago Tribune* (September 25): Sec. 2: 3.

1994a "On Leong, Moy Plead Guilty to Running Longtime Casino." *Chicago Tribune* (February 12): 5.

1994b "Sentencing of 'Chinatown Mayor' Closes On Leong Case." *Chicago Tribune* (May 16): Sec. 2: 1, 4.

O'Connor, Richard

1962 *Gould's Millions.* Garden City, NY: Doubleday.

1958 *Hell's Kitchen.* Philadelphia, PA: Lippincott.

Office of Inspector General

2000 *Semiannual Report to the Congress: October 1, 1999–March 31, 2000.* Washington, DC: U.S. Department of Labor.

Office for the Victims of Crime

n.d. *Anti-Human Trafficking Task Force Strategy of Operations E-Guide.* Washington, DC: U.S. Bureau of Justice Assistance.

Okada, Daniel W.

1992 "Asian Gangs: What Are We Talking About?" Paper presented at the annual meeting of the American Society of Criminology, New Orleans, November.

O'Neil, Gerard and Dick Lehr

1989 *The Underboss: The Rise and Fall of a Mafia Family.* New York: St. Martin's Press.

Onstad, Katrina

2011 "Seeking a New Sicily, Its Dignity Restored." *New York Times* (May 8): TR10.

Orlando, Leoluca

2001 *Fighting the Mafia and Renewing Sicilian Culture.* San Francisco, CA: Encounter Books.

O'Rourke, John J.

1997 Special Agent, Federal Bureau of Investigation, retired. Personal interview.

Orth, Maureen

2002 "Afghanistan's Deadly Habit." *Vanity Fair* (March): 150–52, 165–77.

Ouagrham-Gormley, Sonia Ben

2007 "An Unrealized Nexus? WMD-Related Trafficking, Terrorism, and Organized Crime in the Former Soviet Union." *Arms Control Today* (July/August): Internet.

Overly, Don H. and Theodore H. Schell

1973 *New Effectiveness Measures for Organized Crime Control Efforts.* Washington, DC: U.S. Government Printing Office.

Owen, David

2003 "Concrete Jungle." *New Yorker* (November 10): 62–81.

Pachico, Elyssa

2011 "The Legacy of 9/11 for Latin America." *Christian Science Monitor* (September 12): Internet, 1, 2.

Packer, Herbert L.

1968 *The Limits of the Criminal Sanction.* Stanford, CA: Stanford University Press.

Padgett, Tim

2011 "The War Next Door." *Time* (July 11): 26–30.

2009 "On the Bloody Border." *Time* (May 4): 36–41.

2005 "The Killers Next Door." *Time* (April 18): 140–41.

Padgett Tim and Ioan Grillo

2010 "Mexico's Meth Warriors." *Time* (June 28): 30–33.

2008 "Cocaine Capital." *Time* (August 25): 36–38.

Palacios, Marco

2007 *Between Legitimacy and Violence: A History of Colombia, 1875–2002.* Durham: Duke University Press. Translated by Richard Stoller.

Pallasch, Abdon and Judy Peres

1998 "Abortion Foes Suffer a Big Setback." *Chicago Tribune* (April 21): 1, 8.

Palley, Thomas I.

1996 "The Forces Making for an Economic Collapse." *Atlantic Monthly* (July): 44–45, 58.

Palsey, Fred D.

1971 *Al Capone: The Biography of a Self-Made Man.* Freeport, NY: Books for Libraries Press. Originally published in 1931.

Pantaleone, Michele

1966 *The Mafia and Politics.* New York: Coward and McCann.

Paoli, Letizia

2003 *Mafia Brotherhoods: Organized Crime, Italian Style.* New York: Oxford University Press.

2001 "Crime, Italian Style." *Daedalus* 130 (Summer): 157–70.

1999 "The Political-Criminal Nexus in Italy." *Trends in Organized Crime* 5 (Winter): 15–58.

1994 "An Underestimated Criminal Phenomenon: The Calabrian 'Ndrangheta." *European Journal of Crime, Criminal Law and Criminal Justice* 2(3): 212–38.

Paoli, Letizia and Peter Reuter

2008 "Drug Trafficking and Ethnic Minorities in Western Europe." *European Journal of Criminology* 5(1): 13–37.

Papajohn, George and Tracy Dell'Angela

1995 "Indictments Open Door for Next Gang." *Chicago Tribune* (September 3): 1, 16.

Paradis, Peter

2002 *Nasty Business: One Biker Gang's Bloody War Against the Hells Angels.* Toronto, Canada: HarperCollins.

Paterernostro, Silvana

2011 "Drug Busts." *The Atlantic* (April): 17–18.

2007 *My Colombian War: A Journey Through the Country.* New York: Henry Holt and Co.

Patrinani, Angela

2009 "Counterfeiting: A Global Spread, a Global Threat." *Trends in Organized Crime* 12: 59–77.

Patterson, Orlando

2001 "The Roots of Conflict in Jamaica." *New York Times* (July 23): 21.

PCOC. See President's Commission on Organized Crime

Pennsylvania Crime Commission (PCC)

1990 *Organized Crime in Pennsylvania: A Decade of Change, 1990 Report.* Conshohocken, PA: PCC.

1988 *1988 Report.* Conshohocken, PA: PCC.

Pepper, Daniel

2008 "Aftermath of a Revolt: Myanmar's Lost Years." *New York Times* (October 5): 5.

Permanent Subcommittee on Investigations (PSI)

1983a *Crime and Secrecy: The Use of Offshore Banks and Companies.* Washington, DC: U.S. Government Printing Office.

1983b *Organized Crime in Chicago* (March 4). Washington, DC: U.S. Government Printing Office.

1982 *Hotel Employees and Restaurant Employees International Union: Part I* (June 22, 23). Washington, DC: U.S. Government Printing Office.

1981a *International Narcotics Trafficking.* Washington, DC: U.S. Government Printing Office.

1981b *Waterfront Corruption.* Washington DC: U.S. Government Printing Office.

1981c *Witness Security Program.* Washington, DC: U.S. Government Printing Office.

Petacco, Arrigo

1974 *Joe Petrosino.* New York: Macmillan.

Peters, Alicia W.

2010 *Trafficking in Meaning: Law, Victims, and the State.* Doctoral dissertation, Colombia University Graduate School of Arts and Sciences.

Peterson, Virgil

1983 *The Mob: 200 Years of Organized Crime in New York.* Ottawa, IL: Green Hill Publishers.

1969 *A Report on Chicago Crime for 1968.* Chicago Crime Commission.

1963 "Chicago: Shades of Capone." *Annals* 347 (May): 30–39.

1962 "Career of a Syndicate Boss." *Crime and Delinquency* 8 (October): 339–49.

Pettifor, Tom

2011 "Jamaican Drug Lord Faces 23 Years in Jail for Assault and Racketeering." *Daily Mirror* (September 2): Internet.

Phongpaichit, Pasuk and Chris Baker

2003 "Slaughter in the Name of a Drug War." *New York Times* (May 24): 15.

Physicians' Desk Reference

1988 Oradell, NJ: Medical Economics Co.

1987 Oradell, NJ: Medical Economics Co.

Pietrusza, David

2003 *Rothstein: The Life, Times, and Murder of the Criminal Genius Who Fixed the 1919 World Series.* New York: Carroll and Graf Publishers.

Pileggi, Nicholas

1995 *Casino.* New York: Pocket Books.

1990 *Wise Guy: Life in a Mafia Family.* New York: Pocket Books.

1985 *Wise Guy: Life in a Mafia Family.* New York: Pocket Books.

Pinkerton, James and Ioan Grillo

2005 "The Fight for Nuevo Laredo." *Houston Chronicle* (May 8): Internet.

Pistone, Joseph D.

2004 *The Way of the Wiseguy.* Philadelphia: Running Press.

1992 *The Ceremony: The Mafia Initiation Tapes.* New York: Dell.

1987 *Donnie Brasco: My Undercover Life in the Mafia.* New York: New American Library.

Pitkin, Thomas Monroe and Francesco Cordasco

1977 *The Black Hand: A Chapter in Ethnic Crime.* Totowa, NJ: Littlefield, Adams.

Plate, Thomas and the Editors of *New York*, eds.

1972 *The Mafia at War.* New York: New York Magazine Press.

Polgreen, Lydia

2005 "As Nigeria Tries to Fight Graft, a New Sordid Tale." *New York Times* (November 29): 1, 14.

Polgreen, Lydia and Tim Weiner

2004 "Drug Traffickers Find Haiti a Hospitable Port of Call." *New York Times* (May 16): 6.

"Police Tackle London's Yardies"

1999 *BBC News* (July 20): Internet.

Pomfret, John

2001 "Made Man in China Has Gangland Ties, Party Pals." *Seattle Times* (January 21): Internet.

Popiano, Willie with John Harney

1993 *Godson: A True-Life Account of 20 Years Inside the Mob.* New York: St. Martin's Press.

Porrello, Rick

1995 *The Rise and Fall of the Cleveland Mafia.* Ft. Lee, NJ: Barricade Books.

Posner, Gerald L.

1988 *Warlords of Crime: Chinese Secret Societies—The New Mafia.* New York: McGraw-Hill.

Possley, Maurice

2001 "Union Ousts 3 Leaders for Mob Ties." *Chicago Tribune* (January 12): Sec. 2: 1, 5.

1996 "U.S. Will Help Mole Set Up His New Digs." *Chicago Tribune* (January 22): 1, 16.

Possley, Maurice and Rick Kogan

2001 *"Everybody Pays": Two Men, One Murder, and the Price of Truth.* New York: Putnam.

Post, Henry

1981 "The Whorehouse Sting." *New York* (February 2): 31–34.

Potter, Gary

1994 *Criminal Organizations: Vice, Racketeering, and Politics in an American City.* Prospect Heights, IL: Waveland.

Potter, Gary, Larry Gaines, and Beth Holbrook

1990 "Blowing Smoke: An Evaluation of Marijuana Eradication in Kentucky." *American Journal of Police* 9: 97–116.

Povoledo, Elisabetta

2007 "A Top Sicilian Mafia Boss Is Held, Italy Says." *New York Times* (November 6): 14.

2006 "Police Seize Top Mafioso After 43 Years." *New York Times* (April 12): 3.

Powell, Bill

2007 "The Strange Case of an Afghan Warlord." *Time* (February 19): 28–37.

2005 "Generation Jihad." *Time* (October 3): 56–59.

Powell, Hickman

2000 *Lucky Luciano: The Man Who Organized Crime in America.* Ft. Lee, NJ: Barricade Books. Originally published in 1939.

Prall, Robert H. and Norton Mockridge

1951 *This Is Costello.* New York: Gold Medal.

Préfontaine, D. C. and Yvon Dandurand

2004 "Terrorism and Organized Crime: Reflections on an Illusive Link and Its Implications for Criminal Law Reform." Paper presented at the Annual Meeting of the International Society for Criminal Law Reform, Montreal, August 8–12.

President's Commission on Law Enforcement and Administration of Justice

1968 *The Challenge of Crime in a Free Society.* New York: Avon.

President's Commission on Organized Crime (PCOC)

1986a *America's Habit: Drug Abuse, Drug Trafficking, and Organized Crime.* Washington, DC: U.S. Government Printing Office.

1986b *The Edge: Organized Crime, Business, and Labor Unions.* Washington, DC: U.S. Government Printing Office.

1986c *The Impact: Organized Crime Today.* Washington, DC: U.S. Government Printing Office.

1985a "Materials on Ethical Issues for Lawyers Involved with Organized Crime Figures." Unpublished paper.

1985b *Organized Crime and Labor-Management Racketeering in the United States.* Washington, DC: U.S. Government Printing Office.

1984a *The Cash Connection: Organized Crime, Financial Institutions, and Money Laundering.* Washington, DC: U.S. Government Printing Office.

1984b *Organized Crime of Asian Origin.* Washington, DC: U.S. Government Printing Office.

1984c *Organized Crime and Cocaine Trafficking.* Washington DC: U.S. Government Printing Office.

"Press Release"

2000 U.S. Attorney for the Second District of New York (October 10).

1999 "Operation Impunity Dismantles Nationwide Drug Trafficking Operation." U.S. Department of Justice, September 22.

Preston, Julia and Craig Pyes

1997 "Mexican Tale: Drugs, Crime, Torture and the U.S." *New York Times* (August 18): 1, 5, 6.

"Profaci Dies of Cancer, Led Feuding Brooklyn Mob"

1962 *New York Times* (June 8): 32.

PSI. See Permanent Subcommittee on Investigations Puente, Teresa and Paul de la Garza

1999 "Fear, Loathing and Drugs in Mexico." *Chicago Tribune* (December 5): 6.

Pulley, Brett

1999 "Living Off the Daily Dream of Winning a Lottery Prize." *New York Times* (May 22): 1, 12–13.

1998 "Those Seductive Snake Eyes; Tales of Growing Up Gambling." *New York Times* (June 16): 1, 23.

Putnam, Robert D.

1993 *Making Democracy Work: Civic Traditions in Modern Italy.* Princeton, NJ: Princeton University Press.

Queen, William

2007 *Under and Alone.* New York: Ballantine.

Quinn, James and D. Shane Koch

2003 "The Nature of Criminality Within One-Percent Motorcycle Clubs." *Deviant Behavior* 24(3): 281–305.

Quirk, Matthew

2008 "How to Grow a Gang." *The Atlantic* (May): 23, 25.

Raab, Selwyn

2005 *Five Families: The Rise, Decline, and Resurgence of America's Most Powerful Mafia Empires.* New York: St. Martin's Press.

1997a "Arson Case Led to Inquiry of Mob Cartel." *New York Times* (June 23): 13.

1997b "FBI Agent Runs Brooklyn Club to Sting Mafia Stolen Goods Ring." *New York Times* (January 24): 1, 18.

1997c "Simone DeCavalcante, 84, Former Crime Figure in New Jersey." *New York Times* (February 12): 18.

1997d "Two Convicted as Masterminds of Mob's Hold on Private Garbage Collection." *New York Times* (October 22): 19.

1997e "2 Mob Suspects with Same Name Say U.S. Mixed Them Up." *New York Times* (October 19): 17.

1997f "Longtime Numbers King of New York Goes Public to Clear His Name." *New York Times* (July 6): Internet.

1996a "Crackdowns on Mob Seen as Mixed Blessing by Merchants of Fulton Fish Market." *New York Times* (March 31): 18.

1996b "End Gotti's Reign From Cell, Mafia Bosses Tell Gambinos." *New York Times* (October 26): 20.

1996c "Gotti Files 2d Appeal and Authorities Call It a Power Play." *New York Times* (January 21): 18.

1996d "New Jersey Officials Say Mafia Infiltrated Health-Care Industry." *New York Times* (August 21): 1, C19.

1996e "Trash Haulers Charged with Rigging Bids." *New York Times* (November 13): 17.

1996f "Walkout Disrupts Fish Market." *New York Times* (January 3): B12.

1995a "Brother of Mob Turncoat Is Gunned Down." *New York Times* (October 6): 8.

1995b "Crackdown on Mob Aids Garment Makers." *New York Times* (June 12): B12.

1995c "Jury Convicts Philadelphia Mob Leader." *New York Times* (November 22): 8.

1995d "Mayor Seeks Fulton Fish Market Takeover." *New York Times* (February 1): 16.

1995e "New York Bookies Go Computer Age But Wind Up Being Raided Anyhow." *New York Times* (August 25): 6.

1995f "The Thin Line Between Mole and Manager." *New York Times* (July 2): 15.

1994a "Court Disclosures Expose Mobster Who Died of AIDS as F.B.I. Mole." *New York Times* (November 20): 19.

1994b "New Groups of Russian Gangs Gain Foothold in Brooklyn." *New York Times* (August 23): 1, 3.

1994c "Panel Clears Teamsters' Chief of Mob Ties." *New York Times* (July 12): C20.

1992a "Mafia Family in New York Linked to Newspaper Fraud." *New York Times* (July 8): C3.

1992b "'Most Dangerous Mafioso' Left at Helm of Lucchese Crime Family." *New York Times* (November 28): 14.

1992c "Top Member of Colombo Crime Family Is Ambushed in Brooklyn." *New York Times* (December 30): 13.

1990 "Racketeering Held to Persist at New York's Fish Market." *New York Times* (August 9): B12.

"Racket Chief Slain by Gangster Gunfire"

1931 *New York Times* (April 16): 1.

Rakove, Milton L.

1975 *Don't Make No Waves, Don't Back No Losers*. Bloomington: Indiana University Press.

Randolph, Jennifer G.

1995 "RICO—The Rejection of an Economic Motive Requirement." *Journal of Criminal Law and Criminology* 85 (Spring): 1189–1222.

Rangel, Jesus

1988 "10 Are Convicted for Corruption." *New York Times* (November 20): 25.

Rashbaum, William K.

2011 "Escaping the Law, One Last Time: An Elusive Mobster's End, Double-Checked." *New York Times* (February 2): 19.

2011b "Review of Carpenters' Union Shows Corruption Persists." *New York Times* (January 9): Internet.

2005 "Three Longshoremen Not Guilty of Fraud and Other Charges." *New York Times* (November 9): B1, 12.

2004 "Officials Say Mob Stole $200 Million Using Phone Bills." *New York Times* (February 11): 1, B6.

2002 "Dock Rackets Tied to Gottis, U.S. Charges." *New York Times* (June 5): 21.

2001a "Mob Soldier Faces a Return to Jail for Parole Violations." *New York Times* (July 18): Internet.

2001b "Two Are Charged in Money-Laundering Scheme." *New York Times* (July 18): Internet.

2000 "A Smuggling Operation with a Russian Twist." *New York Times* (August 9): 1, 15.

Rashbaum, William K. and Juan Forero

2005 "Detective in New York vs. Drug Lord in Colombia." *New York Times* (October 5): B1, 5.

Ratliff, Evan

2011 "The Mark." *New Yorker* (May 2): 56–65.

2010 *From Fear to Fraternity: A Russian Tale of Crime, Economy and Modernity*. London: Pluto Press.

Rawlinson, Patricia

1997 "Russian Organized Crime: A Brief History." Pages 28–52 in *Russian Organized Crime: The New Threat?* edited by Phil Williams. London, England: Frank Cass.

Ray, Oakley

1978 *Drugs, Society, and Human Behavior*. St. Louis: Mosby.

Reagan, Ronald

1986 "Declaring War on Organized Crime." *New York Times Magazine* (January 12): 26, 28, 47, 55–57, 62, 65, 84.

Reece, Jack

1973 "Fascism, the Mafia, and the Emergence of Sicilian Separatism." *Journal of Modern History* 45 (June): 261–76.

Reedy, George E.

1991 *From the Ward to the White House: The Irish in American Politics*. New York: Scribner's.

Reid, Ed

1970 *The Grim Reapers*. New York: Bantam.

Reid, Ed and Ovid Demaris

1964 *The Green Felt Jungle*. New York: Cardinal Paperbacks.

1953 *The Shame of New York*. New York: Random House.

Reif, Rita

1984 "Gould Jewels to Be Sold at Auction." *New York Times* (January 3): 21.

Reinhold, Robert

1989 "California Shaken Over an Informer." *New York Times* (February 17): 9.

Remnick, David

1995 "In Stalin's Wake." *New Yorker* (July 24): 46–62.

Renard, Ronald D.

2003 "The Mandalay Connection: Drugs in Myanmar/Burma." Pages 119–132 in *Transnational Organized Crime: Myth, Power, and Profit*, edited by Emilio C. Viano, Jose Magallanes, and Laurent Bridel. Durham, NC: Carolina Academic Press.

Reppetto, Thomas A.

2004 *American Mafia: A History of Its Rise to Power*. New York: Holt.

1978 *The Blue Parade*. New York: Free Press.

Reuter, Peter

1995 "The Decline of the American Mafia." *Public Interest* (Summer): 89–99.

1987 *Racketeering in Legitimate Industries: A Study in the Economics of Intimidation*. Santa Monica, CA: RAND Corporation.

1983 *Disorganized Crime*. Cambridge, MA: MIT Press.

Reuter, Peter and Carol Petrie, eds.

1999 *Transnational Organized Crime: Summary of a Workshop*. Washington, DC: National Academy Press.

Reuter, Peter, Jonathan Rubinstein, and Simon Wynn

1983 *Racketeering in Legitimate Industries: Two Case Studies. Executive Summary*. Washington, DC: U.S. Government Printing Office.

Reuters (News Service)

2004a "Gunmen Free 29 Inmates From Mexico Jail." *New York Times* (January 6): 6.

2004b "Mexican Drug Boss and 2 Others Slain." *New York Times* (September 13): 5.

1999 "Italian Police Capture Calabrian Mafia Boss." (March 11): Internet.

1996 "Hells Angels Convicted in Denmark Slaying." *New York Times* (December 21): 7.

Rey, Guido M. and Ernesto U. Savona

1993 "The Mafia: An International Enterprise?" Pages 69–80 in *Mafia Issues*, edited by Ernesto U. Savona. Milan, Italy: United Nations.

Reynolds, Marylee

1995 *From Gangs to Gangsters: How American Sociology Studied Organized Crime, 1918–1994*. Albany, NY: Harrow and Heston.

Rhodes, Robert P.

1984 *Organized Crime: Crime Control vs. Civil Liberties*. New York: Random House.

Rice, Andrew

2011 "Life on the Line." *New York Times Magazine* (July 31): 20–27.

Richtel, Matt

2011 "Authorities Crack Down on 3 Poker Sites." *New York Times* (April 16): B1, 2.

Riding, Alan

1987a "Colombian Envoy Shot in Budapest." *New York Times* (January 14): 5.

1987b "Colombia Effort Against Drugs Hits Dead End." *New York Times* (August 20): 4.

Riordon, William L.

1963 *Plunkett of Tammany Hall*. New York: Dutton.

Risley, Raymond

1998 Commander, Organized Crime Division, Chicago Police Department. Personal interview.

Roane, Kit R.

2000 "The Mob Goes Downtown." *U.S. News and World Report* (June 26): 16–17.

Robb, Peter

1996 *Midnight in Sicily*. Boston: Faber and Faber.

Robbins, Tom and Jerry Capeci

1994 "Wiseguy Helped: Civil Rights Killings Solved by Snitch." *New York Daily News* (June 21): 12–13.

Roberton, Robert J.

1986 "Designer Drugs: The Analog Game." Pages 91–96 in *Bridging Services: Drug Abuse, Human Services and the Therapeutic Community*," edited by Alfonso Acampora and Ethan Nebelkopf. New York: World Federation of Therapeutic Communities.

Roberts, Sam

2011 "Little Italy, Littler by the Year." *New York Times* (February 22): 20, 22.

Robins, Garry

2009 "Understanding Individual Behaviors Within Covert Networks: The Interplay of Individual Qualities, Psychological Predispositions, and Network Effects." *Trends in Organized Crime* 29 (November): 166–87.

Robinson, Linda

1998a "Is Colombia Lost to Rebels?" *U.S. News and World Report* (May 11): 38–42.

1998b "Land for Peace in Colombia." *U.S. News and World Report* (November 23): 37.

Robinson, Louis N.

1933 "Social Values and Mercenary Crime." Pages 13–31 in *Crime for Profit: A Symposium on Mercenary Crime*, edited by Ernest D. MacDougall. Boston: Stratford Company.

"ROC." See "Russian Organized Crime in the United States"

Rockaway, Robert A.

1993 *But—He Was Good to His Mother: The Lives and Crimes of Jewish Gangsters*. Jerusalem, Israel: Gefen Publishing House.

Roemer, William F., Jr.

1995 *Accardo: The Genuine Godfather*. New York: Donald I. Fine.

1994 *The Enforcer, Spilotro: The Chicago Mob's Man over Las Vegas*. New York: Ivy Books.

Rohde, David

2007 "Taliban Push Poppy Production to a Record Again." *New York Times* (August 26): 3.

Rohter, Larry

1991 "A Cocaine Baron's Tales of Intrigue and Greed Liven Up Noriega's Trial." *New York Times* (November 24): E3.

1989 "Mexico Captures Top Drug Figure and 80 Policemen." *New York Times* (April 11): 1, 6.

Rohter, Larry and Clifford Krauss

1998a "Dominican Drug Traffickers Tighten Grip on the Northeast." *New York Times* (May 11): 12, 17.

1998b "Dominicans Allow Drugs Easy Sailing." *New York Times* (May 10): 1, 6.

Roma, Rafael

2011 "Plan Colombia Revisited: Mixed Result for U.S. Anti-Drug Initiative." *CNN World* (January 11): Internet.

Rome, Florence

1975 *The Tattooed Men*. New York: Delacorte.

Romero, Simon

2011 "In Colombia, Rush for Gold Fuels Conflict." *New York Times* (March 4): 1, 10.

2008a "Union Killings Peril Trade Pact with Colombia." *New York Times* (April 14): 1, 8.

2008b "Ecuador Opposes Outpost in American War on Drugs." *New York Times* (May 12): 8.

2008c "Colombia Extradites 14 Paramilitary Leaders to the United States." *New York Times* (May 14): 6.

2008d "Colombian Warlord Pleads Not Guilty to Drug Charges." *New York Times* (May 15): B3.

2008e "Despite Rebel Losses, Cocaine Sustains War in Rural Colombia." *New York Times* (July 27): 1, 8.

2008f "As U.S. Presses Drug War, Bolivia Is Antagonist and Uneasy Ally." *New York Times* (August 29): 1, 11.

2007 "Cocaine Wars Turn Port into Colombia's Deadliest City." *New York Times* (May 22): 3.

Romoli, Kathleen

1941 *Colombia*. Garden City, NY: Doubleday, Doran.

Rosen, Charles

1978 *Scandals of '51: How the Gamblers Almost Killed College Basketball*. New York: Holt, Rinehart and Winston.

Rosner, Lydia S.

1995 "Preface" to "Organized Crime IV: The Russian Connection." *Contemporary Criminal Justice* 11 (December): vi–viii.

1986 *Soviet Way of Crime*. South Hadley, MA: Bergin and Garvey.

Ross, Irwin

1992 *Shady Business: Confronting Corporate Corruption*. New York: Twentieth Century Fund Press.

Ross, Ron

2003 *Bummy Davis vs. Murder, Inc*. New York: St. Martin's Press.

Rothmiller, Mike and Ivan G. Goldman

1992 *L.A. Secret Police: Inside the LAPD Elite Spy Network*. New York: Pocket Books.

Rubinstein, Jonathan and Peter Reuter

1978a "Fact, Fancy, and Organized Crime." *Public Interest* 53 (Fall): 45–67.

1978b "Bookmaking in New York." New York: Policy Sciences Center. (Preliminary unpublished draft)

1977 "Numbers: The Routine Racket." New York: Policy Sciences Center. (Preliminary unpublished draft)

Rudolph, Robert

1992 *The Boys from New Jersey*. New York: William Morrow.

Ruggiero, Vincenzo

1993 "The Camorra: 'Clean' Capital and Organised Crime." Pages 141–61 in *Global Crime Connections: Dynamics and Control*, edited by Frank Pearce and Michael Woodiwiss. Toronto, Canada: University of Toronto Press.

Rugoff, Milton

1989 *America's Gilded Age: Intimate Portraits from an Era of Extravagance and Change, 1850–1890*. New York: Henry Holt.

Russell, Francis

1975 *A City in Terror—1919—The Boston Police Strike*. New York: Viking.

"Russian Organized Crime in the United States"

1996 Hearing Before the U.S. Senate Permanent Subcommittee on Investigations, May 15. Washington, DC: Committee on Governmental Affairs.

Ryan, Patrick J. and George E. Rush, eds.

1997 *Understanding Organized Crime in Global Perspective: A Reader*. Thousand Oaks, CA: Sage.

Sabbag, Robert

1996 "The Invisible Family." *New York Times Magazine* (February 11): 33–39.

Sack, John

2001 *The Dragonhead*. New York: Crown.

Salerno, Joseph and Stephen J. Rivele

1990 *The Plumber*. New York: Knightsbridge.

Salerno, Ralph and John S. Tompkins

1969 *The Crime Confederation*. Garden City, NY: Doubleday.

Salkowski, Joe

2001 "Encryption on Wrong Side of Law, Officers Say." *Chicago Tribune* (January 29): Sec. 4: 2.

Samuels, David

2008 "The New Dodge City." *Men's Vogue* (February): 20–28.

Sanderson, Thomas M.

2004 "Transnational Terror and Organized Crime: Blurring the Lines." *SAIS Review* 24 (Winter): 49–61.

Sandoval, Ricardo

1998 "19 Mexicans Slain; Drug Feud Is Blamed." *Chicago Tribune* (September 18): 10.

Saney, Parviz

1986 *Crime and Culture in America: A Comparative Perspective*. New York: Greenwood.

Sanger, David E.

1997 "Japanese Near Pact with U.S. on Threat to Bar Their Ships from American Ports." *New York Times* (October 18): 5.

1995 "Money Laundering, New and Improved." *New York Times* (December 24): E4.

1992 "Top Japanese Party Leaders Accused of Links to Mobsters." *New York Times* (September 23): 1, 4.

Sann, Paul

1971 *Kill the Dutchman: The Story of Dutch Schultz*. New York: Popular Library.

Sante, Luc

1991 *Low Life*. New York: Vintage.

Saulny, Susan

2003 "Laundering of Billions Is Alleged." *New York Times* (June 27): B1, 3.

Savage, Charlie

2011 "D.E.A. Squads Extend the Reach of the Drug War." *New York Times* (November 7): 1, 3.

Saviano, Roberto

2007 *Gomorrah: A Personal Journey into the Violent Empire of Naples' Organized Crime System*. New York: Farrar, Strauss and Giroux. Translated by Virginia Jewiss.

Sawyers, June

1988 "A 'King' Who Had Us in His Pocket." *Chicago Tribune Magazine* (October 2): 10.

Saxon, Wolfgang

1990 "Harry Bridges, Docks Leader, Dies at 88." *New York Times* (March 31): 11.

Scalia, Vincenzo

2010 "From the Octopus to te Spider's Web: the Transformation of the Sicilian Mafia Under Postmodernism." *Trends in Organized Crime* 13 (December): 283–98

Scaramella, Gene

1998 Investigator, Cook County (IL) Sheriff's Police. Personal interview.

Schatzberg, Rufus

1994 "African American Organized Crime." Pages 189–212 in *Handbook of Organized Crime in the United States*, edited by Robert J. Kelly, Ko-lin Chin, and Rufus Schatzberg. Westport, CT: Greenwood.

1993 *Black Organized Crime in Harlem: 1920–1930*. New York: Garland.

Schatzberg, Rufus and Robert J. Kelly

1996 *African-American Organized Crime: A Social History*. New York: Garland.

Schelling, Thomas C.

1971 "What Is the Business of Organized Crime?" *American Scholar* 40 (Autumn): 643–52.

Schemo, Diana Jean and Tim Golden

1998 "Bogotá Aid: To Fight Drugs or Rebels?" *New York Times* (June 2): 1, 12.

Schmetzer, Uli

2001 "U.S., China Take Sides in Border Skirmish." *Chicago Tribune* (May 19): 1, 6.

1991a "'Nigerian Connection' Ties Chicago to Asian Drugs." *Chicago Tribune* (December 21): 1, 11.

1991b "Slave Trade Survives, Prospers Across Asia." *Chicago Tribune* (November 15): 1, 18.

1990 "'Prince of Death' Is a Wanted Man." *Chicago Tribune* (March 21): 21.

1985 "A City Whose Kids Are Hired to Kill." *Chicago Tribune* (October 13): 4.

Schmidle, Nicholas

2010 "Inside the Knockoff Factory." *New York Times* Magazine (August 22): 38–45.

Schmidt, John R.

1992 *Mr. Capone*. New York: William Morrow.

Schmitt, Eric

2004 "Afghans' Gains Face Big Threat in Drug Traffic." *New York Times* (December 11): 1, 6.

Schneider, Jane, Peter Schneider, Stanley R. Barrett, Bojan Baskar, Henk Driessen, Chris Hann, Thomas Hauschild, Andrew Kipnis, Lutz Musner, Susana Narotzky, Gustavo Lins Ribeiro

2005 "Mafia, Antimafia, and the Plural Cultures of Sicily." *Current Anthropology* 46 (August–October): 501–521.

Schneider, Stephen

2009 Iced: *The Story of Organized Crime in Canada*. Ontario, Canada: Wiley.

Schoenberg, Robert J.

1992 *Mr. Capone*. New York: William Morrow.

Schorr, Mark

1979 "The .22 Caliber Killings." *New York* (May 7): 43–46.

Schreiber, Amanda J.

2002 "Dealing with the Devil: The FBI's Troubled Relationship with Its Confidential Informants." *Columbia Journal of Law and Social Problems* 301 (Summer): Internet.

Schulte-Bockholt, Alfredo

2006 *The Politics of Organized Crime and the Organized Crime of Politics*. Lexington, MA: Lexington Books.

"Schultz Aide Slain; 7th in Five Months"

1931 *New York Times* (June 22): 2.

"Schultz Product of Dry Law Era"

1933 *New York Times* (January 22): 23.

"Schultz Succumbs to Bullet Wounds Without Naming Slayers"

1933 *New York Times* (October 25): 1.

Schwartz, John

2009 "For a Departed Mobster, Wreaths, Roses but no Tears." *New York Times* (October 14): 6.

2001 "U.S. Declines to Release Data in Trial." *New York Times* (August 25): B1, 2.

Schweich, Thomas

2008 "Is Afghanistan a Narco-State?" *New York Times* (July 27): 44–47, 60–62.

Schwirtz, Michael

2010 "Massacre Shows the Power of Gangs in Rural Russia." *New York Times* (December 12): 20.

Sciascia, Leonard

1963 *Mafia Vendetta*. New York: Knopf.

Sciarrone, Rocco

2010 "Mafia and Civil Society: Economic-criminal Collusion and Territorial Control in Calabria." Pages 173–96 in *Organized Crime and States: The Hidden Face of Politics*, edited by Briquet, Jean-Louis and Gilles Favarel-Garrigues. New York: Palgrave Macmillan.

Sciolino, Elaine and Stephen Engelberg

1988 "Narcotics Effort Foiled by U.S. Security Goals." *New York Times* (April 10): 1, 10.

Scott, W. Richard

1981 *Organizations: Rational, Natural, and Open Systems*. Englewood Cliffs, NJ: Prentice-Hall.

Seedman, Albert A.

1974 *Chief!* New York: Arthur Fields.

SEESAC (South Eastern and Eastern Europe Clearinghouse for the Control of Small Arms and Light Weapons)

2006 *Gun Culture in South Eastern Europe*. Belgrade: SEESAC.

Seguin, Rheal

2005 "Bust Shattered Drug Network, Quebec Police Say." *Globe and Mail* (February 24): 46.

Seidman, Harold

1938 *Labor Czars: A History of Labor Racketeering*. New York: Liveright.

Semple, Kirk

2001 "Colombia's Cocaine Frontier." *Mother Jones* (November/December): 58–63.

Sengupta, Somini

2004 "Violence Jolts the Still Fragile Democracy in Nigeria." *New York Times* (May 24): 3.

Serao, Ernesto

1911a "The Truth about the Camorra." *Outlook* 98 (July 28): 717–26.

1911b "The Truth about the Camorra: Part II." *Outlook* 98 (August 50): 778–87.

Serio, Joseph

2008 *Investigating the Russian Mafia*. Durham, NC: Carolina Academic Press.

1992a "Organized Crime in the Soviet Union and Beyond." *Low Intensity Conflict and Law Enforcement* 1 (Autumn): 127–51.

1992b "Shunning Tradition: Ethnic Organized Crime in the Former Soviet Union." *CJ International* 8 (November–December): 5–6.

Serrin, William

1989 "Jackie Presser's Secret Lives Detailed in Government Files." *New York Times* (March 27): 1, 11.

Servadio, Gaia

1976 *Mafioso: A History of the Mafia from Its Origins to the Present Day*. Briarcliff Manor, NY: Stein and Day.

1974 *Angelo LaBarbera: The Profile of a Mafia Boss*. London: Quartet Books.

Sexton, Joe

1995 "3 Men Accused of Running Chinatown Organized Crime." *New York Times* (June 2): 1, 16.

Seymour, Christopher

1996 *Yakuza Diary*. New York: Atlantic Monthly Press.

Shannon, Elaine

1991 "New Kings of Coke." *Time* (July 1): 29–33.

1988 *Desperados: Latin Drug Lords, U.S. Lawmen, and the War America Can't Win*. New York: Viking.

Shannon, William V.

1989 *The American Irish: A Political and Social Portrait*. Amherst: University of Massachusetts Press.

Shaw, Clifford and Henry D. McKay

1972 *Juvenile Delinquency and Urban Areas*. Chicago: University of Chicago Press. Originally published in 1942.

Shawcross, Tim and Martin Young

1987 *Men of Honour: The Confessions of Tommaso Buscetta*. London: Collins.

Shelley, Louise I.

2010 *Human Trafficking: A Global Perspective*. New York: Cambridge University Press.

2005 "The Unholy Trinity: Transnational Crime, Corruption, and Terrorism." *Brown Journal of World Affairs* 11 (Winter/Spring): 101–11.

2001 "Corruption and Organized Crime in Mexico in the Post-PRI Transition." *Journal of Contemporary Criminal Justice* 17 (August): 213–31.

1997 "Post-Soviet Organized Crime: A New Form of Authoritarianism." Pages 122–38 in *Russian Organized Crime, The New Threat?* edited by Phil Williams. London: Frank Cass.

Shelley, Louise I. and Sharon Melzer

2008 "The Nexus of Organized Crime and Terrorism: Two Case Studies in Cigarette Smuggling." *International Journal of Comparative and Applied Criminal Justice* 32 (Spring): 44–62.

Shelley, Louise I. and John T. Picarelli

2005 "Methods and Motives: Exploring Links Between Transnational Organized Crime and International Terrorism." *Trends in Organized Crime* 9 (Winter): 52–67.

Shelley, Louise I., John T. Picarelli, Allison Irby, Douglas M. Hart, Patricia A. Craig, Phil Williams, Steven Simon, Nabi Abdullaev, Bartosz Stanislawski, and Laura Covill

2005 *Methods and Motives: Exploring Links Between Transnational Organized Crime and International Terrorism*. Washington, DC: U. S. Department of Justice.

Shenon, Philip

1996 "Opium Baron's Rule May End with Surrender in Myanmar." *New York Times* (January 6): 4.

1986 "U.S. Crime Panel: Discord to the End." *New York Times* (April 6): 9.

Sher, Julian and William Marsden

2006 *Angels of Death: Inside the Biker Gang's Crime Empire*. New York: Carroll and Graf.

Sheridan, Michael

1997 "Triads Move on Hong Kong." *London Times* (July 13): 19.

Sheridan, Walter

1972 *The Fall and Rise of Jimmy Hoffa*. New York: Saturday Review Press.

Shimbun, Yomiuri

2011 "Lights, Camera, Corruption/Crime's Longstanding Ties to Showbiz Tough to Untangle." *Daily Yomiuri Online* (August 30): Internet.

Shipp, E. R.

1985 "Former Chief of Teamsters Ordered to Jail Next Month." *New York Times* (April 25): 12.

Shirk, David A.

2011 *The Drug Wart in Mexico: Confronting the Shared Threat*. New York: Council on Foreign Relations.

Shoham, Efrat

2010 "'Signs of Honor' Among Russian Inmates in Israel's Prisons." *International Journal of Offender Therapy and Comparative Criminology* 54: 984–1003.

Short, James F., Jr., ed.

1968 *Gang Delinquency and Delinquent Subcultures*. New York: Harper & Row.

Siciliano, Vincent

1970 *Unless They Kill Me First*. New York: Hawthorn Books.

Siebert, Renate

1996 *Secrets of Life and Death: Women and the Mafia*. London: Verso.

"Siegel, Gangster, Is Slain on Coast."

1947 *New York Times* (June 22): 1.

Silverstein, Ken

2000 "Trillion-Dollar Hideaway." *Mother Jones* (November/December): 38–45, 94–96.

Simpson, Daniel

2002 "In Albanian Politics, Are the Changes Skin-Deep?" *New York Times* (November 21): 4.

Sims, Calvin

2000 "Feeling Pinch, Japan's Mobs Struggle for Control." *New York Times* (April 2): 6.

Sinclair, Andrew

1962 *The Era of Excess: A Social History of the Prohibition Movement*. Boston: Little, Brown.

Singer, Mark

2002 "The Gang's All Here." *New Yorker* (August 12): 56–61.

Sisk, Richard

2004 "Disabling Haiti Drug Cartels Is Job One." *New York Daily News* (March 4): 24.

Skolnick, Jerome H.

2008 "Policing Should Not Be for Profit." *Criminology and Public Policy* 7 (May): 257–62.

Skolnick, Jerome H., Theodore Correl, Elizabeth Navarro, and Roger Rabb

1990 "The Social Structure of Street Drug Dealing." *American Journal of Police* 9: 1–41.

Slind-Flor, Victoria

2011 "Nokia, Firehouse Subs, Winnipeg Jets, Hells Angels: Intellectual Property." *Bloomberg* (September 2): Internet.

Sloane, Arthur A.

1992 *Hoffa*. Cambridge, MA: MIT Press.

Sly, Liz

1999 "In a Hail of Bullets, Island of Macau Awaits a New Master." *Chicago Tribune* (February 18): 8.

Smith, Alson J.

1962 "The Early Chicago Story." Pages 138–46 in *Organized Crime in America*, edited by Gus Tyler. Ann Arbor: University of Michigan Press.

Smith, Craig S.

2005 "Turkey's Growing Sex Trade Snares Many Slavic Women." *New York Times* (June 26): 4.

Smith, David E., ed.

1979 *Amphetamine Use, Misuse, and Abuse*. Boston: G. K. Hall and Co.

Smith, Dwight C., Jr.

1982 "Paragons, Pariahs, and Pirates: A Spectrum-Based Theory of Enterprise." *Crime and Delinquency* 26 (July): 358–86.

1978 "Organized Crime and Entrepreneurship." *International Journal of Criminology and Penology* 6: 161–77.

1974 *The Mafia Mystique*. New York: Basic Books.

Smith, Dwight C., Jr., and Ralph Salerno

1970 "The Use of Strategies in Organized Crime Control." *Journal of Law, Criminology and Police Science* 61: 101–11.

Smith, Greg B.

2005 "Life and Times of New Donnie Brasco." *New York Daily News* (April 18): 20.

2004a "Albanian 'Mafiosi' in Feds' Net." *New York Daily News* (November 1): 24.

2004b "Moving In on the Mob." *New York Daily News* (October 27): 2.

2003 *Made Men*. New York: Berkeley Books.

Smith, John L.

1998 *The Animal in Hollywood: Anthony Fiato's Life in the Mafia*. New York: Barricade Books.

Smith, Peter H.

1999 "Semiorganized International Crime: Drug Trafficking in Mexico." Pages 193–216 in *Transnational Crime in the Americas*, edited by Tom Farer. New York: Routledge.

Smith, Richard Norton

1982 *Thomas E. Dewey and His Times*. New York: Simon and Schuster.

Smith, Sherwin D.

1963 "35 Years Ago Arnold Rothstein Was Mysteriously Murdered and Left a Racket Empire Up for Grabs." *New York Times Magazine* (October 27): 96.

"Smoking Gun, The"

1998 *New York* (November 22): 16.

Snedden, Christopher and John Visser

1994 *Financial and Organised Crime in Italy*. Commonwealth of Australia.

Sniffen, Michael J.

2000 "Mexico-Jamaica Drug Ring Broken." Associated Press (April 13): Internet.

Snyder, Richard and Angelica Duran-Martinez

2009 "Does Illegality Breed Violence? Drug Trafficking and State-Sponsored Protection Rackets." *Crime, Law and Social Change* 52 (March): 253–73.

Society for Neuroscience (SNS)

2002 *Brain Facts: A Primer on the Brain and Nervous system*. Washington, DC: SNS.

Sondern, Frederic, Jr.

1959 *Brotherhood of Evil: The Mafia*. New York: Farrar, Straus and Cudahy.

Song, John Juey-Long

1996 "The Asian Factor: Methodological Barriers to the Study of Asian Gangs and Organized Crime." *American Journal of Criminal Justice* 21(1): 27–41.

South Eastern and Eastern Europe Clearinghouse for the Control of Small Arms and Light Weapons. See SEESAC.

Spadolini, Giovanni

1993 "Foreword." Pages 7–9 in *Mafia Issues*, edited by Ernesto U. Savona. Milan, Italy: United Nations.

Speart, Jessica

1995 "The New Drug Mules." *New York Times Magazine* (June 11): 44–45.

Special Committee to Investigate Organized Crime in Interstate Commerce

1951 *Kefauver Crime Report*. New York: Arco.

Spector, Michael

1995 "Old-Time Boss for Russia's Showcase Port." *New York Times* (August 28): 1, 2.

1994 "New Moscow Mob Terror: Car Bombs." *New York Times* (June 10): 4.

Spergel, Irving

1964 *Racketville, Slumtown, Haulberg*. Chicago: University of Chicago Press.

Spiering, Frank

1976 *The Man Who Got Capone*. Indianapolis, IN: Bobbs-Merrill.

Spinale, Dominic

2004 *G-Men and Gangsters: Partners in Crime*. New York: MJF Books.

"Spotlight" 1981 *Chicago Crime Commission Searchlight* (October): 8.

Stahl, Marc B.

1992 "Asset Forfeiture, Burdens of Proof and the War on Drugs." *Journal of Criminal Law and Criminology* 83: 274–337.

Stanley, Alessandra

2001 "Where Hit Men Better Mean It When They 'Yes Ma'am' to the Boss." *New York Times* (January 11): 11.

1998 "The Army Is Leaving but the Mafia Probably Isn't." *New York Times* (June 26): 4.

1994 "Where Politicians Sometimes Tote Assault Rifles." *New York Times* (May 10): 4.

Starks, Carolyn

1999 "Witness Offers Inside Look at Biker Battle." *Chicago Tribune* (April 6): Sec. 2: 1, 4.

State Commission of Investigation

1989 *Solid Waste Regulation*. Trenton: New Jersey Commission of Investigation.

Steffens, Lincoln

1957 *The Shame of the Cities*. New York: Hill and Wang. Originally published in 1904.

1931 *The Autobiography of Lincoln Steffens*. New York: Chautauqua Press. Reprinted by Harcourt, Brace and World, 1958.

Steinberg, Alfred

1972 *The Bosses*. New York: New American Library.

Steinberg, Allen

2003 "The Public Prosecutor as Representational Image: The 'Lawman' in New York: William Travers Jerome and the Origins of the Modern District Attorney in Turn-of-the-Century New York." *University of Toledo Law Review* 34 (Summer): 753–82.

Sterngold, James

1995 "Organized Crime Puts Its Talent to Helping and Tokyo to Shame." *New York Times* (January 22): 7.

1994 "Gangster Ties to Banks Hurt Japan's Financial Recovery." *New York Times* (October 18): C1, C14.

1992a "Corporate Japan's Unholy Allies." *New York Times* (December 6): 3: 1, 6.

1992b "Japan Takes on Mob, and the Mob Fights Back." *New York Times* (June 15): 1, 6.

1992c "Mob and Politics Intersect, Fueling Cynicism in Japan." *New York Times* (October 21): 1, 4.

Stevens, Jay

1987 *Storming Heaven: LSD and the American Dream*. New York: Atlantic Monthly Press.

Stevenson, James

2006 "Lost and Found New York." *New York Times* (February 25): 15.

Stevenson, Mark

2011 "Mexican Official: 34,612 Drug War Deaths in 4 Years." Associated Press (January 12): Internet.

Stewart, Robert C.

2006 "Reflections on Labor Racketeering and Interdisciplinary Enforcement." *Trends in Organized Crime* 9 (Summer): 60–101.

1980 *Identification and Investigation of Organized Criminal Activity*. Houston, TX: National College of District Attorneys.

Stille, Alexander

1995a *Exquisite Cadavers: The Mafia and the Death of the First Italian Republic*. New York: Pantheon.

1995b "Letter from Sicily: The Fall of Caesar." *New Yorker* (September 11): 68–83.

1993 "Letter from Palermo: The Mafia's Biggest Mistake." *New Yorker* (March 1): 60–73.

Stocckers, Sally W.

2000 "The Rise in Human Trafficking and the Role of Organized Crime." Transnational Crime and Corruption Center, American University. Internet.

Stohl, Rachel

2005 "Fighting the Illicit Trafficking in Small Arms." Center for Defense Information, Internet.

Stolberg, Mary M.

1995 *Fighting Organized Crime: Politics, Justice, and the Legacy of Thomas E. Dewey*. Boston: Northeastern University Press.

Stone, Michael

1992 "After Gotti." *New York* (February 3): 23–30.

Strauss, Neil

2002 "Mafia Songs Break a Code of Silence." *New York Times* (July 22): B1, B4.

Strategy to Combat Transnational Organized Crime

2011 Washington, DC: Office of the President of the United States

Straziuso, Jason

2008 "Marines Ignore Taliban Cash Crop to Not Upset Afghan Locals." *Yahoo News* (May 6): Internet.

Strong, Josiah

1976 "Perils—The Boss, the Machine, the Immigrant: A Nineteenth-Century View." Pages 14–17 in *The City Boss in America: An Interpretive Reader*, edited by Alexander B. Callow, Jr. New York: Oxford University Press.

Sullivan, John and Alex Berenson

2000 "Brokers Charged With Crime Figures in Complex Scheme." *New York Times* (June 15): 1, C27.

Sullivan, Joseph F.

1991 "Casino Union Yields Power as Its Leaders Accept Curbs." *New York Times* (April 13): 7.

1988 "New Jersey Teamster Local Elects Slate Tied to the Mob." *New York Times* (December 8): 16.

Sunderwirth, Stanley G.

1985 "Biological Mechanisms: Neurotransmission and Addiction." Pages 11–19 in *TheAddictions: Multidisciplinary Perspectives and Treatments*, edited by Harvey B. Milkman and Howard J. Shaffer. Lexington, MA: DC Heath.

Suo, Steve

2004 "Unnecessary Epidemic." *The Oregonian* (October 3): Internet.

Supreme Court of the State of New York

1942 *A Presentment Concerning the Enforcement by the Police Department of the City of New York of the Laws Against Gambling.* New York, reprinted by Arno Press, 1974.

Surtees, Rebecca

2008 "Traffickers and Trafficking in Southern and Eastern Europe: Considering the Other Side of Trafficking." *European Journal of Criminology* 5(1): 39–68.

Sutherland, Edwin H.

1973 *Edwin H. Sutherland: On Analyzing Crime,* edited by Karl Schuessler. Chicago: University of Chicago Press.

Suttles, Gerald D.

1968 *The Social Order of the Slum.* Chicago: University of Chicago Press.

Swanberg, W. A.

1959 *Jim Fisk: The Career of an Improbable Rascal.* New York: Scribner's.

Taft, Philip and Philip Ross

1969 "American Labor Violence: Its Causes, Character, and Outcome." Pages 281–395 in *The History of Violence in America,* edited by Hugh Davis Graham and Ted Robert Gurr. New York: Bantam.

Tagliabue, John

1994 "Live by the Rules? An Italian Haven for Cigarette Smugglers Is Fuming." *New York Times* (March 7): 4.

Takahashi, Sadahiko and Carl B. Becker

1985 *Organized Crime in Japan.* Osaka, Japan: Kin'ki University, unpublished paper.

Talese, Gay

1971 *Honor Thy Father.* New York: World Publishing.

1965 *The Overreachers.* New York: Harper & Row.

Talmadge, Eric

1999 "Japanese Mob Raising Fears, Concern." Associated Press (April 20): Internet.

1988 "All Is Not Well Within Japan's Underworld." *Southtown Economist* (December 15): Sec. 2: 4.

Tamayo, Juan O.

2001 "Colombia's Heroin Trade Is Flourishing." *Chicago Tribune* (August 24): 6.

Task Force on Organized Crime

1976 *Organized Crime.* Washington, DC: U.S. Government Printing Office.

1967 *Task Force Report: Organized Crime.* Washington, DC: U.S. Government Printing Office.

Task-Force on Organized Crime in the Baltic Sea Region (TFOCBSR)

2001 *Report on the Fact-Finding Mission Conducted in November 2000 by the National Commissioner of Police for the Baltic Countries Regarding Ttrafficking in Women.* TFOCBSR: Internet.

Tayler, Jefferey

2001 "Russia Is Finished." *Atlantic Monthly* (May): 35–52.

Taylor, Ian, Paul Walton, and Jock Young

1973 *The New Criminology.* New York: Harper & Row.

Tendler, Stewart

2000 "Yardie Gangs Move into the Provinces." *London Times* (August 3): 4.

Teresa, Vincent, and Thomas C. Renner

1973 *My Life in the Mafia.* Greenwich, CT: Fawcett.

Terry, Charles E. and Mildred Pellens

1928 *The Opium Problem.* New York: The Committee on Drug Addictions, in collaboration with the Bureau of Social Hygiene, Inc.

Thomas, Jerry

1994a "Bombings in Chicago, Rockford Linked to Motorcycle Gang Merger." *Chicago Tribune* (November 9): Sec. 2: 4.

1994b "Biker War Erupts in Illinois." *Chicago Tribune* (November 20): Sec. 2: 1, 2.

Thomas, Ralph C.

1977 "Organized Crime in the Construction Industry." *Crime and Delinquency* 23: 304–11.

Thompson, Cheryl W.

2001 "DEA Shielded Tainted Informant." *Washington Post* (July 19): 1.

Thompson, Craig and Allan Raymond

1940 *Gang Rule in New York.* New York: Dial.

Thompson, Ginger

2011 "U.S. Agencies Infiltrating Drug Cartels Across Mexico." *New York Times* (October 24): Internet.

2005a "Drug Violence Paralyzes a City, and Chills the Border." *New York Times* (May 24): 4.

2005b "Mexico's Fallen Party Plans Its Revival with a New Star." *New York Times* (February 6): 12.

2005c "Rival Drug Gangs Turn the Streets of Nuevo Laredo into a War Zone." *New York Times* (December 4): 6.

2004 "Mexico Arrests Leading Figure in Drug Cartel." *New York Times* (August 24): 4.

Thompson, Ginger and James C. McKinley, Jr.

2005 "Mexico's Drug Cartels Wage Fierce Battle for Their Turf." *New York Times* (January 14): 3.

Thompson, Hunter S.

1966 *Hell's Angels: A Strange and Terrible Saga.* New York: Random House.

Thoumi, Francisco E.

2007 "The Rise of Two Drug Tigers: The Development of the Illegal Drugs Industry and Drug Policy Failure in Afghanistan and Colombia. "Pages 125–48 in *The Organized Crime Community.* Edited by Frank Bovenkerk and Michael Levi. New York, NY: Springer.

1995 "The Size of the Illegal Drug Industry." Pages 77–96 in *Drug Trafficking in the Americas*, edited by Bruce M. Bagley and William O. Walker, III. New Brunswick, NJ: Transaction.

Thrasher, Frederic Milton

1968 *The Gang: A Study of 1,313 Gangs in Chicago*, abridged. Chicago: University of Chicago Press. Originally published in 1927.

Tillman, Robert and Henry Pontell

1995 "Organizations and Fraud in the Savings and Loan Industry." *Social Forces* 73 (June): 1439–63.

Tindall, George Brown

1988 *America: A Narrative History*, vol. 2. New York: Norton.

Toby, Jackson

1958 "Hoodlum or Businessman: An American Dilemma." Pages 542–50 in *The Jews: Social Patterns of an American Group*, edited by Marshall Sklare. Glencoe, IL: Free Press.

Tomass, Mark

1998 "Mafianomics: How Did Mob Entrepreneurs Infiltrate and Dominate the Russian Economy?" *Journal of Economic Issues* 32 (June): 565–75.

Tosches, Nick

2005 *King of the Jews.* New York: HarperCollins.

Touhy, Roger

1959 *The Stolen Years.* Cleveland, OH: Pennington.

Toy, Calvin

1992 "A Short History of Asian Gangs in San Francisco." *Justice Quarterly* 9 (December): 647–65.

Train, Arthur

1922 *Courts and Criminals.* New York: Scribner's.

1912 "Imported Crime: The Story of the Camorra in America." *McClure's Magazine* (May): 83–94.

Traub, James

1987 "The Lords of Hell's Kitchen." *New York Times Magazine* (April 5): 38, 40, 42, 44, 85.

Treaster, Joseph B.

1994 "U.S. Arrests Drug 'Laundry.'" *New York Times* (December 1): 1, 18.

1993 "U.S. Says Top Trafficker Is Seized in Puerto Rican Connection." *New York Times* (June 5): 7.

1991 "U.S. Seizes Suspect in New York in 40 Colombian Drug Slayings." *New York Times* (September 27): 1, 7.

Trebach, Arnold S.

1987 *The Great Drug War: Radical Proposals That Could Make America Safe Again.* New York: Macmillan.

Tricarico, Donald

1984 The *Italians of Greenwich Village*. Staten Island, NY: Center for Migration Studies of New York.

Gregory Treverton; Carl Matthies; Karla Cunningham; Jeremiah Goulka; Gregory Ridgeway, and Anny Wong

2009 *Film Piracy, Organized Crime, and Terrorism.* Santa Monica, CA: RAND.

Tri-State Joint Soviet Émigré Organized Crime Project

1997 "An Analysis of Russian Émigré Crime in the Tri-State Region." Pages 177–210 in *Russian Organized Crime, The New Threat?* edited by Phil Williams. London: Frank Cass.

Truong, thanh-Dam

2003 "Organized Crime and Human Trafficking," Pages 53–69 in *Transnational Organized Crime*, edited by Emilio V. Viano, José Magallanes, and Laurent Bridel. Durham, NC: Carolina Academic Press.

Tucker, Richard K.

1991 *The Dragon and the Cross: The Rise and Fall of the Ku Klux Klan in Middle America.* Hamden, CT: Archon Books.

Tuite, James

1978 "Would Benefits of Legalized Betting on Sports Outweigh the Drawbacks?" *New York Times* (December 19): B21.

Tullis, LaMond

1995 *Unintended Consequences: Illegal Drugs and Drug Policies in Nine Countries.* Boulder, CO: Lynne Reinner.

Tully, Andrew

1958 *Treasury Agent: The Inside Story.* New York: Simon and Schuster.

Tulsky, Frederic N.

1987 "U.S. Witness Protection Program Hides a Daughter from Her Father." *Chicago Tribune* (March 5): Sec. 5: 3.

Turbiville, Graham H., Jr.

1995 "Organized Crime and the Russian Armed Forces." *Transnational Organized Crime* 1 (Winter): 57–104.

Turkus, Burton and Sid Feder

1951 *Murder, Inc.: The Story of the Syndicate.* New York: Farrar, Straus and Young.

Turner, Wallace

1984 "U.S. and Nevada Agents Crack Down on Casinos." *New York Times* (January 28): 1, 7.

Tyler, Gus

1975 "Book Review of 'The Black Mafia.'" *Crime and Delinquency* 21 (April): 175–80.

Tyler, Gus, ed.

1962 *Organized Crime in America*. Ann Arbor: University of Michigan Press.

Ungar, Sanford

1975 *The FBI*. Boston: Little, Brown.

"Unger Indicted in Drug Conspiracy"

1928 *New York Times* (December 11): 1.

United Nations

2010 Conference of the Parties to the United Nations Convention Against Transnational *Organized Crime*. Vienna: United Nations.

United Nations Centre for International Crime Prevention

2000 "Assessing Transnational Organized Crime: Results of a Pilot Survey of 40 Selected Organized Criminal Groups in 16 Countries." *Trends in Organized Crime* 6 (Winter): 44–92.

United Nations Office on Drugs and Crime (UNODC)

2010a *The Globalization of Crime: A Transnational Organized Crime Threat Assessment*. Vienna: UNODC.

2010b World Drug Report, 2010. Vienna: UNODC.

2010c *Patterns and Trends of Amphetamine-Type Stimulants and Other Drugs: Asia and the Pacific*. Vienna: UNODC.

2008a *Afghanistan: Opium Winter Rapid Assessment Survey*. UNODC.

2008b *Annual Report: 2008*. UNODC.

2008c *Illicit Drug Trends in the Russian Federation*. Vienna: UNODC.

2007a *Cocaine Trafficking in Western Africa: Situation Report*. Vienna: UNODC.

2007b *Cocaine Trafficking in West Africa: The Threat to Stability and Development (with a special reference to Guinea-Bissau)*. Vienna: UNODC.

2006 *Organized Crime and Irregular Migration from Africa to Europe*. Vienna: UNODC.

2005 *Transnational Organized Crime in the West African Region*. Vienna: UNODC.

UNODC. See United Nations Office on Drugs and Crime

United Press International

2011 "Italian Police Seize $156M in Mob Assets" (August 5): Internet.

U.S. Department of Justice

2010 *The Drug Enforcement Administration's Clandestine Drug Laboratory Cleanup Program*. Washington, DC: Office of the Inspector General.

2008a "Former Top SAS Cargo Group Executive Agrees to Plead Guilty to Participating in Price-Fixing Conspiracy." Press release (July 28).

2008b "LG, Sharp, Chunghwa Agree to Plead Guilty, Pay Total of $585 Million in Fines for Participating in LCD Price-Fixing Conspiracies." Press release (November 12).

2008c *Overview of the Law Enforcement Strategy to Combat International Organized Crime*. Washington, DC: U.S. Department of Justice.

U.S. Department of State (USDOS).

2010 *Trafficking in Persons Report, 10th Edition*. USDOS.

2008 *International Narcotics Control Strategy Report*. USDOS.

2005 *International Narcotics Control Strategy Report*. USDOS.

2004 *Trafficking in Persons Report*. USDOS.

2003 *Southeast Asia*. Internet.

2001 *The Caribbean*. Bureau for International Narcotics and Law Enforcement Affairs. Internet.

1999 *Money Laundering and Financial Crimes*. Washington, DC: Bureau for International Narcotics and Law Enforcement Affairs.

U.S. General Accountability Office (USGAO)

2008 *Drug Control: Cooperation with Many Major Drug Transit Countries Has Improved, but Better Performance Reporting and Sustainability Plans Are Needed*. Washington, DC: USGAO.

Van Devander, Charles W.

1944 *The Big Bosses*. New York: Howell, Soskin.

Van Duyne, Petrus and Alan A. Block

1995 "Organized Cross-Atlantic Crime: Racketeering in Fuels." *Crime, Law and Social Change* 22: 127–47.

van Dyke, Craig and Robert Byck

1982 "Cocaine." *Scientific American* 246 (March): 139–41.

Van Natta, Don, Jr.

1998 "U.S. Indicts 26 Mexican Bankers in Laundering of Drug Funds." *New York Times* (May 19): 6.

1996 "19 Indicted on U.S. Charges in Blow to Genovese Family." *New York Times* (June 12): B12.

Vaquera, Tony and David W. Bailey

2004 "Latin Gang in the Americas: Los Mara Salvatrucha." *Crime and Justice International* 20 (November/December): 4–10.

Varese, Federico

2011 *Mafias on the Move: How Organized Crime Conquers New Territories*. Princeton, NJ: Princeton University Press.

2006 "How Mafias Migrate: The Case of the 'Ndrangheta in Northern Italy." *Law and Society* 40(2): 411–44.

2001 *The Russian Mafia: Private Protection in a New Market Economy*. Oxford, United Kingdom: Oxford University Press.

Väyrynen, Raimo

2003 "Illegal Immigration, Human Trafficking, and Organized Crime." Paper presented at the United Nations University conference on "Poverty, International Migration and Asylum," September 27–28, 2002, Helsinki, Finland.

Veno, Arthur

2009 *The Brotherhoods: Inside the Outlaw Motorcycle Club*, 3rd ed. New South Wells, Australia: Allen & Unwin

2003 *The Brotherhoods: Inside the Outlaw Motorcycle Clubs*. Allen & Unwin: New South Wales, Australia.

Verini, James

2007 "A Budding Invasion." *Men's Vogue* (March/ April): 71, 74, 78, 80, 86.

Vest, Jason

1997 "DEA to Florists: The Poppies Are Unlovely." *U.S. News & World Report* (March 17): 49.

Viano, Emilio C., José Magallanes, and Laurent Bridel, eds.

2003 *Transnational Organized Crime: Myth, Power, and Profit*. Durham, NC: Carolina Academic Press.

Villalón, Carlos

2004 "Cocaine Country." *National Geographic* (July): 34–55.

Villano, Anthony

1978 *Brick Agent*. New York: Ballantine.

Villarreal, Andres

2002 "Political Competition and Violence in Mexico: Hierarchical Social Control in Local Patronage Structures." *American Sociological Review* 67 (August): 477–99.

Violante, Luciano

2000 "Foreword." Pages ix–xi in Alison Jamieson, *The Antimafia: Italy's Fight Against Organized Crime*. New York: St. Martin's Press.

Vitielo, Michael

1995 "Has the Supreme Court Really Turned RICO Upside Down? An Examination of *Now v. Scheidler*." *Journal of Criminal Law and Criminology* 85 (Spring): 1223–57.

Volkman, Ernest

1998 *Gangbusters: The Destruction of America's Last Mafia Dynasty*. Boston: Faber and Faber.

Volkov, Vadim

2002 *Violent Entrepreneurs: The Use of Force in the Making of Russian Capitalism*. Ithaca, NY: Cornell University Press.

2000 "The Political Economy of Protection Rackets in the Past and the Present." *Social Research* 67 (Fall): Internet.

Von Lampe, Klaus and Per Ole Johansen

2004 "Criminal Networks and Trust, On the Importance of Expectations of Loyal Behavior in Criminal Relations." Pages 102–13 in *Organised Crime, Trafficking, Drugs*, edited by Sami Nevala and Kauko Aromaa. Helsinki, Finland: European Institute for Crime Prevention and Control.

Voronin, Yuriy A.

1997 "The Emerging Criminal State: Economic and Political Aspects of Organized Crime in Russia." Pages 53–62 in *Russian Organized Crime, The New Threat?* edited by Phil Williams. London: Frank Cass.

Wahl, Melissa

2000 "Surge Puts Payday Loans Under Scrutiny." *Chicago Tribune* (May 7): 1, 11.

1999a "Hitting a Wall of Opposition." *Chicago Tribune* (February 4): Sec. 3: 1, 4.

1999b "Payday Loans Hit Pay Dirt." *Chicago Tribune* (November 18): 1, 6.

1999c "Suspicions Mount About Secrecy Act." *Chicago Tribune* (March 26): Sec. 3: 1, 4.

Waldman, Amy

2003 "Afghan Group, Once on Top, Again Makes Its Presence Felt." *New York Times* (December 21): 4.

Waldman, Michael and Pamela Gilbert

1989 "RICO Goes to Congress: Keep the Teeth in the White-Collar Law." *New York Times* (March 12): F2.

Walker, Samuel

1980 *Popular Justice: A History of American Criminal Justice*. New York: Oxford University Press.

Wallance, Gregory

1982 *Papa's Game*. New York: Ballantine.

Walsh, Marilyn E.

1977 *The Fence*. Westport, CT: Greenwood.

Walston, James

1986 "See Naples and Die: Organized Crime in Campania." Pages 134–58 in *Organized Crime: A Global Perspective*, edited by Robert J. Kelly. Totowa, NJ: Rowman and Littlefield.

Walter, Ingo

1990 *Secret Money: The World of International Financial Secrecy*. New York: Harper Business.

Walters, John

2003 *Dialogue with John Walters, Director, White House Office of National Drug Control Policy*. Washington, DC: Center for Strategic and International Studies.

Warmbir, Steve, Robert C. Herguth, and Frank Main

2005 "Mob on the Ropes After Indictment." *Chicago Sun-Times* (April 27): 1–2.

Warnick, Mark S.

1997 "City Cop Scandals Dash Drug Trials." *Chicago Tribune* (December 25): Sec. 2: 1, 2.

Washburn, Charles

1934 *Come into My Parlor: Biography of the Aristocratic Everleigh Sisters of Chicago*. New York: Knickerbocker Publishing Co.

Waugh, Daniel

2007 *Eagan's Rats. The Untold Story of the Prohibition Era Gang That Ruled St. Louis*. Nashville, TN: Cumberland House Publishing.

Webster, Barbara and Michael S. McCampbell

1992 *International Money Laundering: Research and Investigation Join Forces*. Washington, DC: National Institute of Justice.

Webster, Donovan

1994 "Chips Are a Thief's Best Friend." *New York Times Magazine* (September 18): 54–59.

Wedel, Janine R.

2001 "Corruption and Organized Crime in Post-Communist States: New Ways of Manifesting Old Patterns." *Trends in Organized Crime* 7 (Fall): 3–61.

Weiner, Tim

2002a "Drug Kingpin, Long Sought, Is Captured by Mexicans." *New York Times* (March 10): 15.

2001 "Mexican Jail Easy to Flee: Just Pay Up." *New York Times* (January 29): 5.

Weinstein, Adam K.

1988 "Prosecuting Attorneys for Money Laundering: A New and Questionable Weapon in the War on Crime." *Law and Contemporary Problems* 51 (Winter): 369–86.

Weiser, Benjamin

2008 "Convictions Reinstated in Mob Case." *New York Times* (September 18): B1, 6.

2002 "Officials Say They Smashed International Ecstasy Ring." *New York Times* (November 6): 21.

1998a "14 Charged in Internet Betting in the First Case of Its Kind." *New York Times* (March 5): 1, 23.

1998b "Reputed Crime Family Head Indicted in Extortion Case." *New York Times* (April 29): Internet.

Weisman, Alan

1989 "Dangerous Days in the Macarena." *New York Times Magazine* (April 23): 40–48.

Weisman, Steven R.

1991 "Is Business Too Cozy with the Mob?" *New York Times* (August 29): 11.

Welch, Dylan

2011 "The Great Bikie Defection." *Sydney Morning Herald* (February 27): Internet.

Wellford, Charles

2001 "When It's No Longer a Game: Pathological Gambling in the United States" National Institute of Justice Journal (April): 14–18.

Wendt, Lloyd and Herman Kogan

1974 *Bosses in Lusty Chicago: The Story of Bathhouse John and Hinky Dink*. Bloomington: Indiana University Press. Originally published in 1943.

Werner, M. R.

1928 *Tammany Hall*. Garden City, NY: Doubleday, Doran.

Wesson, Donald R. and David E. Smith

1985 "Cocaine: Treatment Perspectives." Pages 193–203 in *Cocaine Use in America: Epidemiologic and Clinical Perspectives*, edited by Nicholas J. Kozel and Edgar H. Adams. Rockville, MD: National Institute on Drug Abuse.

1977 *Barbiturates: Their Use, Misuse, and Abuse*. New York: Human Sciences Press.

Wethern, George and Vincent Colnett

1978 *A Wayward Angel*. New York: Marek Publishers.

Whalen, David C.

1995 "Organized Crime and Sports Gambling: Point-Shaving in College Basketball." Pages 19–34 in *Contemporary Issues in Organized Crime*, edited by Jay Albanese. Monsey, NY: Criminal Justice Press.

Wheatley, Joseph

2010 "Evolving Perceptions of Organized Crime: The Use of RICO in the United States." Pages 85–98 in *Defining and Defying Organized Crime*. Edited by Felia Allum, Francesco Longo, Daniela Irrera, and Panos A. Kostakos. London: Routledge.

White, Frank Marshall

1908 "The Bands of Criminals of New York's East Side." *New York Times* (November 8): V 9.

White, Jonathan

2006 *Terrorism and Homeland Security*, 5th ed. Belmont, CA: Wadsworth.

White, Richard

2011 *Railroaded: The Transcontinentals and the Making of Modern America*. New York: Norton.

"Who Are the Yardies?"

1999 *BBC News* (June 19): Internet.

Whymant, Robert

2001 "Crime Bosses Killed in Funeral Attack." *London Times* (September 20): Internet.

Whyte, William Foote

1961 *Street Corner Society*. Chicago: University of Chicago Press.

Williams, Phil

2006 "Trafficking in Women: Markets, Networks and Organized Crime." *Criminal Trafficking and Slavery: The Dark Side of Global and Regional Migration*. Joint Annual Centers Annual Symposium, February 23–25. University of Illinois at Urbana-Champaign.

1997 "Introduction: How Serious a Threat Is Russian Organized Crime?" Pages 1–27 in *Russian Organized Crime, The New Threat?* edited by Phil Williams. London: Frank Cass.

1995a "The Geopolitics of Transnational Organized Crime." Paper presented at the annual meeting of the American Society of Criminology, Boston, November.

1995b "The New Threat: Transnational Criminal Organizations and International Security." *Criminal Organizations* 9 (3 and 4): 3–19.

Williams, T. Harry

1969 *Huey Long.* New York: Bantam.

Wilson, James Q.

1978 *The Investigators.* New York: Basic Books.

1975 *Thinking about Crime.* New York: Basic Books.

Wilson, Michael

2011 "Fake Gucchi's and a Real Cat-and-Mouse Game." *New York Times* (July 16): 15.

Wilson, Michael and William K. Rashbaum

2010 "Real Patients, Real Doctors, Fake Everything Else." *New York Times* (October 14): 31, 37.

Wines, Michael

2002 "Politics in Moscow More Dagger Than Cloak." *New York Times* (August 24): 1, 4.

Winick, Charles and Paul M. Kinsie

1971 *The Lively Commerce.* Chicago: Quadrangle.

Winterhalder, Edward

2005 *Out in Bad Standings: Inside the Bandidos Motorcycle Club—The Making of a Worldwide Dynasty.* Owasso, OK: Blockhead City Press.

Wiretap Commission. *See* National Commission for the Review of Federal and State Laws Relating to Wiretapping and Electronic Surveillance

Wishart, David

1974 "The Opium Poppy: The Forbidden Crop." *Journal of Geography* 73 (January): 14–25.

Withers, Kay

1982 "Cardinal Leads Drive to Crush Sicily's Mafia." *Chicago Tribune* (September 29): 5.

Witkin, Gordon

1991 "The Men Who Created Crack." *U.S. News and World Report* (August 19): 44–53.

Witkin, Gordon with Jennifer Griffen

1994 "The New Opium Wars." *U.S. News and World Report* (October 10): 39–44.

Witt, Howard

1996 "For Russians, Mafia Part of Everyday Life." *Chicago Tribune* (November 24): 1, 14.

1994 "Welcome to Vladivostok, Where Crime Is King." *Chicago Tribune* (November 21): 1, 19.

Woetzel, Robert K.

1963 "An Overview of Organized Crime: Mores versus Morality." *Annals* 347 (May): 1–11.

Wolf, Daniel R.

1991 *The Rebels: A Brotherhood of Outlaw Bikers.* Toronto: University of Toronto Press.

Wolf, Eric R.

1966 "Kinship, Friendship, and Patron-Client Relations in Complex Societies." Pages 1–22 in *The Social Anthropology of Complex Societies,* edited by Michael Banton. London: Tavistock.

Wolfgang, Marvin E. and Franco Ferracuti

1967 *The Subculture of Violence: Toward an Integrated Theory in Criminology.* London: Tavistock.

"Woman, 2 Men, Slain as Gang Raids Home in Coll Feud" 1932 *New York Times* (February 2): 1.

Women's Bureau

2002 *Trafficking in Persons: A Guide for Non-Governmental Organizations.* Washington, DC: U.S. Department of Labor.

Woodham-Smith, Cecil

1962 *The Great Hunger: Ireland 1845–1849.* New York: Old Town Books. Originally published by Harper & Row.

Woodiwiss, Michael

2005 *Gangster Capitalism: The United States and the Global Rise of Organized Crime.* New York: Carroll and Graff.

1988 *Crime, Crusades and Corruption: Prohibitions in the United States, 1900–1987.* Totowa, NJ: Barnes and Noble.

1987 "Capone to Kefauver: Organized Crime in America." *History Today* 37 (June): 8–15.

Worrall, John L. and Tomislav V. Kovandzic

2008 "Is Policing for Profit? Answers from Asset Forfeiture." *Criminology and Public Policy* 7 (May): 219–44.

Worth, Robert F.

2002 "Bank Failed to Question Huge Deposits." *New York Times* (November 28): C1, 9.

Wren, Christopher S.

1999 "Pipeline of Poor Smuggling Heroin." *New York Times* (February 21): 28.

1998a "Afghanistan's Opium Output Drops Sharply, U.N. Survey Shows." *New York Times* (September 27): 11.

1998b "Drug Officials Sense a Shift in Dominicans." *New York Times* (August 14): 16.

1998c "Road to Riches Starts in the Golden Triangle." *New York Times* (May 11): 8.

1997 "29 Held in Drug Smuggling to New York from Mexico." *New York Times* (August 12): C23.

1996 "Mexican Role in Cocaine Is Exposed in U.S. Seizure." *New York Times* (May 3): C19.

Wright, Michael

1979 "Phenix City, Ala., Leaves Ashes of Sin in the Past." *New York Times* (June 18): 14.

WuDunn, Sheryl

1996 "Uproar over a Bad Debt Crisis." *New York Times* (February 14): C1, 4.

Wyler, Liana Sun

2007 *Burma and Transnational Crime*. Washington, DC: Congressional Research Service.

Wyman, Mark

1984 *Immigrants in the Valley: Irish, Germans, and Americans in the Upper Mississippi Country, 1830–1860*. Chicago: Nelson-Hall.

Xia, Ming

2008 "Organizational Formations of Organized Crime in China: Perspectives from the State, Markets, and Networks." *Journal of Contemporary China* 17 (February): 1–23.

Yarmysh, Alexander N.

2001 "A Behavioral Model for Ukrainian Organized Crime Groups." *Transnational Organized Crime* 6 (Spring): 143–49.

Yates, Ronald E.

1987 "Afghanistan Invasion Propels Pakistan to Top in Opium Trade." *Chicago Tribune* (February 12): 32.

1985 "Lawmen's Dispute on Gangs Rages Over Pacific." *Chicago Tribune* (December 8): 5.

Zaitseva, Lyudmila

2010 "Nuclear Trafficking in Ungoverned Spaces and Failed States." Pages 193–211 in *Ungoverned Spaces: Alternatives to State Authority in an Era of Softened Sovereignty*. Edited by Anne L. Clunan and Harold A. Trinkunas. Stanford, CA: Stanford University Press.

2007 "Organized Crime, Terrorism and Nuclear Trafficking." *Strategic Insights* 6 (August): Internet.

Zalisko, Walter

2001 "Russian Organized Crime, Trafficking in Women, and Government's Response." PMC International Inc. (April): Internet.

Zambito, Thomas

2009 "The Digital Wiseguys." *New York Daily News* (June 8): 15.

2005 "Afghani Heroin King Denies Rap." *New York Daily News* (October 25): 8.

Zernike, Kate

2006 "Potent Mexican Meth Floods in as States Curb Domestic Variety." *New York Times* (January 23): 1, 17.

Zimmermann, Tim and Alan Cooperman

1995 "Special Report." *U.S. News and World Report* (October 23): 56–67.

Zorbaugh, Harvey

1929 *The Gold Coast and the Slum*. Chicago: University of Chicago Press.

Name Index

Subject Index